Cambridge Studies in Social Anthropology

General Editor: Jack Goody

63

SOCIAL INEQUALITY IN A PORTUGUESE HAMLET

For other titles in this series see p. 428

Social Inequality in a Portuguese Hamlet

Land, late marriage, and bastardy, 1870–1978

BRIAN JUAN O'NEILL
Lecturer in Social Anthropology
Instituto Superior de Ciências do Trabalho e da Empresa (I.S.C.T.E.)
Lisbon

CAMBRIDGE UNIVERSITY PRESS

Cambridge
New York New Rochelle Melbourne Sydney

Published by the Press Syndicate of the University of Cambridge
The Pitt Building, Trumpington Street, Cambridge CB2 1RP
32 East 57th Street, New York, NY 10022, USA
10 Stamford Road, Oakleigh, Melbourne 3166, Australia

Originally published in Portuguese as *Proprietários, Lavradores e Jornaleiras: Desigualdade Social numa Aldeia Transmontana, 1870–1978* by
Publicações Dom Quixote, Lisbon, 1984 and © Brian Juan O'Neill, 1984

First published in English as *Social Inequality in a Portuguese Hamlet: Land, late marriage, and bastardy, 1870–1978* by
Cambridge University Press, 1987

Printed in Great Britain at the University Press, Cambridge

British Library cataloguing in publication data

O'Neill, Brian Juan
Social Inequality in a Portuguese Hamlet:
land, late marriage and bastardy 1870–1978. –
(Cambridge studies in social anthropology; 63)
1. Portugal – Rural conditions
2. Villages – Portugal – History
3. Social structure – Portugal – History
I. Title II. Proprietários, lavradores
& jornaleiras, *English*
305'0946'9 HN593

Library of Congress cataloguing in publication data

O'Neill, Brian Juan, 1950–
Social inequality in a Portuguese hamlet.
(Cambridge studies in social anthropology; 63)
Translation of: Proprietários, lavradores e jornaleiras.
Bibliography
Includes index.
1. Fontelas (Vila Real, Portugal) – Rural conditions.
2. Fontelas (Vila Real, Portugal) – Economic conditions.
I Title. II. Series: Cambridge studies in social anthropology; no. 63.
HN600.F6605413 1987 305'.09469'2 86-24433

ISBN 0 521 32284 7

SE

To my parents,
Nena and George –
archaeologists
anthropologists
philosophers of modern American marriage

Vou falar-lhes dum Reino Maravilhoso.

Embora muitas pessoas digam que não, sempre houve e haverá reinos maravilhosos neste mundo. O que é preciso, para os ver, é que os olhos não percam a virgindade original diante da realidade, e o coração, depois, não hesite. . .

Miguel Torga, *Um Reino Maravilhoso (Trás-os-Montes)*

A toute famille paysanne se proposent des fins contradictoires, la sauvegarde de l'intégrité du patrimoine et le respect de l'égalité des droits entre les enfants. L'importance relative que l'on accorde à chacune de ces deux fins varie selon les sociétés, ainsi que les méthodes employées pour les atteindre.

Pierre Bourdieu, *Célibat et Condition Paysanne*

Contents

Tables

Figures

Illustrations

Maps

Documents

Plates

Acknowledgements

This book is a slightly revised version of my Ph.D. dissertation in Social Anthropology submitted in 1982 to the London School of Economics and Political Science. The thesis was read and passed by Jonathan Parry (internal examiner) and John Davis (external examiner) in September of 1982, and subsequently published in October 1984 in Portuguese in its original form. Many years have gone into its shaping – since my first immersion in Iberian rural ethnography in 1973 in the Galician region of Northwest Spain, up to my arrival in the Northern Portuguese hamlet of Fontelas in March of 1976. Further back, my earliest influences in both theory and general outlook can be traced to Robert F. Murphy and Morton H. Fried of Columbia University in New York, and to the writings of Eric R. Wolf. One's first introductory anthropology courses frequently leave indelible marks, despite the somewhat circuitous paths along which one passes later through time. Indeed, following a phase of conversion to Lévi-Straussian structuralism in 1969 and 1970, I took a rather different course: thus, the present volume contains a strong dose (however unconscious) of the influence of the latter two scholars. Earlier yet, my childhood and adolescent initiation into archaeology and anthropology is due in great part to my exposure to the rural cultures of Mexico through myriad exploratory trips with my parents George Caracena O'Neill and Nena O'Neill. The latters' unfaltering enthusiasm and interest in my following an anthropological career, geared towards the study of European or Mesoamerican peasant communities, has proved invaluable and realizable in the long run.

Throughout the period of research leading to the publication of this book, a number of individuals and organizations have offered their assistance and support. My greatest appreciation is given to the International Service of the Calouste Gulbenkian Foundation in Lisbon, which granted me a research scholarship in 1976–7 enabling me to carry out the bulk of my fieldwork in rural Portugal. Special thanks are reserved for Maria Clara Farinha and José Blanco for their continuing interest in my work. In London, I received a grant in 1981 from the Radcliffe-Brown Memorial Fund of the Royal Anthropological Institute for aid towards completion of the doctoral thesis.

My greatest debt is to José Cutileiro, who guided my initiation into British social anthropology at the London School of Economics, supervised the initial stages of my research, and helped in the selection of a suitable region for my field study. Julian Pitt-Rivers and Ioan M. Lewis assisted at an early phase of the research, and upon returning from Portugal Jean La Fontaine maintained an inquisitive and interested eye during the course of my writing up. Maurice Bloch's encouragement during my first seminar presentation of field materials at the LSE was also crucial. Warmest gratitude is extended to Peter Loizos, who supervised the project from the latter half of the fieldwork through the conclusion of the dissertation. Both his technical advice and sharp editorial talents as well as his enthusiasm and friendship have proved invaluable throughout. I also extend thanks to many personal friends for their unflinching support and detailed discussions over the years: particularly Frances Pine, Joaquim Pais de Brito, João António Pires, Sandra McAdam Clark, Stuart Brenton, Karen Martin, Rubie Watson, Anna Collard, Raúl Iturra, and Fátima Brandão.

I am very grateful to the LSE Geography Department (Drawing Office) for teaching me the rudiments of map-making. The three maps in this volume were drawn by myself, but none could have been executed without the patient guidance of Barbara Duffy, Jane Pugh, and Alison Fisher. All of the photographs were also taken by myself, and printed especially for the original thesis by Ed Cory and Dave Elsworth of the LSE Photographic Unit. My sincerest thanks are extended to all of the above for their technical expertise and generous advice.

In Portugal, my warmest gratitude is granted to the villagers of Fontelas, who tolerated my innumerable questions and ultimately adopted me temporarily as one of them. Without their at times extreme hospitality and encouragement, the entire project might not have been completed. At the start of my research I was oriented by Benjamim Enes Pereira of the Museu de Etnologia in Lisbon, and in the region studied I was assisted throughout by Padre Antero de Jesus Gomes, Padre Belarmino Afonso, Florêncio Vieira, and Joaquim Lopes de Matos. Indispensable as well was the reception and orientation I obtained in local archives in the nearby town, where consultation and copying of a number of historical sources allowed me to widen diachronically my study of present-day social structure. Warm appreciation is thus granted to the *Conservatória do Registo Civil* (Civil Registry Office), *Administração Florestal* (Forestry Service), *Câmara Municipal* (Town Council), *Grémio da Lavoura* (Landowners' Guild), and the *Tribunal* (Court). My initial acceptance by Fontelas' inhabitants and my knowledge of hamlet customs are due to the friendship and patience of Germano Augusto Fernandes, João António Pires, and Nelson dos Anjos Pires. Their fascination in my work and our long hours of discussion have helped to shape the contours of my portrait of hamlet life.

Finally, my intellectual debt is multiple. On ethnographic matters in the Mediterranean, the work of Carmelo Lisón-Tolosana and John Davis has been particularly stimulating with respect to social stratification, land tenure, and inheritance practices. On historical matters, the guidelines provided by Alan Macfarlane and Peter Laslett for the interpretation of parish records have been especially useful and relevant to my specific case: I hope that this study will constitute a step forward in the development of an historical anthropology of rural Europe. My greatest debt, however, is to the work of Jack Goody and Pierre Bourdieu: their penetrating analyses of strategies of heirship and marriage, patrimony maintenance, and of the links between social relations and property relations have offered constant stimulation and theoretical insight.

Throughout the period following the completion of the original thesis, both in England and in Portugal, a number of further individuals have contributed helpful comments on my work and on specific sections of the ethnography and historical background presented orally in seminar contexts. These include Ernesto Veiga de Oliveira, Manuel Villaverde Cabral, Robert Rowland, José Mariz, José Manuel Sobral, Mary Bouquet, Richard M. Smith, Sarah Harrison, and Joyce Riegelhaupt. I remain deeply grateful for their support and critical vision, although clearly none of them is responsible in any way for the shape of my arguments. A particularly warm appreciation is reserved for Manuel Luiz B. Guimarães of the Gulbenkian Institute of Science in Oeiras, Portugal, for his patient, dedicated, and perfectionist labour in converting my own original genealogies and household diagrams into the visually captivating figures distributed throughout this book. Further thanks are also given to the careful and meticulous efforts of João Freire, who retouched all of the photographs printed here. I am especially appreciative of Robert McC. Netting's critical reading of the thesis with a fine-tooth comb and an ear tuned to the ecological and familial complexities of highland Europe: many of his suggestions have been incorporated in the final revisions of the English text. Finally, my wholehearted thanks for the skilful and patient work on the manuscript by Susan Allen-Mills and Iain White of Cambridge University Press.

One of the goals which I hope this book will achieve is to seduce readers into the fascination that combined anthropological and historical research on rural Europe can spark. Speaking of the rich variety of historical kinship structures in rural Austria, Michael Mitterauer has stated categorically that: 'In order to appraise the breadth of the spectrum of family forms it is hardly necessary to resort to ethnology's treasure of special family forms from distant non-Western cultures. "Old Europe" itself provides historical instances of family forms lacking the spouses' permanent co-residence, which today is considered one of the essential characteristics of the family' (1981:181). The increase in the number of ethnographic studies of rural Europe in recent years now affords us enough material to be able to dispute – or rather modify – Orvar Löfgren's affirmation 13 years ago that 'It can probably be argued that an average 18 or 19th century Scandinavian peasant has left more documentary evidence for posterity than any other European peasant' (1974:46). The abundance of historical material on the Portuguese hamlet analysed in this book – which merely represents the tip of the iceberg – has now rendered Löfgren's comment obsolete.

Continuing research in Portugal, Spain, France, Italy, and other regions of this small but historically rich corner of the Eurasian continent seem to be yielding progressively more data as time goes on. The 'domestic domain' so perceptively stressed as a field of study in Jack Goody's work appears to be one of the areas of most fruitful future inquiry. The pace of publication in the various disciplines that converge upon the topic of rural European kinship structures is intense. I have thus been unable to incorporate within the current format of this monograph a discussion of three recent books which I believe to be directly relevant not only to my own materials but also to any anthropological work on Europe with a historical slant. These are Richard Wall, Peter Laslett, and Jean Robin's edited collection *Family Forms in Historic Europe* (1983), Andrejs Plakans' *Kinship in the Past: An Anthropology of European Family Life 1500–1900* (1984), and Hans Medick and David Sabean's edited volume *Interest and Emotion: Essays on the Study of Family and Kinship* (1984). Although I have included these titles in my bibliography, as this book goes to press they have not been given the close attention which I feel they deserve in relation to my major arguments, and await future comparative treatment.

The most cursory glance at the wealth of relevant historical research on any region of rural Europe, I believe, will almost certainly unearth a cumulative patrimony of raw empirical material quite susceptible to anthropological analysis through short-, medium-, or long-term models. This is one of the fascinations this culture area offers: an incomparable opportunity to follow the development of rural communities through time and social process. Bernard Lewis' captivating account of a peculiar, hostile, and uninteresting European world as viewed through Arab eyes (*The Muslim Discovery of Europe*, 1982) is a marvellous case in point, and illustrates this from an opposite angle. Has anthropology now finally come full circle, only to subject its own geographical and historical cradle to systematic ethnological analysis free of myopic ethnocentrism? The Muslim geographer Masʿūdī had the following to say of the peoples of Europe in the mid-tenth century:

As regards the people of the northern quadrant, they are the ones for whom the sun is distant from the zenith, as they penetrate to the north, such as the Slavs, the Franks, and those nations that are their neighbors. . . . The warm humor is lacking among them; their bodies are large, their natures gross, their manners harsh, their understanding dull, and their tongues heavy. Their color is so excessively white that they look blue;

> their skin is fine and their flesh coarse. Their eyes, too, are blue, matching their coloring; their hair is lank and reddish because of the damp mists. Their religious beliefs lack solidity, and this is because of the nature of cold and the lack of warmth. The farther they are to the north the more stupid, gross, and brutish they are. These qualities increase in them as they go further northward . . . Those who dwell sixty odd miles beyond this latitude are Gog and Magog. They are in the sixth climate and are reckoned among the beasts (Lewis 1982:139).

Can Europe really have remained so repulsive, or simply so outright boring, for over one thousand years to our southerly, Mediterranean neighbours? Perhaps so. But, more subtly, can it be that this 'Arabic' disinterest points to another more serious allergy: a persistent lag of curiosity within anthropology itself with regard to the European land mass as a legitimate object of ethnographic study? Let us hope that the recent surge of interdisciplinary studies will carry on and that this earlier disinterest will rapidly fade. Old Europe constitutes, indeed, one of the last frontiers to be crossed by anthropological knowledge.

Perhaps it is no accident that a New York intellectual, brought up in the bustling 1960s and entering Columbia University in that tumultuous year (1968) – and within a nuclear family whose ultra-liberal core published that provocative analysis of modern American conjugal life *Open Marriage* (1972) – should end up studying one of the most peculiar, archaic, and recondite forms of European marriage imaginable. . . .

Lisbon, Autumn 1985

Map 1. Portugal: Location of Trás-os-Montes province

1

An 'egalitarian' Iberian community?

The problem

This thesis is about internal social distinctions within a Portuguese mountain hamlet. The principal argument is a simple one. I dispute the contention that small, isolated mountain communities in Northern Portugal are necessarily *egalitarian* in social structure. This has indeed been the image created by the major ethnographers working in the region over the past two decades. The inhabitants of such highland villages have everywhere convinced anthropologists that 'we are all equal here' (Davis 1977:71). I also selected a small mountain settlement as my object of study, but have arrived at entirely different conclusions. The epithet 'egalitarian' in this case is totally misleading, and hamlet life is ridden with inequality, internal conflict, and struggles to maintain positions of high economic and social rank.

Despite villagers' initial glosses about their relative equality within the hamlet, distinct social and economic differences emerged from my analysis. My research focused upon three major areas of social life: land tenure, cooperative labour, and forms of marriage and inheritance. Firstly, land is not owned in equal amounts and there is nothing at all egalitarian about its distribution within the community. Secondly, forms of cooperative labour contain conspicuous imbalances in the exchange of labour and time. Thirdly, marriage and inheritance practices reveal fundamental disparities between a few favoured heirs and their excluded siblings: while in ideal legal terms all heirs and heiresses inherit equally, this rarely occurs in practice. Rather than comprising a homogeneous group of peasant farmers, a clear hierarchy of four distinct social groups emerged: radical differences in economic standing, social status, and household structure separate the wealthy, the middling, and the poor. Villagers in this case did *not* paint a self-portrait of Arcadian democracy, nor did they allow me to begin my sketch of them in such tones. In contrast to the accepted image of equality within such mountain villages, most of my informants stressed repeatedly that 'we are all *unequal* here'.

Any discussion of the term *inequality* should of course ideally begin with the origins and genealogy of the word itself, whether we limit ourselves strictly to the European ethnographic literature or search further back in time to its philosophical and sociological roots in Rousseau, Tönnies, or Redfield. This book takes the former course – perhaps a less ambitious one – and seeks to delimit the field of analysis of inequality in a very precise way, in the sense of concentrating solely on local structures and the internal shape of stratification within one rural community (Cancian 1976:235–6). While some classic scholars have erected the 'little community' as an object of supposed homogeneous wholeness (Redfield 1953:4), the omnipresence of the impinging forces of an external society or State upon such isolated villages has also been amply noted, even by Redfield himself (1953:113–31). Nevertheless, what Gilmore has aptly termed a 'village fetish' (1980:3) in Iberian anthropological studies has persisted with remarkable tenacity and continues to perpetuate the myth of the tiny, undifferentiated, *Gemeinschaft*-like rural community (Tönnies 1887:37–73). With notable exceptions in the broad field of peasant studies (for example, the work of Teodor Shanin), the notion that inequality must have penetrated such small collectivities *from outside* continues to dominate ethnological discourse. Alan Macfarlane (1977a; 1977c) has even suggested that the entire conceptual framework revolving around the idea of a 'community' as an object of study may need full-scale revision. As Shanin maintains: 'Rural communities all over the world are known for their relative cohesiveness. But even so, the simple image of an egalitarian and fully cohesive rural community, controlled by a self-sustaining social equilibrium, must be left to the "ideal type" of the sociologists. In reality, rural communities display complex (if frequently elusive) patterns of diversity, power relationships, and conflicts' (Shanin 1972:162). However, recent research directions on forms of status inequality using the Gini coefficient as a standard measure of distribution of wealth (Netting and McGuire 1982; Davis 1977:87–8) are quite promising in their opening up of new and more rigorous approaches to the problem of internal stratification and inequality.

My interest here is somewhat different: I feel that the most essential task at this moment is to provide solid empirical data which will serve to banish once and for all the myth of the egalitarian hamlet community. This means that I will not spill pages or chapters of ink on new or refined definitions of 'inequality' or 'stratification' (despite the calls for such precise definitions by Béteille in 1969 and Berreman in 1981) but rather will rest content if I succeed in providing ample counter-evidence against that incorporeal ghost of rural equality. I take it for granted, following Goody (1976a), that *all* Eurasian village communities are characterized by some form(s) of internal stratification and real differences in wealth and social rank. For instance, one of the most brilliant and sardonic examples of the vast chasm separating villagers in rural Portuguese society can be found in a passing comment by a wealthy latifundist in the Southern Alentejo region of the great estates. After one of that landowner's labourers had been dismissed and proceeded to set fire to one of the former's wheat fields, the latifundist retorted sarcastically – 'The match he used cost him more than the wheat cost me' (Cutileiro 1971:83). It is to this form of social inequality between peasants, with respect to land and other crucial productive resources, that this book is addressed.

Before describing the methodology of my research, let me situate my project within its relevant anthropological context. How has the image of 'mountain equality' in rural Europe been constructed in the ethnographic literature? What specific reasons underlie the conclusions of various ethnographers that the social structures of Northern Iberian communities are so universally egalitarian? A brief look at these questions will lead us into the fundamental problem of this volume – what is meant by the term *social inequality*? If this term is a valid and useful one for the community in question, and I believe this to be the case, then the word 'egalitarian' must either be substantially modified or entirely discarded from our descriptive language.

Four major ethnographies of Northern Iberian communities are of relevance here. The first is a pioneering community-study by a Portuguese ethnologist in 1953, followed by two American studies of small Spanish villages in the 1970s, and the fourth a collection of studies of European villages in a transactionalist vein. All four seem obsessed to varying degrees with concepts of social equality and egalitarianism. Let us look briefly at how each of these authors reifies these concepts. I will not summarize the ethnographies, but rather merely highlight each one's key theoretical statements about equality. Despite this process of selection, the studies are of course all significant landmarks in Iberian ethnography, and I will continue to refer to them for comparison throughout the rest of this book.

In 1953 the extraordinarily detailed ethnography of the tiny border hamlet of Rio de Onor was published by António Jorge Dias: *Rio de Onor: Comunitarismo Agro-pastoril.*[1] Dias succeeded in carrying out, in his own words, 'the first community study . . . to apply the organic and functionalist method . . .' (Dias 1981:11) within the budding anthropology of rural Europe. Rio de Onor was indeed a marvellous incarnation of Eric Wolf's concept of the 'closed corporate community' (Wolf 1957; 1966; 1983). It was geographically isolated within a marginal mountain range in North-east Portugal (Trás-os-Montes province); it had a population of only 228 in 1940, and its extremely strong communal council afforded a perfect example of an independent, self-sufficient peasant economy. This suasive council exerted such an influence over the hamlet's entire productive system that Dias termed Rio de Onor 'a kind of small State . . . that might be called a representative democracy' (1981:82). Dias had found a form of collective village organization which had long since faded into the annals of history in most other regions of rural

[1] Dias' original 1953 ethnography has been reprinted in a second edition in 1981; all page references refer to the latter volume.

Western Europe. Concluding that the social structure of Rio de Onor was nothing but a mummified survival of archaic Germanic pastoral traditions, Dias did indeed succeed in providing a landmark in ethnographic description to which all subsequent community-studies in Portugal still refer today.[2]

But beneath the wealth of descriptive detail, Dias' fundamental theoretical premise emerges. The 'organic, functionalist' method gives him away: the most outstanding feature of Rio de Onor was its extreme social equality. The following passage exemplifies this analytical bent:

> . . . One of the fundamental constants of this culture is its respect for social organization, which until today has oriented all of its collective life. Another constant, related to the former, is the spirit of fraternity and tolerance which leads the villagers to live without friction and in perfect harmony with their neighbours. Everything is done in an atmosphere of celebration, without acrimony or enmities . . . This way of life is reflected in education. Children are brought up in liberty, they take part in festivals, dance and sing alongside adults . . . one generation follows another, equally harmonious, happy and balanced (Dias 1981:329; my translation).

In the same vein, one of Dias' informants emphasized the exceptional equality evident in Rio de Onor as contrasted with neighbouring villages in the area: 'In other villages, there are always two or three wealthy houses which can help the others in moments of need. But here all are equal!' (1981:96). Dias was convinced that he had found a community which was the epitome of rural equality. All members of the hamlet were socially equal and the emergence of great differences in wealth was blocked by the institutionalized council – for instance, no household could graze more than 2 cows and 1 calf on the communal meadows. Yet underneath Dias' use of organic models of social organization hovered the influence of Ruth Benedict: at one point Dias concludes that the personality structure of Rio de Onor's villagers was 'dionysiac' (1981:315). Indeed, in another essay, Dias confesses his debt to Robert Redfield's *The Little Community*: 'The communitarian villages that I had visited in my excursions to the mountain regions of the north offered all the characteristics of the small community as defined by Redfield. They constituted autonomous homogeneous groups, economically self-sufficient, clearly limited, isolated by grazing lands and sowing fields which traditionally belonged to the group' (1961:83).

Both of these points – an organic model of society and a concern with equality – are not in themselves faults within Dias' analysis. But the long-term effects of Dias' study have not been universally positive. Rio de Onor attained such fame in both ethnographic as well as public circles, that the *expectation* of finding such egalitarian social structures in other areas haunted the next three

[2] For instance, to name only a few, see Fontes (1974; 1977), Instituto de Alta Cultura (1974), Bennema (1978), and Polonah (1985). During my fieldwork period, a colleague from Lisbon was simultaneously conducting fieldwork in Rio de Onor along the lines of a re-study of Dias' earlier material. Some preliminary results of his research are available in Pais de Brito (1977).

decades of researchers. Did other hamlets in Northern Portugal also possess such egalitarian structures? Was Rio de Onor merely a lingering example of a uniform past model of collective village organization? The real problem here is not the validity of Dias' analysis, but rather the effects that his conclusions about this special case of rural equality have had subsequently. Rio de Onor thus became the archetype of rural egalitarianism, the last and most perfect survival of an archaic rural tradition against which all other cases were measured. Rio de Onor would have provided a classic example of backwardness for the English traveller Oswald Crawfurd, who in 1880 wrote that 'Farming in Portugal is, as I must admit, at a standstill, and it has moved very little for some fourteen hundred years' (1880:157).

After numerous researchers' visits, many films, and the fame brought about by Dias' ethnography, Rio de Onor's public image leaped far ahead of its actual social identity. The village became an object of exoticism and rural perfection. In fact, Dias' study had such an impact that years later villagers are known to have responded to casual visitors' questions with answers derived straight from the book.[3] In sum then, the picture of rural equality painted by Dias' ethnography has had a lasting influence upon Portuguese ethnology as well as the popular mind. At least in this remote corner of mountainous Portugal, archaic rural equality still survived.

In the 1970s, two American ethnographies dealt with small Spanish communities similar in structure to Rio de Onor. The first of these studies was that of Susan Tax Freeman, entitled *Neighbors: The Social Contract in a Castilian Hamlet* (1970). In her study, Freeman attempted to reach conclusions about the corporate structure of Valdemora (Soria province), a tiny hamlet of 87 people[4] situated to the North-east of Madrid in a mountain range called the Sierra Ministra. The reader is led to believe that the Valdemorans perceive their hamlet to be 'a single coherent world' (Freeman 1970:26) and by the end of the book that there is a perception among villagers of the 'traditions of social harmony' which have accompanied the hamlet's corporate history (1970:204). By stressing elements of Valdemora's public structures of corporate regulation, Freeman deals less completely with the private domain and not at all with internal differences. The community has 'a lack of economic

[3] Personal communication from Joaquim Pais de Brito. One is reminded of Part II of Cervantes' *Don Quixote* (published in 1615) in which Don Quixote and Sancho Panza come upon various people who had already read of the knight's adventures in Part I (published in 1604). Cervantes thus played with his characters' (and his readers') perceptions of fact and fiction. In similar fashion, Rio de Onor's villagers have 'absorbed' features of their own social life filtered back to them through Dias' monograph.

[4] Valdemora had a population of 87 during the first part of Freeman's fieldwork (1963) but this figure dropped to 78 in 1966 (see Freeman 1970:31). But note the same author's fascinating comments on the almost total lack of corporate structures and cooperative activities among the Pasiego shepherds of the Santander region of Northern Spain (1979:94–104). My comments here, however, refer almost exclusively to sedentary agricultural communities in rural Europe with mixed, agro-pastoral farming.

stratification' (1970:152), no internal patron–client ties apart from those established with outside patrons (1970:154), and it has not been subject to 'sharp intrusions or to internal contrasts and discontent' (1970:204). Like Rio de Onor, Valdemora affords another picture of rural harmony and equality.

A good example of this image appears in the early pages of Freeman's study:

> I feel that some contemporary authors have failed to examine Spanish egalitarian traditions closely enough, partly because they worked in centers where hierarchic traditions claimed their attention first. Here, then, is a Castilian hamlet where taking turns – or 'alternating,' as it is called – is the order of the day, and where differences in class and wealth do not separate one family from another, where patronage plays no part in villagers' relations with each other, and relations between families are modeled on the ideal of relations between siblings (Freeman 1970:xv).

Freeman's study thus provides a link with Dias' earlier ethnography of Rio de Onor, and a number of Freeman's footnotes point to similarities between the two communities (1970:32, 33, 65). In an earlier article (1968) Freeman argued that such small corporate settlements constituted an 'Iberian structural type' which characterizes an entire mountain chain extending from Western Portugal through the Pyrenees. Yet a fundamental problem remains: given the focus of both Dias and Freeman on horizontal corporate structures, can we accept the near-total absence in these communities of any forms of vertical hierarchy or social differentiation? John Davis (1977:125) has taken Freeman to task for devoting such minimal attention to internal stratification, and the same criticism could be levelled against Dias. In order to redress an imbalance within the ethnography of rural Spain, Freeman focused upon egalitarian forms of corporate and communal organization. A tiny, isolated hamlet thus provided an excellent context in which to stress harmony and equality.

Yet another ethnography of a Northern Spanish mountain community conveys a similar impression of pervasive equality, although I cannot deal with it in detail here. This is William Christian's *Person and God in a Spanish Valley* (1972). One passage particularly stands out, however:

> The absolute equality within the council is echoed in the customs governing the distribution of property. All land and goods are divided equally among all the children, including daughters. It can be seen also in the uniformity of most outward habits of consumption of the villagers. In these upper villages, a man with seventy cattle lives to all outward appearances in precisely the same fashion as the man who has eight. With the exception of some noblemen and returning emigrants, inconspicuous consumption is the rule (Christian 1972:19).

Although it was not Christian's goal to analyse internal differences in these villages but rather patterns of local religious worship, the background is again set against a landscape of homogeneous equality.[5] Even Pitt-Rivers, in his

[5] William Douglass' brilliant and lucid account of mortuary ritual in a Basque village in Spain (1969) is rather out of step with these studies, whose stress has been on equality. One of Douglass' main concerns was with the very different social positions of selected heirs and

classic monograph on an Andalusian town (which also cannot be dealt with in detail here), obsessively employs an analytical language permeated with concepts of egalitarianism and internal homogeneity. This is all the more perplexing as the town in question is located in an area of Spain recognized by many other scholars as having been rife with class antagonisms, rigid social stratification, extreme economic inequalities, and a long history of anarchist and rural-proletarian agitation and strikes (Hobsbawm 1959; Martinez-Alier 1971; Gilmore 1980). Hierarchy and differentiation are underplayed by Pitt-Rivers as he stresses the factors unifying the various status groups in the town, such as mere co-residence in the *pueblo* – '. . . the equality, in the sense of the identity of nature, of all those who are born in the same place . . .' (1972:49). The author refers later to 'the supremacy of the geographical principle of social integration' (1972:137) and at an earlier point maintains that 'the distinction between pueblo (*plebs*) and the *señoritos* has been made. Otherwise the pueblo has been treated as a culturally homogeneous whole . . .' (1972:76). All of these perspectives lead ultimately towards that mystifying ideal so perfectly expressed in the author's phrase 'the egalitarian values of the pueblo' (1972:71).

Such analyses (and this is not an isolated case in either the Mediterranean or the European ethnographies) which take cultural values as their point of departure are bound to run into quite incongruent situations when statements about purely conceptual equality are misapplied to the very different spheres of economic organization, vast disparities in landownership, and divergent political affiliations. My comments here are not intended as an integral critique of Pitt-Rivers' *The People of the Sierra*, but rather to highlight the extreme stress that has been placed by former anthropological studies of Iberian communities upon the notion of social equality. Nevertheless, of direct relevance to this book is the fact that following Pitt-Rivers' early emphasis on the theme in the South of the peninsula, exactly the same fixation has been reproduced in the monographs on the North.

The third major ethnography of a Spanish mountain community to appear recently is that of Stanley Brandes: *Migration, Kinship, and Community: Tradition and Transition in a Spanish Village* (1975). Becedas is a village of 805 residents located in the Sierra de Béjar mountain range to the West of Madrid. Like many communities in rural Spain, Becedas has been transformed by a wave of migration that has depopulated the village since the 1960s. Brandes' argument is that contrary to theories of modernization current in American

excluded siblings in Murélaga, rather than with questions of egalitarianism. Two further exceptions are Netting's work on the Swiss Alps, where the author warns against our being 'deceived by surface uniformities' suggestive of a 'homogeneous folk community' (1981:40) as well as against confusing the 'comparative independence and autarchy' of Törbel with any mythical or absolute economic isolation (1984:228), and Robert T. Anderson and Gallatin Anderson's rarely quoted but interesting article (1962) stressing the pervasiveness of stratification, hierarchy, and economic inequalities in rural European villages.

anthropology at the time, this rapid process of migration to Madrid did not result in the atomization or total demise of the community. In fact, the village has become more cohesive and new forms of cooperation have emerged, thus giving the community an injection of new life and energy.

While Brandes drills this thesis home throughout the book, however, a fundamental contradiction arises. This contradiction appears in the guise of a false dichotomy between 'the egalitarian present' and 'the unequal past'. Throughout the book there must be well over a hundred references to the fact that villagers in Becedas today are 'more equal than ever before', that they have 'more money than ever before', and that they cooperate 'more than ever before'. Unfortunately, this mysterious historical period of '. . . ever before . . .' is never described in detail, except for 3 pages which deal cursorily with isolated sources from the sixteenth and eighteenth centuries (1975:26–8). Brandes paints a picture of present-day egalitarianism in the village early in the book, stating that 'Unlike many Spanish communities, the Becedas *pueblo* is in many respects homogeneous . . . only under special circumstances does wealth determine social status . . . so that theoretically all villagers have more or less the same access to prestige. This situation provides a high degree of social equality' (1975:38).

Yet throughout we are given numerous hints as to the inequality of Becedas in the past. Brandes speaks of a class of landless labourers, of bitter memories of community divisiveness during the Spanish Civil War of 1936–9 (1975:29), and of former divisions between landowners and day-labourers (1975:44, 71). Even today, it is hard to believe that Becedas is truly egalitarian with its current occupational structure: while the majority of villagers are full-time farmers, there are also several tailors, shoemakers, a blacksmith, a solderer, two barbers, two carpenters, a couple of masons, four construction workers, a State-paid mailman, and medical personnel (1975:47). Yet Brandes insists that equality predominates. Since the wealthiest family lives directly opposite the poorest (the women of these two households having 'an extremely close emotional bond'), Brandes goes as far as to conclude that this proximity is therefore an indication that 'such social equality among neighbors is just one manifestation of the egalitarian ethos of the *pueblo* . . .' (1975:145).

In the past, however, things were different. Here Brandes must construct an image of an 'unequal past' in order to clarify and highlight the 'equal present':

> First and most important is the obvious egalitarianism of the community in comparison with the past. Migration has created a situation in which both land ownership and land control have become more evenly distributed within the community than ever before. The traditional division between *ricos* and *pobres* has become obsolete; while *ricos* have been deprived of the labor supply upon which they depended to sustain their superior position, *pobres* have disappeared altogether. 'Now,' the people say, 'we are all the same.' Everyone shares a middling status as independent proprietor, and the effective interdependence between landless and landed villagers has been totally eliminated (1975:75–6).

A few paragraphs later, Brandes concludes this chapter by stating that 'As Durkheim would put it, there now exists a mutual attraction of the social molecules through similarity and likeness; a state of mechanical solidarity is in evidence' (1975:77). Migration has thus overturned the village entirely and brought about a dominant social atmosphere of equality. Leaving aside the question of the extent of inequality in the past (due to insufficient evidence) the problem of present-day egalitarianism remains: to what extent has Brandes correctly portrayed the apparent equality or levelling within Becedas today? Is the village really as egalitarian as he suggests?[6]

My fourth and final example is the volume on European rural communities edited by F. G. Bailey: *Gifts and Poison: The Politics of Reputation* (1971). This is a collection of essays about small highland villages in France, Spain, Italy, and Austria. It is one of the few volumes to appear recently in British anthropology which has dealt with specifically mountain communities. Perhaps this is so because so much analytical furor about 'honour and shame' in larger Southern European communities had already captivated the attention of an entire generation of anthropologists of the Mediterranean area. After all, how could one study concepts of honour and shame and patterns of patronage in such minuscule mountain settlements? Unfortunately, however, many of the studies in Bailey's book could very well have been carried out anywhere else in the world where tiny villages lie huddled in the mountains. Bailey himself maintains that his pet dichotomy between egoism and altruism will 'allow us to ask questions about communities everywhere' (1971:9).

But Bailey must create a suitable field for the application of his theories about 'small politics' and petty maneuvering – the perfect context for this is the hypothetically egalitarian village.[7] Within such a village community, 'everyone remains equal to everyone else. This is, I suppose, literally democratic society . . .' (1971:23). Equality is a given state of affairs, and inequalities have been injected into these formerly harmonious communities only as a result of the recent modernization of rural Europe. Bailey constructs a fundamentally circular premise in the following terms: 'Equality, in communities like these, is in fact the product of everyone's belief that everyone else is striving to be more than equal. Equality comes about through the mutual cancellation of supposed efforts to be unequal' (1971:20).

But the worst problem created by Bailey's volume is that of the pseudo-romantic notion of the 'community of equals in the past'. Here Bailey

[6] I must repeat that I am being extremely selective here in pointing to the specific theme of equality which links these four studies. The individual merits of each ethnography cannot be dealt with, and I take it for granted that the studies mentioned are of a generally excellent quality. Each of them is filled with detailed descriptions and analyses of the authors' main concerns.

[7] While myriad holes can be found in Bailey's theoretical premises of transactionalism and interactionism, I wish to highlight here only the background of equality which Bailey of necessity was obliged to construct in order to apply his 'game-theory'.

postulates precisely the reverse pattern from that described by Brandes. Where Brandes found an unequal past cancelled out by an egalitarian present, Bailey sees an egalitarian past shattered by present-day inequalities. Bailey views the modernist 'intrusion' of politics and inequality into his communities as destroying the pristine equality of closed, isolated villages. Both views are equally myopic: for both Brandes and Bailey the mysterious past is entirely blurred. While one depicts shades of inequality, the other sees an aura of equality.

Bailey speaks of 'what goes on within a single community, which is not divided into different strata' (1971:17) and of processes through which 'the monolithic uniformity and homogeneity of the community has been broken by separating the leaders above from the followers below' (1971:16). After constructing the image of the 'closed little community'[8] Bailey throws in self-interest and the shady transactions of his patron-like *signori*:

> These comments reveal very clearly the theme of what makes a good community (one in which there is no dissension) and how the new style of *signori* destroy the community by importing the style of the so-called political elections (i.e. provincial and national elections) into the community, where harmony should prevail (1971:251).

Whether such closed and harmonious communities ever existed at all at any time in the European past is itself doubtful,[9] but in order to allow his actors ample theatre space Bailey had to construct a backdrop landscape of equality. Although in rather different terms from the three previous ethnographies I have mentioned, Bailey also insists on the image of mountain communities as characterized essentially by social equality.

Before I began my fieldwork in 1976, I had read all of the studies dealt with above. Dias' and Freeman's ethnographies were in fact quite influential in my selection of a region in which to work in North-east Portugal. Predictably, I began fieldwork in a small mountain hamlet expecting to find relations of social equality everywhere around me. As my fieldwork progressed, precisely the opposite occurred. The more I analysed the hamlet's current social structure, the more I found inequality to pervade social relations. Documents from the hamlet's past confirmed the existence of former inequalities. The combined images of 'mountain equality' were thus in my case quite misleading: none of the authors above had dealt with internal economic differences or with

[8] This point of view filters into the other studies in the volume, one example of which is Paul Adams' analysis of the village of Hogar in the Spanish Pyrenees. Adams maintains that: 'There are no class discriminations in Hogar and there is no tradition of a landed aristocracy . . . All men are thought of as being morally equal, normatively as good as each other (*somos todos iguales aqui*)' (Adams 1971:170–1).

[9] Le Roy Ladurie's fascinating historical ethnography of the French mountain village of Montaillou from 1294 to 1324 (Le Roy Ladurie 1978) should serve to dispel such simplistic notions about the rural past. An extraordinary variety of relationships between villages existed in the Pyrenees at the time, and the internal structure of Montaillou was anything but egalitarian.

social conflicts *within* the rural community. Perhaps this was due, in the case of the American studies, to the concern with community–nation ties. This concept shifted an earlier focus on communities in themselves to an interest in the village community as part of a larger national system. Echoes of this focus can be found in British anthropologists' studies of patronage relations in the Mediterranean area. Yet the studies I have quoted have come almost full circle: Bailey certainly revives the image of the community of equals in the past as another unit of supposed functional, organic cohesion. The fiercely a-historical character of most of this research on highland Europe and its reliance on a wide variety of non-quantitative data have thus contributed to an overall image of stereotyped internal homogeneity in small rural communities; just how much of the stereotype is due to the (unconscious?) ideological stances of the anthropologists in question and their various *milieux* constitutes a rather different methodological and theoretical puzzle. Yet we are confronted in this part of Europe with a situation remarkably similar to that which Jacob Black describes for the Middle East: 'Much of the social anthropological literature on tribal societies in the Middle East is skewed by the tenacious legend that such societies are fundamentally egalitarian in outlook and structure' (1972:614).

My interest in this book is rather different from that of Bailey. I propose to show that even within one small community, an entirely different kind of social relations operates. I deliberately chose a small hamlet with a population of less than 200 people within a region characterized by corporate institutions and traditions of communal property. This indeed placed the hamlet firmly within a comparative Northern Iberian framework. My goal will be to demonstrate that despite its small size and mountain isolation, this community is dominated by distinct social differentiation. I do not propose, however, to discard the concept of equality altogether. Rather, I will use it in a specific fashion to analyse particular moments in the agricultural cycle when masks of equality are worn by villagers. In other words, I will avoid characterizing the hamlet either as totally egalitarian or at the other extreme as totally hierarchical, although my emphasis will be on the latter.

My point is quite another one. Equality and hierarchy can *co-exist* within the same community in different forms and within different contexts. In this sense John Davis is quite right when he points out that the term 'egalitarian' means something very different from 'equal' (1977:110). In the case of this hamlet, isolated moments of equality crystallize *ideals* of social equality, but for the rest of the time marked economic differentiation dominates social life.

But what precisely do I mean by social hierarchy and social inequality? The former concept is rather more difficult to define, but it will lead us towards a clearer perception of the forms of social inequality to be analysed in the chapters to follow. The *Oxford English Dictionary* provides three origins for the first word. Etymologically, the term can be traced back to the Middle

English and Old French *ierarchie*, which in turn was preceded by the medieval Latin *(h)ierarchia*, and yet earlier the Greek *hierarkhia*.[10] Surprisingly, the dictionary lists as the first meaning of the word 'each of three divisions of angels' and the second as 'priestly government; organized priesthood in successive grades'. The third meaning is an 'organization with grades or classes ranked one above another'. I will return to the term *class* below, but here let me stress this aspect of 'grades ranked one above another'. This is the form of economic and social organization I believe to hold the key to analysis of the hamlet of Fontelas.[11] Local historical documents, both civil and ecclesiastical, indicate the internal division of the hamlet into three major social groups. The first of these are called *proprietários* (large landowners), the middle group *lavradores* (peasants) and the lower group *jornaleiros* (day-labourers).[12] Close analysis both of these documents and of present-day distinctions reveals a fourth social group of particularly wealthy peasants, which I have called 'large *lavradores*' (Chapter 3). All of these native terms are still in current use within the hamlet and its surrounding area, and they provide linguistic evidence of a distinct hierarchy of occupational groups. The terms are precise ones and not merely the invention of literate administrative officials or local priests: villagers use them today to classify themselves and others.

But the terms are not only linguistic. These groups are located at different levels within a total hierarchical system: land is distributed unequally among them, 'equal' or balanced cooperative labour exchanges occur only between households of similar standing, and evaluations of social prestige vary considerably from the top of the scale to the bottom. These four groups

[10] For the sake of brevity, I refer here to the *Concise Oxford Dictionary* (1978).

[11] 'Fontelas' is a pseudonym, which I selected from the 1960 Portuguese National Census. There are a number of real villages with this name in Portugal, but they are all quite far from the region I studied. The other three hamlets in the parish are also designated with pseudonyms – Mosteiro (head village), Lousada, and Portelinha. Similarly, following anthropological practice, all names of living persons have been altered, as have those mentioned in historical sources (with a few exceptions from the mid-nineteenth century). However, although the pseudonyms thus retain a slightly archaic twist, they faithfully preserve the sonority of local names as they were chosen almost exclusively from documents referring to this particular parish.

[12] The first and second of these terms are impossible to translate accurately into English using simple one-word equivalents (see Chapter 3 and Glossary). *Proprietários* in this quintessentially European hamlet are not directly comparable in social status or power to the classic absentee landowners or latifundists of Mediterranean agro-towns (although the *proprietários* occupy the highest ranks in Fontelas' hierarchy) and the term *lavrador* could be translated as anything ranging from 'ploughman' or 'tiller' to 'peasant cultivator' or, more precisely in its local meaning, 'peasant with a plough team'. Only the third term – *jornaleiro* – approximates the English 'day-labourer', although the reader is warned not to assume ingenuously either that these labourers are landless or that they are always paid in money. A fourth occupational term appearing in twentieth-century local historical sources – the imprecise feminine classification *doméstica* (approx. 'woman engaged in housework') – also affords a number of irksome interpretative problems. Due to these linguistic subtleties, I have opted for a purist use of these four Portuguese words throughout the text and in all of the diagrams.

constitute the social hierarchy, and each group is distinctly situated in relation to the others. The strength of this hierarchy in ranking villagers is a formidable one, and any attempt to analyse the few egalitarian institutions that do exist in this society must carefully situate these within this hierarchy first. William Christian's statement that in Northern Spain 'a man with 70 cattle lives to all outward appearances in precisely the same fashion as the man who has 8' is totally misplaced in the hamlet studied here, where even the apparently insignificant difference between a day-labourer with *one* cow and a peasant with *two* is in fact a fundamental hierarchical one. The former is doomed to sell his labour or swap his cow with another villager's in order to plough, while the latter is truly a grain-producing 'middle peasant' of a qualitatively different rank.

Let me make it very clear that I do not propose to make the simplistic and reductionist point that although villagers 'see' themselves in emic terms as morally equal, my analysis reveals them in etic terms to be 'really' unequal. The crucial point is that villagers themselves do *not* conceptualize their hamlet as a 'single coherent world' (except perhaps momentarily in church) and that they are constantly manipulating and commenting on the hierarchy in which they are enmeshed. This hierarchy is not solely an economic one: along with differences in landholdings, there are varying patterns of linguistic address, good and bad reputations, distinct kinds of household structure within each social group, and different voting patterns. The hierarchy is comprised of a multiplicity of economic and social signs of differentiation, but I do not think that villagers are necessarily transactionalizing in Baileyan fashion in order to remain equal. During the early months of my fieldwork, my association with poorer families was viewed with suspicion by the priest and his wealthy relatives, whereas a number of poorer women told me that I was 'the first *Senhor Doutor* to come to Fontelas and talk *both to the rich and to the poor*'. This comment itself revealed the continuing presence and power of a real social hierarchy.

My argument, then, will deal with a number of intertwining elements which constitute the villagers' own criteria for classifying themselves and others within the social scale. This is not to say that institutions of equality do not come into play in specific contexts, but simply that these horizontal moments enter the stage, as it were, in front of a vertical, hierarchical background.

By 'hierarchy' I do not mean to imply that there is a rigid and fixed scale of rank through which individuals cannot move. This would be too extreme a theoretical reaction against Bailey's shifty, manipulating actors. Nor do I use the term in a manner directly comparable to either Indian ethnography (Barnes, Coppet, and Parkin 1985) or to James Woodburn's discussion of egalitarianism among the African Hadza.[13] There is of course some movement

[13] A detailed analysis of the term is contained in James Woodburn's Malinowski Memorial Lecture, delivered at the London School of Economics in March 1981 (Woodburn 1982).

upwards and downwards within Fontelas' social hierarchy. A household (or an individual) located in one group may not remain there over succeeding generations. Nor are marriage alliances always contracted within each group, although those between the upper and lower extremes are very rare. The hierarchy is thus to some extent a fluid one.

But this should not suggest that there is no hierarchy or differentiation in the first place. The actions of specific individuals may have repercussions for a social group as a whole. Conversely, the overall position of a social group within the hierarchy may condition particular individuals' actions to a remarkable extent. The key to Fontelas' rather peculiar social structure, particularly with respect to its de-emphasis of marriage and its astronomical rates of illegitimacy, lies precisely in the relation between these ranked hierarchical groups. We cannot search for sociological explanations solely within the framework of isolated transactions between individual actors, but rather within the internal *structural tensions* between composite social groups over the generations. The location of these structural tensions is the primary goal of this book. In this sense, the conceptual image of equality is entirely inadequate as an analytical tool with respect to this community. Within the context of the ethnographies cited above, I plan to add to a melody of equality sung in a major key merely one dissonant note of hierarchy in a minor one. While aware of the definitional and epistemological problems raised by the mere mention of the word 'hierarchy', I do not propose to treat the term conceptually nor to apply it empirically, even less to clarify or resolve any debates. My primary objective is to bury the myth of mountain equality and to demonstrate that in this case, for once, *inequalities* abound and indeed prevail.

I must add here that throughout this study I have deliberately chosen to avoid the use of two concepts: firstly, the concept of 'class' and secondly the idea of 'honour and shame'. There are specific reasons for this decision. Firstly, the concept of class or class structure is an extremely complicated one, and a large body of recent literature has appeared concerning the internal class divisions within the peasantry. If it is generally agreed that peasants are a class in relation to other national classes, it is by now a commonplace to pose the question of to what degree the peasantry is a class in (or for) itself. Within a particular peasantry, are there classes, fractions of classes, strata, or groups? I will not belabour the issue with yet more ink to be spilled over definitions. In his study of a Southern Spanish town in 1954, Pitt-Rivers drew attention to the plethora of varied definitions of social class and social group (Pitt-Rivers 1972: 32, 34). I have thus chosen to speak of *social groups* in this book primarily to avoid such definitional entanglements.

I use the term social group, then, in a loose sense to refer to a series of individuals and households that share a similar position within this social scale of four major levels. These groups are not exclusive in membership, but a household's location in one of them has many repercussions. While within each group there are a certain number of shared life experiences, the relations between the upper and lower groups are always tinged with a note of superiority and subordination. Villagers from the lower groups have been the servants and day-labourers of the wealthy, while the latter have extended their power and influence outside the hamlet through strategic marriage alliances and the maintenance over the generations of high administrative and ecclesiastical posts. These social groups are certainly not corporate groups in the sense of owning joint property of any sort strictly limited to one set of individuals or related kin. But there is a certain degree of continuity between the life-styles of the members of one group and their classification within the social hierarchy. Specific individuals may rise or fall from one group to another, but the basic structure of four layered groups remains quite firm today. In their detailed historical ethnographies of a Spanish town and a Southern Portuguese parish, Lisón-Tolosana (1966) and Cutileiro (1971) have both chosen to use the term 'social group' to analyse the internal stratification of two much larger rural communities: I have followed their lead, and in an even smaller rural settlement, have avoided the use of more misleading terms by preserving their relatively precise phrase.

But why not term them 'classes'? I do not deny that upon the basis of the descriptive data which I provide one *could* define these groups as classes. But this is not my goal, and by rigidly adhering to one or another definition I feel that I would have begun to distort the data to fit a particular model. This is not a neo-Marxist analysis of rural class structure, but I have no objection to future discussions of the materials presented here in such terms. Obviously, the hamlet is inserted within a world system and it probably has been for over two thousand years, but its position within that larger system is not the object of my study. It is crucial to avoid viewing any particular community through foggy glasses clouded by myriad and conflicting definitions and models. If Ernestine Friedl can avoid using the concept of 'peasant' at all in her study of the Greek village of Vasilika (1962:6) due to disagreement among social scientists about its many meanings, then I see no reason why I cannot likewise leave the term 'class' in temporary suspension. It may well be that the social groups I analyse here constitute classes on a regional level, but the hamlet itself is simply too small a field in which to define such larger categories. I must leave this problem aside for the moment. In broad terms, viewed from Lisbon these villagers clearly constitute a 'class' of pitifully small farmers. But examined as it were under the microscope, the concept of class seems too broad and too generalizing. It is these internal, microscopic distinctions that must be viewed with fresh eyes.[14]

[14] This is not to deny that various definitions and preoccupations were not also floating around in my own head prior to, during, and after my fieldwork. I was particularly influenced at an early stage by the methods of Carmelo Lisón-Tolosana (1966) and José Cutileiro (1971) in their studies of social stratification. Both incorporated detailed historical research in local archives within their ethnographic analyses, and this data adds to the richness of their monographs. Many of the sources I consulted are identical to theirs.

The second concept which I explicitly avoid is that ambiguous, elusive phrase unfortunately located at the heart of Mediterranean anthropology – honour and shame. This concept has been reified, along with that of patronage, far beyond its original meaning. One need only think of social occasions in which anthropologists working in Europe are queried: 'Did your village have "honour and shame"?' The concept has attained a life of its own, and has begun to extend its tentacles far beyond its original Mediterranean pool. Even communities like Fontelas, which by all standards is located well outside the limits of the Mediterranean zone, are expected to have patterns of honour and shame. Neither the Romans nor the Arabs left as deep a mark on Northern Portugal as the Visigoths and a number of smaller cultural groups such as the Suevi. Neither Atlantic nor Southern European, the community studied here is more precisely part of *Mountain Europe*, and as such is situated within a culture area and ecological zone quite distinct from that of the Mediterranean. An endless stream of articles have appeared since the definitive text on the topic edited by Peristiany in 1966: *Honour and Shame: The Values of Mediterranean Society*. I will spare the reader an elaborate list but invoke his/her literary suspension of disbelief in taking my word that many of these articles are by now dull, muddled, and say nothing new.[15]

As an analytical tool, the concept of honour and shame is entirely inapplicable to the hamlet I have studied. Compared with other communities in the mainstream of Mediterranean ethnography, Fontelas is really on another planet. It may well be that the concept is best applied in larger centres of population and with a focus on values rather than economics and material wealth. But neither is Fontelas of such a size nor am I interested in values, religion, or ideology in and of themselves. No transfer of property of any kind occurs at marriage in this society, and it is not uncommon for women (if not already pregnant) to have borne several bastard children prior to their marriage. Furthermore, any community with ratios of illegitimacy reaching almost 75 per cent has got to have *something* wrong with its honour code. Or alternatively, a qualitatively different system of moral evaluations must be operative in Fontelas. Any attempt to fit this value system into an honour/shame mould would be fruitless. Square pegs cannot be fitted into circular holes. Throughout 2½ years of fieldwork I heard the word *honra* (honour) used only once unelicited, although the fact that people do not employ this particular word does not necessarily mean in itself that something like 'honour' does not exist (Herzfeld 1980).

[15] One notable exception is Herzfeld, who concludes that 'massive generalisations of "honour" and "shame" have become counter-productive . . .' (1980:349). However, to my knowledge there has been to date no major rethink of the honour/shame topic along the lines of the stimulating collective volume on patronage in the Mediterranean (Gellner and Waterbury 1977), and particularly no dissenting text on honour and shame as lucid, penetrating, and useful as Gilsenan's 'Against Patron-client Relations' in the same volume.

The literature on honour and shame is thus of peripheral interest to my theme, and any concentration upon its development as an analytical tool or its application to this case would be severely misplaced. Like the concept of class, that of honour and shame would only obscure rather than clarify the social processes examined below.

Method of research

The fieldwork upon which this book is based was carried out continuously for a period of $2\frac{1}{2}$ years, from March 1976 through September 1978. Participant observation and informal interviews were my principal means of gathering information. I should stress the word *participant* here, as most of my time during the first year in Fontelas was spent working in the fields. This was the period in which the bulk of my materials on cooperative labour was gathered (Chapter 4). Winter months provided optimum conditions for lengthy interviews with villagers, who were quite insistent that I visit them not only for dinner but for long conversations which lasted hours afterwards well past midnight. Most of my field notes were written down, although I recorded about 25 tapes of songs, verses, and life-histories. Detailed genealogies were also best collected in the winter, through a sequence of two or three successive sessions with the same informant. I made a number of trips out of the hamlet (never for longer than a few weeks) in order to consult archives and libraries in Bragança, Porto, and Lisbon (see Map 1). Otherwise, the vast majority of my time was spent in the hamlet itself.

My entrance to the hamlet was not without its problems. I had carried out a 3-month field study in the Galician region of Spain across the Portuguese border in 1973 and thus arrived unknown in Fontelas three years later speaking Galician: a language historically linked to both Castilian Spanish and Portuguese. I had contacted an ethnologist in Lisbon and a canon in Bragança for orientation and assistance in selecting an appropriate mountain community. In February of 1976 I took one of the local buses in Bragança and got off at the last stop, in front of Fontelas' main *taberna*. My poor luck was that precisely that morning two cows had been stolen from the household of the priest's brother, and the entire hamlet suspected that Galicians had taken them across the border 4 kilometres North of Fontelas. I was thus suspected not merely of being a suspicious student, a government spy, a land surveyor, a professional contrabandist, but also a cattle thief.

My knowledge of Galician did not help in this situation; had I only spoken Castilian Spanish my case might have been more convincing. The entire day was a rather tense one, and no means of transport were available to leave the hamlet as the only villager with a car was the priest. I was allowed to stay the night, but only after several persons had carefully checked my credentials and all of the official stamps throughout my passport. The priest himself months

1 General view of Fontelas, showing some of the hamlet's central sections.

later admitted that my mention of the advice given me by the Lisbon ethnologist and the Bragança canon (formerly his own music teacher) were my only salvation: otherwise I had barely escaped a night in the local town prison. The next morning the cows were indeed found across the border and recovered. I then paid two visits to other hamlets in the area and finally decided to stay in Fontelas, if the inhabitants were sufficiently convinced that I had nothing to do with the cattle theft. By April I had succeeded in becoming 'accepted' in the hamlet, and the Easter period found me well incorporated within the sequence of ritual invitations for Easter cakes and wine.

My fieldwork had a second dimension. This consisted of detailed archival work on local documents. A wealth of parish records were stored within an enormous drawer in the parish church of Fontelas' neighbouring village. These sources refer primarily to the nineteenth and twentieth centuries, but one series of books covered the period from 1703 to 1733. I did not start working with these sources until the middle of my second year in the hamlet, well after a reasonably clear picture of the current social structure had emerged. As Fontelas had no electricity at the time, I had to write at night by candlelight or with kerosene lamps, and later I was obliged to move to the town in order to copy and microfilm some of the documents. During the last year of my fieldwork I returned on weekends and alternate weeks to the hamlet, thus allowing myself time for both archival and continuing ethnographic work. My aim was not, however, to write a social history of the community but rather to check present-day ethnographic materials against a short-term diachronic background. Upon completing the writing of the thesis, most of the forms of hierarchy I observed in the hamlet were indeed clearly reflected in the patterns which had emerged from the sources. Fontelas is neither egalitarian today nor was it so in the recent past.

The parish records provided much of the material for Chapter 5, where I trace three households' recent histories back a number of generations to the mid-nineteenth century. Elsewhere I refer to the records as supplementary information to my contemporary field notes. The records are so rich in detail, and relatively accurate in their recording of names, ages, and kin relationships, that I have merely scratched their surface here. John Davis' assertion in his *People of the Mediterranean* (1977) is absolutely correct: to ignore historical records in European rural communities (*if* they are available) constitutes a serious methodological error. In the case of Fontelas the sources provided an excellent means of testing and checking the conclusions I reached against a time dimension.

My principal goal, then, has been to push the community-study back in time, as it were, by extending the ethnographic present slightly backwards. The reader will note however that this combination of anthropological and historical/demographic methods is not directly comparable to the interdisciplinary methodology used in a number of other recent studies of rural European communities (see Chapter 5, opening pages), particularly those of Laslett (1972; 1980a), Netting (1981), or Augustins (1981). Nor do my data propose merely to extend the classic Fortes/Goody 'developmental cycle' approach into the realm of faded parish registers. My goal is quite another and my model of internal structural tension quite distinct. In the case of marriage ages and illegitimacy rates (Chapters 6 and 7) the Parish Register allows us a far larger field of data than that provided by genealogical materials alone. If I had selected several hamlets rather than one as my locus of study, I feel that the wealth of detail woven below would either have been lost or at least substantially diluted. Nevertheless, I did deal with archival documents for the *four* hamlets in the parish, and I visited all of the neighbouring hamlets in the area for comparison. In this sense, I have worked within the community-study framework despite the methodological problems that choosing a bounded 'community' raises. Macfarlane has pointed to the utility of revised definitions of the community as an object of analysis (1977a): I have followed his tack by attempting to expand the community-study framework diachronically. In this sense, the present study is distinctly not a 'village-outward' analysis, but rather a specific and novel kind of *village-inward* framework which attempts to open out the monographic method by pushing it slightly backwards in time. This study is thus fundamentally ethnographic in nature, although it should be borne in mind that the historical dimension is relevant both to the analysis throughout and to my conclusions at the end.

The format of the book follows a simple pattern. I deal with three major areas of social structure. The first of these is land tenure. Chapter 2 gives an overall description of the geographical characteristics of the region in which Fontelas is located, and contains an analysis of the five main kinds of land cultivated in the hamlet today. Particular attention is given to the open-field system of biennial rotation and to the role of common-land in the hamlet economy. Chapter 3 then provides an analysis of all of the community's landholdings and of the role of land as a fundamental criterion for the definition of social groups. Five case-studies are presented, analysing the situations of five households[16] of different economic levels. Despite the initial levelling effects of a massive wave of emigration to France beginning in the 1960s, I show that the system of land tenure in Fontelas today remains a strictly hierarchical one.

The second area I examine is that of cooperative labour. Here I set out the annual cycle of agricultural activities and discuss the role of the hamlet council in coordinating public works. Chapter 4 deals most extensively, however, with two kinds of cooperative labour: threshing labour-teams and the systematic rotation of turns for the irrigation of kitchen-gardens. Both of these forms of labour, although apparently egalitarian, contain underlying structures of inequality and imbalanced exchanges between villagers at the top and bottom of the social hierarchy.

[16] 'Household' here is virtually synonymous with the anthropological concept of *domestic group* (Goody 1972a: 1972b). The local Portuguese term in question is *casa*, which may be translated as either 'house', 'domestic group', or more precisely as a kind of 'land-house complex'. National censuses and agrarian surveys use, among others, the terms *fogo* and *agregado familiar*, but neither of these are used by villagers themselves. Without entering endless definitional debates and hair-splitting, then, provisionally each household in Fontelas is constituted by a group of persons (not necessarily all related by kinship) residing in the same place with the following factors in common:

(a) *production*: most agricultural/pastoral labour (although not necessarily all) is carried out by the household's members;

(b) *residence*: most meals are eaten together, with sleeping quarters located 'beneath the same roof';

(c) *reproduction*: the domestic group is composed of individuals usually related by kinship ties over a number of generations.

A fourth factor might be added – property – which includes not only the house, movables, and various farm buildings but also the landholding in a wider sense (plots, animals, and equipment) and its inheritance through time. The reader may find the complete array of all of the hamlet's 57 households by glancing at Table 3, Map 3, and the diagrams in Appendix IV. As this book goes to press, I have consulted a more recent, modified anthropological definition of the household (Wilk and Netting 1984:5–21), whose five major characteristics (production/distribution/transmission/reproduction/coresidence) provide an interesting variation and refinement of the elements I have noted above.

The third area concerns customs of marriage and inheritance. Chapters 5, 6, and 7 deal with these topics. Chapter 5 introduces the subject through three extensive case-studies of a representative household from each of the hamlet's major social groups. These case-studies afford empirical evidence of differing patterns of marriage and inheritance within the hierarchy. The wealthy and the landed possess large and complex households, hire servants, and we can trace over the generations a separation between a few favoured heirs and a larger number of tacitly excluded siblings. At the other extreme, poorer households are characterized by small, matrifocal structures of single mothers with several bastard children of separate fathers. Many of these illegitimate children were themselves the servants of the wealthy at various times in their lives. The chapter makes extensive use of the Parish Register and links it with information derived from contemporary genealogies.

Chapter 6 continues the discussion of marriage and opens with a listing of the structure of all of the hamlet's households in 1977. An extremely high age at marriage has characterized the community since 1870 (the date at which the registers begin).[17] A general de-emphasis of the ritual aspects of marriage pervades the entire society. The separate (natolocal) residence of spouses with their respective sets of parents for many years after their marriage suggests a limitation of matrimony in the interests of maintaining unified patrimonies. The opposition between *matrimony* and *patrimony* revealed through the case-studies in Chapter 5 is now further clarified: there is a basic structural tension within this society between the transmission of an undivided patrimony and the countervailing drive towards matrimony and reproduction.

Chapter 7 describes the ritual aspects of death in Fontelas and the various forms of the partition of land. *Post-mortem* inheritance is seen as a key structure within the society and a fundamental nexus around which many other elements revolve. While many Mediterranean communities are frequently obsessed with *marriage*, this mountainous society is preoccupied with *land* and the maintenance of viable patrimonies. Of particular interest is the close link between delayed inheritance, the general limitation of marriage, and the persistence of consistently high proportions of illegitimacy. The unravelling of the long-term effects of this specific form of inheritance reveals its pivotal role in the maintenance of the social hierarchy. This hierarchy is fundamentally conditioned by the transfer of property between the generations at death and not at marriage. The specific timing of this property transfer provides the key to the major features of Fontelas' social structure.

[17] The choice of 1870 as a beginning date for this study was purely for convenience. Although I refer to one listing of parish tithes from 1851, the detailed Parish Register of baptisms, marriages, and deaths referring to Fontelas was available without gaps from 1870 onwards. Apart from one isolated book covering the years 1703–33, additional books compiled from the sixteenth through the nineteenth centuries probably lie uncatalogued in the Bragança District Archive (closed to the public as well as researchers, unfortunately).

Finally, in my concluding remarks in Chapter 8, I situate the study again within its relevant ethnographic context and return to the theme of egalitarian social structures. The data presented in the preceding chapters point emphatically towards a social structure characterized by marked economic and social differentiation.

2

Open fields and communal land

This chapter deals with the various types of land cultivated in Fontelas. Firstly, I describe the major geographical characteristics of the area: aspects of the hamlet's location, climate, vegetation, and soil. Some basic features of the community's spatial organization (streets, houses, shops) are also introduced. Secondly, I look at the open-field system of rye grain cultivation, with its major features of biennial rotation and stubble-grazing. Thirdly, I examine collective rights in the hamlet's common-land, along with a number of local administrative minutes affording historical evidence of the division of small portions of common-land into individual plots. Fourthly, I provide a short description of three further types of land in Fontelas: irrigated meadows, kitchen-gardens, and vineyards. Throughout the chapter, some initial materials on the unequal distribution of land in the hamlet are set forth. These will provide a background for my subsequent analysis of land and social groups in Chapter 3.

Geographical characteristics

The terrain surrounding Fontelas is plateau land characterized by a varied topography of mountains, hills, valleys, and rivers. The *concelho* (municipality) in which Fontelas is located has a total area of 70,328 hectares[1] (703.28 sq km). This area comprises both the land of the *vila* (municipal town) as well as that of its 34 rural *freguesias* (parishes).[2] A crude average would thus yield

[1] This figure is derived from a national survey of all of the common-land in Portugal, carried out in 1936 by the Junta de Colonização Interna (Internal Settlement Board) (JCI 1939:70); 1 sq kilometre = 100 hectares.

[2] I will refer throughout to these approximate English equivalents for Portuguese administrative divisions. The largest entity is the province, which in the case of Trás-os-Montes is comprised of two districts (see Map 1). Each district is composed of a number of municipalities (*concelhos*): Bragança district thus contains 12 (I have deliberately left the name of the municipality in question unidentified for the moment). Each municipality is further divided into a number of parishes (*freguesias*). Although the latter term is actually a civil and not an ecclesiastical one, in most cases the two divisions overlap. For convenience then, I will refer to the 'parish'. Below the parish level are villages (*aldeias*) and hamlets (*lugares*). I have chosen to use the latter term as Fontelas is not the administrative centre of its parish but rather an annex hamlet: it is so tiny and lacking in any sizeable public resources that it barely deserves the appellation 'village'. Most hamlets have their own small church or a chapel, and priests in the area may administer as many as a dozen or more hamlets within the parishes for which they are responsible.

approximately 2,000 hectares (20 sq km) of land per parish, although individual parishes and hamlets clearly vary in their total area due to variations in terrain.

The terrain of the parish of Mosteiro can be approximated at 2,400 hectares (24 sq km). This is a rough calculation of North–South and East–West distances (8 km × 3 km) based on a cartographic map of the area compiled by the Instituto Geográfico e Cadastral in Lisbon (IGC 1960). As no further precise figures were obtainable at the parish level, I arrived at the approximate figure of between 600 and 800 hectares (6–8 sq km) for the land pertaining to Fontelas alone, based on the same map as well as local estimates. Although this is an approximation, it emphasizes the more extensive terrain of this community in comparison with its neighbouring hamlets: although there are four hamlets in the parish, Fontelas' terrain alone accounts for over 1/3 of the parish's total land (see Map 2).[3] For instance, of the 238 hectares of common-land in the parish (JCI 1939) only Fontelas and Portelinha have sections large enough to have merited reforestation. About 108 hectares of these 238 lie within Fontelas' boundaries, while most of the remaining common-land lies within Portelinha's rugged, hilly terrain. All of the hamlets in the area are densely nucleated settlements within distances of 2–5 kilometres of each other. Thus, the three other hamlets in the parish are located at distances of 2½, 3, and 5 kilometres to the West and South-west of Fontelas. To the North and East, it is surrounded by a number of hamlets pertaining to other parishes at distances of about 3–4 kilometres.

Fontelas is located at an altitude of 842 metres, and the three other hamlets in the parish at 760, 740, and 680 metres respectively: Mosteiro, Portelinha, and Lousada. The highest point within the parish is an outcrop of rocks and boulders (1,106 metres) located inside Fontelas' terrain, just under 2 kilometres from the hamlet. Sloping to the North and West of this outcrop lies much of the hamlet's common-land used for pasturage, firewood, and the collection of various kinds of shrub for manure compost mixtures. (Note that the area designated 'commons' on Map 2 indicates the bulk, but not all, of the tracts of common-land within the hamlet's terrain.) Flowing in a South-western direction from this crag are a number of streams and rivulets which lead past the hamlet and through its most fertile meadows. These streams stretch for long distances into the terrain of the neighbouring hamlets and meet the largest local river at two points 2½ and 6½ kilometres distant, to the West and South-west of Fontelas. Due to the marked variability of this plateau terrain, none of the larger streams or nearby rivers are used for transport.

[3] I based Map 2 primarily upon the *Carta Corográfica de Portugal na Escala 1/50,000* (1960) compiled by the Instituto Geográfico e Cadastral in Lisbon (IGC 1960). I supplemented this map with a sketch-map of the hamlet's terrain that I drew with the assistance of two of Fontelas' villagers. Map 3 is also based upon two similar sketch-maps. I am grateful to João António Pires and Nelson dos Anjos Pires for their patient help in drawing the initial plans.

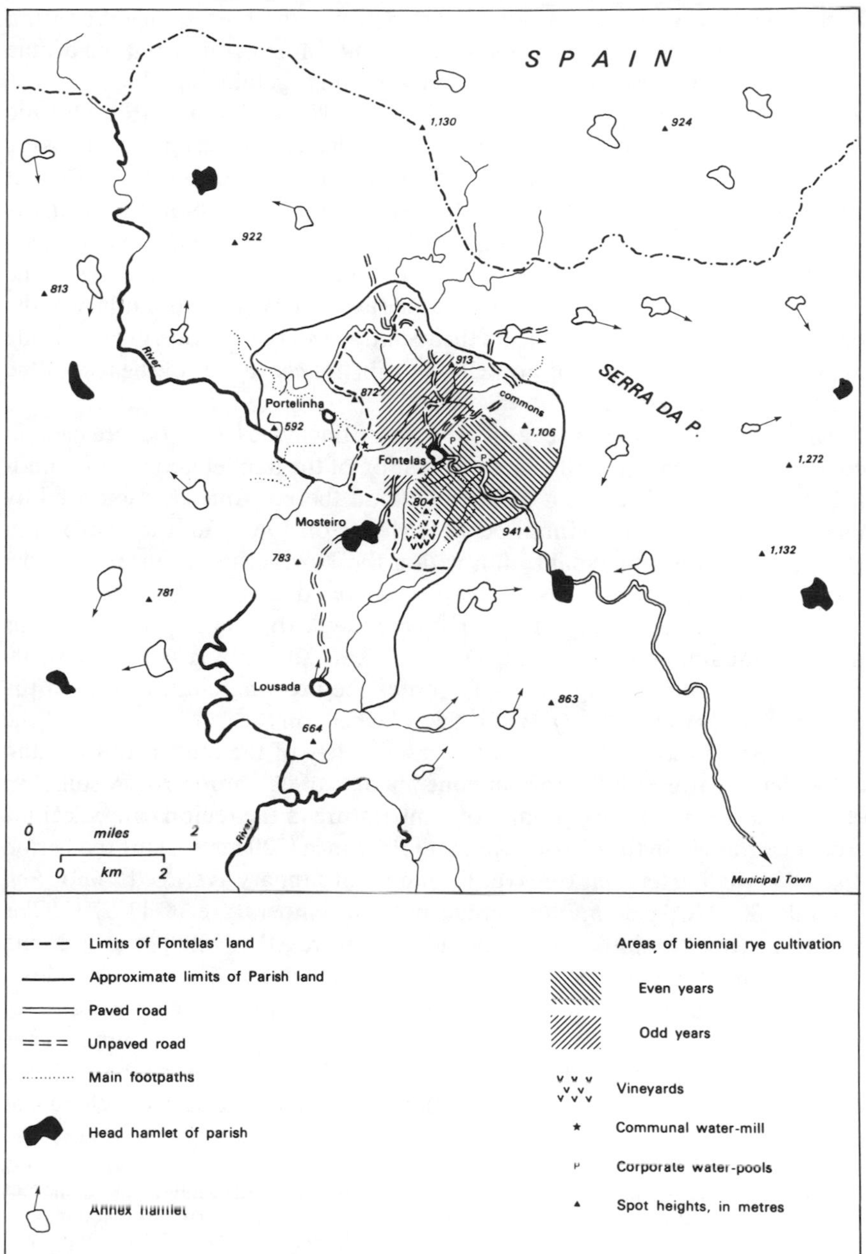

Map 2. Fontelas within its surrounding area

Rather, they serve either as boundaries between the land of neighbouring hamlets and parishes, or for occasional fishing. Most of the irrigated arable fields used for crops such as potatoes, pulses, and vegetables are located close to the hamlet, roughly between the altitudes of 800 and 850 metres. Outside Fontelas' terrain, but only 7 kilometres distant, lies the highest peak in the area – the Serra da P. – at 1,272 metres. Two hamlets lie close to this peak, at altitudes just over 1,000 metres. A few kilometres to the North-east of the Portuguese-Spanish border, four Spanish hamlets lie between 900 and 1,000 metres altitude. The border itself lies 3.7 kilometres North of Fontelas at the closest point. Thus, although the river at the extreme Western boundary of the parish flows in a South-eastern and then South-western direction at an altitude of about 500 metres, most of Fontelas' terrain lies *above* that of the rest of the parish, between 700 and 1,106 metres.

The significance of these altitudes and dimensions can be grasped in connection with the general climatic situation of the hamlet and its surrounding region. Located within a distinctly humid Iberian zone characterized by more than 30 inches of rainfall per year (Houston 1964:136) the hamlet and indeed the entire municipality fall within the Northern section of Trás-os-Montes province known as the *terra fria* (cold land). The *terra fria* is distinguished from the more southerly *terra quente* (hot land) primarily by its more mountainous terrain and higher plateau altitudes (usually over 700 metres). A further distinguishing feature is the predominance of rye on the colder plateaus of the *terra fria* and that of wheat on the warmer plains of the *terra quente*, although this is not the result solely of the higher altitude and colder temperatures of the former zone but also of its poorer, rocky soils. An approximate idea of the extremes of temperature in the region can be gained from recordings[4] in the district capital of Bragança (720 metres) for the period 1938–48. Median temperatures for the month of January averaged 3.66°C and for July 20.18°C, yielding an annual median temperature of 11.57°C. The annual relative humidity for that decade was averaged at 72.3 per cent. Mean annual rainfall in Bragança at the time was 1,184.4 mm. Closer to Fontelas, recordings made in the municipal town[5] registered an average of 63 days of rain per year (1941–8) and a median annual rainfall of 1,095.7 mm. In the 1940s, precipitation ranged from a high of 1,595.7 mm in 1941 to a low of 533.3 mm in 1944. Temperature and rainfall thus characterize the hamlet's climate as

[4] These figures were reported in DGSF (1950:18) – *Posto Meteorológico de Bragança: Médias do Período 1938–1948*. January minimum temperatures for this period averaged 0.30° C and July maximums averaged 27.96° C. Both Ribeiro's and Stanislawski's yearly precipitation maps similarly approximate rainfall in this area of the municipality at 1,000 to 1,500 mm per year (36–54 inches) (Ribeiro 1967: *Mapa II – Precipitação*/Stanislawski 1959: Figure 6 – Yearly Precipitation in the Iberian Peninsula). In addition to these two measurements, Pierre Birot (1950:27) estimates a somewhat lower annual rate of rainfall for the municipality: 700 mm–1 m, with 1 m–2 m (1,000–2,000 mm) estimated further West towards the Minho region.

[5] *Posto Udométrico de M: Resultados das Observações* in DGSF (1950:20).

one influenced more fundamentally by Continental and Atlantic trends than by Mediterranean ones.

These extremes of temperature partly explain the popular saying in the hamlet that the Northern plateaus of Trás-os-Montes suffer *nove meses de inverno e três de inferno* (nine months of winter and three of hell). Summer months are hot and dry, with the exception of occasional thunderstorms, while winter months are cold and wet, accompanied by snowstorms and followed by numerous spring frosts. Interestingly, the *Diccionário Geográfico* of 1758 described the climate of one of Mosteiro's neighbouring parishes as 'freezing, due to the abundance of snow and frosts . . .' The Portuguese geographer Orlando Ribeiro (1967:68) places the altitude limit for the olive-tree ('the best index of the Mediterranean climate') at 600–800 metres. In Fontelas, the only manner in which the few sparse olive-trees in the area are exploited is not for the production of olive oil but for the utility of their branches for the Mass and procession on Palm Sunday. Fontelas thus lies just above Ribeiro's 'olive index' for a Mediterranean climate.[6] Similarly, Ribeiro (1967:71) estimates the altitude limit for vineyards at 800–900 metres in the Northern mountains; the vineyards of Fontelas lie just within this range. Wine production in the *terra fria*, however, is predominantly subsistence-oriented. In general, wine is conserved for household consumption and festive exchanges, and only rarely sold in small surplus quantities. In contrast, one of the prime characteristics of the *terra quente* region further South is its proximity to the Douro river and its large-scale commercial production of Port wine. The classic Mediterranean trio of wheat, wine, and olives is thus absent here, and replaced by the cooler Continental crops of rye, chestnuts, and potatoes.

Throughout this book we shall note a wealth of social and cultural characteristics that echo these fundamental ecological differences between Mediterranean and Central European zones. Whether one adopts a nomenclature based upon Wolf's 'transalpine ecotype' (1966:33–4), Burns' earlier 'circum-Alpine' area (1963), or Laslett's more recent typology of traditional European domestic group organization (1983: 526–7; 1984:360–1) where Fontelas represents a perfect illustration of 'West/central or middle' Europe, it is quite clear that many of the geographical and climatic factors highlighted here are common to other high-altitude regions of Eurasia. Cross-cultural comparisons might be carried even further, along the lines of Rhoades and Thompson's analysis of Alpine environments (1975) and Guillet's comparison of Central Andean and Himalayan mountain ecologies (1983). Within Portugal itself, distinctive regional patterns are evident in geographical, cultural, religious, and political terms, and Rowland's recent demographic

[6] Even as early as 1706, in his *Corografia Portugueza* Carvalho da Costa noted the presence in Fontelas and its higher neighbouring hamlets of rye, butters, wood, and chestnuts. Nearby hamlets at lower altitudes further South were characterized by olive oil, figs, wheat, and hazelnuts.

studies (1984; in press) have detected additional regional distinctions along the same lines. As early as 1955, Dovring (1965: 10–56) had already noted major differences between Southern, Central, and Northwest Iberia with respect to village size, settlement patterns, and farm size, and James Fernandez has reiterated the extreme North/South contrast in rural Spain (1983). Northern Portugal itself cannot be considered a homogeneous ecological zone: there is a profound difference between the Atlantic, maize-oriented Minho province in the North-west and the inland, rye-oriented zone of Trás-os-Montes surrounding Fontelas (Dias 1982 [1948]).

Thus, three decades after both Pitt-Rivers (1954) and Redfield (1956) called attention to the distinctions between Mediterranean and Northwest Iberia with regard to the 'lack of a mystical attitude toward the land' apparent in the Southern portion of the peninsula (Pitt-Rivers 1972:46–7, referred to by Redfield 1973:66), we find exactly the same radical contrast evident between the Southern Portuguese parish studied by Cutileiro (1971) and the Northeastern hamlet described in this book. *Some* kind of enduring historical continuity in regional agrarian systems is obviously at work here. Following both Silverman's elucidative comparison of Central and Southern Italy (1968; 1970) and Macfarlane's discussion of varying regional cultures in Europe (1980a), we should therefore be very careful not to lump Fontelas blindly or prematurely into an inappropriate Mediterranean bag.

Another characteristic of the hamlet's Continental/Atlantic climate is its vegetation. Four major types of tree are common in the area. The most important of these is the sweet chestnut, or *castanheiro*.[7] This deciduous tree is well suited to the cold climate of plateaus and mountains. It is of fundamental significance in the hamlet economy, as it provides large quantities of chestnuts which are used primarily for sale in the autumn, as well as for the fattening of pigs in the winter. Leaves from chestnut-trees and other trees are frequently used to supplement manure compost mixtures within animal stables, as the proper manuring of arable fields is an extremely important element in the hamlet economy and of constant concern to most households. The second type of tree common in the area is the black-oak.[8] This tree provides a source of firewood, leaves, and small quantities of acorns used as feed for pigs. Also present, although in lesser numbers, is the Portuguese oak.[9] Notably uncommon or absent in the area are the holm-oak or evergreen oak and the

[7] Tree names are derived from my field notes, while their corresponding Latin names (see Glossary) are derived from a detailed study of the Northern part of the municipality (DGSF 1950) and a regional geography of Northern Trás-os-Montes (Taborda 1932). These local studies were checked with more general and recent geographical studies of Portugal: Admiralty (1942), Birot (1950), Houston (1964), Ribeiro (1967), Stanislawski (1959), and Way (1962).

[8] *Carvalho da Beira/carvalho negral*: Houston terms this species *Quercus pyrenaica* (1964:98). Stanislawski, however, terms the *Quercus tozza* the Pyrenees Oak, usually found at altitudes of over 1,300 feet (1959:60).

[9] *Carvalho português/carvalho velano* (see Glossary).

cork-oak,[10] both considered as Mediterranean species and more common in warmer zones of permanent foliage or zones of transition between deciduous and non-deciduous vegetation.

Two further types of tree found in the area are the walnut-tree and the cluster pine or maritime pine.[11] Walnut-trees are far less common in the hamlet than chestnut-trees but are highly valued due to the excellent prices offered villagers for their autumn walnuts. Their rarity is attested to by the absence of a term denoting a 'grove of walnut-trees' (*nogueiral*) in the hamlet, in comparison with the large number of *soutos* and *touças* (groves of chestnut-trees) in Fontelas' terrain. These groves are owned by households of all economic levels. However, many of the hamlet's poorer households own no groves at all. Many of these families follow the custom of collecting both chestnuts and walnuts *ao rebusco*, or those 'remaindered' and left underneath wealthier households' trees after their own collection.[12] Pines are a fourth type of tree common in the area. Most of the pines within the hamlet's terrain are not natural to the region but were planted during the government's reforestation programme in the 1950s.

Further types of trees and vegetation in the hamlet include the *olmo* (elm) and *negrilho* (black poplar), usually found along the margins of roads, within the hamlet, and on the borders of meadows. The *freixo* (ash) is also found in and around meadows. The wood from both black poplar and ash trees is used in the region for the construction of ox-carts. The leaves of the black poplar are particularly valued as green feed for pigs, and women can frequently be seen climbing to the higher branches of these trees with numerous sacks to fill.[13] Also found are the *amieiro* (alder), *salgueiro* (willow), *choupo branco* (white or silver poplar) and a number of fruit trees. Further, a variety of rough shrubs are found in hedges and along the banks of streams. The most common of these shrubs is the prickly *silva*, or bramble. A wide variety of wild shrub species (types of furze, gorse, broom, and cistus) are found on the higher common-land (see below), all of which are exploited in different ways for pasturage, firewood, and manure mixtures. All of these kinds of trees and shrubs thus

[10] *Azinheira* (holm-oak/evergreen oak) and *sobreiro* (cork-oak).

[11] *Nogueira* (walnut-tree) and *Pinheiro bravo* (cluster pine/maritime pine). Houston terms the *Pinus pinaster* both 'cluster pine' and 'maritime pine', and mentions the latter as a planted species in humid zones and the former as present with the oak in Northern Portuguese mountain zones (1964:94, 98).

[12] An interesting practice in a nearby hamlet was mentioned to me with regard to firewood and chestnuts. Firewood for the November 1st *magusto* celebration of roasting chestnuts was customarily taken from the wood-piles of the household with the most wood. This is one of many instances in the region wherein the symbolic redistribution of goods and resources could be interpreted as an indication of prior social and economic inequalities. A similar 'redistribution' occurs on Shrove Tuesday in Fontelas, when a group of masked men and boys go around the hamlet playing music and asking for donations of sausages, eggs, and money (Photo 22).

[13] This is only one of many tasks that emphasize the close connection between women and pigs in the hamlet, in contrast with that between men and cattle.

denote a region characterized by inland, mountain forms of vegetation rather than coastal, Mediterranean ones.

It would be an exaggeration to describe the soil of the hamlet's land as simply 'poor and infertile' without qualifying to what degree this is true and in what sense the quality of soil(s) within the hamlet's terrain is uniform or not. Most of the soil surrounding the hamlet is composed of argillaceous (clayey) schists of both archaic-precambrian and silurian formations.[14] To the South of Fontelas lies a zone of the municipality composed predominantly of archaic and precambrian geological formations, while a few kilometres to the North-west and North-east of Fontelas lie two areas of granite intrusion within the terrain of two neighbouring parishes. The hamlet itself is situated between these two regions, within a primarily silurian schist zone. This is apparent, for example, in the composition of the soils of the portions of common-land pertaining to Fontelas, which were described in 1939 (JCI 1939) as 'clayey-sandy schists'. The top-soil in Fontelas' terrain is relatively thin, impermeable, and stony, thus providing difficulties for cultivation due both to its compactness and to the quantities of rock fragments distributed throughout it. While rich in potassium, this type of soil suffers deficiencies of lime and phosphoric acid, two elements essential to fertile land. Soil erosion is a furtheı problem in this humid region. The kind of breaking plough (*arado*) suited to this North-eastern ecological zone has been termed the 'Lusitanian radial' type, as distinct from the two other main types of plough in Portugal – a 'Germanic/Slavic' one in the Atlantic Northwest and the *garganta* type in Mediterranean Southern Portugal (Dias 1982 [1948]; Veiga de Oliveira *et al* 1976: 139–207). A turning mouldboard plough (*charrua*) is also used in Fontelas. Both Portuguese words recall both the medieval Latin *aratrum* and *caruca*, as well as the French *araire* and *charrue* (Smith 1969:200).

As the terrain of the hamlet is so varied, however, the generally poor quality of its soils should not obscure the varied uses to which different plots of land are put. As stated earlier, numerous streams run through the hamlet's terrain and the irrigated soil around these streams is invariably fertile and highly valued. This land is usually devoted to meadows, providing pasturage and hay for cattle. Small sections within these meadows are frequently converted for producing irrigated crops of vegetables and pulses. At the other extreme, high above the hamlet, lie vast expanses of rocky common-land, whose worse sections are suitable only for winter pasturage or for the collection of stones for house construction. Where possible, an occasional plot in this nearly barren land is cleared for the cultivation of rye grain, although this can be a difficult task requiring tractors and bulldozers for the removal of larger stones and boulders. The hamlet's terrain thus follows a general course from the higher

[14] This analysis relies primarily upon the following local studies: DGSF (1950), Taborda (1932), and JCI (1939). The information in all of these studies was checked with more general geographical studies (see Note 7).

reaches of dry common-land through the middle range of arable fields to the lower areas of fertile meadows.

The specific geological and climatic situation of Fontelas to a great extent explain its form of mixed agricultural and pastoral economy. Much of the higher, thinner soil in the hamlet is devoted to dry farming of rye grain. Both the two-course crop rotation system (see below) as well as communal restrictions on individual field enclosures indicate an emphasis upon livestock and grazing-land over land devoted to tillage. The reforestation program beginning in the 1950s has recently contributed to a general reduction of the sizes of the hamlet's flocks of sheep and goats, and to a greater emphasis on arable farming. Despite its mountainous terrain then, agriculture remains very much a continuing way of life for these villagers. But this hilly relief has also placed outer limits upon the consolidation of dispersed plots and the use of large tractors: many villagers stress that small tractors would be more suitable on the more inclined slopes and fields. The hamlet's terrain is thus neither at one extreme Alpine, nor at the other a level plain.

This topography does nevertheless impose constraints upon the possible development of commercial monoculture, and this is markedly attested to by the current system of subsistence *polyculture*. In Fontelas a wide variety of crops is produced primarily for human consumption, animal fodder, and internal hamlet exchanges. Historically, the hamlet has been situated between two of three major local fortifications marking the Northern border of Portugal, each one constructed around a castle. The castles, as well as the mountains separating Portugal from Spain, further denote the region's remote and marginal position. The geographer Vergílio Taborda has emphasized this physical isolation of the Northern plateaus of Trás-os-Montes:

> . . . mountains and hilly plateaus, a rigorous climate of cold winters and hot summers . . . an agricultural and a pastoral economy balancing each other, assisted by the large expanses of natural meadows; an agricultural cycle marked by the predominant crops of rye and the potato; slow and difficult transport routes; a low density of population, composed of small and medium cultivators, leading a primitive life, almost closed to external influences: these are the general aspects of the northern trasmontane region (Taborda 1932:5; my translation).

Similarly, Pierre Birot's map of 'Agrarian Systems and Land Use' in Portugal characterizes the North-west Minho region of Portugal (Map 1) as a maize-producing area, and the Southern Alentejo region as one of 'wheat and olive-trees, covering extensive areas owned by one landowner' (Birot 1950:216–17). But the Northern border region around Fontelas is classified in purely negative terms: it is a *zona inculta* or simply an 'uncultivated zone'.

Finally, a note on peasant 'smallholdings'. Can peasant production in this part of Trás-os-Montes be characterized by the term 'small family farms'? The materials presented and analysed in this book will reveal precisely how, given adequate ethnographic and historical documentation, such a term is entirely inappropriate on three counts.

Firstly, many of this hamlet's 'smallholdings' are in fact quite large in comparative context, given the *extensive* nature of rye cultivation in the area. Further, very large expanses of common-land are devoted to pasturage. While no landholding in the hamlet exceeds 51 hectares in total area, there are four holdings of over 35 hectares, all with substantial amounts of land either uncultivated or rented out to other villagers. In local terms, these large holdings of over 30 hectares are considered enormous. Furthermore, although inheritance is partible between all heirs of both sexes, individual plots are not in all cases divided into successively smaller strips: whole fields of similar value but different sizes are frequently distributed to different heirs (see Chapter 7). This avoids successive partitions of fields into progressively smaller sub-plots. As set forth in Chapter 3, specific measurements of the hamlet's landholdings indicate that neither all nor even most of its farming units are considered by local standards to be 'small', and that it would be a simplification to state that landholdings become progressively minuscule as a result of successive inheritance partitions (see Davis 1973).

Secondly, domestic groups in Fontelas are not necessarily 'family' groups. Many households have historically been composed of small, fragmented, non-nuclear domestic groups of day-labourers working for wages on other villagers' holdings. Other households have had complex and extended stem family structures (Laslett 1972:16–23) with large numbers of resident servants. Mary Bouquet (1982; 1984a; 1984b) has also, in a rather different vein, discussed at length the positions of servants and visitors in Southern England, treating the various meanings of the terms 'family', 'farm', and 'family farm' with great caution. Finally, other households in the hamlet today consist of solitary individuals supported not by their family on the holding but by monetary remittances sent from relatives permanently resident in France. Thus, many of the holdings in the hamlet are too small to support a family group of any size, while some holdings are large enough to support a number of 'families' and employ permanent servants and occasional day-labourers. The term 'small *family* farms' is thus misleading as it implies a uniform nuclear domestic group and a particularly vague notion of the meaning of the word 'family'.

Thirdly, with the exception of a few wealthy, enterprising tractor-owners, landholdings in Fontelas today are not *farms* at all in the sense of being geared towards commercial production of cash crops for the market. I will suggest in Chapter 3, therefore, that these holdings are not uniformly small. Later chapters will show that they are neither farms in the technical sense, nor worked exclusively by family groups. Under the microscope, as it were, these landholdings are clearly not 'small family farms' in any sense.

Nevertheless, regional geographical surveys must of necessity generalize: when compared with the Alentejo region characterized by large *latifúndia* estates of over 500 hectares (Cutileiro 1971:7, 42) Trás-os-Montes must clearly be termed a region of relatively small landholdings. Although Trás-os-Montes is generally referred to as a zone of *minifúndio* smallholdings (Cabral 1978; Rutledge 1977:85) it would be excessive to refer to these holdings as 'microfundia' – a term used by René Dumont (1964:216) for holdings of less than 1/40 acre in Galician Spain. The Galician region of Spain, to the North-west of Fontelas, is also a region of so-called smallholdings. One anecdote from that region states that 'one man's tethered cow will fertilize another man's crops' (Houston 1964:218). The same saying is also known in the Minho region of Portugal to the West of Trás-os-Montes (Birot 1950:68). Further definitions of the *minifúndio*, apart from contrasting it with the *latifundium*, are not standard. The geographer Ruth Way quotes a Spanish census of 1930 which terms *minifúndia* as farms containing less than 2½ acres of land (1962:105), while herself referring to Galician *minifúndia* as 'tiny farms of from two to six acres' (1962:192). Way offers an explanation for the minute Galician subdivisions in 'the ancient Celtic law of equal distribution of land to inheriting sons' (1962:105). Houston has similarly noted the 'tattered patchwork of open field ownership' of the 'excessive *minifúndia*' of the Northern Portuguese and Castilian regions and has linked this pattern of landholdings to gavelkind or equal inheritance among all heirs, as distinct from the Basque practice of primogeniture (Houston 1964: 218–19). No agreement on the precise meaning of the term *minifúndio* is evident among the British geographers of Northern Spain and Portugal. In very general terms, *minifúndio* smallholdings are contrasted with their contraries (*latifúndia* estates) and tend to characterize the mountain and plateau regions of Northern and Central Iberia. It is only from this very generalized perspective, then, that Fontelas' landholdings should be seen as 'smallholdings'.

Fontelas itself is quite a small hamlet. In mid-1977 it had a total population of 187 people in 57 resident households. Most of its houses are grouped into densely nucleated sections called *bairros* (Map 3). There are 11 such named sections spread throughout the hamlet and within each section many houses are physically connected one to another, their walls providing the only separation between the distinct rooms of each adjoining house. With the exception of the five wealthiest houses whose kitchens are spatially removed from the hamlet paths by large courtyards, most smaller houses lie very close to the main thoroughfares. Simply opening their front doors, most villagers reveal their kitchens and living rooms immediately to anyone standing outside in the street (Photo 10). Animal stables are located on the lower street-level of each house, and the main living quarters for villagers on the floor above the stables (Photo 2). Older houses are built of stone, while newer ones are built of brick with their outside walls painted. The interiors of these older houses are quite dark, and the walls and ceilings of their kitchens are usually pitch-black (Photo 3). Hearth fires are kept going throughout most seasons of the year for cooking and heating, and from November through March large portions of salted pork and sausages are smoke-dried above the fireplace.

Houses are so densely huddled that it is virtually impossible to obtain much

2 Old-style house built in stone, with stables on the ground floor and living quarters above.

3 Hearth inside a *lavrador* household.

privacy at any time, and within each section villagers can hear the conversations and watch the activities of their neighbours with great ease. At the Western end of the hamlet lies the cemetery and one of the two small shops (Map 3): the main shop is located on the Eastern end in the *Castelo* section. Both stores are rather dilapidated, musty, and damp in the winter and both also have adjoining rooms that serve as drinking *tabernas*. Neither *taberna* is really a café in any sense, and a few short wooden stools provide the only seating arrangements. The stores are considered to be rather hopeless local supply-shops: women will only purchase an occasional loaf of bread or other household items in them when a trip to town cannot be arranged. The shop on the Eastern side of the hamlet lies opposite the bus-stop: a bus arrives twice in Fontelas each day from the municipal town (a ½-hour ride) and the district city of Bragança (1½ hours).

A closer look at Map 3 shows that many garden plots and threshing-floors lie within this central area of the hamlet. Here many villagers plant household vegetables, construct their grain-stacks and straw-stacks, and let their numerous pigs forage. The main road passing through the upper part of the hamlet was only recently paved (1976) and the remaining paths running through the lower sections are throughout most of the winter veritable quagmires of mud and slush. Some paths leave barely enough room between their walls on either side for an ox-cart to squeeze through. Fontelas thus exhibits all of the features of a classic 'backward' rural community. In 1976–8 it had no electricity, the schoolhouse is located within the schoolteacher's own house in a converted stable (Household 39 on Map 3) and there are only five manual 'crank' telephones in the hamlet. (I will refer to households from now on with my numbering system: H39, H40, etc: see Appendix IV.) The main telephone is in the priest's house (H29) so that in order to reach any of the other four extensions, outside calls must first pass through the priest's phone. His household is the only one in the hamlet with a car (although the bus-driver, a temporary resident, also has one), and also the only one with a functioning television (run by batteries). There are no household industries of any kind in Fontelas. The hamlet's sole blacksmith works only sporadically during the winter months. A former carpenter (currently the hamlet's drunkard) now works for wages at wealthier households' harvests but his 'days' of wage labour rarely last past lunchtime. Only half of the community's households have running water: the rest must fetch water from natural springs or a few taps distributed throughout the hamlet. Washing is done in public water-tanks, one of which I have shown on Map 3 in the centre of Fontelas.

At the outer extremes of the hamlet, beyond the area shown on Map 3, lie the houses of the Forest Guard (North-west) and the stone-mason (South-east), both of whom are non-native residents of Fontelas. Well before reaching these two houses, the central area of the hamlet blends quickly into its surrounding fields and meadows. The dense crowding within the hamlet's huddled sections contrasts sharply with the vast expanses of open fields, stretching for kilometres beyond the hamlet like a distorted chessboard of squares and rectangles. It is here that most of the villagers' time is spent. Out in these fields, only an occasional shout or the penetrating screech of an ox-cart wheel break the monotonous sighs of the wind.

About 14 kilometres to the South-east of Fontelas lies the municipal town, where villagers sell their livestock, shop, pay fees, and obtain much of the machinery and equipment needed for their household-oriented agriculture. The town serves the 34 parishes which comprise the municipality, whose total population in 1970 (INE 1970) was 18,122. This population is distributed throughout the municipality's 95 hamlets. The town itself is rather like an overgrown village, and its population in 1970 was 2,376. It boasts a court, a Town Council, a Tax Bureau, a Civil Registry Office, two secondary schools, a seminary, a few 'noble' houses with coats-of-arms and adjoining chapels, and a variety of other administrative bodies. The 'old quarter' of the town consists of a few narrow, winding streets leading up to the remains of a medieval castle. Many townsfolk themselves consider their town the only local bastion of pseudo-urbanism amidst a vast sea of hopelessly backward peasant hamlets. Yet the entire municipality of 95 hamlets is dependent solely on the town's two doctors and its aging *Misericórdia* hospital. The latter establishment is really a kind of religious welfare institution where villagers are convinced that people only go to die in relative peace. Many peasants simply bypass the town doctors altogether in urgent situations, and go straight to the newly built hospital in the district capital of Bragança.

Although a market (*feira*) is held in the town every two weeks, none of Fontelas' villagers ever sell agricultural produce there. The markets (also a kind of fair) are occasions either to sell livestock, purchase household items, or merely to escape the tedious rural rhythms of work for a leisurely afternoon. These are the days when villagers tend to combine various errands and when they pay their taxes, obtain official certificates, consult a lawyer, or merely amble along the town's main road viewing the many stalls of commercial goods. By late afternoon, the market closes down and by early evening most villagers have completed the short $\frac{1}{2}$-hour bus ride back to Fontelas. After these spring and summer fairs, by the next morning they will be out in the fields again, perhaps as early as 5 or 6 a.m.

The earliest documents to mention Fontelas reveal that it has for quite some time been a very *small* settlement. Table 1 sets forth the population of Fontelas at various dates since 1796, and clearly shows that the hamlet has maintained a population well below 300 inhabitants for most of this period. At the end of the nineteenth century, a particularly good series of parish listings recorded the total number of 'hearths' and 'souls' in the hamlet. As children under the age of first confession were not recorded in the listings, to these figures should be added an estimate of the total number of unrecorded children under the age of

Table 1. *Population of Fontelas since 1796*

Date	Households	Population	Observations
1796	40	181	Not stated whether children were included
1834	39	134	
1886	51	168	Not including children under 8
1888	49	157	
1891	52	182	
1892	53	179	
1894	49	160	
1895	44	153	
1896	45	159	
1898	46	154	
1899	46	159	
1902	50	184	
1905	47	172	
1906	47	167	
1907	47	177	
1908	44	184	
1909	42	173	
1911*	48	229	Including children
1940*	68	241	
1960*	82	284	
1977	57	187	

* These were the only three National Censuses since the first in 1864 to record hamlet and village population and not merely parish totals.

Sources (see Bibliography):
1796 – Ribeiro de Castro
1834 – Carmo
1886–1909 Confessional Rolls
1911–1960 National Censuses (INE 1911–)
1977 – Author's Household Census

8. During this period (1886–1909) Fontelas' population thus hovered around 200.

Following 1964, a massive wave of emigration surged from this region as a whole – large groups of villagers from Fontelas and other neighbouring hamlets emigrated to France and West Germany. The initial effects of this emigration are evident in the hamlet today. New houses are being built with emigrants' remittances, more cash is in circulation within the community, and patterns of conspicuous consumption and extroverted dress styles dominate the month of August each year when most emigrants return temporarily to Fontelas. While an important recent development, emigration has nevertheless not entirely overturned Fontelas' social hierarchy, as we will see in subsequent chapters. One general trend that emigration has reinforced, however, has been the removal of a large number of people from the hamlet with a consequent relaxation of the delicate balance between population and the land. The demographic figures for the parish as a whole[15] also reveal this dramatic decline in resident population. Between 1960 and 1970, the total parish population of 973 dropped abruptly to 566. This constituted a reduction of 42 per cent (INE 1960/1970). In sum then, Fontelas constitutes a conspicuously small unit of population, dedicated entirely to small-scale agriculture and livestock breeding.

The following materials on the five major types of land in Fontelas will help to provide a general view of the ways in which it is cultivated and spatially situated. I have divided the land into five major categories for consideration here: (1) the open fields devoted to rye cultivation, (2) common-land, (3) irrigated meadows, (4) kitchen-gardens, and (5) vineyards. The bulk of this chapter deals with the first two.

The open fields

The great majority of the hamlet's arable land is devoted to dry farming of rye. The system of cultivation followed is that of biennial rotation (*afolhamento bienal*), known also as two-course rotation. The arable land of the hamlet is divided into two sides or courses termed *folhas* (literally 'leaves' or 'pages'). One of these sides lies to the South-east of the hamlet and the other to the North-west (Map 2), one being sown with rye each year while the other remains fallow. For example, in November of 1975 the South-east side was sown with rye. This grain was reaped in June, transported from the fields in July (Photo 9), and threshed in August. From the time the tied sheaves of grain are transported (July 1976) from the fields to each household's threshing-floor, the plots remain fallow for one year and four months until they are sown again

[15] The total parish population (4 hamlets) reported in all of the major National Censuses was as follows:

Year	*Households*	*Population*	*Men*	*Women*
1864	120	607	297	310
1878	139	615	290	325
1890	168	704	342	362
1900	160	724	361	363
1911	151	698	333	365
1920	152	654	312	342
1930	160	734	369	365
1940	188	779	–	–
1950	183	807	424	383
1960	259	973	486	487
1970	162	566	273	293

Source: INE (1864–1970)

(November 1977) with the grain to be reaped in the following spring (June 1978). Once the fields on one side of the hamlet are sown this side is termed a *faceira*, while the area left fallow (the opposite side) is said to lie in *pousio*. The North-west side follows the same pattern in alternating years: while the South-east side remained fallow from July 1976 through November 1977, the North-west side was sown with rye in November 1976 and reaped in June 1977. This side thus remained fallow also for one year and four months from July 1977 through November 1978.

A regular alternating pattern is followed in this fashion every other year. The South-east area is sown in odd years (1975/1977) and reaped in even ones (1976/1978) while the reverse pattern is followed on the North-west side. One half of the hamlet's total arable land devoted to grain is in this way under continual cultivation, and fields are only given a longer period of more permanent fallow after their production declines following 7 to 8 years of constant use. (Actually, the South-east side contains slightly more than half of the total number of grain fields, and we shall see below that seed yields on this side are higher.) During this period of long-term fallow, the plots are left uncultivated and their shrub growth is used for firewood and manure compost mixtures.

A crucial element of this biennial rotation system is its close relation to the practice of collective stubble-grazing. It is stubble-grazing, not the alternating years of fallow, that gives this system the name of 'open-field' cultivation. From the date in July when the sheaves of grain are removed from the fields, any household's flocks of sheep (or goats) are allowed free access to the cut stalks of stubble (*restolho*) remaining after the grain has been reaped (Photos 9 and 12). This stubble can vary in height from 6–12 inches, depending on the deepness of the particular field's furrows and on the height at which the reapers' sickles cut the stalks.[16] The amount of stubble in a specific plot can of course vary with the amount of grain sown and the seed-yield ratio in any one year, but in general most fields provide an important source of nourishment for sheep and the smaller numbers of goats kept in the hamlet. Significantly, Marc Bloch has noted that this system of open fields common to Southern Europe 'was not a regime based of set purpose on individual initiative' (1978:49) because enclosures of individual fields by walls, fences, or hedges were not permitted. Some uniformity of timing in crop rotation had to be followed by villagers in order to leave a certain amount of terrain open (the two alternating *folhas* in this case) for the grazing of their own and others' flocks.

[16] Marc Bloch makes the very apt point that in certain open-field regions of eighteenth-century France, scythes were prohibited from being used to reap grain fields as the stubble would be cut much shorter than with sickles, thus reducing the amount of straw stubble available for free collection (right of gleaning) by other villagers after the harvest (1978:47). Scythes in Fontelas are used exclusively for cutting meadow grass (*erva*) and green rye fodder (*ferrã*), never for reaping the stalks of grain.

The only markers used to separate fields partitioned through inheritance are boundary stones (*marcos*) placed at the imaginary visual borderlines between adjacent plots. The fields remain in this sense 'open'.

The right of stubble-grazing is a prime example of collective constraints upon individual land use. Flocks graze not only on the higher common-land, but also upon roughly half of the hamlet's unirrigated arable land each year. Optimal grazing takes place directly following the June reapings when the stubble is most abundant, and continues through the autumn months. After this, the winter season and the first ploughings of the grain fields in February/March reduce the amounts of weeds and other spontaneous growth. However, flocks may freely graze on the open fallow fields from July through November of the following year when the fields are sown again, although by the second July they will have begun to graze on the stubble of the newly reaped fields on the opposite side. Exceptions to this pattern are the odd field sown in the wrong year – i.e., a grain field sown on the side left fallow that year. In these cases, the owners/users of these fields place a wooden stake with a handful of straw on its tip in the middle of the field, in order to warn shepherds that the field has been sown and to prevent grazing. (Recently some villagers have replaced the straw on the top of the stake with plastic bags, but the effect is the same.) Private rights in the grain fields, however, are no less rigid after the fields are sown than are grazing rights during the fallow period. This is understandable, as the land itself is owned individually, stubble-grazing thus being only a form of partial, temporary usufruct of a portion of the produce in the fields. In other words, what is operative here is a pattern of *alternating* individual and communal usufruct rights in the same field at different points in the agricultural year. Penalties are high for grazing on sown fields at whatever date: either on fields newly sown in the autumn or on fields with green rye fodder in the spring. Republican Guards (*guardas-republicanos*) stationed in the municipal town regularly patrol the hamlets and impose fines on shepherds found grazing their flocks within sown fields, while households without flocks level continual criticism against the abuses of some of the hamlet's shepherds.[17] A number of families (only 12 of 57 households own flocks of sheep) thus regard the 'collective' right to graze animals on the open fields as merely an occasion for the shepherds' 'individualist' abuse of their own sown land.

The preceding description may be clarified further by looking briefly at some of the wider geographical contexts and historical background of open-

[17] The distinction between customary law and the administrative law of the Portuguese Civil Code is not always clear. A lawyer in town clarified the custom of stubble-grazing by citing the abolition of common pasturage on grain fields in Article 2264 of the 1867 Civil Code: in strictly legal terms, permission for grazing on private grain fields must be granted through a written contract between the owner of the plot and the shepherd. Nevertheless, when I put the question to a number of the larger landowners in Fontelas, they responded that neither landowners nor shepherds bother to make written contracts and that on stubble and fallow fields, 'we let them graze'.

field cultivation. One basic characteristic of these open fields, for example, is that they do not take the form of narrow 'strip-fields' common to other areas of open-field cultivation in Central Europe. Grain fields in Fontelas are universally of a square or rectangular shape, many single fields attaining sizes of almost 1 hectare. The largest single grain plot in the hamlet was estimated at 2.9 hectares in area. There does not seem to be any evidence of a shift from two-course to three-course rotation of crops in Fontelas.[18] A three-course system of crop rotation would allow for a greater annual production of grains (the main grains rye and wheat, as well as the lesser barley and oats) but would reduce the area of stubble available for grazing to 1/3 rather than 1/2 of the total dry arable land. Two-course rotation requires a more extensive use of larger portions of land (due to poor and thin soil, hilly terrain, and lower seed yields) than the somewhat more intensive three-course rotation. The latter form of cultivation (also an open-field system) derives its name from the division of the arable area into three courses: the first course being sown with a 'winter corn' of either rye or wheat, the second with a 'spring corn' of either barley or oats, while the third course remains fallow. Each course produces grain for two successive years before reverting to fallow, and 2/3 of the village's grain fields are under cultivation each year. Thus Pounds states that 'conservatism or ignorance' do not account for peasants' failure to adopt three-course rotation systems, but rather that this course of action is firmly blocked by 'the constraints imposed by communal organization . . . and above all the traditional rights of *vaine pâture* . . .' (Pounds 1979:177). In the case of Fontelas, the persistence of a two-course system of cultivation is as much an indication of the emphasis upon retaining community rights in a large area of open grazing land each year as it is of the poor quality of the hamlet's soils. For instance, villagers stressed that manure supplies fall far short of covering all or even the majority of a household's rye grain fields and must be saved for potato plots. Further, it appears to be high altitude – not lack of precipitation – that militates against the cultivation of much maize, wheat, barley, and oats on such infertile soils.

[18] For a detailed analysis of the structure of strip-fields see C.T. Smith (1969:191–259) – Chapter 4 'Agrarian Structures and Field Systems Before 1800', and also Marc Bloch (1978:35–48) and G. East (1966:100–5). For descriptions of the three-course rotation system, see the authors cited above as well as Braudel (1973:74–7), Slicher Van Bath (1963:58–62), and Pounds (1979:35, 175). See also Lynn White's detailed and forceful discussion of the crucial evolutionary shift from two-course to three-course systems: 'The three-field system of crop rotation has been called "the greatest agricultural novelty of the Middle Ages in Western Europe"' (1964:69). White also calls attention to '. . . the practical difficulties of switching a village from the biennial to the triennial rotation. We know of a few cases in which it took place, but unless an entirely new third field could be asserted, or unless by sheer accident individual holdings were so arranged that what had been two could now be cut into three without drastic reallotment of strips, such a change must have run into the opposition of vested rights' (1964:73). The absence of any evidence of such a shift in Fontelas in recent times cannot of course be generalized to other areas of Trás-os-Montes or the Minho province.

Two essential elements of the structure of landholdings in Fontelas are conditioned by the system of open-field rye cultivation described here. The first of these is the 'archaic' nature of two-course rotation, and the second is the central role of rye grain in the hamlet's cycle of production and exchange. Concerning the first point, J. M. Houston describes the open-field system of Trás-os-Montes and Central Spain in terms of survivals:

> A third and the most characteristic system of the Meseta is the collective, biennial rotation of the open fields. This champagne landscape stretches from Trás-os-Montes (which still cultivates over one half of Portugal's common lands) and Beira, throughout Old Castile, and into Aragón and New Castile. Numerous survivals of this agro-pastoral economy have been described. This obligatory biennial rotation grouped the individual holdings into large fields and sometimes the whole area of the commune might be divided into large blocks (Houston 1964:220).

At two other points in his detailed geography, Houston speaks of 'archaic and extensive systems of land use' in the Iberian peninsula, and of the 'rigid conservatism' of the open-field system (1964:126, 221). Houston does not, however, ascribe to theories of the proto-historic origins of the open fields, and emphatically stresses the stamp of municipal authority upon open-field landscapes. He links the open fields to population increase, an intensification of agricultural production, firm divisions between arable and pasture tracts, and the employment of municipal guards to regulate these divisions (1964:221). Both Slicher Van Bath and C. T. Smith also stress, respectively, the dangers of viewing the open-field system or stubble-grazing as expressions of any 'ancient community spirit' (Slicher Van Bath 1963:62) or as a distinctive rural economy 'introduced almost ready-made by a particular culture in prehistory or in the Dark Ages by Celtic, Gallo-Roman or Teutonic influence' (Smith 1969:223). All of the authors quoted present evidence for a later, medieval development of open-field systems of cultivation.

In his classic, detailed study *French Rural History* (1931), Marc Bloch set forth a classification of open-field systems into two broad types. One system, or *régime agraire*, was the Northern one, which was not limited to France but extended throughout Europe and parts of the Mediterranean area. It was characterized by the wheeled plough, long-furlong open fields (strip-fields), and strict collective regulation of both stubble-grazing and triennial crop rotation. Bloch termed the second system the 'Southern type' because it encompassed parts of Southern France and the Mediterranean region. This second system included the features of the wooden plough (*aratrum*), irregular open fields of a square or rectangular shape, and a biennial crop rotation. Bloch suggested no rigid or causal connection between these elements however, and stated that, as in the case of dialect boundaries, 'there are no geographical areas whose limits are exactly coterminous with one particular set of agrarian forms and techniques' (1978:62). A third system, distinct from both types of open-field systems, was that of the enclosures,[19] although again Bloch speaks of this system in broad but not rigid geographical terms: he avoids posing the dichotomy of 'collectivist' open-field systems versus 'individualist' enclosures.[20]

Bloch maintains that both of the two open-field systems he describes are always found in association with collective obligations, of which a number of illustrations will be presented in Chapter 4. Despite these obligations and the wide variety of forms of corporate and communal property in the hamlet, I will demonstrate that no necessary connection exists between collective property or collective obligations and an egalitarian social structure. Firm distinctions must be made in each specific case of 'collective' forms of property or labour, and between truly 'communal' and merely semi-communal institutions. On the one hand there are forms of communal property and communal labour pertaining to or executed by the *totality* of members of the community, and on the other hand corporate property and cooperative labour pertaining to or executed by only a *portion* of the members of that community. The two are frequently confused.

Furthermore, forms of communal property and corporate ownership of resources can *co-exist* with systems of social hierarchy and economic stratification. Bloch noted for the long-furlong open-field system that 'both rich and poor certainly observed their communal obligations, but they were not on an equal footing . . . rural society was composed of clearly defined classes' (1978:47–8). To subsume *all* forms of communal and corporate obligations and activities under the same wide category of 'communal cooperation', as Bennema (1978) has suggested for another hamlet in Trás-os-Montes, may only further obscure the issue and revive the image of the archaic collectivist community. Ample evidence from local historical records will demonstrate that forms of social and economic hierarchy and inequality have characterized this hamlet throughout the eighteenth, nineteenth and twentieth centuries. This evidence does not contradict the results of other empirical studies of Iberian communities which stress continuity in corporate and communal traditions (Freeman, *et al*). Rather, as the data in Chapter 4 show quite clearly, the fallacy here is in our conceptual polarization of social structures as entirely 'egalitarian' or 'hierarchical' in the first place. While they indicate communal rights in *portions* of the hamlet's land, open fields and stubble-grazing do not necessarily have anything to do with equality.

[19] Smith proposes a similar classification for the three major field-system areas of Western Europe: (a) the Atlantic or Celtic system, (b) the open-field, Midland, or *champion* system, and (c) the Mediterranean system (1969:196).

[20] Shades of an embryonic structuralism, however, are evident in one comment of Bloch's concerning the enclosures in North-west France. Speaking of fences, hedges, and in the case of Brittany and Quercy of dry stone walls '. . . which turned the countryside into one huge chequer-board', Bloch states that: 'As in the regions of open-fields, these material manifestations were the outward expression of underlying social realities' (1978:57).

The second element of the open-field system of special interest here is the extremely varied role of rye grain within the hamlet economy. Rye performs a multiplicity of functions throughout the agricultural cycle in Fontelas. As it is a staple in the hamlet diet, the process of production of rye encompasses more tasks and more labour input than any other crop. The major tasks to be carried out include first and second ploughings of the fallow fields (winter and spring), a third ploughing and sowing in the autumn, harrowing, reaping, transporting, and threshing, followed later by storing, grinding, and baking. Most of these tasks involve the recruitment of labour from outside each domestic group, and constitute a large portion of any household's allotment of time and labour for domestic production and consumption. Only small quantities of rye are ever sold, larger portions of total rye production being utilized both as animal fodder and as seed for the following year's crop. In fact, only one individual carries out large-scale production of rye for sale: he is a large *lavrador* (H33 in Table 2) universally ridiculed for his waste of effort and time in producing such a large quantity of unprofitable grain.

Rye is also used as a uniform medium of exchange: the barber from the neighbouring village of Mosteiro charges one *alqueire* (see Glossary) of rye per year for cutting men's hair in the hamlet each Saturday morning. Further, rent for unirrigated grain fields is paid (with few exceptions) in rye grain. The quantity of rent is fixed, and corresponds to the number of *alqueires* that can be sown in the rented field. For instance, a field in which 4 *alqueires* of rye are sown has a fixed rent of 4 *alqueires* per year, regardless of yearly fluctuations in production. (Rent on meadows and highly fertile irrigated plots, however, is always paid in cash.) Smaller quantities of rye are also sown as a fodder crop for cattle – rye fodder is cut with the scythe in spring and fed fresh to cattle. Finally, rye is used as a medium of exchange at religious auctions outside the church, and also at larger regional festivals and pilgrimages (*festas*/*romarias*) as weights carried by women in sacks on their heads around the church in fulfillment of vows to saints.

Rye plays a far greater role in the hamlet economy than wheat, and this can be attributed in large part both to factors of altitude and climate as well as to conditions of the soil. The total production of rye at the hamlet's 45 threshings in 1976 amounted to 9,113 *alqueires*, while wheat totalled only 965. Of the 45 households producing grain that year 41 produced rye: 16 of these 41 households, in addition to rye, also produced wheat (Table 9). The remaining 4 households produced only wheat, and in especially small quantities. A majority of these 45 households thus produced rye alone. Further, the figures indicate that with the exception of the 3 wheat-producing households that year, all 16 households cultivating both cereals produced markedly smaller quantities of wheat than rye. A third grain is also produced in the hamlet, but so rarely and in such minuscule quantities that it barely deserves mention – one large *lavrador* in 1976 produced 7 *alqueires* of barley as fodder.

Table 2 sets forth selected seed-yield ratios for rye in the three successive years 1975–1976–1977. Included are the amounts of grain sown and threshed by 8 households on each side of the hamlet (the 1975 crop was harvested on the North-west *folha*, and the 1976 crop on the South-east). All of the figures of grain threshed in 1976 and 1977 were recorded at the conclusion of each threshing, prior to payments both for the threshing-machine and for land rent. The 1975 figures were retrospective estimates.

Immediately apparent from the information in Table 2 are the lower seed-yield ratios on the North-west side, particularly in the worst of the three years (1977). In contrast, yields on the South-east side were consistently high, attaining a ratio of 17.9 seeds harvested to 1 sown, in the case of Household 49. This may perhaps be attributable to the use of chemical fertilizers in the hamlet in recent decades, as Taborda estimated a seed-yield ratio of only between 1:5 and 1:8 for rye in the *terra fria* region of Trás-os-Montes in 1932 (Taborda 1932:120). Similarly, the DGSF estimated a ratio of 1:6 or 1:7 at best in 1950 (DGSF 1950:32). The seed-yield ratios in Fontelas are thus quite high. Secondly, comparing the 1975 and 1977 results, it is apparent that only a few households sow the same amounts of grain every two years (H20 and H49), and that different amounts sown may indicate the usage of different fields within the same *folha*. This is to be expected, given the two-course rotation of crops and the reversion of some plots at any one time to long-term fallow periods.

Thirdly, these figures must *not* be taken as absolute indicators of wealth in themselves according to the total amounts of rye sown and harvested. For example, although Households 15 and 45 are both poorer smallholders, the figures for H20 and H28 would be highly misleading. H28 is one of the four wealthiest landowning households in the hamlet and receives over 120 *alqueires* of rye each year in rent, yet the figures alone indicate that it sows very little grain. Conversely, H20 is one of the poorest in the hamlet, despite its 38 sown *alqueires* and 298 threshed *alqueires* in 1976. Some of the differences in the figures may also be attributed not only to the quality of the land but also to good and bad farming techniques: the case of H20 is illustrative in its low yields on both sides.

The amount of land devoted to grain cultivation in each household is also a factor of some importance: while H28 has a larger total landholding than H33, it rents out large tracts of its land while the latter rents out none. For instance, the totals of H33's sown land in two consecutive years (1976 and 1977) would yield 113 *alqueires* of sown land or 9.42 hectares (not counting a few plots in long-term fallow). This is quite a substantial amount of grain land in local terms. Three of the largest landholdings in the hamlet have close to 15 hectares of grain land each, while the smallest holdings include only one or two small fields totalling less than 1/3 hectare in area. The amount of grain land cultivated by various households in the hamlet thus reveals substantial inequalities.

Table 2. *Seed-yield ratios in selected households, 1975–1977*

Household	1975 (NW side)			1976 (SE side)			1977 (NW side)		
	Alqueires sown (ha)	*Alqueires* threshed	Seed-yield ratio	*Alqueires* sown (ha)	*Alqueires* threshed	Seed-yield ratio	*Alqueires* sown (ha)	*Alqueires* threshed	Seed-yield ratio
H6	15 (1.25)	160	10.7	17 (1.42)	176	10.4	25 (2.08)	145	5.8
H15	10 (0.83)	100	10.0	10 (0.83)	112	11.2	–* –	–	–
H19	25 (2.08)	300	12.0	30 (2.50)	400	13.3	20 (1.67)	265	13.3
H20	24 (2.00)	140	5.8	38 (3.17)	298	7.8	24 (2.00)	118	4.9
H28	8 (0.67)	75	9.4	8 (0.67)	91	11.4	5 (0.42)	45	9.0
H33	43 (3.58)	400	9.3	65 (5.42)	754	11.6	48 (4.00)	473	9.9
H45	0.5 (0.04)	7	14.0	7 (0.58)	100	14.3	3 (0.25)	20	6.7
H49	10 (0.83)	90	9.0	14 (1.17)	250	17.9	11 (0.92)	65	5.9

* Household 15 sowed no grain in 1977.

The materials above have been presented in order to give some idea of how two-course production of rye grain functions. It is precisely these kinds of specific aspects of small-scale household production, as well as the differences evident between extremes of the social scale, which are of greater significance for this study than the question of whether the open-field system and two-course crop rotation are archaic survivals. Although the three tractors purchased in the 1960s and 1970 have greatly influenced the production of rye in the hamlet, they have by no means replaced former techniques based on manual tools and animal traction: a large number of households still use sickles for reaping as well as draught animals and ox-carts for ploughing and transport. Nevertheless, the villagers do view their system of cereal production as wasteful of labour, unprofitable, and particularly time-consuming in comparison with other crops. Aware that rye is the bread of the poor, villagers are also aware of the constraining factors of soil, terrain, and climate. Fernand Braudel has noted the expenditures involved in cereal production in early modern Europe, and concludes that 'the peasants were as much the slaves of corn as of the nobility' (1973:82). Similarly, in Fontelas a frequent complaint at many points in the cycle of rye production is that: *somos escravos desta terra* — 'we are slaves to this land'.

Common-land

Common-land in Fontelas is termed *baldio*, literally meaning 'uncultivated land'. The word has two further connotations, which remain implicit beneath my provisional translation of *baldio* as 'common-land' or 'commons'. The first, a negative one, implies the useless nature of the land due to any one of many factors (altitude, soil, rocks). The second connotation, in contrast, suggests that this type of land is not necessarily uncultivable, but simply temporarily uncultivated or of such poor quality that only small amounts of rye grain can be grown on its better sections. This second meaning also includes the important implication that common-land (as distinct from completely barren land or wasteland) *does* contain a certain cover of vegetation, whether wild or planted. This is the meaning understood in the hamlet.

Although by and large occupying the highest and poorest land in the hamlet, the crucial significance of the commons lies in their vast stretches of heath and moorland containing wild shrub plants of fundamental use to shepherding and farming households alike. Unlike the shifting, temporary rights of stubble-grazing on the open fields, common rights in the *baldios* are permanent and unlimited. Although national legislation throughout different historical periods has changed aspects of the formal administration of local common-lands, their use by villagers in Fontelas is neither seasonal nor rotational. No household is limited in its usage of *baldio* terrain for the collection of shrub nor in the number of head of sheep, goats, or cattle it may graze.

The Junta de Colonização Interna (Internal Settlement Board) in Lisbon carried out a detailed survey of all the *baldios* in Portugal following its creation in 1936 (JCI 1939). The parish of Mosteiro was registered at the time as having 238.0 hectares of *baldios*.[21] This was quite a large figure for the area, but 185.5 hectares were reserved for reforestation and later planted with pines and other kinds of trees.[22] The 1939 survey is less useful in its estimates of area than for its characterization of the quality of soil on different portions of the commons and the uses to which each local population put specific sections. All of the five *baldios* within the parish[23] were comprised of geological schist formations mostly of 'difficult disaggregation' and the soil composing them was described as 'clayey-sandy'. These soils were mostly reported to be of regular depth but one tract had portions of rock fragments and in another case the soil composing the 90-hectare *baldio* was 'almost without a ploughable layer'. All of the commons were located on slopes and only a few had sections of level terrain and natural springs. In terms of local usage, all of this common-land was exploited communally – the phrase *logradouro comum* (used by the JCI) means not merely 'collective pasturage' but the more general 'common fruition'. This meaning becomes clearer when we note that the commons are used primarily for the collection of shrub and pasturage as well as for firewood. In general then, practically all of this common-land was of extremely poor quality and virtually useless for cultivation.

There are three further uses to which the *baldios* can be put: the first two of these are reforestation and the collection of stones and boulders for house construction. The third use is mentioned in the JCI survey, and concerns the clearing of common-land plots for the cultivation of rye. This process is technically termed *arroteamento* (clearing or assarting), but this word is never used in Fontelas. The process is referred to as an opening or cutting up (*desfazer*) of a portion of the commons, and must not be confused with any form of 'enclosures', as the new field is in no way fenced, hedged, or blocked off from its adjacent terrain. Many of the poorer households in the hamlet today

[21] Indeed, Mosteiro was one of the few parishes with conspicuously large expanses of *baldios*: only five other parishes of the 35 in the municipality contained more common-land than Mosteiro parish. Only two of these 35 parishes had none at all, while the smallest tracts ranged from 0.53 to 4.0 hectares (JCI 1939:70).

[22] The area of *baldio* land to be afforested was estimated by the DGSF in 1950 to be 13,066 hectares within 17 parishes in two municipalities (DGSF 1950:38). Fourteen of these parishes (including Mosteiro) were located within the municipality, and these contained 10,214 hectares of land to be planted. This yields a rough average of 729.6 hectares per parish to be afforested.

[23] Five portions of common-land were listed in the parish, with the sizes of 90, 13, 20, 60, and 55 hectares. The JCI did not specify, however, within which particular hamlets these *baldios* were located. I suspect this figure (238.0 hectares) may have been an underestimate, as the overall calculations by the Forest Guard in Fontelas yield a far larger area and may, conversely, be overestimates: of 550 estimated hectares of commons in Fontelas alone, he stated that 400 were planted. Portelinha was also judged by the Forest Guard as having 'almost 500 hectares' of commons. As I was unable to obtain a precise measurement of all of the portions of *baldios* in Fontelas, I prefer to limit references to the total surface area of the hamlet's common-land to the 1939 estimates.

have converted portions of previous commons into arable fields for the cultivation of rye over the last few decades.Thus, in the 1939 survey the JCI noted that one of the hamlet's *baldios* (20 hectares) was being used for shrub and pasturage, but also that it contained 'a small area of rye'. Although never becoming a full-scale partition of the commons along the lines described by Cutileiro for the Southern Alentejo region of Portugal (1971:15–24), this process of clearing can be traced through local minutes of the Parish Council (*Junta de Freguesia*) throughout the late nineteenth and early twentieth centuries. The clearing of plots on the commons has constituted an important source for supplementing the insufficient arable land owned by the hamlet's smallholders. Thus, the JCI survey mentions a 2-hectare tract in a parish to the South of Fontelas as containing 'crops of rye for the poor'. We should bear in mind nevertheless that this practice of clearing grants nothing but a sort of socially recognized, semi-permanent use right to the newly cleared plots: ultimately any such field on the commons can by definition never constitute private property and its transmission by 'inheritance' is quite problematic in strictly legal terms.

The positive role of the *baldios* in the hamlet economy cannot be overemphasized. The first and foremost use to which they are put is year-round pasturage for sheep and goats, and winter pasturage for cattle. The commons are not, however, used exclusively by the poor as substitutes for more fertile meadowland, but by households of all economic levels. Any household may graze its own flock individually on the common-land, and no system of strictly regulated collective grazing exists whereby successive households rotate shepherding tasks from day to day with a corporate or communal hamlet flock of sheep or goats.[24]

Secondly, the commons are also exploitable as a source of firewood throughout the year. As only one household in the hamlet owns a gas heater, which in fact does not replace but merely supplements the owner's fireplace, the provision of firewood is a constant task, especially during the winter. A major autumn task is the provision of large initial heaps of firewood for the winter months, and this is done by fetching an ox-cart of wood at periodic intervals. Every household without exception uses the fireplace and the hearth for cooking and heating, as well as for the curing of salted pork from December through March. Cooking is generally shifted to butane-gas cookers during the summer months. This is due both to the lesser need for fireplace heating as well as to the necessity for allotment of time to more urgent summer agricultural tasks (hay-making, reaping, and threshing). Thus, for most of the year

[24] This practice is common in many parts of Trás-os-Montes province as well as other mountainous regions of Northern and Central Portugal, and includes the collective pasturage of flocks of sheep, goats, cattle, and pigs, both by household rotation or by payment to an outsider shepherd. The list of monographs describing such livestock pasturage in Portugal is a lengthy one (Dias 1981). No such common pasturage was described to me for the case of Fontelas.

4 Shepherdess leading a flock out to the commons.

firewood must be in constant supply, and it is predominantly gathered from the *baldios*.

Thirdly, the commons provide an important source of shrub plants. Five major types of shrub are found on common-land, although these can also be found on private plots. The first of these is heather (*urze*).[25] Some heather plants also afford large roots, and are used extensively as firewood. The second shrub widely used is a type of broom (*giesta*) which is green in colour, whose branches also provide excellent firewood. The remaining shrub plants are furze or the common gorse (*tojo*), a second kind of broom (*carqueja*), and the cistus or rock-rose (*estêva*). Combinations of these shrubs are referred to by the general term *mato* (shrub/brushwood/undergrowth). Some of these, especially broom and gorse, are occasionally planted in private fallow fields and intermittently cut and used over a period of years as firewood and compost mixtures. A large plot or stretch of land covered with heather is termed an *urzal* (heath/moorland) and an area with a large number of broom plants a *giestal*

[25] Again, the Portuguese names of these shrub species are derived from my notes and the Latin (see Glossary) from the DGSF (1950) and Taborda (1932), which were then checked with regional geographical surveys (see Note 7 to this chapter).

5 *Lavrador* sharpening a scythe.

(broom plantation).[26] Common-land covered with shrub is also referred to as *monte*, a term implying either wild growth, particularly dense scrubland, or the presence of the three local wild animals – wolves, foxes, and less commonly the wild boar (*porco montês*).[27] The term *monte*, however, is used less commonly

[26] I heard no mention of shifting cultivation or swidden utilizing techniques of burning shrub in order to use the ashes as fertilizer, although Taborda (1932:106) mentions the practice (*queimadas*) of clearing natural vegetation for cultivation of the land under it on the commons of Northern Trás-os-Montes.

[27] The extraordinary *Diccionário Geográfico* of 1758, a manuscript consisting of detailed responses by local parish priests to a questionnaire sent to over 500 parishes in Portugal following the Lisbon earthquake of 1755, thus mentioned the terrain of Mosteiro's neighbouring parish as having nothing but 'hills of heather [*montes de urze*] and in some sections they cultivate a little bread [*pam*]'. Another neighbouring parish to the North of Fontelas was described as having 'willows and heather' on its uncultivated land and on the higher mountain slopes of the nearby *serra* as having not only rabbits, hares, and many partridges but also wolves and foxes. Today, a practice still frequent in the area are wolf- and fox-hunts organized by several hamlets in conjunction. In October of 1977 a fox-hunt of about 30 villagers with hunting-rifles was held within the terrain of Fontelas, Mosteiro, and Portelinha.

and usually refers to portions of terrain either of no use at all to the hamlet (except during the hunting season) or spatially more distant from the hamlet than the commons.

The cutting or uprooting of these shrub plants is carried out manually with a long, thick-bladed scythe, or *roçadoura*. The shrub is usually transported to the hamlet's households by ox-cart, but tractors are occasionally used for larger loads. All of these varieties of shrub are laid as litter (*estrume*) on the ground of animal stables to form a kind of mulch or compost along with the animals' dung: all animals are exploited for this purpose – sheep, goats, cattle, and pigs. Lesser quantities of tree leaves, as well as the straw from rye grain stalks, are added periodically to the stable floors to supplement this litter. The final product is a manure compost (*esterco*) of all of these materials collected, combined, and fermented over a period of months. This is then exhaustively removed from the stables with pitchforks and transported by ox-cart or tractor to the household's better fields. The compost is then unloaded in large heaps and later spread thinly over the fields for later ploughing. Irrigated crop fields are manured more extensively, although a number of dry grain fields are also manured – particularly those sown with wheat rather than rye.

The whole process of shrub collection and manuring occupies large quantities of time and labour, especially in the autumn and spring seasons, as manuring constitutes a vital source of fertilizer for the hamlet's arable crops. It is important to note that the wealthier landholders in the hamlet leave large portions of their land uncultivated, due mainly to the shortage of labour and the cost of bringing more land under cultivation given the minimal mechanization of the area. Much of this uncultivated land is either left to wild shrub growth or planted with broom or gorse, thus precluding these households' use of common-land for the collection of shrub. Customary rights of collection on the *baldios*, however, are hamlet-wide and any household irrespective of the size of its landholding or flocks is allowed to collect unrestricted amounts of shrub. There is in Fontelas a very delicate balance in arable farming between land, livestock, and the supply of manure,[28] and no potential threats to this balance seem to have arisen in recent years. In fact, precisely the opposite has occurred. The absence of conspicuous moves to partition any of the commons, or of disputes over collective rights, are an indication of the current lack of population pressure and the contraction of arable farming. This may be a relatively recent trend, brought about by the emigration of large numbers of villagers to France and West Germany in the 1960s. Furthermore, shepherding as a full-time or supplementary occupation (formerly a mark of poverty) is on the increase: this is due both to the excellent income earned on sales of sheep as well as to the abundance of pasturage on both open-field stubble and the commons. Possession of a flock of sheep is today less an indication of low

[28] Slicher Van Bath (1963) deals extensively with this balance in arable farming, and stresses the extreme importance of manuring in the history of Western European agriculture.

social status than a source of steady cash and fresh meat for festivals and larger harvesting meals.

Many of the aspects of common-land use described above can be seen in historical perspective through analysis of the minutes of the *Junta de Parochia* (see Glossary) in the head village of the parish, Mosteiro. For example, one case of the regulation of *baldios* for the collection of firewood and shrub occurred in Mosteiro in 1885. A minute of 17 May mentioned the village's scarcity of shrub, firewood, and timber, and stressed the urgency of restricting individual use of a certain public wood (*Touça da Costa*) to specific days designated by the Junta for collection by everyone. Such collection could only be of shrub for litter and manure composts but not of firewood or larger timber, and fines were to be imposed upon any transgressing individuals. The reasoning behind the restriction was that Mosteiro would have 'a source of revenue' from the wood after a few years.The village would also be self-sufficient in shrub, firewood, and timber rather than having the wood's resources progressively depleted by indiscriminate individual collection. No such restrictions appeared in any of the Junta minutes over the period 1872–1968 pertaining to Fontelas, although this may have been due to Fontelas' much larger expanses of commons. In stark contrast, Mosteiro itself had so little common-land in 1939 that none of it was even proposed for reforestation in the 1950s. As the 1885 minute reveals, even at that time Mosteiro was obliged to limit severely the collective use of its minuscule *baldios*.

More frequently reported in the Junta minutes were restrictions on livestock grazing. In 1900 (21 April) a minute proposed the nomination of a 'field guard for the posted land [*coutos*]' within the limits of the parish. The guard (or his substitute) was to apply fines to anyone found grazing animals within the *coutos*. These areas of land were not specified in the minute, and could have been either common plots or merely cultivated terrain under the administration of the Junta.[29] The fines for animals found grazing on these *coutos*, half of which were to be paid to the guard and the other half towards expenses of the parish church, were stipulated as follows: 40 *réis*[30] for each horse, mule, or cow; 30 *réis* for each goat; 20 *réis* for each head of sheep; and 15 *réis* for each pig. Although not explicit, the minute hints at the encroachment on parish land by villagers outside its limits. Another minute some years later (9 May 1915) restated the need for fines and confirmed the appointment of a new field guard from another hamlet in the parish. This second minute, however, mentions the necessity for the guard to protect the 'agricultural produce' of the parish as well

[29] The word itself (*coutos*) has two meanings. The first is a restricted one and refers to seigneurial land leased out to individuals or hamlets and usually incurring either rent, payments in kind, or labour services. The second meaning is more general, and suggests any portion of land (sown cereal plots, gardens, or a portion of common-land) which is temporarily restricted (*coutado*) and guarded, subjecting to fines any person(s) found using the land during the restricted times. I heard no references in oral tradition to any specific plots of land in the parish termed *coutos*, but this does not of course rule out the possibility of earlier seigneurial tenure.

[30] 1,000 *réis* are equivalent to 1 *escudo*.

as the *coutos*. The minute also designated as restricted (*coutada*) a portion of land pertaining to both Mosteiro and Fontelas and stretching 'a kilometre along the river'. Both minutes point to the role of the Mosteiro Junta in controlling pasturage and public access to the commons.

Yet a more urgent tone characterized a minute in 1921 (29 April): both the commons as well as private land in the parish were being 'constantly assaulted by cattle and flocks without any respect for the property or owners, causing enormous damages'. Four separate restrictions were imposed: two of these limited the grazing of goats to 19 named sections of land within the parish. The third restriction specified five suitable roads for the passage of sheep and goats. Finally, the fourth restriction again limited access to the wood in Mosteiro already restricted in 1885 – this wood was now closed even further both to villagers and flocks from the parish as well as to outsiders. The fines imposed on outsiders were considerably higher than those for parish residents: 5 *centavos*[31] for sheep, 10 for goats, and 15 for horses and cows. Even higher fines were fixed for the removal of shrub plants and firewood. Finally, another minute in 1956 (4 February) clearly excluded the residents of the neighbouring hamlets of Fontelas, Lousada, and Portelinha from using portions of Mosteiro's own common-land.

None of the minutes includes information on the actual imposition of fines or the frequency of infractions, although the minutes themselves attest to the continual concern for community control of common-land and the damages caused by unrestricted grazing.[32] Secondly, a number of minutes stress grazing incursions on various parts of the parish's land, but only *one* hamlet (Mosteiro) had the need to restrict access to commons expressly used for shrub and firewood (the wood referred to in the 1885 and 1921 minutes). This may indicate either that the three annex hamlets in the parish exercised greater autonomy in the control of their own common-land, or that the commons in the other three hamlets were large enough to preclude shortages or formal requests to the Mosteiro Junta for restrictions and fines.

Another process evident from a careful reading of the Junta minutes was the sale of portions of the commons by the Junta. The first minute referring to the sale or auction (*arrematação*) of common-land was that of 27 October 1872. This minute mentions the alienation and disentailment (*desamortização*) of common-land, and specifies the sale of a meadow within the outer boundaries

[31] 1 *centavo* = 10 *réis*. Thus, 5 *centavos* = 50 *réis* or 0.050 *escudo*.

[32] The parish of Mosteiro was elevated to municipal level for 18 years (1837–54) and Mosteiro was designated the central town administering 8 parishes with a total of 34 hamlets. A close examination of the minutes of the Mosteiro *Câmara* (see Glossary) over these years indicates that the institution of field guards was in fact derived from the *Código Administrativo*. The minutes indicate that a field guard (and in some cases a substitute) was normally appointed every one or two years by the Mosteiro Câmara for each hamlet in the municipality: Câmara Minutes, 3 February 1840 (this minute set forth new municipal by-laws), 3 May 1841, 19 March 1843, 2 June 1844, 15 June 1845, 17 June 1846, 10 July 1848, 13 May 1849, 26 April 1852, and 3 May 1853.

of Fontelas and of another portion of land within Fontelas itself. A few years later in Mosteiro (11 May 1875), the Junta decided to sell a series of *baldio* plots and apply the proceeds towards the construction of a schoolhouse. No less than eight further minutes through 1888[33] mention problems concerning the lack of means for constructing this schoolhouse, which required the sale of part of a common meadow in Fontelas whose estimated value in 1881 (15 May) was 50 *escudos*. Two assessors from Mosteiro were appointed by the Junta to determine the exact value of the portion of the meadow to be sold. The temporary building in which the school was housed was moved in 1885 (5 April) but its new building was 'in such a state of ruin' in 1887 that yet another portion of common-land (another part of the meadow in Fontelas) had to be sold to provide sufficient funds for its repair. The minutes do not stipulate to whom these meadow portions were sold.

Another process visible in the minutes was the concession of small *baldio* plots to poor villagers for permanent private cultivation. One of the first requests by individuals for 'a bit of common-land' was mentioned in an 1879 minute (25 May). José dos Santos of Lousada requested that two portions of common-land within Lousada's terrain be granted him. The Junta deliberated, and after concluding that the concession would cause no harm either to 'the public' or to other individuals, decided to grant him the two portions. Not all common-land plots, however, were formally requisitioned in this fashion: an 1880 minute (1 January) mentions another villager in Lousada who had cultivated a *baldio* plot 'for many years without authorization'. The poor economic status of some of the individuals requesting these plots is frequently mentioned in the minutes. For instance, in 1892 (25 December) Manuel Vicente, a widower from Lousada, requested permission to cultivate a portion of land in Lousada with the dimensions 39 metres in length by 30 metres in width (11.7 ares, or 0.117 hectare).[34] Significantly, the Junta decided to grant the portion, 'bearing in mind the poverty of the applicant'. Similarly, six days later (31 December 1892) José Pires of Mosteiro was granted a portion of common-land 1 metre in length by 50 metres in width (0.5 are, or 0.005 hectare). Before granting this concession the Junta had taken note of 'the poverty of the applicant' and noted that this piece of land was conveniently situated immediately next to one of José's own private plots.

Baldio concessions, nevertheless, were not all straightforward encounters between the Junta and individuals: two examples will illustrate problems arising between villagers with contiguous plots. In 1888 (28 October) two requests were made to the Junta, the first by Alfredo Pires of Mosteiro for 2 metres of common terrain next to one of his own fields in the area of *Ribeira pequena*, and the second by Gregório Pires (also of Mosteiro) for a tract of common-land for the planting of chestnut-trees in the area of *Cabos*. Both

[33] Junta Minutes: 1 January 1880, 13 May 1881, 15 May 1881, 6 April 1884, 5 April 1885, 17 May 1885, 17 December 1887, and 20 April 1888.

[34] 1 are = 100 sq metres; 10 ares = 1,000 sq metres; and 100 ares = 1 hectare.

requests were granted after the Junta had considered both of the applicants' poverty and after it had decided that the concessions were of 'great utility' to the applicants and would cause no harm to the other residents of the village. Three days later, however, another minute (1 November 1888) mentions a request by Alfredo Pires of Mosteiro that the Junta impose a fine upon Gregório Pires for having cultivated a small portion of common-land in the area of *Ribeira pequena* and another in the area of *Cabos*. After again noting the poverty of Gregório Pires and recognizing that both portions of Gregório's land had been planted with trees 'years earlier', the Junta decided to refuse Alfredo's request and to allow Gregório continued use of both *baldio* plots.

A second instance occurred in 1891 (5 April) when José Augusto Pires of Mosteiro requested permission to cultivate a plot of 30 square metres (0.3 are, or 0.003 hectare) in the area of *Rio de Algoso*. At the same meeting of the Junta, Manuel Lúcio of Mosteiro protested, and stated that the cultivation of the said plot by José Augusto Pires would cause great damage to his own property in the same area of *Rio de Algoso*, immediately adjacent to the *baldio*. José Augusto Pires' request was refused but Manuel Lúcio's was granted, considering the damage the latter could possibly suffer.

Both of these cases highlight the excessively small size of the portions of common-land in question, as well as the fear of contiguous cultivation of unenclosed plots.

These conflicts between individuals with adjacent plots were by no means the only form of dispute over *baldio* terrain. Plots of common-land to be conceded or cultivated could also give rise to conflicts between public and private spheres of ownership. In 1915 (11 July) the Justice of the Peace of the municipality had to be called in to assist the Junta in recalling 'a large portion of common-land' which had been usurped by two villagers from a neighbouring hamlet. The Junta noted that the land had been cultivated 'for more than 40 years' and had been planted with vine-plants, irrigated, ploughed, and divided into smaller sections. In this case, the Junta demanded that the two villagers abandon the land and return it to its original state. A few months later, however, another minute (26 December 1915) reports one of these two villagers as requesting a small portion of the *baldio* in question. This request was granted, and two witnesses were present at the placing of four boundary stones around the plot. This plot was particularly large: the Junta estimated it as having a capacity of 50 litres of sown rye grain, or approximately 0.42 hectare.[35] But the Junta further included in this concession the condition that

[35] In this region of Trás-os-Montes, 1 hectare of unirrigated land is equivalent to the area in which 12 *alqueires* of rye can be sown (1 *alqueire* = 17 litres). This measurement can vary from 11 to 13 *alqueires*, but is nevertheless a fairly reliable indicator of surface area. Another similar form of measurement in the region is the *jeira*, or the average amount of unirrigated land (in this case 1/3 hectare) that one man can plough in a day with one team of draught animals. This measurement is less commonly used today but it is the form in which the 'ancient' land registers in the town Tax Bureau were originally compiled (see Appendix I).

the plot's new owner would have to pay 15 *escudos* towards repairs of Mosteiro's schoolhouse (a problem obviously not resolved by 1888).

A second case occurred in Mosteiro in 1934 (18 March). The Junta again had to place boundary stones between a tract of common-land and the private land of Domingos dos Ramos Pires. The language of the minute specifically stresses the public/private dichotomy: in this case the Junta was obliged to 'side with the rightful owner, which was the hamlet' (*dando a razão a quem tinha, que era a povoação*). Although the minute was not explicit, the suggestion was that Domingos had encroached upon public terrain.

A number of points can be made on the basis of the information in these minutes. Firstly, the portions of common-land conceded by the Junta for individual cultivation were extremely small and suited in most cases only for dry cereal crops (rye). This land was neither rented nor sold by the Junta but merely 'granted'. In most cases this was done with the explicit purpose of alleviating the poverty of the applicants. Secondly, most of the concessions were granted only in the two hamlets of Mosteiro and Lousada. Although two *baldio* portions pertaining to Fontelas are mentioned (one meadow and one unspecified tract) the minutes do not name the individuals to whom these portions were sold or granted. The fourth hamlet (Portelinha) is not mentioned at all.

The minutes are, however, only one source of information, and we cannot assume (to put the matter crudely) that what did not appear in the minutes did not in fact happen. Throughout my fieldwork in 1976–8 the large amounts of common-land in Fontelas were compared frequently with the sparse and minuscule *baldios* of Mosteiro and Lousada. While large portions of Fontelas' commons were planted with pines by the government's Forestry Service in the late 1950s, none of the smaller commons in Mosteiro and Lousada were planted at all. Nevertheless, a large number of Fontelas' current residents have cleared plots on the *baldios* for rye cultivation over the past decades, and none of these clearings are recorded anywhere in the Junta minutes.[36] Of the 55 landholdings in Fontelas, I gathered 52 detailed estimates of the amount of cleared common-land included in each holding. Of these 52 households, 29 have cleared terrain ranging from 0.08 hectare to 4.16 hectares (see Table 3 in Chapter 3). These areas are considerably larger than any of those mentioned in the Junta minutes for *baldio* plots in Mosteiro and Lousada. The essential point here, then, is that these portions of common-land are of different size and serve different purposes, and are *not* distributed evenly among separate hamlets in the parish. Mosteiro's tracts have been exceedingly small, while at the other extreme, Fontelas' *baldios* are vast even today, and they constitute an important source of supplementary land for rye cultivation.

[36] As none of these clearings of *baldios* were recorded in the Junta minutes, it is possible either that their registration was carried out by the town Câmara, or that they were not recorded at all.

A third point concerning the commons arising from these materials is the distinction between purely 'communal' land and municipal land under the administration of the Junta. This distinction is not always clear either locally or in the numerous historical debates over changes in legislation concerning the *baldios*.[37] Thus a classic article on forms of communal tenure in Portugal (Peixoto 1908) mentions the 'tens of thousands of hectares of *terra baldia*' under the general administration of parish Juntas, but notes that in fact their actual modes of use are determined not by the hierarchically dominant Juntas but by local assemblies of villagers. Referring to this statement, Cabral notes that at this time (the early twentieth century) the national administration of the Juntas was reflected in a 'perfect bureaucratization of Portuguese local life' symbolized by the figure of the *regedor* (Junta chairman) appointed not locally but in the district capital or in Lisbon (Cabral 1974:404). Nevertheless Cabral accepts that in 'certain corners of the country' administrative authority may still concede some amount of autonomy to such local assemblies of villagers.[38] A number of authors have also noted the role of the 1867 Civil Code in abolishing communal pastures[39] and converting them into municipal land (*bens do concelho*) under the control of the Juntas and thus susceptible to division and sale. The timing of this legislation seems consistent with the first mention of the alienation of *baldios* in the Junta minutes of Mosteiro in 1872, and with subsequent sales and concessions through the early twentieth century. However, the actual legal status of the commons over time, as either municipal, parish, or truly communal land is quite difficult to pin down accurately.

The process of the partitioning of common-land in Portugal continued with added impetus from the central administration from 1925 through 1957 (Castro 1973:278) and culminated in the reforestation program requiring large tracts of commons in Northern Portugal for pine plantation. The extent to which local hamlet developments in *baldio* use conformed to a regional and national pattern is difficult to determine in the absence of records at the hamlet level. The commons have nevertheless attained a key symbolic position within

[37] The Junta is far clearer in its definition of roads, bridges, buildings, and non-*baldio* land as strictly municipal or parish property. The minutes abound with instances of repairs, reconstruction, and the general upkeep of these forms of municipal property. Thus one minute of the short-lived Mosteiro Câmara in 1840 (8 October) refers to (a) a bridge under construction, (b) the Câmara meeting house, and (c) the prison of the municipality all as truly municipal property (*bens municipaes*). Similarly, the Mosteiro Câmara referred on 18 July 1841 to 'the public ground of this town'. The word *baldio* was not mentioned in any of these cases.

[38] In 1933 the French sociologist Paul Descamps (1935:6) described a series of hamlets in the Serra da Cabreira to the West of this municipality and noted: 'Les *baldîos* (communaux) appartiennent au municipe de Vieira qui en répartit l'usage entre les paroisses ou les consigne aux services forestiers de l'État.' Again, the precise meaning of 'communaux' below the parish level at the hamlet level is not entirely clear.

[39] On the abolition of communal pasturage, see Cabral (1974:51–2), Cabral (1976:227–8), and Veloso (1953).

some of the Portuguese literature concerning definitions of the 'closed peasant community' and its dissolution in the face of the development of rural capitalism. Thus in 1935 Descamps, speaking of Trás-os-Montes, stated that: 'L'état social que nous décrivons en ce moment n'est pas basé sur un système capitaliste, car la monnaie est rare . . .' (Descamps 1935:63). On the other hand, Cabral (1976:236) maintains that the partitions of common-land for rye cultivation in Northern Portugal indicated a seigneurial regime with aspects of strong 'communitarian' vestiges which post-1820 Liberal legislation attacked. In this sense, the *baldios* have become symbolic representations of primitive communal forms of property besieged by the onslaught of modern capitalism and the destruction of the older 'autonomous' communities.

Differences in regional developments are striking, particularly with respect to the North and South of the country. In 1939 the Junta de Colonização Interna recorded a total of 210,707 hectares of commons in the province of Trás-os-Montes alone: this accounted for almost half of the national total of 531,441 hectares. In contrast, the two sectors of the Southern Alentejo province (Alto Alentejo/Baixo Alentejo) had only 613 and 669 hectares of commons respectively. A local reflection of these extreme regional differences is reported by Cutileiro (1971:13) for the parish of Vila Velha in the Alentejo province. In Vila Velha, full-scale partition of the parish's common-lands had already been completed prior to 1820.[40] Not only did the partitions (actually a form of semi-permanent concession or usufruct) occur much later in the North, but also on a much smaller scale. Further, not all of the Northern *baldios* were partitioned, as the case of Fontelas has shown, and the designation 'enclosures' would be entirely inappropriate in this case, as nothing is really fenced or closed off at all.

Highly relevant here is the position of Fontelas as an annex hamlet within the parish. Fontelas' commons were thus registered by the JCI in 1939 as being under common usage (*logradouro comum*) despite their technical definition as parish land under parish administration.[41] Two outstanding factors are evident concerning Fontelas' position as an annex hamlet. Firstly, there is a

[40] Note also Cutileiro's comment on the absence of open-field pasturage in Vila Velha in the early nineteenth century: '*Vaîne pature* in private property, if it ever existed locally, was no longer found by the end of the *ancien régime*' (1971:17). This is merely one example of the large number of striking differences between the Northern communities examined here and the Southern parish of Vila Velha studied by Cutileiro.

[41] Veloso (1953) discusses at length the various changes in legal definitions of communal land, parish land, municipal land *per se*, and municipal land under the administration of the parish Juntas. Veloso notes the sometimes deliberate confusion in legislative language between communal property and 'corporative' property purportedly pertaining to the 'moral person' of the municipality or parish (1953:142). For instance, in the case of the corporate hamlet of Vilarinho da Furna studied by Jorge Dias (1948), Veloso notes (1953:129) that '. . . despite the presumption of the *Código Administrativo*' the Junta never intervened in practice in the affairs of the hamlet leaders (*zeladores*). See also Cutileiro's note on the communal (not municipal) *baldios* in Vila Velha (1971:15–16).

long tradition of hostility between Fontelas and Mosteiro. This tradition includes both material and symbolic dimensions of competition and conflict. While Fontelas' landholdings, and especially its fertile meadows, are generally larger and more productive than those of Mosteiro, Mosteiro boasts its history as a town and market centre (1837–54) and its administrative centrality today as the seat of the Junta and the parish church. Extremely few marriages have been contracted between the inhabitants of Mosteiro and Fontelas for the period covered by the parish marriage records (Chapter 6), while villagers in both hamlets have tended to marry more frequently within each hamlet or with other surrounding hamlets. One dramatic instance of conflict occurred a few years ago, in which youths from Fontelas armed with pitchforks entered Mosteiro 'threatening to kill' some of the latter village's residents. The event necessitated the calling of the Republican Guards from the town in order to stop a potential riot.

Further, in 1978 a large reservoir of water was constructed by the *Câmara Municipal* (see Glossary) for irrigation purposes in Fontelas and Mosteiro, and was located a few yards from one of Fontelas' households. Mistrust was so great between the two communities that rather than divide the timing and rotation of irrigation turns from the reservoir, both hamlets agreed to divide the reservoir itself into two halves separated by a cement wall. No one in either place trusted the inhabitants of the other. The cement division thus relegated potential disagreements over water to the internal hamlet level rather than risk a larger Fontelas/Mosteiro dispute.

A similar distinction is clear with regard to the *baldios*. Whether in fact this land legally pertains to the municipality or comes under the administration of parish officials in Mosteiro, the commons within Fontelas' terrain are today very much thought of as 'ours' and exploited only by 'the people of our hamlet'. The following events illustrate this point quite clearly. Recent legislation (1976) has returned the commons to their original owners – each local hamlet – thereby superseding previous legislation concerning parish and municipal administration. Thus, the *Lei dos Baldios* of 19 January 1976[42] explicitly states that tracts of common-land will be reinstated as 'institutionalized forms of local democratic organization' under the control of local assemblies. On 15 June 1976, a meeting was held in Fontelas with regard to this particular law and to Fontelas' commons previously appropriated for reforestation. (Significantly, the meeting was held on a small section of common-land on the Western side of the hamlet formerly used as a forage meadow for the hamlet's pigs.) Two representatives of the town Forestry Service were present and convoked the meeting. All hamlet residents over 18 years of age were allowed one vote. They could vote either in favour of total

[42] *Decreto-Lei* (Law by decree) No. 39/76 of 19 January 1976 (*Lei dos Baldios*), and *Portaria* (Decree) No. 117/76 of 1 March 1976.

hamlet administration (not parish administration) of the future timber resources of the pines and other trees planted on the hamlet's commons, or for joint State/hamlet exploitation of the resources on the basis of a 60%–40% division of the proceeds.[43] The 61 villagers present (men and women) voted unanimously for State/hamlet joint exploitation, with no votes for total hamlet control and no abstentions. A *comissão directiva* (executive or managing committee) of four elected co-leaders was formed. Composing this committee are the four men who received the highest number of votes at the meeting (25, 8, 6, and 6 votes respectively).

Expressly stated at the meeting was the fact that the Junta of Mosteiro possessed no substantial commons and that Mosteiro had 'never suffered from the reforestation program'. Mosteiro therefore had no say in the future timber benefits to be gained from Fontelas' own afforested common-land. This legislation and its local implementation have firmly placed control of the commons (for pasturage, clearing, and shrub and firewood collection) in the hands of Fontelas' households and not the Junta of Mosteiro. The 1976 law has also legalized the status of the *baldios* as truly 'communal' land administered by the hamlet's own local residents. Hamlet response to the law was universally favourable in Fontelas, as the devolution of the commons clarified local rights previously obscure amidst a plethora of changing historical and legal definitions. Recent national legislation had effected a positive change in a process formerly viewed by villagers solely as encroachment by hostile external agencies: whether the State, the plundering Forestry Service, or the favouritism of Junta presidents in Mosteiro.[44] While for decades coveted by the residents of Mosteiro and legally administered by the Mosteiro Junta, the immense expanses of Fontelas' *baldios* were now reinstated as truly communal land exploitable by Fontelas' villagers alone.

Meadows, gardens, and vineyards

I have dealt in some detail with two types of land subject to various forms of community control. Two further types of land which play important roles in Fontelas' economy are meadows and kitchen-gardens. Both of these kinds of land are predominantly farmed on an individual basis, but forms of corporate organization are nevertheless also evident here. In the case of kitchen-gardens, a system of irrigation by turns is brought into play during the spring and summer months for the watering of garden plots lying close to the hamlet's households (Chapter 4). A similar system of alternating irrigation turns is used, although on a smaller scale, for the watering of meadows. By no means of lesser importance to the hamlet economy than the open fields and the

[43] The Decree of 1976 (see Note 42) explicitly stipulates as voters all adults of both sexes over 18 years of age, and stresses local rights in the use of *baldios* 'according to the customs and habits recognized by the community' (Macedo dos Santos *et al* 1978:161).

commons, meadowland provides a highly valued source of pasturage and green fodder for cattle. Similarly, kitchen-gardens provide extremely fertile plots for the cultivation of household vegetables, pulses, and some root crops.

Most of the hamlet's fertile meadows (*lameiros*) are located close to the hamlet along the banks of the shallow streams passing from the higher North-east areas of the hamlet's terrain to the South-west, towards Mosteiro (Map 2). There are a number of further meadows distributed in other areas, especially on some of the slopes between the hamlet and the rock outcrop located at 1,106 metres. Meadows are of two general types. Firstly, most highly valued are irrigated meadows providing a major harvest of hay in June as well as smaller amounts of autumn grass. Secondly, unirrigated meadows termed *lameiros de secadal* (dry meadows) provide much smaller amounts of hay of a thinner, finer quality than that on the irrigated meadows. Both types of meadow are used exclusively as private pasturage.

The quality of the hamlet's meadows contributes to the area's fame as one of the best regions of Trás-os-Montes province for the raising of cattle. Taborda (1932:132–7) has noted the excellent pasturage conditions of the municipality's meadows due to the region's humid climate, its hilly and mountainous terrain, and the abundance of natural springs. Even earlier historical reports on these hamlets have stressed the quality of their meadows and pastures. In 1706 Carvalho da Costa noted the 'good butters' produced in Mosteiro and its neighbouring parishes. Similarly, in the *Diccionário Geográfico* of 1758 the priest of a parish to the North-east of Fontelas emphasized that all of that parish's six hamlets produced butter in abundance 'because the land has many pastures'. Although butter and cheese are not produced today in these hamlets, sales of young livestock are a major source of income and this livestock continues to depend upon good pasturage.

The sizes of the total amounts of meadowland owned and rented by various households afford a good indication of social differentiation within the hamlet. While two of the hamlet's four largest holdings include approximately 10 and 15 hectares of meadowland each (much of which is rented out) five other large holdings contain portions of meadowland between 3.2 and 7.1

[44] Although the word *patrão* (patron/boss) is frequently employed in the hamlet to refer to influential individuals outside the community, I never heard the words *cacique* or *caciquismo* used by villagers themselves. Fontelans maintain a view of the Mosteiro Junta as a kind of favour-factory: the inhabitants of Mosteiro thus 'do what they like' simply due to their proximity (residentially and socially) to the Junta president. One glaring example of favouritism by the Câmara in Mosteiro occurred in 1852 (26 April), when a priest from a neighbouring hamlet requested the concession of a small portion of common-land on the banks of the local river in order to open a water-course for irrigating 'a large piece of terrain that he possesses' within Mosteiro's confines. Invoking the 'improvement of agriculture' which would result from this act, the Câmara granted the priest the land, but upheld the right of the public to the free passage of ox-carts through the common-land plot to the river. The Câmara went even further by forbidding anyone to obstruct the priest's passage of water through this portion of (former) common-land under penalty of a fine of 6 *mil réis* (6 *escudos*).

hectares in area. Households with smaller holdings combine both owned and rented meadowland of between 1 and 3 hectares, while the tiniest holdings contain no meadows at all or smaller fractions of 1 hectare. The largest rented meadow in the hamlet (2.25 hectares) is rented out by a wealthy household to a poorer one, the latter household paying a rent of 120 *alqueires* of rye grain (2,040 litres) per year for its use. This rent constitutes almost 1/3 of that household's total grain production in 1976. The value of specific meadows is measured by the number of ox-carts of hay they can produce. For instance, one wealthy villager owns an irrigated meadow of approximately 0.9 hectare in area that produces 8–9 carts of hay in a good year. In contrast, one of the hamlet's shepherds obtains only a small cart of hay on a rented meadow of approximately 0.37 hectare. His wife's own minuscule dry meadow of 0.04 hectare yields only 'one or two bundles of hay for the pigs'.

The productivity of meadows is extremely variable and to a large extent dependent not only upon size but also upon water resources. Important factors are the location and amounts of water provided by underground springs and external pools, the number of persons sharing the same water and irrigation channels, and the care and timing of each household's watering of its own meadows. The value of meadows is further attested to by their high rental prices in cash and by their crucial role in the maintenance of cattle. Without a minimum of 1.5 hectares of meadowland (owned or rented) no villager can maintain a plough team of two draught animals: we will see in Chapter 3 that possession of a plough team constitutes a fundamental criterion of economic ranking within the hamlet's social hierarchy.

Although providing pasturage for cattle and precious green fodder for the winter months, some portions of meadows are also used as irrigated furrows for vegetables, pulses, and fodder crops. Other portions are ploughed, manured, and planted with a number of crops which are irrigated with the water pertaining to that particular meadow. For example, H1 owns a meadow of approximately 21 by 10 metres in area (2.1 ares, or 0.02 hectare) of which about one half is used for pasturage and hay for the household's donkey and heifer. The other half is devoted to the following crops: winter-sown barley as spring fodder for the household's heifer, donkey, and pigs; turnips and calabashes for pig fodder; and smaller portions of cabbages, haricot beans, carrots, and peppers for household consumption. This household shares the irrigation water pertaining to this meadow with three other households on the following basis: it can water the meadow and crops once every two weeks (Tuesdays) alternating every other Tuesday with H14. The remaining days of each week are split between two other households in the hamlet, the first watering on Wednesdays, Thursdays, and Fridays, and the second on Saturdays, Sundays, and Mondays. Entire meadows as well as these cultivated portions are thus regulated through rotating systems of corporate water use by various households.

Although almost all meadows are privately owned, a very small portion of the hamlet's meadowland is common-land available for public use. We recall that the Junta in Mosteiro referred to a portion of Fontelas' *baldios* as meadowland in a number of minutes from 1872 through 1888, with reference to the sale of a portion of that meadow towards the construction of Mosteiro's schoolhouse. Another Junta minute in 1879 (25 May) refers to a section of Mosteiro's commons as 'meadowland'. João Lopez was refused his request for the concession of a plot precisely because it was not merely of use only for dry cultivation of rye but for 'any crop, and principally rye, wine, vegetables, and meadow'. The plot thus provided a more valuable source of future revenue for the parish. The ethnographic literature on Trás-os-Montes offers many further examples of cases of common pasturage on meadows. Two cases reported very near Fontelas are illustrative. In 1939, one of Fontelas' neighbouring hamlets was listed as having reserved a portion of irrigated meadow 0.0250 hectare in area for 'public use' (JCI 1939). Similarly, another nearby hamlet mentioned by Martins (1939) possessed a number of 'common pasture meadows' regulated by its parish Junta for communal pasturage on festive days. These references provide further evidence that meadowland in the area has generally been a highly fertile and useful public resource.

Within Fontelas, another type of smaller and less valuable meadow is termed a *poulo*. There are three such tiny meadows in the hamlet, which according to all of my informants constituted properly communal (not municipal or parish) land in former years. All three *poulos* afforded common pasturage for the pigs of poorer households. In recent decades two of these plots have come under church ownership, and are currently rented out to individual households for an annual payment in rye grain. Thus, the Fontelas Church Accounts Book (1951–78) mentions these two meadows in 1955 among its few rented plots: they provided 9 and 2 *alqueires* of rent in grain to the church. These two meadows are now termed 'saint's meadows' as the rent payments contribute towards the expenses of the yearly patron saint's festival in honour of Saint Anthony. Two poorer households today cultivate the *poulos* and pay the rather minimal total rent of 5 *alqueires* of rye to the patron saint's festival committee.[45]

The third *poulo* has remained purely communal property, although it was the source of a fierce public/private conflict a number of years ago. A small portion of this meadow bordering a dirt road at one of the hamlet's exits (Map 3) was 'appropriated' by one of the larger landowners of the hamlet for the construction of a warehouse and garage for the storage of his tractor, agricultural equipment, and potatoes. It was not sufficiently clear where the borders of the meadow ended and the landowner's contiguous private plot

[45] The disparity in rent between the 1955 and 1977 amounts (11 *alqueires* and 5 *alqueires* respectively) may be a sign of the recent shift in festival expenses from grain to higher cash contributions, due to emigration since 1964.

began. Public opinion nevertheless stressed the dangers of uncontrolled individual encroachment and the drive for 'seizing' the property of the hamlet. The meadow is not currently used for grazing pigs, but was the site of the hamlet meeting discussed earlier concerning recent changes in the 1976 legislation on common-land. This same *poulo* is also the site of the annual dance occurring in the afternoon and evening of the patron saint's festival on 13 June.

The second major type of irrigated land in Fontelas is the small kitchen-garden, or *cortinha*. In these gardens are grown the major portions of household vegetables, and they must be irrigated regularly. Most gardens lie directly outside or around their owners' houses, but many households also possess some additional garden plots quite distant from the hamlet. The definition of *cortinha* thus depends not upon the proximity of the gardens to the household, but on the nature of this kind of land as small in area, highly fertile, and the fact that it is worked by hand (hoeing, weeding) for human consumption. Virtually all of the gardens in the hamlet centre (Map 3) are irrigated through a complex system of rotating turns during the summer, and as they are so fertile, much of the garden-land in this area has been split up through inheritance divisions into myriad contiguous square and rectangular plots, much like a miniature checker-board. Kitchen-gardens are in fact the most indispensable type of land for every household in the hamlet: very poor smallholders may own or rent no grain fields, no meadows, and no vineyards, but possession of or access to a garden is vital. Thus Eufémia, a widow who married into the hamlet, described the size of her landholding as *nada* (nothing). The 1.13 hectares of land which she had usufruct rights to upon her first husband's death were inherited by one of her sons upon her second marriage to a husband no wealthier than her first. Widowed again, Eufémia now has access only to a small garden which is in fact lent to her, and which must be hoed and planted for her by another villager (not kin) as a favour. Eufémia is thus the only truly 'landless' villager in Fontelas, and she is particularly pitied for not owning even a few square metres of garden land.

Gardens give a somewhat less clear indication of differences in land ownership as a whole, although my analysis in Chapter 4 does reveal large disparities in the ownership of gardens of different sizes. The largest landholdings in the hamlet have between 0.38 and 1.13 hectares of garden land (combining various garden plots) and the smallest gardens I recorded were approximately 0.02 hectare and 0.04 hectare in area. As most villagers own *some* garden plots however small in size, the rental of gardens is extremely rare: of all of the households in the hamlet, not one enumerated a garden either rented by themselves or rented out to others. However, it is common practice to convert a small section of a tract of meadowland into a garden plot. Occasionally a household may thus cultivate a few furrows of a rented meadow in order to supplement its own meagre gardens.

Fontelas' abundant water has long been a source of envy and competition on the part of the inhabitants of Mosteiro. The decision in 1978 to divide the cement tank of water in Fontelas into two separate sections for each hamlet was the most recent expression of this hostility, although its origins are more remote. Around 1957, a number of villagers from Mosteiro attempted (or at least desired) to redirect the water emanating from one of Fontelas' natural water-pools into Mosteiro. In response, one of Fontelas' largest landowners wrote a letter of protest to the President of the town Câmara. She insisted that Mosteiro be refused permission effectively to 'steal' any part of the water pertaining to the hamlet of Fontelas. The contents of this letter are translated below:

Most Excellent Mr President:

The undersigned plead Your Excellency to heed their rightful request and to take precautionary measures, standing up for their most legitimate interests.

They ask if it is just to benefit one hamlet at the expense of another?

Well, it is precisely this that the hamlet of Mosteiro intends to do to Fontelas, usurp the irrigation water which by law belongs to us and has always belonged to us through inheritance from our ancestors. The water which they intend to direct into Mosteiro is the water which the majority of the inhabitants of Fontelas use for the irrigation of their *cortinhas* and *hortas** during the summer, and if they remove this water the *cortinhas* will become dry fields or sterile terrain unsuitable for vegetables.

This same water, during the winter months, pertains to two meadows and is the only water these meadows have.

And further, when in the summer the aridity is great and the public springs dry up, this water is used at the spring by the villagers nearest to it for household consumption; as even now occurs and which can be proved.

There is much water above the hamlet in the hills, which has not yet been exploited and which does not pertain to individual owners. Why don't they exploit those?

For these reasons, Mr President, we beseech that Your Excellency deign to carry out the necessary measures with the greatest haste in order to put a stop to such abuse.

* vegetable gardens, located further outside the hamlet than the nearer *cortinhas*.

In addition to revealing disagreements between the two neighbouring hamlets with regard to ownership and use of an unequally distributed resource (water), the letter also affords an instance of community action in the face of an external threat. Whether rights in the use of local water were legally defined as subject to municipal or parish control, the letter demonstrates the continuing strength of customary law: the writer refers to the irrigation water 'which by law belongs to us'.[46] The request was successful, and the town Câmara responded by formally prohibiting any of Fontelas' irrigation water from being directed into Mosteiro's terrain.

[46] Susan Tax Freeman has noted a similar distinction in the Spanish hamlet of Valdemora between water within the public domain by law, but administered freely in local terms: 'Although the water supply is public by law, the fountain and lavadero are común-owned structures and the común considers all who use them liable for their maintenance and repair' (1970:121, 36).

The fifth major type of land in Fontelas are its vineyards. While there are a number of small private vineyards scattered throughout the terrain of Fontelas, the majority of vineyards are contiguous plots located at the South-east extreme of the hamlet terrain (Map 2) in a block of land termed *o Vinhago* (the large Vineyard). This Vineyard constitutes one of the more sandy, drier stretches of land in the hamlet and is situated on a gentle slope exposed to maximum sunlight. All of the sub-sections of the Vineyard are privately owned plots separated only by single boundary stones, narrow footpaths, or an occasional larger path for the passage of ox-carts. There are no enclosed or constructed bowers in or around the Vineyard, nor any kind of arbours of climbing plants, vines, or trees anywhere in the hamlet's terrain (we recall that wine is not a cash crop in Fontelas).

Apart from forms of cooperative labour between households for the execution of the two spring vineyard-diggings and the autumn vintages, the Vineyard is not subject to any form of corporate or communal regulation. Most households perform tasks in their separate plots at approximately the same time during each season, although there are of course a few early starters and late followers. None of the dates for either the diggings or the first vintages are set by Fontelas' hamlet council (Chapter 4) nor are they expected to take place on any specific date. However, in 1841 (29 August) the Mosteiro Câmara had to fix the date of 29 September, prior to which no one was permitted to begin their vintage due to the 'inconveniences and havoc' caused by a few villagers collecting their grapes before the generally agreed time. A by-law set a fine of 1,200 *réis* for anyone found collecting grapes before that date, and each parish chairman was obliged to post a notice so as to avoid the possible excuse of 'ignorance of the law'. Even a year earlier, another Câmara minute in Mosteiro (6 September 1840) stressed the fact that the wines made from grapes collected prior to 24 September 'did not acquire the degree of perfection which Nature offers in this municipality'. This was an isolated case, however, and I heard of no such restriction in recent years in Fontelas.

An approximation of the size of the vineyards in Fontelas can be gained from my landholding survey. Two of the largest holdings in the hamlet had totals of 2.63 and 1.88 hectares of vineyard land, while at the other extreme a large number of households own between 1/4 and 1/2 of a hectare. As most households own at least some vineyards, if only a few rows of vine-plants, rental of vineyard plots is extremely rare. No one mentioned rental of vineyards of any size to me, although a few households have bought small portions of vineyard land in recent years.

There are three further types of land in Fontelas. The first of these is the chestnut-grove or coppice (*souto*). The latter word can refer to (a) a portion of land with a large number of wild or planted chestnut-trees (a Junta minute in 1882 – 19 November – specified an item of property pertaining to the parish church as a *souto de castanheiros*, or 'grove of chestnut-trees'), or equally to (b) a coppice of shrub (also with some chestnut-trees) grown for periodical cutting for litter. The latter type of wood is termed locally a *touça*, and tends to blend in with rye grain fields: many grain fields have merely one or two chestnut-trees within their boundaries and are left fallow occasionally for a few years as a *touça* to provide firewood and shrub. The two largest chestnut-groves in the hamlet were estimated at 3.7 and 5.3 hectares in area. In contrast, many poorer households own neither chestnut-groves nor any chestnut-trees; others own only small groves of between 0.2 and 0.4 hectare in area. As *soutos* are also frequently integral parts of grain fields or adjoin the latter, they are rented along with them.

Two further types of land in Fontelas are threshing-floors (Chapter 4) and roads. Rights of passage within and alongside fields are of crucial importance in a hamlet so heavily dependent on manual agriculture, ox-cart transport, and livestock rearing. The myriad paths and roads passing within and around fields and meadows are thus of great significance to all resident villagers. References to conflicts over passageways between adjacent properties are numerous in the Junta minutes, as well as in a number of legal disputes reaching the town court. Further, roads and paths within the hamlets are frequently in need of repairs and reconstruction, and the hamlet council must be called together in order to coordinate such large public works. In addition to the *baldios* and the three small *poulos*, roads are thus the only other form of truly communal or public land in Fontelas.

This chapter has set forth a description of the major types of land owned and cultivated in Fontelas. I have included some initial information on differences in the proportions of these kinds of land owned and rented by households of varying wealth at the top and bottom of the social hierarchy. In Chapter 3 we will now examine the extent to which these types of land are unequally distributed among the distinct social groups of *proprietários*, *lavradores*, and *jornaleiros*.

3
Social groups

As in many other Southern European communities, land forms the basis of social differentiation in Fontelas.While the system of hierarchy within the hamlet involves a multiplicity of economic and social factors granting higher positions to some households and lower ones to others, the fundamental criterion of this differentiation in villagers' eyes is still the ownership of land. All households are directly engaged in agricultural or pastoral production to some extent – this is a thoroughly *rural* community in all senses of the term. Only 8 adults of the hamlet's total population of 187 derive regular incomes from non-agricultural occupations: these are the two shopkeepers, two schoolteachers, the priest, a stone-mason, a Border Guard (*guarda-fiscal*), and a Forest Guard (*guarda-florestal*). All of these specialists nevertheless also engage in some form of agriculture, however minimal. Despite this universal dependence on farming, neither direct ownership nor indirect access to land are in any way equally distributed within the hamlet. These 'crude material differences in wealth' (Davis 1977:81–9) are the subject of this chapter.

Although inequalities in the size and structure of landholdings form the core of a much broader field of ranked social groups, I do not wish to maintain that such inequalities constitute totally determinant forces. As Pierre Bourdieu has noted for the villages of Béarn in South-west France: 'An 'important' family was recognized not only by the extent of its landholdings but also by a whole set of signs, among them the external appearance of its house . . .' (1976:123). It is this whole set of signs which forms the overall pattern of the social hierarchy within the peasantry in Fontelas. These signs include both economic and material factors such as land, house size, income, and number of livestock owned, as well as various linguistic and social factors: forms of address, titles, education, and social prestige. The essential form of this hierarchical pattern, however, is firmly grounded in the differential ownership of land.

My primary aim is to show how villagers' categories of social ranking coincide with my own analysis of crude material differences in their landed wealth. One central problem arising from these materials is the definition of the so-called 'middle peasantry'. In this chapter I will present information suggesting that such a category obscures rather than illuminates the structure of tenurial and productive relations between different social groups. In Fontelas a small core of wealthy households owns and controls large quantities of land, while a large number of smallholders continue to depend upon insufficient holdings, wage labour, and rental of land from this core of owners. For the village of Becedas in Central Spain, Brandes has maintained that: 'Everyone shares *a middling status as independent proprietor*, and the effective interdependence between landless and landed villagers has been totally eliminated' (Brandes 1975:75–6; my emphasis). Despite recent emigration from both regions, an entirely different process seems to be taking place in Fontelas. This interdependence has not been eliminated and the majority of villagers do not view themselves as middling in status. Wealthy landowning households are the only ones to stress that 'we are all equal here' (thereby understating their superior status) while most villagers consistently point to internal inequalities and their own inferior positions.[1]

Land and social groups

Table 3 presents a detailed analysis of the size and structure of all of Fontelas' landholdings. Appendix 1 describes the method used to obtain these figures. A close examination of this table is worthwhile at this point, as it sets out the basic pattern of hierarchy in the hamlet to which I will refer throughout the rest of this book.

The first column in Table 3 lists all of the households in the hamlet (minus the bus-driver's – H17) according to the total size of each holding farmed. This total is then broken down into the amounts of land owned, land cleared on the commons, land rented, and land rented out. For example, in the middle of the table, Ricardo farms a total holding of 9.58 hectares, of which 6.75 are owned by himself and his wife. Included in these 6.75 owned are the 2.67 hectares that Ricardo has cleared on the *baldios*. A further 2.83 hectares of land are rented from others, while none of this household's land is rented out. For most households then, the total amount of land farmed can be obtained by adding the total amounts owned and rented. For those households that rent land out, the total amount of land farmed can be obtained by subtracting the amount rented out from the amount owned. The form in which the table is organized

[1] I refer here specifically to the perception of this inferior position by the poorer groups *within* the hamlet community, and not to the wider sense of the 'underdog position of the peasantry' *vis-à-vis* the State (Shanin 1973:15). The domination of the peasantry by outsiders (of course also evident in Fontelas) should not obscure parallel patterns of domination by insiders: a somewhat different kind of underdog position and inferiority perception is noticeable among many of the smallholders in Fontelas with respect to the hamlet's large landowners. Until very recently, the collective position of many of these smallholders was that of day-labourers within the hamlet and temporary migrant labourers in other parts of Trás-os-Montes province. This life-style has defined them more precisely as mobile semi-proletarians rather than as independent landowning peasants.

Table 3. *Landholdings, 1978*

Social Groups & Households	Total size of holding farmed (hectares)	Total owned	*Baldios* cleared (included in total owned)	Land rented	Land rented out	House-hold size	(*Avg.*)	Plough team (P)	Occupation
4 Proprietários (> 30 ha)									
H38 – D. Elvira	48.08	50.83	0	0	2.75	9		tractor 2	proprietária
29 – P. Gregório	41.25	43.33	0	0	2.08	4		–	priest & schoolteacher
39 – D. Sofia	27.08	40.83	0	0	13.75	3	5.0	tractor 3	proprietária/schoolteacher
28 – Cláudio	30.61	35.42	0	0	4.81	4		P	proprietário
	147.02	170.41	0	0	23.39				
	28.1%	*33.2%*			*58.0%*				
7 Large lavradores (20–30 ha)									
40 – Delfim	29.17	29.17	0	0	0	6		P + tractor 1	lavrador
30 – Miguel	27.29	28.75	4.16	0	1.46	4		P	lavrador
19 – Julião	27.80	26.72	0.33	1.08	0	10		P	lavrador/chief of police
32 – Bento						2	4.7	P	lavrador
31 – Bernardo	22.00	22.25	0	0	0.25	5		P	lavrador/chief of police
34 – Daniel	21.58	21.58	0	0	0	3		P	lavrador
33 – Gabriel	20.21	20.54	0	0	0.33	3		P	lavrador
	148.05	149.01	4.49	1.08	2.04				
	28.3%	*29.0%*	*14.1%*	*2.7%*	*5.1%*				
14 Lavradores (6–20 ha)									
6 – Juliana	16.67	16.67	0.83	0	0	8		P	lavradora
12 – Benigno	15.00	13.33	1.67	1.67	0	1		–	–
14 – Lourenço	14.33	14.33	2.50	0	0	6		P	lavrador
36 – André	12.66	12.37	1.67	0.29	0	4		P	lavrador
21 – Elias	11.56	4.31*	0.83	7.25	0	5		P	lavrador/shepherd
11 – Leopoldina	11.25	10.25	0	1.00	0	4		P	lavradora
23 – Fortunato	10.75[a]	0.33	0.33	10.42	0	4		tractor 3	sharecropper
13 – Ricardo	9.58	6.75	2.67	2.83	0	3	4.6	P	lavrador
10 – Rosa	8.95	8.25	0	0.83	0.13	3		–	–
9 – Cristina	7.21	7.21	0.58	0	0	7		–	Border Guard
20 – Jacinto	7.16	4.58	1.25	2.58	0	3		P	lavrador
8 – Amaro	7.00	6.83	0.67	0.17	0	6		P	lavrador/shepherd
3 – Romão	6.83	6.00	1.17	0.83	0	5		P	lavrador/shepherd
47 – Claudina	6.63	4.00	0.25	2.63	0	6		P	lavrador/shepherdess
	145.58	115.21	14.42	30.50	0.13				
	27.8%	*22.4%*	*45.3%*	*75.6%*	*0.3%*				
31 Smallholders (0–6 ha)									
22 – Eduardo	5.87	2.46	0.08	3.41	0	6		–	shepherd
1 – Silvério	5.66	4.41	1.33	1.25	0	4		–	shepherd

15 – Duarte	4.71	4.71	1.67	0	0	1		–	–
42 – Paulo	4.31	3.00	1.08	1.31	0	3		–	–
25 – Balbina	4.29	3.62	0	0.67	0	3	*2.6*	–	–
26 – Aurélio	4.21	4.21	0	0	0	3		–	–
49 – Inácio	4.00	3.33	3.00	0.67	0	2		–	–
46 – Diogo	1.83	3.33	1.25	0	1.50	1		–	–
45 – Pedro	3.16	2.83	1.50	0.33	0	2		–	–
51 – Vitorino	2.83[b]	3.08	1.00	0	0.25	1		–	–
2 – Lucrécia	3.00	3.00	0	0	0	4		–	–
37 – Águeda	3.00	3.00	0.25	0	0	1		–	–
	60.78	56.14	11.66	8.22	3.58				
	11.6%	*10.9%*	*36.6%*	*20.4%*	*8.9%*				
48 – Narciso	2.92	2.92	?	0	0	1		–	-
53 – Sebastião	2.75	2.75	0	0	0	2		–	shopkeeper
27 – Sância	1.25	2.58	0	0	1.33	1		–	–
5 – Helena	1.96	2.50	0.08	0	0.54	3		–	–
54 – Afonso	2.08	2.08	0.42	0	0	2		–	–
44 – Engrácia	2.00	1.71*	0	0.29	0	3		–	–
43 – Vilfredo	1.67	1.42	0	0.25	0	2		–	jornaleiro
16 – Vigailde	1.25	1.58	0	0	0.33	2		–	–
41 – Jerónimo	1.50	1.50	?	?	0	1	*1.9*	–	jornaleiro
4 – Ezequiel	1.25	1.25	0.58	0	0	4		–	jornaleiro
35 – Tomé	1.00	1.00	0.17	0	0	1		–	jornaleiro
57 – Hermínio	0.75	0.75	0	0	0	4		–	Forest Guard
56 – Floriano	0.67	0.67	0	0	0	1		–	stone-mason
55 – Simão	0.25	0.25	?	0	0	1		–	shoemaker
18 – Marcos	0.17[c]	0.17	0	0	0	1		–	–
52 – Eufémia	0.02	0.02*	0	0	0	1		–	–
	21.49	23.15	1.25	0.54	2.20				
	4.1%	*4.5%*	*3.9%*	*1.3%*	*5.4%*				
Others	–	–	–	–	9.00				
					22.3%				
55 Landholdings	522.92	513.92	31.82	40.34	40.34	187	18		

Notes to Table 3:

* These individuals are lent the following plots (included in their amounts of land owned):
Elias – 0.25 hectare
Matias – 1.25 hectares
Engrácia – 0.13 hectare arable field
Eufémia – 0.02 hectare garden

a – Fortunato is Dona Sofia's sharecropper and former servant. He cultivates 20.84 hectares for the latter's and his own household, so I have approximated his own holding at one half of this amount as he and Dona Sofia split all of their crops in half. The rest of Dona Sofia's land is either rented out or temporarily uncultivated.
b – Vitorino leases a number of plots to co-villagers on a sharecropping basis; he is elderly and lives alone.
c – Marcos has bought some land in a neighbouring hamlet and cultivates it there.

Source: Author's Landholding Survey (Appendix I).

thus provides comprehensive information on both land ownership as well as land usage.

The four major social groups in the hamlet can be categorized either according to the total size of the holdings they farm, or the total size of the holdings they own. For example, most of the *lavradores* rent land from others and have cleared large amounts of land on the commons – their position is thus defined by the total size of the holdings they farm, although they own substantially smaller quantities of land. In contrast, the position of the 11 wealthier households is defined by the size of the holdings they own, as they rent out considerable amounts of land and have cleared very little common-land.

Also included in the table are the size of each household (permanent resident members), possession of a plough team, and the occupation of the head of household. Where no specific occupation is listed 'agriculture' is understood, although more will be said below about the particular kinds of farming and wage labour engaged in by these smallholders. Where two occupations are listed, such as *lavrador*/shepherd, this indicates a dual orientation within the household with a predominance of the first.

The amount of land owned by resident villagers is 513,92 hectares.[2] Of this total (which includes the 31.82 hectares of cleared common-land) 31.34 are rented by villagers to other residents within Fontelas. There are three further sources of rented land which account for the discrepancy (9.0 hectares) between the total amount of land rented and the total rented out. These sources are: (a) 5.42 hectares rented out by seven emigrant villagers resident in France; (b) 2.66 hectares rented to villagers but from unspecified owners who are probably resident villagers; and (c) 0.92 hectare (two small *poulos*) rented out by the Church. Thus the total amount of land farmed in Fontelas includes the total amount owned by resident villagers plus 9.0 additional hectares, or 522.92 hectares. This figure also includes all plots owned but temporarily uncultivated by residents. Thus, the total amount of land rented by villagers accounts for only 7.8 per cent of the total land owned.

To this total we should add the 93 hectares of non-arable common-land currently used for pasturage and the collection of shrub and firewood, thus bringing the total area of arable and pasture land *used* by hamlet residents to 615.92 hectares. The total amount of land cleared on the *baldios* accounts for only 6.2 per cent of the total amount owned. Taken together, the amounts of land rented and cleared (72.16 hectares) account for 14 per cent of the total land owned. This pattern of land tenure reveals that Fontelas is predominantly a hamlet of owner-cultivators.

One additional source of land used for rental is that owned by villagers who

[2] Comparing this total with the size of large *latifúndia* estates in Southern Portugal (Cutileiro 1971:42) the amount of land owned by the entire hamlet of Fontelas is equivalent to the size of only *one* of Vila Velha's latifundist's own holdings!

are emigrants in France, Germany, and Spain, or resident in other areas of Portugal. A systematic survey of these villagers' holdings was not carried out, but a number of resident households enumerated plots owned by emigrant siblings which were entrusted to them temporarily. For example, the smallholder Matias and his wife Bernarda have been lent 7.75 hectares (they cultivate 1.25 of these) owned by Bernarda's four siblings in Lisbon, Brazil, Spain, and France.[3] These cases of emigrants' lending or entrusting of land are the only exceptions to an entirely internal system of land tenure in Fontelas. No one rents any land from any of Fontelas' neighbouring hamlets, nor vice versa. Only one villager (the smallholder Marcos) has bought land in a neighbouring hamlet which he farms there. The total amount of land farmed in Fontelas is thus likely to be an underestimate of the total amount of *cultivable* land in the community. Also to be taken into account are those plots cleared on the commons by non-residents, and some plots mentioned by current residents which they had cleared but which were subsequently abandoned as they produced negligible crops of rye. Much of this land could theoretically be brought back into cultivation. A guarded estimate would thus place the total amount of currently cultivated and cultivable land in the hamlet (both private and commons) at about 700 hectares.[4]

I have divided the hamlet's households in Table 3 into four main social groups according to the size of their landholdings. What other criteria of differentiation are used by villagers to define these social groups, and how are these definitions related to the varying sizes of their landholdings?

1. Smallholders. I have termed the first group 'smallholders'. These households currently farm landholdings of between 0 and 6 hectares. Formerly, most of these villagers were *jornaleiros* (day-labourers) and were listed as such in administrative and parish records from the mid-nineteenth century through the 1960s. Today the word *jornaleiro* is rarely used in Fontelas due not only to the small number of villagers (5) performing wage labour on a regular basis, but also to the connotations of dependence and poverty that the term implies. Smallholders do nevertheless use the term to describe the occupations of relatives in their genealogies. Another word no longer used today but present in the historical records is *cabaneiro* (cottager) denoting a smallholding cultivator who neither worked for a daily wage nor possessed sufficient land to

[3] In her analysis of landholdings in the Castilian hamlet of Valdemora, Susan Tax Freeman also excludes the holdings of emigrant siblings (1970:17).

[4] Compare this total with the much larger amounts of land cultivated in Pisticci in Southern Italy (22,216 hectares), Genuardo in Sicily (13,648 hectares), and Vila Velha in Southern Portugal (8,900 hectares) (see Davis 1977:82–4). Much closer in scale are the totals of land farmed in the Central Spanish town of Belmonte de los Caballeros, with 2,182 hectares (Lisón-Tolosana 1966:20) and in Valdemora, with 87.61 hectares (Freeman 1970:17). Fontelas does of course exhibit many structural features more comparable to the two latter Spanish communities than to the southern Portuguese Vila Velha.

support a plough team. The word suggests both cottage (*cabana*) as well as the verb to dig (*cavar*). The latter meaning is the most frequent in Fontelas. Villagers describe these individuals as defined not by their dwellings or cottages but by their characteristic form of labour – digging rather than ploughing. Their only tools were hoes and picks, and they were hired for their manual labour and paid in wages or kind. While the term *jornaleiro* is still occasionally used today in the hamlet, the word *cabaneiro* is never used except in reference to the past.

A variety of words are used by other villagers with larger holdings to refer to this group: one reason I have called them smallholders is precisely because there is no accepted term for them which is consistently used today. These households are spoken of as farming very small holdings or just 'a few little fields'. The owners of dwarfholdings (less than 3 hectares) are particularly pitied and even on occasion ridiculed by others. Quite frequent is the comment: 'he/she has only a tiny garden and a few plots – nothing'. Another saying often quoted by villagers in discussions about property is the following: *Muito tens, muito vales/Nada tens, nada vales* (Owning a lot, you're worth a lot/Owning nothing, you're worth nothing). Again, the term 'dwarfholder' is my own and does not have a current equivalent in the hamlet, and although it may be a rather clumsy term linguistically (suggestive of a person grasping a dwarf!) it is the most precise word available for referring to a minuscule, almost miserable, farm holding. The division between the dwarfholders (0–3 hectares) and smallholders (3–6 hectares) is thus somewhat arbitrary. Note however (Table 3) that it is only the smallholders with more than 3 hectares who begin systematically to rent land from others and to clear land on the commons. A few of the households in this group however (3 smallholders and 3 dwarfholders) rent out some of their land to others. Unless otherwise stated, by 'smallholders' I will thus refer as a whole to all 31 of these households; specific references will then be made to the 16 dwarfholders and the 15 smallholders.

Conspicuous among the dwarfholders is the very minimal amount of land rented from other villagers – only two of these households rent land (Vilfredo and Engrácia). Seven smallholders with slightly larger holdings, however, rent more and larger portions of land. For example, Eduardo rents 3.41 hectares to supplement his own household's 2.46 hectares. While the dwarfholders rent only 0.54 hectare from others, the 15 smallholders rent the much larger quantity of 8.22 hectares. As a whole, the 31 smallholders rent 21.7 per cent of the total land rented. Further, much larger portions of common-land have been cleared by the 15 smallholders than by the dwarfholders. While the latter have cleared only 1.25 hectares, the former have cleared 11.66. The figures indicate that the slight margin of a few more hectares possessed by the 15 smallholders is associated with the renting, clearing, and farming of substantially larger portions of land than the dwarfholders.

Occupationally most of the current smallholders, as well as their parents and grandparents, were formerly either day-labourers or resident servants in wealthier households. The present occupations of the dwarfholders and smallholders can be summarized as follows. Today, only four dwarfholders (and one smallholder) work for other villagers for daily wages: these wages were 200 *escudos* in 1976, rising to 500 in 1978 (£3.33 and £6.10 respectively).[5] Even today, elderly smallholders recall their childhood years and mention daily wages of 'only 7 *escudos*' (about £0.11) or merely 'a bit of bread or wine'. Two dwarfholders (the stone-mason and the Forest Guard) have steady incomes, respectively, from house construction and the town Forestry Service, but both of these specialists also cultivate small garden plots and one or two grain and potato fields. They are both outsiders to the hamlet and bought their land in Fontelas a number of years ago. The former shoemaker Simão, pitifully poor by hamlet standards, manages to cultivate a tiny garden plot despite his age and poor health.[6] Also among the smallholders are the hamlet's two shopkeepers, both of whom also farm a number of fields as supplements to their cash incomes from shop sales. Finally, the hamlet's blacksmith only works on a part-time basis during the winter months, and two households (Silvério and Eduardo) herd flocks of sheep co-owned in each case by two wealthy *proprietário* households (Dona Elvira and Dona Sofia respectively). As both of these shepherd households have little land of their own, both flocks are grazed on the meadows of the two wealthier households. The remaining smallholders and dwarfholders eke out a living on their tiny holdings with the help of other villagers.

None of the smallholders owns a plough team of draught animals. In a few cases, two smallholders will pool a cow or mule with another smallholder's in order to form a joint plough team. Consequently, most of these households depend on other villagers with cows or tractors for the ploughing of their few grain and crop fields. These ploughing services are described (by the ploughers) as 'favours for the poor' but are usually repaid with the smallholders' return labour and sometimes with cash. The dwarfholders' landholdings are so small that it is virtually impossible for them to engage in equal exchanges of labour or goods with any of the wealthier households. Many dwarfholders thus work not for wages but for meals and donations of small quantities of food. The general economic situation of the 15 smallholders is poor, and were it not for the recent improvements in State welfare payments and the advent of emigrants' remittances following 1964, most of them would

[5] I have calculated these wage equivalents according to the following three exchange rates for British currency during my fieldwork: mid-1976: £1 = 60 *escudos*/mid-1977: 66 *escudos*/mid-1978: 82 *escudos* (Banco Borges e Irmão, municipal town).

[6] Simão's funeral in 1977 was a particularly sad one. Not only did he have no kin in Fontelas or nearby (a distant relative was called from Spain to attend the funeral), but a number of villagers spoke of his abject poverty and lack of cleanliness. One comment evoked a popular local saying that some people are so dirty physically that it seems that they have taken 'only two baths in their entire life – the first when they were baptized and the second when they die'.

6 The indispensable plough team: a *lavrador* cultivates a rye field.

be below the near-destitute state of the dwarfholders. Eight of the 15 smallholder households have emigrant siblings or children in France and six also have siblings or children emigrant in Spain and Brazil. In contrast, only four of the 16 dwarfholder households have siblings or children emigrant in France, and another four have relatives in Spain and Brazil. Twelve of the 31 smallholder households consist of solitary individuals: only two of these twelve are widows and one is a widower. One married man's wife is not resident in the hamlet, and the remaining 8 are all elderly and unmarried (7 men and 1 woman).

Of the total amount of land owned in the hamlet, the 31 smallholders as a whole own only 79.29 hectares, or 15.4 per cent. The 16 dwarfholders alone own only 23.15 hectares, or 4.5 per cent. The average size of holding in this group as a whole is only $2\frac{1}{2}$ hectares. The figures are revealing, as the smallholding households constitute 31 of the hamlet's 57 households. More than half of the hamlet's households thus own only about 1/6 of the land.

2. Lavradores. Members of this group are set apart from the smallholders by the size of their holdings (between 6 and 20 hectares) and by their possession of a plough team. It is important to note that the term *lavrador* is used today by villagers in the hamlet to refer to other villagers: it is a currently employed native term and not the invention of the ethnographer. No villager without a plough team is termed a *lavrador*. (The word literally means 'plougher' and stresses the meaning of the verb *lavrar* – to plough.) Even those smallholders who do own a plough and who pool an animal with another household's animal are not termed *lavradores*. The word implies in the strictest sense the ownership of a plough team and not merely a plough or one draught animal. The term is an old one, and comparable terms have been reported for many other parts of Southern Europe. Georges Duby (1978:187) has noted for the French peasantry that: 'the fundamental social distinction apparent in rural France as early as the tenth century finally split the peasantry into two distinct groups: those that had to work the land by hand, and, vastly superior to them, the *laboratores*, those rich enough to possess a plough team'.[7]

As is evident in Table 3, three households not owning plough teams have been classified within this group due to the size of their holdings and their general socio-economic situation. Cristina's son-in-law is a Border Guard in a nearby hamlet and spends part of each week there and part in Fontelas; for its ploughing this household pays for the tractor services of one of the hamlet's wealthy *proprietários*. Similarly, Rosa's husband is an emigrant in France and her household consists of herself and their two young children. Rosa's brother, resident in a neighbouring hamlet, comes to Fontelas to plough her fields with his tractor. Finally, the elderly Benigno lives alone and his two sons are emigrants in France and Germany. Benigno's daughter-in-law Juliana has her eldest son plough the few plots needed by her father-in-law. All three of these households have owned plough teams in the recent past and their holdings are considered medium-sized by other villagers. Although they do not own plough teams at the present moment and are not technically *lavradores*, they are clearly viewed as members of this group by other villagers.

Comparing the *lavradores* with the smallholders, a number of sharp contrasts immediately appear. Firstly, the size of holding needed to support a plough team is 6 or more hectares. This minimum of 6 hectares need not be

[7] A similar contrast between ploughing peasants (*laboureurs*) as distinct from manual workers (*manouvriers*) has been noted by Marc Bloch in rural France: 'Ever since the Middle Ages a careful distinction had been drawn between two categories of peasant: one group (clearly the wealthier) owned teams of draught-animals – horses, oxen, donkeys – the other had to rely on the strength of their own right arms. The antithesis was between *cultivateurs*, ploughmen who "had horses to do their labouring" and manual workers, *laboureurs de bras*, *brassiers* or husbandmen *ménagers*. Medieval lists of labour services make a distinction between the two . . . it is obvious that the essential cleavage was between *manouvriers*, manual workers, and *laboureurs*' (Bloch 1978:193–4).

owned, but the household must have *access* to a total of 6 hectares in order to maintain two draught animals. The 6 hectares may of course be a combination of land owned, land rented, and land cleared on the commons, but they must include at least 1.5 hectares of meadowland: this is the minimum amount needed to feed two cows or oxen. Three of the households in this group (Claudina, Jacinto, and Elias) own substantially less than the minimum but rent supplementary land, bringing their total holdings to more than 6 hectares. There is one exception to this pattern: Fortunato is a former servant and current sharecropper on Dona Sofia's large holding of 40.83 hectares. Although Fortunato operates Dona Sofia's tractor, villagers constantly stress his non-ownership of both the tractor and the land he sharecrops. He is still termed a *lavrador*, however, as no specific word for 'sharecropper' exists in the hamlet.[8] I measured the size of the holding Fortunato cultivates for Dona Sofia at 20.84 hectares, thus estimating the land cultivated for his own household alone at 10.42 hectares (Note a to Table 3). Part of Dona Sofia's remaining 20 hectares are rented to others and the rest is currently left uncultivated. Fortunato's case further illustrates that the term *lavrador* refers less to the ownership of land than to the activity of ploughing, whether that ploughing occurs on one's own or another villager's land.

Secondly, the *lavradores* rent far more land from others than do the smallholders. The figures are striking: these 14 households rent 30.50 hectares in all, or 75.6 per cent of the total land rented. These households have also cleared large amounts of common-land: 14.42 hectares, or 45.3 per cent of the total amount cleared. Every one of these 14 households has enlarged its holding either by clearing or rental, and 9 of the 14 have done both. However, the *lavradores* do not as a rule rent out any land to others – their pattern of land usage is so intense that they cultivate virtually every bit of land they manage to acquire.

Thirdly, four of these households supplement arable farming with shepherding. In contrast to the shepherd/smallholders Silvério and Eduardo, these four households' flocks constitute only a source of supplementary income and not their primary livelihood. Fourthly, the size of these 14 households is larger than the size of the smallholding households. A number of these households have 6, 7, and 8 resident members. The mean household size among this group is 4.6 members, well above the average size of 2.6 among the smallholders and 1.9 among the dwarfholders. This correlation between landed wealth and household size is a very common feature of many peasant societies, as noted by Netting: 'Wherever recorded data on wealth and household size are present,

[8] Again the comparison with Vila Velha is revealing. The word *seareiro*, approximating the English 'sharecropper', is used in the latter community (Cutileiro 1971:54–9) but is completely unknown in Fontelas. Also never used in the hamlet is another term for sharecropper – *quinteiro* – reported by Jenkins (1979) for the Serra de Monchique in the Western Algarve as well as by Iturra (1985:77) for the Central region of Nelas.

the two indices apparently vary together. With the advent of reliable census figures along with accounts of taxable property in European historical records, a regular relationship can be shown to exist' (1982:641–2).

Possession of a plough team thus places these households in an entirely different niche within the productive system of the community. These 14 households own 115.21 hectares of land, or 22.4 per cent of the total land owned. The average size of holding in this group is about 8 hectares. About 1/4 of the hamlet's households, this group owns just under 1/4 of the land. They *farm* a somewhat larger amount of land, however, if we include the 30.50 hectares they rent from others. In fact, the land they rent and the land they have cleared account together for 31 per cent of the 145.58 hectares they farm. In other words, this group is very dependent upon rented and cleared land. Yet compared to the smallholders, through the use of their plough teams the *lavradores* can cultivate more land, grow larger crops, transport more firewood and shrub, and sell more young livestock.

The general economic situation of this group is substantially better than that of the smallholders. This is due not only to their plough teams, their larger households and therefore greater labour resources, but also to emigrants' remittances. Eleven of these 14 households currently have siblings or children emigrant in France, and members of three of these eleven households have bought small portions of land with the savings from migrant periods abroad. It would be excessive, however, to term this group an ideally 'middle' peasantry. They are in fact (as the 'rented' column shows) more dependent on rented land than the entire smallholder group. Further, many individuals in this group contain in their genealogies a large proportion of relatives who were by occupation *jornaleiros* in the past, and a few have served for a number of years as servants or shepherds within wealthy households in poorer times. Many villagers in this group have thus only become *lavradores* recently through a combination of factors including land rental, land purchase, and the clearing of common-land.

The crucial defining characteristic of this group – a plough team – provides them with a modicum of self-sufficiency: no one in this group performs wage labour today. But the plough team does *not* grant them a position of any particular wealth or status within the hamlet's social hierarchy. Given the choice of defining themselves as either wealthy or poor, most would choose the latter.

3. Large lavradores. The third major social group are the 'large *lavradores*', owning between 20 and 30 hectares of land each. There are two specific terms used to refer to these housholds: *lavradores remediados* and *lavradores abastados*, meaning respectively 'well-off' or 'wealthy' *lavradores*. Again, Table 3 shows that unlike the 14 *lavrador* households, these 7 households do *not* rent land from others (with one exception) but rather rent land out. The figures are small (2.04 hectares rented out) but taken together with the minimal amount of land these households rent from others and the smaller portions of land cleared on the commons (4.49 hectares) an image of the truly self-sufficient peasant household begins to emerge. These households, more so than the *lavradores*, are the real *owner*-cultivators.

Almost all of the land owned by 6 of these 7 households was inherited: Daniel bought most of his household's land, and Delfim bought a substantial portion of land (8.3 hectares) before he married. While Miguel has cleared 4.16 hectares of common-land, both he and Delfim have inherited far more land than they have bought or cleared. Many of these households are related by kinship or marriage to the four wealthier *proprietário* households and tend to cooperate more frequently within their own group or with the latter households than with the rest of the hamlet. One extreme case illustrating this pattern is Gabriel, a religious fanatic who divides his time between his fields, the Church, and conversations with his neighbour the priest. Gabriel is consistently ridiculed for his occasionally crooked ploughing into the furrows of adjacent fields, a practice seen as indicative of this group's excessive love of private property and constant attempts to increment their already large crops and holdings.

Their occupations and preference for mechanized farming also distinguish these households from the *lavradores*. Two individuals (Julião and Bernardo) occupy the positions of *cabos de polícia* (chiefs of police). The title is more impressive in word than in deed, but nevertheless confers some minimal administrative authority on these individuals delegated to them from the Junta in Mosteiro, by whom they are appointed (see Note 7, Chapter 4). Delfim was the first villager in Fontelas to buy a tractor (1965). Delfim's household does not therefore use a plough team regularly, although two of its seven cows are occasionally used as a back-up team (in addition to the tractor) by one of Delfim's daughters during periods of heavy or rushed ploughing. Most of these households consequently produce larger crops than the *lavradores* and smallholders, and tend to use tractors more frequently than draught animals for ploughing and transport. Julião, in fact, formally applied to an administrative body in town for a loan to buy a tractor in 1978. While the four *proprietário* households could be termed 'family capitalists' (Franklin 1969:74),[9] these households could be seen as rich peasants or aspiring capitalist farmers.

The general economic situation of this group is markedly better than that of the *lavradores*. Only two men from this group (Bernardo and Julião) emigrated temporarily to France in the 1960s, and both returned after short periods there. None of the children of the current adult generation in these households are emigrants, while two of Daniel's four children have become Border Guards in other hamlets in the municipality rather than emigrants. The large amounts

[9] The two *proprietário* households with tractors and other agricultural machinery are frequently referred to by other villagers, in a somewhat jocular tone, as the *capitalistas* of the hamlet.

of land owned and inherited by these households are all well over the minimum of 6 hectares needed to support a plough team. They are consequently less dependent upon rental of land, the clearing of common-land, or emigrants' remittances. Where the *lavradores* have as a rule consolidated their current holdings through a variety of means, these households have not needed to.

A glance at the '*baldio*' and 'rental' columns in Table 3 reveals an abrupt change in patterns of land usage between the 14 *lavradores* and these 7 households. Along with the *proprietários*, these households also have larger garden plots and consequently longer irrigation turns. The genealogies of individuals in this group contain many more relatives who were *lavradores* or *proprietários* than those who were *jornaleiros*, and in the case of Daniel's wife Vitória, an enormous number of relatives with military occupations. These households also tend not to own flocks of sheep, as from their point of view the occupation of shepherd (like that of *jornaleiro*) retains connotations of poverty and dependence. Never servants themselves, large *lavradores* are more likely to hire servants to work in their own households.

Quite aware of their greater amounts of landed wealth than those of the smallholders and *lavradores*, members of this group will on occasion direct a derisive laugh at (to their eyes) the ridiculously small amounts of land owned by dwarfholders and smallholders. Wealthier *proprietários*, in contrast, always manage to inject their comments on the poor with a note of Christian pity. Large *lavradores* view their positions as patrons of the poor rather than their equals. As a whole these 7 households own 149.01 hectares, or 29.0 per cent of the total land owned in the hamlet. The average size of holding in this group is about 25 hectares. None of the members of this group would even remotely consider engaging in wage labour, and if given the choice would define themselves as wealthy rather than poor.

4. Proprietários. *Proprietários* constitute the fourth major social group and own holdings of more than 30 hectares each. The word *proprietário*[10] does not translate correctly as 'proprietor' but rather, in its local meaning in Fontelas, as 'large landowner'. The word refers in the hamlet specifically to the owner of a very substantial landholding (by local standards) and should not be confused with the more general meaning of the standard Portuguese term *proprietário*, designating the owner or possessor of any piece of property of unspecified size or value. These four households constitute the hamlet's élite of notables, firmly

[10] Although the word is the same as that used in Vila Velha in Southern Portugal for the social group located between the wealthiest latifundists and the poorer *seareiros* (Cultileiro 1971:50–4), its meaning in Fontelas is quite different. Both today as well as historically, the *proprietários* of Fontelas have occupied the highest positions of wealth and social prestige in the hamlet. Although not absentee landowners they are more comparable in some respects to the latifundists than to the less prosperous group of *proprietários* in Vila Velha. However, the gulf dividing the latifundists from the masses of landless labourers in Vila Velha is of course not as wide in such a small community as Fontelas.

located at the top of the social hierarchy due to the size of their holdings and to the maintenance of their households' past positions of administrative influence, political power, and high moral standing.

Like the large *lavradores*, the *proprietários* have inherited virtually all of their land. The households of Cláudio and Padre Gregório, along with those of Bernardo and his father Bento, formerly farmed the same holding before its partition. Many villagers refer to this former household (called the *Casa do Conselho*) as having owned 'half of the land of the hamlet'. A number of smallholders and *lavradores* worked within this household as servants and shepherds in their younger years. Today the original Conselho household (the priest's) owns the only functioning television (battery-operated) in the hamlet, and the hamlet's only car. It is an imposing structure (Map 3 – H29) and with its adjacent household (H28) it constitutes the largest house-complex in the entire hamlet.

Dona Elvira's holding (50.83 hectares) has not been partitioned as she is an only child. Both Dona Elvira and Dona Sofia purchased tractors in 1970 and these are operated respectively by Valentim and the latter's sharecropper Fortunato. Dona Sofia owns the hamlet's only threshing-machine, which is also operated by Fortunato and rented out to other villagers. Both households (as well as Delfim's) own motor-mowers for haymaking, and they hire out or rent these mechanized implements to co-villagers on a regular basis. Most of these households have either a plough team or agricultural machinery (tractors) that precludes their use of animal traction. (The priest's land is ploughed by his brother Valentim, the owner and driver of the second tractor.) Along with the large *lavrador* Delfim, two of these four households thus own all of the agricultural machinery in the hamlet.

Table 3 allows us to confirm that these four households neither rent land nor have they cleared any on the commons. Rather, they rent out the largest portions of land in the hamlet to others: 23.39 hectares, or over 1/2 of all the land rented. Dona Elvira rents a meadow of 2.25 hectares in area to the *lavrador* Ricardo, for which she receives the highest single rent payment in the hamlet – an annual sum of 120 *alqueires* of rye grain (equivalent to 6,400 *escudos*, or £98). Only two men from this group have emigrated to France: one of these (Valentim) went briefly for two years when emigration increased in the mid-1960s. Others have attained educational training or entered military or ecclesiastical professions. For instance, Dona Sofia is the hamlet's current primary school teacher and her brother, Doutor Custódio, heads a secondary school in Lisbon. The priest's sister Dona Prudência is a schoolteacher in a neighbouring hamlet, while her sister Dona Constância married a Border Guard Sergeant in town. The retired Border Guard Cláudio completes the picture: he married into the hamlet and into the *proprietário* group. Most of the individuals in this group are set apart from the rest of the community not only occupationally but also linguistically through the deferential terms of address *Doutor*, *Dona*, and *Padre*.[11]

Physically, the households of this group are also set apart: their houses are far larger than those of the *lavradores* and smallholders, and their kitchens are without exception separated spatially from the hamlet roads by large courtyards. The rooms and hallways within them are also larger and more numerous than those of other households in the hamlet. During his yearly Easter visit to most of the households in the community (some deliberately shut their doors to the priest) Padre Gregório and his accompanying boys invariably pause, sit down, and eat a snack for conspicuously longer periods within his own and the three other *proprietário* households. This group is also viewed as more religious than the rest of the hamlet, and their attendance at masses and participation in special Church activities is especially good. Many villagers, however, explain this participation by stressing that most of the *proprietários* are in fact relatives of the priest. Further, the women of this group do not perform much manual labour, and when they do so this is limited to garden tasks physically close to the household. *Proprietário* women, particularly when married, do not perform any of the heavier physical tasks executed so frequently by *lavrador* and smallholder women.

The genealogies of *proprietários* reveal marriage alliances predominantly with other members of this group and with some *lavradores*, but rarely with *jornaleiros* or individuals of less prestigious occupations. The history of these individuals' kin groups and households also demonstrates a pattern of large stem-family households (Laslett 1972:16–23) as well as large numbers of resident servants drawn from poorer smallholder households. With regard to the hiring of day-labourers and servants, this group occupies an inverse position to that of the smallholders: never servants or labourers themselves, *proprietários* are normally the hirers of others' labour.

Marriage alliances within this group remain strictly controlled. Due to the system of partible *post-mortem* inheritance, property is not transferred through dowries at marriage but only upon the deaths of both parents (Chapter 7). In this sense, a new household is not normally formed upon marriage and the married couple do not obtain a portion of land or other resources centred upon the new conjugal unit. In fact, there is no new conjugal unit at all, as a frequent practice has been for both spouses to reside after the marriage with each of their respective sets of parents (natolocal residence), the husband sleeping with his wife but returning early the next morning to his own

[11] Anyone who has completed a *licenciatura* university degree (B.A./B.Sc.) is automatically termed a *Doutor* or *Doutora* by villagers. The equivalent feminine term *Dona* is employed for women who have not studied at a university but who nevertheless have some minimal educational qualifications. It is also a respectful term of address for wealthy women of high social status (married or single) and particularly those in the *proprietário* group.

parents' household. No means of inheriting land were open to the spouses until their parents died, and thus each set of parents retained their married child for labour within the natal household.[12]

Thus unless a *proprietário* marries a *proprietária* the portions of land owned by both spouses may eventually diminish in size through partition (if there are a number of other siblings). Two such cases have occurred in Fontelas in recent years. The large *lavrador* Bento was a *proprietário* earlier in his life within the large Conselho household. However, his marriage to the servant Tomásia (originally from another hamlet) and his inheritance of 1/4 of his natal household's original holding places him today within the large *lavrador* group. Similarly, the priest's sister Angelina married the large *lavrador* Miguel: although still quite large in size, Angelina's land (1/6 of her mother's holding) along with her husband's is not of the magnitude of the other *poprietário* holdings, and the couple are not termed *proprietários*. Both cases illustrate a pattern within the top of the social hierarchy: it is easier to be born into the *proprietário* group than to stay within it, unless carefully controlled marriage alliances maintain the positions of both spouses in landed wealth as well as social prestige. It is important to note here that these marriage strategies are *not* merely economic ones aimed at maintaining large, intact, and economically viable holdings, but also social and political strategies aimed at maintaining the high rank of each *proprietário* household within the hierarchy (I will return to this point in Chapter 7). Each partition of a large holding within this group, or a series of 'downward' marriages, may lower the position not only of the individuals involved but that of the entire *proprietário* group.

Far from being absentee landlords universally resented by local labourers, the *proprietários* are nevertheless land *owners* in the strictest sense. They rent land out to others and hire labourers and servants to work on their own large holdings, but their position as hamlet residents obliges them to maintain a distance and poise tinged with a personalized note. In other words, these landowners do not constitute an abstract class of absentee exploiters: they all live in the hamlet and come into daily contact with other villagers. Yet some

[12] This form of natolocal residence (Fox 1978) is another indication of the stress in Fontelas on 'vertical' ties of descent and filiation rather than the 'horizontal' matrimonial tie (Chapters 6 and 7). The latter tie is even less firm among the poorer groups due to the absence of sizeable portions of landed property. The formation of a new house and neolocal residence are *not* the rule in Fontelas although these are sometimes stated as ideals. Partible *post-mortem* inheritance and the absence of dowries at marriage together have favoured natolocal, uxorilocal, or virilocal residence. Susan Tax Freeman reports a similar but more temporary form of natolocal residence for the Spanish hamlet of Valdemora, where both spouses customarily remain for one year with their respective parents until after the first harvest (1970:75–7). While legally the partition of a landholding can take place in Fontelas upon the death of the first parent, this is rarer than the later partition following the death of the surviving spouse. Both delayed partitions as well as natolocal residence point to strategies aimed at maintaining the natal household and landholding intact both in terms of maximum labour resources as well as the retention of a unified patrimony.

form of social distance is maintained. This distance, however, is frequently broken down within the confines of these households in cases of the adoption of poorer servants. The epitome of the landowner/servant relationship is not a cut and dried one between hirer and employee, but rather a labour relationship conceptually converted into a form of fictive kinship. Long-standing servants thus become 'like family members' (*como família*). Ironically, the cases of adopted servants reveal that the only way of entering the *proprietário* group is either from the top of the hierarchy or from the very bottom: either one is born into this group or one marries into it. The only exceptions are adopted servants rising from the poor to the wealthy: no one has 'bought' himself or herself into this group.

The general economic situation of these four households is very good, despite their attempts to portray themselves as 'equally poor' with the rest of the hamlet's households or as equally victims of monetary inflation. Underlying this sense of participation in hard times lies a deeper feeling of displacement, in large part due to the *proprietários*' decline as representatives of a formerly dominant rural aristocracy. The 1974 Revolution affected this municipality very minimally with regard to any aspects of agrarian reform, and very few of the measures adopted elsewhere in Portugal were applicable to such smallholding regions. No estates in the area were expropriated, and the words *herdade* (estate) and *latifúndio* are never employed by villagers in Fontelas. A number of *proprietários* in Fontelas and environs nevertheless feared that national political developments (commonly personalized as 'the communists') would in the course of time 'take away our property'. One minor change affecting the hamlet was the cancellation after 1975 of all taxes on land valued at less than 2,000 *escudos* in taxable wealth. In other words, all those paying an annual tax (19 per cent of this taxable wealth) of less than 380 *escudos* (£5.75) were exempt. This change affected only the hamlet's smallholders and some *lavradores*, but none of the large *lavradores* or *proprietários*.

This group today owns 170.41 hectares of land. Only four households thus own 33.2 per cent of the total land owned in the hamlet. The average size of holding in this group is about 43 hectares. Although their ability to recruit labour within the community is suffering setbacks, these households still maintain direct control of a large part (1/3) of the hamlet's land and own virtually all of the available agricultural machinery. Anxious to portray their situation as closer to those below them in the hierarchy or as part of a marginal community of oppressed underdog peasants stuck in a forgotten corner of the country, the *proprietários* are viewed internally as a core of wealthy *ricos* at the top.

I have dealt extensively with Table 3 in order to set out clearly the differences in the sizes of landholdings owned by various households and social groups. The classification does present analytical problems: to what extent are these groups defined not merely by differences in material (landed) wealth but also by accompanying forms of social differentiation? How rigid or flexible are the lines dividing smallholders and *lavradores*, or those separating large *lavradores* and *proprietários*? Can individuals in one group move up in the hierarchy, or down, on the basis of long-term changes in land tenure and emigration, or due to individual placement within favourable or unfavourable inheritance positions?

I do not wish to present these figures on landholdings as totally fixed or determinant. Yet the role of land cannot be underplayed. Rather than constituting static numbers frozen in the present, each particular landholding could be seen as the temporary result of a continuing series of individual and group decisions concerning land, labour, marriage, and inheritance. These decisions vary widely, however, according to the position of particular individuals and households within the social scale. In the following case-studies, as in those in Chapter 5, I will show that this social hierarchy does not constitute a fluid system in which upward or downward mobility is principally a function of individual initiative or failure. Rather, the hierarchy rests upon a historically conditioned system of unequal stratification separating the land-rich from the land-poor.

Table 4 presents a summary of the totals in Table 3 and includes the average size of holding owned by each social group. Taken together with Table 3, this table will allow us to make a number of further points. In the second table we find that each group owns greater portions of land than the group beneath it in the hierarchy. But these portions are concentrated within a smaller number of increasingly larger holdings as we move up the scale.

Immediately apparent is the problem of classification of the two *lavrador* groups as a 'middle' peasantry. A glance at Table 4 reveals that both of these groups could be seen together as a middle group owning 20 medium-sized holdings totaling 264.22 hectares, accounting for 51.4 per cent of the total land owned. The households of both of these groups are large, most of them have plough teams, and the same term is used by others to refer to them. However, it would be equally feasible to join the large *lavradores* with the *proprietários*, both groups thus constituting an upper group owning 319.42 hectares, or 62.2 per cent of the total land owned. Grouped in this way, 11 households (less than 1/5 of the hamlet) control nearly 2/3 of the hamlet's land.

It is significant that there is a concentration of 8 large landowning households in the central sections of the hamlet (Map 3). Four of these 8 households are those of the *proprietários* and the remaining four all pertain to large *lavradores*. Six of these 8 households are related by kinship or marriage. Spatially as well as socially, then, the large *lavradores* are closely linked to the *proprietários*. Furthermore, the pattern of land tenure among this group bears far more similarity to that of the *proprietários* than to that of the *lavradores*. These seven households rent far less land and have cleared fewer common-land plots than either of the two poorer groups. Like the four wealthiest

Table 4. *Land ownership, 1978*

Size of holding owned		Number of holdings	Social groups
Less than 6 ha:	<1	6	
	1–2	6	
	2–3	7	31 Smallholders
	3–4	7	(+ 4 Lavradores)*
	4–5	7	
	5–6	2	
6–20:	6–10	5	
	10–15	4	10 Lavradores (14)
	15–20	1	
20–30:	20–25	3	6 Large lavradores
	25–30	3	
More than 30:	30–40	1	
	40–50	2	4 Proprietários
	>50	1	
		55	

* A number of households are defined by the size of the holdings they *farm*, not own. Thus the total of 14 *lavradores* includes 3 who own only 4–5 hectares each, and the sharecropper Fortunato.

Social group	Size of holding owned (ha)		No. of holdings	Total owned by each group		Avg. size of holding (ha)
Smallholders	dwarf	<3	16	23.15	*4.5%*	1.45
	small	3–6	15	56.14	*10.9%*	3.74
			31	79.29	*15.4%*	2.56
Lavradores	medium	6–20	14	115.21	*22.4%*	8.23**
Large lavradores	large	20–30	6	149.01	*29.0%*	24.84
Proprietários	very large	>30	4	170.41	*33.2%*	42.60
Totals			55	513.92	*100%*	9.34

** Due to the *lavradores*' rental of large portions of land, the average size of holding they farm would be 10.40 hectares.

households, these seven households rent out more land. The 'rented' column in Table 3 is particularly striking. For instance, considered together these two upper groups account for only one of the 21 households that pay rent on land. Further, both groups account for only two of the 25 households that have cleared common-land. Is there, then, more meaning in the hamlet term *lavrador remediado* than is at first apparent?

This form of division would then join the *lavrador* group with the 31 smallholding households, constituting a larger group of 45 households (almost 80 per cent of the hamlet) together owning 194.50 hectares, or still only 37.8 per cent of the land. There is more to this division than the shifting of figures and percentages.[13] In contrast to the clustering of wealthy households in the centre of the hamlet, the spatial distribution of smallholder and some *lavrador* households occurs outside the centre and particularly in the Eastern and Western sections at opposite extremes of the hamlet (Map 3). It is precisely these poorer sections that will be seen in Chapter 4 to possess the smallest turns in irrigation rotations: their minuscule gardens in fact reflect the small total sizes of their landholdings.

This chapter as well as those to follow will show that historically the position of the *lavradores* has been one not of independent cultivators (they are barely that today) but rather of dependent wage labourers. Rather than constituting a ready-made category of middle peasants whose ideal image they poorly fit, the *lavradores* and smallholders constitute 'the poor' of the hamlet. While the poor of Fontelas are certainly not directly comparable in position to the much larger proletariat of rural labourers in the Alentejan parish of Vila Velha (Cutileiro 1971), structures of material and social inequality are nevertheless present in this smallholding community. But these forms of inequality are articulated within the social structure in quite a different way. The hamlet's small size must not divert our attention from its own distinct divisions between varying social categories. Although the community as a whole appears to be one of owner-cultivators, this is not strictly true for the majority of its households. Just as the term 'small family farms' gives a false impression of uniformity within the hypothetical *minifúndio* peasant community, so the term 'middle peasantry' suggests a misleading continuity within a social structure which is itself far more differentiated internally.

Although dramatically affecting the hamlet in a number of ways, emigration during the 1960s has not radically altered the hamlet's system of land tenure. Nor has it eliminated inequalities in landholdings or the divisions between social groups: divisions which are still viewed by many villagers as a dichotomy between the few wealthy and the many poor. These perceptions are not unrelated to the actual distribution of land: the crucial cleavage within the

[13] Voting patterns have also varied among these social groups. I was present in Fontelas on the dates of three major national elections: 25 April 1976 for the National Assembly, 27 June 1976 for the Presidency, and 12 December 1976 for Municipal Bodies (*Autarquias Locais*). At the time of two of these elections (25 April & 12 December) discussions in Fontelas indicated a general trend of party preference: *proprietários* tended to support the right-of-centre Party *Centro Democrático Social* (CDS), some large *lavradores* the centrist *Partido Popular Democrático* (PPD), and a number of the *lavradores* and smallholders the left-of-centre *Partido Socialista* (PS). Very few votes in the parish were cast in any of the three elections for candidates of the Communist Party (PCP) or far-Left parties (see Ministério da Administração Interna 1976; 1977).

hamlet hierarchy is not that between the smallholders and the somewhat more successful *lavradores*, who have attained a measure of well-being through land rental, land purchase, clearing, and emigration. It is rather between the *lavradores* on the one hand, whose life-histories have been those of poor day-labourers, and the large *lavradores* on the other, whose ancestors have (like the *proprietários*') always owned and controlled greater landed wealth. These two groups together (the *proprietários* and large *lavradores*) constitute the dominant élite of the hamlet. The crucial division of Table 3 is thus the 20-hectare line, splitting the hamlet between two large groups of villagers – one with abundant land and the other without. Grouped in this way, the *lavradores*' and smallholders' perception of the social hierarchy is not one of rich, middling, and poor but rather one of 'the rich and the rest'. There is here, then, no proper middle peasantry.

Five case-studies

To what degree are the divisions within the peasantry described above visible in particular individual cases? I have selected five different households – one from each of the four major social groups (plus one dwarfholder) – and provide below a brief summary of their positions *vis-à-vis* land and social rank. The case-studies are intentionally short, as they are meant primarily to provide only an initial picture prior to the longer case-studies in Chapter 5. Here I wish to stress the role of land as the primary criterion of social ranking while at the same time highlighting the villagers' own categories of differentiation, varying subjective meanings attached to the major criteria of stratification, and specific cases of upward and downward peasant mobility.

Throughout the five case-studies, the reader may find it helpful to refer back to Table 5, which contains further internal breakdowns of the landholdings of these selected households. Before examining each case, a brief comparison of the holdings reveals the following initial points. Especially apparent is the wide margin between Dona Elvira's and Bento's holdings and the other three. In turn, every type of land (except vineyards) owned by the former is more than twice the size of all those owned by Bento. Some of Dona Elvira's types of land are well over three times the size of those of the *lavrador* André. Both Dona Elvira and Bento rent out portions of land to others. The latter's holding is still in turn twice as large as Andre's. Bento's 5.0 hectares of meadowland provide both his own and his son's households with ample land for the upkeep of their two plough teams. Further, neither Dona Elvira nor Bento rent any land from others, and neither household has cleared plots on the commons.

The holdings of the other three households are extremely small in contrast. Ten of the 15 different portions of land owned by these households are less than 1 hectare in area. Both André and Eduardo have cleared land on the *baldios*, and all three households rent land from others. André rents 0.29

Table 5. *Internal structure of five landholdings, 1978*

	Dona Elvira Proprietária	*Bento* Large lavrador	*André* Lavrador	*Eduardo* Small-holder	*Engrácia* Dwarf-holder
Total size of holding farmed (ha)	48.08	22.00	12.66	5.87	2.00
Total size of holding owned	50.83	22.25	12.37	2.46	1.71
Types of land owned					
Arable fields	25.67	12.50	8.33	1.71	1.54
Meadows	13.75	5.00	1.62	0.37	0
Groves	7.50	2.50	1.42	0.17	0.13
Vineyards	2.33	1.42	0.58	0.04	0
Gardens	1.58	0.83	0.42	0.17	0.04
Baldios cleared (included in arable fields)	0	0	(1.67)	(0.08)	0
Land rented	0	0	0.29[a]	3.41[b]	0.29[c]
Land rented out	2.75[d]	0.25[e]	0	0	0
Ploughing method	1 tractor	2 plough teams	1 plough team	1 mule	–

a – Rents 0.25 hectare meadow from sister-in-law (a smallholder) and 0.04 hectare communal meadow from Our Lady of Carmo.

b – Rents 0.83 hectare meadow from dwarfholder Sância and 2.58 hectares of fields from 5 owners (smallholder Diogo, dwarfholder Sância, large *lavrador* Gabriel, and 2 non-resident smallholders).

c – Rents 0.08 hectare meadow, 0.08 hectare garden, and 0.13 hectare field all from smallholder Vitorino, and is lent 0.13 hectare field by her half-sister (dwarfholder Helena).

d – Rents out 2.25 hectare meadow to *lavrador* Ricardo.

e – Rents out 0.25 hectare field to dwarfholder Vilfredo.

hectare of meadowland in order to supplement his own household's meagre 1.62 hectares of meadows, thus bringing his total meadowland farmed to 1.91, just above the minimal amount needed to support a plough team. This household's total holding (12.66 hectares) is considered a medium-sized holding by other villagers. About 2/3 of André's holding is composed of arable grain fields, shrubland, and some chestnut-groves, only half of which can be cultivated each year due to the two-course open-field system. Without renting this additional 0.29 hectare of meadow, André's meadowland would be only just above the 1.5 hectares necessary to maintain a plough team. With any less meadowland, André would be forced to hire one of the tractors to plough his fields, or to exchange his labour for the ploughing services of another *lavrador*.

Yet more land is rented by the smallholder Eduardo – more than half (3.41) of the total land comprising his holding of 5.87 hectares is rented from others. Were it not for this rented land, Eduardo's own holding (actually his wife's) would only comprise the dwarfholding size of 2.46 hectares. A full-time shepherd for Dona Sofia, Eduardo occasionally pools his mule with his neighbour's (the smallholder Matias) for joint ploughing as his wife owns only 0.37 hectare of meadowland. This is well below the minimum amount needed for a plough team.

Finally, the smallest holding – that of the dwarfholder Engrácia – is minuscule by hamlet standards. It provides neither enough land to support even one draught animal nor sufficient crops to support all of Engrácia's four illegitimate[14] sons. Engrácia owns no meadows, no vineyards, and has not cleared any land on the commons. Barely subsisting, Engrácia does not exchange labour with her economic equals but rather obtains sporadic help and favours from kin or other co-villagers who pity her. Unmarried and short of labour within her own household, Engrácia must have her few small grain fields ploughed by her *lavrador* brother Elias. These factors once prompted her brother to state: 'My sister Engrácia must be the poorest person in the entire hamlet.'

1. Dona Elvira's household. Dona Elvira's household (Map 3 – H38) presents a number of characteristics which constitute the epitome of the *proprietário* group. Herself an only child, Dona Elvira (aged 74) occupies an uncontested position as sole heir to her parents' wealth. All of her land was inherited and none of it purchased: in fact, a few plots were sold to villagers in Mosteiro a number of years ago. Although unmarried but addressed in person with the respectful *Senhora Dona Elvira* due to her high rank, Dona Elvira is also referred to within Fontelas by the nickname *a fidalga*, or 'the gentlewoman'. Educated, literate, and possessing high prestige within Fontelas as well as in the eyes of many of the neighbouring hamlets, Dona Elvira is one of the last of a continuing line of local notables. Despite her laudatory nickname, however, she does not belong to the regional nobility. Very wealthy noble and ecclesiastical houses in the region are usually identifiable by a coat-of-arms and an adjoining chapel. Neither of these markers set apart Dona Elvira's or any other *proprietário* house in the parish (there are a few such houses in the nearby town).

[14] I should clarify here that none of my references to illegitimacy (or indeed to that apparently charged term 'bastard', used here scientifically) or other similar liaisons should be viewed as a value judgement of either the individuals in question (whether living or mentioned in parish records) or their social group or hamlet. The problems under study are human realities with varied historical and sociological roots, which I have analysed with the greatest objectivity possible. Perhaps 'natural child' would be a preferable designation. In any case, the term 'illegitimacy' is simply too all-encompassing and I have chosen therefore to retain 'bastardy' instead, despite the strong moralistic undertones characterizing the latter word's social connotations. To avoid repetition, however, I use the three terms interchangeably.

7 Young woman ploughing a field.

There is ample evidence that historically this household was one of the most influential within the entire parish. Both Dona Elvira's father and grandfather sat as aldermen on the town Câmara, and her great-grandfather Miguel Pires served as an alderman on the Mosteiro Câmara during the years when Mosteiro was elevated to municipal level (1837–54). When an electoral census of adult males in the extinct municipality of Mosteiro was conducted in 1851, Miguel Pires was listed as one of the wealthiest *lavradores* in the parish, paying the third highest tithe of the 91 registered men. Also on the list was Miguel's nephew, the Reverend Venâncio Pires (Dona Elvira's great-uncle).

The parish records to be examined in Chapter 5 reveal that Dona Elvira's household has had a permanent structure of resident servants since the late

8 Chestnut collection (November): three sisters from a large *lavrador* household carry sacks on their heads.

nineteenth century. This pattern continues today. Figure 1 below sets forth the structure of his household in 1977, and includes selected individuals from Dona Elvira's genealogy.[15]

The servant Lucas (Generation 3 – person g) as well as his common-law wife[16] Leónida (3h) reside today within Dona Elvira's household (Lucas had

[15] Not *all* of the marriage relationships of individuals outside the household in question have been included: for instance, Bento (3a) is married and has children and grandchildren. Occupations are either those given to individuals today or those listed in parish or administrative records.

[16] I shall use the terms 'common-law wife/common-law husband' for individuals living in a consensual union. There were four such unions in Fontelas in 1976–8, and the parish records reveal further cases in past times. Locally, villagers use the terms *amigados* (literally, 'befriended'), *amantizados* (literally, 'to be tied to one's lover'), or simply *juntaram-se* ('they got together') to refer to such couples. Only local priests and some *proprietário* families use the strictly ecclesiastical term for concubinage (*amancebados*), and it is only they who view this type of relationship in a depreciative way. Other villagers accept these unions as *de facto* marriages.

resided in the household many more years than Leónida). The younger servant Gracinda (2g) has through time become 'like a daughter' to Dona Elvira. This was partly due to the servant Lucas' long years of service in the household; it is Gracinda and not her mother Leónida who directs most of the internal household economy. Gracinda married the *proprietário* Valentim, a brother of the current parish priest Padre Gregório (2c), who is himself a *proprietário* and also resident in Fontelas. Prior to their marriage, Valentim emigrated briefly for two years to France in the mid-1960s. Upon returning to Fontelas and marrying Gracinda, Valentim purchased a tractor with his savings and some assistance from Dona Elvira. At this time he continued to reside in his own parents' household for about five years, only coming to Dona Elvira's household to sleep at night (Chapter 6). Valentim's own inheritance of 1/6 (10.83 hectares) of his mother's very large landholding (65 hectares) was thus joined finally with Dona Elvira's own 38.33 hectares when Valentim moved into the latter's household. Along with Leónida's own 1.67 hectares, the current size of this landholding is 50.83 hectares. Hamlet rumour stresses that all of Dona Elvira's land has been willed to her servant Gracinda and the latter's brother Mateus (2h), currently a university student in the city of Porto. Like his sister Gracinda, Mateus has also been adopted[17] through time by Dona Elvira, who was chosen as his baptismal godmother (*madrinha*).

Valentim's marriage to Gracinda in fact merely reproduced already existent ties of kinship and marriage between Dona Elvira's household and that of the priest, as the latter's mother Manuela (3b) was Dona Elvira's second cousin (FMBSD). Gracinda's marriage to the *proprietário* Valentim was the culmination of Gracinda's own upward mobility within the hamlet hierarchy: an illegitimate daughter of a poor servant, Gracinda's long residence within her father's hirer's household placed her in a favourable pseudo-kinship relation to the aging and heirless Dona Elvira. This is one of a number of examples of female servants rising from the bottom of the hierarchy to the top. Unlike his sister Angelina (2d) who married the large *lavrador* Miguel and thus married down, Valentim stayed within the *proprietário* group through his marriage to Dona Elvira's adopted servant. This close tie between marriage and landed wealth is constantly stressed among the *proprietários* and large *lavradores*. In fact, some villagers point to Valentim's cleverness by stating that 'he married not his wife but Dona Elvira's fields'.

The scale of farming in this household is considerably larger than that of

[17] Formal adoption in Fontelas is extremely rare, but there are a few cases of the 'social adoption' of servants by *proprietários*. In this case, Gracinda has become 'like a daughter' to Dona Elvira although no legal adoption process took place. Gracinda's brother Mateus, however, is Dona Elvira's godson – thus the hirer/servant tie between Dona Elvira and Gracinda was extended in Mateus' case to one of spiritual kinship. Because they are not legally adopted, long-standing servants cannot inherit property directly from their hirers on an equal footing with the latter's legitimate descendants, but they may be recipients of a portion of their hirer's property through a will.

most other households in Fontelas. Owning not only a tractor but also a mechanical reaper and a motor-mower, Valentim hires his tractor services out to other villagers. The household sells large quantities of potatoes, chestnuts, grapes, wine, and livestock, as well as milk from its three dairy cows. Its flock of 150 head of sheep, tended by Leónida's brother-in-law, the smallholder/shepherd Silvério (3j), provides an estimated £606 profit each year to be divided between the two households. A rough estimate of Dona Elvira's total earnings was calculated at £2,197 in 1978. In addition, Dona Elvira occasionally hires one of Fontelas' five wage labourers for periods of a few consecutive days during peak agricultural activity.

This household's good economic situation is further reflected in its favourable reputation as a 'wealthy but generous household' in contrast to the pejorative phrase 'a rich household' used frequently by many villagers to refer to other *proprietário* households in Fontelas and other hamlets. This ambivalent and almost scornful attitude is particularly evident in the cases of a few villagers who have risen from their position as servants in their employers' households to the status of *proprietários*. Not wholly responsible themselves, these servants-turned-*proprietários* are viewed as having in turn adopted the stingy mannerisms of their masters. Villagers constantly stress the infamous reputations of such servants by quoting the phrase: *Nunca sirvas a quem serviu* (Never serve one who has served). Underlying its literal meaning, the saying implies that 'former servants are the worst masters'. No suggestion of this reputation is apparent in the case of Dona Elvira's household or the servant Gracinda. In fact, Valentim himself shares in the very high prestige of the household he married into: at the 1976 election of the committee of four villagers to administer future common-land resources, three other villagers received 8, 6, and 6 votes each while Valentim received a clear majority of 25.

Firmly aware of its high position economically as well as socially within the community, Dona Elvira's household views its role not as an exploiter but rather as a helper of the poor, and not as wealthy but rather as 'less poorly endowed'. This attitude is manifest in its donations to volunteer helpers at its harvesting tasks. The same attitude is also evident in Dona Elvira's Christian comments on the value of honest, hard work, and the 'bad luck' of those poor villagers not possessed of sufficient resources to be able to work. The absence or lack of property among the poor is never accounted for or explained by *proprietários* in terms other than personalized, individualized ones: 'they have little because their parents had little'. This circular reasoning among the wealthy supports the view that poverty simply reproduces itself over the generations, the fault lying exclusively with these specific individuals who 'don't want to work' (*não querem trabalhar*).

But from another perspective, Dona Elvira as well as Valentim and other *proprietários* constantly stress the general poverty of *all* of the hamlet's households *vis-à-vis* wealthier and more developed regions within Portugal. In

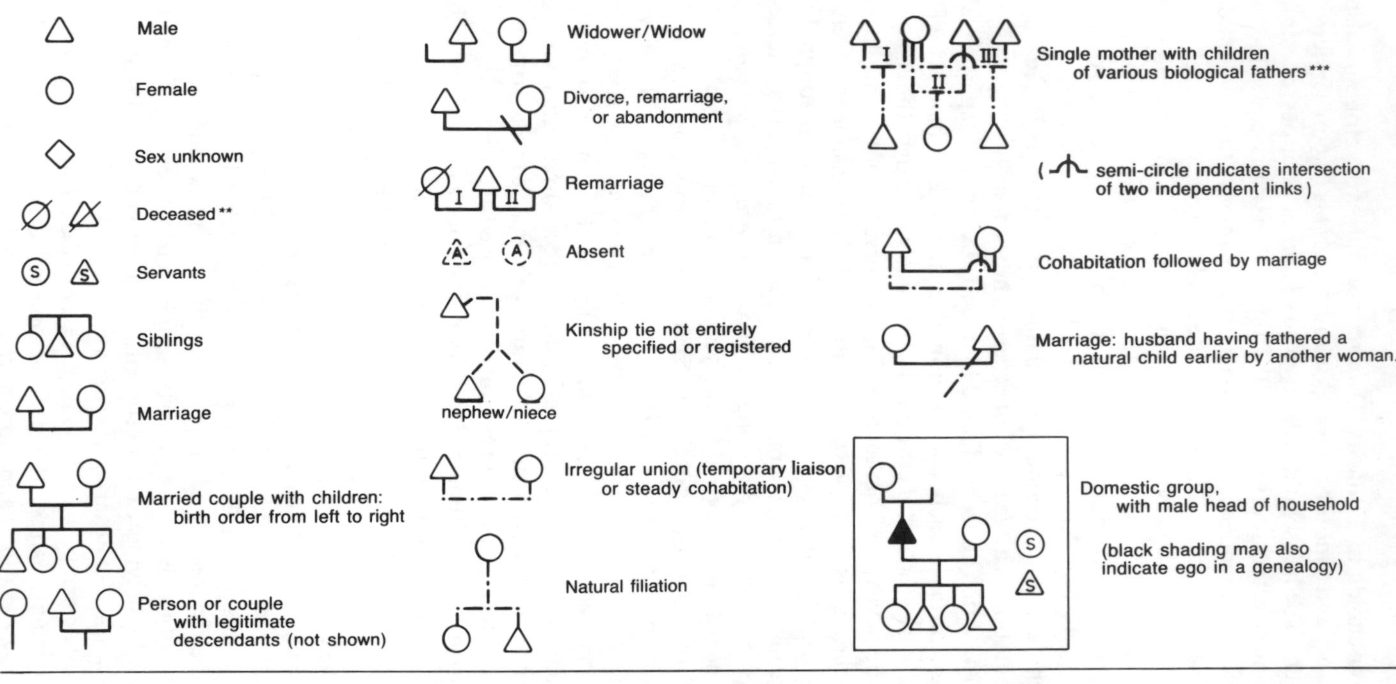

* This visual system for the illustration of kinship links should not be regarded as rigid or definitive: it is an adaptation of various ideographic conventions standardized in Social Anthropology for the representation of a wide variety of interpersonal relations. The diagrams (either genealogies or domestic groups) constitute analytical tools, and as such are susceptible to modification according to the specific features of the society in question. In order to avoid serious distortion of the human realities under study, the reader is thus warned against any form of obsessive fetishism with regard to the legend in and of itself.

** In some genealogies, particularly those reconstructed through the use of historical records, the diagonal lines are dispensed with in the case of deceased persons.

*** In Portuguese, half-siblings sharing the same mother but different fathers are termed *meios-irmãos uterinos;*
half-siblings having the same father but different mothers are called *meios-irmãos consanguíneos;*
full siblings (illegitimate or not) sharing the same mother and father are termed *irmãos germanos.*

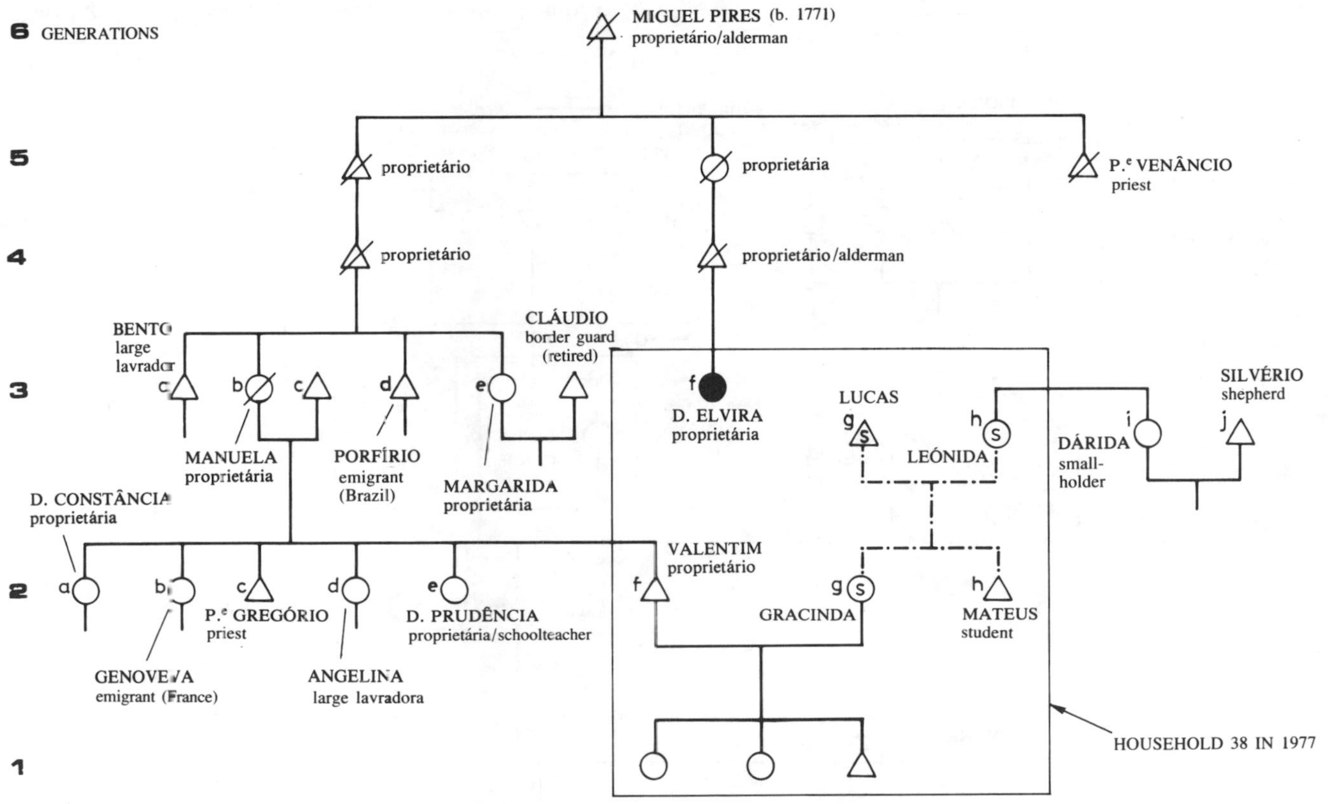

Figure 1. Partial genealogy of the *proprietária* Elvira, 1977

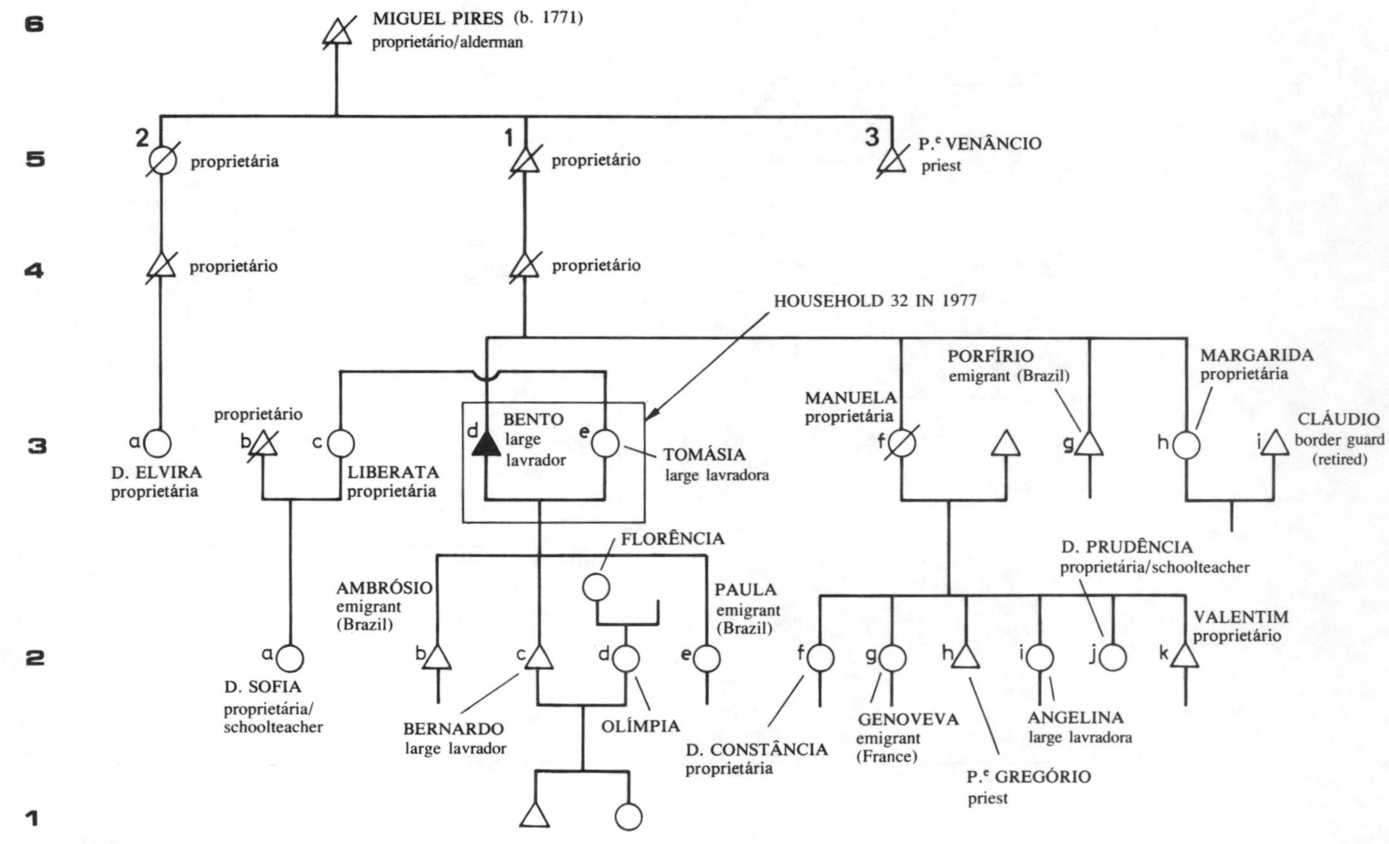

Figure 2. Partial genealogy of the large *lavrador* Bento, 1977

the classic Marxian sense, the *proprietários* are anxious to emphasize not their internal position as a distinct class but rather their common peasant mode of life as one class of 'homologous magnitudes, much as potatoes in a sack form a sack of potatoes' (Marx 1852:172). Clearly unequal to others in its wealth and prestige, this household nevertheless attempts to paint a picture of uniform peasant suffering by stating that 'we are all equally poor here'.

2. Bento's household. Figure 2 presents a partial genealogy of the large *lavrador* Bento. The elderly Bento (3d) and his son Bernardo (2c) are both wealthy *lavradores* who farm the same holding but reside in adjacent households. Bento lives with his wife Tomásia, while Bernardo lives with his wife Olímpia (2d), their two young children, and Olímpia's mother Florência. As inheritance in Fontelas is partible between all siblings, but rarely effective until both members of the parental generation have died, Bento's holding remains intact and is ample enough to support two plough teams and two separate households. A second cousin of Dona Elvira's, Bento is also related by kinship to all of the other three *proprietário* households in Fontelas. Bento is the brother of Manuela (3f) and Margarida (3h), and thus the maternal uncle of the priest (2h). His son Bernardo is thus the priest's first cousin (a fact repeatedly stressed by the latter). In addition to being related to the two *proprietário* households of his two sisters, Bento is also related to Dona Sofia's household through his marriage to the latter's maternal aunt, Tomásia (3e). Significantly, both Tomásia and her sister Liberata (3c) came to Fontelas as child servants but fared better than their two brothers (not shown), who are today poor smallholders both living with common-law wives and their wives' previous illegitimate children (Figure 18). Thus both Liberata and her sister Tomásia afford two further examples of poor women climbing through the social hierarchy through their marriages to wealthy men.

Bento and Bernardo reside in separate houses belonging to the older Conselho household of Bento's parents (Map 3 – H31 and 32). Neither Bento's nor Bernardo's house has a separate courtyard, although both dwellings share a large private threshing-floor with the priest's sister Angelina (H30). The eldest of four siblings, only one of whom emigrated to Brazil (Porfírio: 3g), Bento inherited a portion of land substantial enough to preclude his clearing of *baldios* or renting any land from others. His marriage, however, was distinctly downwards in the social scale, as his wife Tomásia had been a child servant in Fontelas brought in from another hamlet. Bringing no land to the marriage (a rare occurrence anyway given the system of inheritance and the frequency of natolocal residence) Tomásia nevertheless married up into a large *lavrador* household. In the next generation, Bento's son Bernardo is the second of three siblings: his elder brother Ambrósio (2b) and younger sister Paula (2e) both married and had left for Brazil prior to the 1960s emigration to France. Similar to his father's choice, Bernardo also married a woman from another hamlet (a *lavradora*) who brought no land to the marriage. Nevertheless, Bernardo's father's holding (22.25 hectares) is still large enough to support both couples, Olímpia's mother, and Bernardo's two young children: 7 people in all.

Unlike Dona Elvira's household, this household has not consolidated separate individuals' shares into one larger landholding, but has merely maintained intact Bento's portion of his parents' very large former *proprietário* holding. Bento's holding is somewhat smaller than those of his two sisters, both of which include land willed to them by Manuela's father's unmarried siblings (Chapter 5). Very little of Bento's land is uncultivated, and even less (only 0.25 hectare) is rented out to others than by Dona Elvira. Neither Bento nor his son ever hire occasional wage labourers or resident servants.

While Bento and his wife maintain a slow rhythm of relatively independent farming, the younger Bernardo divides his own household's farming between the use of his plough team and the tractor services of his first cousin – the *proprietário* Valentim. Although a fairly prosperous pair of households, the amounts of crops sold by Bernardo are somewhat smaller than those sold by Dona Elvira and Valentim. Although he also emigrated briefly to France in the 1960s, Bernardo did not invest savings in either agricultural machinery or land purchases. Also elected to the executive committee for common-land exploitation, Bernardo obtained 8 votes. He is one of the hamlet's two chiefs of police in charge of reporting minor offences and infractions to the Mosteiro Junta, and in general is supposed to 'maintain public order'.

Unlike many of the *lavradores* and smallholders, Bernardo's orientation towards farming is one of internal improvement rather than external emigration. With a holding of ample size for two households, Bernardo keeps a keen ear tuned to national agricultural and political developments with a view to future changes in credit facilities, loans, mechanization, and the general improvement of the lot of small farmers. In contrast to the smallholders and *lavradores*, Bernardo and others of this group are not caught within a circle of diminishing returns on steadily shrinking and insufficient holdings. On the contrary, the seven large *lavrador* households are interested in and possess the means adequate for technical expansion and innovations in farming methods. For example, another large *lavrador* (Delfim: H40) cultivates a holding of 29.17 hectares with a tractor, and Julião (H19) awaits a loan to buy a tractor for use on his holding of 27.80 hectares. In fact, whenever large cooperative labour-teams are formed to execute semi-communal tasks (the cleaning of irrigation ditches, roadworks) Bernardo and his friend Julião (also his co-godparent) always manage to end up in heated debate over the general economic and social situation in Portugal. Other villagers regularly scoff at them as *políticos* more interested in verbal arguments over abstract national politics than in more practical local repairs. In other words, rather than desert the hamlet altogether (as the poor have done) the large *lavradores* seek to improve their standard of living through channels already available.

They thus pay close attention to wider economic and political developments.

The reason for this attitude lies principally in the distribution of land, which has placed the large *lavradores* in a particularly favourable position. Rather than striving like the *lavradores* and smallholders to attain a reasonable rural standard of living through permanent emigration and greater sources of monetary wealth, Bernardo and others of this group have maintained a higher standard of living because greater sources of landed wealth were already available to them through inheritance. Like the *proprietários*, these households seek to maintain control of the large portions of land they already own. They are unlikely to lose control of this land except in cases of the partition of a holding into numerous smaller portions (a rare occurrence as some siblings usually marry out or remain single) or in cases of a series of large *lavradores* marrying down in succession over the generations. Along with the *proprietários*, members of this group are quite aware of their wealth but seek to portray a picture of common peasant poverty. They also tend to stress that 'we are all equally poor here'.

3. André's household. Although a *lavrador* with a plough team, André occupies an entirely different position from that of Bento or Bernardo (Map 3 – H36). Most of André's and his wife's land was inherited (9.08 hectares) but a substantial portion was obtained through other means: 0.29 hectare is rented from others, 1.67 hectares were cleared, and another 1.67 were bought. (Note in Table 3 that most of the other *lavradores* rent much larger portions of land than does André.) None of either spouse's sets of parents are alive today: although André's parents were *jornaleiros* and Joaquina's *lavradores* (Figure 3), André inherited more land than his wife as his parents' holding was partitioned solely between himself and his only brother, the blacksmith Justino (2d). Joaquina obtained 1/4 of her parents' holding, which was divided between herself and her three siblings. Both André's and Joaquina's households were of relatively similar standing – neither of them married up or down.

André and Joaquina have five children – the three eldest have left Fontelas and the two youngest brothers have remained. Their first daughter Umbelina (1f) married into a neighbouring hamlet and had two children. Umbelina and her husband and children visit Fontelas frequently and contact between her household and that of her parents is close. The second sibling (Crispim: 1g) married a woman from another neighbouring hamlet and emigrated to Brazil, where he established a bakery. This couple also have two children, but their visits to Fontelas are less frequent. The third sibling (Lídia: 1h) married a husband from a smallholding household in Fontelas, who emigrated in 1966 to Germany. Lídia and their daughter followed in 1969 while their son remained with Umbelina in the latter's hamlet. Lídia's husband works in an ironware factory and has bought a number of meadows in Fontelas which are looked after by Lídia's parents but not cultivated by them. Visits to Fontelas by this

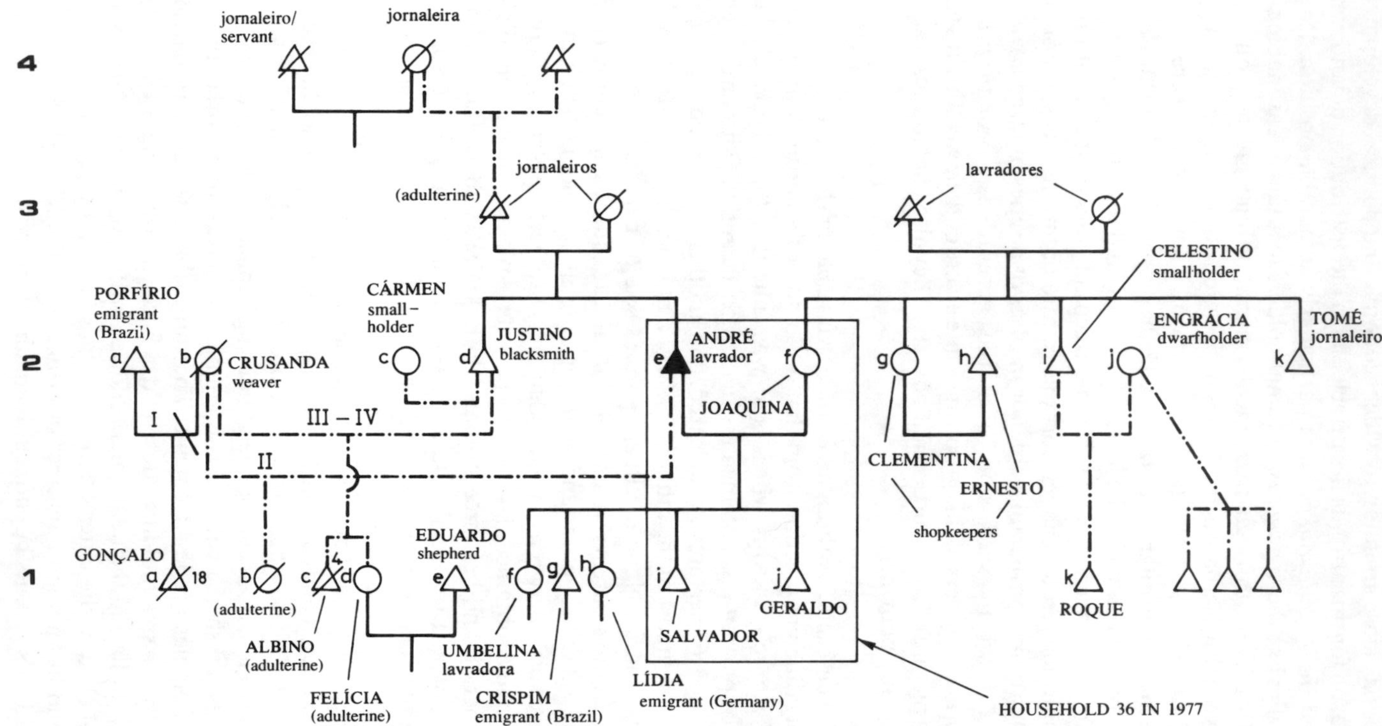

Figure 3. Partial genealogy of the *lavrador* André, 1977

couple are also frequent: they returned for a few weeks during two of the three summers I spent in the hamlet. Finally, the younger brothers Salvador and Geraldo (1i/1j) are both still resident within the household. Salvador's three years of military service during the colonial war in Mozambique have given him experience of the outside world and a desire to escape from the small-scale farming of Fontelas. At the conclusion of my fieldwork, Salvador was preparing for the entrance examination for training as a Border Guard. The youngest son Geraldo is earmarked as the child who will continue farming, stay in the household, and look after his parents as they grow older.

Note that in the case of this household it is not the eldest sibling that remains in the household but rather one or more of the younger ones. Further, a pattern of two kinds of emigration appears in the case of André and Joaquina's children. The first of these is an older long-term emigration to Brazil, implying only occasional return visits to the hamlet and a *de facto* (although not *de jure*) relinquishment of rights to the natal landholding upon its partition. In contrast, the second is a more recent long-term emigration to France or Germany, which implies more frequent return visits, possible purchases of land, and the retention of *de facto* rights to portions of the natal landholding (although these portions are frequently lent to kin or rented out to co-villagers). In contrast to the children of *proprietários* and large *lavradores*, the children of these households tend not to emigrate temporarily with a view to returning to Fontelas and investing in mechanized improvements in farming. Rather, they emigrate permanently. Further, their marriages are contracted within their own group or with poorer smallholders rather than with *proprietários* or individuals with professional or military occupations. While members of the two upper groups tend to remain within the hamlet and marry either individuals with land or 'the land itself', the *lavradores* tend either to marry out or hurry out.

While Bernardo's exchange relationships involve two of the four *proprietário* households in Fontelas, André's exchanges are more frequently contracted with the households of his neighbour, the large *lavrador* Daniel (Map 3 – H34) and the *lavradora* Claudina (H47). Significantly, Daniel's household is the only one of seven households in his group to have bought its way into the large *lavrador* group through continual purchases of land over the years, but due to his household's small size (3 persons) much of its land remains uncultivated. As their scale of farming is similar, André's household and those of Claudina and Daniel engage in frequent exchanges of unpaid labour throughout the agricultural cycle. Neither André nor his wife ever perform labour for a wage. Socially, André is regarded as a rather quiet villager who goes about his business independently and respectably.

Neither André's own brother nor any of Joaquina's siblings are in similar positions. Joaquina's sister Clementina (2g) married one of the two shopkeepers in the hamlet. Although the shop provides a reasonable but by no means wealthy standard of living, Clementina (H7) points more hopefully to the future profits from her daughter's emigration to France. These profits are already materialized in the latter's recently constructed house in Fontelas (far left of Map 3). Joaquina's two brothers have both fared less well. Celestino (2i) resides with his sister Clementina and her shopkeeper husband, and years ago suffered an illness incapacitating him for any sort of agriculture. Celestino is also the natural father of the dwarfholder Engrácia's first illegitimate son Roque (1k). Joaquina's youngest brother Tomé (2k), an occasional day-labourer and once a carpenter, lives alone (H35) and is a chronic alcoholic. Thus, none of Joaquina's three siblings has managed to rise from the smallholder or dwarfholder groups.

None of André's siblings have fared very well either. André's brother Justino (2d) is the hamlet's part-time blacksmith, a smallholder who lives with his common-law wife, originally from Asturias in Northern Spain. While living with the latter, and well after the births of their three children (not shown), Justino fathered another two children: an adulterine son Albino (1c) who died at the age of 4, and an adulterine daughter Felícia (1d) both by the weaver Crusanda (2b). Crusanda was formerly married but abandoned by her husband – the *proprietário* Porfírio (2a) – who left for Brazil less than one year after their marriage. Felícia remained in the hamlet, marrying the smallholder Eduardo (1e), originally from another hamlet nearby and today a smallholder/shepherd.

In fact, illegitimacy has characterized a number of other relationships in André's kindred group. André's father was himself an adulterine child of a *jornaleira* living separately from her husband (this was explicitly stated in André's father's baptismal entry in the Parish Register in 1880). Before marrying, André himself had fathered an adulterine daughter (1b) by the same woman (Crusanda) his brother Justino later came to live with (this child died a few months after birth). This fact was mentioned by Joaquina as a point of contention affecting her own subsequent marriage to André: Joaquina's parents considered her prospective husband's illegitimate child a negative mark jeopardizing André's marital desirability. Thus, although they are *lavradores* today, both André's and Joaquina's siblings exhibit characteristics of the poorer *jornaleiro* group: consensual unions, abandonments, illegitimacy, and adulterous liaisons.

The scale of farming in André's household is markedly smaller than that of the large *lavrador* Bernardo, and smaller still than that of the *proprietário* Valentim. An estimate of another *lavrador* household's annual earnings (Lourenço's slightly larger holding of 14.33 hectares) yielded the approximate figure of £758 per year. This amount is substantially lower than Valentim's earnings of £2,197. André's earnings are likely to be even smaller than the former figure for Lourenço's household (not including remittances from André's son-in-law in Germany). André's outlook on farming is not a positive one like Bernardo's: he looks toward a future of subsistence rather than mechanized improvements or further expansion of his holding. The size of his holding is also problematic – upon his and his wife's deaths it is likely to be partitioned among their five children. It is quite common in such situations for non-resident heirs to lend or sell their shares of land and other property to the sibling(s) remaining on the holding (two of the priest's sisters have done this). Although two of these children (Umbelina and Crispim) are not likely to need their portion of the 12.37 hectare inheritance, the holding's final partition into five portions of 2.47 hectares each will still afford none of the three younger heirs an ample farming unit.

Unlike the large *lavrador* Bento, whose size of holding provides in itself sufficient land to support the labour and draught animals of two separate households, André's holding barely provides enough land to enable him to plough at all. Only a combination of land rental, land purchase, the clearing of common-land, and the joining of both spouses' inheritances have enabled André and Joaquina to consolidate enough resources to place them in the *lavrador* group. Unlike members of the two upper groups, André and other villagers in similar situations stress that 'we are all quite *unequal* here'.

4. Eduardo's household. Eduardo and his wife Felícia are smallholders (Map 3 – H22). The total size of the holding they farm (5.87 hectares) is only just under the 6 hectares needed to support a plough team. Only 2.46 of the 5.87 hectares they farm are owned, however; the remaining 3.41 hectares are rented from six other households (Note b to Table 5). All of their own land belongs to Felícia, as Eduardo was originally a smallholder from a neighbouring hamlet. Appendix 1 contains a plot-by-plot listing of all of the parcels of land comprising this holding: of the 27 parcels farmed, 17 are owned by Felícia. In addition to their minimal farming activities, Eduardo is a shepherd for the *proprietária* Dona Sofia and thus has access to 2.17 hectares of the latter's meadowland for the pasturage of their 'share-herded' flock of sheep. All of these meadows (6 separate plots) are used exclusively for the grazing of sheep and not for the upkeep of plough animals. Eduardo and Felícia supplement Felícia's two small meadows (0.37 hectare in all) with another meadow (0.83 hectare) rented from the dwarfholder Sância. These meadows are used to provide feed for the household's mule and pigs and are not sufficiently large for maintaining a plough team. In order to plough their small amount of arable land (1.71 hectares) Eduardo pools his mule with the smallholder Matias' mule to form a joint plough team. Eduardo's mother, twice a widow in Fontelas, owns no land of her own (her husbands were both dwarfholders) and she is lent a small garden plot (0.02 hectare) by Felícia.

The scale of farming in Eduardo's household is quite a bit smaller than that of André's, and minuscule in comparison with either Valentim's or Bernardo's. Eduardo's main source of livelihood derives from the flock of sheep

9 Rye transports (July): two youths cart sheaves of grain from a rye field.

he tends for Dona Sofia. The earnings from sales of these sheep are split equally between Eduardo and Dona Sofia, whose own portion is again halved between her household and that of her sharecropper Fortunato. In 1977 Eduardo's sale of 30 large and 12 small sheep brought earnings of £1,689. This sum was already a good bit less than the *proprietário* Valentim's total yearly earnings, but only half (£845) was kept by Eduardo. A large portion of these £845 was used to pay off outstanding debts. Eduardo's earnings from occasional wage labour in the same year only totalled £91 for 30 days of work at £3 per day. In addition to these earnings, Eduardo and Felícia receive social security payments for two of their three children (those under 14): £3.64 per month, or in this case £87.27 per year. Including the sales of sheep, wage labour, and social security payments, Eduardo's total earnings in 1977 thus amounted to £1,023. Without the sales of sheep, this household obtains substantially lower earnings (£178) than the *lavrador* household of Lourenço (£758).

In mid-1978 a decision on the part of Dona Sofia to sell her entire flock resulted in a bitter argument between Eduardo and Dona Sofia's sharecropper Fortunato (Eduardo's nextdoor neighbour – H23). Eduardo had tended Dona Sofia's flock for one year. In order to repay her original capital (£1,700) Eduardo sold most of the flock and repaid £1,651, remaining with a small flock

10 *Lavradores* and smallholders resting on a summer afternoon during the hay harvest.

of his own. Once this division was accomplished, Dona Sofia immediately prohibited Eduardo from grazing his own remaining flock of 30 head on her 2.17 hectares of meadowland which were originally used for the grazing of the larger shared flock. Legally, Dona Sofia acted correctly, although Eduardo remained resentful because the hay from the 2.17 hectares of meadowland was given to Fortunato, with whom Eduardo and his wife were already on poor terms. Fortunato's wife (originally from a large *lavrador* houschold) had at this point begun to direct drainage water from her roof into Felícia's stables, and Felícia was on the brink of severing all relations with her. Deprived of his principal source of monetary income (a large flock) Eduardo was obliged to return to more frequent wage labour.

The case was viewed by many villagers as one of the indirect abuse of smallholders by large landowners. Also stressed was Dona Sofia's favouritism towards her sharecropper, already infamous for charging hourly rates for incomplete 50-minute periods of tractor ploughing. Others pointed to Eduardo's initial mistake of not demanding that the original oral agreement be sealed in a written contract, thus ensuring Eduardo's usufruct of Dona Sofia's meadows after the partition of the joint flock. Many villagers also quoted the phrase 'Never serve one who has served': both Dona Sofia's mother as well as

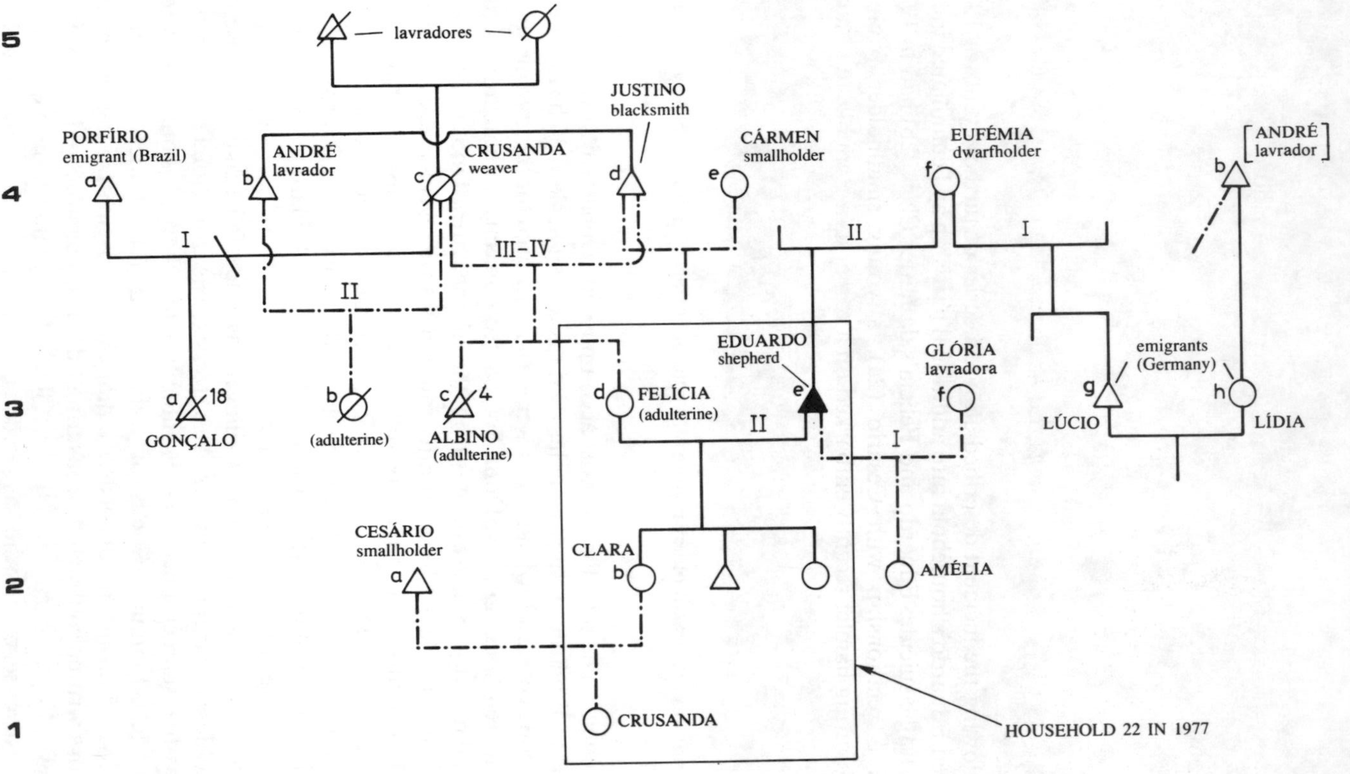

Figure 4. Partial genealogy of the smallholder Eduardo, 1977

the sharecropper Fortunato had been child servants adopted into Dona Sofia's father's household. They were thus less likely to offer and cooperate than to 'grasp and exploit'.[18]

Eduardo's household is related to that of the *lavrador* André. Eduardo's two stepbrothers (by his mother's first marriage) emigrated to France and Germany: the latter is Lúcio (3g), the husband of André's daughter Lídia (3h). Eduardo's two full brothers and two full sisters (not shown) all left Fontelas: two went to Spain, one to the local town, and one to Lisbon. Eduardo himself (3e) attempted to emigrate to France after his marriage to Felícia, but the death of Felícia's mother brought him back to Fontelas and prevented his definitive return to France. Of seven siblings, Eduardo was the only one to remain in Fontelas.

Following the incident described above, a series of further events in 1978 plunged Eduardo's household into additional hardship and culminated in his wife's tragic suicide. Eduardo and Felícia's daughter Clara (2b) had in 1977 begun a relationship with Cesário (2a), a young smallholder from a neighbouring hamlet recently embarked on a career as a Republican Guard. Although their future marriage was spoken of by other villagers, neither of the two themselves mentioned concrete plans. In late 1977 it became evident that Clara was pregnant. Villagers stressed Clara's delicate position by stating that with little property, an unassuming personal appearance, and now pregnant, she provided not a very attractive bride for Cesário and even less for any subsequent suitor. The child was born illegitimately, but this did not cause any particular scandal in the hamlet. Clara continued to reside in her parents' household, and the child was named after her grandmother, Crusanda. In fact, the child's baptism took place under these conditions, although the father of the child was the only individual from his own hamlet who attended the celebration. The baptism itself was no less opulent and festive than that of any legitimately born child. Only months later did the marriage take place, both spouses remaining in their respective parents' households in their own natal hamlets.

Cesário's visits to Clara's parents' household grew more frequent, and the two couples, along with Eduardo and Felícia's two younger children, spent many winter evenings by the hearth through early 1978. On one occasion, however, Eduardo apparently reported seeing his wife Felícia and his son-in-law Cesário embracing each other alone by the fireside. Eduardo was incredulous and shouted, while Felícia, in what was later to become 'proof of her guilt', immediately fled the household with Cesário and crossed the border

[18] Fortunato's ascent from the status of a child servant to that of the management of a *proprietário* household's farm is viewed by other villagers with great suspicion. This attitude itself is further evidence of the functioning of a social hierarchy which places great stress upon ascribed status linked to land, rather than upon achieved status acquired through personal effort.

into Spain. The next day, Eduardo and a number of his relatives crossed the border and found them in one of the major towns of Orense province.

What ensued was not a series of 'honour crimes'. Although Eduardo stressed his possession of a pistol and his intent to use it upon Cesário's next setting foot in Fontelas, Felícia returned to the household and continued to reside with Eduardo. Although they were known to have shouted frequently at each other for a period of months, mention by other villagers of physical violence between them was infrequent and limited to unverified rumours. Hamlet opinions varied in placing the blame either on Felícia for admitting her guilt by fleeing to Spain with her son-in-law 'to sleep with him there', or on Eduardo who was said to have imagined the entire scene in a moment of 'craziness' (*loucura*) and afterwards to have 'gone mad'. The latter explanation had little foundation in past behaviour, as Eduardo's reputation was one of an entirely honest, quiet, and respectable shepherd. No one placed any particular blame on Cesário himself, as his supposed advances to Felícia were understandable due to their frequent contact and the closeness of their ages. Eduardo and Felícia continued to live together for months afterwards, while after a period their daughter Clara moved to Cesário's parents' household in the latter's own hamlet. No break occurred in either marriage. Although co-villagers speculated as to whether Eduardo and Felícia would divide their own acquired possessions and part company (the house and landholding were all Felícia's) this did not occur, nor did Eduardo demand that Felícia leave the household. For a while the couple were known to have slept in the same bed with their heads and feet at opposite ends.

At this point villagers began to stress that in Felícia's case 'adultery ran in the family'. Felícia herself had been a second adulterine child of the weaver Crusanda (4c) and the blacksmith Justino (4d) (André's brother). We have seen earlier that Crusanda had also borne a first adulterine daughter by André. Crusanda's own original marriage had been to one of the *proprietários* of the large Conselho household (Porfírio: 4a), but we recall that less than a year after their civil marriage, Crusanda's husband left Fontelas permanently for Brazil. Villagers disagree even now as to whether this man died later in Brazil or whether he is still alive today. A son Gonçalo (3a) had been born legitimately to the couple but died later at the age of 18. Consequently, Felícia was the only one of two half-siblings and two full siblings to survive into adulthood. All of her siblings had died earlier: one legitimate son (her half-brother Gonçalo), one adulterine daughter (her half-sister), and another adulterine son (her full brother Albino). Felícia thus inherited all of her mother's (not very substantial) property but none of that of her mother's legal husband Porfírio, which was retained by the *proprietários* of the Conselho household (Figure 2: 3d, 3f, 3h).

Further, Eduardo himself was the father, shortly before his marriage, of an illegitimate daughter (Amélia) of the *lavradora* Glória (3f). Glória had suffered an attack of meningitis as a child and is consequently deaf and unable to speak properly. She currently lives in her mother's household (the *lavradora* Cristina). Eduardo refused to affiliate the child legally, and the case went to court (see Glossary – *perfilhação*). Although it could not be proved that Eduardo was the child's father, villagers today still stress the physical resemblance of Amélia to Eduardo. Neither Glória nor anyone in her household are on speaking terms with him.

We recall that Felícia has two more half-siblings through her biological father's consensual union with the Spanish Cármen.

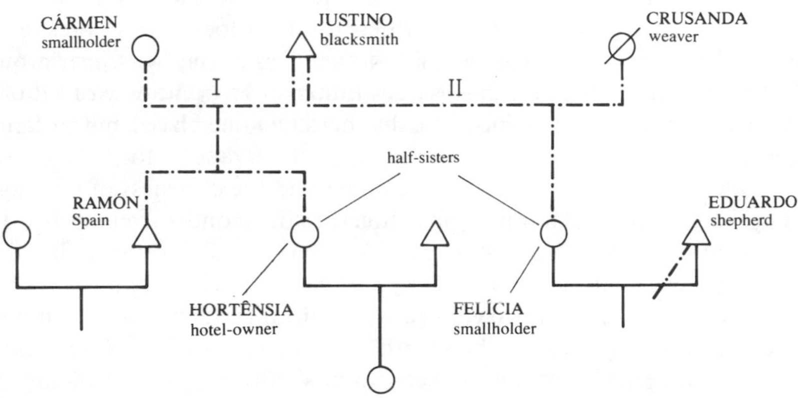

Figure 5. Half-sisters in the smallholder group

Relations between Felícia and her father Justino are distant and infrequent – Justino did not affiliate Felícia. Justino himself had two children by Cármen (Ramón and Hortênsia). In 1978 Hortênsia caused another adultery scandal in town, where she and her husband (from the town) run a small hotel and restaurant. One night Hortênsia was apparently caught by her husband in bed with another man. Hortênsia and the man were said to have fled, although Hortênsia returned to the household, left yet again months later, and finally returned again. While her husband began divorce proceedings in the town court, Hortênsia's second return has suspended the break-up of the marriage. This second case of adultery caused a far greater scandal than that of Felícia's fleeing with her son-in-law, due to the former couple's more public position in the municipal town.

Both cases of marital infidelity by 'the women of Fontelas' (both are half-sisters) created a somewhat infamous reputation for the hamlet in 1978. By letter I was notified in 1979 that Eduardo's wife Felícia had committed suicide in one of her fields by drinking a bottle of potato pesticide. Eduardo's daughter Clara currently resides in her husband's natal hamlet with her parents-in-law, leaving Eduardo the task of bringing up his two younger children on his own.

Eduardo is known to have recently moved into the household (H24) of the smallholder Bernarda,[19] a close neighbour of Eduardo's and herself the mother of four bastard children by three different fathers.

These incidents point not only to the frequency of irregular (and in some cases adulterous) unions within this group, but also to the tenuous nature of the marital tie among the poor. Both of these patterns are related to these households' lack of landed property and low position in the hamlet's scale of prestige. While among the *proprietários* and large *lavradores* every marriage is based upon one (or both) partner's possession of large amounts of land and high social standing, neither of the latter are common to any great degree among the smallholders. In the absence of property, the prestige of smallholders is never as secure as that of members of the two upper groups. When even that minimal prestige is questioned, or as in the case of Eduardo and Felícia entirely undermined, smallholders have no choice but to fall yet lower.

5. Engrácia's household. Engrácia's household is one of the poorest in Fontelas by a number of standards (Map 3 – H44). The size of her landholding, even including the land she rents, is only 2.00 hectares. This is barely enough to provide for herself and her two younger children and is far below the minimum needed for a plough team. The fourth child of seven illegitimate siblings, Engrácia's inherited portion of her parents' already small holding was negligible. Inheriting only 0.66 hectare of land, Engrácia rents a meadow, garden, and field totalling only 0.29 hectare from the smallholder Vitorino (Note c to Table 5). In addition she is lent one small field of 0.13 hectare from her half-sister Helena. Joining all of these minuscule plots, Engrácia still farms far less than an average smallholder's holding of 2.5 hectares.

Engrácia's elder brother Elias, a *lavrador*, performs the few ploughing tasks needed by Engrácia and also lends her one of his small garden plots of 0.02 hectare. Rather than exchange her labour with kin and co-villagers, an impractical possibility as her holding is so tiny, Engrácia volunteers her help at many of the wealthier households' harvesting tasks in exchange for an immediate meal and some small donations of food and wine. Occasionally, she is paid a daily wage. She also receives £3.64 per month for each of her three youngest sons (aged 16, 13, and 10). Most of the rest of Engrácia's tasks are performed for her by her other brothers and sisters as favours. Neither of the

[19] I was able to observe this change in residence during a brief return visit to the hamlet in March of 1981: Bernarda's husband Matias (by whom she bore no children) had died in 1979. Although not without some reservation, the term *irregular union* will refer to a relationship with characteristics somehow anomalous to the official and ecclesiastical local models, and includes both permanent cohabitation as well as temporary sexual liaisons. 'Irregular' obviously does not refer to any form of frequency in time, but is used merely in order to avoid even more imprecise adjectives such as 'illegitimate', 'illicit', or 'abnormal'.

two sons who reside with her are old enough to begin ploughing and her other two sons live in other sections of the hamlet. Even upon reaching ages of ploughing and greater agricultural activity, none of Engrácia's four sons will be able to support a plough team on her paltry 2-hectare holding without borrowing, renting, and clearing at least an additional 4 hectares of land.

Engrácia's natal household (H47) is located in another section of the hamlet, where her elder sister Júlia (2b) and younger siblings Claudina (2h) and Inocêncio (2j) continue to live jointly. Engrácia's elder brother Elias (2d) lives in another section. Elias remained in this natal household for about 6 years after his marriage to the smallholder Leocádia (2e), moving to Leocádia's father's household (H21) only following the death of both of Elias' parents and the subsequent partition of the holding. (This was also the point at which Engrácia left the natal household for her own.)[20] Engrácia's siblings' household is also a *lavrador* household, although her siblings must rent a large portion of land (2.63 hectares) in order to supplement their own joined portions of only 4.0 hectares.

Engrácia's eldest sister (the deceased Marcelina: 2a) was formerly a *jornaleira* in Fontelas, as were both of Engrácia's parents and both of her grandmothers (4a/4d). Only one of Engrácia's five living siblings (the next-to-youngest Antónia: 2i) has emigrated permanently from Fontelas. Antónia married a *lavrador* from the town and both are resident today in France. Engrácia's elder sister Júlia is the shepherdess of her natal household, while Inocêncio (2j) does the ploughing and heavy agricultural work and Claudina (2h) most of the cooking and household chores. Engrácia as well as Elias pay frequent visits to this household, and harvesting tasks as well as family celebrations are frequently carried out jointly. Both Júlia and Claudina have bastard children resident within the household: one of Júlia's three illegitimate children (Hermenegildo: 1b) and Claudina's one illegitimate son (David: 1j). Engrácia in turn has borne four illegitimate sons, by four different fathers. The eldest (Roque: 1f) is a servant in a large *lavrador* household, while the third son (Vicente: 1h) resides in Engrácia's natal household with his aunts and uncle. Finally, an illegitimate daughter (Albina: 1a) of Engrácia's eldest sister Marcelina moved into the household in late 1977.

The illegitimacy apparent in the case of Engrácia and her sisters is typical of the smallholder group and particularly of the former group of single *jornaleira* women in Fontelas. Chapter 5 will examine the pattern in detail, but here I wish to stress the connection between illegitimacy, small landholdings, and the lower social groups. Neither Engrácia nor her two resident sisters Júlia and Claudina nor her brother Inocêncio have married. Elias married the smallholder Leocádia (2e) but he as well as his wife had *both* had bastard

[20] This form of natolocal residence appears to be linked closely to the strictly *post-mortem* transfer of land in Fontelas. I will return to this point in Chapter 6.

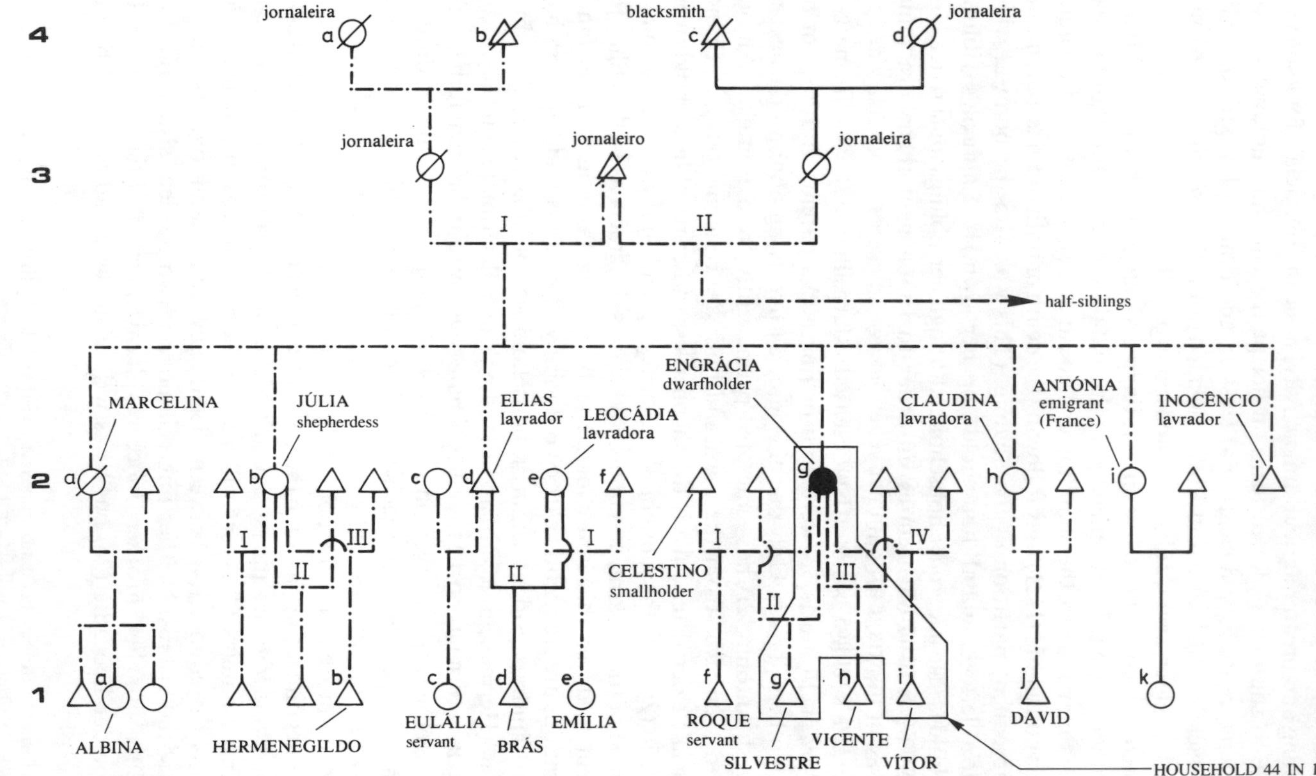

Figure 6. Partial genealogy of the dwarfholder Engrácia, 1977

children before they married each other. Elias fathered an illegitimate daughter Eulália (1c) by the smallholder Bernarda, and Leocádia had borne the illegitimate Emília (1e) before her marriage to Elias. Emília lives in her mother's household, Elias being referred to as her *padrasto*, or stepfather (although the relationship is not technically one of remarriage). Engrácia's eldest sister Marcelina (2a) bore three illegitimate children by the same father, while Júlia (2b) had three illegitimate children each by a different father. The only sibling of the seven to have married 'honourably' was the next-to-youngest Antónia, who emigrated to France. The youngest brother, Inocêncio, remains unmarried and without any natural children. None of these three sisters resident in Fontelas is likely to marry, and other villagers lament that the 41 year-old Claudia (a servant and cook for many years in town) will also stand little chance of marrying prestigiously with her illegitimate son.

Engrácia's situation is even worse. With four illegitimate children her chances for marriage are slimmer yet as her age advances. (Engrácia was 45 in 1977.) The youngest of these four children, in fact, was the result of a union between close kin (Figure 7). Vítor is the son of Engrácia and her 'half-nephew'

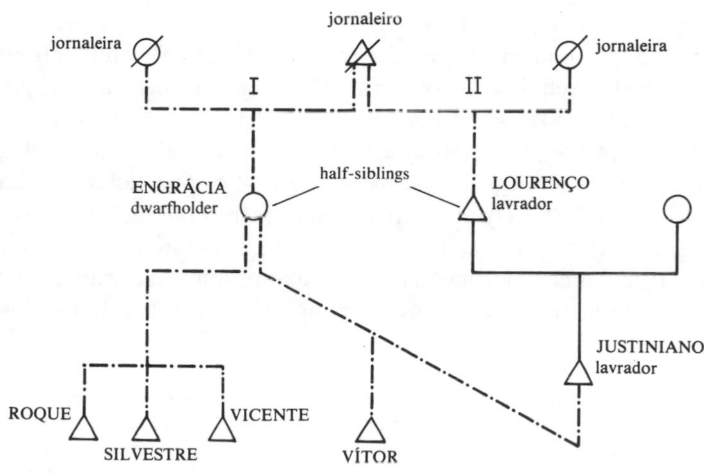

Figure 7. Natural kin of Engrácia (bastard children and half-nephew)

Justiniano (aged 35 in 1977). Justiniano is the son of Engrácia's paternal half-brother Lourenço. Although this sibling relationship is not technically one of full siblings of legal parentage, the children (legitimate or not) of half-siblings are considered first cousins (*primos carnais*) in Fontelas in the same manner as first cousins traced through legitimate marriage ties. In this case, through the union with his 'half-aunt', the *lavrador* Justiniano is simultaneously the father and first cousin of Vítor.[21]

Unlike the series of unusual events occurring in the case of Eduardo examined earlier, the history of Engrácia and her siblings is quite typical of the *jornaleiro* group. One could argue that illegitimacy is here the rule rather than the exception. This is so among the smallholders and dwarfholders, as well as some of the *lavradores*. Inheriting little land of their own, and forced to become servants, cooks, and wage labourers within Fontelas as well as outside it, the children of servants and labourers reproduce patterns of illegitimacy and low social prestige over the generations, a pattern somewhat suggestive of what Peter Laslett (1980b) has termed the 'bastardy prone sub-society' (see Chapter 7, section c). Some (Elias) manage to move upward in the social hierarchy and even to achieve the position of *lavrador*. Others (Engrácia) never rise above the level of the dwarfholding, never marry, and are incapable of maintaining anything but a minimal level of agricultural production.[22] Unable to obtain sufficient quantities of land, many of the dwarfholders remain dependent siblings or sellers of their own or their children's labour, and their current situation remains precarious.

Although all smallholders in Fontelas are considered substantially poorer than the two upper groups of the *proprietários* and large *lavradores*, the position of dwarfholders such as Engrácia is particularly lamentable. The 16 dwarfholding households (1/4 of the hamlet) together own only 4.5 per cent of the land. Neither possessing the means to support a plough team nor the household labour necessary for maintaining a reasonable standard of living, the dwarfholders remain at the very bottom of the ladder. Villagers in Engrácia's plight lie barely above the level of poverty of local gypsies, tinkers, and beggars. Prior to the emigration of the 1960s the only way out of this situation (for women particularly) was to become a servant in a wealthy household and hope to be adopted through time. Yet beside the few female

[21] The father/son relationship is in this case the one most frequently used to refer to the tie between Justiniano and Vítor, rather than the first cousin link. The relationship is a distant one though, and no joint celebrations occur nor are there any exchanges between the two households. Even Engrácia and Lourenço (paternal half-siblings) are not themselves particularly close.

[22] See the fascinating work on Austrian illegitimacy and inheritance patterns carried out by Sigrid Khera (1972a; 1972b; 1973; 1981) which presents astounding similarities to my Portuguese materials: 'Late marriage and celibacy were responsible for a considerable number of illegitimate children, who were totally excluded from any inheritance and as a result remained at the level of agricultural laborers throughout their lives' (1972a:32). Note also the parallels between the *proprietários* and the Austrian *Bauers* – independent landowners who formerly constituted the highest social stratum (now in decline) and who formed 'a tight solidarity group, which is not connected by any but distant and therefore socially unimportant kin ties to the social strata of small plot owners and landless people' (1972b:362). Mitterauer and Sieder (1979) also afford Austrian data on family structures and social groups directly comparable to mine.

11 Gypsies passing through Fontelas.

servants who are adopted by *proprietário* households, the vast majority of smallholder women have remained in Engrácia's plight.

Emigration has not substantially altered this picture among the dwarfholders, who are considered either economic or moral failures (or both). They are a distinctly marginal group of individuals who are pitied and assisted by kin, friends, and other co-villagers willing to help them along with occasional favours. Life-histories of illegitimacy and dependence as labourers and servants have provided these households with few chances for obtaining even minimal social prestige. Dwarfholders possess neither the means of production nor abundant labour resources for the maintenance of a landholding or household sufficient to support themselves. While feeling somehow cheated by the upper groups of 'the wealthy', their perception of precisely how they arrived in this situation is neither clearly understood nor coherently expressed.

Some of the smallholders generally possess just enough land (at least 3 hectares) to enable them to shift at different times between reliance on wage labour or share-herding, and on cultivation of their own private plots. This is a position of partial flexibility stressed by Cabral (1976) as exemplary not of a landowning peasantry but of a semi-proletariat.[23] In contrast, dwarfholders remain a particularly impoverished sub-group at the lowest level of the social hierarchy. Few recent developments, including both emigration or the 1974 Revolution, have offered them satisfactory solutions.

[23] Not entirely *landless* proletarians depending primarily upon the regular wages of one or more household members, the *jornaleiros* could fall back upon their tiny holdings in times of crisis and engage in additional but occasional wage labour. They were thus neither peasants living solely from labour on the land, nor rural proletarians *tout court* who depended predominantly upon salaried wage labour, but rather combined both of these work patterns in varying combinations. Rather than peasants in the strictest sense, they were thus semi-proletarians. This group possessed few material means in either land, equipment, or labour with which to rise to the level of the ploughing *lavradores*. They were hardly peasants 'tied to their little plots of land' because their relation to that land has probably been a tenuous one from the very start.

4

Cooperative labour

This chapter deals with the organization of labour in Fontelas. Two aspects of this area of social life stand out clearly: the first of these is the large number of agricultural activities which require the recruitment of additional labour from *outside* the household. In Fontelas the truly self-sufficient peasant household is non-existent. The second aspect concerns the imbalanced and unequal exchanges of labour at large harvesting tasks. I deal with each of these topics in turn.

The first section describes the annual cycle of production and forms of *household labour* involving only the members of the domestic group. Some mention is made of simple exchange labour involving small labour-teams with a few recruited helpers. Secondly, I deal with *communal labour-teams* formed for the repair or reconstruction of public property. The third section contains two descriptons of conspicuously large tasks requiring the complex coordination of labour, time, and the rotation of house-by-house turns. These are examples of *intermediate* forms of agricultural labour, located between the two extremes of the individual household and the entire hamlet. In the last section, I formulate an analytical question concerning all three of these forms of cooperation: to what extent can labour exchanges in Fontelas be termed 'egalitarian'? Further, do these work exchanges in fact reveal underlying structures of social hierarchy and inequality?

Household labour

Each household in Fontelas confronts common problems of production within this mountainous region of Trás-os-Montes. But it would be misleading to term the household the 'basic unit of production'. Each household is in reality *insufficient* in equipment, animal traction, and labour resources and cannot act entirely on its own. Only a very few domestic groups could ideally produce enough crops to support themselves, and even these must still recruit extra labour for their four major harvesting tasks each year. The real productive units are thus a series of continually shifting teams whose membership overlaps as successive households exchange personnel and labour throughout the year. I was struck by the large number of such labour-teams in Fontelas during the first months of my fieldwork, and my participation in them did indeed lead to my general acceptance in the hamlet.

No household is an island unto itself: each must depend on a number of others in order to subsist. As advanced agricultural technology is quite scarce, the crucial element in Fontelas' productive system are 'labouring arms' or *braços para trabalhar*. Thus, three of the four principal kinds of work in Fontelas necessitate extra-household relationships of exchange:

1. Household labour;
2. Simple exchange labour;
3. Large harvests;
4. Communal tasks.

While many of the minor daily tasks throughout the year are executed by household members, some require one or two extra persons. Others may require up to 40 or 50 people. A fifth kind of labour – wage labour – is not dealt with here as it plays a relatively minor role in Fontelas today. Most of the hamlet's households are virtually unanimous in their preference for unpaid exchanges of labour and time. Let us look first at the annual agricultural cycle and the first two kinds of labour enumerated above (1 and 2), before turning to the more complex forms of cooperation involved in threshings and irrigation rotations.

As I have shown, three of Fontelas' major crops are rye, potatoes, and wine. The cycle of productive activities needed to grow these crops requires large labour inputs. Somewhat less effort is needed to produce and gather lesser crops: wheat, maize, chestnuts and walnuts, garden vegetables, pulses, and root crops. Very few families sell any of their crops, and those that do are principally the wealthier *proprietários* and large *lavradores*: depending on annual yields, these may sell reasonable quantities of surplus wine and potatoes. But even these households systematically complain that their minimal sales at the end of each year barely compensate for production costs. Only one villager sells rye grain in any quantity – virtually all of the hamlet's households produce grain exclusively for domestic consumption or internal hamlet exchanges. Thus the only crops that are sold by a large number of the hamlet's households for cash are potatoes and chestnuts.[1]

The general pattern is thus one of 'subsistence' production: that is, production of a large variety of crops for household consumption. Small

[1] Not all households sell these two crops, though, and sales can also depend on the particular agricultural year. For example, in 1976 the *lavrador* Elias produced 93 sacks of potatoes (80 kilos per sack) of which 78 sacks were kept for household consumption and 15 given as feed to the animals: not one of these sacks of potatoes was sold that year. Similarly, Elias' production of wine in 1976 amounted to 20 *almudes*, or 500 litres. This was not sufficient even for household consumption, and Elias had to purchase an extra $5\frac{1}{2}$ *almudes*. No wine was sold.

quantities of most crops (rye, potatoes) must also be stored for the next year's sowing or planting. Furthermore, much of a household's produce is consumed by kin, neighbours, and other co-villagers at large harvesting tasks, and this requires continual reserves of extra stored food for such occasions. Cash is seen as a necessary supplement when the household reserves begin to dwindle. Only a few wealthy households maintain more complex market-oriented rhythms of production, yet even these engage only in a kind of incipient capitalism on a relatively small scale. Their own harvests are so big that the cost of feeding their teams of helpers and providing abundant wine is enormous. On the whole then, peasants in Fontelas do not produce 'for the market' but rather for themselves.

Livestock provides the principal source of cash income. Twelve households own shares in or whole flocks of sheep (there are 8 flocks) and sales of these animals are lucrative. Their sizes range from the smaller flocks of about 20 head to the largest flock (2 owners) of 150. Most households also own one or two head of cattle – even some smallholders own one cow which may be paired with another villager's in order to plough. Sales of young calves are quite profitable and many villagers pay great attention to their animals with such sales in view. A few goats are kept, but in much smaller proportions than sheep. In addition to these animals reared primarily for sale, a number of household animals are also raised.[2] Women are particularly affectionate with their young piglets, and great care is taken throughout the autumn to fatten one or two large pigs for the winter pig-killing (Photo 13).[3] Pork is the hamlet's staple meat, and barely a day goes by each year without some form of pork being eaten in practically every household in the hamlet. Sales of pork are almost unheard of. Even in the few cases I know of concerning sales to outsiders of the area's famous meat and loin sausages (*chouriça/salpicão*), thé prices were exorbitant.

Agricultural technology in Fontelas is markedly poor and predominantly manual in operation. The five principal tools used are the sickle, scythe, pick, pitchfork, and hoe. These are a household's primary equipment. Most families of course own a number of such tools in order that various household members may work in conjunction at the same task. Grain is reaped manually with sickles (Photo 12) and hay is cut with scythes. Hoes and picks are used for weeding, digging vineyards, and the cleaning of irrigation ditches, and

[2] Elias' *lavrador* household thus had a flock of 39 sheep and 2 rams in 1977, along with 4 cows and 2 donkeys. In addition to their 2 dogs and 3 cats, the household kept 3 grown pigs (for slaughtering in November), 4 piglets, 3 hens and a rooster, 1 goat, 3 beehives, and 35 rabbits. All of the latter animals are kept for household consumption and are very rarely sold.

[3] An extensive analysis of the labour exchanges involved in pig-slaughters in Fontelas is contained in my Final Field Report submitted to the Calouste Gulbenkian Foundation in Lisbon (1977). The weights of fattened pigs frequently reach the extraordinary figures of up to 250 kilos each, and the opulent meals accompanying the occasion attain truly Breughelian proportions.

pitchforks for manuring as well as for lifting and stacking large sheaves of grain. For ploughing, we recall that two kinds of wooden plough are used, and the ox-cart is the major transport vehicle for large loads of hay, grain sheaves, and firewood (Photo 9). However, as we have seen, many households do not own either of these two major pieces of equipment, and do not possess sufficient land to maintain a team of plough animals.

Only over the last few decades has advanced machinery come into use. The first chemical fertilizers used in Fontelas were introduced in the 1930s, while in the late 1940s the first mechanical threshing-machines were rented from outside in order to thresh the hamlet's grain. (Formerly, two alternating 'bands' of men threshed the grain manually with wooden flails called *malhos*.) More recently three tractors have been purchased: the first in 1965 and the remaining two in 1970. These tractors were then equipped with motor-mowers for haymaking as well as mechanical reapers for the cutting of rye and wheat stalks. However, as the hamlet's terrain is steep, many fields are inaccessible to the tractors and must be harvested by hand. Further, the three tractors and their respective reapers and mowers cannot be used by all of the hamlet's households at the same time: the best each owner can do is to harvest his own crops first and then help some kin and close friends. After this, other co-villagers can rent the machines' services. Inevitably, some villagers are left out and must harvest manually. Others actually prefer manual labour to machine cultivation as the latter is more costly. In general then, agricultural technology has modified the hamlet's productive system in recent years, but it has certainly not supplanted manual tools entirely. Sickles and scythes are not yet 'things of the past', as townsfolk tried to convince me upon my arrival in the region. Indeed, upon the entrance of the first tractor in a neighbouring hamlet a few years ago, the story goes that an elderly woman approached it and fed it a bundle of hay.

In Table 6 I have set out a simple list of the major agricultural tasks carried out in the four seasons of each year. There are of course a large number of minor jobs executed, but those listed are only the major activities characteristic of each season of the year. Some of these tasks (ploughing, sowing) are either successive steps or peak harvests within an entire cycle of production of a particular crop. Rye is thus a crop requiring continual year-long activity: in the winter the fields on the fallow side of the hamlet are given their first ploughing (the *decrua*), in the spring a second ploughing (the *vima*), and in the autumn a third ploughing at which time the fields are sown. Meanwhile, the harvesting stage takes place on the sown fields on the alternate side: in the summer these fields are reaped, the grain is transported to the threshing-floors, and finally threshed and stored in August. Other tasks in the table, such as the spring sheep-shearing, are executed only once each year.

The principal pattern emerging from Table 6 indicates a separation between strictly household tasks and larger tasks requiring extra-household teams. It is the latter tasks that are most urgent and which must be executed as quickly and efficiently as possible: even the smallest of these requires at least 15 or so helpers. The jobs are concentrated in the months from May through August when the heaviest labour inputs are needed, principally for haymaking as well as for the haulage and threshing of rye. Slightly less urgent are the spring cleanings of irrigation channels as well as the autumn vintages and winter pig-slaughters. But even these tasks are conspicuously large, and in the case of vintages and pig-slaughters they take on a distinctly festive character as 'work-parties' in celebration of the final phases of the farming year.

There are specific reasons for the recruitment of these very large labour-teams. Firstly, poor technology requires that these momentary peaks of labour input during the agricultural year be executed very fast, so that no household is delayed in its own weekly or daily calendar: to carry out any of the six largest tasks with smaller groups of villagers for longer hours or days would also be disproportionately exhausting for all of the participants (and probably somewhat less boisterous and animated). Both Veiga de Oliveira (1955) and Fernandez (1981:41) have stressed this last point concerning the festive and convivial aspects of large gatherings of villagers working together, the latter author using the phrase 'social euphoria' to refer to the general atmosphere at such occasions in Asturias, Northern Spain. Secondly, the scheduling of large events such as the threshings – which are dependent upon *one* available machine for the whole hamlet – is quite complicated. Without informal collective consensus or a strictly ordered rotation system, individual disagreements or disputes over precedence could result in endless discussion and delays. Of course at the smaller and more household-oriented tasks such as the grain transports or vintages, both of which require tractors, this problem is less acute and the hamlet's three tractors circulate between different groups of households independently. Thirdly, and again in contrast to the more family-oriented vintages and pig-slaughters, at corporate and communal tasks (public works/ditch cleanings) there is also a crucial element of social control: extending the task over a number of days with smaller teams would totally eliminate the careful and often critical observation by co-owners of the quality of work performed by each other. At all such large events which I attended, the pace was extremely intense. Most villagers were literally vultures with respect to their co-participants: they quite intently invigilated each others' efforts and rapidly censured any lazy movements or individuals lagging behind.

Throughout the year, all women but the very wealthy work closely alongside men or on their own in the fields. Women and young girls are total participants in Fontelas' agriculture and their spheres of activity are in no way limited to household and kitchen chores (O'Neill 1982a). I have seen young women ploughing at various times with a standard team of two draught animals (Photo 7), and one young woman of 25 also drives her father's tractor on occasion. Work in the fields is not considered demeaning or in any sense

Table 6. *Major agricultural tasks by season*

Spring (March–May)	*Summer* (June–August)	*Autumn* (Sept.–November)	*Winter* (Dec.–February)
Pruning of vineyards	*2nd vineyard-digging	*Potato harvest	**Pig-slaughters
*Manuring (crop fields)	Irrigation of gardens	Fruit collection	Irrigation of meadows
*1st vineyard-digging	**Haymaking	Maize harvest	1st ploughing (fallow fields)
Potato planting	Reapings (rye)	*Maize husking	Firewood collection
*Sheep-shearing	*Transports (rye)	**Vintages	Shrub collection
2nd ploughing (fallow fields)[a]	**Threshings (rye)	Liqueur distilling[c]	Carpentry, household repairs, etc.
**Public works/communal tasks[b]		3rd ploughing & sowing (fallow fields)	Blacksmith opens forge
**Cleaning of irrigation ditches		Chestnut collection	

* Tasks requiring the recruitment of between 1 and 10 extra helpers.

** Tasks requiring the recruitment of up to 50 extra helpers.

a – These 1st, 2nd, and 3rd ploughings refer to the *fallow* side of the hamlet. The cereal on the side sown in November grows in this way until the following summer, when it is reaped. The fields on each side are thus ploughed three times each year and sown every alternate year.

b – These may take place at any time of the year, but as the grain cycle is so rushed in the summer, public works usually occur in the spring.

c – *Aguardente* (fire-water): a clear drink distilled from the grape-branches and seeds remaining after the treaded liquid is removed from the wine-press tank (*lagar*) to the wine-barrels.

'dishonourable' for women, but quite the contrary. The greater women's participation in outdoor work, the greater are their contributions to total household production. This may not have been true of women in the *jornaleiro* group in former decades, when the latter worked for wages or payment in kind: but today no women in Fontelas ever work for anyone else for wages.

No household possesses the adequate labour or technical resources to accomplish large harvesting tasks on its own. The tractors have alleviated some of the effort needed for these jobs and have hastened the timing of their execution. But even the tractor-owning households are forced to recruit enormous teams to turn and dry their hay in the fields, load it onto the tractors, to transport their grain, and to cut, collect, and tread their grapes. Cash rarely enters these exchanges of labour, except in cases of payment for tractor or mowing services. It is far more frequent for a tractor-owner to plough other villagers' fields or transport their grain in exchange for the latters' labour at the formers' much larger harvests. Thus when the *lavrador* Elias offered to pay tractor-owner Delfim (a large *lavrador*) for the cost of driving a tractor-full of guests to his cousin's baptismal banquet at a nearby river site, Delfim refused the money three times at the end of the day. He explained: 'I don't need Elias' money, but I do need him to dig my vineyard.'

Most of Fontelas' households are involved in this way in a large number of labour-teams (their own as well as others') throughout the agricultural year. The membership of these teams is continually shifting from household to household as each in turn organizes its own harvesting labour. Each household (even the wealthiest ones) to a certain extent thus possesses 'insufficient means of production'. Villagers must either borrow or exchange animals, tools, or 'labouring arms' in order to reach production targets.

One typical task usually carried out only by small teams using domestic labour are the summer reapings. A close look at this task will give us an idea of household labour patterns in the summer season. The reapings (*segadas*) begin in late June, and working days may start as early as 4 or 5 a.m. If the fields are far from the hamlet, the first three of the day's four meals are carried out and eaten there – breakfast (*mata-bicho*) around 9 a.m., lunch (*almoço*) around 2 p.m., and an afternoon snack (*merenda*) around 5 p.m. Dinner (*ceia*) is then eaten at home and can be as late as 11 p.m. on days of heavy labour. A full day's reaping comprises up to 10 or 11 hours of work per person. Only occasionally are an extra person or two recruited to help. Meals on these days are usually larger and frequently include generous servings of fresh meat: normally roast lamb or kid. The first few days of reaping may start with a large household team (4 or 5 people) after which the remaining days follow with 2 or 3 household members finishing the job at a more leisurely pace. The work is generally quite strenuous and physically exhausting.

In each field the work to be done is the same. First the stalks of rye must be cut: reapers work at distances of about one metre apart, to allow room for the sweep of their sickles. Some individuals (including myself) use leather finger-guards on their left hands to avoid being cut by upsweeps of the blade. Five to six sweeps of the sickle in a semicircle from left to right leave a large handful of stalks in the reaper's left hand, which is then put on the ground. A few of these handfuls are piled upon each other as the stalks are progressively cut. Once all of the cutting is completed in the field, three or four of these loose piles are tied together to form large sheaves (*molhos*), which are left lying on the ground. If the grain is at all wet the tied sheaves are joined together into compact vertical piles of four sheaves each, leaning against each other: four such sheaves form a *pousada* (Table 7). Once dry, the sheaves are stacked carefully into larger conical structures called *morneiras*: each of these conical mounds provides just about one cart-load of grain sheaves, or 25 *pousadas*. A tractor-load is roughly equivalent to just over two loads of an ox-cart, but only about one half of the hamlet's grain is transported from the fields by the three tractors.

Each of a household's rye fields is reaped in this way in succession beginning in late June. The reapings usually begin following St John's Day (24 June) and end in mid-July when all of the sheaves are taken from the fields to the threshing-floors within the centre of the hamlet. Reaping is an exhausting process and it occupies some of the longest and hottest days of the year. The task has its own folklore: there are a wide variety of songs sung specifically during reapings. One of these stresses the length of the reaping day,[4] and the return of the reapers to their host's house in the darkness:

Oh Lady our hostess, Come out for the evening-party, Come out for the evening-party.	*Oh Senhora nossa ama,* *Saia cá para o serão,* *Saia cá para o serão.*
If you want to see your reapers, Who have reaped your bread, Who have reaped your bread.	*Se quer ver os seus segadores,* *Que segaram no seu pão,* *Que segaram no seu pão.*
Oh Lady our hostess, Put the oil-lamp in the living-room, Put the oil-lamp in the living-room.	*Oh Senhora nossa ama,* *Ponha a candeia na sala,* *Ponha a candeia na sala.*
If you want to see your reapers, Arriving from your reapings, Arriving from your reapings.	*Se quer ver os seus segadores,* *Que vêm da sua segada,* *Que vêm da sua segada.*

One household's sequence of reapings is set out in Table 7, which contains all of the fields cultivated by the *lavrador* Elias on the South-east side of the

[4] Another type of reaping song involves a picturesque alternating structure in which a man reaping on one hill sings to a woman reaping on another: the woman replies and the song continues with each reaper exchanging verses. These *cantigas ao desafio*, or 'competitive songs', are falling into disuse. A number of elderly villagers sung them on request, but complained of 'the exodus of the young' and the effects of mechanical reapers in reducing the sizes of their formerly enormous manual reaping teams (*camaradas*). These larger teams were more colourful, they maintained, and reapers in those days expressed a fiercer competitive spirit. Only fragments of these former songs are remembered today.

12 Rye harvest (June): a large *lavrador* reaps rye stalks with a sickle.

hamlet. The most striking pattern that emerges is that of the predominance of household labour at these tasks. On only one day (30 June) were extra helpers recruited: three of these were paid a daily wage of 200 *escudos* (£3.33) and given four free meals each. Two of the household's largest fields were reaped on this day: all of the remaining ones were reaped by Elias, his wife, and his widowed father-in-law. Towards the end of the cycle, a mechanical reaper was hired to reap the grain in four medium-sized fields. Thus 10 consecutive days of reaping completed the bulk of the job and the remaining 6 plots were reaped in a few additional hours. Note that on the whole the largest fields were tackled first and its smaller ones last, thus concentrating the household's greatest physical efforts towards the beginning of the cycle.

Another means of looking at household labour is to compare the activities of all of the members of one household on the same day. On a number of days throughout the year, I recorded all of the tasks executed by the members of various households, listing their entire daily schedules of chores and the time it took to complete each of them. In some cases I spent the entire day with the

Table 7. *One household's reapings (Household 21)*

Date (1976)	Time of day	Field	No. of people working	Hours worked	Yield in *pousadas**
24 June	morning	Field 1	3	4½	25
24 June	afternoon	Field 2	3	1	
25 June	morning	Field 2	3	7	50
25 June	afternoon	cloudy weather			
26 June	morning	Field 3	3	6	
26 June	afternoon	Field 3	3	5	50
27 June	morning	Field 4	3	6	
27 June	afternoon	Field 4	3	5	50
27 June	afternoon	Field 5	3	1	
28 June	morning	Field 5	3	4	30
28 June	afternoon	rain			
29 June	morning	Field 6	3	6	22
29 June	afternoon	Field 7	3	2	14
30 June	morning	Field 8	6	7	70
30 June	afternoon	Field 9	8	5	50
30 June	afternoon	Field 10	8	1	13
1 July	morning	Field 11	3	4	14
1 July	afternoon	Field 12	3	5	35
2 July	morning	Field 13	3	3	
2 July	afternoon	rain			
3 July	morning	Field 13	3	5	40
3 July	afternoon	Field 14	reaper	½	25
3 July	afternoon	Field 15	reaper	½	25
?	–	Field 16	reaper	½	25
?	–	Field 17	reaper	½	30
?	–	Field 18	3	1	14
?	–	Field 19	3	¾	12
12 days		19 fields		81.75	594

* Dry capacity measure which facilitates calculation of the cereal harvest prior to threshing; a *pousada* is equivalent to about 13½ litres, thus a bit smaller than the *alqueire* (17 litres).

family, and in others I had dinner with them and wrote down their schedules that evening. The tasks of Household 14 on 6 May 1977 provide a good example.

In this household reside Lourenço and Sebastiana (aged 62 and 56), their married daughter Benta and her husband Avelino (aged 33 and 38), their unmarried son Justiniano (aged 35), and a granddaughter Leonarda (aged 9). The elder couple participates fully in the day's work – they have in no sense retired from farming. For instance, Lourenço took breakfast at 7:30 a.m. and worked for most of the day (10 hours including an hour for lunch) on the installation of a large water pipe along the road to Mosteiro. (While this work lasted for about four months that year, Lourenço worked for daily wages.) After a snack at home at 6:30 p.m., Lourenço dug part of a kitchen-garden for half an hour before returning home at 7:30 p.m.

Lourenço's wife Sebastiana tends to vary her working rhythms between jobs out in the fields and household chores, which are done with more routine by her daughter Benta. Sebastiana rose at 6:30 a.m. and helped with fixing breakfast. The morning meal consisted of dried codfish (*bacalhau*) fried in olive oil, eggs, home-baked rye bread and purchased wheat bread, wine, coffee with milk, and the distilled liqueur *aguardente*. After breakfast, Sebastiana assisted her son in ploughing a field from 8:30 a.m. until 2 p.m. They returned home for lunch, which was prepared by Sebastiana's daughter Benta. Lunch consisted of chick-pea soup with potatoes and noodles, dried codfish with potatoes, bread, and wine. After lunch, Sebastiana fed the household's rabbits and then went to a distant field to cut and collect a large bundle of fresh grass for the cows. This task lasted from 3 o'clock until around 5:30 p.m. Around 7 p.m. she fed the household's goat. Both Sebastiana and her daughter are quite strong physically and it is not unusual to see either of them (or both together) carrying heavy sacks on their heads or chopping enormous logs of firewood.

Before breakfast the younger Benta milked the household's dairy cow, and afterwards she prepared the morning meal for the household's pigs: this consisted of cooked cabbages and flour. This is not an easy task, as the pigs are fed huge quantities of food, particularly in the autumn. This food is heated over the fireplace in large black cauldrons. Benta then fixed the beds, swept the floors, washed the dishes, and went to the fountain to gather water (this household does not have running water). After a brief trip to the shop, Benta washed some clothing and began to prepare lunch. During the afternoon Benta also assisted in the cutting of grass from 3 until 5:30 p.m., and returned home to prepare the 6:30 snack (really a kind of dinner). This meal consisted again of dried codfish, but also of roast chicken, salted pork fat (*toucinho*), rashers, smoked ham (*presunto*), meat sausages, bread, and wine. Benta then milked the dairy cow again and fed the pigs a second meal. Even the young Leonarda participates in tasks out in the fields following her afternoon session at school. On this day she left school at 4 p.m. and helped her mother and grandmother in cutting and collecting grass until 5:30 p.m. Leonarda and her mother paid a visit to a friend's house from 8:30 to 9:30 that evening, after which Benta and Sebastiana took a bit of bread and milk before going to bed at 10:30.

Finally, note that Justiniano took care of the cows' meals in the early morning (6:30–7:30 a.m.) and evening (7:30–8 p.m.) and ploughed a field from 8:30 a.m. until 2 p.m. He also assisted with the cutting of grass in the afternoon. However, Avelino spent 9 hours of the day working *outside* his own household at another villager's vineyard-digging. Counting meals and walking time between the vineyard and the hamlet, Avelino dedicated almost 11 hours of his day to a friend's labour-team. Later of course, this friend will return a day's work in exchange for Avelino's, probably at Avelino's household's own subsequent vineyard-digging. In addition to the bulk of his day spent in the vineyard, Avelino rose at 5:30 a.m. to irrigate a meadow in another section of the hamlet's terrain before returning home for breakfast at 7:30 a.m., just prior to his going to the vineyard. He returned to the same meadow again in the early evening for two hours between 7 and 9 p.m.

The day is typical of the mid-spring period when tasks increase in number and pace. Lourenço's household provides a good example of a middle-level *lavrador* household which, if not exceptionally wealthy in land or livestock, is nevertheless quite wealthy in labour: an extraordinary number and variety of tasks can be executed by these six household members on any one day. Villagers lament the predicament of wealthy *proprietário* households with excesses of land and shortages of labour: they have no large work group within their households and find difficulty in hiring day-labourers. The times when a wealthy family could maintain four or five resident servants have gone, as many of the poor who worked formerly as servants and day-labourers have emigrated. Villagers sigh sadly: 'all that land and no one to work it – what a waste'. Much of these households' land lies uncultivated and covered with brush. It is land *and* labour that count in Fontelas and neither of these alone. Lourenço's household, on the other hand, has an optimum labour supply neatly balanced with its 14 hectares of land. Six persons (3 men and 3 women) can distribute domestic tasks well and avoid excessive and multiple exchanges of labour with other households. This does not mean that they can dispense with the four very large harvesting teams needed for haymaking, threshings, vintages, and pig-slaughters. But they are the closest example of a 'self-sufficient' peasant household in Fontelas. Few other households are in similar situations, and few have so many 'labouring arms'.

Many other households in Fontelas must pool their labour as well as their animals and tools in order to produce at all. In these cases simple exchange labour is decisive. One pertinent example is provided by four households who pooled their efforts and tools for the planting of potatoes.

H36 ANDRÉ – *lavrador*
Joaquina – wife
Salvador – son
Geraldo – son

H50 JUSTINO – André's brother (blacksmith)

H7 CLEMENTINA – Joaquina's sister
Ernesto – husband (shopkeeper)

H27 SÂNCIA – Clementina's first cousin

Task: 19 May 1976, morning and afternoon; near the church. André ploughs all three plots, while various persons plant potatoes in their respective furrows.

The household (H36) providing the plough and animal team was a middle-level *lavrador* household farming a holding of 12½ hectares. The other three households were all smallholders without plough teams. Justino lives with his common-law wife farming a holding of 5 hectares, Ernesto and his wife Clementina (and her incapacitated unmarried brother) farm a holding of 3½ hectares; Sância lives alone and farms a mere 1.25 hectares. These three poorer households are extreme contrasts to Lourenço's *lavrador* household examined above: none of them has abundant sources of labour, agricultural tools, nor the crucial team of draught animals.

The rationale for this pooling was simple. The first three of these households have contiguous plots in which they plant potatoes: the plots are owned by André, Justino, and Clementina. André simply ploughed all three plots together while each of the owners planted their own potatoes. Labour was temporarily pooled while the use of the plough team was lent by André to the others (Sância was recruited to assist her cousin Clementina). To plough each field separately would involve various separate loans of ploughs, animals, and people, so this simple coordination accomplished the tasks together at one go. Many of the hamlet's poorer households must pool their efforts and resources in this way in order to produce even the most minimal crops. In the absence of such pooling one would be forced to hire a tractor or a day-labourer. But these are problematic options anyway, as the tractors are always over-booked in advance and most residents are reluctant to work for wages for their co-villagers. We have seen that more than half of the hamlet's households own less than the 6 hectares of land necessary to maintain two cows. Once again, the example above reveals households with only 'insufficient means of production' for standard subsistence crops.

Labour in Fontelas is best envisaged as a continual process rather than as finite quantifiable units of time. This is in fact precisely how villagers themselves view work – as an unending cycle of shifting relations between people, land, animals, tools, and the weather. In striking contrast to the notion of *trabalho* (work) among rural wage labourers in Southern Portugal (Cutileiro 1971:60–8), in Fontelas an entirely different notion exists: *trabalhar* is best translated as a verb (to work) or yet more precisely as the present participle form 'working'. A day's work is not governed in Fontelas by hours, wages, or a particular chronological pace but rather by the broader confines of sunrise to sunset. Even *jornaleiros* hired for a day's wages today do not work for 8 hours but rather (especially at reapings) for up to 10 or 11. No rural strikes have been recorded anywhere in local documents throughout the last century, and even the idea of a strike presupposes a system of relations between hirer and labourers totally out of place within the household-oriented, unpaid work rhythms of Fontelas. Day-labourers in and around the hamlet were not always paid with wages but in kind, and their days of wage labour did not constitute year-long patterns. In Fontelas it is the completion of a specific seasonal task that counts, not the number of hours worked. Not to be actually seen physically working brings immediate criticism and indirect chastisement. *Está na boa vida* (you're enjoying the good life) is a frequent comment levelled at any person pausing on a road, sitting, or not visibly applying their hands or arms to a specific end.

Intellectual work does not count, of course, as I soon learned. The priest and myself were consistently compared as individuals clever enough to have somehow escaped the bad life of manual labour. All attempts to justify 'working with the brain' or writing with the pen were fruitless. This was not really work, either because the body is not seen to sweat nor the product to grow tangibly from the ground. As with lawyers, town clerks, and politicians, villagers place priests (and anthropologists) among the lucky few who have managed to wangle their way out of the peasant's lot. Indeed, one of the most common criticisms directed by villagers against all political figures is that 'they don't want to work' (*não querem trabalhar*). National political figures in Lisbon offices are particularly despised, and peasants view them as fundamentally corrupt and lazy: 'they should come to Fontelas and sweat in the fields like us'. But as these officials are immersed in useless *política* their paths are not those of real work but rather of feeding their bellies and filling their pockets. No one sitting at a desk in an office anywhere, even in the local town, ever really 'works'. Furthermore, the wealthy of Fontelas are convinced that the poverty of the local poor is the direct result of an ingrained lack of desire to work: the poor are poor not because specific conditions prevent them from working, but rather because they are simply lazy.

Each household maintains a delicate balance between the size and quality of its land and the labour resources available to work that land. Even Fontelas' two retarded villagers and one boy with a case of mild epilepsy participate fully in working rhythms. These two women suffered attacks of cerebral meningitis in childhood, but both do household chores and some occasional work in the fields. The same is true of the epileptic youth. While one of these women is deaf but barely understandable when she speaks, the other is totally deaf and dumb: despite this fact, the latter woman (living with her sister and brother-in-law) can frequently be seen washing dishes, feeding animals, or carrying large loads of firewood. Even a prospective marriage partner in Fontelas may be valued more for a reputation as a hard worker or a serious, responsible farmer than as the owner of a large amount of land. Labour is a vital asset which can outweigh other kinds of wealth. Fontelas' system of production is essentially labour-intensive not capital-intensive, and this is why at peak harvests there are never enough arms to go round.

No household in Fontelas is an isolate, or a basic cell of independent production. Despite the many minor tasks that can be carried out by three or four household members, key harvesting tasks force each domestic group to expand momentarily to bring the harvest in. The major currency of labour exchange in Fontelas' agricultural cycle is thus not cash but labouring arms. Each household is to a greater or lesser degree dependent on perhaps five or six other households with which it maintains continual exchanges of labour, tools, animals, and meals. Thus, one worries not only about one's own crops and production targets but about others' as well, because every household also has a stake in the productive cycles of their cooperators' households. The basic unit of production in Fontelas is thus not technically the household itself, but *a series of cooperating households* linked through multiple harvesting exchanges.

Communal labour

All of the examples above provide only a partial picture of the labour process in Fontelas. Let us turn from the area of specifically household labour to the other extreme of communal labour involving the entire hamlet. These are occasions for which large labour-teams are organized for pubic works.

A specific institution is brought into play in Fontelas for communal tasks – this is the *conselho*, or hamlet council. The *conselho*[5] is an entirely hamlet-centred body and has no links of any kind with administrative entities at the parish or municipal levels. There are only two fixed and rigid elements in the functioning of the council: (a) equal participation in repairs of communal

[5] The council's complete designation is *conselho de vizinhos* (council of neighbours) – the word 'neighbours' here understood in its classic Northern Iberian meaning as not merely one's proximal next-door neighbours but *all* co-residents of the community. However, villagers simply call the council *o conselho* in most cases. The term refers to a public meeting or assembly of villagers in a small rural settlement, and should not be confused with the strictly administrative term *concelho* (municipality). Similar hamlet councils have been reported for many regions of mountain Europe. The closest parallels outside Northern Portugal itself are with the *concelho* and *xunta de veciños* of Galician Spain (Lisón-Tolosana 1971:115–17) and the *común de vecinos* in Castilian Spain (Freeman 1968; 1970).

property, and (b) the right on the part of the collectivity to exclude individual owners. Apart from these two rules, all the rest is a question of consensus and informal discussion. The sole purpose of the *conselho* is to organize large labour-teams for repairs and reconstruction of communal property. There are five such forms of property in Fontelas: the *baldios*, small communal meadows (the *poulos*), public walls and roads, the cemetery, and the hamlet's four communal water-mills.[6] Although only one of these four mills presently functions, all of these forms of property are used by virtually every household in the hamlet at some time or other. The communal mill may be used by any of the hamlet's households to grind grain for animal feed or less frequently for human consumption. The term *moinho do povo* (people's mill/hamlet mill) is itself suggestive: the mill belongs to everyone in Fontelas and it is not formally registered in anyone's name anywhere.

For repairs and the general upkeep of any of these forms of property, the council must meet and discuss prospective plans jointly. These meetings are seen as processes rather than as discrete events. Villagers meet to *fazer conselho*: to 'take council' or to consult with each other – in standard Portuguese, the word *conselho* also has the general meaning of advice. Every household which uses the specific property in question on anything like a regular basis is ideally required to send one male family member to assist in the repairs. In fact, it is rarely the case that *all* households send a representative as there are never any tasks that would require more than 40 or so men. Failure to send a representative without good reason, however, incurs criticism and may lead to demands for a monetary fine. In extreme cases a household may be completely excluded from further use of the property.

The following four meetings of the council took place during my fieldwork, and in 1981 I was told of two further meetings which took place in 1980.

Common-land: (15 June 1976) Election of four villagers to an executive committee in charge of future exploitation and sales of timber from Fontelas' common-land.

Wall Construction: (6 October 1976) Extension of a stone wall to the right of the church, opposite H32 (Map 3).

Road to Communal Mill: (7 March 1977) Hiring of a bulldozer to widen and smooth out the dirt road leading to one of the hamlet's communal water-mills.

[6] In addition to the 4 communal water-mills, there are also 3 private mills. Two of the latter belong to *proprietário* households (H28 and H39). The third private mill is owned jointly by H28, 29, and 32 – two of the latter are *proprietário* households and the third a large *lavrador*. However, none of the private mills functions at present and each of them is in a rather dilapidated condition. This is probably due to the villagers' use of a mechanical mill installed in a neighbouring hamlet (5 kilometres from Fontelas) around 1972. Villagers from Fontelas and other nearby hamlets carry their grain to and from the mechanical mill by mule or tractor.

Dispute over Communal Plot: (15 April 1978) Discussion of two households' individual usurpation of portions of the *Campo* communal plot.

Dispute over Communal Plot: (January 1980) Further discussion and court action against two households usurping part of the *Campo* communal plot.

Cemetery Enlargement: (April 1980) Northern wall of cemetery extended about 20 metres.

Only one of these meetings was in any way unusual. At the second meeting over disputed rights to the communal plot (January 1980), a decision was arrived at on the part of a group of households to take the two transgressing villagers to court in town. The latter had a number of years ago constructed a hay-loft and a garage within the bounds of the *Campo* communal plot (top left of Map 3). The council was unanimous in demanding that the two buildings be removed in order to create space for a new schoolhouse and a Border Guard barracks soon to be built in Fontelas. The two villagers refused to move their buildings, and the case is still pending a court ruling.

A number of households have borne grudges against these two families for years due to the latters' individual appropriation of hamlet property: what belongs to *o povo* (the hamlet) cannot be treated as individually owned property. This is why the households decided to carry the dispute to court, but they were somewhat resigned that the case would take time to resolve and that ultimately all four buildings (including the new school and the barracks) would end up crowding the plot. In former years, the meadow was used as pasturage for the pigs of the hamlet's poorer households, but today it is used solely as the dance floor at the patron saint's festival on 13 June of each year.

The other four meetings listed above were similar, and a brief description of one of these will complete our picture of how the council normally functions.

In February of 1977 a number of villagers had begun talking of the difficulty of reaching the hamlet's communal water-mill along a rather narrow dirt path. This mill is located to the North-west of Fontelas (Map 2) on the banks of a large stream. The dirt path leading to the mill was not only narrow but quite curvy and cluttered with stones and boulders. The only means of carrying sacks of grain and flour to and from the mill was by tying the sacks onto a pack animal or alternatively by ox-cart. At this time, a bulldozer was widening a dirt road connecting Fontelas with Mosteiro: this 3-kilometre road was soon to be paved. Consensus was reached that the time had come to widen the mill path into a road so as to allow the hamlet's three tractors to pass, as well as to smooth the way for ox-carts and mules. A meeting of the council was in order, both to discuss the matter and to set a date for beginning the work. Prior to the meeting, one villager approached the driver of the bulldozer to request his services for two days. The driver agreed, and his reply was communicated informally to a number of other villagers.

13 Pig-slaughter (November/December): a group of kin and neighbours assists a host household of wealthy *lavradores*.

The council met on 7 March. Around 9 a.m. the church bells were rung by one of Fontelas' two chiefs of police.[7] The chimes are simply rung a few times in rapid succession with no specific pattern, so as to let people know that an assembly is about to take place. About 25 men gathered in the current meeting-place for the council: this lies on a central hamlet path just outside H32 (Map 3 below). As the day was rainy, two groups of men gathered, one next to the uninhabited household to the right of H32 and the other underneath an extended roof of H32. Ideally, each household in Fontelas must send one male

[7] The post of *cabo de polícia* is a rather undefined one in Fontelas in social terms, despite the formal administrative duties granted to these men by Portuguese law. As mentioned earlier, the *cabos* are the lowest public office at the level of the hamlet, and they are appointed directly by the Junta in Mosteiro. Their duties are merely to report to these higher authorities (the Junta and the town Câmara) any legal irregularity occurring within their hamlets, such as disputes over public thoroughfares, minor trangressions, and brawls. Each hamlet has two *cabos*. In Fontelas, one of these has held the post for 9 years, having been appointed by the President of the Mosteiro Junta. The second was appointed by the first in 1975. Throughout my $2\frac{1}{2}$ years of fieldwork, neither of the chiefs of police lodged formal reports or complaints of any kind either to the Junta or the town Câmara about anything.

representative to *conselho* meetings, but this is not a rigid rule.[8] Those households who do not send a member are told of the discussion later and their views on the matter are consulted before any final decision is taken. If necessary, a second meeting may be called to carry discussion further or to resolve any disagreements. Attendance at the assembly is thus not an absolute requirement, but participation in some part of the repair work is.

The men present at this meeting discussed plans to enlarge the road to the mill: these plans included the cost of hiring the bulldozer, the distribution of this total cost by household, the date when work would start, and the number of men needed. It was decided that 20 men could complete the job, working in teams of 5 men each for two morning shifts and two afternoon shifts on the 8th and 9th of March. These men would walk along the path ahead of the bulldozer in order to assist with the removal of large stones and small boulders. They would also clear some of the rubble left on the edges of the road. It was estimated that the job could be completed by working four sessions of $2\frac{1}{2}$ hours each, or a total of about 10 hours of work. The total cost of the bulldozer hire at £14.50 per hour would thus be £145. It was decided that each household using the mill should contribute 200 *escudos* (£3) towards the total cost, irrespective of whether each of these sent one of the 20 working men. Nine smallholding households who do not use the mill were excused from this payment, thus bringing the total to £145 through contributions averaging £3 from 48 of the hamlet's households. The next day the bulldozer began the job, and I accompanied one team of 5 men on the first morning. One of the chiefs of police then collected the money from the remaining 47 households immediately following the completion of the roadworks. The task was executed in this fashion: quickly, efficiently, with minimum deliberation and no major disagreements.

As in other cases of public repairs directed by the *conselho*, households which are particularly poor in money or labour resources are exempted from the work or even from contributory payments. They are not criticized nor are they fined, and their rights in the mill thus remain latent. Such households are not even likely to use the mill (or other communal property) with any regularity. Thus, a number of other smallholding households did pay the £3 contribution towards the new mill road: although they do not have plough teams and consequently cannot produce their own bread, they purchase rye grain and find it cheaper to grind in the communal mill than in the mechanical mill in the neighbouring hamlet. But a recalcitrant villager of reasonable

[8] In Mosteiro I attended a *conselho* meeting at which many of that hamlet's women also attended and voiced opinions. Also in Mosteiro – as is the case in Fontelas – the meeting place for the council is located conspicuously away from the church (about 50 metres distant) although the meeting was held on a Sunday morning immediately after mass. My queries about such assemblies in other hamlets yielded no set rules: in some communities only men attend and in others women do as well. Women heads of household (single women, widows, or those with emigrant husbands) are always consulted later in hamlets where only men attend the meetings.

economic standing may be prohibited from using the property by all of the other owners. However, redefinitions of the property rights invested in the council – such as the current court case over the communal plot – are quite infrequent. Total exclusion of a co-owner is rare, and I heard of no fines actually imposed during my fieldwork.

There are a few links between the council and the Church, but the former should not be seen as in any sense a 'religious' institution. Aside from the chimes to announce meetings, the council is also called together for repairs of the cemetery or for reconstruction of public walls around the church or the churchyard. But there the links end, and no further coordination between the two institutions occurs. Any reconstruction or improvements within the church, however, are the concern exclusively of the priest and outside ecclesiastical bodies. The annual patron saint's festival in honour of St Anthony is organized on a rotating basis each year by three youths termed *mordomos*, who coordinate the construction of the wooden platforms (*andores*) on which each of the saints' images are placed. Prior to the festival these three youths go around the hamlet collecting each household's financial contribution towards the costs of the construction of these platforms, fireworks, and other festival expenses. But these youths have no tie whatsoever with the council and the annual religious festival is in no way seen as lying within the secular field of the council's activities. Teams formed to reconstruct churchyard or cemetery walls are seen as contributing to *public* property and not to solely religious structures, and the use of the church's bells is purely a matter of convenience.

Religious processions and auctions are further examples of levelling events which usually involve the entire hamlet. Note however that these processions and auctions also have no links with the council and fall exclusively within the domain of the Church. Even the actual physical site of hamlet auctions (centre of Map 3) is itself located outside the church doors, in a distinctly different place from that of council meetings. Religious and economic forms of 'levelling' are of course quite separate spheres of social life and as such, I fear, not legitimately comparable. The kinds of levelling of wealth differences I describe in this chapter are qualitatively different from those Aguilera speaks of for religious celebrations in South-Central Spain: 'This festival cycle can be seen as a series of ceremonies each of which completes a phase of the dual process of dissipation of tension and hostility, and the reassertion of group identity and integration' (1978:103). The multiplicity of occasions in the religious calendar of yearly Catholic celebrations (in either Spain or Portugal) which stress the idea of human beings being 'equal in the eyes of God' probably vastly outnumbers the rare instances in Fontelas when villagers are forced to acknowledge that their reciprocal economic obligations to each other must also be 'equal'. Much more relevant to my argument is yet a third kind of levelling mechanism analysed by Shanin (1972) for the Russian peasantry, and by Weigandt (1977) and Netting and McGuire (1982) for the Swiss Alps, which emphasizes land distribution, differences in total wealth, and the rise or fall of individuals and households over the generations (in regions of partible inheritance) due to considerations of fragmentation through partition, number of inheriting siblings, and the potential reconsolidation of property through marriage. The latter studies are also concerned, unlike Aguilera, with diachronic dimensions of relative equality or differentiation between households of different economic standing: to repeat, this is quite a distinct object of analysis ('real wealth') from the conceptual unity and integration involved in festive or other ecclesiastical ceremonies.

It is important to note that the *conselho* is a relatively flexible institution. When a large task is called for, the council is organized in order to facilitate collective action. No officials are ever elected as there are in fact no offices. No rotation of leaders exists in the council, and no kind of formal written minutes are ever kept. Among all the documentary sources I examined for the eighteenth, nineteenth, and twentieth centuries at the hamlet, parish, and municipal levels, not one mention of any hamlet council in the area ever appeared. In the absence of such written evidence or even minimal lists, it is very easy to speculate about whether Fontelas' council in former years was any 'more cohesive' than it is today. I found no means of verifying this, and older villagers provided mixed views. Some pointed to the current 'lack of community spirit' due to a growing individualism (so they affirmed) while others stressed that in former years even the council was dominated indirectly by wealthy *proprietários* whose opinions and decisions always carried more weight.

Although the topic is beyond the scope of this book, a number of social historians have suggested that medieval village councils should not be seen as truly communal or egalitarian social institutions. Hoffman has noted that for Central European common-field villages, corporate control of resources or an open-field system were not necessarily indicative of village equality. In this sense, 'the common-field system . . . was not simply egalitarian. Communal control of limited resources rested not in the hands of all inhabitants nor, with exceptions, even in those of all heads of households. The assembly of cultivators was everywhere dominated, if not monopolized, by the better-off peasants' (Hoffman 1975:62). Clearly, the actual functioning of village assemblies should not be assumed to correspond precisely with their apparent levelling of all villagers in the face of a communal task: powerful villagers may have gained the upper hand even *within* the council structure itself. Similar suggestions were made decades ago by the French historian Marc Bloch, in this case concerning the external link between the corporate community and an outside political system:

> The very fields that they cultivated were not held to be theirs in full ownership, nor was their community – at least in most cases – the full owner of those lands over which

common rights were exercised. Both were said to be 'held' of the lord, which meant that as landowner he had a superior right over them, recognized by dues owned to him, and capable in certain circumstances of overriding the concurrent rights of the individual cultivators and of the community (Bloch 1941:235–6).

The suggestion therefore is that open fields as well as ovens, mills, and even roads were only nominally communal in practice: in legal terms they remained part of a larger ('feudal'?) system of ownership. Although a wider coverage of the topic in economic and social history would undoubtedly reveal further references to this point (Blum 1971), these two quotations alone are provocative in that they challenge simplistic interpretations of village institutions of corporate regulation. Forms of communal property, as well as the village councils activated for their use or repair, have not sprung out of abstract ideas of rural equality. However isolated geographically, such communal institutions may well have been merely local extensions of larger regional systems of stratification and economic control.

Today the council in Fontelas constitutes a purely instrumental means of organizing labour for *sporadic* repairs and reconstruction. Even on these occasions, the number of men needed and the labour-time required are flexible.[9] If 20 men are needed, then 20 will do: if 40 men are needed, then 20 more will be recruited. No specific rules are codified at any time or in any formal structure: the council is an entirely consensual institution. At those moments in any particular year when large teams of men are required (to move boulders, build walls, or extend the cemetery) a temporary levelling of all households occurs. At these times, all households (except the very poor) are equally responsible for the hamlet's communal property: each one must participate either by attending the assembly, sending a man to work, or contributing to the total costs. In abstract terms, all co-owners are equal and their individual differences in economic and social standing are momentarily obliterated. These differences are as it were forgotten during the temporary levelling required to pool collective labour and get the task done. Whether this was so in former historical periods must remain unanswered for the moment. Today a wealthy household of *proprietários* as well as a smallholding household must both send one man, and their economic differences are 'hidden' temporarily within the collective obligation to repair the communal

[9] It should be noted that the legal definition of 'public property' within the hamlet terrain is a complicated one, as we have seen in Chapter 2 with regard to the *baldios*. The council really functions within an extremely small sphere in that it organizes specifically minor repairs or reconstructions at the hamlet level. Major public works, which also usually require more labour and money than even the council could bring together, fall within the jurisdiction of the Junta in Mosteiro or the town Câmara. For instance, a few months before I left the community in 1978, a number of large piles of square stones were brought to Fontelas for conversion of the hamlet's main dirt paths into cobblestone roads. The council had no formal meetings over the matter. This entire roadwork project was begun through the town Câmara, and it was this administrative body that eventually (in 1979) had the cobblestones placed and bore the total expenses.

property. The former household may use the mill for two full days to grind its grain, while the latter may use it only for two hours. But even so, the obligation to discuss and to assist in the repairs and their costs is strictly the same, and is divided equally among all participating villagers.

The *conselho* is thus a kind of abstract 'corporate person' (Freeman 1970) to whom labour, duties, and payments are owed. It is a centripetal body consisting of myriad household/council ties: the ties between each individual household and the corporate person are the key links, not the ties between each member household. No specific person has any formal voice of greater authority than any other. Even the two chiefs of police hold relatively powerless posts. Both men have a very loose role in calling council assemblies together: they are merely in charge of ringing the church bells to announce meetings and in most cases it is they who collect the money needed from each household. But their voice in hamlet decisions about public works has no priority over that of any other resident villager. If either or both *cabos* were sick or temporarily absent, the council would function perfectly well without them. Both come from wealthy *lavrador* households, but villagers view their actual legal authority as laughable.

Council repair teams are thus not work groups consisting of reciprocal dyadic exchanges of labour: each household does not exchange labour with others but rather contributes labour to the communal whole. In this sense, disparities between wealthy and poor households are temporarily suspended in the interest of getting the large task done. As such, the *conselho* is virtually the only social institution in Fontelas which is truly egalitarian.

Threshing teams and irrigation turns

There are three kinds of semi-communal property in Fontelas: (a) sectional baking ovens, (b) threshing-floors, and (c) corporate water-pools used for the irrigation of kitchen-gardens. This section will deal with the latter two and with the corresponding labour-teams organized in relation to them at key points in the agricultural cycle. It is in these intermediate tasks between the levels of the individual household and the entire hamlet that inequalities in the exchange of labour are most prominent. This is so despite the presence in both cases of social rules of apparent equality. The existence in the hamlet of a few kinds of communal and corporate property does not necessarily mean that the entire social structure should be termed communal or egalitarian as a whole. This would be a serious error of interpretation. Let us see why this is the case.

Before beginning, a brief note on the corporate baking ovens is in order. There are three such ovens (*fornos do bairro*) in Fontelas, located in three separate sections of the hamlet. Note that these ovens are located in three of the poorer sections of the community: none of them is physically close to any of the wealthiest households (Map 3). The buildings which house these ovens are rectangular in shape and relatively small: two are constructed of stone and the third of bricks. Each oven itself (Photo 14) is a round or oval structure built of stone in order to withstand high temperatures. But in addition to these three corporate ovens, there are also 20 private ovens in Fontelas: these are located mostly inside one of the rooms of their owners' households. Those individuals without either private ovens or rights in one of the three corporate ovens must pair off with other villagers or buy bread in one of the shops.

A list of all of the hamlet's ovens and their owners is included in Table 8. Note that there is no direct correspondence between ownership rights and locality. That is to say, some villagers move households, but their rights in their corporate oven remain unchanged. For example, H42 bakes in the *Fundo da Aldeia* section although that oven is not physically near it. Similarly, H53 (a shopkeeper) has rights in two corporate ovens but only uses the closer *Castelo* one once each year at Easter: this household's rights in the *Fundo da Aldeia* oven nevertheless remain unless it desists or refuses to contribute to repairs. Other households retain rights in corporate ovens but do not use them as they do not currently produce grain. Bernardo (H31) uses the private oven in his parents' household (H32), while H1 and H42 bake regularly in their friends' ovens as these are closer to their houses. An average household bakes well over a dozen loaves of rye about every fortnight, increasing this amount at peak seasons and during low seasons supplementing these loaves with an occasional loaf of non-local wheat purchased from one of the hamlet's shops.

The co-owners of each corporate oven are termed *herdeiros* (literally, heirs) of the oven and they may refuse entry and usage rights to another villager if the latter does not participate in costs and repairs. Each owner is an 'heir' of the property and enjoys strictly equal rights and duties. In one case, a villager described to me that the use of a corporate oven had been requested by a woman who was not a co-owner. The woman asked 7 of the 8 co-owners if she could bake in the oven, and these 7 agreed. While her loaves were ready to be placed inside the heated oven, the eighth co-owner appeared and objected vehemently. The non-owner was forced to remove her loaves immediately and forbidden to bake there ever again. Although such disputes are rare, when they occur the actual force of co-ownership is expressed. Particularly at Easter and prior to the patron saint's festival in June, the corporate ovens become quite crowded and the bustle of baking creates a lively and sociable atmosphere. At these times, two or three women will pool firewood and bake their loaves and cakes jointly. Each oven-house, or *casa do forno*, also provides temporary living quarters for groups of travelling gypsies passing through the hamlet.

In sum then, although there are three corporate baking ovens in the hamlet there are also 20 private ones currently in use. To place undue emphasis on the corporate ovens at the expense of the private ones would distort the actual state of affairs. While 23 households regularly bake in the hamlet's 20 private ovens, another 18 must all bake in the 3 corporate ones. A further 14 households buy

14 Corporate oven in the *Fundo da Aldeia* section of the hamlet: co-owner women often bake jointly.

their bread and thus rarely if ever use either the corporate ovens or any of their co-villagers' private ones. Both private as well as semi-communal property co-exist in Fontelas, but there is a distinct pattern of spatial distribution. In the case of ovens, private ovens are concentrated within the wealthy centre of the hamlet and the three corporate ones on the poorer margins.

Both the rye threshings in August and the cleaning of irrigation ditches in the spring are accomplished through the operation of two institutionalized

Table 8. *Corporate and private ovens*

Corporate ovens (3)

Cimo da Aldeia (8 co-owners)	– Households 1, 7, 9, 10, 12, 13, 14, & 1 family in France (H5).
*Fundo da Aldeia** (11 co-owners)	– Households 16, 19, 20, 21, 22, 23, 24, 25, 26, 42, 53. (H27 excluded for non-participation in 1972)
*Castelo*** (9 co-owners)	– Households 44, 47, 49, 50, 51, 52, 53, & 2 families in Brazil. (Also lent for use to H17)

Private ovens (20)

H2	H32 (used also by H31)
H3 (used occasionally by H1)	H33
H4	H34 (used also by H42)
H6	H36 (used also by H27)
H8	H37
H11	H38
H15	H39
H28	H40
H29	H46
H30	H57

Buyers of bread (14) – Households 16, 18, 35, 41, 43, 45, 48, 50, 51, 52, 53, 54, 55, 56.

* Reconstructed in 1972: the cost of stones and cement was 1,500 *escudos* (£22.60 at the 1972 exchange rate) and was split by the 11 co-owning households.

** Constructed anew in 1962: the 7 co-owning households split the cost of construction of 4,000 *escudos*.

systems of rotation and sequential turns.[10] While only four council meetings took place throughout my entire fieldwork period, each year between 40 and 50 households must thresh their grain. In addition, the same number of households will have to recruit further labour-teams for their haymaking, vintages, and pig-slaughters. Thus, in any one year as many as 200 large labour-teams will at varying times work (some simultaneously) for successive households' harvests. If we include the smaller groups needed for tasks such as potato-planting and vineyard-diggings, then we could observe some 400 teams working throughout each year in cooperation. Forms of intermediate corporate property (e.g., sectional ovens) are comparable to these large harvesting teams: the teams necessitate extra-household labour but they do

[10] Some of the materials presented here formed part of a conference paper I delivered in Oxford (September 1981) at the SSRC Conference on 'Institutionalized Forms of Cooperation and Reciprocity in Europe', organized by Sandra Ott and John Campbell. They have nevertheless been modified in this chapter, as the thematic interests of the conference were substantially different from the argument proposed here.

not involve *all* of the households in Fontelas. These teams are in this sense a form of communal labour on a smaller scale. The entire productive system of the hamlet is dominated by these shifting labour-teams, and my notes on them are copious. Let us look in detail at two of them.

The threshings (*malhas*) of rye grain in Fontelas are the culmination of an exhaustive year-long cycle of cereal production. Of the hamlet's 57 households, 45 threshed grain in 1976 and 1977. Virtually all of the hamlet's households produce rye except for those composed of individuals either too poor or too old to engage in heavy agricultural production. Although one mechanical threshing-machine is used to thresh all of the hamlet's grain, a team of at least 20 or so people is required to coordinate all of the accompanying tasks at each threshing. A *proprietário* household (H39) owns the machine and rents it to other villagers: it was purchased in 1950 but other similar machines had been rented since about 1945. The threshings constitute the hamlet's last collective effort each year in pooling labour and resources towards the common goal of safely stored grain. For about two and a half weeks at the end of each summer, the entire life of the community is dominated by this time-consuming and labour-intensive job. The last two or three threshings each year always attain heights of festivity, joking, and drunkenness as weeks of arduous threshing labour come to an end. Nightly dances at this time last into the early hours of the morning. A general atmosphere of calm then pervades the hamlet in early September, as villagers recover from the work and begin the much slower rhythm of the autumn harvests (potatoes, grapes, and chestnuts).

Table 9 sets out the sequence of threshings as they took place in 1976. The numbering of the households is my own, and corresponds to a general West–East sequence of household location which I mapped out in the early months of fieldwork. No such fixed numbers are ever used by villagers themselves to refer to other households.[11] The table lists the date on which each of the hamlet's threshings took place and the form of labour-team recruited: this was done either by means of unpaid day-labour exchange (*tornajeira*) or by hiring a group of men who were paid a flat sum. Only 5 threshings were paid for in cash: for instance, on 13 September H39 threshed by paying a team of 12 men the total sum of 1,200 *escudos* (£20) to complete its four-hour threshing. The quantities of rye and wheat threshed by each household are also included (minus those of Marcos: Note c). A percentage of each household's total grain threshed was paid (in *alqueires*) to the owner of the threshing-machine at the end of each threshing (7 per cent in 1976 and 1977, rising to 9 per cent in 1978) but the totals here precede this fee and all land-rent payments. Finally, in the

[11] This general West–East direction is nevertheless followed at a number of other times when rotating collections or processions take place, but no fixed order of households seemed evident to me on these occasions. I have deliberately *not* changed my own numbering system here to fit the order of the threshings, as such a change would be highly misleading and would imply a house-order of 1, 2, 3, etc. which in fact does not determine the sequence of the threshings.

left-hand column are the hamlet's threshing-floors, on which various households' grain-stacks are located prior to the threshings and where their conical straw-stacks remain afterwards.

A word on these threshing-floors is necessary here before proceeding to Map 3, which sets out the circular sequence of the threshings. The location of these threshing-floors provides the key to the system of rotation which is brought into play on this occasion. There are 13 threshing-floors (*eiras*) in the hamlet, of which 5 are entirely private property and 8 the corporate property of various households. Each corporate threshing-floor is named after the section of the hamlet in which it is located, while private threshing-floors are referred to by the names of their respective owners (for example: 'Gabriel's threshing-floor'). There is no threshing-floor which is entirely communal property in the sense of being owned by *all* of the hamlet's households. Each corporate threshing-floor is termed the property of the co-owners (*herdeiros*) who have the right to place their grain-stacks and straw-stacks within its boundaries. No physical markers delimit any area within threshing-floors such as the boundary stones which are placed at the corners of many privately owned arable fields.

Rights in threshing-floors are inherited equally by all heirs following the lines of partible inheritance. It is important to note that the *use right* is inherited and not any actual plot of land. Overcrowding does not occur, however, as not all of an individual's heirs remain in the hamlet nor do they all set up new households upon marriage (Chapter 6). *De jure* rights are nevertheless held, and any individual may place grain- or straw-stacks within the threshing-floors 'owned' by his/her mother or father. Each household may theoretically place its stacks on one threshing-floor one year and on another the next, or it may shift the location of its stacks within the same threshing-floor from year to year. Nevertheless, each household's stacks usually occupy the same positions year after year within the same threshing-floor. In other words, although it is individuals who possess *de jure* property rights as 'co-heirs' of threshing-floors, a much smaller number of grain-producing households are the actual units which exercise *de facto* use of them. Because of the system of partible inheritance and the overall structure of such dispersed corporate property, there is a certain amount of flexibility in any household's choice (or habit) of location for its stacks. No formal rule exists obliging anyone's stacks to be placed on any particular threshing-floor.

Each year the sequence of threshings occurs in a roughly circular direction. In 1976 the threshings rotated in a clockwise direction around the hamlet from threshing-floor to threshing-floor, roughly following the pattern of South–West–North–East–South. The reverse pattern is followed in odd years when the rotation is counter-clockwise, moving in the direction South–East–North–West–South. Map 3 illustrates these two patterns: the sequence is best followed using both the map and Table 9.

Table 9. *Threshings, 1976*

Threshing-floors	Household	Date	Type of labour	Rye (*alqueires*)	Wheat (*alqueires*)	Duration of some threshings
Caniteiro	36 – André	30 July	tornajeira	450	52	(1 day)
	34 – Daniel	31 July	tornajeira	418	0	
Private	33 – Gabriel	31 July	tornajeira			
	,,	1 August	tornajeira	754	0	(1½ days)
Conselho	31 – Bernardo	2 August	tornajeira	245	5	
	32 – Bento	2 August	tornajeira	70	30	
	30 – Miguel	2 August	tornajeira	210	127	
Conselho	29 – P. Gregório	3 August	tornajeira	79	0	
	28 – Cláudio	3 August	tornajeira	91	0	
Outeiro	22 – Eduardo	3 August	tornajeira	170	0	
	23 – Fortunato	3 August	tornajeira	350	0	
	24 – Matias	4 August	tornajeira	164	29	
	14 – Lourenço	4 August	tornajeira	310	0	
	19 – Julião	5 August	tornajeira	318	82	
	20 – Jacinto	5 August	tornajeira	298	0	
	21 – Elias	6 August	tornajeira	500	0	(9 hours)
	26 – Aurélio	6 August	tornajeira	120	0	
	27 – Sância	6 August	tornajeira	0	25	
	25 – Balbina	7 August	tornajeira	45	0	
Campo	3 – Romão	7 August	tornajeira	272	0	
	2 – Lucrécia	7 August	tornajeira	66	0	
	1 – Silvério	7 August	tornajeira	326	15	
	7 – Ernesto	7 August	tornajeira	60	0	
	8 – Amaro	9 August	tornajeira	250	54	
Cimo da Aldeia	15 – Duarte	10 August	paid	112	0	(2 hours)
	10 – Rosa	10 August	tornajeira	208	52	
	11 – Leopoldina	10 August	tornajeira	250	0	
	43 – Vilfredo	11 August	tornajeira	75	0	(1½ hours)
	9 – Cristina	11 August	tornajeira	61	0	
	13 – Ricardo	11 August	tornajeira	323	45	
	– – Etelvina[a]	11 August	paid	15	0	(½ hour)
Private	6 – Juliana	12 August	tornajeira	176	0	
Private	57 – Hermínio	12 August	paid	40	0	
Private	38 – D. Elvira	12 August	tornajeira	370	70	
Ribeira	49 – Inácio	13 August	tornajeira	250	0	
	47 – Claudina	13 August	tornajeira	455	40	
	44 – Engrácia	13 August	tornajeira	20	0	
	35 – Tomé	13 August	tornajeira	0	61	
	50 – Justino	15 August	tornajeira	90	70	
	41 – Jerónimo	15 August	tornajeira	0	50	
	42 – Paulo	15 August	tornajeira	140	0	
Private	40 – Delfim	17 August	tornajeira	639	48	
	53 – Sebastião[b]	?	tornajeira	23	0	
	(18) – Marcos[c]	?	paid	(330)	(60)	
Portela	39 – D. Sofia	13 Sept.	paid	200	100	
	45 – Pedro	13 Sept.	tornajeira	100	10	
	45 Households[d]	16 days		9,113	965	

a – Emigrant in Germany who sent money to have her threshing carried out.
b – The elderly Sebastião's threshing took place on a plot outside his house (not on a threshing-floor) a few days prior to 13 September.
c – Threshed in a nearby hamlet; Marcos' grain is not included in the totals.
d No threshing: Hs. 4, 5, 12, 16, 17, 37, 46, 48, 51, 52, 54, 55, 56.

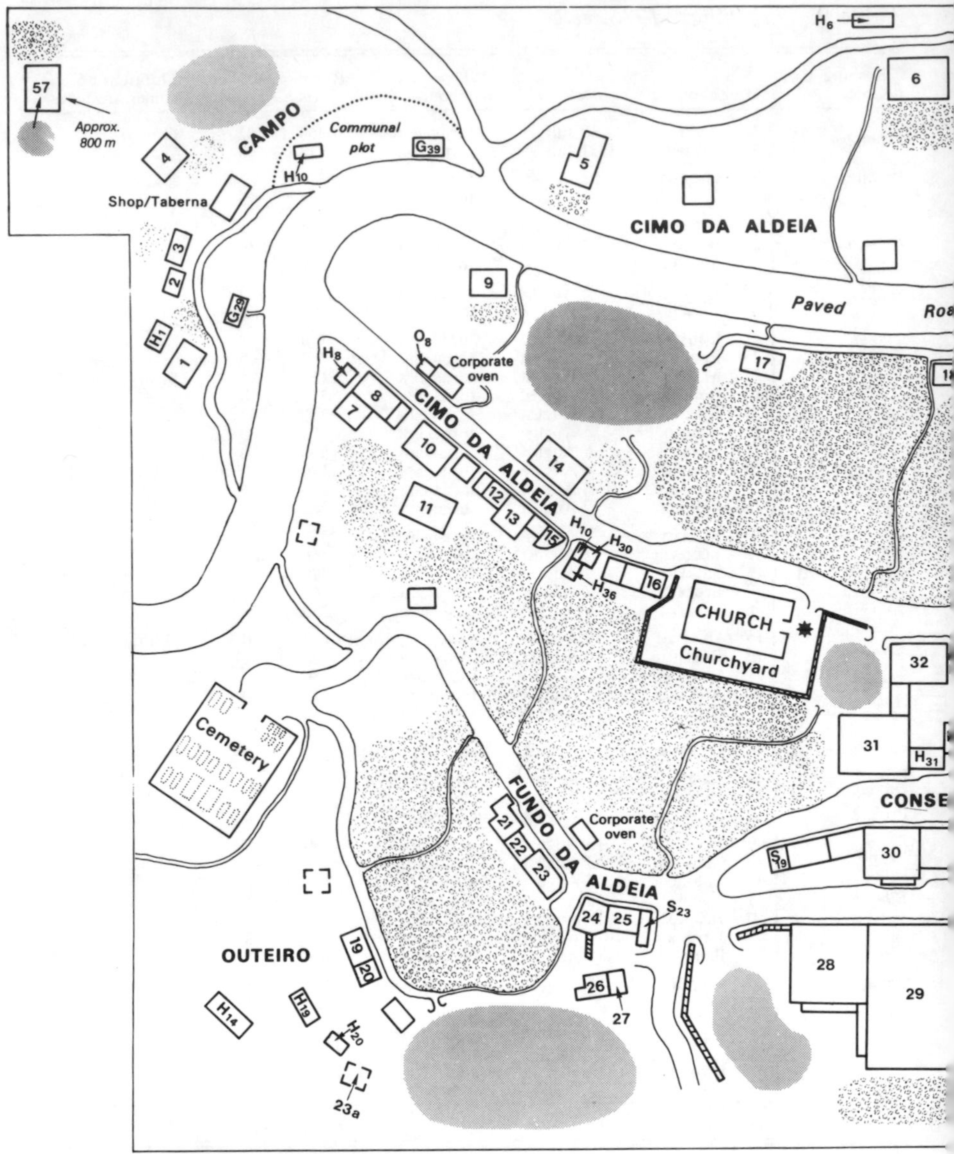

Map 3. Sketch-map of Fontelas, 1977

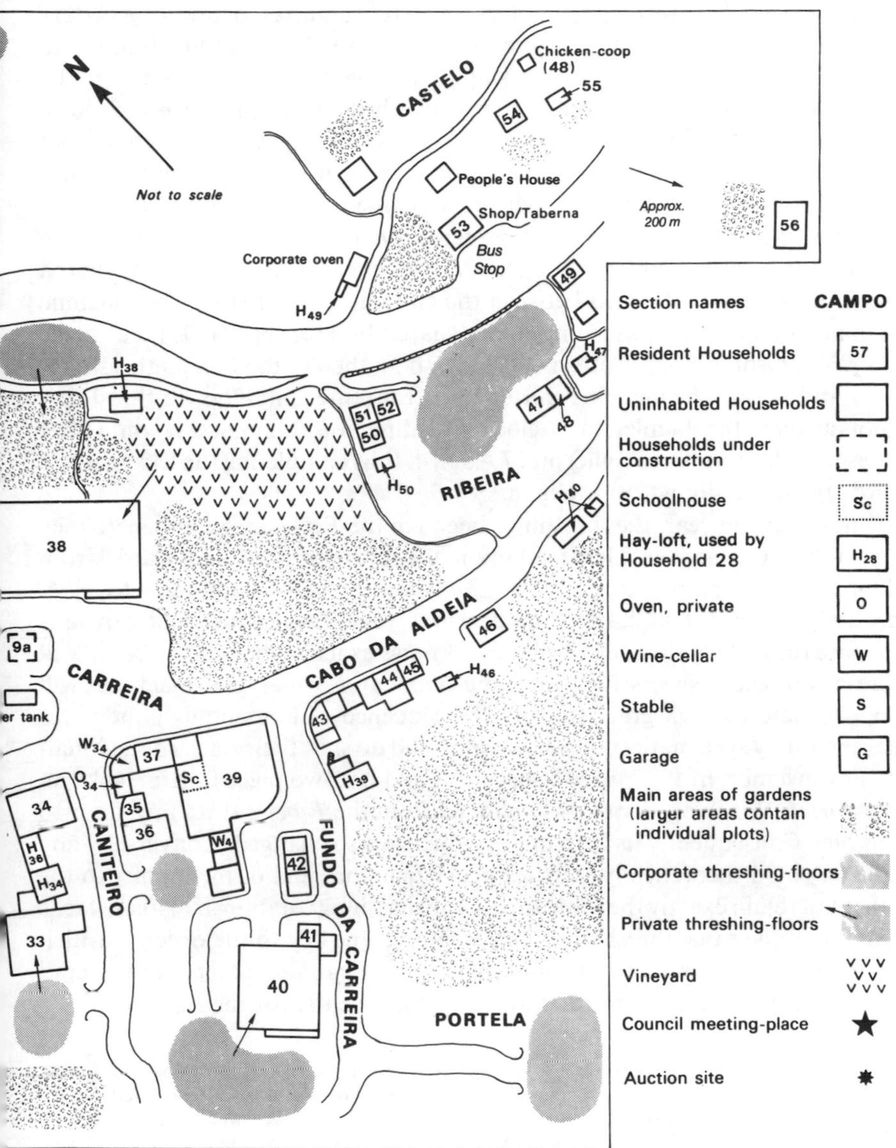
N
Not to scale
CASTELO
Chicken-coop (48)
55
54
People's House
Shop/Taberna
53
Bus Stop
Approx. 200 m
56
Corporate oven
H49
49
H47
47
48
H38
51
52
50
H50
RIBEIRA
H40
38
CABO DA ALDEIA
46
H46
44
45
43
9a
CARREIRA
er tank
W34
O34
37
Sc
39
H39
34
35
36
W4
H36
H34
CANITEIRO
FUNDO DA CARREIRA
42
41
33
40
PORTELA
Section names
CAMPO
Resident Households
57
Uninhabited Households
Households under construction
Schoolhouse
Sc
Hay-loft, used by Household 28
H28
Oven, private
O
Wine-cellar
W
Stable
S
Garage
G
Main areas of gardens (larger areas contain individual plots)
Corporate threshing-floors
Private threshing-floors
Vineyard
Council meeting-place
Auction site

In 1976 the first threshing took place on 30 July and was followed by 16 days of continual threshing, with the exception of two Sundays. The first household to thresh was H36, and the threshing-machine began to operate on the threshing-floor in the *Caniteiro* section shared by H36 and H34 (right of centre on Map 3). On the second day (31 July) H34's threshing was completed. That same day the machine was moved across the path to the wealthy *lavrador* Gabriel's threshing-floor (H33), where it remained throughout the next day as his threshing was the longest in the sequence. On the fourth day (2 August) the machine moved towards the centre of the hamlet to the threshing-floor shared by H30, 31, and 32, located between the churchyard and H32. The machine then moved on to the threshing-floors shared by H28 and H29, then to the *Outeiro* threshing-floor (bottom left of Map 3), then to the *Campo* threshing-floor and so on. The machine shifted thus from threshing-floor to threshing-floor around the hamlet in a clockwise direction, culminating on H40's threshing-floor (bottom right) on 17 August, thus completing the 'circle' a few yards from the site where it began.[12]

The following year, the threshings began in the *Portela* section, where they ended the previous year. The threshing-machine thus moved 'backwards' from floor to floor, culminating on the *Caniteiro* threshing-floor next to H36, precisely where it had started the previous year. Each household can thus prepare for its own threshing because it knows exactly when the machine will thresh on each successive threshing-floor and when the machine will approximate its own grain-stacks. The sequence of households is however never entirely systematic: households may and do shift their stacks occasionally. For instance, in 1977 three households and not two placed their stacks on the *Portela* threshing-floor: H47 changed from the *Ribeira* threshing-floor to this one. Consequently its turn in the sequence also changed. Conversely, any villager could theoretically shift residence from one end of the hamlet to the other but retain exactly the same turn in the threshing rotation, if his/her stacks remain on the same threshing-floor as before. The key to the order in which households thresh is thus *the location of the threshing-floors* and not any overall house-order or rotation around an imaginary 'centre' of the hamlet.

[12] There were only two exceptions to this roughly circular pattern. These were H53 (which threshed on a small plot outside its house) and the two households (H39/H45) that use the *Portela* threshing-floor (bottom right of Map 3). In H39 reside the owner of the threshing-machine (Dona Sofia: the hamlet's schoolteacher) and her widowed mother and widowed paternal aunt. The machine is operated by this household's sharecropper in H23, whose threshing occurred earlier on 3 August. It is this sharecropper (Fortunato) who runs the machine throughout the threshing cycle and collects the fees for its use. Almost an entire month passed after the last threshing in the 'circle' (17 August) before Dona Sofia's grain was finally threshed: significantly, this threshing employed hired labour and did not follow the standard system of unpaid labour exchanges. The second late threshing was that of Dona Sofia's elderly uncle Pedro, who also uses the *Portela* threshing-floor. Only a very small team was needed for Pedro's threshing, which lasted less than two hours. Both of these threshings, then, lay considerably outside the temporal sequence of the hamlet's clockwise rotation.

The process of rotation as a whole is termed a *roda* by villagers. The same term, as well as a wealth of further rotation mechanisms, has been reported by Pais de Brito (1981; 1983) for another hamlet in Trás-os-Montes, thus suggesting that the word has an extensive regional distribution. *Roda* means literally 'wheel' but it can also mean any kind of circle or rotation involving most or all of the hamlet's households. In this sense the *roda das malhas*, or wheel of threshings, is turned in one direction one year and the reverse direction the next. Villagers explicitly describe this process as one of the threshings 'turning around the hamlet' – they proceed *à roda da aldeia*. This phrase implies less a sequence of rigidly prescribed component turns than a more general circle which eventually encompasses all of the households involved. I must emphasize here that in the case of the threshings the term *roda* is explicitly used by villagers to denote a formally ordered system. In this sense the threshing rotation is a specific kind of wheel as distinct from other less systematic circular activities (collections and processions) which also move 'around the hamlet' but which start randomly with one household and end with another without any fixed order or sequence. The word is also used to refer to physical wheels such as those of an ox-cart or the wooden revolving-hatch of the municipality's Foundling Home (*Roda dos Expostos*) in former years. Finally, there are other forms of circular activities which evoke the term *roda*: for instance, dances termed *jogos de roda* (circular dancing games) as well as festival processions which also proceed in a somewhat circular fashion around the hamlet.

Where now do dyadic exchanges of labour come into play? The structure of the labour-teams formed at threshings involves a specific kind of labour exchange: the *tornajeira*. This term combines the words *torna* (an exchange or a return) and *jeira* (a day's labour). The essence of the term lies in its discrete reference to the task-specific, unpaid exchange of labour. A threshing is exchanged for a threshing, and a day (approximately) for a day. A day-labourer who works for wages is termed either a *jornaleiro* or a *jeireiro* because he works for payment on a daily basis: the latter word derives from the local term *jeira* and the former from the more general Portuguese term *jorna*, both denoting 'a day's paid labour'. The joining of the two terms in the word *tornajeira*, however, has the very precise meaning of 'a day-labour exchange' between two villagers which does not involve any monetary transaction. It is labour and time that are swapped and not money. This is why the term *torna* (suggesting here 'a return') is used. Thus all but five of the threshings in 1976 (that is, 40 out of 45) were carried out using unpaid *tornajeira* exchanges.

Dyadic exchanges form the individual component links within a wider system of rotation. As the community is so small, many labour-teams overlap in membership as successive teams are formed. If a considerable number of households opted for paid labour to execute their threshings the entire system would break down, as this would reduce the size of the large labour pool necessary for the formation of successive working teams around the hamlet. Metaphorically, dyadic *tornajeira* exchanges thus constitute the indispensable spokes within a *roda* and the smooth functioning – or turning – of the wheel as a whole depends directly upon the number, strength, and internal coherence of its component spokes.

The structures of specific threshing teams are remarkably similar, and each team usually comprises a total working group of about 35 people. Optimally, a threshing should have about 40 people (25 men and 15 women) to proceed quickly and without undue effort on the part of those stuck with the heaviest tasks. In some cases there may be more than 50 or 60 people present, if we include the odd observer as well as all of the younger children who run errands and provide the team with steady sources of water and wine. No one is explicitly invited or recruited to any particular threshing: one just goes, and by working one establishes a counter-obligation. Thus any one household *must* send at least one helper to assist at up to 30 other threshings or it will not itself be able to thresh adequately. There is never any preference for an adult man to represent a household over an adult woman. As at other agricultural tasks, the labour of women is considered as equal to that of men. Only the very heaviest of tasks are ever regarded as exclusively 'male' ones.

Any threshing team smaller than 30 (except in cases of poorer households with very short threshings) is an indication of hosts who do not return the labour of their helpers in the prescribed fashion. For instance, because Julião (H19) assisted at comparatively few threshings and infrequently sent one of his young daughters in his place, he ended up with a rather small and sluggish team of 28 at his own long threshing (5 August). Conversely, a few individuals with special skills (particularly two men who are adept at constructing straw-stacks) are usually present at most threshings and always have large teams at their own. Men generally perform the heavier tasks of throwing the sheaves of grain onto the machine with pitchforks, operating the machine, and forming the straw-stack. Women generally form two separate groups for cooking and for gathering the fallen straw and chaff into piles.[13] Threshing meals are extremely opulent, and invariably include fresh meat of lamb, kid or piglets slaughtered expressly for the occasion. At each threshing, the male and female heads of household are termed *patrão* and *patroa* respectively: the words appear to translate literally as 'patron' but more specifically in this case they mean task organizer or merely host. Hosts always participate in the threshing: there are no foremen or managers in even the wealthiest of households.

Table 10 sets forth the structure of one threshing team in 1976 (3 August). I

[13] A more detailed analysis of the various tasks performed by men, women, and children during threshings can be found in my paper 'Work-parties in a Northern Portuguese Hamlet', awarded the Raymond Firth Prize for 1979 *ex aequo* by the Department of Anthropology, London School of Economics. This paper has been published in Portuguese (O'Neill 1982a).

15 Threshing (August): one of the key moments in the agricultural cycle at which forms of *tornajeira* reciprocal labour are brought into play between co-villagers.

have grouped the labour-team into three sub-groups. Firstly, there was the host household itself (H22) composed of five individuals. The house and landholding are Felícia's as her husband Eduardo married into the hamlet from a neighbouring community. Secondly, there was a group of regular cooperators with whom this household exchanges labour, tools, and meals throughout the year: these individuals are usually but not necessarily a few of the host household's field of kin and neighbours. Thirdly, we find a large group of co-villagers who appear solely for the purpose of the threshing, with whom the host household does *not* normally maintain further cooperation throughout the rest of the agricultural cycle. Let us look first at the structure of exchanges within this group of co-villagers.

It is not necessary for any of these individuals to reappear each year at a particular threshing, but each *household* involved in the exchange must be represented. For example, if Gualter (H1) appears as a helper at this threshing, Felícia herself or someone from her household must return the assistance at Gualter's threshing. Conversely, no threshing exchange normally occurs between Felícia's household and those other households in the hamlet which did not send a helper to hers. The rigidity of the *tornajeira* system lies not in any fixed membership in the labour-teams but rather in this strict reciprocity between households. Thus, some domestic groups were represented by different members in successive years (H6, 11, and 38 for instance), while others assisted in only one of these two years (H10, 26, 43, and 47 in 1976, and H4 and 9 in 1977). This may occur for a number of reasons: two of the most common are either the sickness of the person usually representing a household as its main threshing helper (Note to Table 10) or the breaking of social relations. In the latter case, H22 and H23 severed all relations in early 1977 (they are nextdoor neighbours) and no one from either household appeared at the other's threshing in August of 1977 or 1978.

At Felícia's threshings, in these successive years two members from H19 and two from H6 assisted rather than merely one (Julião and his daughter Bela in 1976, and Juliana and her son Clemente in 1977). This occurs rather infrequently, and is usually due to a household head's decision to participate alongside the household's younger representative. An adult for an adult is the usual exchange but a young boy or girl under the age of 16 or so may be seen as 'half a helper', thus suggesting the presence in these cases of one-and-a-half helpers. In general then, the large group of co-villagers who help at any particular threshing is a relatively flexible one as far as who represents a household as well as which of the hamlet's households are involved as helpers. The most rigid and prescribed element in these exchanges is that of the *tornajeira*: every household which helps must be helped in return. The only exceptions to this pattern are a few individuals who are seen as capable of returning a favour in another form at a later date: the two shopkeepers (H7 &

Table 10. *Threshing teams for Household 22, 1976 & 1977*

Helpers in 1976	Helpers in 1977	Relation to Host (Felícia)
H22 Felícia*	H22 Felícia	host
22 Eduardo	22 Eduardo	husband
22 Clara	22 Clara	daughter
22 Crisóstomo	22 Crisóstomo	son
22 Petronilha	22 Petronilha	daughter
H8 Amaro	—	(Contância's husband)
—	H8 Constância	1st cousin (MZD)
—	H8 Jorge	2nd cousin (MZDS)
14 Avelino	14 Avelino	1st cousin (MZS)
21 Leocádia	21 Leocádia	2nd cousin (MMZSD)
21 Elias	21 Elias	(Leocádia's husband)
–	21 Crisóstomo	2nd cousin (MMZS)
–	21 Brás	3rd cousin (MMZSDS)
24 Matias	24 Matias	friend/neighbour
24 Bernarda	—	friend/neighbour
–	24 Bebiana	friend/neighbour
25 Estêvão	25 Estêvão	friend/neighbour
52 Eufémia	52 Eufémia	mother-in-law
1 Gualter	1 Gualter	co-villager
2 Lucrécia	2 Lucrécia	co-villager
3 Romão	3 Romão	co-villager
–	4 Ezequiel	co-villager
6 Ângelo	–	co-villager
–	6 Juliana	co-villager
–	6 Clemente	co-villager
–	9 Justina	co-villager
10 Rosa	–	co-villager
11 Clemente	–	co-villager
–	11 Patrício	co-villager
16 Cristela	16 Cristela	co-villager
19 Julião	19 Julião	co-villager
19 Bela	–	co-villager
20 Jacinto	20 Jacinto	co-villager
26 Aurélio	–	co-villager
27 Sância	27 Sância	co-villager
30 Miguel	30 Miguel	co-villager
31 Bernardo	31 Bernardo	co-villager
33 Gabriel	33 Gabriel	co-villager
34 Silvino	34 Silvino	co-villager
38 Valentim	–	co-villager
–	38 Mateus	co-villager
40 Manuela	40 Manuela	co-villager
41 Jerónimo	41 Jerónimo	co-villager
42 Prudência	42 Prudência	co-villager
43 Vilfredo	–	co-villager
45 Pedro	45 Pedro	co-villager
47 Hermenegildo	–	co-villager
49 Inácio	49 Inácio	co-villager
50 Justino	50 Justino	co-villager

* Unexchanged threshings at which Felícia (1976) and Eduardo (1977) helped:

1976	1977
7 Ernesto (shopkeeper)	7 Ernesto (shopkeeper)
23 Fortunato (temporarily ill)	28 Cláudio (retired Border Guard)
53 Sebastião (shopkeeper)	29 P. Gregório (priest)
	47 Claudina (temporarily ill)
	57 Hermínio (temporarily ill)

H53) and the priest (H29).[14] Otherwise, an individual whose household threshed early in the cycle can predict exactly which subsequent threshings it will be obliged to help at and which ones to skip.

Exchanges within the smaller group of this household's regular cooperators are markedly different. While co-villagers are distinctly short-term cooperators involved in one exchange, this group of kin, neighbours, and friends are long-term cooperators engaged in many varied exchanges throughout the year (Bloch 1973). There is much assistance between these households and continual borrowing and lending of agricultural equipment. These individuals are sometimes present as almost complete households at Felícia's threshings, and they assist with tasks both before and after the threshing. This is very clear in Table 10: H8, 21, and 24 sent various individuals as helpers, while among the co-villagers we have seen that only one household in each year sent more than one person (H19 in 1976 and H6 in 1977). In stark contrast to these regular cooperators, co-villagers consistently arrive only following the first sound of the threshing-machine's motor, and they conspicuously leave immediately following the final meal. Some may on occasion even arrive late or leave slightly early.

The essence of the *tornajeira* system lies not in the exchanges between the host household and these regular cooperators but in those contracted with its co-villagers. If only one member of a regular cooperator's household helped in one year and the whole household in the next year, this flexibility would be tolerated within the repeated and loosely calculated exchanges between these domestic groups. The *tornajeira*, however, is a strict one-shot exchange of one person's labour for another's, of one threshing for another threshing. It must be employed as a mechanism for ensuring the adequate succession of reciprocating helpers at all of the constituent threshings in the rotation. No household can thresh on its own, nor even with its core of regular cooperators (kin, close neighbours, and friends): the threshing is simply too big and too complicated a task. A failure to fulfil one's obligations of helping an adequate number of households is sure to provide a hopelessly tiny, overburdened, and fatigued team in return. Regular cooperators maintain constant exchanges of agricultural tasks (and also of festivities) suggestive of Sahlins' concept of generalized reciprocity (1965). In contrast, the threshing *tornajeiras* between a host household and its co-villager helpers are more akin to a strictly balanced reciprocity involving minimally delayed exchanges of like for like. Most of the

[14] There are of course a few further exceptions within the threshing rotation. One of these (13 August) was termed jokingly by some a 'pity threshing' as it was performed by an already mobilized team for the hamlet drunk, Tomé (H35). A semblance of balanced *tornajeira* exchanges was nevertheless upheld, even though Tomé's assistance at other households' threshings rarely lasted past mid-afternoon. A second exception was Cristela (H16), a poor single mother of a bastard child who lives with her 89-year-old mother. Although her household does not produce grain, Cristela appeared at most of the hamlet's threshings in order to exchange her labour for the right to pick an occasional bundle of straw from each host's straw-stack for her pig-pen.

dyadic labour exchanges at threshings thus link villagers who do *not* cooperate at any other time of the year.

While *tornajeira* exchanges are also employed for a few other heavy agricultural tasks (haymaking and vintages, for example) it is during the threshings that they are most visible. No other unpaid exchanges are ever so rigidly calculated. The threshing is simply too important, too large, and too urgent (there is always danger of fire or rain) to be left to each household's normal daily pattern of labour exchanges. A special form of institutionalized, systematic cooperation marked by a specific term (the *tornajeira*) must be brought into play in order to achieve the community-wide goal of quick, efficient threshing and storage of the grain. As most of the hamlet's households produce grain and are involved in most of the threshings, another term (the *roda*) is used to refer to the sequence of rotation of the threshings around the hamlet from threshing-floor to threshing-floor. Both of these specific forms of exchange and rotation appear *at a particular moment in the productive cycle* at which very large labour-teams are required and during which virtually all of the hamlet's efforts are urgently needed.

A second example of a rotation system is that of the irrigation of kitchen-gardens. These plots (*cortinhas*) are one of the most fertile kinds of land in Fontelas. They lie mostly within the central hamlet area and many are located directly next to their owners' houses (Map 3). The gardens are watered through the use of three large water-pools called *poças*, all of which are situated at different points above the hamlet roughly to the West, North-east, and East (Map 2). All three pools are natural formations without any enclosures of cement, and they are opened and closed for irrigation through the use of a hoe and various piles of earth and shrub. The largest pool is about 10 metres in diameter.

All three pools, as well as the ditches through which their water is directed for irrigation, are strictly regulated in their modes of use during the summer months by the households owning shares in them. As with corporate ovens and threshing-floors, co-owners of water-pools are also termed *herdeiros*. Each household whose garden(s) is watered by one of the pools has a right to a specified amount of time during which it can use the pool's water. It is crucial to note that this amount of time is directly proportional to the size of the garden. When a garden is lent, sold, or partitioned through inheritance, the new owner is guaranteed rights to the garden's water in proportion to its new size. Each turn or sub-turn is called an *abridura*.[15] The standard amount of

[15] A number of references suggest that another term (*torna*) refers to a very old system of water regulation in Northern Portugal. A minute of the Mosteiro Junta in 1943 (15 February) mentions 'conflicts of certain gravity' occurring in a neighbouring hamlet due to 'the ancient and already abolished system of *torna-tornará*'. Further to the West in Trás-os-Montes province, Sampaio (1923:31) has mentioned the existence of '. . . undivided waters, termed *torno tornas* or *torna tornas*; this system, unknown to the Civil Code or the previous Ordenações, has been maintained in spite of Portuguese laws' (my translation). Yet another author (Veloso 1953:128) has noted that similar irrigation rotations are also called *tapa-tapa* as well as *torna-tornarás*.

time for each turn is theoretically 12 hours. Each turn usually provides one full pool of water during the summer months, but variations in weather (humidity/rain) may provide as much as one and a half pools on a long 16-hour summer day. Some households have rights to over four 'days' of water within one rotation, while households with smaller gardens may have rights to only 1/4 of a day (3–4 hours).

Disagreements over the timing of irrigation turns necessitated the drawing up of a written list of households and their respective turns in 1965 for one of the hamlet's three water-pools. This was the *Ribeira* pool, named after the section of the hamlet to which the pool's water is directed. The list itself is extremely revealing and is reproduced below along with an English translation. While the two remaining ponds follow roughly the same system of rotation, this was the only one to have its schedule set down in writing. The sequence of households described here and based on the 1965 list is still followed in the hamlet today.

Note that the word *roda* was explicitly used at the bottom of the list: 'The *roda* ends, inserting the respective Sundays.' In this sense the 'wheel' revolves completely four times within the period from May through September. The *Ribeira* pond is used only on weekdays and Saturdays in the summer by 34 households for the watering of their gardens: at night and on Sundays in the summer, it reverts to corporate regulation between a smaller group of 12 households for the irrigation of their privately owned meadows along the ditches. During the winter, the use of the pool is rotated between these 12 co-owning households at all times: on weekdays, Saturdays, Sundays, and at night.[16] In this fashion, the turns constantly alternate through the summer between (a) nights and Sundays when the pool is used by a corporate group of 12 households for their meadows, and (b) weekdays and Saturdays when a larger corporate group of 34 households waters their gardens. Some of the 12 households with night-turns also have gardens watered by this pool, and are thus members of both corporate groups.

Formerly, there were fixed dates at which each pool was turned over to summer regulation. Today these dates are not rigidly set, but villagers stressed that all three rotations used to stop around 8 September[17] which marks the date of a religious festival and pilgrimage (*romaria*) in a neighbouring hamlet

[16] The other two water-pools have a similar winter/summer alternating regulation. The *Tojal* pool has 31 co-owning households in the summer but reverts to private use for the rest of the year by one household (H28) for its large meadow along the ditches just below the pool. The *Falgueiras* pool has 28 co-owning households in the summer, while only two households (H30 and H38) use it privately for their meadows during the remaining eight months of the year.

[17] The smaller *Tojal* pool was formerly transferred to corporate summer rotation on 29 June, the Saints' Day of *São Pedro e Paulo*. Today this date is not fixed, and the pool is used for only three months to irrigate gardens from around 15 June through mid-September. The *Falgueiras* pool was formerly transferred to summer regulation on 3 May, but in 1976 and 1977 this date was 12 May. Any or all of the pools may be delayed in their transferral to summer schedules due to other more urgent spring tasks (haymaking, for instance).

in honour of *Nossa Senhora de Remédios* (Our Lady of Remedies). No fixed dates or days of the week thus constitute the referents for the '1st day' or the '2nd day' in the list for the summer rotation, as the starting date may vary from year to year. Thus, summer irrigation from the *Ribeira* pool began on 26 May in 1976 and on 23 May in 1977. Contrary to that which occurs in other corporate communities described in the Iberian ethnographic literature, neither the Church nor the hamlet council determines which day will mark the start of the rotation; this decision is arrived at through informal consensus between the 34 co-owning households. If we assume, for example, that Day 1 were a Monday (see the irrigation list) then Day 6 would be a Saturday and Day 7 the following Monday (skipping Sunday). Each full rotation thus comprises 27 weekdays and 4 Sundays, or $27 \times 4 = 108$ days. Adding 16 Sundays, the total number of days in the four summer rotations would be 124, or precisely four months.

Some turns combine a number of successive days, while others comprise fractions of a day. Each 12-hour turn usually spans the period from dawn to dusk in the summer months. Each turn tends to start between 5 and 7 a.m. and end around 8 or 9 p.m., thus giving each 'day' a period of around 14–16 hours. Each household must communicate to the next in order when it has finished watering. Unlike the system of rotating *aguadores* (water-men) in the Spanish village of Becedas (Brandes 1975:90–2) there is in Fontelas no institutionalized structure designating an appointed person to coordinate irrigation turns, nor was I told of any in former years. Like the setting of the date for the beginning of the summer rotation, all decisions concerning irrigation and the timing of turns are discussed and implemented directly between the co-owners of a particular pool.

The sequence of turns proceeds as follows; let us first consider a simple turn of a full day. Towards dusk on Day 11, Dona Elvira's household (H38) will irrigate its very large garden outside its house at around 8 p.m. Valentim (this household's usual irrigator) goes to the pool and conducts the water along the channels: it takes about an hour for a full pool of water to be opened and directed along the ditches into the garden. After the water supply has ended, Valentim must let the holder of the night-turn know that Valentim's day-turn has ended. This may be done by Valentim himself or by message. A member of the household holding the night-turn then walks up to the pool at around 9 p.m. and closes it (*tapar a poça*) with earth and shrub. Early the next morning the pool is opened by the holder of the night-turn and its water directed into his/her private meadow which lies alongside the ditches. When this is completed (around 5 or 6 a.m.) this household must let Mário know that his day-turn has begun (Day 12) and that Mário may now go to the pool and close it. During the day the pool fills with water and later that evening Mário waters his garden, and so on.

A number of days in the rotation are divided into smaller sub-turns with

Agua da rega da Ribeira

Azevedo-Leiria, 28 - Porto - Modelo N.º 214 — DEVE — HAVER

1.º dia da casa dos da Angelina
2.º dia dos do Concelho
3.º dia da Piedade e irmão
4.º dia da tia Ermelinda
5.º dia nossa (traço da Al[illegible]
6.º dia nossa até meio dia e depois dos [illegible] do
7.º do Trepeda
8.º dia das raparigas do fundo da Aldeia até às 4 depois [illegible]
9.º dia do Concelho e Trepeda
10.º dia do Brasileiro Matilde e Maria Vermelha
11.º dia nossa o dia inteiro
12.º do Mario o dia inteiro
13.º do Mario e do Pequeno
14.º nossa até meio dia e depois do Brasileiro
15.º do Manuel Afonso Guilherme Augusto do C. e Cantar[illegible]
16.º do Luiz
17.º do Jaime do fundo da Aldeia e do Brasileiro [illegible]
18.º da Ermelinda Veiga
19.º da Ermelinda até ao meio dia, depois do Trepeda
20.º nossa o dia inteiro
21.º da casa do Concelho
22.º da casa do Concelho
23.º da casa do Concelho
24.º do Manuel Afonso Guilherme e Bobela (fundo [illegible]
25.º nossa até ao meio dia e depois do Mario e das outras [illegible]
26.º do Luiz ... etc ...
27.º dos da Ribeira Graciano .. etc ...
Acaba a roda metendo-se os respectivos domingos

Document 1. List of irrigation turns, 1965

List of irrigation turns, 1965*

1st day for the household of Angelina's descendants
2nd day for those of the Concelho[a]
3rd day for Piedade and siblings
4th day for aunt Ermelinda
5th day ours[b]
6th day ours until noon, and then for the gardens of (*Cabo da Al[deia]*
7th for Cepeda
8th day for the little girls of *Fundo da Aldeia* until 4, then for Er[melinda]
9th day for Concelho and Cepeda
10th day for the Brazilian, Matilde, and Maria Vermelha
11th day ours the entire day
12th for Mário the entire day
13th for Mário and for Joaquim
14th ours until noon, and then for the Brazilian
15th for Manuel Afonso, Guilherme Augusto of the C. and Constan[tino]
16th for Luiz
17th for Jaime of *Fundo da Aldeia* and for the Brazilian [. . . Ma . . .]
18th for Ermelinda Veiga
19th for Ermelinda ,, until noon, then for Cepeda
20th ours the entire day
21st for the Concelho household
22nd for the Concelho household
23rd for the Concelho household
24th for Manuel Afonso, Guilherme, and Cobelas
25th ours until noon, then for Mário and the plots[c] in the *Fundo da Car[reira]*
26th for Luiz . . . etc . . .
27th for those of *Ribeira*, Graciano . . . etc . . .
The *roda* ends, inserting the respective Sundays[d]

* The names in this list refer to real individuals, but this is the only place in this book where reference to them cannot be avoided. Elsewhere, the same people are referred to with pseudonyms.

a – House name for the adjoining Households 28, 29, 31, and 32, formerly two very large households in Fontelas. The *conselho* meets outside H32.
b – 'Ours' refers to the household which compiled the list (Dona Elvira of H38): one of the wealthiest in the hamlet.
c – The Portuguese word *sortes* refers to the shares or lots acquired through inheritance divisions.
d – The complete rotation thus revolves four times from May through September, skipping four Sundays each month.

fixed hours as points of division (Days 6, 8, 14, 19, and 25). For instance, noon on Day 6 and 4 p.m. on Day 8. In the first case (Day 6) the pool is used by H38 until around noon or 1 p.m. when it is given over to the gardens of the *Cabo da Aldeia* section until the evening.[18] If the pond does not provide a full pool of water during these half-days then that is 'tough luck' – the household in question irrigates with however much water it happens to contain.

Another pattern may be followed, however, and this is the division of a day into a number of smaller sub-turns *without* any fixed hours of division. There are ten days in the rotation on which this form of partition occurs. In these cases a number of co-owners may voluntarily divide these days' water as above by hours, but much more common is the sequential watering of gardens all at once at the end of the day. In Piedade's case (Day 3) this proceeds as follows. Piedade is married and lives with her husband and their two children: she also has one unmarried brother living in a separate household next to hers, and a married sister in another section of the hamlet. All three individuals own portions (*sortes*) of their parents' former garden: when the plot was partitioned each sibling automatically acquired rights to 1/3 of the garden's water from the *Ribeira* pool. At the end of the day, Piedade (or someone from her household) opens the pool and directs the water to her portion of the garden. Her brother and sister will be there or appear shortly afterwards, and about twenty minutes into the 'watering hour' Piedade's brother takes up his sub-turn by directing the water into his own portion of the garden. Piedade's sister then waters with the remaining third of the water, and notifies the holder of the night-turn that the day-turn has ended. If the pool is particularly depleted, the three sub-turns will last for rather short periods of 15 minutes each, or for about 30 minutes each if the pool is quite full. In other cases, instead of irrigating in succession, the co-owners in question divide the running water simultaneously from the start of the watering hour, each one guiding his or her rillet into their respective gardens.

Thirdly, a number of days apportion water into even smaller sub-turns held by groups of households in the poorer sections of the hamlet (Days 6, 8, 25, and 27). These households also tend to water together at the end of their joint turn as division of the already short sub-turn into even smaller turns would be virtually impractical as the pool would fill negligibly in only a few hours. In extreme cases these sub-sub-turns may provide minuscule amounts of barely 5–10 minutes of water each.[19]

[18] Geertz has described a similar system of day- and night-turns for Moroccan villages (1972:35–6). I am grateful to Robert Netting for having called my attention to Geertz' article in 1984, as well as to his own treatment of Alpine village irrigation (1974).

[19] There are of course limits to uneconomic partitions: not all garden plots (or other kinds of land) are divided but rather distributed whole to different heirs (Chapter 7). If an individual owns three garden plots, for example, each of his/her three heirs may receive one. In other cases, a small garden plus an irrigated arable field may comprise one share equivalent to, say, five dry grain fields and a small meadow. Thus garden plots and their respective water-turns are not always partitioned into steadily decreasing sizes.

It is important to note here that those days which comprise a number of sub-turns link the pool's water to *adjacent* gardens: here lies the principle determining the rotation of turns. The only way a number of gardens may be watered effectively is not by filling and emptying the pool three or four times a day, but by watering *only once* at the end of the day in unison or in rapid succession. This avoids not only repeated openings and closings of the pool, but also the wasteful time and effort that would be needed to direct the water through additional ditches from one set of gardens to another in a different area of the hamlet. Sub-turns are thus held by the owners of contiguous or nearby gardens: these may of course be kin or simply unrelated co-villagers, as the gardens comprising any joint turn may be adjacent but not necessarily as a result of an inheritance partition. Thus, the key to the system of rotation is *the physical location of the garden plots.*[20]

As in the threshing rotation, each household knows approximately when its turn will come as the turns of the households before it approach. All households using the pool know precisely which families precede and follow them in order, although some do not know the exact order of turns very far before or after them in the rotation. Of course, conflicts do arise – particularly over 'thefts' of water at night. In one extreme case involving such a theft in the early hours of the morning, one villager poked another's eye out with a hoe. The case went to court, but the blinded villager only obtained a minimal monetary compensation after some years of legal dispute. None of the members of the two households have spoken to each other for the last two decades. Another type of conflict arises when an individual fails to notify the next in turn. This not only minimizes the second household's time and water, but also provides the garden (or meadow) of the first with precious extra minutes of trickles from the pool through the ditches into the garden. This angers not only the second household but the following ones as well, as the third household will want the rotation times kept at the expense of the second household's loss. Otherwise a series of such delays would throw the whole sequence off balance. If a turn is delayed very long, it is simply missed, and the following household in order picks up the rotation at the correct time. Like the threshing rotation, the irrigation *roda* is akin to a wheel with its spokes – the component turns – and all of these 'spokes' must be secure and relatively punctual for the wheel to turn properly.

Although a number of comparative analyses of rotating water-turns similar to those described here have also stressed a lack of formal, institutionalized structures in irrigation, I do not think this fact is necessarily the most important nor the most illuminating aspect of such forms of property-holding.

[20] Two comparable systems are reported for Castile, firstly by Freeman for Valdemora where the term *sortía* is used to refer to plot-order rotation (1970:33), and secondly by Brandes for the Sierra de Béjar where irrigation is carried out 'by neighbors' (*por vecinos*) and 'adjacent fields are irrigated in turn' (1975:92).

For instance, Geertz has emphasized the absence of a 'superordinate political structure of any significance connected with irrigation' in the Moroccan communities he studied (1972:34–5), but his comparison of the latter with the elaborate corporate and ritual irrigation systems of Bali leads him to stress an abstract principle of 'agonistic individualism' in Morocco purportedly expressive of a highly complex (Mediterranean?) system of ownership of private property. This tells us little of the social relations between co-owners of corporate water resources, and his interesting but brief description of water-turns remains as it were hanging within his essay and therefore not very useful for more detailed comparisons with other European or Mediterranean irrigation systems. Netting's analysis also offers us an example of weak institutionalization in the Swiss Alps: 'Water rights are not publicly recorded, and no one knows even in outline the entire pattern of water distribution. Indeed informants universally deny the possibility of comprehending the total system. Each individual can supply information on when and where he is entitled to water, but no one can accurately list the shares for a whole day, much less an entire cycle' (1974:69). While again this is strikingly similar to the Portuguese system I describe, I would hesitate in employing the phrase 'an acephalous system of ordered anarchy in irrigation' (Netting 1974:72) because this also leads us almost unwittingly towards conclusions concerning village equality based erroneously upon judgements about an apparently *ad hoc* or 'loose' system of water control. This is all the more surprising when much of Netting's own data reveal clear inequalities in *time* per unit of land watered, although these inequalities do not constitute the central focus of the latter's analysis.

For Southwest Portugal, Jenkins has also mentioned in passing irrigation turns similar to those of Fontelas: 'The irrigation system is made more complex by land inheritance laws that have resulted in the constant splitting of family plots and even more complicated sharing of rights over existing tanks . . . When the water starts to get scarce, the formal "partilhas d'agua" or water divisions are made; after that it is a serious offence to use water at the wrong time. Every piece of land has its particular water rights . . .' (1979:71). Again we are confronted with a kind of 'anthropologists' allergy' to the apparently impenetrable intricacies of irrigation rotations. Suffice it to say here that although the three authors cited describe water-rotations from very diverse perspectives and within different theoretical frameworks, what strikes us at first are the cross-cultural similarities in watering activities. Let us return, however, to our theme of inequality in water-rights.

Once each year in Fontelas, the ditches (*agueiras*) conducting the water for irrigation are cleaned with hoes by a large labour-team composed of one male representative of each household that uses them. As is the practice before council meetings, the church bells are rung a number of times on the cleaning day in the early morning or early afternoon. This is done in order to let the pool's co-owners know that the task is about to start. The ditch-cleanings have nothing to do with the council, however, as each group of co-owners using the water-pools has a different membership. On the designated day, the men gather in a group and begin cleaning the ditches from the gardens upwards towards the water-pool (Photo 16). The cleanings may be completed that evening, or they may continue through part of the next day. Households not participating in this job incur either the criticism of the working participants or, in some cases, demands for compensation in money or wine. Households unable to send a male representative must hire another villager for a wage to take their place, while those with very small gardens are excused from the task. Criticism and complaints about non-participating co-owners are more vehement in the case of these ditch-cleanings than at public works involving the whole hamlet. At one ditch-cleaning in 1976 three men were so angry that one particular household did not send a man to work (or a replacement) that they threatened the household with total exclusion from further rights in the water.

This is an important point. These three annual ditch-cleanings are not communal tasks in that none of them involves all of the households in the hamlet. The three water-pools are corporate resources, neither privately nor communally owned. As is the case with the threshing-floors, rights in each pool are held by co-owners (*herdeiros*) and the pools are thus a form of semi-communal resource owned and used by hamlet sub-groups of varying numbers of households. While some households have rights to the water from all three pools, others use only one or two. Also like the threshings, the irrigation rotations involve the majority of the hamlet's households: this is one reason that a systematic rotation with discretely divided component turns comes into play.

A final point of interest here is the unequal distribution of time in the turns, itself a function of the widely varying sizes of different households' garden plots. While many of the smallest gardens in Fontelas are merely a few square metres in surface area, some of the wealthiest houscholds own combinations of garden plots totalling over one hectare of garden land each (see Table 11, derived from the 1965 list discussed above). Note that two of the hamlet's wealthiest households (Dona Elvira's and the Conselho households) have the largest totals of time in which to irrigate their various garden plots: 4½ days each. Five further households have rights to more than one full day of water. At the other extreme, a number of households have turns of only 1/3 or 1/4 of a day. One of the poorest sections of the hamlet (*Cabo da Aldeia*) must divide half a day of watering time between three households: this is barely enough time for a full pool of water in the summer. At the end of their half day, these three households will have only about 30 minutes of running water, which must be divided between them into roughly 10 minutes each.

Map 3 also reveals a general pattern of the concentration of wealthy

16 Ditch-cleaning (May): some of the men forming a large work-team clean the irrigation channels leading from a corporate water-pool to their kitchen-gardens.

households in the centre of the hamlet, while a number of poorer households are located in sections at the outer extremes (West, South, and East). A pattern of stratification emerges – the wealthier households' longer turns are reflections of their bigger garden plots and larger overall landholdings, while the reverse is true for the hamlet's poorer households. As in the case of the three corporate ovens, here the largest gardens and longest water-turns are generally found in the 'wealthy centre' of the hamlet and the smaller gardens on the outer edges.

Table 11. *Irrigation turns, 1965*

Households (U = uninhabited)	No. of turns or sub-turns held	Duration of each turn (in 'days')	Total 'days'
38 –Dona Elvira ('ours')	6	1, $\frac{1}{2}$, 1, $\frac{1}{2}$, 1, $\frac{1}{2}$	4 + $\frac{1}{2}$
28/29 31/32 –*Conselho*	5	1, $\frac{1}{2}$, 1, 1, 1	4 + $\frac{1}{2}$
33 –Ermelinda (Gabriel)[a]	4	1, $\frac{1}{6}$, 1, $\frac{1}{2}$	2 + $\frac{2}{3}$
39 –Cepeda (Dona Sofia)	3	1, $\frac{1}{2}$, $\frac{1}{2}$	2
34 –Luiz	2	1, 1	2
30 –Mário (Miguel)	3	1, $\frac{1}{2}$, $\frac{1}{4}$	1 + $\frac{3}{4}$
40 –Brazilian (Delfim)	3	$\frac{1}{3}$, $\frac{1}{2}$, $\frac{1}{2}$	1 + $\frac{1}{3}$
U/U –Angelina's descendants[b]	1	1 (shared by 2)	1
7/35/36 –Piedade & siblings	1	1 (shared by 3)	1 ($\frac{1}{3}$ each)
47/48 49/50/51 –*Ribeira* (Graciano . . . etc)	1	1 (shared by 5)	1 ($\frac{1}{5}$ each)
21 –Matilde & Jaime	2	$\frac{1}{3}$, $\frac{1}{2}$	$\frac{5}{6}$
U/27 –*Fundo da Aldeia*[b]	1	$\frac{5}{6}$	$\frac{5}{6}$
11 –Manuel Afonso	2	$\frac{1}{3}$, $\frac{1}{3}$	$\frac{2}{3}$
U –Guilherme[c]	2	$\frac{1}{3}$, $\frac{1}{3}$	$\frac{2}{3}$
26 –Joaquim	1	$\frac{1}{2}$	$\frac{1}{2}$
9/43/47 –*Cabo da Aldeia*	1	$\frac{1}{2}$ (shared by 3)	$\frac{1}{2}$ ($\frac{1}{6}$ each)
41 –Maria Vermelha (Jerónimo)	1	$\frac{1}{3}$	$\frac{1}{3}$
54 –Cobelas	1	$\frac{1}{3}$	$\frac{1}{3}$
17 –Constantino	1	$\frac{1}{3}$	$\frac{1}{3}$
41/42 –*Fundo da Carreira*	1	$\frac{1}{4}$ (shared by 2)	$\frac{1}{4}$ ($\frac{1}{8}$ each)
34 Households	42	13 Full 'day' turns 39 Sub-turns (fractions of a 'day')	27 days

a – Names in parentheses are those of current heads of households who have inherited their parents' gardens and corresponding water rights.

b – The gardens and water pertaining to these three uninhabited households (two are opposite H42, and the other next to H20) have been lent temporarily to kin: their owners are currently not resident in Fontelas but they plan to return in the future.

c – Guilherme (whose uninhabited household is opposite H11) is resident in the district city, and he has rented out his two separate garden plots to H16.

The point I wish to stress here is that the rotation itself is systematically organized, but that this organization is not one of house-order and still less of any order of priority either of seniority or a sequence of households from wealthy to poor. Each turn is strictly calculated by the size of the garden which is irrigated. Large gardens merit full day turns (or multiple days) while medium gardens have 1/2 or 1/3 of a day and the smallest gardens only a few hours. Neither households nor individuals possess equal turns, except in cases of the division of a turn into several smaller sub-turns, when a kind of 'equality in poverty' grants each tiny garden a roughly equivalent amount of water. While only 13 turns are held for a full day, a larger number of 39 sub-turns divide one day's water between up to two and five different households. The essential pattern is not only that various households have rights to a few days of water and others to only a few hours, but that most of the turns in the rotation require careful division of running water at the end of the day. While the expenditure of labour and time by co-owning households at the ditch-cleanings is strictly equal, there is nothing at all equal about the specific division of total water-time between wealthy and poorer households.[21]

Unlike the alternating direction of threshing rotations, irrigation sequences do not have any particular spatial pattern following a circular movement. The sense in which this irrigation *roda* is very similar to the threshing cycle is in its defining factor: the location of the gardens. I am not making a reductionist point here, but merely one concerning the *practical* organization of these villagers' specific apportioning of water to gardens in different locations. A very general direction is followed from gardens on the Eastern side of the hamlet to those on the Western side (which could be easily shown through mapping the various garden plots in the hamlet's central area). I have no idea why the gardens of 'Angelina's descendants' are the first in order and those of the *Ribeira* section last. The internal order of the rotation itself is quite strict, however. The sale or loan of a garden plot grants the purchaser or borrower automatic rights to the appropriate turn in the rotation, but the new owner cannot change the order of this turn or its duration (Notes b and c to Table 11). If two villagers were to swap two garden plots in different areas of the hamlet, they would have to swap irrigation turns as well.

All of the gardens in one area of the hamlet are irrigated in succession, after which another area nearby is irrigated. There is no specific house-order fixed at any time either by the council or purely by custom, and no form of lottery (as reported for other Iberian rural communities) ever orders any of the hamlet's irrigation rotations. Furthermore, no formal rules tie any particular plot of land to any specific household, although of course a preference for avoiding excessive partitions of land tends to keep most of a household's land intact over the generations through the informal selection of a favoured heir or heiress (Chapter 5). In other words, there is always a certain amount of flexibility in the system because property-holding individuals may and do move around, thus precluding any rigid entailment of garden plots to households. While both individuals as well as households may shift places

[21] Even the language used in Dona Elvira's list of the *Ribeira* Irrigation Turns is itself indicative of villagers' conceptualizations of wealthy/poor distinctions. Her use of the term *raparigas* (little girls/maids) in referring to the *Fundo da Aldeia* section (Day 8) is quite suggestive: there has been a long-term relationship between the hamlet's wealthier households and the poorer villagers in this section. Many of these 'little girls' have served as maids within *proprietário* households for long periods of time (Chapter 5).

within the rotations, the turns themselves and the garden plots to which each turn is linked are the fixed elements within the rotation. The key factor ordering the *roda* is thus the location of the garden plots.

The 'collective lie' of egalitarian rotation

A general definition of the terms *roda* and *torna* can now be drawn up as follows, based on the examples analysed above:

roda (wheel/circle) – a circular rotation involving most or all of the households in the hamlet;
torna (turn/exchange) – an individual turn or dyadic exchange within a wider systematic rotation;
ajudar (to help/to assist) – any form of non-systematic help between individuals or households.

The third of these terms is of course a more general one referring to a wide variety of exchanges and reciprocal ties, which are visible throughout most of the year at smaller harvesting tasks. It is significant, however, that the terms *roda* and *torna* are both nouns while the term *ajudar* is a verb. No smaller labour-team of villagers working together in Fontelas is ever termed an *ajuda* (noun) but merely described as individuals 'helping each other out'.[22] In contrast, it is only irrigation turns and the specific form of *tornajeira* threshing exchanges that are distinctly institutionalized within wider systematic rotations.

This brings me to my final point. Let me stress again that beneath the apparently egalitarian structures of turns and rotations lie significant differences in the ownership of landed property. For instance, at threshings it is obvious that helpers producing less grain on their own landholdings will work more hours for villagers with larger harvests than the latter will in return. Vilfredo, a day-labourer and threshing only 75 *alqueires* of rye in less than two hours (11 August) will clearly work longer at prosperous Gabriel's threshing of 754 *alqueires* for a day and a half (31 July–1 August) than Gabriel will in return. Due to the strict system of *tornajeira* exchanges (a threshing for a threshing) Vilfredo's extra labour for Gabriel is lost within the general pool of hamlet-wide threshing labour: no further obligation remains for Gabriel to repay Vilfredo's surplus effort. The more I pestered villagers with my questions concerning these unequal exchanges, the more adamantly they emphasized

[22] In the Galician region of North-west Spain, however, the term *axuda* is used as a noun to refer to 'a traditional institution in rural Galicia' whose principal aspect is 'the absence of payment either in money or kind, and the maintenance of reciprocity by the return of an equal amount of work' (Iturra 1977:78). Iturra's detailed analysis of the structure of one *axuda* team offers an excellent point of comparison with the Northern Portuguese *tornajeira* work-groups.

that these differences were tolerated: Vilfredo's excess effort is never repaid in any form by Gabriel, nor is the *expectation* of ideal repayment ever stressed. In this sense 'reciprocal' exchanges of labour at threshings function in the long run economically in favour of wealthier households at the expense of poorer households' labour (although the former incur greater expenses of food and wine). The poorer families are partially compensated socially by the greater quantities of food and the more festive atmosphere at prosperous villagers' threshings (Erasmus 1956). While labour is 'paid' upwards in the social scale, festivity and food are reimbursed or 'repaid' downwards.[23] This is not a conscious exploitation of labour on the part of the wealthier households, but rather a form of inequality masked by an ideology of equality: each household is considered, only momentarily, as equal within the harvesting rotation. Pierre Bourdieu (1977:60, 192) quite rightly terms these minor inequalities found in marginal, relatively unstratified communities a form of disguised *corvée* or a kind of 'gentle, hidden exploitation'.

Apart from the generalized reciprocity among regular cooperators, *tornajeira* threshing exchanges between co-villagers may be divided into two types: (a) relatively equivalent exchanges between households of similar economic standing, and (b) conspicuously unequal exchanges between the fringes of wealthier landed households and poorer labouring ones. The inequalities of labour exchanged within the latter type of *tornajeira* are conveniently dissolved within the wider threshing rotation, under the disguised appearance of equal exchanges. Threshings are thus a kind of *temporary suspension of inequality*, a hiatus of theoretical equality in an otherwise unequal system of social and productive relations. The same sort of imbalance is also evident in the irrigation rotations, particularly at the annual ditch-cleanings. Possessing larger gardens and consequently longer turns, the wealthy gain more help in the long run and the poor work more. A *proprietário* household with four days of water and a poorer household with only a few hours must both send one man to work equal amounts of time to clean the ditches. Of course, this is a question merely of hours, but the temporary levelling that occurs at the ditch-cleanings tends to mask the actual disparities between landholdings. Each man must nevertheless work until the task is completed. While in both the threshing and irrigation rotations each individual's *obligations* are the same as everyone else's, the actual *quantities* of time and labour expended at threshings (and the amounts of land owned by each member of the rotation) are distinctly unequal.

[23] Benjamin Orlove has also noted a similar phenomenon in rural Peru: 'Certain individuals are able to use social forms of reciprocal exchange for their personal advantage. They receive more than they give' (1977:211). The wider implications of this apparently heretical view of reciprocity are quite clear: Orlove maintains that 'the examination of reciprocity as a basis for inequality is important, since this sort of exchange has frequently been seen as one of the bases of the homogeneous egalitarian nature of peasant society' (1977:202).

Both rotation systems are excellent examples of John Davis' point that egalitarian institutions are a means through which 'the reality of differentiation is socially destroyed' (1977:111). Speaking of Valdemora and other communities in the Mediterranean, Davis states that 'there are institutional means of preventing any one person or group from acquiring permanent domination over others – segmentation, complementarity and rotating elections, hagiarchy, lottery, *initia* – all these tend to destroy crude material differences' (1977:125). The threshing and irrigation rotations in Fontelas thus temporarily suspend more pervasive inequalities by imposing an obligation of 'one representative per household'. Other events similarly level all of the hamlet's households by demanding that each be represented by at least one person: vigils, funerals, and public works organized by the council. Both threshings and the ditch-cleanings invoke this rule, and both events are the antithesis of the smaller and more intimate agricultural and festive exchanges between closely cooperating households, where the rule of 'one representative per household' is not operative. This is precisely why *tornajeira* exchanges at threshings are *not* really a form of generalized reciprocity tolerant of imbalanced and delayed exchanges. Threshings only momentarily unite individuals who may pass the entire year without ever cooperating at any other task. The threshings and ditch-cleanings must be executed with large labour-teams and with the greatest of speed. The means by which each rotation accomplishes this urgent pooling of labour is by temporarily equalizing all participant households and subordinating individual differences in wealth to the common goal.

Along with Davis, Pierre Bourdieu also points to the underlying structure of large communal tasks. In the case of Fontelas, the law of self-interest is put into abeyance in favour of the common good but in the process each *roda* becomes an 'institutionally organized and guaranteed misrecognition' of material differences in wealth (Bourdieu 1977:171 – *la méconnaissance institutionnellement organisée et garantie*). In other words, each rotation is a form of 'collective lie' through which villagers who are otherwise unequal delude themselves temporarily that all may contribute equally towards a common goal. This also happens at public works. But the minute the desired goal is achieved, the 'misrecognized' equality of rotation disappears. Only in those special cases of tasks requiring the efforts of enormous labour-teams are both rotations as well as systematically ordered turns employed. These tasks may either involve the upkeep or repairs of a corporate resource such as ditches, water, ovens, mills, and roads or they may concern a resource produced by virtually the entire hamlet, such as rye grain. As we have seen earlier, no household could accomplish any of these tasks entirely on its own, nor even with the limited scale of assistance provided by its core-group of regular cooperators. A very large group of co-villagers must be recruited, and the means of organizing these teams is through an institutionalized rotation of rigidly calculated turns and exchanges. The threshings thus involve almost the entire hamlet in a 'communal' effort, although the actual resource (rye grain) is owned individually and in quite varying quantities.

While public works and ditch-cleanings are relatively infrequent, each year there are a very large number of threshings and other harvesting tasks at which large teams must exchange labour. The potential for asymmetric trading of labour at these times is particularly great. The *tornajeira* exchange is thus a social 'mask' of equality concealing essentially unequal economic relations – the illusion that everyone is equal and that everyone will contribute equally to the task is institutionalized within the misrecognized egalitarian rotation of equal turns and equal exchanges. This is precisely why wealthy/poor disparities in threshing labour-time are never recovered, but rather dissolved within the institution itself.

Analyses of circular rotation may tell us *how* villagers conceive of these ramified forms of community-wide cooperation, but they may not reveal *why* such systematic forms exist in some communities and not in others. In the case of Fontelas, and I suspect in other small Iberian corporate communities as well (Freeman 1968), it is the location of corporate property which provides the basis for rotating systems. This is so in Fontelas both for threshing-floors as well as for the sequence of irrigation turns which connect a water-pool with the successive groups of adjacent gardens which it waters. In both cases, the fulcrum of each cycle is the physical location of corporate property (threshing-floors and gardens). Both *rodas* I have described are thus 'plot-order' systems of rotation – the underlying principle which shapes the basic form of both types of rotation is the particular geographical layout of landed property. In this sense, it is my hunch that villagers in Fontelas do not entirely 'control' certain key elements within their system of production (grain and water) but that it is these elements which control them. Rather than dominating their own forms of corporate property it is that property itself, through the mediating systems of *roda* and *torna*, which dominates them.[24]

The functioning of these forms of corporate property requires the successive recruitment of enormous teams of villagers, and this is achieved through complex systems of rotation and turns. But neither process (threshings or irrigation) is entirely communal nor are they truly egalitarian. Once each task is completed, the masks of social equality immediately vanish. Economic inequality re-emerges, and the hamlet's social hierarchy again reigns supreme.

[24] I am grateful to Tim Ingold for pointing out the similarity of this point about property to the major argument in Edmund Leach's *Pul Eliya* (1961). However, as I had not yet read the latter book when I wrote this analysis, the two arguments are entirely independent. My treatment of the 'temporary suspension of economic inequalities' and of the 'collective misrecognition' of egalitarian rotation has derived much inspiration from specific sections of John Davis' *People of the Mediterranean* (1977) and Pierre Bourdieu's *Outline of a Theory of Practice* (1977).

5

Matrimony and patrimony

In the first half of this book we have looked at the composition of Fontelas' social hierarchy with respect to landholdings, social groups, and cooperative labour. The second half will now deal with household structure, marriage, and inheritance: do we also find aspects of differentiation and inequality in these areas of social life?

The following three chapters will deal with aspects of matrimony and patrimony in Fontelas. By 'matrimony' I mean the complex of elements defining the whole process of marriage: courtship, wedding ritual, post-marital residence, child-rearing, and the establishment of affinal ties. By 'patrimony' I mean firstly the overall sum of a specific individual's or household's material property: land, house, and movables (tools, furniture, and livestock). The second meaning implies the larger structures of the inheritance of property and the transmission of patrimony (primarily land) over the generations. No suggestion of emphasis respectively on women and men is intended by the two terms. Following the minute analysis of three case-studies in this chapter, Chapters 6 and 7 will afford some conclusions concerning this society's general orientation towards patrimony and descent and its extreme de-emphasis of marriage and conjugal ties.

It is my contention that a major structural tension exists in this community between these two complexes. While dominant strategies attempt to maintain a unified patrimony and a large labour group within the natal household for as long as possible, each occasion of matrimony threatens to disperse individuals and to divide that patrimony ultimately in the second and third generations. One means of resolving this tension, or at least of delaying potential conflicts, is the selection of a favoured heir or heiress who marries and stays on the landholding. This appointment itself imposes informal pressures on other siblings either to emigrate, marry out, or remain celibate. Although this selection process operates on a practical level despite the legal rule of equal partition between all siblings, it is never elevated to an institutionalized system of primogeniture or unigeniture. Thus the interests of matrimony and those of patrimony are in constant conflict, but much of the material presented here indicates the prevalence of one dominant mechanism – *the maintenance of a unified patrimony over time*. Marriage may join both individuals and groups, but it may also do the reverse: in this society the prevailing power of patrimony separates the 'chosen few' who may marry from the 'many damned' who may not. Case after case indicates that despite the existence of a formal rule of equality between heirs, on a practical level there is a distinct inequality between one favoured heir and many secondary, tacitly excluded heirs.

This chapter is comprised solely of three detailed case-studies of the developmental cycle over four generations within the households of a *proprietário*, a *lavrador*, and a *jornaleira*. The analysis is triply complicated in its combined use of genealogies, the Parish Register, and the Confessional Rolls, and the case-studies may border on the dense and tedious. I have thus attempted in each case to expand the internal analysis of household structure through the selection of 'typical' households representative of each social group, thereby allowing a certain degree of generalization. The case-studies should be seen therefore not only as individual cases but models for more general processes within each of the three major social groups.[1] A sequence of pictorial diagrams (based partially on Laslett 1972:41–4) is included at the beginning of each section, each diagram representing the exact structure of the household as listed in each of the 15 successive Confessional Rolls from 1886 through 1909.[2] The somewhat skeletal nature of this chapter will be amplified in the two following chapters, where I consider broader comparative aspects of marriage and inheritance, and some of the major cultural values placed upon them.

To my knowledge, no such analysis of this type of documentary source has been carried out in the social anthropology of Southern Europe. I refer of course only to published works on Southern European communities in anthropology: there are a number of analyses of Confessional Rolls and other similar household listings in Laslett (1972) as well as other works in historical demography. There are also references to parish records in Lisón-Tolosana's study of a Spanish town (1966), but the ecclesiastical records alone do not constitute a principal focus of that author's analysis.[3] The directions proposed

[1] The fourth social group (the large *lavradores*) presented a minor problem: households in this group resembled both *proprietário* and *lavrador* households in structure and developmental process. For the sake of brevity I have only dealt in this chapter with three typical domestic groups: the reader may assume that to a certain degree large *lavrador* households blend with both social groups.

[2] There were 15 Confessional Rolls archived in the sacristy of the parish church in Mosteiro, covering the years 1886, 1888, 1891, 1892, 1894, 1895, 1896, 1898, 1899, 1902, 1905, 1906, 1907, 1908, and 1909. I was unable to determine whether other Rolls were lost, archived elsewhere, or simply never compiled in the first place.

[3] As this book goes to press, we should note a number of other studies which have also concentrated recently upon similar documentary sources. Firstly, the classic debate on household developmental cycles between Laslett (1972) and Berkner (1972a; 1975) has been developed and given new direction by Segalen (1977), Netting (1979b), and Verdon (1979), all of whom point to the advantages of more diachronic and dynamic theoretical analyses of family cycles. Secondly, an impressive array of multiple sources (notarial, cadastral and census

here should thus be judged as initial suggestions, preceding any future conclusions which may be arrived at through more sophisticated demographic and historical techniques. John Davis (1977:5–7) has argued that one of the major failures of Mediterranean anthropology has been its neglect of history. An attempt is made here to reset this imbalance: what is lost in accuracy through analysis of the records examined below will be gained through a reincorporation of *process* and the dimension of time.

Proprietário household

The Confessional Rolls (*Róis de Confessados*) are one of the most detailed and meticulously compiled series of documents available in the parish for the late nineteenth and early twentieth centuries. This kind of listing is of course a very old one in the Catholic tradition, and was originally destined to provide a series of local checks on the observance (or lack of such) of the major religious rituals of confession, communion, and confirmation. Following the *Rituale Romanum* in 1614, these soul listings were further formalized with regard to the actual recording of this information about parishioners (Hajnal 1982:483). A sample page of the 1895 Roll for the parish of Mosteiro is reproduced below along with a translation of its key Portuguese terms and abbreviations. The Rolls provide a wide range of information on all resident domestic groups in the parish's four hamlets, each one consisting of numbered households with the name, marital status, occupation, and age of each of the individuals in every household in the parish. After each name comes an abbreviation (wife, son, servant) indicating the relation of each person to the head of household,

records as well as vital event registration) has been used effectively by Siddle and Jones (1982; 1983) to trace the continuity of family structures and patrilines in a rural community of Haute Savoie for over 400 years, while Diskin (1979) has noted some novel sources in Mexico and Brandão and Feijó (1984) have provided a useful survey of many historical sources for community-studies in Portugal. David Gaunt also offers a convenient overview of historical records of use to anthropologists in his survey-memoir (1982), and Augustins (1981) has developed an excellent and convincing means of analysing the transfer of property over a number of generations through the combined use of genealogies and land Cadasters in the French Pyrenees. Thirdly, a number of authors have made use of *Libri Status Animarum* listings for the study of family structures: see Viazzo (1986) for a limited use of 5 lists in the Italian Alps, Hanssen (1979/80) for a fascinating long-term study of Swedish household processes over 300 years using 'Books of Communion', John Hajnal's comments on the *Status Animarum* as a demographic and historical source (1982:483), and finally an analysis of Austrian household structures over time – through examination of consecutive 'soul descriptions' which affords the closest similarities in both methodology and theory to my own study (Mitterauer and Sieder 1979). It should be borne in mind, however, that the uses of Confessional Rolls (or other forms of household listings and historical sources containing information on individuals and households) made by historians and demographers are manifold, and may be quite tangential to some of the key problems which anthropologists may be seeking to illuminate through the same documentary sources. Only the most careful delineation of the ethnological problem to be tackled, the method(s) to be used, and the reliability of the available records will afford the most productive interdisciplinary results.

and following each age one or two letters (*c* or *cc*) denoting respectively 'confession' or 'confession and communion' and a cross indicating confirmation. Children under the age of first confession (8) were not normally registered. The Confessional Rolls were compiled by the parish priest at Easter time: they were printed first on a standard form and then sent to parish priests for completion. The fact that a relatively consecutive series of such listings is available at 1–3 year intervals affords an extraordinary opportunity to observe changes in the developmental cycle of various households over a period of 23 years.

This kind of analysis is thus quite distinct from that used in prior studies of parish and tax records in that its prime focus is *process* over time, rather than the synchronic tabulation of household type and membership at one specific date or the calculation of aggregate demographic totals. The 'household histories' analysed by Carter (1984) are fundamentally different from my case-studies here, although the former's major point concerning the general utility of longitudinal materials is well taken. Such collections of consecutive Confessional Rolls or *Status Animarum* lists are thought to be rare: further research in Portuguese and Iberian local ecclesiastical archives may well prove the contrary in future years.

As we look at the household diagrammed below (Figure 8) we should bear in mind the overall proportions of households in the hamlet which were headed by *proprietários*, *lavradores*, and *jornaleiros* at the time. For instance, in 1896 Fontelas had 6 *proprietário* households, 14 *lavrador* households, and 24 *jornaleiro* households; the household examined here was one of these 6. Also in 1896 there were 19 servants (11 men and 8 women). I will present a more complete picture of these proportions for 1886–1909 towards the end of this chapter. Note that in all diagrams from Figure 8 onwards, domestic groups referred to in historical documents will appear as 'House 3, House 27' etc., in order to distinguish them from the households I enumerated in 1976–8. The order in which these houses were listed by successive priests does not correspond precisely, therefore, to the sequences of household rotation described in Chapter 4.

The structure of this domestic group in the Confessional Roll of 1886 included first the head of household, Rodrigo Manuel Borges.[4] Rodrigo was

[4] I have changed the names of all living individuals in the Confessional Rolls and Parish Register, and have substituted them randomly with pseudonyms. The pseudonyms retain some note of reality, however, as I selected most of them from the names of other individuals in other hamlets of the parish, as well as a few from a demographic study by Amorim (1973) of the parish records (seventeenth and eighteenth centuries) of a village in the same district. Nevertheless, I have everywhere been careful to reproduce the *number* and *order* of names: for example, a real Manuel Alberto I give the pseudonym João António, but in every case where he is listed only as Manuel, I have listed him only as João. Individuals frequently appear with only one Christian name in one listing, but with their surname in another. In this sense, apart from my changing the names, the actual patterns of the ways in which various priests have listed individuals' names have been exactly reproduced.

listed as a *lavrador* aged 35, and his name was followed by those of his two maternal aunts, Catarina and Doroteia (aged 62 and 60). Their relationship to Rodrigo is only stated later in the 1891 Roll as *thias*, or aunts, and Rodrigo's genealogy tells us that they were his maternal aunts (the Rolls do not state this explicitly). Along with these three individuals, the household included three servants, termed *criados*. These three servants were Policarpo (aged 18), Quitéria (aged 48), and Teresa (aged 30). None of these six household members was married at the time: the Roll explicitly refers to each of these individual's marital status as 'single'. All six individuals were listed as having taken both confession and communion. Note that this was the case throughout the years 1886–1909 except in 1898 and 1907, when two younger servants took only confession.

In 1888 the structure of Rodrigo's household was the same but only five individuals were listed, the servant Teresa having moved out. We are unable of course to determine why this servant left the household: she may have found another employer, moved in with kin, or have been asked to leave. Thus when I mention that servants 'move in' or 'move out' of a household, I refer only to those movements visible to us through the documents, not to the various reasons or motivations behind such changes of residence. Further, other servants may have moved in and out of the household between the dates of compilation (1886 and 1888) and thus may have remained unrecorded. Ultimately, we know only that these individuals were *listed* by the parish priest as household residents at the time the Confessional Roll was compiled (April–June). In other words, we cannot be absolutely certain that they were in fact there throughout the entire year.[5]

In 1891 a different priest compiled the Roll (Padre Morais) and continued to do so for all of the following Rolls with the exception of those compiled in 1905 and 1906. Rodrigo was listed from now on as a *proprietário*, and his aunts' full names were recorded. The actual listing of villagers' occupations by the three parish priests who compiled the Rolls are of course subject to error: there are no objective criteria written in the listings (size of landholdings, amounts of taxes) indicating specifically why some individuals were listed as *proprietários* and others as *lavradores*. But we can provisionally assume that some form of uniform classification of occupations was shared by priests and villagers alike.

[5] The Rolls do not state *where* these servants lived: I was told during my fieldwork that servants sometimes resided within the household of their employer and sometimes in adjacent buildings. But irrespective of their place of residence, servants always ate meals and worked within their employers' households. They were resident members of the *household* as distinct from lodgers forming part of a larger physical unit termed the *houseful* (Laslett 1972:34–9) and merely using part of a household's spatial quarters for sleeping. Servants were thus to all intents and purposes full members of their hirers' households: while in some cases they may have slept in adjoining buildings, they participated in two of the major characteristics of the household as defined by Goody (1972b:111–22): working and eating together with their employers (see p. 20, n. 16).

Rol dos confessados da freguezia de =1895=

Moradas	Nomes dos chefes de familia e pessoas que a compõem	Estados	Profissões	Annos a que diz respeito e signal de desobriga—C				
				189	189	189	189	189
33	Fran.co do Rio Pinheiro	casado	lavrador	48 cc				+
	Belisanda Eugenia Pires, m.er	"	"	38 cc				+
	Antonio Pires, f.	Solt.o	"	19 cc				
	Manuel f.	"	"	17 cc				
	Francisco f.	"	"	14 cc				
	Verato f.	"	"	10 c				
	Barbara de Moraes, sogra	Viuva	"	66 cc				+
34	Joanna de Jesus	Viuva	Jorn.a	50 cc				
35	José Joaquim Pires	Casado	Jorn.o	38				
	Maria das Dores, m.er	"	"	33				
	Carolina Pires, f.	Solt.a	"	9 c				
36	M.el do Espirito Santo Pires	Casado	Jorn.o	36				
	Delfina Leita, m.er	"	"	34				+
	José, f.	Solt.o	"	10 c				+
37	Bernarda Pires	Solt.a	Jorn.a	33 cc				
	Domingas Pires, irmã	"	"	40 cc				
	Laurinda dos Anjos, f.a	"	"	18 cc				
	Maria José f.a	"	"	12 c				
38	Sebastião Affonso	Casado	lavrador	59 cc				+
	Maria Agostinha Gomes,	"	"	58 cc				+
	Maria Joanna, f.a	Solt.a	"	19 cc				
	João Evangelista, genro	Casado	"	38 cc				+
	Justina da Purificação, m.er	"	"	28 cc				+
	Maria	Solt.a	Criada	36 cc				/
	Manuel	"	"	11 c				
39	Barbara Affonso	Viuva	Prop.a	58 cc				+
	Jeronymo Ferreira, genro	Casado	"	33 cc				+
	Albina do Nascimento, m.er	"	"	31 cc				+
	José f.	Solt.o	"	16 cc				
40	Fran.co J.e Pires Quintella	Viuvo	lavrador	61 cc				+
	Maria Isabel, f.	Solt.a	"	23 cc				
	Antonio Pires, f.	"	"	20 cc				

Document 2. Confessional Roll, 1895

In 1891 the number of servants in the household was particularly large – there were three male and three female servants, only one of whom (Policarpo) had remained since 1886. The same servants were resident in the household in 1892, although there was some inconsistency between Clemente's listed ages. We are unable to tell whether the Teresa (aged 51) listed in 1892 was the same individual as the Teresa (aged 30) listed in 1886.[6]

At some point between 1891 and 1892, Rodrigo married a *proprietária* from a neighbouring hamlet – Madalena de Sousa. (The marriage entry is not listed in the Mosteiro Parish Register, thus suggesting that it was registered in Madalena's parish.) Note the ages of Rodrigo and Madalena at the time of their marriage: Rodrigo was 39 and Madalena 34 or 35. The household at this point was at its largest size (10 resident members) during the 23-year phase of its developmental cycle visible to us through the Rolls. The household did not comprise the structure of a 'nuclear family' strictly defined as a conjugal unit of husband, wife, and children: although a marriage took place, the structure of additional resident kin (aunts) and servants was maintained throughout the years in question. In fact, a permanent structure of resident servants (characteristic only of the *proprietário* and large *lavrador* groups) has been maintained within this household until today: in 1940 two servants were listed, and even in 1978 Rodrigo's daughter Dona Elvira still has three resident servants within the household.

In 1894 the household was somewhat smaller – since 1892 four servants moved out and one moved in, while Rodrigo's aunt Doroteia was no longer listed. The Parish Register (death entries) allows us to confirm that Doroteia

1895 CONFESSIONAL ROLL – PORTUGUESE TERMS

Annos a que diz respeito e signal de desobriga – C: Respective years and mark of performance of paschal duty – C
Casado: Married
Chrisma (+): Confirmation
Creada: Servant
Estados: Marital status
fª (*filha*): Daughter
fº (*filho*): Son
Genro: Son-in-law
Irmã: Sister
Jornº (*Jornaleiro*): Day-labourer
Lavrador: Peasant
Moradas: Addresses
mr. (*mulher*): Wife
Nomes dos chefes de família e pessoas que a compôem: Names of heads of household and persons composing them
Profissões: Occupations
Propª (*Proprietária*): Large landowner
Sogra: Mother-in-law
Soltª (*Solteira*): Single
Viúva: Widow

[6] Inaccuracies in the registration of ages, particularly the ages of servants, are a constant problem in the Confessional Rolls and must be checked where possible with individuals' baptismal entries in the Parish Register. This is not always possible, as not all servants resident at any particular date in Fontelas were necessarily born there, but rather in neighbouring hamlets. Thus their baptismal entries will not be listed in the Mosteiro Parish Register.

Figure 8. *Proprietário* household (17 diagrams)

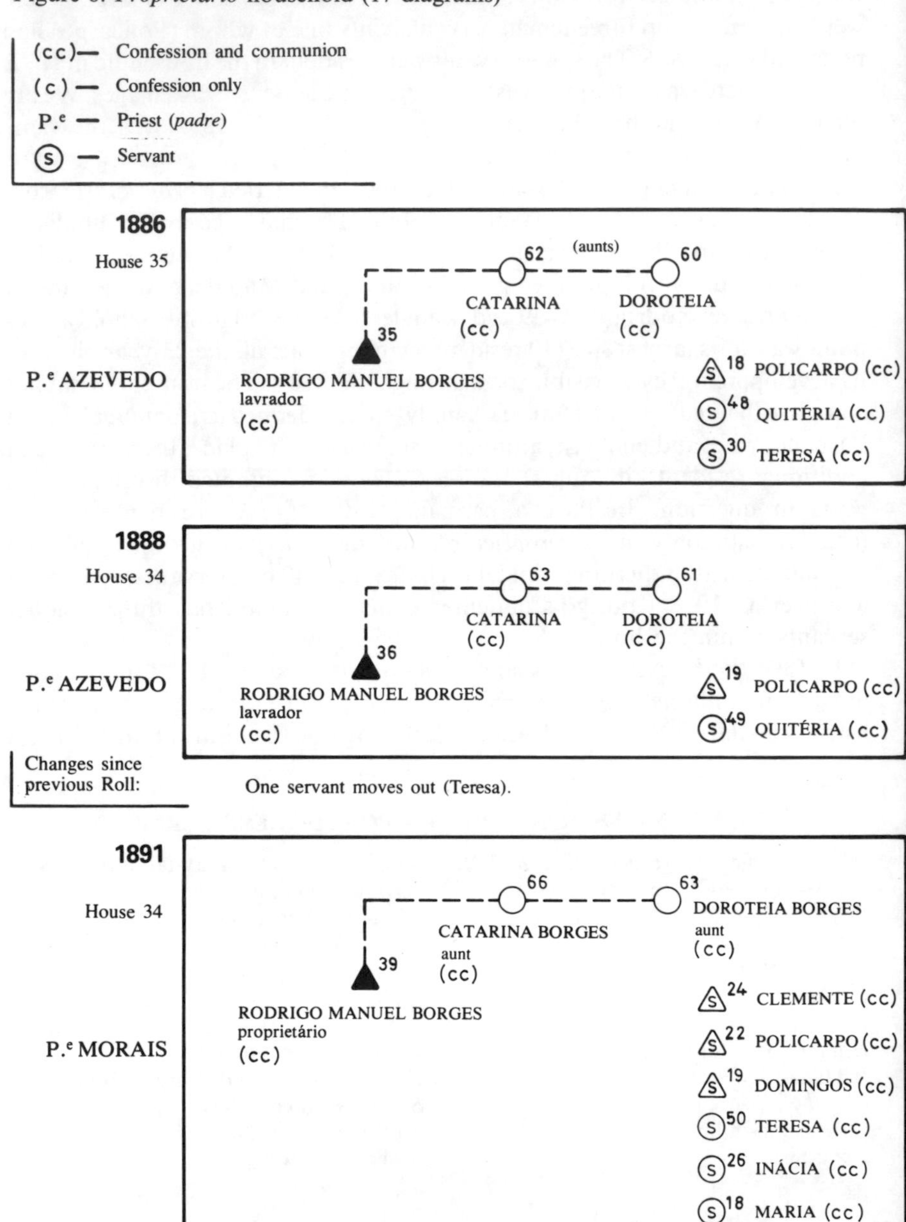

Four servants move in.

Rodrigo is listed as a *proprietário* from now on.

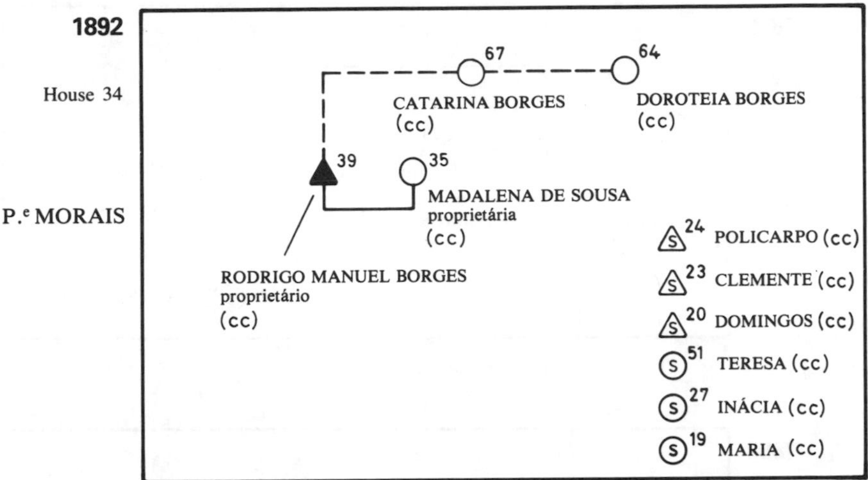

Rodrigo marries a *proprietária* from a neighbouring parish (in 1891 or 1892).

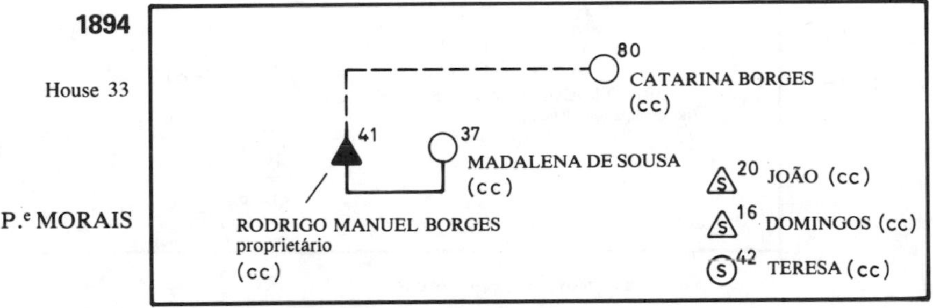

Doroteia dies (aged 76) on 29 May 1894, leaving a will but no children.

Four servants move out; one moves in.

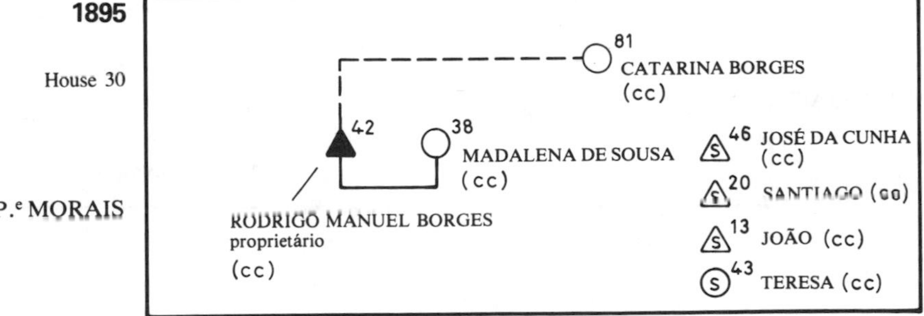

Two servants move out; three move in.

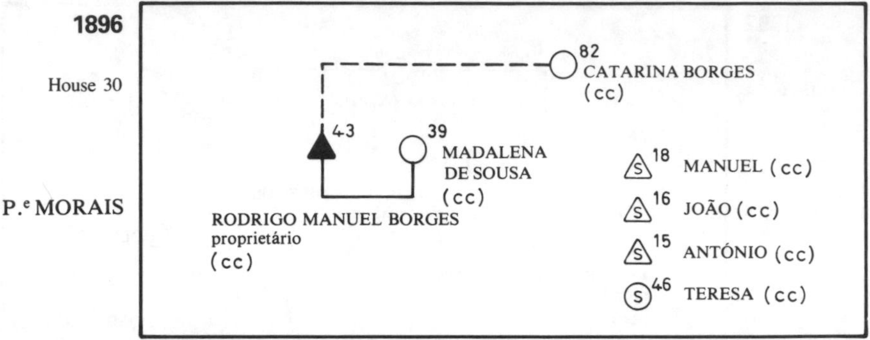

Two servants move out; two move in.

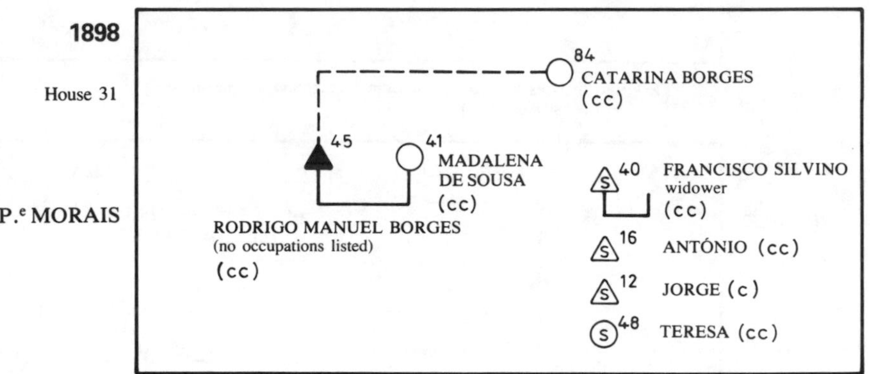

Two servants move out; two move in.

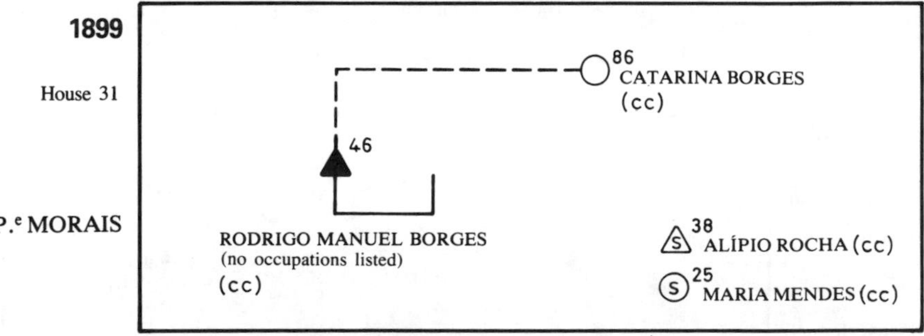

Madalena dies (aged 42) on 30 March 1899,
leaving no will and no children.

Four servants move out; two move in.

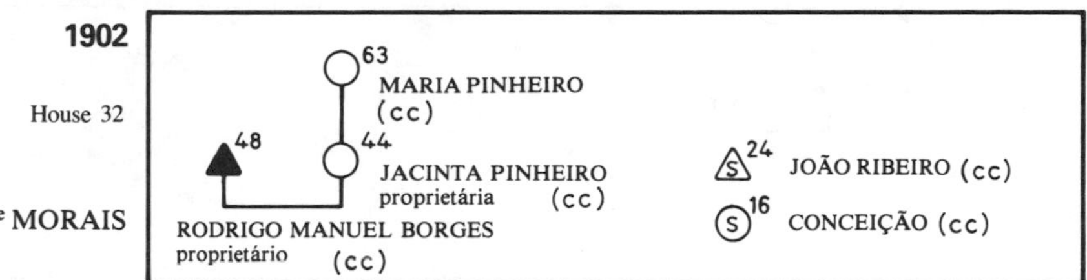

Catarina dies (aged 86) on 7 November 1899, leaving a will but no children.

Rodrigo remarries a *proprietária* from the town (1900?).

Two servants move out; two move in.

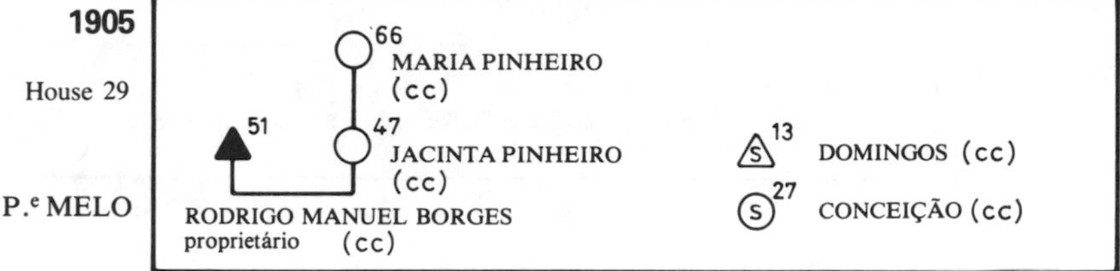

Two servants move out; two move in.

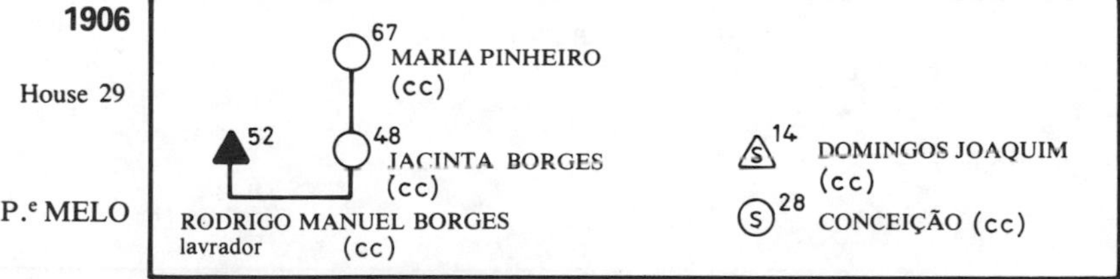

Rodrigo is listed as a *lavrador*.

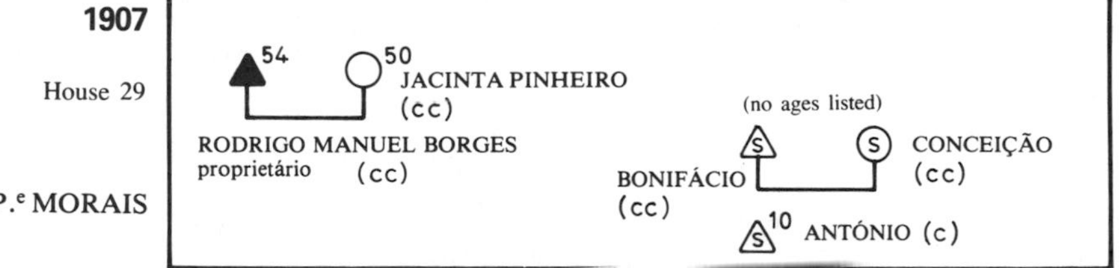

Maria Pinheiro dies (aged 74) on 22 October 1906, leaving no will but leaving children (siblings of Jacinta?). Sacraments administered by Rodrigo, not the priest.

Two servants move out; three move in.

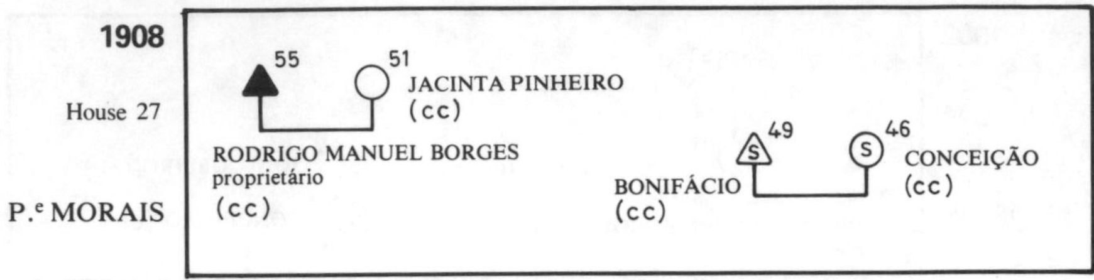

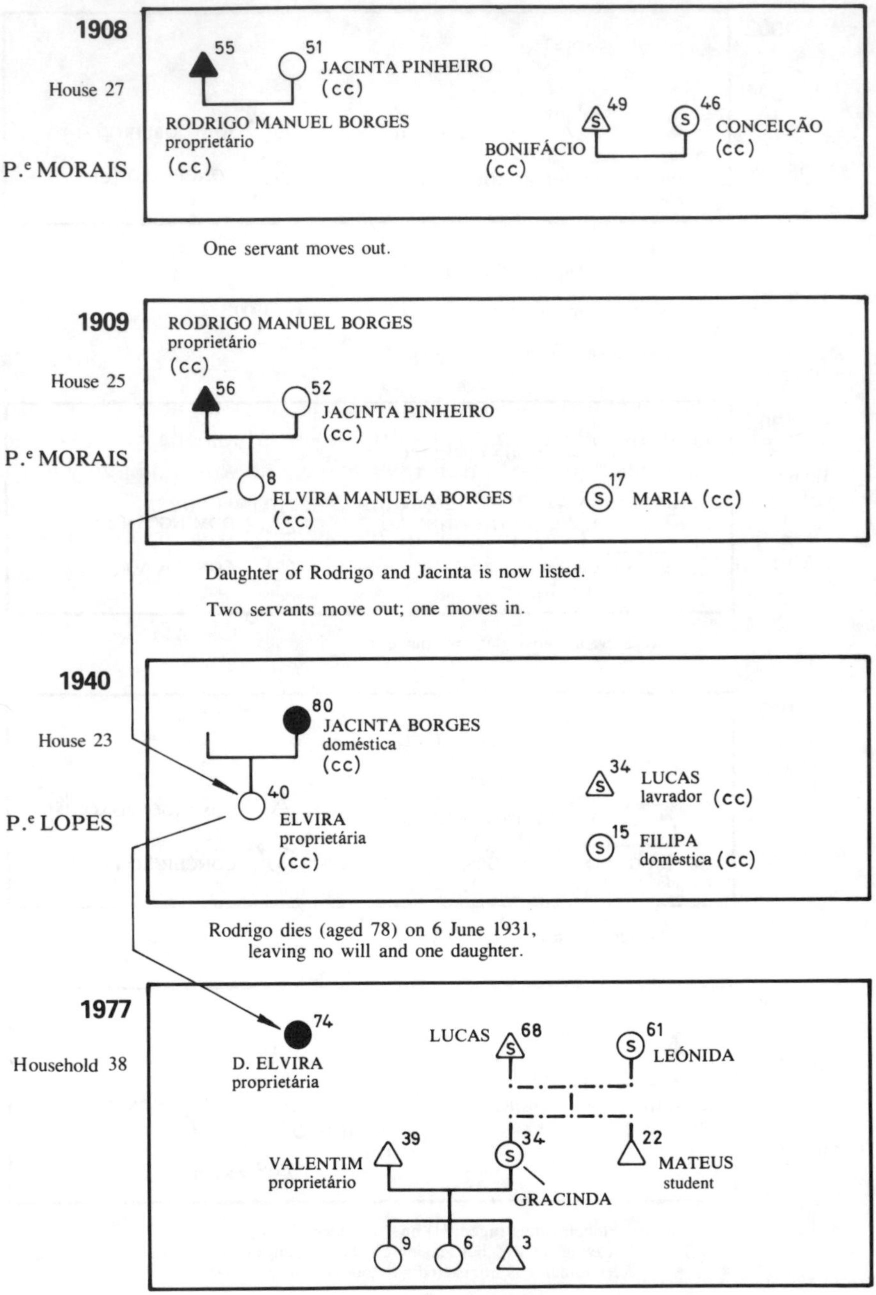

1908
House 27
P.e MORAIS
55
51
JACINTA PINHEIRO
(cc)
RODRIGO MANUEL BORGES
proprietário
(cc)
49
46
BONIFÁCIO
(cc)
CONCEIÇÃO
(cc)
One servant moves out.
1909
House 25
P.e MORAIS
RODRIGO MANUEL BORGES
proprietário
(cc)
56
52
JACINTA PINHEIRO
(cc)
8
ELVIRA MANUELA BORGES
(cc)
17
MARIA (cc)
Daughter of Rodrigo and Jacinta is now listed.
Two servants move out; one moves in.
1940
House 23
P.e LOPES
80
JACINTA BORGES
doméstica
(cc)
40
ELVIRA
proprietária
(cc)
34
LUCAS
lavrador (cc)
15
FILIPA
doméstica (cc)
Rodrigo dies (aged 78) on 6 June 1931,
leaving no will and one daughter.
1977
Household 38
74
D. ELVIRA
proprietária
LUCAS
68
61
LEÓNIDA
39
VALENTIM
proprietário
34
GRACINDA
22
MATEUS
student
9
6
3

(1977 Source: author's Household Census)

died (aged 76) on 29 May 1894, leaving a will but no children.[7] The death entry states only whether or not the deceased left a will, but no further details are given concerning the legatee(s) or property mentioned in the will. Inaccuracies in the recording of ages are particularly evident here: while the same priest compiled the Confessional Rolls and the Parish Register at this time, Doroteia was listed as 64 years of age in 1892 but as 76 at her death in 1894. Similarly, Catarina was listed as 67 in 1892 but as 80 (!) in 1894. Further, the age of the servant Teresa has dropped from 51 in 1892 to 42 in 1894 (presuming this is the same person, which may not have been the case). It is of course possible that elderly individuals did not remember their ages, or that the head of the household or the priest incorrectly estimated some individuals' ages.

From 1895 through 1898 the basic structure of the household as well as its size (7 persons) remained constant, although again a number of servants moved in and out. In 1899, however, Rodrigo's wife Madalena was no longer listed: she died (aged 42) on 30 March 1899, leaving no will and having borne no children. In the same year, Rodrigo's aunt Catarina also died (7 November 1899): she was 86 years of age, childless, and she left a will. Significantly, by 1902 Rodrigo had remarried. His second wife, Jacinta Pinheiro, was a *proprietária* from the nearby town, and both she and her mother were now listed as residents of Rodrigo's household. Note that Jacinta's age at the time of her marriage (between 1899 and 1902) was quite high: between 41 and 44.[8]

From 1902 through 1906 no major changes occurred in the structure of the household, although in 1906 Rodrigo was listed as a *lavrador* (this change in his listed occupation may be explained by the fact that a different priest compiled the 1905 and 1906 Rolls). In 1907, Rodrigo's mother-in-law was not listed: she had died on 22 October 1906 (aged 74) leaving no will. Her death entry states that she was administered 'the sacraments' in the household by Rodrigo and not by the parish priest (suggesting sudden death).[9] In the 1907 Roll the two

[7] A detailed description of the Parish Register is contained in Appendix III, along with translations of some sample entries of births, marriages, and deaths.

[8] Like Rodrigo's first marriage, this one was also not entered in the Mosteiro Parish Register. It is customary in this region for the bride's parents to provide the wedding banquet; in cases of inter-hamlet marriages, the wedding ceremony usually takes place either in the chapel (or church) of the bride's hamlet or alternatively in the bride's parish church. This may explain the absence of this marriage entry in the Mosteiro Parish Register: it would have been entered in the records of Rodrigo's bride's parish.

[9] All death entries in the Parish Register explicitly state whether the deceased received the sacraments or not. In many cases, particularly those of sudden infant deaths, the entry states that the sacraments were administered by someone other than the parish priest: many such lay baptisms were carried out by mothers due to their child's being 'in danger of life' (*em perigo de vida*) anywhere from a few hours to a few months following their birth. Others died without receiving the sacrament, whether administered by a priest or a lay person. One extreme case occurred in 1875 in Mosteiro, when Manuel Pires (aged 49) and his son (aged 16) did not receive the sacraments because 'they died suddenly under the ruins of their house, which collapsed over them'.

servants Bonifácio and Conceição were explicitly listed as 'married' although their ages were not recorded until 1908.

The final Roll in 1909 included a daughter of Rodrigo and Jacinta: Elvira Manuela Borges, aged 8. The married servants Bonifácio and Conceição had moved out of the household and a young female servant (Maria) moved in. The domestic group at this time was the closest in any of the Rolls to the nuclear form, and it comprised a married couple, one child, and one servant.

The next household listing available in the Parish Records was the *Status Animarum* of 1940, almost identical in form to the earlier Confessional Rolls. In 1940 the household consisted of Jacinta Borges (aged 80), her daughter Elvira (aged 40), and two servants: the *lavrador* Lucas (aged 34) and Filipa (aged 15) who was listed as a *doméstica* (see Glossary). Rodrigo had died (aged 78) on 6 June 1931, leaving no will and an only child (Elvira). Note however that although Jacinta was listed as a *doméstica* and head of the household, it was her daughter Elvira who was listed as a *proprietária*. The term is suggestive here of the process of inheritance in Fontelas: upon his death (if he had left no will) half of Rodrigo's property was inherited by his wife and the other half by his descendant(s), in this case Elvira. Legally, Elvira becomes the sole heir of her father's property, while Jacinta obtains legal usufruct of half of her husband's property and the right to material support by her daughter (a form of jointure: Goody 1976b:25). The occupational term *proprietária* for Elvira and not her mother is thus properly chosen and points to the legal property-owner in the household (Elvira), although Jacinta was listed formally as the household head.

By 1977 the household had changed again in structure. Jacinta died (age not stated) on 16 February 1943. The death entry did not state whether a will was left, although the priest noted the cause of death as 'apoplexy'.[10] The servant Lucas, listed also in 1940, had remained in the household as Dona Elvira's servant and main *lavrador*. The structure of the household again indicates a number of servants: these are Lucas' common-law wife Leónida and their daughter Gracinda, whom in Chapter 3 we noted has become Dona Elvira's adopted heiress. Also resident in the household are Gracinda's husband Valentim and the latter's three young children, along with Gracinda's brother Mateus. The household is the second largest in Fontelas today, with 9 resident members.

We have now constructed a series of 'snapshots' revealing the structure of

[10] From 1940 through 1945, the 72 death entries in the Parish Register include the priest's recording of the cause of death. These are the only years when this was done, but unfortunately Padre Lopes and Padre Jerónimo did not over these six years include the age of the deceased at the time of death. There were a number of cases of apoplexy, pneumonia, tuberculosis, intestinal fever, old age, and infantile rickets, along with one case of a woman dying during childbirth and one of a woman (a domestic servant) dying of syphilis. When I inquired in the Civil Registry Office in town about these recorded causes I was promptly laughed at, and told to disregard them entirely as merely the priests' suppositions as to the real causes of the deaths.

17 *Proprietária*, ca. 1895 (enlargement of an old photograph).

Dona Elvira's father's household over time, with a particularly clear consecutive sequence between 1886 and 1909. This cycle offers an extremely novel method for examining the specific timing of marriage and inheritance as these events occurred within the changing structure of a domestic group through the years. What broader patterns are revealed by these specific changes (or lack of changes) in this household's structure from year to year? How representative is this household's developmental cycle of the *proprietário* group as a whole?

An excellent way to examine long-term patterns in the structure of Rodrigo's household is to compare it with another household of high rank within the social hierarchy. As the two households are related by kinship and control much of the hamlet's landed wealth today, this comparison provides the added advantage of examining not only two households but specifically two *proprietário* households at the very top of the hamlet pyramid. Both Rodrigo's as well as Inácio Ferreira's households owned some of the highest amounts of taxable wealth in the hamlet in 1892. The Parish Tax Listing of that year (Appendix II) listed Rodrigo and his uncle (Padre Venâncio) as owning combined taxable wealth of 58,800 *réis* (41,360 + 17,440 in Table 21) and Inácio Ferreira as owning taxable wealth of 90,430 *réis*. These were two of the three highest figures in Fontelas at the time.[11] Three diagrams will suffice here for the purpose of comparison.

Apart from its enormous size in 1905, a striking characteristic of this household was the presence of a number of unmarried siblings of advanced age: three of Inácio's four children were unmarried at the ages of 58, 56, and 40. The third sibling (Cândido) had married his first wife in 1896, when the structure of the household (not diagrammed here) was that of a stem family. Both of Cândido's parents were resident within the household along with the new conjugal group of Cândido and his in-marrying wife. At some date prior to the 1905 Roll, Rosa Rodrigues (Cândido's second wife) brought her elder brother João Rodrigues into the household (we cannot determine precisely when). João remained unmarried at the age of 58 at the date of the last Roll in which he appeared in 1909. Similarly, Cândido's younger brother Silvestre also remained unmarried in the 1909 Roll, at the age of 44. In the Parish Register (death entries) I was able to date Manuel José's death in 1922 and Antónia's in 1931. Neither Manuel José nor Antónia left children, while Antónia left a will. Similar to the positions of Rodrigo's two elderly and unmarried aunts Catarina and Doroteia, Inácio's three unmarried children tended to remain within the natal household in secondary roles as dependent kin (Wolf and Cole 1974:200–2).

The positions of these elderly unmarried individuals are particularly interesting. In the six cases of unmarried individuals in the two households examined here, information was available on four of them through the Parish Register's death entries. Of these four (Catarina, Doroteia, Antónia, and Manuel José) three left wills. According to Portuguese law (Chapter 7) in the

[11] Again we encounter the problem of overlap between the occupations of *proprietário* and *lavrador*. Inácio was consistently listed as a *lavrador* throughout the Rolls, but both of his parents as well as his wife's parents were listed elswhere (Parish Register entries) as *proprietários*. Further, Inácio's great-grandson is Fontelas' current priest: the epitome of the wealthy, élite *proprietário* group. The difference in taxable wealth owned by Inácio and Rodrigo may of course indicate that these occupations had less to do with actual differences in wealth than with what each landowner actually did in terms of 'working their own land' or hiring servants.

Figure 9. *Proprietário* household (3 diagrams)

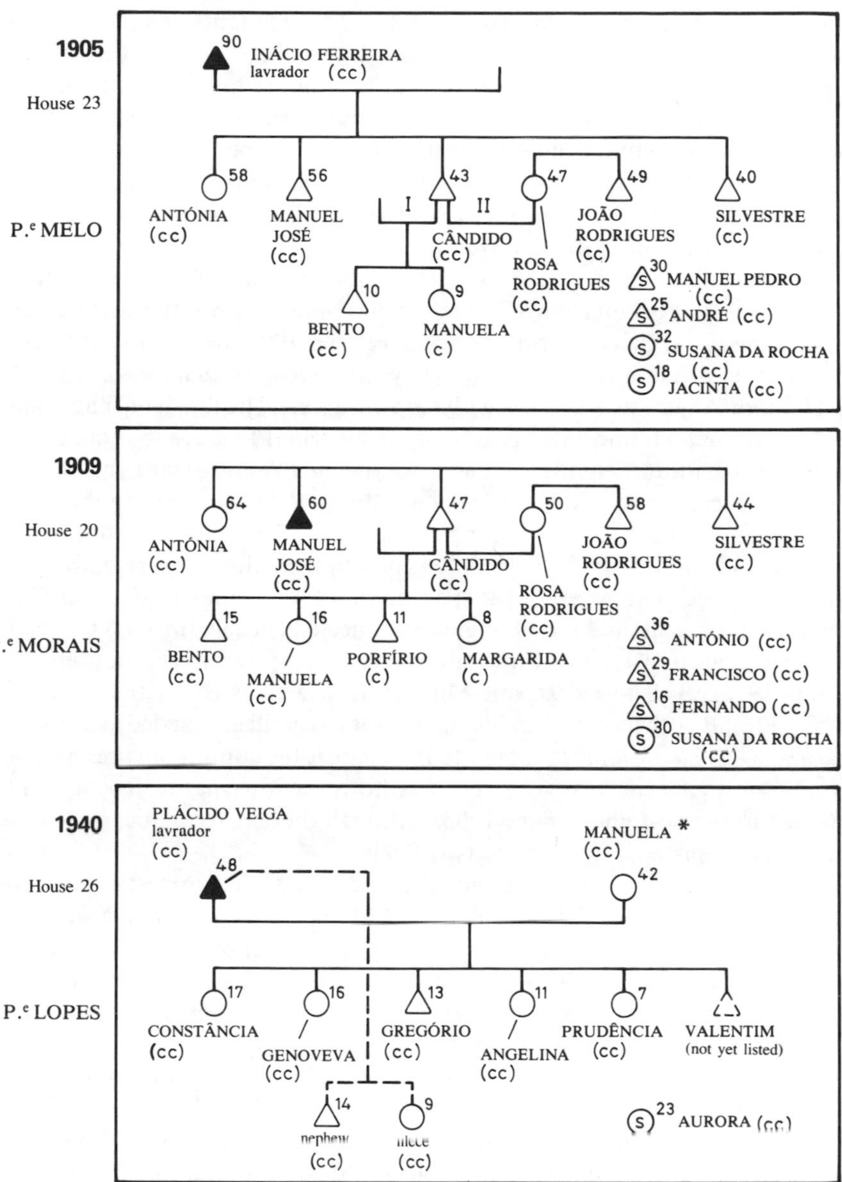

* All of the women in this listing were registered as *domésticas*. Gregório (later to become the parish priest) was listed as a student *(estudante)*.

absence of direct descendants these individuals could legally bequeath half of their total property to any chosen legatee(s). The other half must remain the 'legitimate inheritance' (*legítima*) of the testator's ascendants or siblings-and-descendants, in that order. In Antónia's case (1905 diagram) a portion of her property was willed to her niece Manuela, who remained in the natal household and was the mother of the current parish priest. In other words, in Antónia's case we have definite information that property was re-directed through a will into what was to become the main line of property transmission among Inácio's children: first the favoured heir Cândido and in the next generation the favoured heiress Manuela.[12]

The second diagram above represents the same household four years later in 1909: the most important change in its structure since 1905 was the death of the head of household Inácio Ferreira on 3 December 1905 (he left no will). It is significant that in this Roll in 1909, four years following Inácio's death, the natal household was still intact as a kinship grouping. The death of Inácio did *not* bring about an immediate break-up or dispersal of Inácio's four children. Whether a partition actually occurred following Inácio's death (or earlier following Inácio's wife's death in 1891) we cannot determine, but in this case such a partition did not imply a fragmentation of the natal household as a residence and labour unit. The adult generation at this time resembled a *frérèche* arrangement wherein 'no parent or other member of an earlier generation is present, and the siblings are connected entirely through the filial linkage of each to a conjugal unit no longer represented in the household' (Laslett 1972:30). The eldest son Manuel José was listed as the head of household, and both he as well as his elder sister were still unmarried at the ages of 60 and 64. Also of significance in the 1909 Roll is the continuing presence of servants: only one of these four servants however (Susana da Rocha) had remained in the household since 1905, although there is some inconsistency between her registered ages in the two Rolls.

The third diagram above represents the structure of this domestic group in 1940. The natal household was resided in by Manuela, who married a wealthy *lavrador* from another hamlet (Plácido Veiga) who moved into Fontelas, residing uxorilocally. Like Rodrigo's household, this was a very large one: it comprised 13 members in 1905 and 10 in 1940. As we have seen in Chapter 3, of Manuela's six children two have remained celibate today (Padre Gregório and the schoolteacher Dona Prudência). Of the remaining four siblings, the two eldest sisters Constância and Genoveva married out of the hamlet, while the younger Angelina and Valentim both married spouses natural to Fontelas. The structure of the household in 1940 was distinctly non-nuclear: it was composed of a married couple, six children, a nephew and niece of unspecified parentage, and one female servant.

[12] Henceforth I will use the term 'heir' for convenience to mean both male heirs and female heiresses. Inheritance and kin reckoning in Fontelas are strictly bilateral and there is no legal preference for either male or female heirs. I will return to this point in Chapter 7.

Another factor in the structure of this household is important here: both Antónia and her younger brother Silvestre were chosen as godparents (*madrinha* and *padrinho*) of all four of their nephews and nieces (1909 diagram). Thus in this case the tie of *compadrio* (coparenthood) was established within the household rather than outside it. In addition, Antónia's death entry indicates that she left a will, and I was able to confer that this will granted property to her god-daughter Manuela. In the case of Inácio's household, then, both this internal selection of godparents as well as the transmission of property from an unmarried sibling (Antónia) through *one* line of descent within the natal household (Cândido's children) suggest a pattern of property consolidation despite the legal rule of equal partition. In the case of Rodrigo's household, in contrast, this consolidation was unnecessary as his only child Elvira became his sole heir. In other words, although Cândido and his three siblings legally inherited equal shares of their parents' patrimony, a portion (perhaps all?) of Antónia's property was directed through Cândido's children, specifically through Manuela, who was both Antónia's niece as well as her god-daughter. While all four of Cândido's children married, it was Manuela who remained in the natal household, and who even today retains the larger landholding. Both the presence of elderly celibate siblings as well as this example of the vertical and internal effects of spiritual kinship (in contrast to the usually stressed horizontal, external functions of the godparenthood tie) indicate a focus upon the unity of a patrimony and efforts to avoid that patrimony's division. This avoidance is achieved through the informal selection of a favoured heir: these were Cândido in the earlier generation and Manuela in the next.

What patterns of marriage occurred in both of these households? Rodrigo's two marriages were with *proprietárias* from neighbouring hamlets and in both cases his wives resided virilocally. Rodrigo's first marriage of 9 years to Madalena was childless.[13] By 1902 Rodrigo had remarried. Elvira's listed ages in the 1909 and 1940 Rolls suggest that she was born in 1900–1, thus indicating Rodrigo's quite rapid remarriage. Similarly in the case of the second household (Figure 9), Cândido remarried quickly on 21 March 1904, only five months after the death of his first wife (23 October 1903). Both of Cândido's wives were also originally from neighbouring hamlets, and both resided virilocally after their marriages.[14] Both households' histories thus indicate

[13] Two documents allow us to confirm this. Firstly, no children appear born to Madalena in the baptismal entries of the Parish Register between the time she married Rodrigo (1891–?) and the date of her death (1899). Secondly, Madalena's death entry itself explicitly states that she died 'without leaving any children'.

[14] I would hesitate in calling the pattern of virilocal residence in these cases a *rule*, as many cases of uxorilocal and natolocal residence (Chapter 6) are also evident from an analysis of the genealogies I collected. For instance, in Cândido's household (1909) both of his daughters, Manuela and Margarida, later married *proprietário* husbands from other hamlets who resided uxorilocally in Fontelas. Only a complete analysis of all of the marriages listed in the Parish Register using more detailed methods of family reconstitution would provide a definitive series of statistics. Only an initial suggestion of such a method is attempted here.

extra-hamlet marriages suggestive of prestige alliances contracted outside the limits of the community (Bourdieu 1976:122/1977:52–8). These prestigious 'distant marriages', as Bourdieu terms them, are specific in Fontelas to the upper group of *proprietários* and the wealthier *lavradores*.

Another similarity between these two households is evident in the high ages at marriage and sibling order. We have noted that Rodrigo's age at the time of his first marriage was 39, and at the time of his second marriage, 47–8. Likewise, at the date of his first marriage in 1896, Cândido was 37 and his wife 30, while at his second marriage Cândido was 45 and his wife 47 (marriage entries). In all four of these marriages, then, every spouse was over 30 years of age and some were well over 40.

Sibling order at marriage is also of significance. Rodrigo himself was the third of three siblings: both his elder brother (a Justice of the Peace) and his elder sister married out of the hamlet. In the case of Cândido's household (Figure 9:1905), note that Cândido was the only one of four siblings to marry but that he was the third in order of birth. In the next generation, Cândido's own four children all married in the following order, at the noted ages.

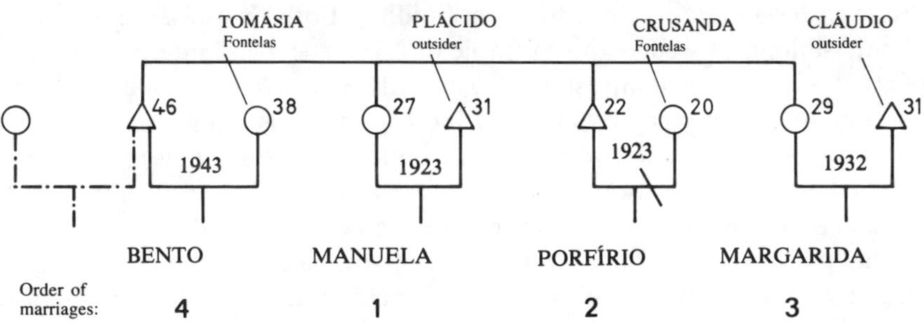

Figure 10. Marriage order of four *proprietário* siblings

Of all four marriages, *only one* (Porfírio's) was comprised of spouses with conspicuously low ages. Manuela was the first sibling to marry: she remained in the natal household and two of her six children (the priest and Dona Prudência) still reside in the natal household today. As stated above, Manuela's aunt Antónia willed some of her property to Manuela and her children: this is evident today in the somewhat larger size of the priest's landholding (43.33 hectares) than that of his uncle Bento (22.25 hectares) and that of his aunt Margarida (35.42 hectares). We noted in Chapter 3 that Porfírio's marriage to the weaver Crusanda was short-lived, Porfírio emigrating alone shortly afterwards to Brazil (the priest's household rarely speak today of this uncle of theirs). The third sibling to marry was Margarida, resident today in a partitioned section of the natal household (H28) with her husband and their two unmarried daughters, aged 43 and 42.

The fourth sibling to marry was the eldest son, Bento. Bento's marriage was particularly revealing for a number of reasons. Ten years prior to his marriage to the servant Tomásia, a first child had been born to this couple illegitimately. (Bento had earlier fathered another bastard child by a woman in a neighbouring hamlet.) Three of their children were legitimated at the time of their marriage in 1943 – the youngest of these three (18 months of age) was baptized immediately following the wedding ceremony. The marriages of Manuela and Bento thus constitute a stark contrast: while Manuela married a 'distant' and prestigious *proprietário*, married first, and remained within the natal household, Bento married downwards socially, at an advanced age, having already fathered four natural children, and he moved out of the natal household.

These materials suggest a certain stress upon the transmission of property through a favoured heir. This person tends to be the sibling who marries first, brings a husband or wife into the household, and produces children. There may of course be other siblings who marry first but leave the domestic group. In the first household examined above, this favoured heir was Rodrigo and in the second it was Cândido. In the generation following Cândido's, Manuela was the favoured child. It was she who married first and attained a special position in continuing the household's 'line of descent' and maintaining a concentration of its patrimony. Those siblings not attaining this strategic, favoured position within the natal household's main line of property transmission either never marry (Rodrigo's two aunts and Cândido's three siblings) or marry very late and move out of the natal household (Bento). However, precisely as reported for the Swiss Alpine village of Törbel by Netting (1981:178–85), there is no way to predict which sibling will be the one to marry and stay within the household simply by sex or birth order.

Although subject to a legal rule of equal partition among all siblings, the actual processes of marriage and inheritance within these two households suggest the conscious avoidance of partition. This is achieved through attempts to obstruct or delay marriage and the threats to the break-up of the natal patrimony that each marriage potentially implies. It is important to note that this potential division of the patrimony is not linked in the case of Fontelas to the provision of dowries at marriage, but rather to the ultimate future division in cases of many siblings marrying, staying in the hamlet, and producing children. In this sense, strategies among members of the parental generation are directed towards maintaining *some* children within the household as a source of labour. Optimally, only one of these children will marry, stay within the natal household, and produce children, but the rest must either remain unmarried or leave. In contrast, strategies on the part of an early-marrying sibling remaining in the household (Cândido for instance) may be directed towards the prevention or deferral of other siblings' marriages in the name of a unified patrimony. Underlying these strategies[15] is the rigid rule of *post-mortem* inheritance (Chapter 7) which in any case delays the acquisition of landed property by the younger generation until the deaths of their parents. In a very literal sense, in this community aging parents retain control of their property until their dying day.

This continual dialectic of strategies and counter-strategies between the elder and younger generations must, however, not be granted excessive volitional importance: while much of Bourdieu's analysis of marriage strategies (1976) focuses on such conscious moves and parries, both he as well as Goody stress the local context of inheritance traditions and property relations. It is this total historical, legal, and cultural context – rather than a vaguely defined set of *noumenal normative rules* (Laslett 1984:364) in fact quite reminiscent of Bourdieu's already developed concept of *doxa* (1977) – which sets the stage for a tragic or a comic play, beyond and above the individual gestures of the actors themselves. According to both Goody and Bourdieu, it is the overall context of particular marriage and inheritance systems that will to a large extent set the limits within which specific personal strategies may operate. Within these authors' theoretical models, therefore, the Portuguese pattern examined here – with its stress upon *post-mortem* division and the maintenance of unified patrimonies at all costs – provides a test-case illustrative of the forms through which an overarching 'structure' conditions or indeed almost determines the choices and actions of its component individuals.

This concern with avoiding the partition of landholdings may also clarify the presence of servants within wealthy households. Looking at Rodrigo's household, one is prompted to ask the question: why so many servants? In both 1891 and 1892, six servants were listed as residents of Rodrigo's household. This was the largest number of servants recorded for any household at any date covered by the Confessional Rolls. Following 1892, the number of female servants in Rodrigo's household decreased from three to one. Until 1909, and even in 1940, only one female servant was listed although the number of male servants varied from one to three. There is a suggestion in these figures that when Rodrigo's first wife entered the household (1891–2), fewer female servants were needed for domestic chores. Thus, following Rodrigo's marriage, the number of servants decreased from six in 1892 to three in 1894. In

[15] I use the term 'strategy' here as directly derived from the work of Pierre Bourdieu on Southwest France (1976) and Kabylia in Algeria (1977). The term has two major drawbacks, however. Firstly, it suggests a certain militarism of strategic tactics, and secondly it can be taken to imply an excessive focus upon the behaviour of isolated individuals as maximizers, thus exhibiting aspects of interactionism and transactionalism. Bourdieu's meaning ultimately suggests neither of these possible interpretations, but rather uses the term as a means of linking and *mediating* between the two levels of individual 'choice' and societal 'structure' without placing excessive emphasis upon either one.

1894 Rodrigo's aunt Doroteia died and his elder aunt, Catarina, was listed as being 80 years of age. In this sense, servants could thus be seen as a source of *temporary* labour within the household (female servants) and on the landholding (male servants) in cases of a small resident kin group such as Rodrigo and his two aunts. Servants would be hired during periods of family labour shortage within the household and leave when the household's own labour resources increased (kin moving in, or children growing up).[16]

There are two further possibilities, however. The first is that the presence of servants may be a direct indication of the wealthy household's social welfare role in providing employment and temporary homes for the poor. This is especially apparent if we recall the position of many of the *jornaleira* women initially described in Chapter 3; unable to support large households, young illegitimate children (as well as legitimate ones) from the *jornaleiro* group could serve for varying periods within wealthy households. Informants today consistently stress the positive, advantageous conditions of child servants within wealthy households (good food, gifts in the form of clothing and other goods, perhaps some minimal wages) as contrasted with the shifting, insecure positions of seasonally hired day-labourers. The hiring household also gained a certain amount of prestige: the presence of many servants was an indication of a large landholding, high production levels, and the provision of some margin of leisure time for household members whose menial tasks were thus taken care of by their servants. In this sense, the broader social hierarchy of the hamlet, with the *proprietários* located at the top and the *jornaleiros* at the bottom, is reflected and reproduced within the structure of the wealthy household through an internal hierarchy and division of labour between the hirers and the hired.

A case in point is that of the servant Francisco Silvino, who was listed within Rodrigo's household in the 1898 Roll (Figure 8) as a widower aged 40. In the 892 Roll, Francisco (aged 31) was resident in House 29 (not shown) with his wife (aged 24) and mother-in-law (aged 39). All three individuals were listed as *jornaleiros/as*, and significantly Francisco's mother-in-law was listed as 'single', indicating that Francisco's wife had been born illegitimately. By 1895, Francisco was listed again as a *jornaleiro* but this time with his wife and their newly listed daughter (aged 10). In 1896, immediately prior to the Roll in which we find him as a servant in Rodrigo's household (1898), Francisco was listed as a widower residing only with his daughter (his wife died on 23 January 1896). In other words, shortly following the deaths of his mother-in-law and his wife, Francisco was taken on as a servant in Rodrigo's household for some period

[16] Inácio's household does not indicate this process, however. Throughout its developmental cycle visible to us through the Rolls there were a number of servants resident within the household *along with* a large number of Inácio's children (1909 Roll). See Kussmaul's detailed analysis of servants in England (1981) for some wider comparative points on the position of servants in rural households, and Mitterauer and Sieder (1979:261) for comments on the rapid turnover and circulation of servants in rural Austrian households.

between 1896 and 1899. He reappears (aged 51) in the 1902 Roll residing again with his daughter, in a separate household and by occupation still a *jornaleiro*. Thus Francisco's period as a servant was a short one, and he shifted occupationally from *jornaleiro* to servant and back to *jornaleiro* again over a period of a few years.

The documents are suggestive concerning the possible reasons influencing specific individuals' changes of residence. The case of Francisco is illuminating for two reasons. Firstly, it indicates that not all servants were young and unmarried, but that some (of both sexes) were of advanced ages and in some cases either married or widowed. Secondly, it reveals that wealthy households may have hired both young as well as older servants from the poorer *jornaleiro* group as a form of social assistance and the temporary provision of employment.

But there is a third possibility for the presence of these large numbers of servants. In this case, the hiring of servants may be seen not only as a form of birth-control but more importantly as a kind of *heir-control*. From the point of view of the wealthy hiring households, servants were a means of carrying on large-scale household production without ultimately threatening the unity of the landholding. Servants thus provided a resident source of labour but ultimately had no claims upon the hiring household's patrimony. Significantly, in most hiring households, and Rodrigo's is an excellent example, there is a continual turnover of servants hired for short periods of a few years at a time. The essential structure is one of a permanent servantry regardless of which specific individuals occupy the roles of servants in each consecutive year. In other words, one means through which the wealthy hiring household maximizes both production levels and social prestige is by maintaining a permanent *structure* of servantry producing within the domestic group.

The presence in the hamlet of a large labour-pool of almost landless *jornaleiros* ensured this source of servant labour. Further, there was an added attraction to becoming attached to a wealthy household as a servant: there was always a possibility (however distant) of becoming adopted in time. For a female servant, however, this option was accompanied by the ever-present danger of exploitation by her male employer(s), or indeed by other male farmhands. While for the female servant, an illegitimate child fathered by a wealthy male implied a negative social stigma for both the mother and the child, for the wealthy household itself the long-term effects could be indirectly positive. Through avoiding the multiplication of *legitimate* children within his own household, the wealthy married male also avoided the reproduction of more future heirs to the family's patrimony. Thus a sort of hirer/servant 'concubinage' ensured a limitation of heirs within the wealthy household at the cost of bastard births among servant women, who could at any moment be asked to leave the hirer's household. A number of such cases of illegitimate births were mentioned to me in Fontelas and neighbouring hamlets, and of the three major types of relationship culminating in bastard births (see section below) this was considered by villagers to be the most odious.

Such forms of indirect heir-control do not always constitute contributing elements to the hirer/servant relationship: servants are in most cases hired for their labour alone. In this sense, Rodrigo's household limited the number of potential heirs with claims to the family's patrimony by maintaining a constant, almost institutionalized system of servants moving in and out of the domestic group. As we have seen, only in the case of Dona Elvira in the next generation did the household, out of necessity, adopt the servant Gracinda as its legitimate future heiress. Yet the second household we have examined also maintained a similar structure of a permanent servantry of 3–4 helpers throughout its developmental cycle from 1886 through 1909, despite the presence of many children. With four children as heirs in the younger generation in 1886, another four heirs in the following generation in 1905, and six heirs in the subsequent generation today (the priest and his five siblings), Cândido's household was provided with successive series of heirs and consequently none of its servants were adopted. In other words, while both Rodrigo's and Cândido's households hired servants regularly, Rodrigo's had too few heirs and Cândido's had too many.

A look at a more complete version of Rodrigo's genealogy (Figure 11) may clarify some of these points concerning marriage, inheritance, and servants within the *proprietário* group, particularly as both of the households we have examined through the Confessional Rolls are related and can be traced within the same kindred group.

The genealogy goes back to Dona Elvira's great-grandfather Miguel Pires (6c), who paid the second highest tithe in the parish in 1851. In Generation 5 we note the eldest members of the two households examined above: Inácio Ferreira (5e) appeared in the 1905 Roll diagrammed earlier, and Rodrigo's aunts Catarina and Doroteia (5h and 5i) appeared in listings of Rodrigo's household following 1886. Two of Rodrigo's maternal uncles never married: one became a priest (5f) and the other (Patrício: 5g) had an illegitimate child by Rodrigo's paternal aunt (5a). No further details were given to me concerning this relationship by Dona Elvira (my informant for the genealogy) except that the child later married a *proprietário* from a hamlet in another part of the municipality. Rodrigo's paternal uncle (5b) married out of Fontelas into a neighbouring hamlet. He was termed a *lavrador* by Dona Elvira, while her grandfather (5c) was termed a *proprietário* in addition to his occupation as an alderman on the town Câmara. Thus of Rodrigo's father's siblings, one married and one remained unmarried but had an illegitimate child. On Rodrigo's mother's side only two of six siblings married, and one of these four 'celibate' siblings (5g) fathered a bastard child.

In Generation 4 we find Rodrigo himself (4c) and his two elder siblings (4a & 4b) who both married out of the hamlet. 4a became a Justice of the Peace in a

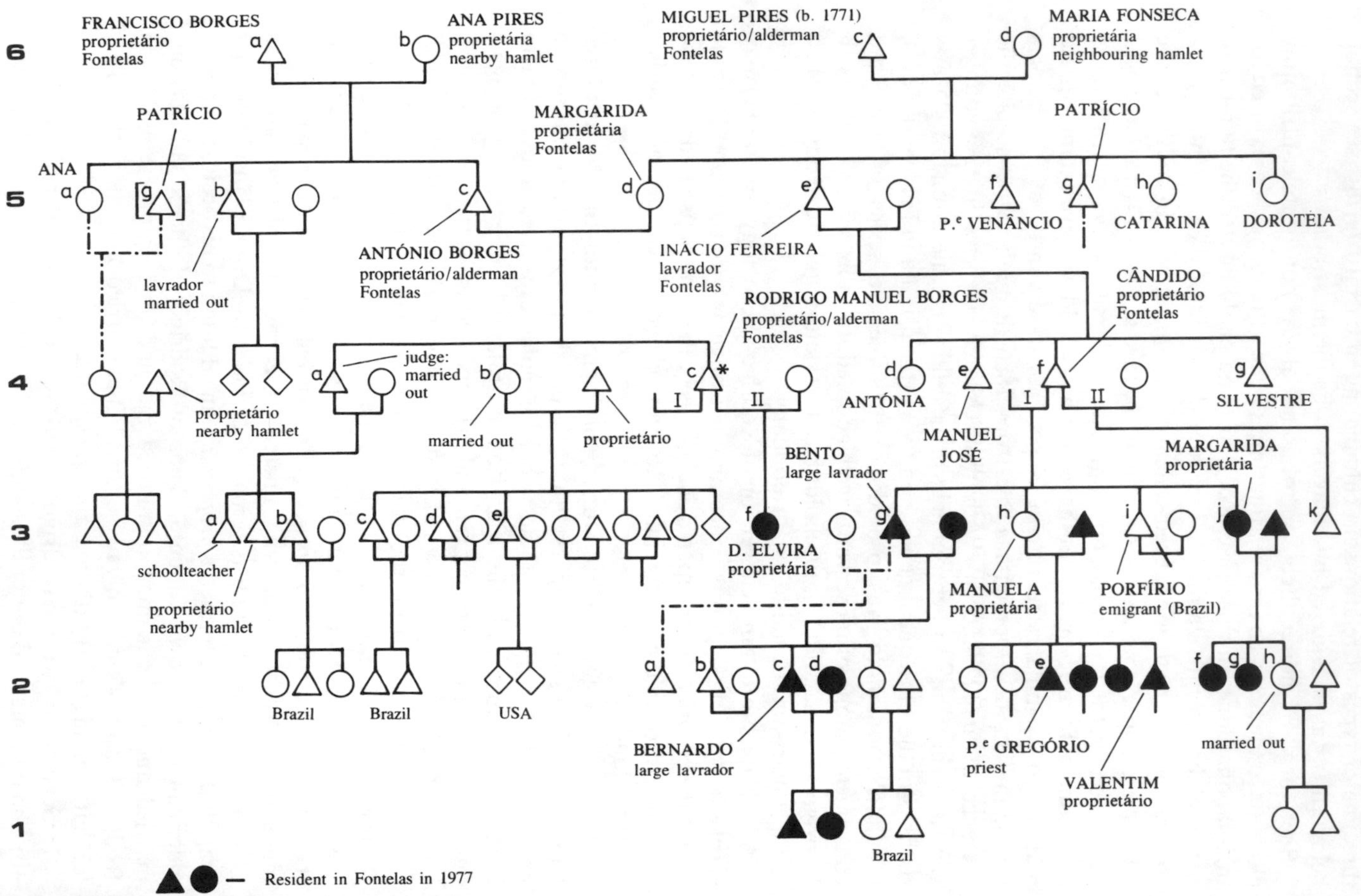

6
FRANCISCO BORGES
proprietário
Fontelas
a
ANA PIRES
b
proprietária
nearby hamlet
MIGUEL PIRES (b. 1771)
proprietário/alderman
Fontelas
c
MARIA FONSECA
d
proprietária
neighbouring hamlet
5
PATRÍCIO
ANA
a
[g]
b
lavrador
married out
c
ANTÓNIO BORGES
proprietário/alderman
Fontelas
MARGARIDA
proprietária
Fontelas
d
e
INÁCIO FERREIRA
lavrador
Fontelas
f
P.e VENÂNCIO
PATRÍCIO
g
h
CATARINA
i
DOROTEIA
4
proprietário
nearby hamlet
a
judge:
married
out
b
married out
proprietário
c*
I
II
RODRIGO MANUEL BORGES
proprietário/alderman
Fontelas
d
ANTÓNIA
e
MANUEL
JOSÉ
CÂNDIDO
proprietário
Fontelas
f
I
II
g
SILVESTRE
3
a
schoolteacher
proprietário
nearby hamlet
b
c
d
e
f
D. ELVIRA
proprietária
BENTO
large lavrador
g
h
MANUELA
proprietária
i
PORFÍRIO
emigrant (Brazil)
MARGARIDA
proprietária
j
k
2
Brazil
Brazil
USA
a
b
c
d
BERNARDO
large lavrador
e
P.e GREGÓRIO
priest
VALENTIM
proprietário
f
g
h
married out
1
Brazil
— Resident in Fontelas in 1977

nearby parish and married a *proprietária* from that parish. Their eldest son (3a) became a primary school teacher, while the children of their youngest son (also a *proprietário*: 3b) emigrated to Brazil. Rodrigo's elder sister (4b) married a *proprietário* from another municipality in the Northern part of Trás-os-Montes, and none of their children returned to Fontelas (the children of 3c emigrated to Brazil and those of 3e to the USA). Thus Rodrigo himself was the only one of three siblings to remain in Fontelas and it was he who remained in the natal household.

Also in Generation 4 were Rodrigo's four first cousins (mother's brother's children) whom we recognize from the 1905 and 1940 listings as Inácio's children: 4d, 4e, 4f, and 4g. In Generation 3 were Cândido's four children, who are second cousins of Dona Elvira: Bento (3g), Manuela (3h), Porfírio (3i), and Margarida (3j). A child born to Cândido's second wife (3k) died unmarried. Finally, in Generation 2 we find the priest (2e), his five siblings, and their seven first cousins. A general pattern appears within the cycles of the two households of Rodrigo and Cândido: while most of Rodrigo's relatives left the hamlet, most of Cândido's kin remained within it.

In terms of inheritance, a striking contrast appears between the heirless Dona Elvira and the multiple heirs of the patrimony concentrated in Cândido's line in Generation 3. On this side of Dona Elvira's kindred group, the patrimony passed in Generation 5 predominantly through Margarida (5d) and Inácio (5e) and not through the unmarried priest (5f) nor Inácio's three younger siblings (5g, 5h, and 5i). The daughter of Ana (5a), unless affiliated or legitimated, would have no claim to any of her natural father's property. As the Confessional Rolls have shown, in the following generation (Generation 4) Cândido (4f) was the only one of four siblings to marry and have children. Consequently, the patrimony passed to his four descendants in Generation 3, the household being occupied today by the priest, one of the priest's sisters, their father, and a young female servant. Although in Generation 3 all four siblings married and had children, in the current Generation 2 four individuals have remained unmarried. In other words, in three of four generations within Cândido's 'family line' there were a number of individuals who never married.

The pattern emerging is that in each generation *some* siblings either never marry or marry very late in life, and in the case of Bento (3g) some have children well prior to legal marriage. An attempt is thus made to avoid the dispersal of property through heir-control and the transmission of patrimony through *as few married children as possible*. Cândido's four children in Generation 3 represent a failure to accomplish this concentration of property, while Dona Elvira herself represents the opposite extreme. A sole heir, she never married, and it was necessary to adopt another heir to prevent her property (in the absence of descendants, ascendants, and siblings-and-their-descendants) from reverting to distant kin whose contact with the hamlet and with Dona Elvira had long since been minimal (Dona Elvira's paternal first cousins in Generation 3). Both Dona Elvira's father's household as well as Cândido's had permanent structures of resident servants, but it was only the aging and unmarried Dona Elvira who was finally forced to adopt one.

In general terms, then, Rodrigo did an excellent job of maintaining his patrimony intact but a poor job of biological reproduction: only his second wife provided him with an heir (Dona Elvira), who herself never married nor bore any children. In contrast, Cândido's children and grandchildren did an excellent job of biological reproduction but a poor job of maintaining Cândido's original patrimony intact. While one household had a lack of heirs threatening extinction of the family line, the other had a surplus of heirs ultimately threatening uneconomic multiple divisions of its patrimony. As we have seen in Chapter 3, this division in fact took place upon the death of Manuela (3h), and the priest and his five siblings now own fractions of this patrimony inherited from two generations earlier. Both Dona Elvira's and Cândido's households, nevertheless, ultimately provided well for the *social reproduction* of the *proprietário* group. Here a strictly materialist analysis might fail to take into account the concomitant social and political strategies of wealthy landed households in the long term: these strategies aim not only at the preservation of an undivided patrimony but also at the maintenance of high social rank and prestige. By adopting a servant who later married her own distant cousin Valentim, Dona Elvira secured an heiress as well as a male heir with high economic standing and a good reputation. In other words, following her great-grandfather, grandfather, and father, all of whom sat on local Câmaras and Juntas, Dona Elvira maintained a household with a large quantity of material capital (land) as well as a long tradition of 'symbolic capital' in the form of ascendants with prestige and high administrative positions (Bourdieu 1977:171–83). Similarly, while the priest and his five siblings partitioned their parents' holding, every one of them has compensated by attaining occupations of high social status: three siblings are addressed as *Dona* or *Padre*, one is a prosperous emigrant, one a wealthy *lavradora*, and Valentim a highly respected and popular *proprietário*. All of these siblings have thus conserved the *proprietário* group's large quantities of symbolic capital in the form of prestigious occupations.

The processes delineated here seem to stand in complete contradiction to those described by Weigandt for the Swiss Alps, where '. . . there is a diffusion of wealth throughout the community over time. This implies that the rich do not pass on their status to their children but then, neither do the poor. We should expect to find that children of the wealthy have relatively less than their parents and children from poor families improve their standing . . .' (1977:143). This relatively eclectic view of the levelling process is repeated at further points in Weigandt's brief analysis: she maintains that '. . . wealth does not remain concentrated among a few families through time but rather . . . there is an up and down movement. In extreme terms, the rich of one generation produce the poor of the next and vice versa' (1977:145). Where are we to locate the circularity of this purported levelling – within the specific Alpine village under study or within Weigandt's own model? All sorts of peasant strategies for the reconsolidation of land plots (supposedly dispersed and fragmented at inheritance) seem to be ignored by the author. Large numbers of siblings do not – in *any* inheritance system – necessarily lead ineluctibly to multiple partitions and the descent of a family to future poverty, nor do poor families generally have fewer children or necessarily rise in status. Thus, for the Russian peasantry, Shanin suggests in a more convincing fashion that 'the cyclical mobility displayed by many households does not presuppose the operation of any mystic equilibrium mechanism or necessary averaging of the prosperity of peasant households over time' (1972:120).

Further data on levelling mechanisms in the Swiss Alps (not corroborative of all of Weigandt's findings) is provided by Netting and McGuire (1982:281–2), and much of the Portuguese material dissected in this chapter indicates inheritance processes (within a nominally partible system) which over many generations have had precisely the opposite effect as those described by Weigandt. There is little if any diffusion of wealth within Fontelas, families tend either to remain in the same wealth-niche as their parents and grandparents or to *descend* in the scale, and as we shall see later the apparently destructive consequences of inheritance divisions are subtly but effectively bypassed through the selection of favoured heirs and the consequent exclusion of secondary co-heirs via late marriage, celibacy, or bastardy.

Ideally, each *proprietário* household must attempt to achieve a balance between an optimum labour supply and a minimization of threats to divide its patrimony. One means of achieving this balance between one extreme (too many children and multiple marriages) and the other (no children and no marriages) is to exert some form of heir-control. With one child and many servants, Rodrigo tipped the balance towards the preservation of the patrimony. In contrast, Cândido's children shifted the balance in the other direction towards a large labour-force. This consequently implied a diminished patrimony through successive marriages and inheritance partitions. It is as if every occasion of matrimony in this society provided a future threat to the patrimony. This threat is materialized in cases of marriages producing children, particularly the marriages following that contracted by *the first in order to marry and stay within the household.* There does not seem to be any rule of preference for which sibling marries first in terms either of sex or birth order, but there is most definitely some evidence of a hindering or even thwarting of the marriages of the subsequent siblings. In some cases this postponement, in the name of the undivided patrimony, implies either celibacy (Rodrigo's aunts and Cândido's siblings) or late marriage (Bento). Further, the early 'strategic marriage' of a favoured heir is usually a prestige marriage in Bourdieu's sense in that it brings into the household an outsider, whereas later 'secondary marriages' tend to be less prestigious and to be contracted between spouses both from the same hamlet.

The rare illegitimacies occurring to wealthy women threaten *both* the material capital (primarily land) and the symbolic capital (prestige) of a wealthy household. This was the case with regard to Ana, Rodrigo's paternal aunt (5a). Natural children always inherit from their mothers but not from their fathers unless they are formally affiliated or legitimated. In contrast, illegitimacies originating from unions between wealthy males (Bento) and poor women may place a dent in the father's prestige but provide no threats to the latter's patrimony. There is thus an emphasis upon the transmission of patrimony through the line of one or two descendants who are strategically those who marry first and stay within the natal household. Of course, some siblings may marry early but marry out, thus easing potential threats to the patrimony. Besides, not all siblings may desire the favoured position in the first place, especially if this position involves a strictly controlled marriage. In other words, among the *proprietários*, the chosen few connect property, marriage, and sexuality. In contrast, secondary heirs remain locked out of the main line of property transmission, may never marry, or may marry very late in life. Further, these informally excluded heirs may be barred from sexual relations altogether (the case of wealthy women) or forced by conditions to engage in irregular, non-marital sexuality (particularly men) with women from the poorer social groups.

Two other *proprietário* households in Fontelas today have also found themselves in similar situations to that of Dona Elvira. In the first case, the schoolteacher Dona Sofia has remained unmarried (aged 53) but her brother heads a school in Lisbon, is married, and has children. With no direct heirs in Fontelas, villagers constantly stress the probability of some of Dona Sofia's property being ultimately willed to her sharecropper Fortunato: a situation similar to Dona Elvira's adoption of the servant Gracinda. In the second case, only one of Margarida's three daughters (Figure 11: 2h) has married and this daughter has left the hamlet. Both of Margarida's elder daughters (2f/2g) remain unmarried at the ages of 43 and 42, and villagers do not view them as likely to marry in the future. This household has no servants and has not adopted anyone in the hamlet as its heir. Unlike Dona Elvira and Dona Sofia who have both provided adopted heirs within Fontelas, Margarida's household and patrimony will become an extinct branch of the family line. Villagers lament the 'waste of women' who never marry in such wealthy households.[17]

[17] An interesting comment by villagers throughout my fieldwork was the following: 'Senhor Brian, why don't you marry Dona Sofia or the priest's sister Dona Prudência? They're both educated, *and they have lots of land*.' My attempts at laughing off these comments due to Dona Sofia's age (53) and Dona Prudência's (42) (I was 26 to 28 during the fieldwork) were consistently parried by villagers' insistence that in Fontelas 'one marries not only a person but their land as well'.

Women at the top of the social hierarchy tend to remain unmarried rather than marrying downwards. Many *proprietário* marriages are contracted across hamlet and parish boundaries. As we have seen, both Rodrigo and Cândido each married twice: all four of their wives were either from immediately neighbouring hamlets or other hamlets in the municipality. Although not entirely analogous, some of these marriages are suggestive of the 'distant prestige marriages' in Kabylia (Bourdieu 1977:52–8) contracted by those with high positions in the social hierarchy. In Fontelas, not to marry at all (in the case of wealthy women) is seen as preferable to marrying down or marrying 'close'. Again, the *proprietário* group seeks to minimize possible threats to the symbolic capital possessed by the kindred group and specifically focused on the position and marriageability of its women. At the expense of celibacy, implying for women a form of non-participation in both marriage and sexuality, some wealthy women remain permanently and exclusively dedicated to their natal household and its patrimony. Blocked from matrimony, Dona Sofia and others in her position are entirely dominated by the interests of patrimony. In the short term they provide labour and assistance for their natal households as well as support for the prestigious positions of those domestic groups and of the *proprietário* group. Although celibate, Dona Sofia is nevertheless a prestigious *proprietária* and schoolteacher. In the long term, however, the absence of heirs will discontinue her family line.

This section has dealt with specific features of household structure within the *proprietário* group as they relate to processes of marriage and inheritance over the generations. Although the sources used present inconsistencies in individuals' names, ages, and occupations, the Confessional Rolls plus the Parish Register plus current genealogies together afford a unique set of multiple references to particular individuals and households over time. However, it is obvious that not all individuals in Fontelas can be traced in all of these three sources: marriages outside the parish, emigration, and other changes in residence may all be invisible and thus leave many individuals unrecorded at certain dates. However, I do propose a cautious use of the records along with contemporary ethnographic materials, rather than dismissing the statistical data in the records as 'virtually useless' or terming the compilers' criteria for occupational classification as 'totally subjective', as Brandes does (1975:71). This analysis should be seen, then, as contributing to methods of reconstruction of 'the entire matrimonial history of the family' (Bourdieu 1976:136) – i.e., each family which contracts a specific marriage at a particular point in time.

The data suggest that despite the existence of a formal ideal of equality between heirs, among the *proprietários* there is a distinct hierarchy of heirs. This hierarchy has less to do with any formal rule of primogeniture or unigeniture than with the privileged position within the natal household of the sibling (of either sex) who marries and stays on the holding. This favoured heir can be either an eldest sibling, a middle sibling, or a younger one, but not all siblings are encouraged to marry and remain in the hamlet.

In an illuminating analysis of matrimonial arrangements in Béarn (Southwest France) Pierre Bourdieu criticizes legalistic analyses which see specific individual practices or strategies of marriage and inheritance as merely mechanical executions of codified laws. Bourdieu states that:

> The only evidence that counts is the practices, and they indicate that all means were justified when it came to protecting the integrity of the patrimony by forestalling the potential division of both the property and the family as a network of competing claims to the ownership of the patrimony, for this threat arose with every marriage (Bourdieu 1976:127–8).

It is precisely this *avoidance of partition* that explains in great part the large number of celibate individuals found in both the Confessional Rolls and the genealogies, as well as the high ages at marriage. Matrimony becomes subordinated to the dominant interest of maintaining a unified patrimony.

It is important to note that these processes of marriage and inheritance do not constitute a 'game' situation in which all individuals may simply strive to maximize their gains and minimize their losses. Chapter 3 and Appendix II show that landed wealth is concentrated in greater quantities among the *proprietários* and large *lavradores* and in conspicuously smaller quantities among the *jornaleiros*. The 'hand of cards' (Bourdieu 1976:122) dealt to the wealthy is already stacked in their favour from the start, while the opposite is true for the poor. Each individual's strategies in marriage and inheritance (among the landed groups) are thus obviously open to individual skill and initiative, but these are put into operation within certain limits already set by 'the entire matrimonial history' of that person's household and social group. This matrimonial history, as the two cases above have shown, involves a structure of *inequality between heirs* which is reproduced over the generations in the interests of the integrity of the patrimony.

A rigid application of the formal rule of equal partition would ultimately (except in cases of sole heirs) plunge multiple descendants into complete impoverishment, much as Cutileiro has maintained at another level that in Portugal: 'If all regulations were observed, the life of the country would be paralysed within twenty-four hours' (1971:199). This is of course an extreme prediction,[18] and in the case of the *proprietários* even a partition among many siblings (e.g., the priest and his five siblings) may not necessarily despoil or pauperize each heir as the sizes of the partitioned holdings may themselves

18 John Davis (1973) provides an excellent treatment of this problem in his study of the South Italian town of Pisticci. Davis dismisses the simplistic reasoning which views partible inheritance as inevitably dwarfing the size of landholdings through consecutive generations of division. Not only are landholdings *not* in all cases partitioned, but a whole series of countervailing processes of land *consolidation* occur which partially offset inheritance partitions.

remain relatively large. As we will see below, the dangers of partition among the *lavradores* and *jornaleiros* are distinctly more acute. Strategies directed towards maintaining an undivided patrimony obviously involve more valuable stakes in land among the upper groups. In contrast, strategies among the land-poor are usually directed either towards the clearing or purchase of land, the consolidation of a large household as a labour unit, or alternatively – permanent emigration. While the wealthy in Fontelas have simply held onto their land, the poor have been struggling to acquire it.

Thus not only is the formal rule of equal partition consistently avoided or postponed – the rule itself affects different social groups to differing degrees. Consequently, among the landed groups a hierarchy of heirs separates a favoured sibling from his or her dependent siblings, who are forced into positions of relative exclusion from the natal patrimony.[19] A strict equality of heirs is difficult to maintain in practice, and the balance is tipped in favour of an informal preference for one heir and one line of property transmission.

Lavrador household

Let us compare the case examined above with the developmental cycle of a *lavrador* household over the same years. The sources used here are the same as those referred to in the last section. The household I have selected is that of the *lavrador* João Pires da Silva, who in the 1892 Parish Tax Listing was registered as owning taxable wealth of 9,960 *réis* (Table 21), a substantially lower sum than those of both Inácio (90,430) and Rodrigo (58,800).

The structure of this domestic group in 1886 (Figure 12) was strictly 'nuclear'. Its residents were the head of household João Pires da Silva, his wife Carolina Pires, and their five children. In 1891 a sixth son (Pedro) was listed, thus giving the household eight resident members. Through 1892 this structure remained strictly nuclear.

By 1894 three changes had occurred. Firstly, the head of household (João) died on 21 July 1892, leaving no will. The Confessional Rolls of course offer no information as to whether the holding was formally partitioned at this time between the six children or whether it remained undivided until the death of Carolina, although the household's structure over the following years suggests the latter. Secondly, an elder sister of Carolina (the widow Maria, aged 50) moved into the household at some time between 1892 and 1894. Finally, it was the third sibling in order of birth (Susana) who married first and at a relatively

19 I must emphasize the adjective in the phrase '*relative* exclusion', as clearly these unmarried or late-marrying siblings nevertheless retain *legal* rights to their shares of the patrimony. But once the favoured heir is established and has borne children, his/her *de facto* control of the patrimony and of household activities overshadows the diminished roles of these other siblings. The latter are obviously not totally excluded, but rather relegated to secondary positions within the household. I will return to this point in Chapter 7.

Figure 12. *Lavrador* household (16 diagrams)

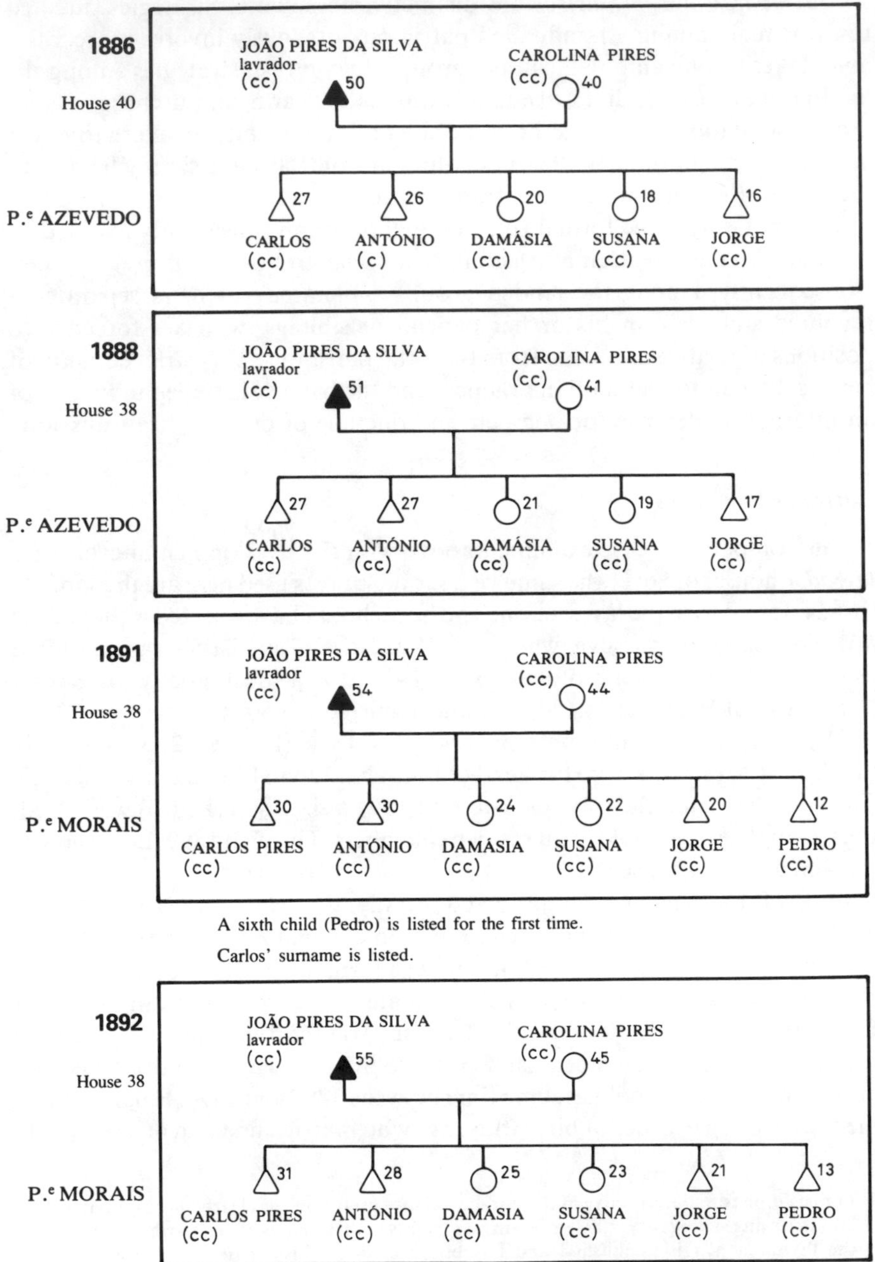

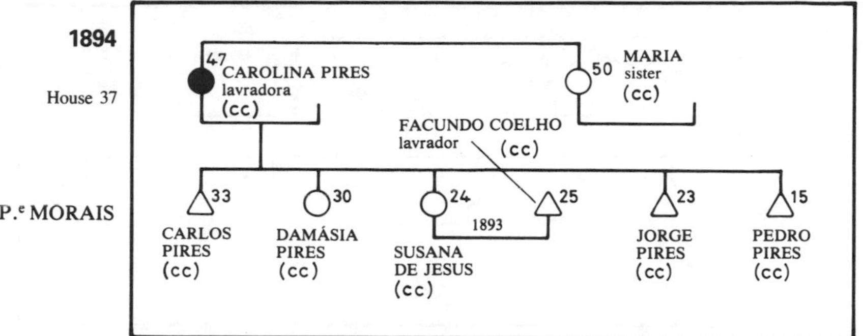

João dies (aged 60) on 21 July 1892, leaving no will.

Carolina's sister Maria moves into the household.

Susana marries a *lavrador* from a neighbouring parish on 14 May 1893.

Surnames of children are listed.

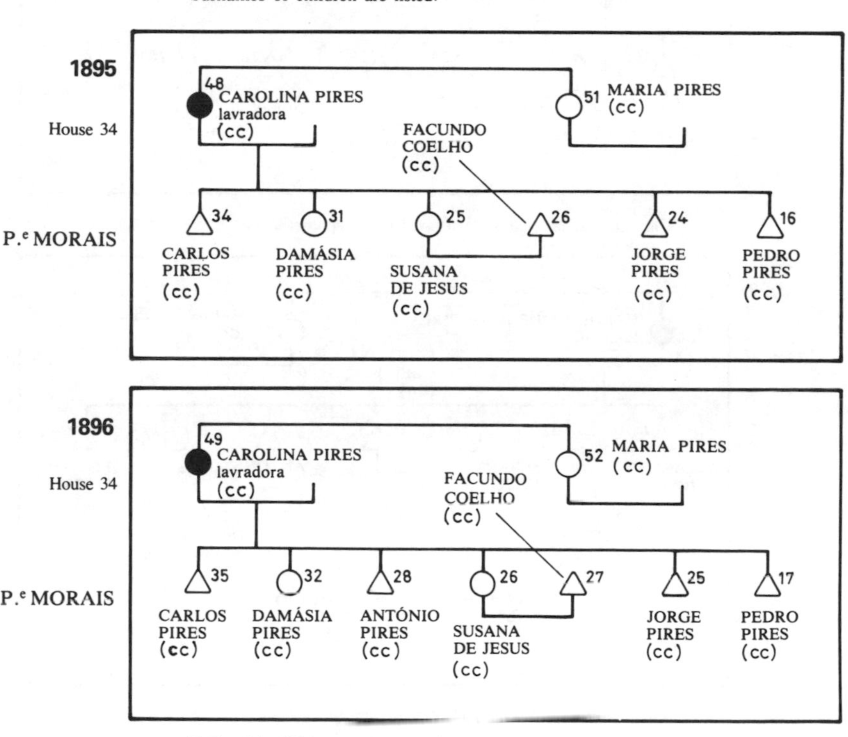

Unlisted in 1894 and 1895, António now reappears.

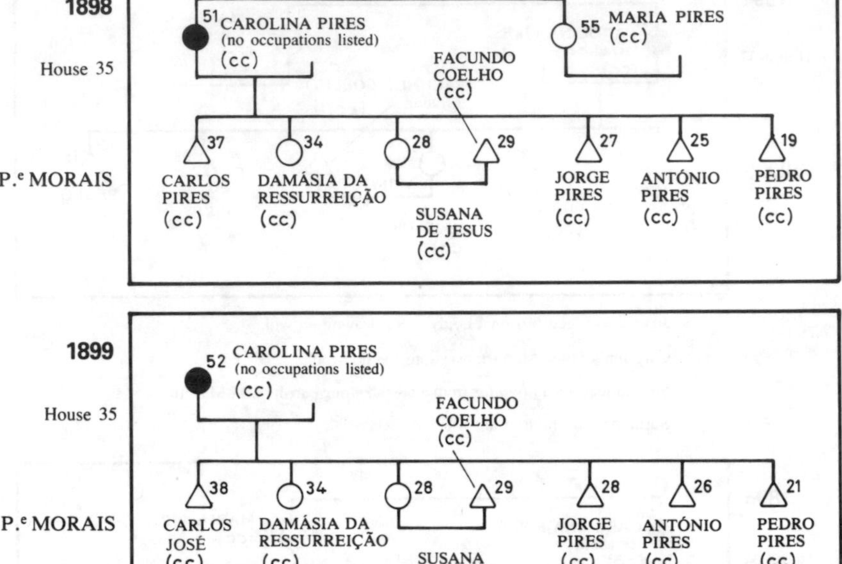

Carolina's sister Maria is not listed (she reappears in 1902).

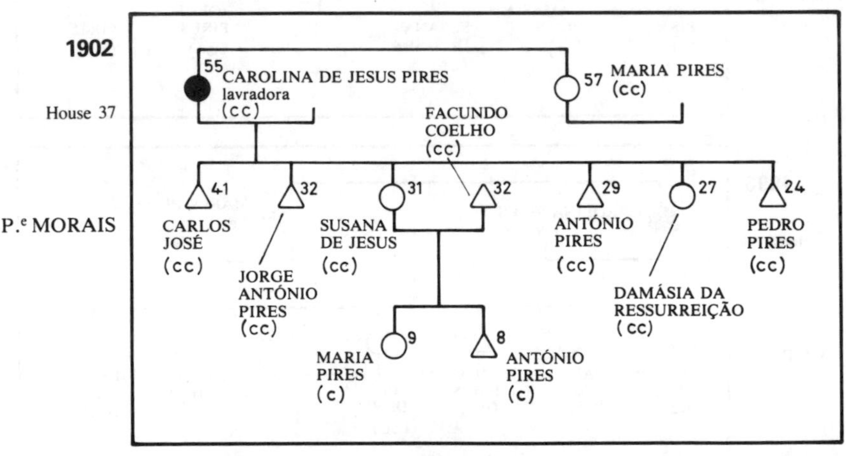

Two children of Susana and Facundo are listed.

Inconsistency in Damásia's age from 1899 to 1902.

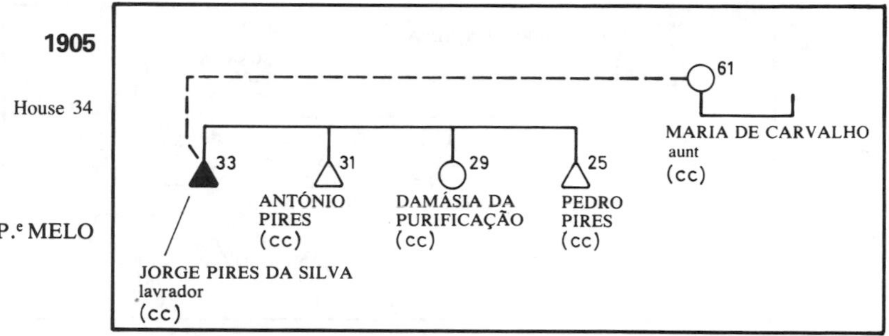

Carolina, Carlos, and the nuclear group of Susana/Facundo/children move out of the household.

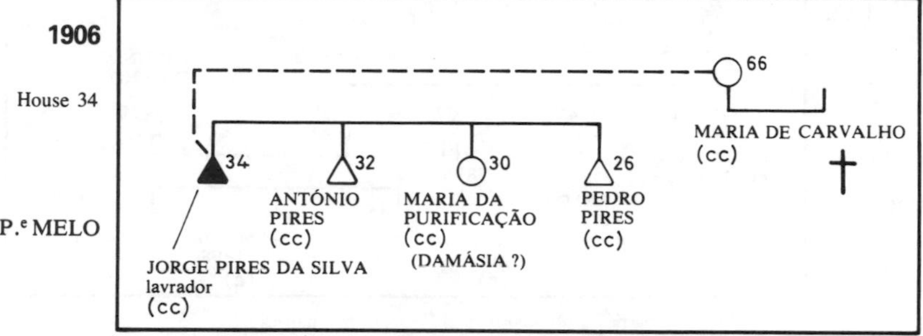

Maria de Carvalho dies (aged 72) on 7 June 1905; although she is still listed in 1906, a cross is drawn following her name.

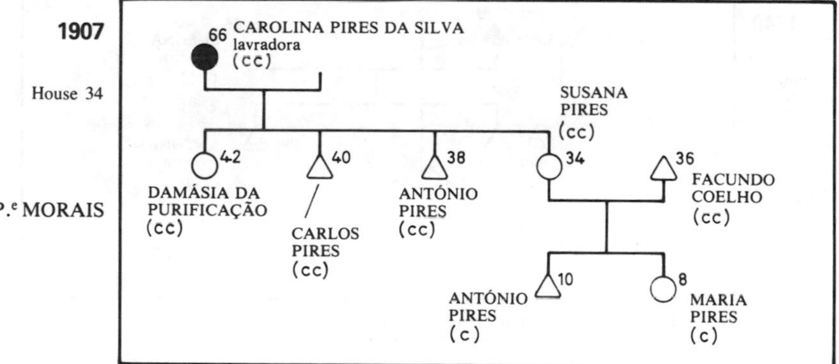

Carolina, Carlos, and the nuclear group of Susana/Facundo/children move back into the household.

Pedro marries in 1906 and moves out.

Jorge is not listed, but he reappears in 1908.

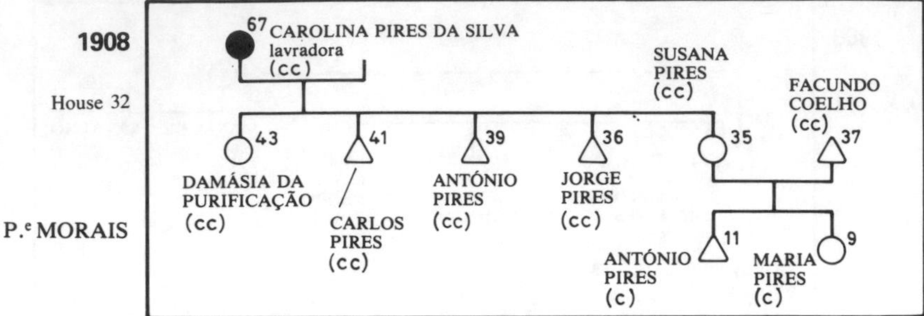

Jorge is listed again.

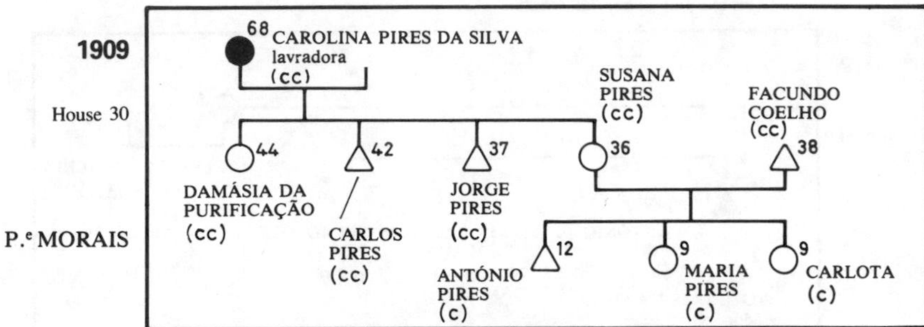

António marries a *lavradora* from Fontelas, and moves out of the household (marriage: 25 January 1909).

A third child of Susana and Facundo (Carlota) is listed.

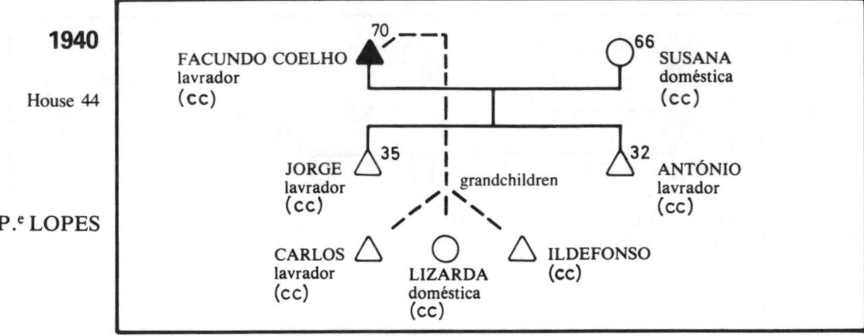

Two sons of Susana and Facundo are listed (note that they have the same names as their uncles — Jorge and António).

Three grandchildren of Facundo are listed (of unspecified parentage).

Susana dies (no age given) on 14 April 1945 of «old age» (no information on will in the death entry).

Facundo dies (aged 82) on 12 April 1951 (no information on will).

young age: she married a *lavrador* (Facundo Coelho) originally from a neighbouring parish but resident in Fontelas at the date of the marriage (14 May 1893). The structure of the domestic group at this point was no longer nuclear, and it held constant through 1899 with only two minor changes: (a) António (aged 28 in 1892) was not listed in 1894 or 1895 but reappeared as a member of the household in 1896,[20] and (b) Carolina's sister Maria was not listed in 1899 but reappeared in the following listing. Throughout this period from 1886 through 1899, the household had between seven and nine resident members.

In contrast to the household of Rodrigo, we note first the complete absence of recorded servants. Further, this domestic group had a larger number of children than Rodrigo's, thus presenting a structure more similar to that of the second household dealt with above: that of Inácio Ferreira. Note also that by 1899 only one of the six siblings in this household had married. Further, the in-marrying Facundo took up residence within his wife's parents' household following his marriage to Susana.

The household's structure following 1894 was distinctly non-nuclear: it was composed of a female head of household (Carolina) and her elderly sister (both were widows) as well as a younger married couple and five unmarried siblings. Thus at the termination of the elder generation's conjugal tie (João's death in 1892) a new conjugal tie was established in the younger generation in 1893, but neither of these changes brought about the break-up of either the natal landholding or the natal household's resident labour group. The large natal household remained the focus of residence and labour: none of its members were listed as *jornaleiros* and it is probable that none of them worked for wages outside the holding. The occupations of *lavradores* as well as the size of the household's taxable wealth suggest (although we cannot prove this) that it worked its own land predominantly with its own labour.

What additional changes occurred in this household's structure from 1899 through 1909, and later by 1940? In 1902 two young children of Susana and Facundo were listed for the first time, probably because they had by now reached the age of 8. In this year the household was at its largest recorded size (11 members) between 1886 and 1909. Further, Susana's two children listed in 1902 only took confession, not communion. Of special significance in the 1902 Roll is the fact that Susana's five siblings were still unmarried: the eldest of these (Carlos) was 41 years of age.[21]

[20] António occupied a rather peculiar position throughout the Rolls. He was constantly shifted in order of birth, and his age was frequently inconsistent from one Roll to the next. Although in the early Rolls (1886 onwards) he was listed as the second eldest, his name was in fact written below those of his younger siblings (??). Through 1892 he was the second sibling in age, but in 1898 he was the fifth. These shifts in age have been reproduced precisely as they appear in the Rolls (although I cannot explain them). The Parish Register of baptisms, always a more reliable source for specific ages, lists António as the *fifth* sibling in order of birth.

[21] Two inconsistencies in ages are evident in these Rolls: Damásia's listed age of 27 did not correspond with her noted ages in 1899 and later in 1907, and António's age from 1906 through 1907 jumped from 32 to 38.

A major change occurred in 1905–6 when Carolina, her eldest son Carlos, and the nuclear group of Susana/Facundo/children moved out of the household. (I could not locate the latter individuals in other households in the hamlet in either of the 1905 or 1906 Rolls.) Remaining in the natal household in 1905 and 1906 were four unmarried siblings and their widowed aunt, Maria de Carvalho.[22] In 1907 Carolina, her son Carlos, and the nuclear group of Susana/Facundo/children had returned to the household. Carolina's elder sister Maria de Carvalho was no longer listed: she had died (aged 72 in the death entry) on 7 June 1905, leaving no will and no children. Jorge disappeared from the 1907 Roll but reappeared in 1908, this time as the fourth sibling, which he had in fact been listed as in earlier Rolls by Padre Morais (1894, 1895, 1898, and 1899).

In 1907, however, Susana's youngest brother Pedro was no longer listed. He had married a *lavradora* (Maria) from Fontelas on 4 January 1906 and moved out of the household. This marriage was particularly revealing when I followed up on Pedro's and his wife's post-marital residence in subsequent Rolls. Like Susana and Facundo, this couple did not immediately reside neolocally, but rather within the household of an aunt of Maria's who was married but childless.

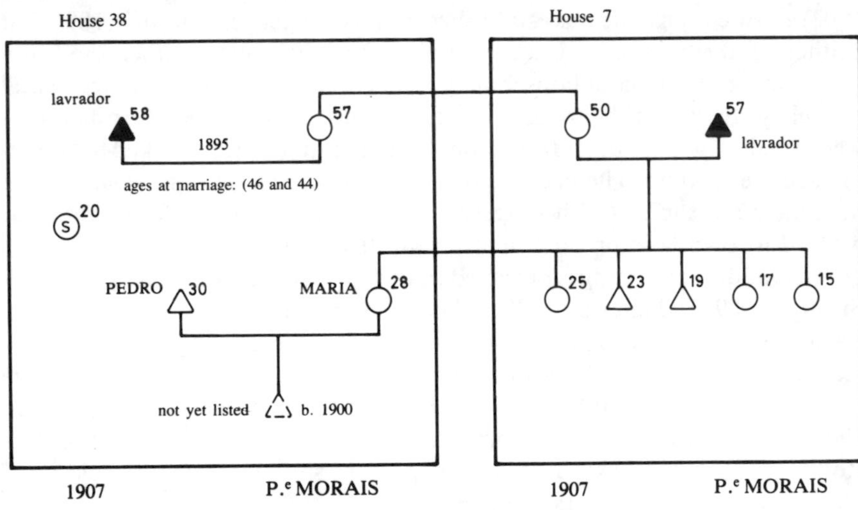

Figure 13. Two *lavrador* households

[22] Maria's name changed from Maria Pires during 1895–1902 to Maria de Carvalho in 1905 and 1906. This may have occurred due to Padre Melo's compiling of the Rolls in the latter two years. Also in 1905, Jorge was listed as the head of household and the eldest sibling, although earlier Rolls placed him as a younger sibling. The change of priests in 1905–6 could have accounted for these discrepancies.

As Maria's natal household was a large household of *lavradores* (both of her parents were resident along with five of Maria's siblings) Maria and Pedro moved into the former's aunt's household (Figure 13) along with a servant. This shift in residence (we can only speculate) indicates a possible emphasis upon assistance for elderly individuals in the form of labour performed by kin or servants. It also suggests a wider preference for the continuing functioning of large natal households over the formation of smaller, neolocal households at each marriage (Chapter 6). Note also that Maria's aunt and the latter's husband were both in their 40s at the time of their marriage (neither spouse had been married before).

Meanwhile, Pedro's natal household in 1908 continued to include only one married sibling (Susana) along with four older unmarried siblings still resident within the household at the ages of 43, 41, 39, and 36. By 1909 one of these siblings (António) had married (on 25 January 1909) and moved out of the household. This time, however, neolocal residence was established, and António and his wife (aged 32 and 34 in the marriage entry) were listed as resident in a separate household elsewhere in Fontelas in the 1909 Roll. Thus, remaining in the natal household in 1909 were Susana, her mother, and Susana's three unmarried siblings aged 44, 42, and 37.

Throughout the latter part of this household's developmental cycle, the nuclear group of Susana/Facundo/children appears as the elder generation's favoured heirs. By the time the last Roll was compiled in 1909, two of Susana's younger brothers (António and Pedro) had married and moved out of the household. Neither of Susana's brothers Carlos or Jorge ever married: I found no marriage or death entries for them referring to their marital status. Although they could conceivably have married out of the hamlet, this does not seem probable, as out-marrying individuals usually have the date and place of their marriage written in the margin of their baptismal entry in the Parish Register: these annotations are meticulously recorded. Susana's sister Damásia did marry but she married a *lavrador* from Fontelas (8 September 1915) at the very late age of 51. In other words, only Susana's marriage was an early one and a strategic one in that it quickly placed her in a special position within the natal household.

By 1940 we find that Susana and Facundo have in fact remained within the natal household and carried on the family line. Two of Susana's and Facundo's children were resident with them (again, *unmarried* at ages 35 and 32) as well as three grandchildren of unspecified parentage, the eldest of whom was listed as a *lavrador*. From 1886 through 1940, we have followed (albeit with a gap from 1909 to 1940) the development of four successive generations of *lavradores* within the same household. The 1940 Roll affords the last picture available to us of the continuing developmental cycle within this domestic group.[23]

[23] None of Susana's and Facundo's children or grandchildren are currently resident in Fontelas.

To what extent can we view the evidence in the Confessional Rolls as conclusive? When the Rolls are supplemented by cross-references to the Parish Register, we learn even more about Susana's household. Of the four marriages contracted by Susana and her siblings, in two cases a child had been born prior to the marriage, and one further case was of a bridal pregnancy. The order of these siblings' marriages and their ages at marriage were as follows (Figure 14): two marrying relatively early, two relatively late, and another two never marrying. The Parish Register is an indispensable and precise source for these crucial dates of births, baptisms, and marriages. For instance, Susana and Facundo were married in the parish church of Mosteiro on 14 May 1893, but their first child had already been born (in Fontelas) only two weeks earlier on 28 April 1893. Significantly, the baptismal entry always notes the date and place of a child's birth as well as the date and place of baptism: in this case Susana's and Facundo's child was baptized on the same day as the wedding, in the same parish church.[24]

Two similar cases occurred at the marriages of both António and Pedro. While Pedro and Maria married on 4 January 1906, the marriage entry explicitly states that the ceremony formally legitimated 'their own true child' born six years earlier on 25 May 1900 and baptized on 13 June 1900 (Figure 14). Despite the birth of this child, Pedro's future wife (and the child presumably) continued to reside for six years in her own natal household with her parents and siblings, while Pedro resided in turn in his own natal household. Only following the marriage in 1907 did Pedro and Maria move into the household of Maria's aunt (Figure 13 above). In other words, the Confessional Rolls alone do not indicate that Maria was in fact an unwed mother for six years: it is only *both* sources (the Rolls and the Parish Register) that reveal this.

In the case of the third sibling to marry (António) a bridal pregnancy occurred. While António and Emília were married on 25 January 1909, their first child was born exactly six months later, on 27 July 1909. The couple formed a new household at this time and were listed as a separate conjugal group of husband and wife in the 1909 Roll. (We do not of course know whether the house in which they took up residence was owned, borrowed, or rented.)

The only marriage of these four siblings which was entirely normal was the last one: that of Susana's elder sister Damásia. Damásia married in 1915 (8 September) and had no children on the date of her marriage nor afterwards. In the 1940 listing we find her residing with her husband and a nephew (aged 13)

[24] Normally, in cases of illegitimate births the phrase *pai incógnito* (unknown father) is used to denote the paternity of the child. In this case, the baptismal entry listed Facundo as the child's legitimate father because the baptism took place immediately following Facundo and Susana's marriage. Therefore, although the child was technically 'illegitimate' for two weeks, on the actual date of the baptism the child was formally legitimated by her parents' marriage.

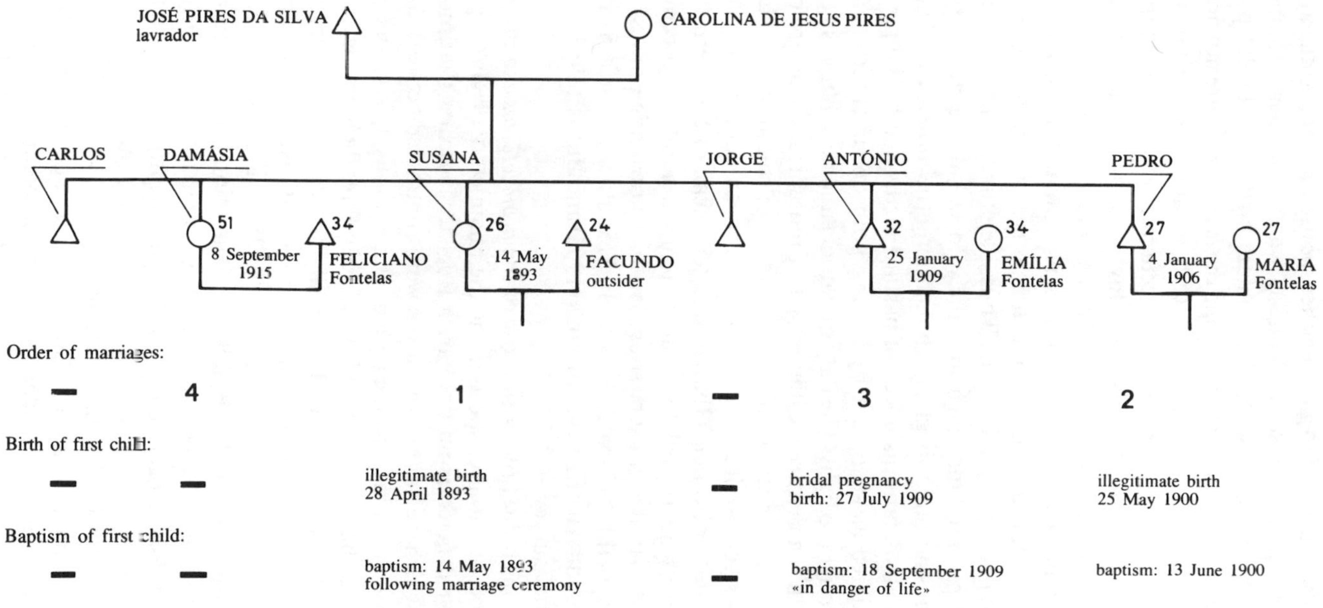

Figure 14. Order of *lavrador* marriages

who was listed as a shepherd. Again, neither spouse was very young at the time of the marriage: as we have seen, Damásia was 51 and her husband 34.

All three of the above cases of illegitimate births and bridal pregnancy suggest that the actual relationships among the *lavradores* were not necessarily as straightforward as the Confessional Rolls would imply. While there are cases such as these of illegitimate births occurring within this group, by and large the illegitimacy ratios have been far lower among them than among the *jornaleiros* (Chapter 7). Situated in the shifting 'middle' of the social hierarchy, the mechanisms and social pressures operative among the *lavradores* place a greater stress upon legitimating unofficial unions and natural children than is the case for the poorer day-labourers. Thus, illegitimate births and pregnancies occurring prior to marriage are likely to culminate more quickly in legitimate unions among this group than among the *jornaleiros*. These three cases were not all blatant instances of bastard births and bridal pregnancies explicitly registered as such, but by linking both documentary sources the patterns are brought to light. The data on Susana and her siblings suggest, at a broader level, that an entirely different set of moral standards are operative here than we would expect in other Mediterranean communities. Here again we note that a circum-Alpine or Central European comparative context is more appropriate for Fontelas than a Mediterranean or Southern European one, in this case with regard to value systems in addition to ecology and economy. Closer parallels must be sought within rural communities located in the southern tier of this Central European area (Southern France, Switzerland, Northern Italy, and Austria) – see Pitkin's (1963) and Burns' (1963) still highly relevant regional surveys.

Comparing this household with those of the *proprietários* examined above, what were the occupations of spouses and their hamlets of origin? A genealogy of Susana reconstructed from the Parish Register indicates that most of the marriages for which we have information were contracted between *lavradores* and other *lavradores*. This was the case in Generations 2, 3, 4, and 5 (Figure 15). In the cases of both José Pires (4a) and João Pires da Silva (3a), two wives married into the hamlet and resided virilocally. In Susana's case (2c), however, the husband married into Fontelas and resided uxorilocally. The three following marriages of Susana's siblings (2b, 2f, and 2g) were all contracted with spouses within the hamlet. Finally, in Generation 1 we have information that 1c and 1f both left Fontelas and that they died in the neighbouring parish of P. in 1963 and 1948 respectively, while 1e married into that parish. 1b and 1d both died at the respective ages of 18 months (in 1896) and 9 months (in 1900); I was unable to obtain further information on 1a.

Here again we note the pattern also evident among the *proprietários*: early marriages usually bring an outsider spouse into the natal household, while late marriages are usually between two spouses *both* natural to Fontelas. The marriages in Generations 2, 3, and 4 exhibit this pattern. It is significant in the

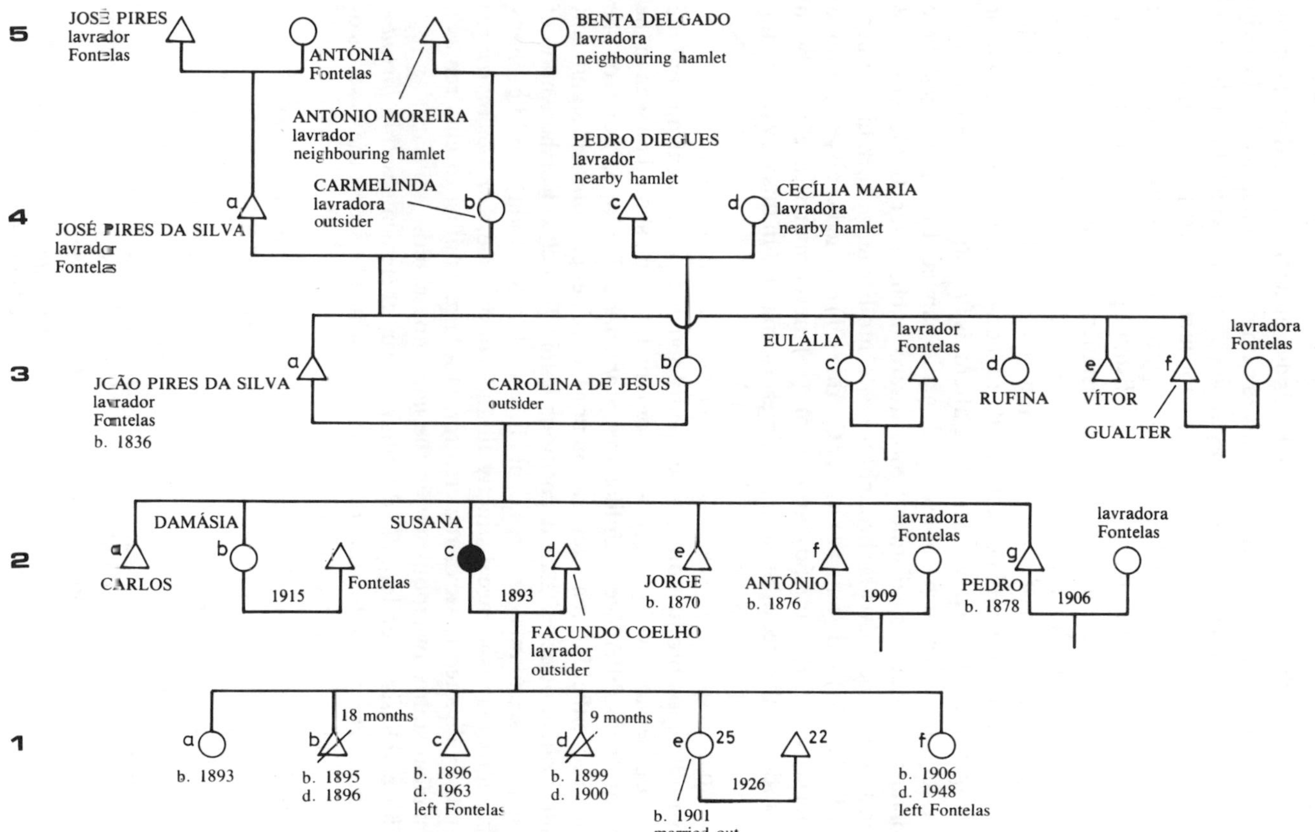

Figure 15. Genealogy of the *lavradora* Susana

cases of both of the *proprietário* households as well as Susana's, that the early strategic marriage of the sibling who stayed within the natal household was in each case a marriage across hamlet or parish boundaries which brought in an outsider affine. Both Susana's father (also the first to marry) and grandfather married in this way: both brought wives into Fontelas from outside the community. This pattern suggests the distant prestige marriages of the *proprietários* as well as the *de facto* relinquishment by in-marrying spouses of rights to their natal holdings in their own hamlets. (An in-marrying spouse such as Facundo would of course legally inherit land and other property in his natal hamlet, but he would be likely to sell, rent out, or lend that land to kin or co-villagers there.) Marriages occurring after this first strategic one tend to be late and usually between spouses within the hamlet. In some cases these secondary marriages are distinctly 'downward' in character. In Generation 3 for instance, while João (3a) brought his wife into Fontelas, both his younger sister Eulália (3c) and younger brother Gualter (3f) married spouses natural to Fontelas, while Rufina (3d) and Vítor (3e) never married. Similarly in Generation 2, all three of Susana's siblings also married in this way (marrying late and with spouses natural to Fontelas).

Compared with the *proprietários*, the *lavradores* confront a different set of constraints upon production. Consequently marriage, child-bearing, and the absence of servants within most households in this group should be seen in the light of these differences. Unlike the *proprietário* Rodrigo, none of the members of either Susana's generation nor that of her parents held significant administrative or ecclesiastical positions within Fontelas. Further, none of Susana's descendants are resident in the hamlet today. While many *proprietário* marriages are distinctly alliances of prestige, *lavrador* marriages are mostly directed towards the creation of a large number of children as a permanent source of labour within the natal household.

This emphasis on children and labour as crucial elements within *lavrador* households is expressed in the following song, which lists a mother's series of possible choices for her daughter's marriage:

1 Oh Joaquina, Oh Joaquininha, Behind that hill, You're in love, you're in love, Over there with a carpenter.	*1 Ó Joaquina, Ó Joaquininha, Trás daquele outeiro, Andas em namoro, andas em namoro, Lá com um carpinteiro.*
2 Carpenter – no, carpenter – no, He'll bolt our door, Rather a soldier, rather a soldier, Who marches in the army.	*2 Carpinteiro não, carpinteiro não, Que nos tranca a porta, Antes soldadinho, antes soldadinho, Que marcha na tropa.*
3 Soldier – no, soldier – no, He might not know how to march, Rather a barber, rather a barber, Who knows how to shave.	*3 Soldadinho não, soldadinho não, Não sabe marchar, Antes barbeirinho, antes barbeirinho, Sabe barbear.*

4 Barber – no, barber – no, He sharpens knives, Rather a tailor, rather a tailor, Who will make our skirts.	*4 Barbeirinho não, barbeirinho não, Que amola as navalhas, Antes alfaiate, antes alfaiate, Que nos talha as saias.*
5 Tailor – no, tailor – no, He might be a liar, Rather a student, rather a student, Who's more of a lover.	*5 Alfaiate não, alfaiate não, Que é min* mentiroso, Antes estudantinho, antes estudantinho, Que é mais amoroso.*
6 Student – no, student – no, He might mess up the bran, Rather a blacksmith, rather a blacksmith, Who can strike an iron.	*6 Estudantinho não, estudantinho não, Que amassa o farelo, Antes ferreirinho, antes ferreirinho, Que malha no ferro.*
7 Blacksmith – no, blacksmith – no, He would get all black, Rather a mason, rather a mason, Who can split stones.	*7 Ferreirinho não, ferreirinho não, Que anda muito negro, Antes pedreirinho, antes pedreirinho, Que escacha o penedo.*
8 Mason – no, mason – no, He'd make too much noise, Rather a peasant, rather a peasant, Who can plough our land.	*8 Pedreirinho não, pedreirinho não, Causa muita guerra, Antes lavrador, antes lavrador, Que nos lavra a terra.*
Sung 18/5/1976	* i.e., *muito*

Each one among the list of occupations of possible husbands is discarded in favour of the final choice of a *lavrador* 'who can plough our land'. In three of the verses (2, 4, and 8) the mother speaks significantly of '*our* door', '*our* skirts', and '*our* land' thus stressing the utility of the in-marrying husband within the wife's parents' household.

In a thoroughly rural community in which almost everyone engages in full-time agriculture, an extreme emphasis is placed upon labour and the value of such vital activities as ploughing and harvesting. Ideally, every *lavrador* household strives to work its own land with its own labour: members of this group rarely engage in wage labour and they do not normally hire labourers or servants. Unlike the *proprietários*, these individuals are not seen as actual or even potential helpers of the poor, and the expectation of social welfare or humanitarian assistance from them is nowhere visible either in the form of donations of food or the hiring of child servants. While today the *lavradores* rent large quantities of land, their ideal is that of the self-sufficient peasant located between the extremes of the hiring *proprietários* and the semi-proletarian *jornaleiros*. Their marriage strategies are thus directed towards providing abundant sources of labour (in-marrying sons– or daughters-in-law) and large numbers of children. The song above quite rightly stresses their concern with labour.

Throughout the Confessional Rolls, it is among the *lavradores* that we consistently find the biggest domestic groups and the largest numbers of children. These are also the households with the most frequent cases of stem family structures of two conjugal pairs. Susana's household is thus similar in size to Inácio's household, although in structure it never contained a comparable permanent supply of resident servants. Unlike the wealthiest domestic groups, most households in this group did not use the hiring of servants as an indirect form of heir-control. In this sense, it is crucial to supplement data on household size with information on household structure. While both *proprietário* and *lavrador* households were large in size in the Confessional Rolls, their structures were very different with respect to the presence or absence of servants. My examples clearly reveal this difference.

A *lavrador* household was thus confronted with a more acute tension between the goals of maintaining its patrimony intact and providing a large labour group for household production. While a partitioned *proprietário* holding may not impoverish a large number of heirs, a smaller holding is constantly in danger of doing so. Each *lavrador* household attempts to enlarge its labour supply by rearing many children from a single conjugal pair, which in turn ensures that one or more of these children will assist their parents as they age. This emphasis on child-bearing occurs at an early stage in the household's developmental cycle, and is followed by the starting of a second reproductive group through the marriage and continued residence of *one* of its children. Again, secondary marriages are either delayed or never occur, and as we have seen in the genealogy above these secondary marriages tend to produce fewer children. The first and strategic match of the favoured child must thus optimally be an early one, thereby beginning the bride's reproductive cycle at a young age.

The ultimate conclusion of this cycle is final partition. For instance, while Susana's parents did an excellent job of biological reproduction (6 children), some form of heir-control must have been exerted in the interests of maintaining a viable holding. Two possible means of achieving this (apart from Rodrigo's example of an only child and many servants) were to stall the marriages of some siblings and to block the marriages of others. Again, each occasion of matrimony *following* the first strategic marriage tends to pose a potential future threat to the patrimony. When these strategies directed towards maintaining a unified patrimony are not entirely successful, some of the household's members must inevitably leave the holding or marry down. This is precisely what occurred in Generation 3 in the case of João's siblings (Figure 15), as we will see in the section below. While João himself remained a *lavrador*, two of his siblings became *jornaleiros* and one a *cabaneira*, or cottager. It was João who attained the strategic position in his natal household by marrying early and staying put, while each of his siblings remained to a certain degree excluded.

To summarize, the characteristic features of *lavrador* households are the following: large households with many children from one couple, the absence of servants, few prestige marriages, and some form of heir-control through the separation of a favoured sibling who marries early from secondary heirs who marry late if at all. While in general terms it could be stated that *proprietários* marry for rank, in contrast *lavradores* marry for labour. This emphasis on the household as a labour unit is constantly emphasized today in verses, songs, and statements stressing the value of prospective spouses' abilities to work and to produce. The phrase *é muito trabalhador* (he works a lot) stresses the value of hard work and is a compliment to a boy's or a man's reputation. Precisely the same phrase is used for women: *é muito trabalhadora.* A household is regarded as *forte* (strong) and 'wealthy in labour' if it has many children who have good working habits. One villager thus stated that the large *lavrador* Delfim was 'the richest man in Fontelas' due to his large and hard-working household of six (husband, wife, three daughters, and one son). Most *lavrador* households are thus judged primarily by both the quantity and the quality of their labour resources.

Although some *lavradores* will occasionally hire servants, this is rarely done on a permanent basis, and is usually limited to one or two servants but never as many as five or six. Thus in 1977 the large *lavrador* Miguel hired the young servant Eulália (aged 20) neither out of a desire to assist the latter's mother (the wife of a *jornaleiro*) nor as a means of minimizing threats to his household's patrimony through heir-control. Rather, Eulália was hired primarily as a source of labour and as 'an extra hand around the house': Miguel's wife's only child was deformed at birth and confined for life to a crib. Further, while the relationship between a *proprietário* and his servant could be seen as a kind of patron/client tie, the smaller size of most *lavradores*' landholdings and the minimal number of servants hired by them do not suggest this sort of relationship. The prestigious position of having a sizeable team of male and female servants working on an extensive landholding is reserved solely for the *proprietários.*

How then have the *lavradores* confronted the inevitable conflict between a multiplicity of heirs and the goal of delaying or avoiding the division of a patrimony? Like the *proprietários*, this group is obliged to exert some form of heir-control through selection of a favoured heir who marries early and stays on the holding. The parental generation exerts strategies of control over the labour of their children and their childrens' timing and choice of marriage. It is important to note here that these strategies are directed *informally* towards the reproduction of the household labour group through a preferred child. This is often quite a prolonged process and it usually begins while the children move from childhood into adolescence, as the parents watch the growth of each sibling and the potential of each of them for responsible and effective farm management. Among the very wealthy – particularly *proprietária* women – celibacy constitutes an entirely respectable and honourable alternative to conjugal life, and in effect kills two birds with one stone by avoiding yet another sibling's marriage and reproduction while at the same time maintaining the celibate's own (and the household's) high social rank. Further, marriages are not effected through the simplistic 'arrangement of marriages by the elder generation' thereby obliterating any power held by the younger generation. *Both* generations employ different kinds of strategies, thus generating a constant dialectic inside each domestic group. These strategies are extremely difficult to pin down clearly, but the data presented so far indicate that a definite pattern is operative among both of these landed groups. The marriages of many of a household's children are either severely trammelled or entirely thwarted, but the means through which this is accomplished (the strategies) are extremely subtle. I will return to this point in Chapter 7.

The prime goal is to delay the final *legal* partition of the holding which grants each heir an equal share. Strategies of delay tend to take place during a specific phase of the developmental cycle, usually at the point that some of the children reach marriageable ages. These strategies continue after the death of one of the parents, which is the first point at which the heirs may legally choose to effect a partition. In this sense, the rule of *post-mortem* inheritance itself contains a built-in mechanism further delaying the acquisition of property by the younger generation: no one can inherit anything until one or both parents have died. The actual outcome of inheritance partitions is another matter: the residence locations, marital statuses, and individual claims of the heirs upon the natal holding obviously vary with the particular circumstances of each heir at the time of the partition. But it is precisely this ultimate division that both parents (and later the surviving spouse) attempt to forestall. Even after the death of the surviving parent (e.g., Inácio's household following 1905: Figure 9) although a partition may occur between the heirs, the latter may remain together within the same producing household for many years afterwards.

The *lavrador* household thus faces an optimum phase of high labour resources until a second conjugal pair (Susana and Facundo) begins to take on the principal role in household production as well as biological reproduction. It is crucial to note here that at no point do the aging parents physically move out of their households into adjoining rooms or buildings as they retire from farming. In no sense do they hand over *de jure* direction of the household (labour) and the holding (land) to the younger generation until the actual dates of their deaths, although of course a kind of *de facto* shift in household authority may take place as the parents grow very old and particularly following the death of either parent. As first one and then the second parent dies, attempts *by the parents* to delay partition may shift to attempts *by the favoured heir* (Susana for instance) to retain unmarried siblings and their shares of the patrimony within the natal household group. Both the division of the patrimony and the dispersal of the household labour group are thus avoided. The future threats to the patrimony viewed from afar by the parents

18 *Lavradores*, ca. 1954 (enlargement of an old photograph).

are thus sharpened and heightened between the inheriting siblings at the moment of partition. By this time the favoured heir has long since married, produced children, and informally taken over the natal household. This was the pattern in the case of Susana and Facundo, although we have no concrete information on what actually took place in terms of inheritance following Susana's mother's death (post-1909).

Another point of relevance here is the use or avoidance of wills. In Susana's situation, either of her parents could theoretically have left her 1/3 of their total property in a will (Chapter 7). Wills by a parent to any of his/her children are extremely unpopular and are frequently the cause of bitterness and severed relations between the favoured recipient of property and his/her secondary heirs. Such a will of course formally installs a particular sibling as a chosen legatee and thereby institutionalizes a real and formal inequality between siblings. Cases in which some heirs suspect that a will has been illegally 'fudged' in favour of one child are usually taken to court, where the legitimate heirs dispute the will in order to effect a proper division. However, by and large most married individuals with descendants do not leave wills and the situation described above of the informally privileged position of a favoured sibling is far more common.

The significant point here is that *lavrador* households must try to achieve a balance between (a) maximizing their labour resources, and (b) minimizing future divisive threats to the patrimony. Unfortunately, bearing many children (which is what in fact most *lavradores* do) shifts this balance towards the former (a large labour group) thereby guaranteeing future problems with the latter (many competing heirs). In broad terms, the parental generation does a good job of biological reproduction and installs a favoured heir, but it leaves the concomitant future conflict between multiple heirs to be faced between the siblings *after* both parents' deaths.

Unlike the situation among the *proprietários*, fewer possibilities for heir-control are open to this group. Firstly, servants are not employed on a regular basis and thus do not generally serve as substitute labourers without inheritance claims. Secondly, while very wealthy women who remain celibate retain high social positions as property-holders or professionals, this is not the case for *lavrador* women. Unmarried or celibate women in this group are distinctly pitied. They occupy a peculiarly ambiguous position, possessing neither the high status of *proprietárias* nor the low status of *jornaleiras*, and they are in constant danger of becoming part of the latter group by falling lower in the social hierarchy. Unless they marry early, they will find it either difficult to marry up or undesirable to remain secondary members of a married sibling's household.

In contrast to the situation faced by celibate *proprietárias* (no marriage is better than a bad marriage) the *lavradora* faces a different set of choices: for her, any marriage is better than no marriage at all. Two courses are usually followed – either marrying late (Susana's elder sister Damásia) or bearing natural children outside legal marriage altogether. As we will see in the section below, the latter course carries the imminent danger of some measure of social ostracism through illegitimacy, and it constitutes a process whereby a *lavradora* may 'fall into the proletariat' through her position as an excluded heir (Le Roy Ladurie 1976:62–3). Blocked from the main line of property transmission by the favoured heir (male or female), these secondary female heirs are likely to descend in the hierarchy both through the delay in their acquisition of inherited property as well as through their irregular, non-marital unions. This is precisely what occurred in the case of Rufina examined below, a *jornaleira* whose elder brother was in fact the *lavrador* João Pires da Silva.

Lavrador men occupy a distinctly different position. Although secondary male heirs may be victims of heir-control, they certainly do not as a rule engage in any regular form of birth-control.[25] My argument in Chapter 7 will stress that the high proportions of illegitimacy in Fontelas cannot be explained satisfactorily by the absence of birth-control, nor solely by cases of exploitation of poor women by wealthy landowners, nor by the failure of the Church to raise the low moral standards of the local population.[26] Rather, illegitimacy is linked closely to *post-mortem* inheritance and to the avoidance of partition through the informal institution of separating one favoured heir from many secondary ones. The latter (particularly male heirs) are locked out of the main line of property transmission which descends through their married sibling (the favoured heir) but they are not entirely denied all sexual relations. Thus, as is the case among the *proprietários*, a few individuals are chosen as those who may join marriage, property, and legitimate sexuality. The rest must remain celibate, marry late, or establish sexual relationships outside legal marriage. It is this surplus of unmarried men who are in fact the 'unknown fathers' of the bastard children of a small number of *jornaleira* women. Much of the information in the Confessional Rolls, the Parish Register, and the genealogies I have collected points toward this conclusion.

Lavrador households are faced with a particularly acute tension between the

25 Although a number of wealthier women today use the pill (*pílula*) as a form of contraception, I was told that the most common form of birth-control in Fontelas formerly was *coitus interruptus*.

26 I return to this point briefly in Chapter 7, but here I wish to emphasize that illegitimacy may not be solely linked to the strong (or weak) role of the Church or particular individual priests. There is a tradition of anticlericalism in Fontelas, although this is by and large a Catholic community in which most villagers pay at least minimal, token respect to the Church. This can be seen in their regular mass attendance, their participation in patron saints' festivals, and their at least tacit acceptance of the religious ceremonies accompanying baptisms, weddings, and burials. My argument is that *despite* the far stronger role of the Church here than in Vila Velha (Cutileiro 1971), the high ratios of illegitimacy here are linked to a particular form of property transfer which either delays or ultimately prevents the marriage of many of the hamlet's inhabitants.

interests of matrimony (many children) and those of patrimony (an undivided holding). This conflict is sharper partially due to the smaller amounts of landed property owned by this group in comparison with the *proprietários*. The same system of favoured and secondary heirs is operative nevertheless, although with different results. *Lavrador* households must produce many children in order to maximize labour returns and to provide exchange partners for cooperative tasks with other domestic groups. Produce children, marry one child and produce grandchildren, maximize labour: but by no means allow *all* of one's children to pursue this course or the ultimate result will be mass impoverishment.

The basic structural tension between the interests of matrimony and those of patrimony is expressed in the real conflict between the favoured heir and secondary heirs at the moment of partition. Who will receive what, and who will remain within or leave the natal household? As we will see, this underlying tension is never entirely resolved in structural terms: the *thesis* of the parental generation's maintenance of the patrimony is challenged by the younger generation's *antithesis* of marriage and reproduction, which pose ultimate threats to the patrimony. The tension between the older generation's strategies of maintenance and the younger generation's counter-strategies of marriage are mediated and temporarily delayed through the selection of a favoured heir. Patrimony and matrimony are structural opposites, but the rule of *post-mortem* inheritance appears to be a game which places a good hand of cards with the parents and a poor hand with the tacitly excluded children. The only *synthesis* of this opposition on a larger structural level is the social reproduction of a large number of bastard children locked out of both patrimony and matrimony.

Jornaleira household

The third and final case-study is that of the *jornaleira* Rufina, the unmarried mother of four illegitimate children by 'unknown fathers'. Rufina probably occupied a position far lower in the social hierarchy than the *lavradora* Susana. While the latter's father had taxable wealth of 9,960 *réis* in the 1892 Tax Listing, Rufina was not even registered. This suggests either that Rufina owned so little property as to preclude her inclusion on the list of parish taxpayers, or that she was not present at the time the Tax Listing was compiled. The latter possibility is contradicted by Rufina's presence in all of the Confessional Rolls prior to and following 1892. Like Rufina, 13 other *jornaleira* women were listed in the Confessional Rolls but not in the 1892 Tax Listing (Table 21), suggesting that their property was negligible. Some may of course have been entirely landless.

Some idea of the context from which I have chosen Rufina as an example can be derived from the following figures. In the 1896 Roll, for instance, there were

45 households listed in Fontelas. Six of these households were headed by *proprietários*, one by a blacksmith, 14 by *lavradores*, and 24 by male or female *jornaleiros/as*. Thus in 1896 more than half of the hamlet's households were headed by either a male or a female day-labourer. Within this group, of the 11 male heads of household two were widowers, six were married (one without his wife present) and three were single. The figures for adult women in this group (heads of household or wives of heads) in the same year are more revealing, however: of the 19 adult women in the *jornaleiro* group, five women were widows, five were married, while nine were single. One of the latter was resident with a single man in a consensual union. In other words, a large number of households within this group were headed by an unmarried, day-labouring woman. Usually these women resided alone or with one or more of their illegitimate children. An analysis of all of the households in this group in the 15 Confessional Rolls reveals two major types of *jornaleiro* household: (a) a predominantly nuclear structure of a married couple with children, and (b) a 'matrifocal' unit of a single mother with bastard children. Rufina's case most clearly represents the latter type, and it is this type of domestic group that I will concentrate on here. Rufina's household thus provides a striking contrast to the *proprietário* and *lavrador* households examined above.

The first Confessional Roll of 1886 listed Rufina Pires as an unmarried *jornaleira*, aged 30 and living alone (Figure 16). In 1888 the household's structure was identical – Rufina was again living alone. In 1891, however, a daughter appears in the listing, Carmelinda (aged 9). The Confessional Rolls alone would suggest that this was Rufina's first child, now appearing in the Rolls once she had reached or passed the age of 8.

Again, the value of two documentary sources is here beautifully illustrated: the Parish Register of baptisms indicates that Carmelinda was in fact Rufina's *second* illegitimate child. Another daughter had been born to Rufina on 25 May 1877, five years prior to Carmelinda's birth on 23 August 1882. (This elder daughter reappears later in the 1898 Roll.) Each of Rufina's two daughters was explicitly registered in her baptismal entry as a *filha natural*, or 'natural child'. Carmelinda's baptismal entry stated that she was the daughter of Rufina and an unknown father (*pai incógnito*).[27] In other words, the Confessional Roll alone listed Carmelinda as the daughter of an unmarried woman (Rufina was listed as single), but our second source (the Parish Register) allows us to confirm that this daughter was in fact an illegitimate child. Further, the two sources together tell us not only which individuals resided inside the household over the years in question, but also which ones resided outside it as well.

[27] In the majority of cases, this formula of *pai incógnito* is explicitly stated in the baptismal entry, but it is a strictly legalistic term, quite distinct from the moral values held and expressed by villagers in everyday life. Of course, the biological father may in fact have been known to the priest, and in most recent cases of illegitimacy in Fontelas the entire hamlet knows who the 'unknown fathers' of bastards really are.

Figure 16. *Jornaleira* household (18 diagrams)

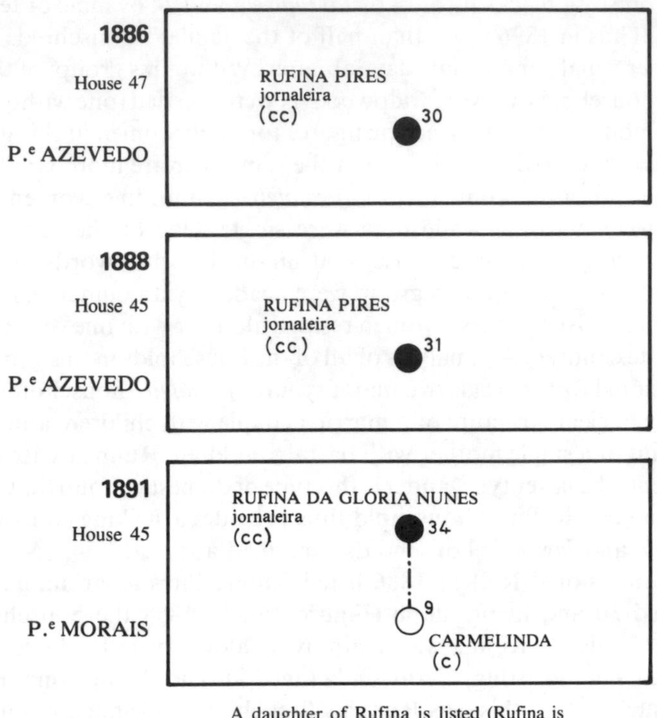

A daughter of Rufina is listed (Rufina is explicitly listed as *solteira*, or 'single').

Different surname listed for Rufina (?): the surname 'Pires' was her father's, but 'Nunes' was not her mother's.

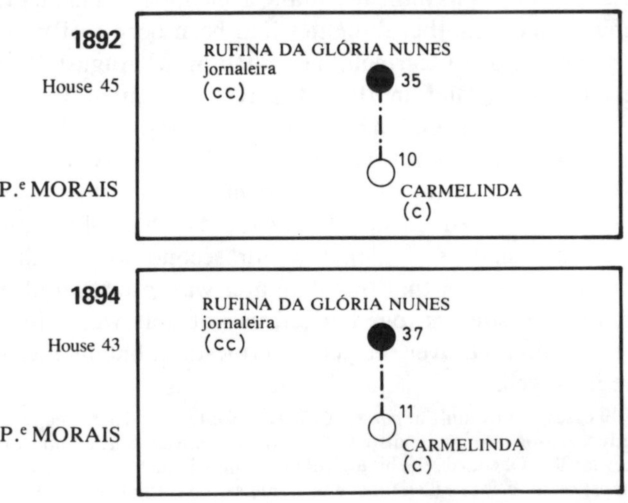

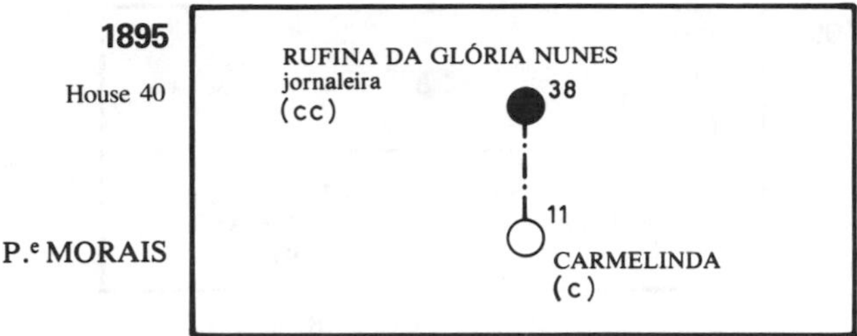

Inconsistency in Carmelinda's age from 1894 to 1896.

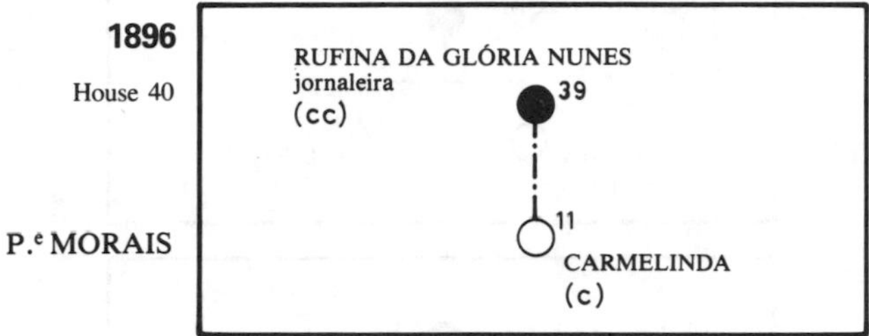

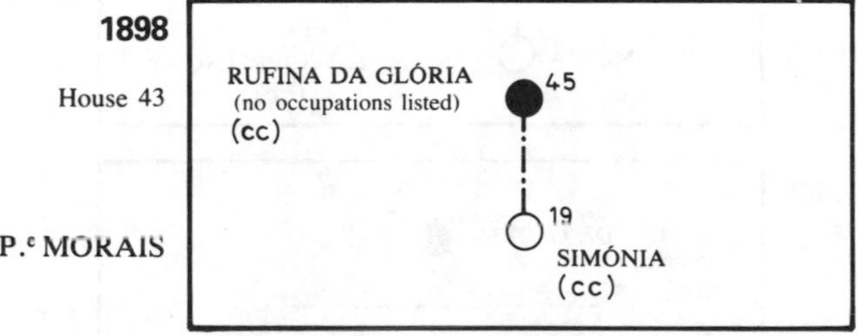

Carmelinda moves out of the household, and another of Rufina's daughters (Simónia) moves in.

Rufina's surname is no longer listed.

Inconsistency in Rufina's age since 1896.

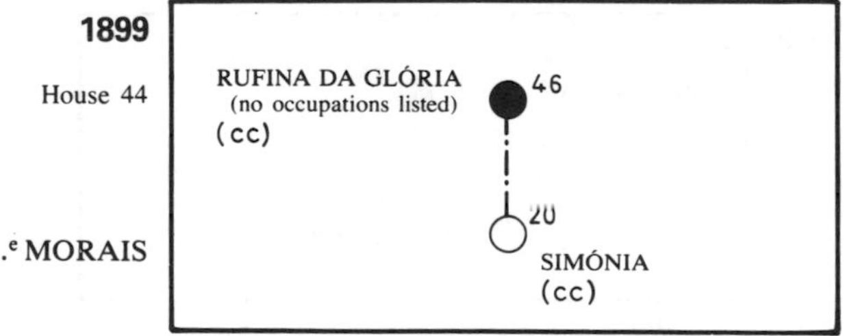

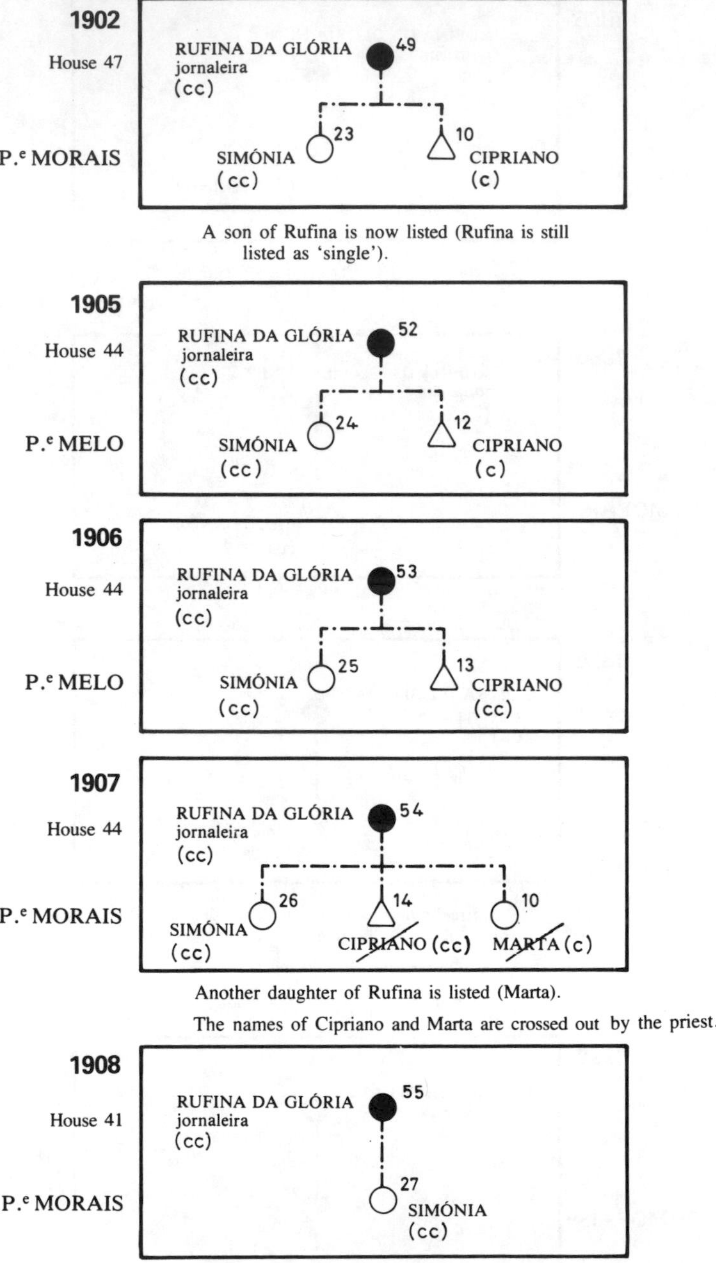

Cipriano and Marta move out of the household (possibly prior to the date of compilation of the 1907 Roll).

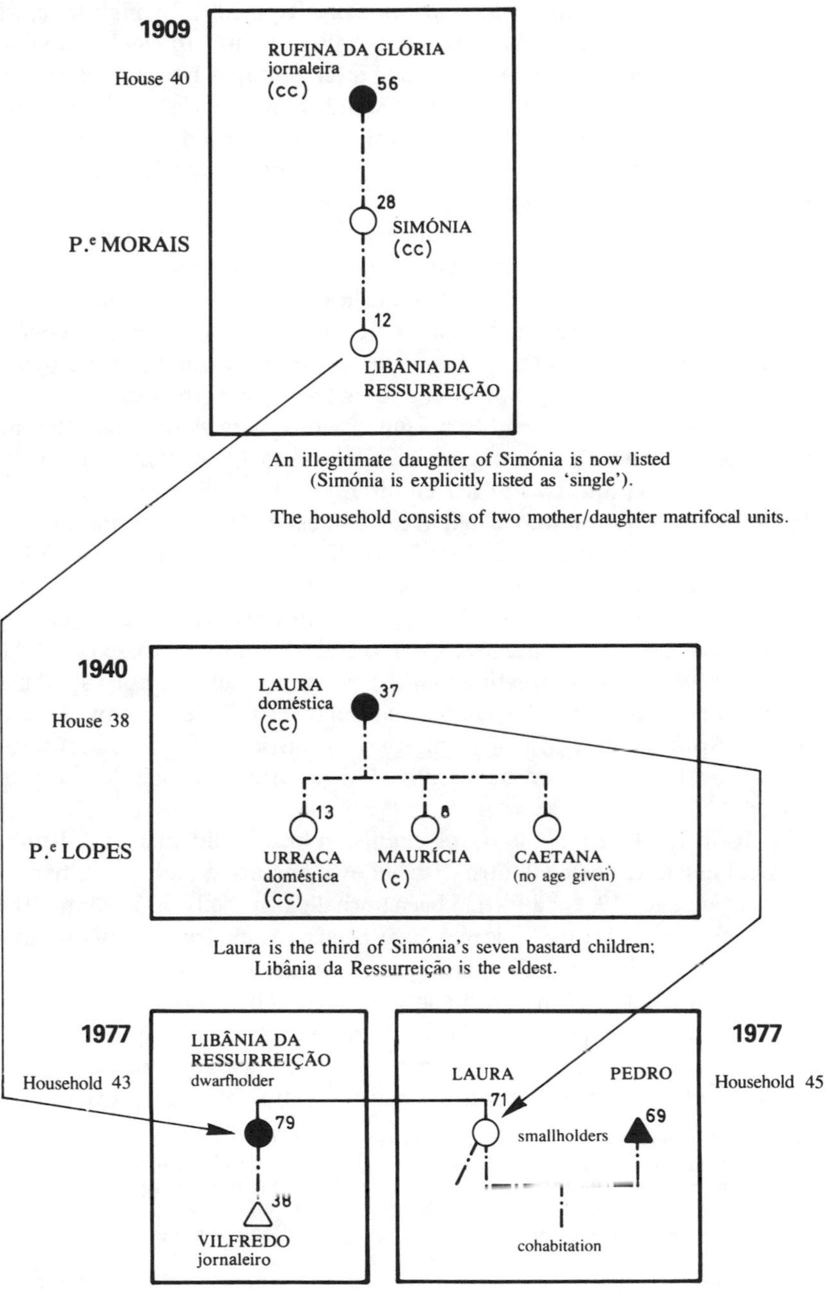

An illegitimate daughter of Simónia is now listed (Simónia is explicitly listed as 'single').

The household consists of two mother/daughter matrifocal units.

Laura is the third of Simónia's seven bastard children; Libânia da Ressurreição is the eldest.

The household's structure remained the same from 1891 through 1896, with Rufina and her daughter Carmelinda as its only residents. In 1898 Carmelinda was no longer listed: Rufina's eldest daughter Simónia had moved into the household with her mother. Rufina's second daughter Carmelinda became 'invisible': she was not listed in her mother's household at any later date covered by the Rolls, nor did she appear as a servant in any other household in Fontelas in 1896 (nor in the death entries following 1896). Imprecise recording of ages again presents a minor problem: there are inconsistencies in both Carmelinda's age from 1894 through 1896, and in Rufina's age from 1896 to 1898. By 1902 a third child was listed in the household: Cipriano (aged 10) was born to Rufina on 19 February 1888. Cipriano was also a 'natural child' of Rufina and an unknown father. There is no way of determining from either the Confessional Rolls or the baptismal entries (or even both sources together) whether any of these three children's unknown fathers were in fact the same man.[28] The household's structure remained the same from 1902 through 1906, comprising Rufina and two of her children.

In 1907 three children were listed in the domestic group, this time including Rufina's fourth child Marta, aged 10. Marta had been born on 29 March 1891, and she was listed also as the illegitimate daughter of an unknown father. In 1908 the household became smaller again, with only Rufina and her eldest daughter as residents. The names Cipriano and Marta were crossed out by the priest in the 1907 Roll, suggesting that they may have left the household prior to its date of compilation. We can only speculate as to where the two younger children Cipriano and Marta went: they could have become servants in Fontelas or elsewhere, or have moved into other households or other hamlets.[29]

Finally, in 1909 we find a striking change in household structure. Rufina's daughter herself was listed in turn with her own bastard daughter – Libânia da Ressurreição, aged 12. Libânia had been born illegitimately on 15 March 1898, also of an unknown father. This may have been a reason for Simónia's moving into her mother's household in the same year that her child was born (1898), which was the first Roll in which she was listed. The household at this time consisted of not one but two matrifocal units, each one comprising a single mother with an illegitimate daughter by an unknown and absent father.

By 1940 yet another generation of bastard children had been born to two of

[28] Occasionally, there is a baptismal entry in which the name of the father of an illegitimate child is listed. These are usually cases in which the child's parents were cohabiting or intended to marry, and in which their later marriage legitimated the child. One particularly revealing case of registered paternity occurred in 1729. A natural daughter was born to a woman from Fontelas, but the father was explicitly named as 'Padre B.' by the priest compiling the Parish Register (Padre C.). Such cases of priests being registered as the fathers of the bastard children of servants or poor women are quite rare, although there are innumerable jokes and sayings about this pattern in Fontelas today.

[29] It is difficult to follow changes in the residence of servants as many of those in wealthy households were listed with only one Christian name, thus making their full identification problematic.

Rufina's granddaughters, Libânia and Laura. Libânia gave birth to an illegitimate son (Vilfredo) on 17 July 1936. Today she and her only son (one of Fontelas' five *jornaleiros*) live together in the same household. Vilfredo's current age is 38 and his mother's, 79. Further, prior to Vilfredo's brith, Libânia's younger sister Laura had already given birth to the first four of her eight illegitimate children in 1927, 1929, 1932, and 1934. Three of these children were listed in the 1940 Roll: Urraca, Maurícia, and Caetana. Today, none of Laura's eight children live in Fontelas, and Laura (aged 71) lives alone with her common-law husband Pedro (aged 69), now a smallholder but formerly a child servant in Fontelas.

The 15 Confessional Rolls again afford us a sequential look at one portion of the developmental cycle within the household of a *jornaleira*. This 'skeleton' of generational change, however, can be amplified and combined with genealogical information derived from both the Parish Register and contemporary informants. Figure 17 presents this additional information.

Two characteristics are immediately apparent from a glance at this genealogy: the large number of illegitimate children born to unmarried mothers, and the small number of marriages. For example, in Generation 3 it can be stated with reasonable certainty that only one of Rufina's four children ever married. Simónia (3a) had seven bastard children but never appeared in the marriage entries of the Parish Register. Carmelinda (3b) also never appeared in either the marriage entries or the baptismal entries as a mother: it is probable that she never had any children. Cipriano (3c) died unmarried on 29 May 1913 (aged 24) leaving no will and no children. However, Rufina's fourth child married in 1933: Marta (3d) married a *jornaleiro* from Fontelas but subsequently bore no children. Marta's and her husband's ages at the date of their marriage were 41 and 30 respectively. No information is available on inheritance partitions between these four siblings, although there was not likely to have been much property to divide in the first place considering Rufina's generally low economic position. Rufina died on 22 December 1925 (aged 68), an unmarried *jornaleira*, leaving children but no will. The household was resided in successively by her daughter Simónia and then in turn by the latter's daughter Laura (2c). The building itself is small and cramped, and is located at the end of a row of four connected stone houses (Map 3 – H45). At the other end of this row reside Laura's sister Libânia (2a) and her son Vilfredo (1a), in an equally small and unassuming house (H43).[30]

[30] Yet another irregular relationship is evident here in the case of Libânia's son Vilfredo. Following Libânia's death in early 1978, the hamlet spoke much of Vilfredo's relationship with a dwarfholder woman in Fontelas, herself the unmarried mother of seven illegitimate children by four different fathers. While Vilfredo lives alone, his 'girlfriend' Lucrécia lives with her two youngest children in a tiny house on the edge of the Western side of the hamlet (Map 3 – H2). Although the tie is not one of cohabitation, Lucrécia can be seen frequently entering and leaving Vilfredo's household. Villagers laughed at the prospect of their marrying – Vilfredo is 38 and Lucrécia 50 – and compared the couple to the other four couples in Fontelas who currently live together in cohabitation. A number of villagers commented that 'they're "married" just the same'.

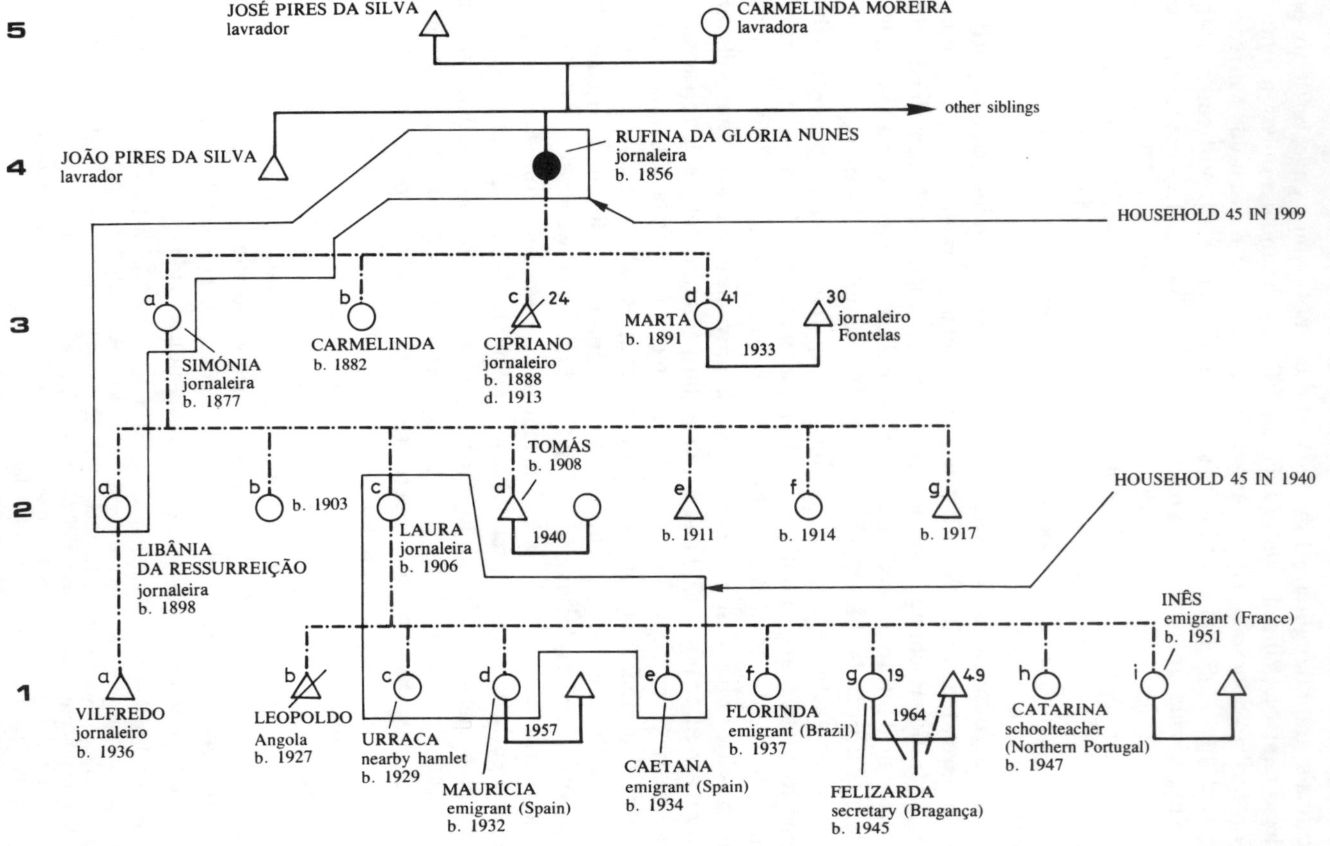

Figure 17. Genealogy of the *jornaleira* Rufina

The movements of the individuals in Generation 2 were more difficult to follow. For four of these seven siblings, I was able only to locate birth and baptismal dates (2b, 2e, 2f, and 2g), suggesting either migration or marriage outside the hamlet. Tomás (2d) married in the district city of Bragança in 1940. None of these five individuals nor any of their children were resident in Fontelas at the time of my fieldwork. Finally, both Libânia and Laura have remained in Fontelas and both have borne illegitimate children. Most of the individuals in Generation 2, then, have either left Fontelas or have become otherwise invisible in the records.

These details indicate a particular problem with the location of specific individuals from the *jornaleiro* group in the records: they are highly mobile and are not easily traced. In contrast to the *proprietários* and *lavradores*, many members of this group do not remain in their natal households as unmarried siblings. This is due principally to the smaller sizes of landholdings within this group as well as the smaller sizes of domestic groups: a *jornaleiro* household simply could not support a large group of resident kin. Further, many of these villagers have shifted residence at one time or another as day-labourers within Fontelas, servants, or seasonal migrant labourers outside the parish. While many of the *proprietários* and *lavradores* tend to remain within their natal households (married or celibate) and 'tied to the land', the reverse is true of this poorer group: they are neither tied to the land nor necessarily permanent residents in their natal households. Although the succession of children born within wealthier landed households can usually be followed chronologically through the Confessional Rolls, in the case of the *jornaleiros* this is far more difficult. Various children appear, disappear, and reappear within the household at different times. This pattern suggests frequent changes in household structure and high mobility, similar and often linked to the movements of servants in and out of *proprietário* households.

A number of other studies using historical sources on the poor have noted the same problem. Kussmaul, for example, has perceptively pointed to the invisibility of servants in early modern England:

> Farm servants were, in many respects, invisible to the state. While under contract, they were submerged beneath the broadly circumscribed authority of their masters . . . The normal relation of servants to the state was indirect, mediated through their masters. They were subject to personal taxes, such as the subsidy, poll tax, and marriage tax, but their masters were either responsible for paying the tax, deducting it from wages, or liable to pay the tax in case of default (1981:33).

Mitterauer and Sieder (1979) have also noted high mobility among Austrian rural servants, and McArdle has reported a similar pattern for rural Tuscany: 'Different family behavior has already been noted in the registration of births and marriages, in the formation of last names, and between rich and poor generally; these differences may even extend to domestic relations. Different family cultures at Altopascio only reinforce what other indicators already underline: the real differences in the villagers' lifestyles according to class and social structure' (McArdle 1978:155). In addition to highlighting the dangers (1978:56–7) of limiting family reconstitution studies to the non-mobile families of a community (possibly an a-typical minority within the local context), McArdle goes on to suggest that this high mobility among the poorer social classes constituted one element of 'the multiplicity of the obstacles to the creation of a sentimental family line' (1978:142). This comment alone opens McArdle's passing mention of semi-proletarians (1978:128) to a much wider sphere concerning the affective links (or lack of such) of peasants to the land. By confronting the annoying problem of tracing the mobility of the landless or land-poor rural groups, McArdle has keenly tuned our documentary attention to the implicit necessity for following the movements of this shifting labour-force which – although invisible through the prism of many historical sources – remains a crucial pivot within many a rural class system.

Continuing with Rufina's genealogy in Generation 1, of Laura's eight children, one died at a relatively young age (Leopoldo: 1b) while three of her seven daughters have married. Maurícia (1d) married a Spanish husband and is permanently resident in Barcelona, while Inês (1i) married a husband from another hamlet in the area and both currently reside in France. Felizarda (1g) married a smallholder in Fontelas (himself the father of an earlier illegitimate child) but this marriage had broken a number of years ago and is currently in court as a formal divorce proceeding. Laura's remaining four daughters are unmarried (1c, 1e, 1f, and 1h). During my fieldwork, all of Laura's six younger children (with the exception of Florinda: 1f) paid at least one visit to Fontelas and stayed in their mother's household. Visits by Felizarda (1g) and Catarina (1h) are particularly frequent as the district city of Bragança is only a short 1½ hour bus ride away, while the region where Catarina teaches is also only a few hours away by bus. Significantly, all eight of Laura's children have left the hamlet and each time they return, these trips are seen as 'visits to kin' and short-term assistance around the house. The scale of Laura's agriculture is so small that no form of assisting labour is needed by Laura's two sons-in-law when they visit. Neither Laura nor her common-law husband owns a plough team and between them they own only 2.83 hectares of land (some additional land is rented). In this sense, in contrast to the holding of the *lavradora* Susana, there was very little land of Laura's for any of her children to remain on in the first place. Thus in both Generations 1 and 2, very few individuals actually remained in the hamlet in their natal households. This pattern is quite the opposite to that visible in Rodrigo's genealogy, where most of Inácio's descendants have remained.

Laura's own marriage was a particularly unusual event, and her secret wedding provides a striking contrast to the customarily grandiose and public weddings of *lavradores* and *proprietários*. Laura's nuptial ceremony was in fact a perfect negation of Fontelas' ideal of a large public ritual. It took place on 19

December 1977 at 7 a.m., in secret, with the minimal individuals necessary for the ceremony: these were Laura, Pedro (her cohabitor), the priest, and two witnesses (one of Laura's daughters and Pedro's niece Dona Sofia). Further, the wedding took place many years after all of Laura's children had been born. But why all this secrecy? A wedding at dawn, no banquet, a minimal ceremony, and a conspiracy of silence.

I did not attend the wedding (in fact no one was invited apart from the priest and the two witnesses) and I was told the next day by the priest as well as by Laura's daughter that 'the hamlet did not even know of the marriage'. I was also asked not to mention the wedding in order to avoid embarrassing the newly married couple. Only many weeks later did it become public knowledge in the hamlet, and villagers' comments were both humorous and matter-of-fact. Pressure from the priest as well as from a number of Laura's daughters led the couple to their decision to marry. As neither spouse owns much land or other property (they farm a total holding of less than 4 hectares) there was little material reason underlying the match in relation to inheritance. Pedro, the natural father only of Laura's four younger children, had already been living with Laura in her household for many years in a consensual union. The ages of the two spouses at the time of their marriage were particularly striking: Laura was 71 and Pedro 69.

In fact, *all three* of Pedro's siblings have also lived in consensual unions for a time in Fontelas, both of Pedro's sisters bearing illegitimate children prior to their marriages. A brief look at this sibling group will illustrate further aspects of these irregular relationships among the *jornaleiro* group: Figure 18 presents these ties. Firstly, Tomásia (3c) had borne her first son Ambrósio (2b) ten years before marrying the large *lavrador* Bento (3b) – the biological father of all three of Tomásia's children. (We recall that Bento had fathered an illegitimate child – 2a – earlier by a woman in a neighbouring hamlet.) In the 1940 Roll, Bento and Tomásia were both listed as living within the same household. However, over the words stating their marital statuses (single in both cases) was written the word 'married' (*casado*). In this case, the Roll explicitly registered the *actual* legal relationship between the two individuals: prior to their wedding on 12 August 1943 they were in fact not yet married but cohabiting. Significantly, their third child Paula (2d) was baptized immediately following the marriage ceremony. Again the documents are extremely detailed and revealing: the marriage entry explicitly states that at the time of the ceremony, Tomásia and Bento recognized and legitimated 'their own true children'.

The second sibling, Liberata (3e), married the *proprietário* Lázaro (3d) following the death of the latter's first wife in 1922. However, Lázaro had already had a child (2e) by Liberata, who herself was a child servant in his household in 1923, three years prior to their marriage. Liberata was 16 at the time, and 19 at the date of their wedding. The legitimation of the child through the subsequent marriage of her biological parents proved significant in later

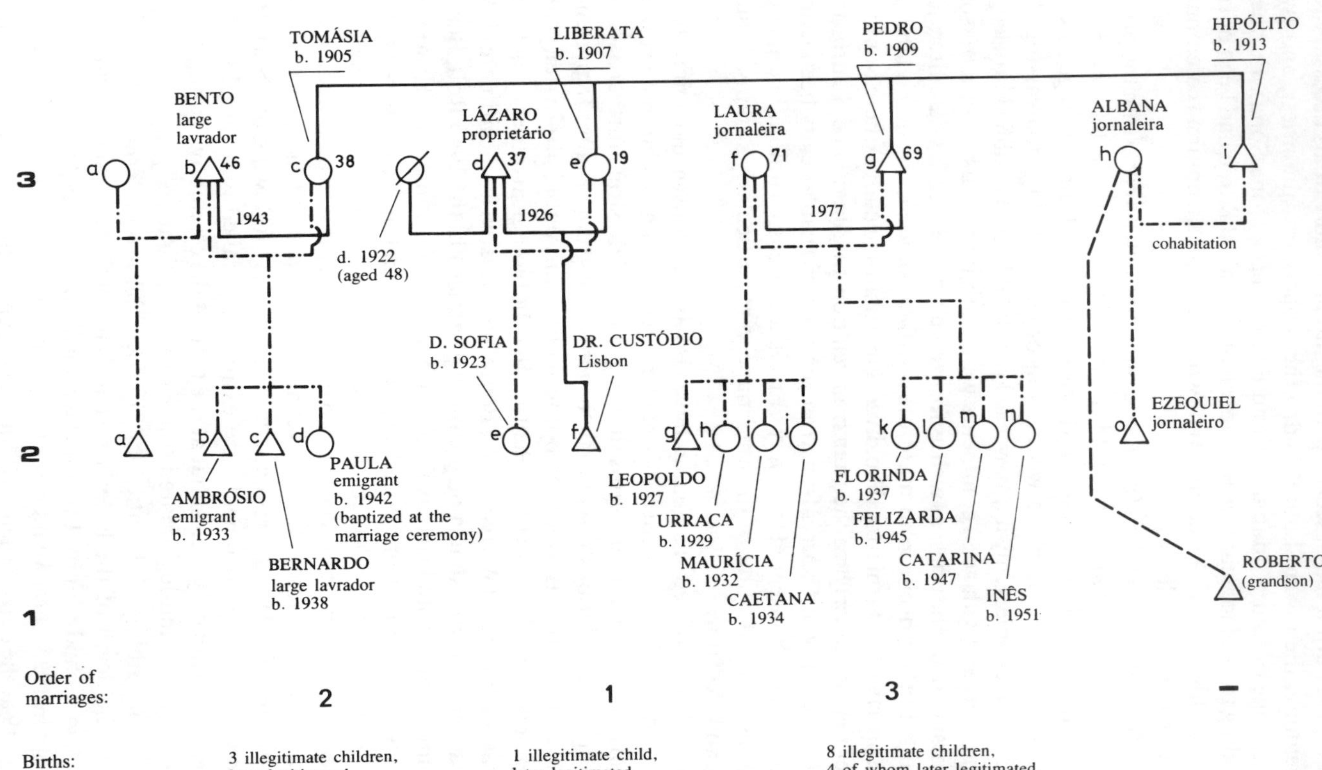

Figure 18. Consensual unions among *jornaleiros*

years: the child was to become the hamlet's current schoolteacher, Dona Sofia. The fourth sibling, Hipólito (3i), has been living for a number of years with the single mother Albana (3h). In 1977 Hipólito's age was 65 and Albana's 80. Also resident in the latter's household are one of her illegitimate children (2o) (not by Hipólito) and her young grandson Roberto, also a natural child. Both Hipólito and Ezequiel are *jornaleiros*, although the younger Ezequiel works for wages on a somewhat more regular basis than the elderly Hipólito. No specific kin terms exist for the relationships in this domestic group: only in the event of Hipólito and Albana's marriage would Hipólito formally become Ezequiel's *padrasto*, or stepfather. Towards the end of my fieldwork, Roberto left the household for a while as a servant in Mosteiro, and Albana died. No marriage took place prior to her death, and Hipólito moved out of the household into a rented house in another section of the hamlet, leaving Ezequiel (aged 48) in the household on his own.

Three of these four siblings, then, lived for some time in consensual unions and one (a child servant) married her *proprietário* employer. Further, three of the four had natural children prior to their marriages. In all three cases, marriages legitimated the children of the respective mothers.[31] Of the four siblings, one married young, one late, one very late, and one never married. While the two brothers Pedro and Hipólito have remained extremely poor, their sisters Tomásia and Liberata constitute two of the hamlet's three cases of female servants rising in the hierarchy through marriage or adoption, Liberata having borne a bastard (D. Sofia) to her *proprietário* employer at the age of 16. The most frequent contact between these four households occurs at agricultural tasks, particularly on occasions when Bento's son Bernardo (2c) assists his uncle Pedro (3g) and (more rarely) when Pedro returns Bernardo's assistance. Laura's daughters Felizarda (2l) and Catarina (2m) pay frequent visits to the hamlet as we have seen, when mutual invitations are exchanged by Catarina (a schoolteacher) and her first cousin Dona Sofia (2e). Otherwise there is little contact between the households, and villagers comment on both the luck and cleverness of Tomásia and Liberata for having married up into such good fortunes. However, many other villagers are extremely ambivalent (and even hostile) towards these two women who have 'jumped' from the bottom of the social hierarchy to the top.[32] These womens' successful upward

[31] Pedro of course legitimated only his own four daughters, and not Laura's previous four children by other unknown fathers. These four eldest children remain legally illegitimate unless they are formerly affiliated (see Glossary: *perfilhação*) by their biological fathers, but their social relationship to Pedro within the hamlet is referred to as one of stepchildren/stepfather (*filharascos*/*padrasto*).

[32] Like the attitude toward the sharecropper Fortunato (who also rose from rags to riches) these villagers' ambivalence towards these upwardly mobile women is yet another indication of the power of a social hierarchy which stresses the ascribed quality of land ownership rather than the achieved status of land acquisition. Villagers thus repeatedly pointed out to me that these women 'really aren't true *proprietárias* because they weren't born in that group'.

mobility nevertheless only further amplifies the conspicuous, continuing poverty of their two younger brothers. The case of these four siblings is illustrative in that it reveals patterns of illegitimacy and irregular unions among members of the *jornaleiro* group but on close analysis we find that these characteristics were not entirely internal to this social group. Outside help from wealthier villagers was needed. While both brothers remained poor, both sisters rose in the hierarchy through ties with *proprietário* men.

Returning to Rufina's case-study, we can now make a number of comparisons between marriage and inheritance among the *jornaleiro* group on the one hand and among the *proprietários* and *lavradores* on the other. But what proportion of the hamlet's total households did the day-labourers constitute over these years? Table 12 gives us a clearer idea. The overall proportion of these households was quite high throughout the period covered by the Confessional Rolls. Combining the total number of individual servants with the *jornaleiros* would yield an even clearer picture of the proportions of villagers from each social group at the time. In 1902, for example, the number of *individuals* listed as living in the 30 *jornaleiro* households was 92: along with the 14 servants, all of these individuals accounted for 106 of the hamlet's 184 residents over the age of 8. The *jornaleiro* group was thus even larger than the figures reveal: following 1902 this group constituted well over 1/2 of the hamlet's population.

The especially salient characteristics of households in this group are the following: small households, nuclear or matrifocal structures with few co-resident celibate siblings, very rare instances of stem structures of two conjugal pairs, no servants, a high frequency of cohabitation outside legal marriage, and high illegitimacy ratios. These characteristics are radically different from those exhibited by the domestic groups of the two wealthier groups. The absence of substantial quantities of landed property among the *jornaleiros* is likely to have been a major factor underlying these differences. For instance, on a total landholding of only 3.16 hectares today, Laura and Pedro simply could not support more than one or two of their children on a regular basis. None of Laura's children ever remain visiting within their mother's household for more than a few weeks at a time. Pedro himself does not work for wages but exchanges his labour for occasional tractor services on his few sparse plots, and he is assisted in agricultural tasks by his nephew Bernardo and a few other villagers with whom he maintains reciprocal exchanges. In this sense Laura's household is today somewhat less reliant on wages than in the past, although its current size (2) is still quite small.

As stated above, two types of *jornaleiro* household appear regularly in the documents, and it is important to distinguish between the two. The nuclear type not dealt with here blends to some extent with the structure of the households of poorer *lavradores*: these had an occasional stem structure of two conjugal pairs, and were commonly comprised of a married couple with

Table 12. *Households and occupations in Fontelas, 1886–1909*

Year	Occupation of household head: *Proprietário*	*Lavrador*	*Jornaleiro*[a]	Total households	Individual servants[b]	Total 'souls' (>8 years of age)
1886[c]	4	17	27	51	17 – 6 M / 11 F	168
1888[c]	3	16	27	49	12 – 1 / 11	157
1891	9	11	27	52	25 – 9 / 16	182
1892	10	13	27	53	22 – 7 / 15	179
1894	9	12	26	49	20 – 7 / 13	160
1895	6	14	23	44	16 – 9 / 7	153
1896	6	14	24	45	19 – 11 / 8	159
1902	9	11	30	50	14 – 7 / 7	184
1905[d]	6	11	30	47	10 – 3 / 7	172
1906[d]	7	11	29	47	10 – 3 / 7	167
1907	8	10	29	47	12 – 6 / 6	177
1908	5	13	26	44	11 – 4 / 7	184
1909[e]	10	6	26	42	10 – 6 / 4	173

Source: Confessional Rolls.

a – There were also a few households in various years (1886–1896) headed by blacksmiths, a stonemason, a tailor, a weaver, and a shoemaker.

b – Most of these servants were resident in *proprietário* households and a few in *lavrador* households.

c – Compiled by Padre Azevedo

d – Compiled by Padre Melo (All other Rolls were compiled by Padre Morais)

e – The 1898 and 1899 Rolls have been omitted from this table, as no occupations were listed in them.

This table was originally published in *Peasant Studies*, Vol. 12, No. 3 (Spring 1985): p. 210.

legitimate children. They were also normally larger in size (4–6 persons in some cases) than the fragmented, matrifocal households of unmarried women such as Rufina. The former type of nuclear household was more likely to exhibit problems in classification, or to have its residents listed at one time as *jornaleiros* and at another as *lavradores*. This is to be expected, as we have seen that day-labourers may shift at different times between reliance upon wage labour or upon cultivation of their own land.

The second type of household in this group is typified by the case of Engrácia in Chapter 3 as well as Rufina and Laura above. These matrifocal structures stress a predominance of ties through women and relations of filiation and siblingship over those of marriage and affinity, and they are usually characterized either by the absence of men or the presence of stepfathers rather than biological fathers. In the case of Rufina's household, the structure of a mother and her illegitimate children was repeated over three generations as her successive daughters and granddaughters bore further bastard children. Unlike the respectable positions of *jornaleiro* households which attain nuclear structures through legitimate marriage and child-rearing, these women remain marginal and only one step above the abject poverty of foundlings (*expostos*) or wandering beggars.

The position of these women within the social hierarchy is somewhat similar to that of secondary heirs and celibate siblings within wealthier landed households: they remain *outside* the main lines of property transmission and favoured marriage alliances. There is a major difference, however. While secondary heirs among the landed groups may fall into lower positions in the hierarchy, *jornaleira* women are already low from the start. Excluded from both matrimony and patrimony, these women have remained on the fringes of the local social structure. Inheriting little from their mothers and in most cases nothing from their unknown fathers, these women have few chances for prestigious marriage within a society which already hinders and obstructs the marriage of a large proportion of its members. In some cases (Laura) bastard children are later legitimated by the subsequent marriage of their biological parents, but even then neither the wedding ceremony itself nor the change in status that marriage implies are sufficient to lift *jornaleiro* spouses from their low social ranks. From the start these individuals are dealt a 'bad hand of cards' in that their group as a whole has long been debarred from the main sources of landed wealth in Fontelas. A detachment from landed patrimony thus already creates the initial conditions for an exclusion from prestigious matrimony. Women such as Laura thus 'inherit' nothing but this marginal role of non-inheritance.

In the absence of abundant landed property there thus seems little reason for forms of heir-control among the *jornaleiros*. Consequently, we do not find here the structures of competing heirs evident among the two landed groups, nor the pattern of selection of a favoured heir. The absence of widowed parents living with one of their children, as well as the absence of a stem structure of clustered conjugal pairs are perhaps both structural indications of the lack of landed property around which such clustering usually occurs. Further, it is extremely rare for these households to hire a servant, even in the absence of children or other resident kin. While many women in this group produce large numbers of children, many of these children are continually moving out of their natal households as servants, migrant labourers, or common-law spouses of others in this group; more recently they have moved out simply by emigrating permanently to France. While *proprietária* women (particularly celibate ones) will at times stress their removal from the physical aspects of childbearing, *lavrador* and *jornaleira* women tend to bear many children through extended reproductive cycles. In contrast to the wealthiest women, *lavradoras* are thus frequently admired for the large number of children they have borne. There is a crucial difference, nevertheless, between the destinies of the children of a *lavradora* and the children of a *jornaleira*: while the former usually remain in the natal household and work on the landholding, the latter generally leave the natal household and work for wages *outside* it.

In other words, among the two wealthier groups, landed patrimony forms the nexus of competing claims to a strategic position within the domestic group. The favoured heir who attains this strategic position will optimally prevent this patrimony from being dispersed among his or her siblings. But this patrimony is so minimal among the *jornaleiros* that such competition and selection is almost entirely absent. Very few aunts, uncles, or unmarried siblings ever remain on these holdings for purposes of re-directing property by wills through a favoured heir and a single line of inheritance. In fact, an initial analysis of the death entries in the Parish Register over the decades since 1870 reveals that very few adult *jornaleiros* (men or women) have ever left wills at all. Women in this group, then, are continually producing children who will of necessity be forced to leave the natal holding. Whereas among the landed groups many siblings may remain for years within the natal household following the marriage of a favoured brother or sister, only to marry very late or move out of the household at the moment of final partition, none of these patterns are evident within the developmental cycles of *jornaleiro* households.[33]

[33] For further analysis of the differences in behaviour between distinct wealth groups, although in a very different context, see Barlett for Costa Rica – particularly her discussion of rural strata defined by the 7-*manzana* dividing line in landholding area (1982:54), somewhat similar to the 6-hectare division between smallholders and *lavradores* in Fontelas. For a manor in medieval England Richard Smith (1979) locates four different 'quartiles', each with a distinct socioeconomic status, and for Tuscany McArdle has once again hit the nail on the head by emphasizing the need to analyse different social strata as distinct categories: 'The final verdict should stress that, for social history, terms like "depression", "recovery", and "crisis" are relatively useless as research tools unless they are anchored in a concrete reference to classes and income groups' (1978:217).

Unlike secondary heirs among the landed groups, however, individuals in this group cannot compensate for their exclusion from property through the acquisition of a respected occupation nor through a prestige marriage out of the natal holding into another hamlet. While households in the two wealthier groups place a high value upon labour, this labour has been predominantly *household labour* performed for domestic purposes. Among this group it has been *wage labour* and servant labour that have defined these households' predominant orientations, and these forms of labour have been performed for others and not on one's own landholding. The emigration of the 1960s has granted this group access to cash (not land) as a form of economic advancement and has provided them with their only respectable exit.

Two points concerning illegitimacy should be made here within the bounds of this case-study. The first is that there are three main forms of this phenomenon that should be distinguished, and the second is the connection between bastardy and the 'celibacy' of excluded heirs. The three forms of illegitimacy can be classified as follows:

(a) a relationship between one woman and one unmarried man, leading (eventually) to marriage and the legitimation of their children;
(b) a relationship(s) between one woman and one or more unmarried men, *not* culminating in marriage or legitimation;
(c) exploitation of a poor woman by a wealthy man (married or single), *not* culminating in marriage or legitimation.

We have seen in the case of Susana and her siblings that the first type of relationship (a) may also occur even among the *lavrador* group, and that included within this type would be cases of bridal pregnancies and near-illegitimate births. Bento and his wife Tomásia (Figure 18) also illustrate the first type: their marriage and simultaneous baptism of their three children not only legitimated them but it legalized their prior cohabitation as well. Laura illustrates both types (a) and (b), as her first four children (Figure 18) were born of unknown fathers but her four youngest were later legitimated by their natural father Pedro. Another example of type (b) is the dwarfholder Engrácia, whose four illegitimate sons were born of four distinct fathers none of whom either lived with Engrácia nor later legitimated them.

There are also examples in Fontelas of the third type of relationship, by far the most criticized form of bastardy in villagers' eyes. One such case was described to me by a smallholder woman, who stated that both she as well as her mother were born illegitimately as the result of relations forced upon them by powerful employers. 'What could they do? The *proprietário* controlled their jobs and could throw them out at will.' This kind of relationship is frequently referred to in cases of women servants, and codified in the phrase *criadas para todo o serviço* (servants for all services). Very few of these instances ever reach the town court, and when they do it is usually in cases of young girls still legally

19 *Jornaleira* with niece and two children, ca. 1956 (enlargement of an old photograph).

under the protection of their mothers (or parents). Some cases have also involved seductions or promises of marriage which were subsequently broken. A specific phrase is used to refer to this form of illegitimacy: *arranjou-lhe um filho* means 'he gave her a child' or more literally, 'he burdened her with a child'. The phrase suggests either rape or a relation implying economic control on the part of the male, rather than mutual consent between a man and a woman, and is repeatedly employed to refer to cases of wealthy men 'using' poor women. However, I found in Fontelas no examples today nor in recent years of the almost institutionalized adultery reported by Cutileiro (1971:144–5) for the Alentejo province, where women were encouraged by their husbands to sleep with their wealthy latifundist employers in order to maintain job security.

It is important to note here that in types (b) and (c) an illegitimate child legally inherits property only from the mother.[34] This is a significant legal point because it reveals the marginal position of the illegitimate child *vis-à-vis* the patrimony of the child's unknown father. In type (a) once the children are formally legitimated by the marriage of their parents, they enjoy full inheritance rights to both parents' property. At the other extreme, in the case of children born to relationships of type (b) and particularly of type (c), affiliation is extremely rare and the social relationship between the father and the child is a distant one.[35]

Between these two extremes lies a third course. Although rare, there are occasional cases of legal recognition of paternity by fathers who do not consequently marry the child's mother. One such case occurred recently in Fontelas, and involved one of Laura's daughters. Laura's fifth daughter (Felizarda) married the smallholder/shopkeeper Sebastião in 1964 (5 September). Prior to the marriage villagers forewarned both spouses of the dangers inherent in their union: Felizarda (aged 19) was a generation younger than Sebastião (aged 49) and the latter had already fathered an illegitimate son (Dionísio) in the local town. Some villagers mentioned the craziness and infatuation which had 'entered Sebastião's head' when he used to admire the young Felizarda as she took a flock of sheep out to pasture. Others maintained that the final result of this union merely confirmed the saying: 'old men and younger women always make poor matches'. Within a number of years the marriage broke down, and Felizarda left the hamlet for Bragança taking their legitimate daughter Assunção with her. The case went to court as a divorce proceeding some years ago (ca. 1972) and is still pending a second hearing.

[34] Following the 1974 Revolution, a number of substantial alterations were made in the Portuguese Civil Code of 1966 (see *Código Civil Português* 1977). Many of these changes were far-reaching, and in the case of inheritance provided a much more favourable position for the surviving spouse than was the case before. The existence of 'illegitimate' children has been entirely eradicated on paper: all children whether legitimate or not now share strictly equal rights to both parents' property. Very few of these legal changes, however, were perceived as such in Fontelas during my fieldwork and many have been implemented very slowly. For most of the period considered in this study (1870–1978) these recent legal changes did not apply. These alterations in national law and their interpretation by the customary law of rural communities such as Fontelas is of course a fascinating topic.

[35] This is the usual case, but there are exceptions. One woman in Fontelas had an illegitimate son by a bus-driver a number of years ago. The father later married another woman in the district city, but the mother in Fontelas did not sever relations with him altogether. While the mother and father are not on speaking terms, the child attends school in his father's city, spending weekdays with his father and 'stepmother' there and weekends (and summers) with his mother in Fontelas.

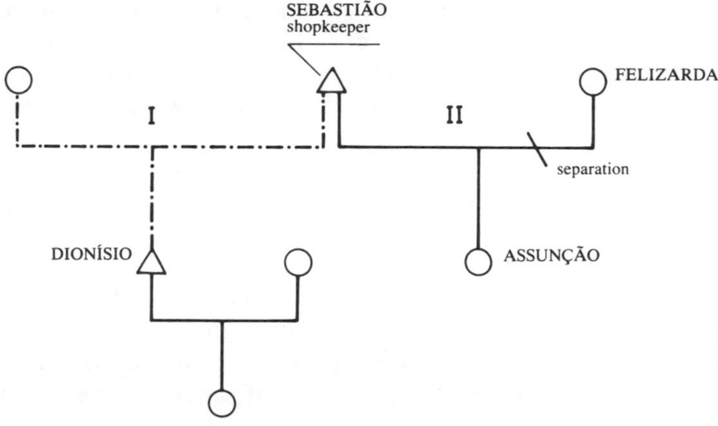

Figure 19. Sebastião and children

An entire series of non-speaking relationships began at the first hearing when bitterness surfaced between witnesses supporting either Sebastião or Felizarda. For most of the duration of my fieldwork, Felizarda's parents Laura and Pedro (as yet unmarried) never set foot in Sebastião's shop (Map 3 – H53). Two close friends of Felizarda's parents (neighbours of Sebastião across the road) also completely severed relations with the shopkeeper and avoided entering his shop by sending younger children for minor purchases. When conversations occurred outside the store, conspicuous avoidances could be heard in these individuals' mutual silences. Felizarda's parents themselves rarely even passed within sight of the shop. Individuals from both of these households remained in a formal relationship of evasion with Sebastião, of rigid enmity rather than friendship or neighbourship.

A second legal counter-action was initiated by Sebastião. Although during visits by Felizarda to Fontelas their daughter Assunção would customarily spend a few hours with her father alone, Sebastião's judicial move was to affiliate his previous illegitimate son Dionísio. Upon legal recognition of paternity, a bastard child's rights to the father's patrimony are equivalent to half of the portion pertaining to a legitimate child. In the event of Sebastião's death, the affiliated Dionísio would thus inherit one-third of the share pertaining to Assunção (who in turn would inherit one half of the patrimony and Felizarda the other half). Thus Dionísio would inherit 1/6 of the total patrimony and Assunção 2/6.

But a further means of transferring property was attempted through the divorce. Should the divorce be granted, a larger portion of Sebastião's property would revert to Dionísio (1/3 of the total patrimony), once affiliated, than to Assunção. A particularly valued piece of property in this case was Sebastião's house, which is located at the entrance to the hamlet and ideally situated for purposes of both transport and business. Over the years, in contrast to Sebastião's strict avoidance of his wife and her kin, his relations with his natural son Dionísio and Dionísio's mother in town very distinctly warmed. Frequent visits to Fontelas by the latter were made during my fieldwork, and Sebastião was invited to the town baptism of Dionísio's daughter in the role of the child's legitimate grandfather. In fact, villagers lamented the fact that Sebastião did not finally settle down and (upon the divorce) marry his first son's mother.

The case illustrates a rather uncommon pattern of the legitimation of a bastard child outside the legal marriage tie. An illegitimate child can be re-incorporated into a 'legitimate' social role, although a certain number of legal steps must be taken to bring this about. The case also illustrates the importance of the act of legal affiliation for the inheritance of paternal property by natural children.

Most cases of illegitimacy, however, leave bastard children effectively excluded forever from any property rights in their fathers' lines. Is it possible, then, to examine processes of marriage and inheritance among the *jornaleiro* group along the same lines as marriage and inheritance among the landed groups? My answer is, emphatically, no. A distinctly different set of strategies, rules, and patterns are operative among the land-poor, and the key to this difference lies again in modes of property transmission.

To elucidate these patterns, let me now turn to the second and final point concerning illegitimacy: the connection between illegitimacy and the celibacy of excluded heirs. We have seen that the *proprietários* and *lavradores* tend to select a favoured heir who marries, stays in the natal household, and (in the long term) carries on the patrimony of the family line. The cost of this preference, however, is the exclusion of secondary siblings. Many of these secondary heirs are in fact the 'unknown fathers' of the bastard children of unmarried *jornaleiras*.[36] One extremely clear example of this is the dwarfholder Engrácia, examined in Chapter 3 (Figure 20).

The four unknown fathers of Engrácia's illegitimate children turn out to be the following individuals (all natural to Fontelas). Father A is an incapacitated middle-aged man living in Fontelas with his smallholder sister and her husband; Father B is an emigrant in France married to a woman from a nearby parish; C is an emigrant in France married to the daughter of a smallholder woman from Fontelas; and D we have seen is Engrácia's half-nephew, an unmarried *lavrador* today. None of Engrácia's four bastard children has been affiliated, and none of them will inherit anything from their unknown fathers. They will, however, each inherit 1/4 shares of their mother's property upon her death.

36 Of course, not *all* unknown fathers are secondary heirs from *proprietário* or *lavrador* households. Many illegitimacies have also resulted from unions between unmarried *jornaleira* women and unmarried male *jornaleiros*.

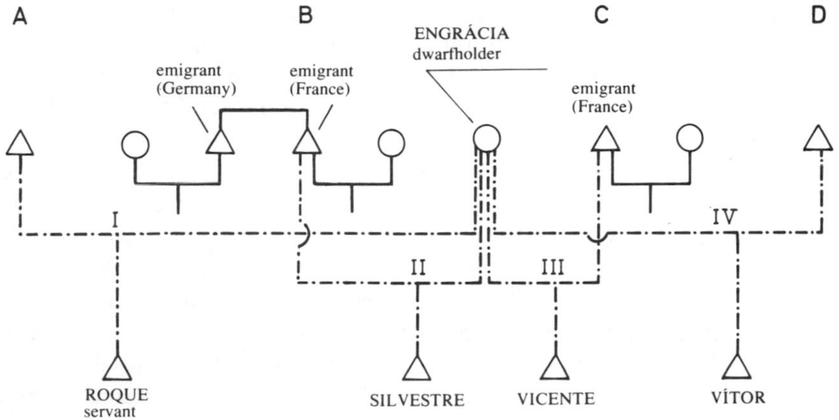

Figure 20. Natural fathers of Engrácia's children

The essential point here is that *all four* of the fathers were unmarried at the time of their relations with Engrácia and all four remained outside the main lines of property transmission within their own natal households. Further, none of these men were either conspicuously wealthy nor particularly poor. While B and C later married, both have left the hamlet permanently. B's brother is also an emigrant (in Germany) but it is B's brother's wife who has remained on the natal holding and it is she who looks after B's father. While B and his wife have constructed a new house in Fontelas, the house remains an investment in the future: a future which B has built outside the hamlet and outside his father's landholding. Similarly, it is not C but his stepbrother Eduardo who has remained in the hamlet and looks after their aging mother, the dwarfholder Eufémia. Finally, both the incapacitated A as well as Engrácia's half-nephew D live today in Fontelas as dependent kin: secondary heirs attached to the households of their sisters, they are unlikely to marry or set up new domestic groups which would later pose threats to their natal households' patrimonies.

In other words, all four of these fathers have been excluded to some degree from the main sources of patrimony within their natal households. While only two of the four have married, both of these have abandoned the community. All four are thus secondary heirs to hamlet patrimony, and participants in matrimony strictly *external* to Fontelas' local context.

Engrácia herself has remained in Fontelas and she occupies a position similar to that of Laura, although even a very late marriage and its token social recognition have not as yet appeared likely in her case. Like the position of secondary heirs within landed households, the position of these poor, unmarried women lies outside the central spheres of matrimony and patrimony. As a group, *jornaleira* women and their illegitimate children are excluded not only from favoured marriages but also from inheritance: their mothers own little and from their unknown fathers they inherit nothing. (I am of course stressing here the position of unmarried labouring women and not that of labouring women who marry and bear legitimate children.) While two of the fathers of Engrácia's four children have emigrated, the two other fathers as well as Engrácia herself have remained in Fontelas and their positions are of marginal, dependent kin. While these men may remain dependent upon their particular households, in contrast women such as Engrácia remain as it were dependent on the entire community for donations, pity, and other forms of economic assistance. The result of this skewed, asymmetrical situation – which places women like Engrácia and Laura in a position diametrically opposite to that of *proprietária* women – is the reproduction over the generations of a sector of marginal low-status women burdened with the reproduction of a surplus of excluded children.

A day-labouring woman in most cases retains the already low position of her mother, who herself was also frequently an illegitimate daughter of an unmarried labouring woman. This structure is reproduced over the generations: her illegitimate children then in turn inherit further social identities of exclusion. The term universally used to refer to bastard children (*zorro* or *zorra*) has a double meaning. Firstly, it suggests the role of a 'rascal' or mischief-maker, and this is in fact how many adults view their activities: always directed towards some form of roguery or deceit. The second meaning of *zorro* is 'fox', suggestive of the excluded position and extra-human role of the natural child. Both meanings stress the marginal status of bastards within both a social structure where they are morally inferior and disruptive as well as within a fragmented household and family in which their rights to property are either partial or non-existent. While I shall return to the meaning of the term *zorro* in Chapter 7, it is important to note here the intimate link between the negative connotation of the word and its almost exclusive incidence within the *jornaleiro* group. Like secondary heirs among the landed groups, *jornaleiras* and their bastard children remain debarred from both matrimony and patrimony but not from 'illicit love' (Laslett 1977) or sexual reproduction.

The predominance of this pattern of irregular sexual relationships between excluded, marginal individuals does not deny the occurrence of the exploitation of poor women by wealthy men. Such cases merely attest to the existence of a social hierarchy which grants a high (and largely unchallenged) position to wealthy males and a low and virtually powerless one to poor women. I do not, however, think that this form of relationship is sufficient to account for the extremely high ratios of illegitimacy in Fontelas (Table 18). Rather, the process of informal preferential inheritance along with the general delay of marriage together account for the pattern. Both of these factors (late marriage and the selection of favoured heirs) necessarily imply the exclusion of many individuals from the acquisition of landed property and a favoured marital position. In other words, it is illegitimacy of the types (a) and (b) listed earlier which reveal the underlying pattern of bastardy as linked to a specific form of inheritance, and not solely to the exploitation of poor women by wealthy men. It is not the specific cases of exploitation of servant women by *proprietário* men that underlies this community's abnormally high proportions of illegitimacy, but rather the inheritance system itself that generates the social reproduction of a 'bastard group' over the generations.

This is a rather different explanation from that offered by Laslett (1980b), in that a local cultural pattern itself is not seen here as the key to the persistence of illegitimacy – i.e., a marginalized and self-reproducing 'bastardy prone sub-society' somewhat like Oscar Lewis' culture of poverty. The crucial clue to my analytical explanation (system of inheritance plus an endemic, almost parasitic link between the very top and the very bottom of the social hierarchy) is the circulation of bastards from poor households to wealthy ones and back again. This form of explanation, rather than granting a sub-society of bastard-bearing women a sort of life of its own within but simultaneously apart from the rural community, would view the continual dynamic between this bastard group (actually not marginal at all) and the *proprietário* families as a central nexus of social reproduction at the very heart of the social structure.

A perfect illustration of this selection process is that of the *jornaleira* Rufina examined earlier. It is now possible to show how the second case-study above relates directly to that of Rufina. The latter was the sister of João Pires da Silva and thus a paternal aunt of Susana (Figure 21). While our second case-study dealt with João's *lavrador* descendants (Figure 15), let us focus for a moment on the relations between this João and his sister Rufina. We have noted that three of these five siblings married and had children, while Rufina and Vítor remained unmarried. We have also seen that Rufina bore four illegitimate children, while Vítor died unmarried and with no children. Of special interest were the occupations of these siblings as listed both in the Confessional Rolls and the Parish Register: João consistently remained a *lavrador* throughout the listings, while Eulália and her husband were consistently registered as *jornaleiros*, as was Vítor. However, Gualter and his wife were registered as *lavradores* in 1883 at the birth of their first child, but as *jornaleiros* in 1889 and 1892 at the births of later children. Similarly, Rufina herself was listed upon the births of her children as a *lavradora* (1877), then as a cottager (1882). This constituted a drastic descent in the social scale. From the date of the first Confessional Roll (1886) onwards, Rufina was consistently listed as a *jornaleira*. In other words, if we can rely this time upon the relative accuracy of various priests' recordings of occupations, two of these five siblings remained *jornaleiros* while two others fell downwards in the social hierarchy from the occupation of *lavrador* to that of *jornaleiro*. In contrast, the eldest brother João remained throughout a *lavrador*.

Could Rufina as well as her other siblings have 'fallen out' of the main line of

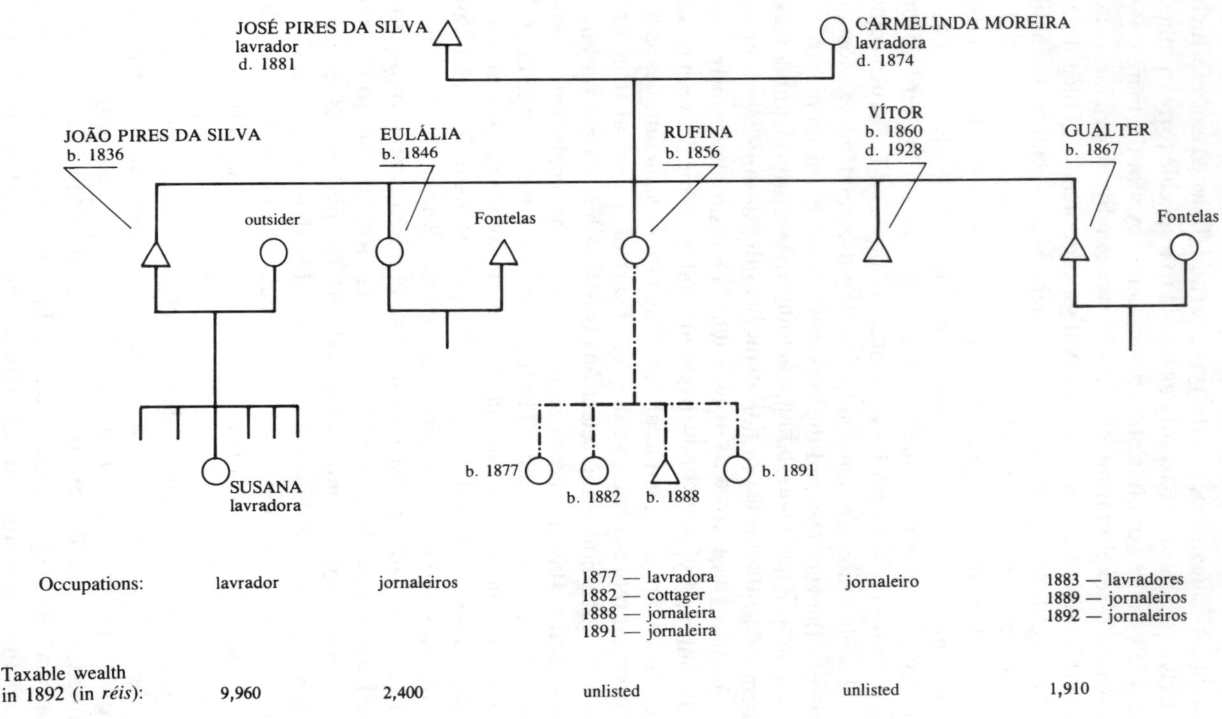

Figure 21. Rufina and siblings

property transmission in their parents' household? The documents suggest that this may have occurred, as we piece together two further bits of evidence. Firstly, the 1892 Tax Listing registered only three of these siblings, and each one of these three with very different amounts of taxable wealth. While the *lavrador* João owned taxable wealth of 9,960 *réis* (bottom of Figure 21), Eulália's husband owned only 2,400 *réis*, and João's younger brother Gualter owned the yet smaller quantity of 1,910 *réis*. Rufina and Vítor were not even listed.

Yet even by the date of the first Confessional Roll (1886) all five siblings were resident in separate households, and as we have seen, João's household was a very large one which supported his six children for a long period of time. But a crucial factor was the date of death of each of the parents of these siblings – Carmelinda died in 1874, but José died seven years later in 1881. It is conceivable that Rufina was in fact a *lavradora* within her natal household in 1877 *prior* to her father's death. Following her father's death, however, in 1882 Rufina was listed as a 'cottager' and from 1886 on as a *jornaleira*. Could the partition of José and Carmelinda's natal holding have been effected following the death of the second parent José in 1881? This was extremely likely. However, the absence of Parish Register entries prior to 1870 as well as the lack of notarial documents prevent us from affirming this course of events. The occupations and dates are nevertheless suggestive: most of the natal household's patrimony remained within the line of transmission through João and not through his four younger siblings.

In an essay on inheritance customs in early modern France, the French historian Le Roy Ladurie has pointed to regional differences between the egalitarian divisions of property in the North-west of France and preferential divisions in the South. One passage from this essay is particularly relevant here:

> . . . the southern paterfamilias fights against fragmentation by using the right to advantage, *préciput*, donation *inter vivos*, and the testamentary absolutism of statute law, all of which were aimed at securing a larger share for one of the children, not necessarily the eldest. So this favoured descendant will succeed to virtually the whole of the family land or plot (often after a period of co-residence during his parents' lifetime). Whereas the other children must be satisfied with portions of varying degrees of meagreness, with crumbs distributed in the will, or with a *légitime* or legal share that is merely a custom-prescribed hand-out of a few sous. At this point, these underprivileged offspring run the risk of falling into the proletariat, if they are of the people; or into the church, if they come from the middle or upper classes.
>
> (Le Roy Ladurie 1976:62–3)

While the formal institutions of *pre-mortem* property transmission through dowries or the French *préciput* are absent in this region of Portugal and wills in favour of a preferred heir are not very common, much of my data points towards the occurrence of the same forms of preference and exclusion described by Le Roy Ladurie for the South of France. This selection process is operative at the practical level of concrete strategies of marriage and inheritance, and is brought into play at crucial moments of potential conflict between heirs.

The selection of a favoured heir occurs despite the formal rule of equal partition, and its results are wide-ranging. In the case I have just described, Rufina did indeed fall into the proletariat. Further, both her children as well as her grandchildren remained there, the entire cycle being broken only in the 1960s when Laura's children managed to leave the hamlet entirely as migrants or to emigrate externally to France. Again, the main line of property transmission in Rufina's generation was directed through one heir (the *lavrador* João) while this heir's four siblings remained to greater or lesser degrees excluded. While for some this did not necessarily mean further exclusion from marriage or the bringing up of a family, for others (Rufina) it meant a distinct decline towards the bottom of the social scale.

A remarkably similar process of social descent has been reported for Austria by Khera: 'Not even the best of marriage arrangements can prevent some members of a rich family from eventually descending to a lower stratum, however. Those who have to establish independent households are frequently at a disadvantage compared to those who start out with the parental farm' (1972b:355). In another article, Khera stresses the inevitable fall of some individuals, in a region of partible inheritance, over the course of 3 or 4 generations to the level of cottagers or landless labourers (1981:311). Such downward social mobility seems to be institutionalized in regions of impartible inheritance (most of Austria) while also occurring in partible inheritance areas with some form of heir selection (the Eastern Austrian province of Burgenland/Northeast Portugal), and Khera's fine analyses suggest a more complex and satisfactory explanation of predominantly downward mobility than the circular upward–downward movement analysed for Switzerland by Weigandt (1977). Note also Löfgren's perception of this problem for Scandinavian peasantries: '. . . we need a complete picture of the measures taken to secure the social position of the next generation. Decisions concerning inheritance and concerning the timing of marriage and retirement were but parts of a complicated strategy . . . We may find that the strategies vary but the goal remains the same: to stop the family from moving downwards on the social ladder' (1974:44). What further proof should we need for confirmation of Goody's affirmation (1976a) that *all* European rural communities, however small, are characterized by internal stratification and delicate systems of property devolution intimately linked to fine local gradations of social status?

Among the *jornaleiros* there is little reason for a favoured heir to be selected at all, as the amounts of property owned by this group are so small. Thus many of the day-labourers are effectively out of the race for marriage and property as they are dealt a bad hand of cards from the start. Strategies are thus directed neither towards maintenance of the (already minimal) patrimony, nor towards a maximum labour group of many children, which in any case a *jornaleiro* household would be unable to support. Formerly, strategies carried out by day-labouring men may have been directed towards the acquisition of steady wages or good employment relations with wealthier landowners. A wide field of employing households might thus have ensured that day-labourers would be able to work at major harvesting tasks, during which a series of a few days' labour for various *proprietário* households may have provided relatively steady wages. More recently, this group's skill in manipulating their poor initial life-chances has been exercised in escaping from the hamlet altogether and obtaining permanent work in France.

For *jornaleiras*, however, this course of action was not so easy. Already low in status, these women formed the escape-valve for those male heirs unable to obtain favoured positions within their natal households. As the case of Rufina and her descendants has shown, the low position of *jornaleiras* can be reproduced over the generations through an entire line of bastard-bearing women. This low status itself attests to a social hierarchy which separates those possessing land and those forced to sell their labour. But it also reveals a structure of inheritance which although granting formal equality to all heirs, persists in dividing the chosen few from the many disadvantaged. The structural tension (among the landed groups) between the competing forces of matrimony and patrimony is resolved only through the illicit unions of excluded male heirs and poorer *jornaleira* women.

True 'celibacy' is reserved only for very wealthy women, while a large number of unmarried men (usually secondary heirs) have relations with a small group of single *jornaleiras*. It is this surplus of secondary heirs who are in fact the 'unknown fathers' of bastard children. Underlying the formal equality of heirs lies a rigid inequality in inheritance: this inequality between individual heirs is mirrored by the larger social gap separating the two landed groups from the land-poor *jornaleiros*. The final 'heirs' to this general structural inequality are a marginal group of poor women and their bastard children.

In the three case-studies examined in this chapter I have concentrated almost exclusively on the *internal* structure of three households over the generations. I am quite aware that there is a danger in this kind of hermetic analysis of specific domestic groups: households and their resident individuals may appear merely as isolated units within the larger social system of which they form a part. Major links between the individual household and the larger social structure may remain hidden beneath such detailed, microscopic analysis of part-elements. For instance, I have followed the developmental cycles of these three households from 1886 through 1909, but have then jumped from 1909 to the 1940 listing and then jumped again from 1940 to the ethnographic present in 1977: significant changes in household structure may obviously have occurred *between* the dates for which we have documentary sources. In this sense, the above analysis has told us little about the relations between households and even less about the general social and economic conditions *outside* the hamlet which have doubtless affected it in various ways at different times.

Part of the explanation for this situation lies in the nature of the documents assessed and another part in the specific form of analysis adopted by the author. Firstly, throughout this chapter I have deliberately examined the sources in enough detail so that both their utility as well as their imperfections have been clearly revealed. Despite their inaccuracies with regard to the recording of names, ages, and occupations, the Confessional Rolls and the Parish Register together offer a unique sequential set of documents for the analysis of changes in the structure of domestic groups over time. These ecclesiastical sources do not, however, explicitly tell us much about the economic, political, or administrative structure of the surrounding parishes in the area. While some amount of speculation and inference is necessary for the specifics of their interpretation, the basic thrust of my analysis has used the sources to confirm the existence in Fontelas of a ranked social hierarchy of three major social groups.[37] Some very different elements of household structure, marriage strategies, and inheritance processes have characterized the three family lines of a *proprietário*, a *lavrador*, and a *jornaleira*. These characteristics within each group have maintained a surprising continuity over the generations, and ethnographic evidence has been used in conjunction with the documents to confirm this social continuity. While earlier chapters have revealed inequalities *at the hamlet level* between landed social groups and those with little land, this chapter has concentrated on inequalities *at the household level* between individual heirs.

Secondly, I have consciously tried to further one form of analysis of historical materials and not two. In this sense I have worked within the framework of the community-study in that I have severely limited the scope of my sample population. As stated in Chapter 1, no detailed attempt has been made to place this community within its wider regional or international context since the late nineteenth century. This does not mean that I do not think the latter is necessary or useful, but rather that the materials I have presented lend themselves less to this kind of analysis than to that of the community-study. An examination of the links between Fontelas and its wider contexts would not, I think, contradict most of the conclusions arrived at here.

However, I *am* suggesting that the community-study framework itself can be modified and enlarged through the incorporation of process and the

[37] Again, due to restrictions of length, I have not included a case-study here of a large *lavrador* household, but this should not imply that the tripartite hierarchy examined in this chapter is in any way inconsistent with the four social groups analysed earlier in Chapter 3.

dimension of *time*.[38] The generational method adopted here has shown how revealing this dimension of time can be. It is thus a particular kind of local historical document (continuous series of Confessional Rolls and Parish Registers) that has been used to telescope processes of marriage and inheritance backwards in time. The approach proposed here should therefore be seen as one step towards the incorporation by social anthropology of one of its long-neglected but kindred disciplines – social history (Davis 1977:239–51). Throughout my analysis this suggestion has been implicit, but prior to the analysis itself I had already favoured joint anthropological/historical research. Rather than carrying out a purely synchronic community-study focused exclusively upon the ethnographic present, I have attempted to introduce such a time dimension into the community-study model.

[38] Three anthropologists' work on various dimensions of 'time' are of direct relevance here, each in their own way: Lisón-Tolosana (1966), Bourdieu (1976; 1977), and Macfarlane (1977c). See also Philip Abrams' discussion of the concept of 'generations' (1982:240–66), the comments by Orlove (1980:245–61) on the utility of processual approaches for ecological anthropology, and those of Netting (1981:xiii–xiv) concerning the use of continuous and complete historical and demographic sources as well as the construction of interpretative models of process and change which necessarily rely on a time depth of some sort.

6
Minimal marriage

Marriage is a very odd institution in Fontelas. The essence of this oddness lies in the overall weak role of *matrimony* in comparison with this society's far greater stress upon the elements of *patrimony*, or the inheritance and transmission of property at death. Given its ecological setting and the form of agriculture practiced, rigid limits must be set for the size of individual households and the overall population of the hamlet. As in the Swiss and Italian Alpine communities studied by Wolf and Cole (1974), Friedl (1974), and Netting (1979a), in Fontelas also severe restrictions are placed upon villagers' marriages in the interests of maintaining unified landholdings and households of manageable size. While the interests of the parents (preserving such landholdings intact) may in these cases conflict with those of the children (the assemblage of a viable household property of land, animals, and buildings through inheritance, marriage, and purchase), in the Northeast Portuguese case the conditions for constructing or accumulating the latter assemblage of goods are extremely confining. Common also to both the Alpine and highland Portuguese marriage systems is a severe limitation on the number of new households formed in each generation. Unlike many Mediterranean communities described in the ethnographic literature, this community does not place particular emphasis upon marriage or the conjugal tie. In fact, it does its best to prevent or postpone the marriages of most of its member individuals. Matrimony is systematically subordinated to the predominant power of patrimony.

In Chapter 5 I have shown how three major social groups in Fontelas exhibit different patterns of marriage and inheritance. In this chapter I will conclude this discussion of matrimony by placing those case-studies within a wider context: how representative are they of the hamlet as a whole? Do they reveal historical patterns alone, or do they apply equally to the ethnographic present in 1976–8? A broader question may also be posed – why in fact is marriage such a peculiar arrangement in Fontelas and why is it so carefully controlled?

To answer these questions, in the section that follows I give an overview of nuptiality in Fontelas, stressing the high age at marriage and the large proportion of villagers never marrying. I will show that Fontelas constitutes a perfect example of John Hajnal's classic 'European marriage pattern' (1965).

The next section describes the pattern of natolocal residence. I conclude that this form of residence is not solely a result of a shortage of housing but indicative of a general cultural stress on 'descent' and filiation at the expense of marriage and affinity. Finally, Chapter 7 deals with the process of inheritance and the practical arrangements occurring after death. There I show that a particular mode of *post-mortem* inheritance underlies and shapes an entire fabric of social and marital relations.

The de-emphasis of marriage

A convenient place to start here is to look at the exact composition of all resident households in Fontelas in 1977. This will allow us to place marriage within its contemporary context. I have diagrammed each household's structure in Appendix IV, to which I shall refer throughout this chapter: Table 13 presents a summary of the materials in this appendix, and provides an overall view of the kinds of domestic group which currently comprise the hamlet's 57 households. A perusal of the diagrams in Appendix IV along with Table 13 reveals the following general picture.

Firstly, it is particularly striking that only a very small number of households in 1977 were strictly nuclear in form. Only 13 households (Type 3b) were composed of a husband, wife, and child(ren). Similarly, the category of Simple Family Households as a whole accounted for 26 domestic groups, or less than half of the hamlet's total. It is important to note that the nuclear family of husband/wife/child(ren) is only one of seven types of household arrangement constituting Laslett's classification of Simple Family Households (Laslett 1972:41–2). Two of these 26 households consisted of a married couple living alone, three of 'nuclear' structures with an emigrant husband, and one of a widower and children. Further, 7 of the 26 (3e/3f) consisted of either consensual unions between unmarried persons or of a single mother with a bastard child(ren). In the hamlet as a whole, there were 16 households (in various categories) which contained some form of irregular or illegitimate tie, that is to say, relations viewed through the ideal model of the Church as irregular. The 'folk model' of course views these ties as socially acceptable to a certain degree. This proportion of households with extra-legal social ties outside formal marriage is particularly high, and is consistent with the historical and genealogical materials examined in Chapter 5. Even today, Fontelas continues to afford examples of illegitimacy and irregular common-law unions.[1] Strictly nuclear structures do not account for even 1/4 of the hamlet's households.

[1] A complete tabulation of illegitimacy ratios in Fontelas since 1870 is presented in Chapter 7 (Table 18). The essential point here is that however much some villagers attempt to dismiss illegitimacy as 'a thing of the past', it has not entirely disappeared from the social scene and has left quite a clear mark on contemporary household structure.

Secondly, we find that 13 households are 'extended' in some form.[2] Some of these households include a widowed parent (extended upwards), co-resident grandchildren or nephews/nieces (extended downwards), or co-resident siblings or affines (extended laterally). Illegitimate ties also account for some of these extensions outward from the nuclear structure (H4 & 22 for example – see Appendix IV). Yet more complex are the structures of the five Multiple Family Households. While two of these (H8 & 14) are perfect examples of stem family arrangements comprising two conjugal pairs, the remaining three (H9, 38, & 47) fit into no convenient category at all within Laslett's scheme. (H47, for instance, contained three co-resident siblings along with four bastard children of four different mothers.) In other words, a total of 18 (almost 1/3) of the hamlet's domestic groups were extended or multiple to some degree.

Thirdly, there were another 13 households composed of solitary individuals. Only three of these were widowed (H12, 37, & 52). Of the remaining individuals, 8 were unmarried (7 men and 1 woman) and 2 men were living separately from their wives and children (one pending a divorce). Thus, Table

[2] For the time being, I have adopted Laslett's classification of households proposed in *Household and Family in Past Time* (1972:28–44), although there remain a number of differences between that classificatory system and the manner in which I have drawn the kinship relations within Fontelas' domestic groups (Appendix IV). While endless debates concerning the meaning of 'extended family' could arise from this categorization, I have followed it in order to achieve consistency between the diagrams in Chapter 5 and those in Appendix IV. An Extended Family Household in this sense implies the presence of at least one household member (however distantly related) from outside the nuclear conjugal group. In Laslett's schema, the presence of a servant does not substantially change a nuclear structure into an extended one. With respect to the proportions of household types in Fontelas, we find very similar figures by enlarging the sample to include the four hamlets in the parish. According to the 1896 Confessional Roll, these proportions were as follows:

1. *Solitaries*	1a:	5		
	1b:	20	25	17.1%
2. *No family*	2a:	7		
	2b:	4	11	7.5%
	2c:	—		
3. *Simple family households*	3a:	26		
	3b:	22		
	3c:	6	79	54.1%
	3d:	15		
	3e:	10		
4. *Extended family households*	4a:	9		
	4b:	2	26	17.8%
	4c:	12		
	4d:	3		
5. *Multiple family households*	5a:	—		
	5b(i):	1	5	3.4%
	5b(ii):	4		
Total		146		99.9%

Table 13. *Types of household in Fontelas, 1977*
[based on Laslett (1972:28–32) and Rowland (1981:217–20)]

Categories	Classes	No. of Households	Total	Observations
1. *Solitaries*	1a: Widowed	3	13	a – 2 men separated
	1b: Single, or of unknown marital status	10[a]		
2. *No family*	2a: Coresident siblings	–		
	2b: Coresident relatives of other kinds	–	–	
	2c: Persons not evidently related	–		
3. *Simple family households*	3a: Married couples alone	2		b – 3 households with absent emigrant husbands
	3b: Married couples with child(ren)	16[b]		
	3c: Widowers with child(ren)	1		
	3d: Widows with child(ren)	–	26	
	*3e: Single mother with child(ren)	5(12)**		
	*3f: Consensual unions	2(4)		
4. *Extended family households*	4a: Extended upwards	3		c – Multiple illegitimacies in H4
	4b: Extended downwards	6[c]	13	
	4c: Extended laterally	4		
	4d: Combinations of 4a–4c	–		
5. *Multiple family households*	5a: Secondary unit(s) UP	–		d – Multiple illegitimacies in H47
	5b: (i) Secondary unit(s) DOWN (male line)	1		
	(ii) Secondary unit(s) DOWN (female line)	1	5	
	5c: Units all on one level	–		
	5d: *Frérèches*	–		
	5e: Other multiple families	3[d]		
6. *Indeterminate*		–		
Total:		57***		

*I have had to add these two categories (3e/3f) to Laslett's scheme due to the high frequency of irregular unions and illegitimate births in Fontelas.

**Two further consensual unions exist within households in other categories (H4, H38), and there are 7 further households in which an illegitimate mother/child tie exists.

***This total includes three men living alone (H12, H46, H55) who died shortly prior to my Census of 1 July 1977.

13 indicates that just as many households were composed of solitary individuals as were strictly nuclear or extended.

In summary, the structures of Fontelas' domestic groups in 1977 provide a wide range of solitary, nuclear, extended, and multiple family households none of which dominates entirely. Roughly half of these households are Simple Family Households approximating a nuclear structure. But perhaps more striking is the large number containing irregular relationships. Emigration since the 1960s has not reduced Fontelas to a ghost-town of the idling elderly, and younger villagers (particularly women) continue to marry and remain in agriculture. This variety of domestic arrangements suggests that, at least in 1976–78, there was no universal norm of household structure. Whether stem family structures constituted an 'ideal' household arrangement (Laslett 1972:13–23) or nuclear structures a norm, certainly very few families in Fontelas managed to achieve either of these.

Perhaps the small number of stem family arrangements is itself more surprising than the lack of predominance of nuclear family households: a number of authors have drawn attention recently to the enduring pattern of association between stem family forms and the specifically Northern Iberian geographical zone. Northeast Portugal could very well be included within the area John Hajnal refers to as being characterized by a 'Northwest European household formation system', particularly with reference to late marriage ages for both sexes and to the circulation of servants (Hajnal 1982). Both Rowland (1984) and Medeiros (1985) have called attention to a number of early monographic studies of Northern Portuguese rural regions carried out at the beginning of the twentieth century by a group of French scholars influenced by Frédéric Le Play. The fact that in 1977 only two households in Fontelas were strictly 'stem' in form should not obscure this larger geographical and historical context, nor the fact that stem family arrangements do appear to have been common among Fontelas' wealthier strata.

Let us look specifically at the marriages of individuals currently resident in Fontelas. These basic statistics will allow us to place marriage within a wider comparative context. All of the marriages shown in the household diagrams in Appendix IV (including widowed individuals and remarriages) amount to a total of 55. Of this total, 38 involved two living spouses in 1977.[3] However, 2 of these 38 marriages involved separations, one an abandoned wife, and one was a civil marriage.[4] Of the remaining 14 marriages shown, in 10 of these a widow

[3] I have pushed this date forward one year in order to include two marriages which took place in 1978, after my 1977 Household Census. These marriages (in H9, H22, and H40) are not diagrammed in Appendix IV, but I have made note of them in each of the households concerned.

[4] This marriage is considered by other villagers to be rather more akin to the four cases of consensual unions than to 'respectable Catholic marriages'. Civil marriage implies a failure (whether deliberate or not) to follow the precepts of the Church. Although according to

has survived and in 4 a widower. In only 2 of the total of 55 marriages did widows remarry a second husband. In another 2, widowers remarried second wives.

The general pattern of intra- and extra-hamlet marriage revealed by this sample is as follows. Almost half of the total marriages (25) were between spouses both natural to Fontelas. About the same number (24) involved one outside spouse. (Of these 24 marriages, 12 brides and 12 grooms married spouses from Fontelas.) Finally, 6 marriages involved spouses who were both outsiders by birth but two subsequently took up permanent residence in Fontelas. These individuals include three widows who moved into Fontelas with kin, and three specialists: the Forest Guard, bus-driver, and stone-mason. In other words, of the community's current marriages about half were hamlet-endogamous.[5]

By and large, marriages across hamlet and parish boundaries involve the 20 or so hamlets immediately surrounding Fontelas (Map 2). For example, of the 24 unions involving one spouse from outside Fontelas, a majority of 18 in-marrying spouses came from these surrounding communities. Only 2 individuals came from more distant hamlets in the municipality, and only one from the municipal town. Quite surprising is the minimal number of marriages occurring within the boundaries of the parish: only 3 were contracted between spouses from Fontelas and two of the other hamlets in the parish (Lousada and Portelinha). Predictably, *not one* of these 55 unions linked Fontelas with its rival neighbouring hamlet, Mosteiro, with which Fontelas has maintained an enmity long rooted in history. The pattern revealed by this small sample of recent marriages indicates that just about as many villagers have married within the community as outside it. Further, when marriages are contracted across hamlet boundaries, they are more likely to involve any neighbouring or nearby settlement. There is no preference whatever for intra-parish marriages. The trend is thus definitely one of marriages between a relatively small radius of local hamlets.

ecclesiastical law the parish priest could entirely omit households with consensual unions or civil marriages during his Easter visit, he does not. The blessing given to these households is no different textually from that given to other households. After having unsuccessfully attempted at various times in former years to 'marry them in the proper way', the priest simply gave up, concluding that the couple were stubborn and staunchly anticlerical. For some interesting comparative points on civil marriages in the Alentejo province, see Livi Bacci (1971).

5 There is of course a problem in all of these marriage materials in deciding whether to consider the spouses' hamlets of *birth* or their hamlets of *residence* at the time of their marriage. I have considered as an outsider any person born and brought up in another hamlet. This means that individuals moving into Fontelas as children or adolescents are still regarded as outsiders (as they are in fact considered by villagers themselves). A person born in a neighbouring hamlet and moving into Fontelas permanently at the age of 5 or 6, for instance, is always referred to as 'from hamlet X', and not as 'one of our own hamlet'. The only exceptions are those persons whose marriage entries state that they have been 'resident in Fontelas from infancy'. Thus a day-labourer from outside, resident in this community for a number of years at the time of his marriage to a Fontelas bride, would still be regarded socially very much as an outsider.

We can supplement this sample with the marriage entries in the Parish Register from 1870 through 1978. This will allow us to push our sample somewhat further back in time and also to enlarge the field of cases studied. Table 14 sets forth the essential information contained in all of these marriage entries.

A total of 105 marriages were listed for Fontelas alone, thus yielding an average of about one marriage per year. Most of the 55 marriages I have mentioned above were also recorded in the Parish Register. Some, however, were of course not listed: these would be widowed persons moving into the hamlet, or out-marrying husbands. Alternatively, some couples listed in the entries may have died or moved elsewhere. Thus the Register is useful merely for information on where and when the weddings took place and *not* for information on post-marital residence. In this sense, the figures above and those in Table 14 link two sources of marriage data but they do not entirely overlap.

We can summarize the information in Table 14 as follows: there are four main types of marriages according to the origins of spouses.

Intra-hamlet (both spouses from Fontelas)	–	41		
Hamlet + parish (one spouse from another hamlet in the parish)	–	12	63	44 in-marrying grooms 19 in-marrying brides
Hamlet + outsider (one spouse from outside the parish)	–	51		
Both outsiders (residents of Fontelas)	–	1		
Total marriages		105		

From these figures we can conclude that in 85 of these 105 marriages the bride was from Fontelas (41 + 44), and in 60 the groom (41 + 19). These figures over the past century indicate that a somewhat larger number of marriages (63) were hamlet-endogamous than hamlet-exogamous (41). But too many marriages of villagers from Fontelas may be invisible due to their registration in other parishes, and so we must use the figures only as guides to general trends.

Nevertheless, a clear pattern is discernible with regard to out-marriage. Of the 51 marriages involving outsiders the overwhelming majority (37) of spouses came from Fontelas' neighbouring hamlets shown on Map 2. Further outside this radius, 7 spouses came from other hamlets in the municipality, 4 from the municipal town, 1 from a nearby city in Trás-os-Montes province, and 2 from Spain.[6] As a whole, the entries clearly duplicate the pattern of out-marriage revealed by the 55 current unions discussed above. The range of this out-marriage takes place predominantly within a small area of surrounding hamlets.

In the absence of a larger sample,[7] we can conclude that since the late nineteenth century, between a third and half of the marriages examined were hamlet-endogamous and that approximately half to two-thirds were hamlet-exogamous. The overall trend, despite a considerable proportion of intra-hamlet unions, has been one of marriage *across* both hamlet and parish boundaries.

Two further patterns emerge from the household diagrams in Appendix IV and these marriage entries: (a) an extraordinarily high age at marriage, and (b) a large proportion of adults never marrying. It is here that the indelible stamp of Hajnal's 'European marriage pattern' is most evident. Let us look closely at these ages before setting Fontelas within this wider European context. Our first figure is a simple sum of all adults resident in Fontelas in 1977, according to marital status. I have calculated these figures from a complete count of ages on 1 July 1977, checking these ages where possible with each person's baptismal entry.[8] As a whole, there were 143 resident adults of both sexes over the age of 15, and the proportions who were single, married, or widowed were as follows:

Number of adults single:	68	(48%)
Number of adults married:	62	(43%)
Number of adults widowed:	13	(9%)
Total adults	143	(100%)

Quite striking is the high proportion of adults who are currently unmarried (48 per cent). But how are these proportions distributed within different age

6 There may be a tendency here towards under-registration of out-marrying males. Most marriages are recorded in the Parish Register of the bride's hamlet, where it is customary for the wedding to be held. This does not mean that the groom in these cases resided thereafter in the bride's parents' household. The marriage entry may be recorded in the Parish Register of the bride's hamlet, but this entry itself may be totally misleading as regards residence. The bride may (although this is not very common) have returned to the groom's hamlet and resided virilocally, or the couple may have resided neolocally elsewhere.

7 I could of course count the marriages of the other three hamlets in the parish (which I also copied) in order to enlarge the sample. But this would be a rather laborious task and, judging from my perusal of the entries, the parish figures do not appear substantially different from the data on Fontelas alone.

8 Where no baptismal entry was available, I recorded the age stated on an individual's *cédula* or identity card. In the absence of even this record or any marriage entry (where ages are always given) in a few cases I had to rely entirely on the person's stated age. This was not always a correct estimate. For most villagers, however, baptismal entries were available and the ages are thus by and large accurate to the day.

Table 14. *Marriages in Fontelas, 1870–1978*

Year	Groom's occupation	Hamlet of origin	Age	Bride's occupation	Hamlet of origin	Age	Observations
1870	Field labourer	Fontelas	36	Housework	Lousada	28	
	*Lavrador	Fontelas	38	Lavradora	Portelinha	52	Dispensation
	Lavrador	Nearby hamlet	27	Lavradora	Fontelas	37	
1871	Jornaleiro	Fontelas	21	Jornaleira	Town	23	
1872	Jornaleiro	Distant hamlet	33	Lavradora	Fontelas	32	
1873	Jornaleiro	Nearby hamlet	31	Jornaleira	Fontelas	23	
	Sawyer	Spain	42	Lavradora	Fontelas	35	
1874	Lavrador	Nearby city	26	Housework	Fontelas	23	
1875	Lavrador	Neigh. hamlet	27	Lavradora	Fontelas	25	
1876	Lavrador	Nearby hamlet	28	Lavradora	Fontelas	27	
1877	Lavrador	Fontelas	42	Lavradora	Fontelas	27	
1878	Lavrador	Fontelas	49	Lavradora	Fontelas	35	
	*Shoemaker	Fontelas	40	–	Spanish hamlet	47	(–) Occupation not recorded
	Blacksmith	Fontelas	25	Cottager	Neigh. hamlet	28	
1879	*Jornaleiro	Fontelas	49	Cottager	Fontelas	48	
	Jornaleiro	Neigh. hamlet	30	Lavradora	Fontelas	60	
1880							No marriages
1881							
1882	Lavrador	Fontelas	29	Lavradora	Fontelas	35	
1883	Jornaleiro	Lousada	37	Lavradora	Fontelas	35	
	Jornaleiro	Portelinha	29	Lavradora	Fontelas	27	
1884	Lavrador	Fontelas	25	Lavradora	Neigh. hamlet	23	
	Jornaleiro	Fontelas	42	Jornaleira	Fontelas	48	
1885	*–	Nearby hamlet	41	–	Fontelas	31	
1886	Tailor	Neigh. hamlet	49	Jornaleira	Fontelas	41	
1887	*Lavrador	Fontelas	69	*–	Nearby hamlet	51	
	Jornaleiro	Fontelas	35	Jornaleira	Fontelas	25	Dispensation
	Jornaleiro	Fontelas	35	Jornaleira	Fontelas	30	1 child legitimated
1888	Jornaleiro	Nearby hamlet	36	Jornaleira	Fontelas	24	1 child legitimated
1889	Jornaleiro	Neigh. hamlet	36	Jornaleira	Fontelas	35	
1890							
1891	Jornaleiro	Fontelas	26	Jornaleira	Fontelas	20	
1892							
1893	–	Nearby hamlet	24	–	Fontelas	26	
1894	–	Neigh. hamlet	30	–	Fontelas	23	1 child legitimated
1895	–	Fontelas	27	–	Fontelas	17	
	–	Fontelas	28	–	Fontelas	23	1 child legitimated
		Fontelas	46	–	Fontelas	44	Dispensation

		[illegible]	[illegible]		Fontelas	37	4 children legitimated
1897	–	**Parish	27	–	Fontelas	22	1 child legitimated
1898							
1899	–	Town	26	–	Fontelas	29	1 child legitimated
1900							
1901							
1902	–	Fontelas	25	–	Nearby hamlet	24	
1903	*–	Fontelas	32	–	Neigh. hamlet	33	
1904	*–	Fontelas	45	–	Nearby hamlet	47	
	–	Fontelas	41	–	Portelinha	43	5 children legitimated
1905							
1906	–	Fontelas	27	–	Fontelas	27	1 child legitimated
1907							
1908	–	Fontelas	27	–	Portelinha	28	
1909	–	Fontelas	32	–	Fontelas	34	
	*–	Nearby hamlet	54	–	Fontelas	47	
1910							
1911							
1912							
1913							
1914	–	Neigh. hamlet	22	–	Fontelas	24	
	–	Fontelas	32	–	Neigh. hamlet	23	
	–	Fontelas	19	–	Neigh. hamlet	18	
1915	Jornaleiro	Fontelas	43	–	Fontelas	27	
	–	Fontelas	34	–	Fontelas	51	Dispensation
1916							
1917	*–	Fontelas	47	–	Fontelas	38	
1918	–	Fontelas	37	–	Nearby hamlet	32	
1919	–	Fontelas	21	–	Fontelas	26	
	–	Neigh. hamlet	30	*–	Nearby hamlet	35	
1920							
1921	–	Distant hamlet	42	–	Fontelas	40	
	–	Fontelas	26	–	Fontelas	28	
	–	Lousada	32	–	Fontelas	26	
1922	–	Fontelas	38	–	Fontelas	33	
1923	–	Nearby hamlet	20	–	Fontelas	19	
	–	Fontelas	23	–	Fontelas	18	
1924	–	Fontelas	31	–	Fontelas	16	
1925	–	Fontelas	24	–	Fontelas	17	
1926	–	Fontelas	31	–	Neigh. hamlet	22	
	*–	Neigh. hamlet	37	–	Fontelas	19	Dispensation
	–	Nearby hamlet	22	–	Fontelas	25	
1927							
1928							
1929							

Table 14 (*cont.*) *Marriages in Fontelas, 1870–1978*

Year	Groom's occupation	Hamlet of origin	Age	Bride's occupation	Hamlet of origin	Age	Observations
1930							
1931							
1932	Border Guard	Nearby hamlet	31	Proprietária	Fontelas	29	
1933	Jornaleiro	Fontelas	30	–	Fontelas	41	
1934							
1935							
1936	Lavrador	Neigh. hamlet	27	–	Fontelas	22	
1937							
1938							
1939							
1940							
1941	Jornaleiro	Fontelas	25	Doméstica	Fontelas	20	
	Jornaleiro	Fontelas	25	Doméstica	Fontelas	23	
1942							
1943	Jornaleiro	Lousada	34	Doméstica	Fontelas	53	1 child legitimated
	Jornaleiro	Fontelas	33	Doméstica	Neigh. hamlet	22	
	*Lavrador	Fontelas	46	Doméstica	Fontelas	38	3 children legitimated
1944							
1945	Jornaleiro	Mosteiro	34	Doméstica	Fontelas	22	
1946	Jornaleiro	Fontelas	40	Doméstica	Fontelas	26	
	Border Guard	Neigh. hamlet	43	Doméstica	Fontelas	43	
	Jornaleiro	Fontelas	63	Doméstica	Fontelas	56	8 children legitimated
1947							
1948	Jornaleiro	Fontelas	29	Doméstica	Fontelas	26	1 child legitimated
1949							
1950	Lavrador	Fontelas	24	Doméstica	Fontelas	23	
1951							
1952	Jornaleiro	Nearby hamlet	22	Doméstica	Fontelas	20	
	Jornaleiro	Nearby hamlet	23	Doméstica	Fontelas	25	
	Jornaleiro	Nearby hamlet	27	Doméstica	Fontelas	22	
1953							
1954	Shopkeeper	Fontelas	30	Doméstica	Fontelas	33	
1955	Jornaleiro	Fontelas	29	Doméstica	Fontelas	18	
1956							
1957							
1958							

1960							
1961	Lavrador	Neigh. hamlet	26	Doméstica	Fontelas	18	
1962	Jornaleiro	Fontelas	39	Doméstica	Fontelas	28	
	Lavrador	Fontelas	75	Doméstica	Fontelas	65	3 children legitimated
	Motorist	Nearby hamlet	34	Doméstica	Fontelas	31	
	Jornaleiro	Fontelas	34	Doméstica	Fontelas	25	
	Lavrador	Fontelas	23	Doméstica	Fontelas	18	
1963							
1964	Shopkeeper	Fontelas	49	Doméstica	Fontelas	19	
1965	Police officer	Town	27	Doméstica	Fontelas	21	
	Jornaleiro	Fontelas	61	*Doméstica	Nearby hamlet	64	
1966	Clerk	Portelinha	29	Doméstica	Fontelas	24	
1967	Jornaleiro	Neigh. hamlet	25	Doméstica	Fontelas	26	
1968							
1969							
1970	Lavrador	Fontelas	60	Doméstica	Fontelas	74	
	*Jornaleiro	Lousada	49	Doméstica	Fontelas	41	3 children legitimated
1971	–	Neigh. hamlet	55	–	Fontelas	51	4 children legitimated
	–	Town	25	–	Fontelas	27	
1972	–	Distant hamlet	33	–	Fontelas	35	
1973							
1974							
1975	–	Fontelas	56	*–	Fontelas	56	
1976	–	Distant hamlet	24	–	Fontelas	17	
	–	Fontelas	20	–	Fontelas	16	
1977	–	Fontelas	69	–	Fontelas	71	
1978							
	Total men marrying for the first time	– 93		Total women marrying for the first time	– 101		5 Dispensations
	Men re-marrying	– 12		Women re-marrying	– 4		39 children legitimated
	Total marriages:	105		Total marriages:	105		

Source: Parish Register – Marriage entries.

* Re-marriage
** This groom in 1897 was listed only as coming from 'the parish of Mosteiro', thus not indicating his hamlet of origin.

Table 15. *Marital status of adults, 1977*

	Single	Married	Widowed	Total
Men				
15–19	16	2	–	18
30–39	3	6	–	9
>40	14 (16)*	22	4	40
Total men:	33	30	4	67
Women				
15–29	12	4	–	16
30–39	3	9	–	12
>40	20	19	9	48
Total women:	35	32	9	76
Total adults:	68	62	13	143

* Note that shortly prior to my Age Census of 1 July 1977, three men all over the age of 40 died, two of whom were unmarried.

groups? Table 15 presents a more detailed breakdown of marital status by age groups and sex.

As a whole, in the two higher age groups (> 40) women outnumber men. But the most illuminating trend is the large proportion of single men and single women in Fontelas: single adults outnumber married ones. The proportions within the over-40 age group are most interesting: 22 men were married but 14 single, while 19 married women were balanced by 20 single women. Clearly the trend is *not* towards early marriage, but rather towards celibacy or the late marriage of spouses in their 30s or older. The total number of married villagers was merely 43 per cent, or less than half of the hamlet's adults. In his study of the European marriage pattern, John Hajnal has concluded that 'If over 30 per cent of women 15 or over are single one may be certain that the population had a marriage pattern of the European type' (1965:136). In Fontelas this percentage is strikingly high and well over 30 per cent: of all of the adult women in Fontelas over the age of 15, unmarried women account for 46.1 per cent. Also of interest here is one of the myriad figures that can be calculated from the Confessional Rolls: in 1896 the proportion of single villagers was enormous. Among women over 14, the proportion unmarried was 52.8 per cent and that of married women merely 34.9 per cent (53.2 per cent of men were single and 40.5 per cent married).

Late marriage is a second pattern that emerges from these figures. From the 105 marriages listed in the Parish Register since 1870, the mean age of men marrying for the first time was 33.2 and of women, 31.0. If we include 12 remarriages in this calculation, these mean ages would be even higher: 34.6 for men and 31.8 for women. These are surprisingly high figures, comparable to those reported in recent ethnographies of Swiss and Italian Alpine communi-

Table 16. *Mean age at first marriage in Fontelas, 1870–1978*

Years	*Number of marriages recorded	Mean age of groom	Mean age of bride
1870–1879	16	32.1	34.4
1880–1889	12	35.3	32.2
1890–1899	10	30.9	27.1
1900–1909	8	30.4	35.4
1910–1919	9	29.8	29.9
1920–1929	11	28.9	23.9**
1930–1939	3	29.3	30.7
1940–1949	10	36.2	32.9
1950–1959	6	25.8	23.5
1960–1969	11	38.4	27.5
1970–1978	9	42.8	41.5
Totals	105	33.2	31.0

Source: Parish Register – Marriage entries.

* These are the *total* numbers of marriages recorded in each decade. The totals thus include 16 re-marriages, but the ages of these re-marrying spouses (12 widowers and 4 widows) have been omitted from the calculations of mean ages.

** Five teenage brides who married during this decade were aged 16–19.

ties.[9] How was this figure obtained, and further, how is such a high age at marriage to be explained? Additional breakdowns of male and female ages at first marriage since 1870 are presented above in our last series of figures in Table 16.

The general trend of the figures indicates a high age at marriage for both men and women. In only 4 of the 11 decades did the mean age at marriage for men drop below 30, and in the 1970s it actually rose to almost 43 (!). Similarly, in only 5 of the 11 decades did the mean age at marriage for women drop below 30. For both sexes, in the decades from 1910 to 1930 and again in the 1950s these average ages were particularly low.[10] However, there appears to be no

[9] See Wolf and Cole (1974) for the Italian Alps, where the median ages at marriage for men from 1900 to 1949 were respectively 34 in St Felix and 38 in Tret, and for women 28 in St Felix and 24 in Tret. Friedl (1974:27) also reports average marriage ages of late 20s and early 30s for Kippel in Switzerland, as does Netting (1979a:152) also for the Swiss Alps. Stanley Brandes (1975:118) reports for Central Spain that 'the overwhelming majority of persons of both sexes marry at age 25 or over', thus providing 'conformity with the overall European pattern of postponed marriage'.

[10] There may of course be a link between these drops in marriage ages and the general trend of population at these times. As Note 15 in Chapter 2 has shown, both the 1920s and the 1950s saw rapid rises in population at the parish level (no hamlet figures are available in the national censuses for these years). For example, from 1920 to 1930 the total parish population rose from 654 to 734 while from 1950 to 1960 it rose from 808 to 973, but the disproportion between the sexes at these times was not extreme. As these figures do not apply to the hamlet of Fontelas alone, I have not been able to deal with the demographic statistics in detail. The situation is further complicated by the hamlet's high rates of illegitimacy: varying proportions of the population are born outside legal marriage and thus *marital* fertility does not provide a uniform guide to *total* fertility.

substantial direction of change in recent decades indicative of the lowering of the average age at marriage. A number of recent weddings were mentioned in Chapter 5 and might be attributable to pressure from the parish priest (resident in Fontelas since 1964) upon unmarried couples to 'marry within the Church' and legitimate their bastard children. For instance, one couple marrying in 1970 (both in their 40s) legitimated their 3 children, and another couple marrying in 1971 (both in their 50s) legitimated 4 children (Table 14). Of the nine men marrying in the 1970s two were aged 60 and 69, while of the women two were in their 50s and two others were 74 and 71. We recall that the latter (Laura) married Pedro in 1977, at dawn; their marriage legitimated 4 of Laura's 8 bastard children (although in this case the marriage entry did not explicitly state this fact).

As a whole then, the table indicates a consistently high age at first marriage for both men and women. Villagers in Fontelas have been marrying for the past century at mean ages somewhere between their late 20s and their mid-30s.

A brief description of a wedding and of some of the rich folklore about the dangers of marriage may lead us further towards an explanation. I attended only four weddings during my fieldwork,[11] but the structure of each of these was similar enough to allow for some provisional generalization. The marriage in question was between two spouses both natural to Fontelas – Zeferina of H40 (aged 26) and Gaspar of H34 (aged 24). Two of Gaspar's elder siblings had married out of the hamlet while his younger brother Silvino (aged 21) remains with his parents. Similarly, Zeferina's elder sister had already married a man from Fontelas a few years earlier while her three younger siblings remain with their parents. Both spouses were thus middle siblings, both had younger unmarried brothers or sisters, and neither of the two was the first sibling in their household to marry. At the time of the wedding, Zeferina was resident in her parents' household, while Gaspar was a Border Guard stationed in a hamlet a few kilometres to the North-east of Fontelas. Both spouses came from wealthy *lavrador* households and they are third cousins.

The wedding (*boda*) was quite small in size – 40 people were present including the priest and myself. The ceremony took place in the summer of 1978 in the district capital at a church overlooking the city from a hill. This rather fashionable choice of location was the only departure from the standard wedding procedure according to other villagers' descriptions. Weddings are usually announced only once in church by the parish priest, at the end of a Sunday mass shortly preceding the date of the wedding. This announcement did not take place in this case, as an outside priest from the city officiated. The religious ceremony itself was fairly short and to the point. The bride and groom stood close to the front of the church with their two chosen witnesses

[11] Two of these weddings involved brides from Fontelas, the third took place in a neighbouring hamlet, and the fourth in the town.

(*testemunhas*) on either side. After the exchange of rings, a brief communion service follows along with some final prayers of blessing. Following the service, a number of group photographs were taken by myself at the spouses' request: after this the married couple and all of the guests were driven to the city for the banquet. This took place in a hall rented for the purpose by the bride's father. Prior to a wedding, the groom pays for the minimal legal fees involved in arranging the preliminaries for the marriage at the Civil Registry Office in the municipal town, while it is customary for the bride's father to provide (or pay for) the repast and accompanying dance. At this wedding, patterns of dress were not particularly ornate: the bride's white gown was clearly the most outstanding sight, while men's suits and women's clothes bore little difference to those worn for an ordinary Sunday mass. No bells were rung before, during, or after the ceremony, and no procession took place at any point.[12]

All of the food provided for the banquet was spread out along three long tables in a U-shape (Photo 21). This arrangement is called a *copo d'água* or 'water-glass': the term refers to the cold meats and drinks spread out on the tables, quite distinct from the roasted and boiled meats and soups eaten at the feasts following baptisms and patron saints' festivals. All four weddings I attended had banquets of this type. Wines and liqueurs are served, while cold meats (kid, lamb, pork, chicken) are laid out beside cakes, rolls, pastries, and assorted sweets. The room rental and the meal cost the bride's father 8,000 *escudos* (£98) and was somewhat smaller in scale than a comparable hamlet banquet. Later that evening a dance was held in Fontelas in a large room in the bride's parents' household. These wedding dances are loosely structured: the bride as well as the groom dance with many others, and no formal sequence of partners is followed at any time. In fact, the dance is little different from those held in each of Fontelas' neighbouring hamlets during the summer, following patron saints' festivals. All of the wedding guests are automatically invited to the dance, which is also open to all other hamlet residents. Music is played on battery-operated record-players, and usually lasts until around 2 or 3 a.m.

Although the wedding day as a whole includes a rather lavish repast, it is nevertheless only a one-day occasion. Furthermore, a wedding does not stand out as significantly different from the equally opulent household celebrations and feasts on the occasions of baptisms or winter pig-slaughters. The months following the nuptials were equally lacking in novel developments. Following

[12] The wedding I attended in a neighbouring hamlet did however have a procession following the church ceremony. Two large decorated hoops (*arcos*) were held above the married couple and their witnesses as they led a procession from the church to the bride's parents' household (see p. 277, Photo 20). At the entrance to the house any and all villagers were allowed to gather, and large plates of 'wedding almonds' were offered. Two other aspects of wedding ritual I came across in nearby hamlets (neither of them ever mentioned to me in Fontelas) were (a) a tall, thin pine tree planted outside the household of the bride's parents on the day of her wedding, and (b) a golden thread or string held across the doorway of the bride's parents' house for the bride and groom to pass under (Martins 1939:427).

a brief honeymoon (*lua de mel*) of a few weeks spent in another region of Portugal, Zeferina returned to her natal household while Gaspar obtained a change of post from Northern to Southern Portugal. Following the honeymoon (itself a recent innovation), the couple visited each other a number of times for a period of $2\frac{1}{2}$ years (Gaspar's visits to Fontelas were more frequent than Zeferina's trips abroad).[13] In the second year following the wedding, a child was born to Zeferina while she was still residing with her parents. Only by early 1981 had the couple established their own (rented) household in a neighbouring hamlet to which Gaspar had again been re-stationed. A kind of variant of the pattern of the 'visiting husband' to be discussed below in the next section, Gaspar's quasi-military occupation (high in local status but middling financially) did not allow the couple to set up neolocal residence immediately.

Apart from the ceremony and banquet, what other transactions occurred between the spouses or their two respective households? Here again, the structure of wedding exchanges in Fontelas is markedly scant. A few days later, I visited Zeferina's parents' household and made an inventory with Zeferina of the gifts offered to herself and Gaspar on the day of the wedding (Table 17).

It is clear that with the exception of one cash gift,[14] all of the objects were household items for future joint use by the married couple. These gifts are called *pinhas*, or less frequently *prendas* or *presentes*. It is an obligation for every household (not each individual) to give the couple at least one gift. A gift may of course be given a few days prior to the marriage or on the wedding day itself: no formal rule exists concerning the timing of these gifts. As in this case no new household was set up at the time of the marriage, the gifts were stored temporarily in the bride's parents' household. When I visited the hamlet in 1981, the couple had only a few months earlier established their own household in a neighbouring hamlet. The wedding gifts are thus an initial *household* investment consisting mainly of cooking utensils, kitchen-ware, and some bedclothes.

There seems little major difference between the kind and value of the gifts given by close kin, more distant kin, and friends. In fact, a number of households duplicated the choice of a wine tankard and six glasses. Most households donated one gift although a few gave two. The groom's sister (6 gifts) and the bride's godfather (5 gifts) went overboard in their large variety of multiple donations. Particularly notable was the absence of a trousseau of linens and clothing apart from the two blankets and quilt given by the bride's mother. Although the word *enxoval* is occasionally used to refer to a trousseau of clothes, linens, and other household items given to the bride by her parents, villagers did not talk much of the contents of trousseaux either in casual

[13] I gathered this information while visiting Fontelas briefly in March of 1981.

[14] I found no evidence currently, nor in villagers' accounts of weddings in the past, of the kind of ostentatious and competitive *ofrecijo* (offering) payments described by Brandes for Becedas in Central Spain (1975:164–71).

20 Wedding procession in a neighbouring hamlet: two hoops are held respectively above the newlyweds and their witnesses.

conversation or at weddings themselves. I did not gather detailed information on the matter, but I do not think that this was due either to embarrassment or a reluctance to enumerate personal possessions. Rather, I suspect that the reason is merely indifference: trousseaus are simply not of overwhelming significance either materially or symbolically. Because four other brides in recent years (like Zeferina) have continued to reside within their parents' households for a few years following their marriages, it is not unlikely that the donation of a large trousseau is simply postponed until the couple later establish their own residence.

Similarly, all of my questions concerning dowries were uniformly answered in the negative. Villagers insisted that no kind of dowry in the form of land, a house, or a large sum of cash is given to a bride. The only occasional mention of the word *dote* (dowry) which I came across was among the wealthier *proprietário* group, but even in these cases, dowries were said to have been given 'only in the past, and only among the very wealthiest of families'. The

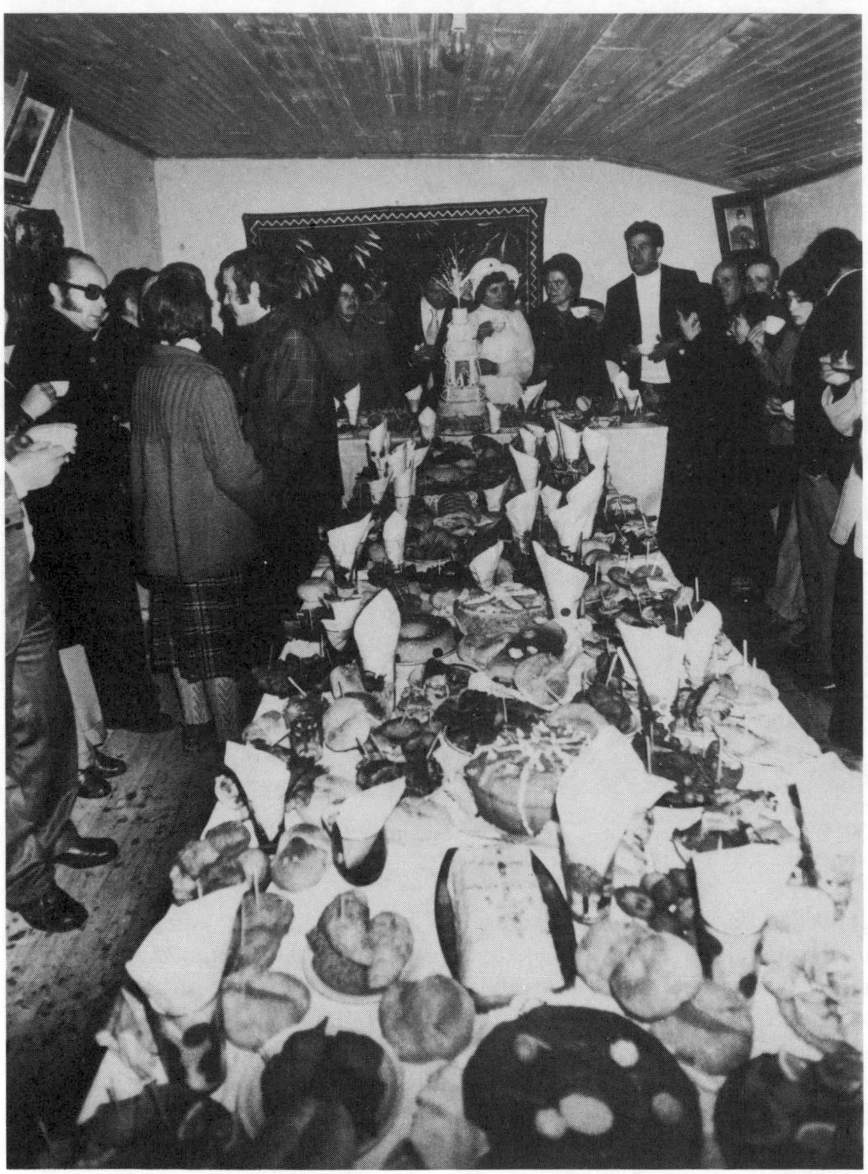

21 Wedding banquet: meats, cakes, pastries, and drinks are spread out on large tables in a number of rooms in the bride's parents' household.

Table 17. *Wedding gifts, 1978*

Guests	No. of guests	Residence	Gifts (*pinhas*)
Bride's parents & 3 of bride's siblings	5	Fontelas (H40)	2 woolen blankets (factory-made) 1 wool and cotton quilt (hand-made in a nearby hamlet)
Groom's parents	(2)	Fontelas (H34)	No gifts (refused to attend wedding)
Bride's sister (+ husband)	2	Fontelas (H23)	1 earthenware coffee-set: 1 pot with 6 cups
Groom's sister	1	Porto	7 glass dessert bowls (1 large & 6 small), 1 glassware wine tankard with 6 glasses, 2 breakfast bowls, 1 toasting-grill, 1 cruet-stand (with salt, pepper, & oil containers), 1 tray
Groom's brother (+ wife & son)	3	Municipal town	1 cotton quilt
Bride's uncle: half-brother of bride's mother	1	Fontelas (H19)	1 glassware wine tankard with 6 glasses
1st cousin of groom (+ husband)	2	Fontelas (H38)	1 earthenware coffee-set 1 pot with 12 cups
1st cousin of bride's mother (+ sister)	2	Fontelas (H28)	2 towels
1st cousin of bride's father (+ wife & 2 children)	4	Distant city	Cash by post
1st cousin of bride's father* (+ daughter)	2	Fontelas (returned to hamlet in 1978)	1 glassware wine tankard with 6 glasses
2nd cousin of groom	1	Portelinha	1 porcelain tea set
3rd cousin of bride's mother (+ husband & daughter)	3	Nearby hamlet	1 pressure-cooker
3rd cousin of bride's mother	1	Nearby hamlet	1 set of silver cutlery (12 knives, 12 forks, & 12 spoons)
Godfather of bride: also distant cousin of bride (+ mother & daughter)	3	Neighbouring hamlet	24 plates (12 large, 12 small) 24 bowls (12 large, 12 small) 2 trays 1 large fruit-salad bowl 1 soup tureen
Friend (+ wife & mother)	3	Neighbouring hamlet	2 electric lamps
Friend (+ daughter)	2	Nearby hamlet	1 glassware wine tankard with 6 glasses
Friend	1	District capital city (orig. from H45)	7 glass dessert bowls(1 large & 6 small), 1 cruet-stand (with salt, pepper, & oil containers)
38 Guests (including bride & groom)			

* The bride's mother is the godmother (*madrinha*) of this guest's daughter.

industrious folklorist and ethnographer of this region, Padre Firmino Martins, had also noted the absence of dowries in these hamlets in the 1930s: 'There are no dowries or *arras*.'[15] In only one case in Fontelas did I encounter an example suggestive of a dowry: upon her marriage, one of the priest's sisters was given a meadow and field by her parents, and her husband was given two cows by his. Both gifts were considered rather more as advances on inheritance than as outright wedding dowries, much akin to the 'marriage portions' (as distinct from both the trousseau or the dowry) donated by both sets of parents to each spouse among the Northern Spanish shepherds studied by Susan Tax Freeman (1979: 118–19). While I tried to elicit the word *dote* from both spouses, each of them staunchly resisted applying the term. It took about 15 years following their marriage for the latter couple to set up an independent household. Until then they resided natolocally, the husband visiting his wife only at night (see below, pp. 289–91). New households at marriage, as well as dowries, have certainly not been the norm in Fontelas.

This is not a society in which a rule or preference for virilocal or neolocal residence necessitates successive parental contributions to daughters who will leave the household upon marriage. This pattern provides a stark contrast to that reported by Jane Schneider for Sicily, where 'From the time she [the bride] was born, her father and brothers labored to purchase the materials of which a respectable *corredo* was made . . .' (1980:325). The stress upon dowry and trousseaux in rural Sicily is virtually nonexistent in this area of North-east Portugal, and the process quoted below (sale of land in order to buy bedclothes) would be quite unthinkable in Fontelas: 'One could always marry without land, houses or money, but never without trousseau, and several informants spontaneously recalled exemplary families who had recently sold off land to acquire their daughter's linens' (Schneider 1980:327). There is nothing at all 'patrilineal' or 'patrilocal' about Fontelas' social structure nor any particular bias within its strictly bilateral kinship system. No institutionalized system of payments or donations to either the bride herself or the couple as a unit is intended to help establish themselves immediately. In fact, there is very often quite a long period of waiting until such independent households are set up (if at all). One reason for this may be that daughters as well as sons inherit property in equal shares. As Chapter 5 has shown, one heir may be favoured socially, but legally there are no fixed rules granting sons any greater rights to property than daughters. Hence, there is no system of compensation payments offered to sons or daughters in order to push them off the parental landholding. Younger sons do not all emigrate, enter military

[15] *Arras* in Portuguese means some form of pledge or token, but Martins' short passage on marriage and weddings does not specify in any detail what kind of pledges or payments he had in mind. I suspect that the term suggests a form of gift given directly by the groom to his bride. Martins' major point was of course to stress the absence of any such groom-to-bride payments or dowries in these hamlets (Martins 1939:429).

service, or religious careers, nor do they relinquish claims to their shares of the natal patrimony. Younger daughters do not normally receive cash payments or land as advances on inheritance. Thus, major transfers of property do not occur in Fontelas *inter vivos* at marriage, but rather *post-mortem*, only following the death of a parent.[16]

Given these conditions, it is not surprising that dowry payments are entirely absent. In fact, the whole system seems to conspire *against* the formation of new households at marriage. No major conjugal fund of any kind is focused on the marrying couple, except for that provided by the wedding gifts. None of these gifts constitute large capital investments of land, cash, or agricultural equipment. The formation of new household units is de-emphasized, and one reason for this, stated by villagers themselves, is to maintain the spouses as dependent children for as long as possible after their marriages. As the groom's mother in the case above forcefully phrased it: 'I would like to see all of my children unmarried forever – my own rather than someone else's.' Despite the cousin link between the two households and the slightly higher economic position of the bride's household, the groom's mother remained opposed to the marriage. As the wedding date approached, she repeatedly spoke of her future daughter-in-law as *aquela peste* (that pest/that swine). In the end, she refused to attend the wedding and forbade her husband to as well. No gifts of any kind were given by these parents to the marrying couple. In Fontelas there is no 'house-property complex' (Loizos 1975a). Rather, it is natal households and not new ones that retain the balance of domestic power.

The folklore of marriage and courtship is a rich and varied one in Fontelas, but its dominant tone is lugubrious. Most of the verses and songs dealing with lovers or newlyweds convey messages of moralistic warning. The drawbacks of conjugal life and the dangers of marrying the 'wrong person' are constantly stressed. There are also verses and sayings extolling the virtues of marriage and youthful love: in fact, a specific form of 4-line verses which are called *loas* (wedding carols) were the customary laudatory songs sung before and after the nuptial ceremony. Only a few of these lyrics were sung at the wedding I attended in a neighbouring hamlet, and I recorded none in Fontelas.[17]

One quite common form of music sung in the hamlet, however, is the

[16] William Douglass' comments on the sparse ritual elements in rural Basque weddings are particularly germane here: 'We noted that marriage in rural Basque society is a process rather than an event. However, we have not examined the ceremonial aspects of marriage. Presently, the ceremony entails a minimum of ritual. A simple church service, attended by relatively few kinsmen and neighbors, is followed by a small banquet in a local tavern' (1969:215–16).

[17] This brings up the possibility that at the time of my fieldwork I may have been witnessing an aging population at a particular point in a cycle of emigration and depopulation. This would hence tend to present a mere fossil of former structures of weddings. I do not think this was the case, however. Firstly, there have been a low number of marriages per decade anyway throughout the twentieth century. Secondly, villagers themselves did not consistently describe more elaborate former celebrations in comparison with contemporary ones.

romance, or ballad. These are invariably tragic in theme and are mostly sung in minor keys. Such ballads were not normally songs originally of hamlet oral tradition. Rather, they were learned by younger villagers 'while up on the hills with the flocks' and based upon oral texts chanted by travelling blind men called *cegos*, who moved from hamlet to hamlet earning donations for their singing. While in this sense the *romances* were imported into Fontelas' oral literature, they were the type of song I found most completely remembered and re-sung by various villagers.[18] Two examples of such ballads are the following:

I warned you well, oh Ilda, You didn't want to hear, Armando's love was false, It was only to deceive you.	*Eu bem te avisei, ó Ilda,* *Não me quisestes ouvir,* *Amor de Armando era falso,* *Ele era só para te iludir.*
I warned you well, oh Ilda, You didn't want to listen, Armando's love was false, It was only to deceive you.	*Eu bem te avisei, ó Ilda,* *Não me quisestes escutar,* *Amor de Armando era falso,* *Ele era só para te iludir.*
I swear to you, oh my mother, And I will explain to you, Armando will not marry me, But he'll marry no one else.	*Eu juro-lhe, ó minha mãe,* *E eu lhe vou a explicar,* *Armando comigo não casa,* *Com outra não vai casar.*
I'll dress myself in rags, As a beggar in the street, Only to see Armando, By the light of the moon.	*Hei-de-me vestir de pobre,* *Tirar esmola na rua,* *Só para ver o Armando,* *Na claridade da lua.*
It was exactly midnight, When her mother called, If you want to see Armando dead, Here is the one who killed him.	*Era meia-noite em ponto,* *Quando a sua mãe chamou,* *Se queres ver Armando morto,* *Aquí está quem o matou.*
Oh how painful it was, Armando! To see you dead on the table, Take from me this funeral wreath, And I will now be imprisoned.	*Que assim me custou, Armando!* *Em te ver morto na mesa,* *Tira um botão de grinalda,* *E eu agora já vou presa.*
Oh how painful it was, Armando! To see you in that coffin, And in passing by my door You made my heart tremble.	*Que assim me custou, Armando!* *Em te ver nesse caixão,* *E ao passar à minha porta,* *Fez tremer meu coração.*

[18] The question is perhaps poorly phrased in this manner, erecting a false dichotomy between oral literary texts which are either 'internal' or 'external' to a particular hamlet's oral tradition. Variant versions of many ballads are sung in the region, and there is a local influence from Spain. Further, *romances* were usually printed on ballad sheets (*folhetins*) which were handed out by the blind men, so some interplay between oral and printed sources has characterized their development and diffusion. Perhaps a more pertinent phrasing of the problem would consider, irrespective of the origins or literary history of the ballad form, why in the first place this particular type of song has caught and held the attention of villagers in Fontelas so well?

Oh how painful it was, Armando!
To see you going to the cemetery,
You go to swallow the earth,
And I to the iron bars.

Que assim me custou, Armando!
Ver-te ir para o cemitério,
Tu vais a tragar a terra,
E eu vou p'rás grades de ferro.

There, Dona Ângela is married,
There, my wife is married,
By the will of her parents,
Rather than her own.

Lá se casa Dona Ângela,
Lá se casa, esposa minha,
À vontade de seus pais,
Pois à dela não seria.

From the church to the house,
She said only this:
God grant that you do not enjoy me,
Not for an hour, not for a day.

Da igreja para a casa,
Ela só isto dizia:
Deus queira que me não logres,
Nem uma hora, nem um dia.

It was the middle of the dinner,
Dona Ângela was not eating,
Everyone ate and drank,
Dona Ângela fell to the floor.

Era o meio do jantar,
Dona Ângela não comia,
Todos comiam e bebiam,
Dona Ângela ao chão caía.

They took her for a walk,
Only to distract her,
In the middle of the walk,
Again she fell to the floor.

Foram co'ela ao passeio,
Só para ver se a distraía,
Chegaram ao meio do passeio,
De volta ao chão caía.

They took her to the doctor,
To see what illness caused her death,
Her heart had been upturned,
With the bottom towards the top.

Foram co'ela ao doutor,
Para ver do que mal morria,
Tinha o coração revolto,
Com o de baixo para acima.

And within her heart,
Two golden mottos she had,
And one was: Goodbye Dom João,
And the other: Love of my life.

E dentro do coração,
Duas letras d'ouro tinha,
E um era: Adeus Dom João,
E a outra: Amor da minha vida.

There goes Dona Ângela,
There goes my wife,
There she goes to the high altar,
To the feet of the Virgin Mary.

Lá se vai a Dona Ângela,
Lá se vai, esposa minha,
Lá se vair para o altar-mor,
Para os pés da Virgem Maria.

To the feet of the Virgin Mary,
To the feet of Our Lady,
Let us give her a kiss,
Before she's eaten by the earth.

Para os pés da Virgem Maria,
Para os pés de Nossa Senhora,
Vamos-lhe dar um beijo,
Antes que a terra a coma.

Both *romances* refer to relationships preceding marriage and both culminate in death. In the first song a woman kills her false lover (thus preventing his marriage to another) and in the second Dona Ângela dies with her lover's name 'inscribed in her heart' after having married her parents' chosen suitor. These ballads, always tinged with a rather morbid note, usually relate stories of blocked or doomed matches. The most common themes in the songs are either those of a prospective marriage ending in death or murder, or of a mother's lament on the departure of a son to war (where the son is invariably killed).

Many songs also relate the death of a parent.

Numerous shorter verses also warn young women of the dangers of falling prey to the advances of men, whose false promises may lead to everything but marriage:

Young girl, don't fall in love, With a married man; that's risky, Court a single man, Who can marry you.	*Menina, não se namore,* *De um homem casado; é perigo,* *Namore-se de um solteiro,* *Que possa casar contigo.*
Young girl, don't fall in love, With a servant boy, The year will end, and he will go, Young girl, you'll watch him leave.	*Menina, não se namore,* *De um criado de servir,* *Acaba o ano, vai-se embora,* *Menina, vêde-lo ir.*

Further, there are a whole series of verses concerned with post-marital situations. These usually heighten the sense of careful choice in spouses, but they also draw attention to practical considerations which may be hidden from a prospective bride possessed only by the ideals of youthful love:

Marry, marry, God will give bread, After marrying, He may or may not.	*Casar, casar,* *Que Deus dará pão,* *Depois de casar,* *Dará ou não.*
My mother, before I married, Promised me all that she had, After I had married, She gave me a needle without threads.	*Minha mãe por me casar,* *Prometeu-me tudo quanto tinha,* *Depois de me casar,* *Deu-me uma agulha sem linhas.*
My mother, before I married, Promised me three sheep, One lame, another blind, And another deaf without ears.	*Minha mãe por me casar,* *Prometeu-me três ovelhas,* *Uma manca, outra cega,* *E outra soxa sem orelhas.*

Whether these forms of literature merely reflect social patterns or on an unconscious level attempt to invert them,[19] the message behind the verses is clear. Marriage is a tricky business and it can lead to uncomfortable economic situations or tragic death. The verses also hint that marriage can imply a severing or cooling of parent/child relations when a child marries against parental wishes.

Courtship is another area in which little rigid structuring of social relationships is evident. The term *namoro* is occasionally used to refer to courtship in general and the terms *namorado* and *namorada* to speak of 'boyfriend' and 'girlfriend'. *Namoro* can also be used (although less frequently) to refer to the state of being in love. Rather more commonly employed by

[19] Although these songs are clearly not myths, the text that comes to mind here (among others) is Lévi-Strauss' 'The Story of Asdiwal' (1973). For an analysis of inversions in the moral and sexual conduct of rural priests in Galician Spain through satirical oral tales, see my own earlier work on the topic (O'Neill 1974; 1984a).

villagers is the phrase *andar com* meaning 'going with' or literally 'walking with'. The phrase is applied equally to both boys and girls: a girl may also be, for instance, *andando com João* (going with João). To be going with someone in Fontelas does not necessarily imply a relationship which will proceed to marriage, nor is this the stated ideal. Any form of relationship, from an initially interested acquaintance to a more advanced stage of courtship, may invoke the phrase *andar com.* The two partners may only talk together at dances or they may have been seeing each other for a number of years. Many liaisons merely stop, with either or both partners taking up successive relationships with others later.[20]

Thus two young villagers had stopped seeing each other shortly before my fieldwork began. Carmina was a younger sister of the bride Zeferina discussed above (H40) and Salvador was a middle sibling from H36, a somewhat less wealthy family but quite respectable. The relationship did not lead to marriage, but neither partner took up with anyone else immediately after their break. Both were seen at dances and festivals, sometimes dancing together and sometimes with others. Towards the end of 1978, rumours spread that Carmina was *andando com* Silvino (H34), the younger brother of the groom in the wedding described above. Carmina's former boyfriend Salvador had passed the entrance examination to be a Border Guard and had obtained a good post in Lisbon. Although all three of the individuals concerned were from relatively wealthy *lavrador* households, no particular stigma was attached to the break-up of Carmina with Salvador, and each went their way respectably.

This pattern is somewhat different at the top and bottom of the social hierarchy. Only among the *proprietários* do we find a greater stress upon the position of women and the virtuous reputations of daughters prior to marriage. In H28, for instance, two elderly *proprietários* live with their two celibate daughters aged 43 and 42. The younger of these daughters was many years ago betrothed to an elder brother of the groom discussed earlier (Gaspar). This relationship did not lead to marriage. While the boy involved later married out, and is today a Border Guard Sergeant in the municipal town, the *proprietária* remains unmarried. Villagers lament her celibate status and many say that 'once that *namoro* ended, she vowed never to have another'. As first cousins of the priest, both daughters lead quiet lives and spend much of their time around the house or in church. The younger daughter is viewed as rather bookish and intelligent, while the elder one (regarded as somewhat of a religious fanatic) tends to assist her father with more 'masculine' agricultural tasks and has never been known to have had a *namoro* with anyone.

[20] Precisely the same pattern has been reported for the Barroso region further West of Fontelas in Trás-os-Montes province. There, Lourenço Fontes found that 'the boy as well as the girl can have more than one *namoro*, a number of times, with the consent of the partner, or others without the partner's consent. But there are girls who have only one. Boys always have more' (Fontes 1974:106; my translation).

It is among the *proprietários* that a young woman's first courtship is liable either to lead to marriage or to permanent celibacy. There is of course a suggestion here that virginity and high status are closely linked, and also that there is (for the wealthy) a respectable path *not* leading to marriage or child-rearing. In contrast to the *lavradores* and *jornaleiros* this group watches its daughters and their prospective mates with great caution and distrust. The stakes are obviously higher, and this is why villagers lament not only the 'loss' of two eligible women who will never marry but also the waste of their large amounts of land. Even the vocabulary of courtship is employed with more precision by the *proprietários*: the word *namoro* is used more frequently as are the terms for those betrothed (*prometidos*) and fiancé/fiancée (*noivo/noiva*). There is some difference here between the situations of favoured heirs who marry young and their co-heirs who usually marry late if at all: formal courtship may be quick and to the point for the former while for the latter it may drag on for decades. The real question is whether this diluted form of prolonged relationship should be termed 'courtship' at all.

Wealthy men occupy a rather different position. Both before and following their marriage, there is ample room for a variety of relationships which, although not openly sanctioned, may be reluctantly tolerated. Should a wealthy man break off with a wealthy *noiva* the latter's position may be somewhat delicate (although not necessarily hopeless) but the man's reputation may remain unscathed. A later marriage to another girlfriend may take place, the first relationship implying no necessary fall in the man's prestige. Even following his marriage, a *proprietário* may proceed unchallenged in 'getting a poor servant woman pregnant' and then 'throwing her out of the house' with impunity.

Among the poor a different situation exists. The words *namoro* and *noivo/a* are less frequently employed in conversation, the courtship relation itself is taken less seriously, and the terms of discussion are quite distinct. Here villagers not only refer to a couple as going together but occasionally as even 'sleeping together'. Elaborate gossip abounds concerning the details of relationships between couples in this group. This manner of conversation alone would itself shock most *proprietários*, and when villagers talk of such matters in public places a passing *proprietário* or the priest will simply turn a deaf ear. Large landowners as a whole (and priests) view the amorous habits of the poor as morally aberrant and incorrigible, and in extreme moments will blame these habits on 'their blood'. In contrast to the pattern among the wealthy, young women in this group may have a series of boyfriends and yet marry relatively respectably later on. Indeed, we have seen that many *jornaleiras* marry many years after they have borne several bastard children. As illegitimate births are so frequent within this group, a somewhat looser set of pressures operates, indicative of a kind of 'alternative' sexual code.

A case in point was the courtship of a smallholder girl and a *lavrador* boy, the boy's household being distinctly wealthier in this case. Bebiana (H24) and Patrício (H11) had been going together for a few months in 1978 when Bebiana's mother (herself having borne 4 daughters by 3 different fathers) began to speak of their possible future marriage. This would of course be in the rather distant future, as at the time (1978) Patrício was only 20 and Bebiana 17. Patrício's mother, however, was categorically opposed to the match. A third household (H10) then became involved indirectly – that of Rosa, a nextdoor neighbour of Patrício's. Rosa wanted the latter to break off relations with Bebiana and start 'walking with' her own daughter Albertina, also aged 17.

By the end of my fieldwork, things had changed quite dramatically. Bebiana and Patrício had stopped seeing each other, while Rosa's daughter had had a relationship of her own initiative with a boy from Mosteiro (a rare and doomed choice anyway as Fontelas and Mosteiro are ritual rivals) which also broke off fairly soon after it began. After her first *namoro*, Albertina married someone entirely different in 1980, from yet another hamlet. Patrício began his military service and returned only occasionally to the hamlet, while Bebiana remained with her mother and stepfather: unattached but certainly not prohibited or excluded in any way from further relationships in the future. The case is not atypical. It is among the *jornaleiros* that the following verse has its most frequent referents:

The little stars in the sky hasten, They all go down little paths, Lovers also hasten, From your hands into mine.	*As estrelinhas do céu correm,* *Todas vão às carreirinhas,* *Também os amores correm,* *Das suas mãos para as minhas.*

No one seemed particularly upset about any of these breaks, and in Bebiana's section of the hamlet gossip about her relationship with Patrício centred not upon *whether* the two had slept together but rather on *when* Bebiana might be likely to find herself pregnant. On one occasion, I was returning on a late summer afternoon from Mosteiro on my bicycle, and along the main road came upon Bebiana and Patrício emerging from a bush while pulling up their trousers. They casually asked me the time, after which we exchanged a few words and I rode on. Neither of them seemed at all concerned that I (or anyone else for that matter) had seen them together nor about what might be said about them later. Again, the general pattern of courtship among the *jornaleiros* and some of the *lavradores* seems quite loosely structured as successive 'suitors' begin and end relationships with other partners. Neither the choice of partners nor the details of sexual conduct follow the more rigid rules operative among the very wealthy.

In general then, it is only among the *proprietários* that we find a somewhat elaborate code of values concerning formal courtship. Even among this group, however, I did not find much evidence of as strict a system of values as that described by Cutileiro for wealthy latifundists in Southern Portugal (1971:93–

9). I have never heard of any cases of abduction or elopement in or around Fontelas, nor does the figure of the go-between appear in either villagers' conversation or their folklore. Although the households and relatives of prospective spouses will endlessly discuss the relative economic and moral standing of the two families in private, elaborate financial negotiations preceding a wedding are simply non-existent.

This is not to say that relationships do not exist, but rather that because so many individuals in Fontelas are prevented from marrying, these relationships do not follow a prescribed *process* of formal courtship leading to marriage. I did not hear any mention of distinct phases of courting from an informal stage of going together through a transitional one ('at the corner/at the door') to a final formal one ('inside the house') similar to those described by Price and Price (1966a) for the Central Spanish region of Extremadura. It is of course possible (but doubtful) that I observed only the first of the three phases of courtship described by Price and Price. However, in Fontelas no word is used for any of these phases such as 'at the door' or 'in the house'. Especially among the poor, no formal stages were evident between walking together and sleeping together. Intermediate phases are simply bypassed. Furthermore, a humorous phrase is used to refer to unmarried couples of any age, particularly those involved in temporary or consensual unions. These are said to have *casado nas giestas*, or 'married in the broom shrubs'.[21]

Far more comparable with Fontelas are the villages of Galician Spain immediately North of the hamlet: for these Lisón-Tolosana (1971:237) has reported that 'courtship hardly exists'. As with weddings and the related structures of matrimony, in this society the preliminaries of courtship and betrothal are also consistently de-emphasized.

Natolocal residence

The residence pattern I describe below caught my attention towards the end of my fieldwork in 1978. On my return visit to Fontelas in 1981 I gathered some further information on the topic. The following section therefore constitutes some initial notes towards the study of natolocal residence. Further visits will, I am sure, provide additional details for completing a quite novel picture of a residence pattern which is rather rare within the European ethnographic literature. Indeed, one notes a certain survivalist tone in the demographer Livi Bacci's comment that 'customs restrictive of marriage have survived until relatively recent times in Trás-os-Montes' (1971:52). Natolocal residence

[21] Another metaphor used to refer to such unions is that of 'gypsy marriage' (*casamento à cigana*). Gypsies frequently pass through Fontelas or on occasion camp out for a few weeks in one of the hamlet's three corporate oven-houses, exchanging their own hand-made articles (usually straw or wicker household items) for food or money. Although not utter outcasts, these groups of gypsies are nevertheless viewed as morally and socially 'different'. Among the *proprietários*, the sexual conduct of poor, bastard-bearing women is occasionally compared with that of gypsies: these women are located well below them in the social hierarchy and distinctly outside the bounds of respectable society.

affords yet another particularly clear example of the general limitation and suppression of marriage in Fontelas.

Natolocal residence[22] proceeds in the following manner. After their marriage, both spouses remain within the natal households of their respective sets of parents. The bride and groom are given the use of a room within the bride's parents' household – this is where the couple sleep. The 'visiting husband' (Fox 1979) thus retires to this room in his wife's parents' house only at night to sleep, after taking his evening meal with his own parents. Early the following morning, he then returns immediately to his own parents' household for daily labour. Informants repeatedly stressed to me that the husband's morning breakfast was not taken in his wife's parents' household but rather in his own natal household. In this sense, it was meals which constituted the key boundaries between the husband's allotted time in each separate domestic group. After the evening meal (particularly in winter) it was of course a matter of choice where the husband spent some time by the hearth before bedtime: this could be in his natal household or in his wife's. However, lunch was always taken in his own natal household, and the only occasions on which the two families would all take meals together were at peak agricultural harvests or celebrations such as threshings, vintages, pig-slaughters, or baptisms.

The marriage thus itself implied merely a minor adjustment of sleeping arrangements, but no major changes in patterns of work or consumption. It was the married couple, not their natal households, who were obliged to accommodate themselves after the marriage. In other words, it was the newlyweds who must adapt to their respective households' rhythms of daily labour. Under this arrangement, the husband was indeed merely a night-time visitor in his wife's natal household.

In my brief survey of this residence pattern, I encountered 11 cases of currently married couples who resided natolocally for some time in the past. By 1981 two more younger women had married and were also residing in their own natal households, their husbands (both Border Guards) paying brief weekend visits at sporadic dates months apart.[23] In addition, I was told of a number of cases in neighbouring hamlets, and even of a few in which the spouses were from different communities. These might best be termed 'weekend' marriages, as it was usually only at weekends that the husband left

[22] I have continued to use the term *natolocal* residence, following Lisón-Tolosana (1971) and Robin Fox (1978). Fox himself states that the term was 'originally coined by Professor John Barnes of Cambridge' (Fox 1978:203). In a recent introductory text, Robert Murphy mentions 'a rare variation' on the theme of residence and speaks of natolocal arrangements as *duolocality* (Murphy 1979:89). Murphy concludes that among the Ashanti and on Tory Island this form of residence is 'a sort of "half-marriage" and a way of beating the Irish pattern of interminable courtships and middle-aged weddings' (1979:93).

[23] Yet another couple was residing natolocally in early 1982 in Fontelas, following their marriage in mid-1981. I was told of this arrangement by another villager in Porto while on a brief visit to Portugal in February 1982, and later in 1983 the couple was still residing separately. Clearly, when I employ the synonym 'separate' residence, no suggestion of legal separation or divorce is intended.

his natal household and hamlet to spend a night with his wife. The duration of such residence arrangements in the 11 cases I examined lasted from 1 to 15 years. For instance, six couples resided in this way respectively for 7 months, 1 year, 2 years (2 couples), $2\frac{1}{2}$ years, and 3 years. A further five arrangements lasted for the longer periods of 5, 6, 8, and 15 years (2 couples). The most extreme case I was told of occurred in Fontelas' neighbouring hamlet of Portelinha, where a husband and wife resided natolocally for 23 years: the wife already had grandchildren before her own husband moved in permanently with her, following the deaths of his own parents. Significantly, it was only this latter case that seemed to the villagers I questioned to be definitely 'too long' a period to reside apart. A shorter period of 5–10 years was not considered unusual. Although some villagers were slightly embarrassed about their own earlier years of separate residence, most considered it an acceptable arrangement necessary within a specific set of limiting circumstances.

In all of the cases described to me, the children of the newly married couple were brought up initially in the wife's parents' household. At least one parent of each spouse was still alive at the time of the marriage. Thus, at the time of her first child's birth the wife's household was three-generational, but not technically a stem or multiple family household because each of the younger spouses resided separately and not under the same roof. One interesting characteristic of this arrangement was the specific usage of kin terms by the wife's children when addressing their maternal grandparents. Here a child would, for instance, call her mother Maria *mãe* (mother) but would prefix her grandmother's name with 'mother' as well: thus a grandmother Amélia would be called *mãe Amélia* (mother Amélia). The same extension applied when grandchildren addressed their mother's father. In this case a grandfather André would be called *pai André* (father André) while the term *pai* (father) would be used to address the child's own father. (We recall that the latter would not be a daily resident in his wife's household.) It was the *father's* parents who were more frequently referred to as grandfather and grandmother (*avô*/*avó*) rather than the mother's parents with whom the children were living. In these cases, then, there is a suggestion of closer kin ties through continual residence as well as through stronger maternal links: it is with the mother's parents that grandchildren live and not the father's. The kin term extension suggests a minimization of the generational distance between grandchildren and grandparents in the mother's household: in one sense these grandparents are just like parents.[24]

[24] Precisely the same kin term extension of 'mother' and 'father' to the maternal grandparents has been reported by Lisón-Tolosana for villages in Orense province in Galician Spain, just across the border to the Northwest of Fontelas. One of the latter's informants stated: 'The grandparents with whom they live . . . [maternal] . . . they call *papá* and *mamá*, because it is with these that they grow up; . . . the "grandparents" are the others, those that are outside, in another house, the paternal ones. Here it has always been like that' (1971:327–8; my translation).

Only when natolocal residence terminates at some later date will the children reside (perhaps already teenagers) with both of their parents. Significantly, while natolocal arrangements persist, it is always the grandparents who retain near-complete control of the natal landholding and who (except if quite senile) direct the agricultural tasks and apportion household funds. No couple residing separately mentioned any major financial contributions of the husband either towards his wife's household or towards the upkeep of their children, and to my knowledge no conjugal fund is collected or stored towards a future neolocal household. As with land and other kinds of property, it is the elder generation which maintains practical control over the residence patterns of their married children. Once again, matrimony is severely limited. Although legally coupled and already bearing children, each spouse is retained 'as if he/she were a single child' and had not in fact married. Matrimony in Fontelas is not only limited through celibacy and late marriage but also through such post-marital restrictions. The visiting husband and his wife-who-is-still-a-child reduce wedlock to the role of a distinctly part-time activity. Each spouse's time and labour during the day are devoted to their own parents and not to each other, and the conjugal tie is banished to the shadows of the night.

Two examples of natolocal residence will illustrate some of these points. The first is that of two relatively poor *jornaleiro* households, and the second of three very wealthy *proprietário* households. In Figure 22 (the first case) we find both spouses' households a few years following their 1948 marriage, in other words around 1950. Both spouses remained in their natal households following the marriage. Dárida continued to live with her mother, her two half-siblings, and her 'half-niece', while in the second household Silvério stayed with his widowed mother Fabiana. (The first of Dárida's four children had been born illegitimately in 1945, three years prior to the marriage.) This arrangement lasted for some 8 years. Dárida's half-brother Ernesto (who later in his life opened a shop) was the household's main day-labourer, while both Leónida and Dárida worked around the house or also occasionally as day-labourers. Silvério's elder sister Sebastiana had married a number of years earlier and moved in with her husband (neolocally). Silvério thus continued to work for wages and do the heavier agricultural tasks in his mother's household.

But why the separate residence? Couldn't Dárida have moved into Silvério's mother's household, or vice versa? When confronted with these questions, the spouses' responses were unanimous: 'each of us had members of our own household to look after'. Both informants stressed that their primary obligations were to their natal households and not to their spouse's, and that parents and siblings always 'needed them more' than did their husband or wife. For Silvério to leave his mother alone to fend for herself, with only occasional assistance from her son, was unthinkable – indeed, by local standards, such behaviour would be tantamount to a form of family treason. The fact that the couple had married, and even the fact that they had already borne children, did

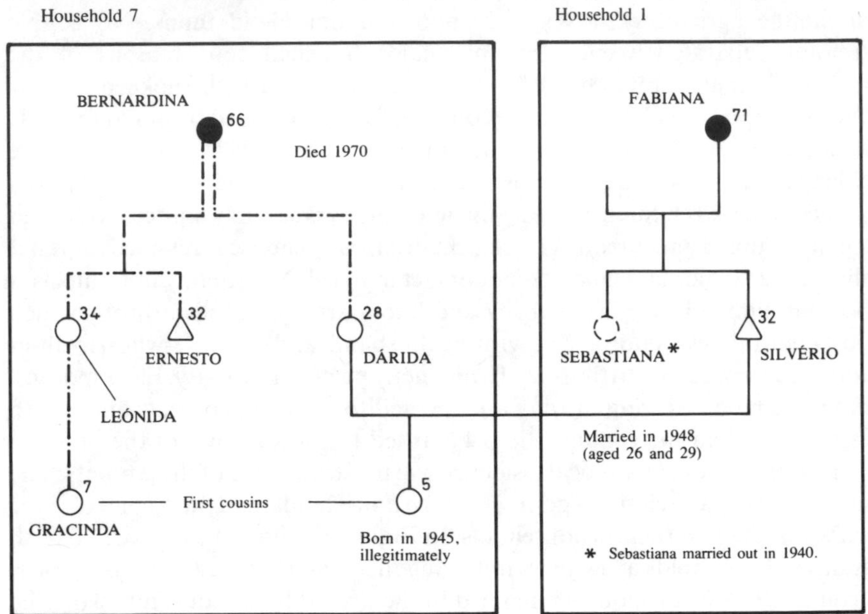

Figure 22. Natolocal residence, ca. 1950

not constitute sufficient reason for breaking up the domestic group in either natal household.

In the long term, both domestic groups eventually changed in structure. Today, Silvério, Dárida, and their two youngest sons live in Silvério's mother's house, while Ernesto lives with his wife and her elderly unmarried brother in his own natal house. Leónida later moved into Dona Elvira's household after her daughter Gracinda had become Dona Elvira's favourite servant. When Bernardina died in 1970, her few plots of land were divided between her three children, the house remaining with Ernesto as both of his sisters had moved elsewhere. The first point at which Dárida and Silvério moved in together followed closely after the date (ca. 1956) when Silvério's mother moved into her daughter Sebastiana's household upon the birth of her first grandchild. When Silvério's mother died her landholding (not a very large one) was partitioned between Silvério and Sebastiana. As the latter had already established a new household upon her marriage, Silvério remained in his mother's household with his wife and children.

There is of course a suggestion that both households originally feared or disliked the presence of an in-marrying affine as a 'stranger' within the natal household. Conflicts between mothers and their daughters-in-law are classic elements in Fontelas' folklore, and this may well be a major factor militating against virilocal residence. One saying cautions specifically against such tense affinal relations: *Vai-te minha filha, bem casada/Onde não vejas cunhada nem sogra* (Go my daughter, well married/Where you will see neither sister-in-law nor mother-in-law). But both spouses in the case above repeatedly stressed that each one's labour was needed by their natal household and that this was the decisive factor. The case illustrates the strength of kin ties of descent and siblingship within natal households, as contrasted with the comparatively weak conjugal tie between husband and wife after the marriage. The latter tie is subordinated, if only temporarily, to the dominant and long-established rhythms of each spouse's own natal household.

A second example duplicates some of the points revealed by the first, albeit in a more complicated fashion. Figure 23 shows that in this case two siblings within the same household were both residing natolocally, thus simultaneously connecting three households and four spouses through separate residence arrangements. The household on the right is that of Dona Elvira and the middle one that of the parish priest, who like his three sisters was not resident in their natal household at this time. The household on the left is that of one of the hamlet's wealthiest *lavradores*. The first marriage involving separate residence was that of Miguel and Angelina. This couple had only one child – a son who is today confined to a crib due to a problematic Caesarian birth. Again, the major reason stated for this couple's separate residence was in each case that 'my parents needed me to look after them'. In all three domestic groups, the individuals in the elder generation were well into their 60s and 70s.

In the first household, it was pointed out to me by Miguel himself that he was the principal farmer in the household and was responsible for carrying out the major agricultural tasks. Until 1961, his younger sister helped their mother with household and garden chores, while the youngest brother had his eyes on a military career as a Border Guard. The sister (* in Fig. 23) married out and left the hamlet in 1961. Around 1972–3 the household underwent a major change: after Agostinha's death in 1972, Evangelista moved to Brazil and the youngest brother (** in Fig. 23) married and moved into his wife's parents' household (H9) in another section of the hamlet. Miguel finally moved into a new household with his wife and child, but only after 15 years of separate residence. Note that when they established their new abode (actually part of the old Conselho household: H30 on Map 3) in 1973, Angelina's mother Manuela had also died. This landholding (a very large one) was immediately partitioned and each of the six siblings received a share. The widowed Plaćido remained in the natal household to be cared for by his son (the priest) and his daughter (a schoolteacher), who then returned to the household.

Also in 1973, the second couple (Valentim and Gracinda) moved in together

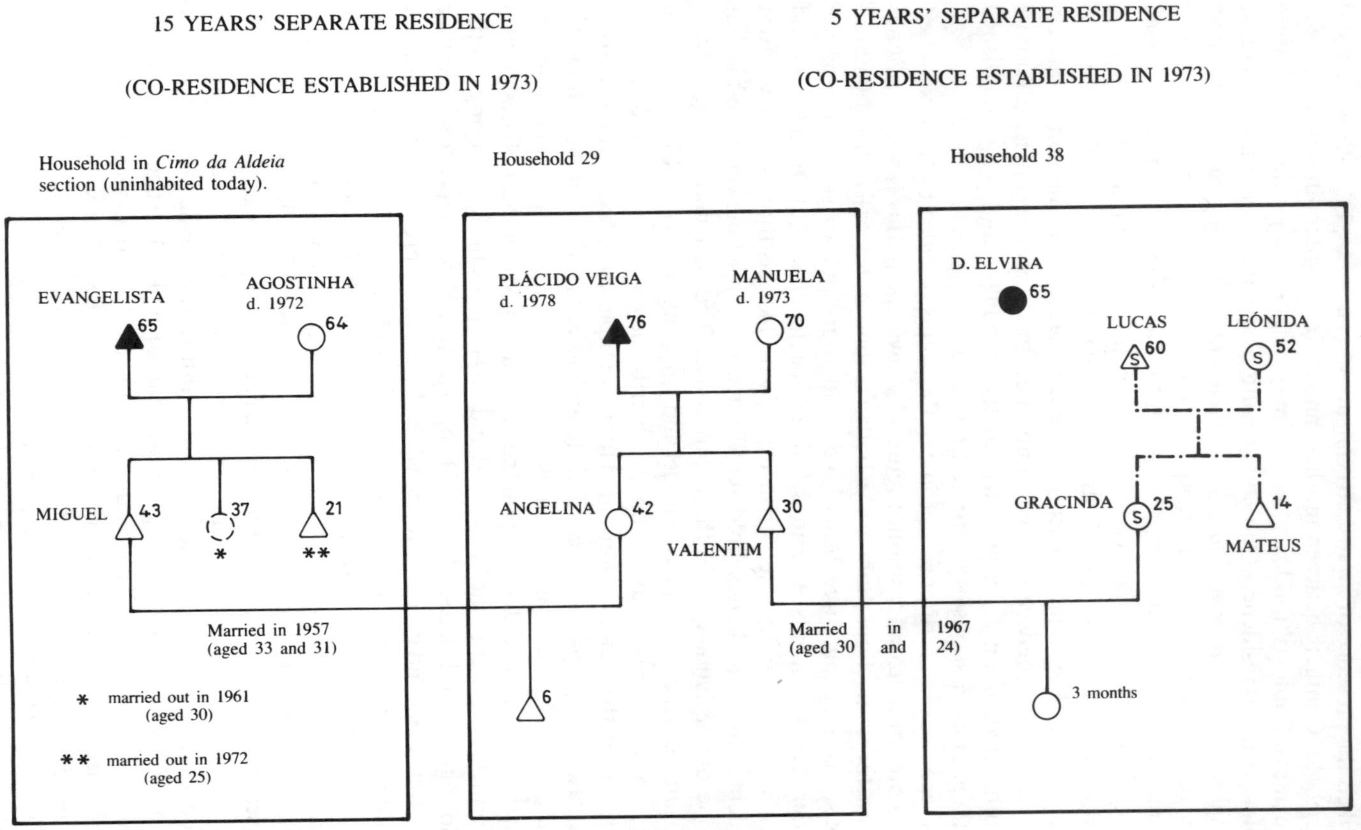

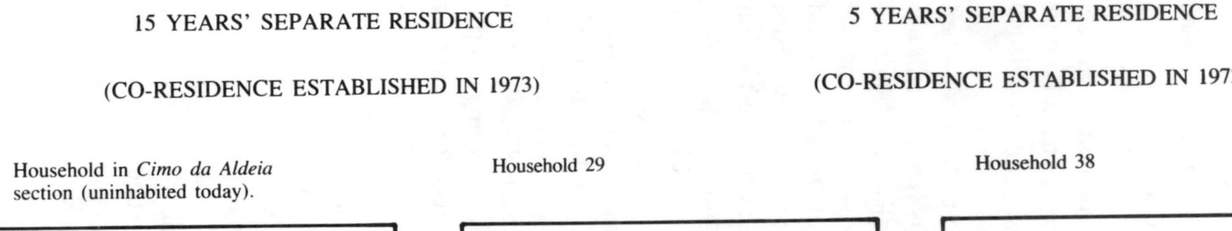

Figure 23. Two natolocal marriages, ca. 1968

following 5 years of separate residence. Precisely the same explanations for natolocal residence were given by Angelina, Valentim, and Gracinda. Angelina and Valentim were both 'still needed by their parents'. Similarly, as Gracinda was by now Dona Elvira's permanently adopted servant, there was no possibility that she could move into her husband's parents' household.[25] So in this case, *three* domestic groups were connected by part-time marriages in which women stayed put day and night. In contrast, men worked in one household during the day and slept in another at night. Both men were thus 'visiting husbands'.

All of the individuals involved once again stressed the need for their labour in their natal households rather than emphasizing potential in-law conflicts. In the case of the middle household in Figure 23, no favoured heir appeared: all six siblings divided their mother's landholding in six shares as the latter left no will (Plácido had married into Fontelas thus bringing no land to the marriage). Today the priest and his younger sister (both celibate) remain in the household, yet neither is seen as a favoured heir to land but rather as holding high-status professional occupations. In the other two households, however, Miguel and Gracinda were each distinctly favoured. Yet the natolocal residence pattern indicates that even despite a favoured heir's match, the domestic group of the latter's spouse may still put a brake on the marriage. This is done by their demanding that married children remain within their natal households: as it were, 'married only by night'. All three households concerned, however, were quite close in physical terms (Map 3) and some daily encounters were of course to be expected. This residence pattern thus suggests that it is not only the transmission of property through a favoured heir that is of import here, but also a very strict organization of precisely *who* remains (even after marriage) within the natal household as productive labour. Both land as well as the structure of the domestic group are the crucial factors at work here: a balance between land and labour must be maintained at all costs and in spite of the potential rearrangements that marriage implies. It is this delicate land/labour balance that wins out and not the conjugal tie.

There is, therefore, a disjunction here between households as productive and reproductive units. While natolocal arrangements last, both married men and women remain as productive labour within each of their natal households: the marriage does not bring about major changes in the structure of either household's domestic labour group. Yet only the woman's household functions as a reproductive unit. It is here that grandchildren are initially brought up and not with the husband's kin. Marriage then, under these circumstances, does *not* constitute a key point in any of these individuals' lives

[25] Note that of the four marriages shown in the middle generation in Figure 23, in the end one wife married out of Fontelas, one couple established neolocal residence (after 15 years apart), and two husbands reside uxorilocally.

at which new arrangements of cooperation or residence occur.[26] Rather, marriage is simply adapted to the ongoing patterns of each of the domestic groups concerned. As many of these individuals themselves remarked: 'things continued as if nothing had happened – *as if no one had married at all*'.

The basic contours of natolocal residence are now clear. But how do villagers explain the underlying reasons for this kind of residence, and how do their explanations relate to my theme of matrimony and patrimony? The following three interpretations, in the order listed, were those most consistently given to me with regard to separate residence. I questioned both those who resided in this way as well as many who did not. From the villagers' own point of view, natolocal residence occurred due to:

1. The need to retain the child's labour;
2. The difficulty of constructing new houses;
3. Sentimental attachment;
4. A 'descent principle' linked to *post-mortem* inheritance.

I have added a fourth explanation of my own which I have found underlying the other three, and will return to it below.

Firstly, let me repeat that all of the individuals I questioned stressed their roles as important sources of labour within their natal households. Marriage did nothing to alter these roles: or at least, this is the social fiction aimed at through natolocal arrangements. Each child is simply kept 'as a child' within the parental household. Separate residence usually occurs in cases of younger siblings' marriages, especially after elder siblings have already married out or emigrated permanently (see the middle household in Figure 23). Further, natolocal residence can occur when both parents of each spouse are still alive. This was the case in all of the households shown in Figure 23, whereas in Figure 22 each spouse had only one surviving parent. Natolocal residence can also occur, although I have only one example, when both parents of a spouse have died but when one or more of the spouse's unmarried siblings are still alive and resident in the natal household. The essential point is that for this kind of residence to occur, the marrying child need not be the only child left in the domestic group. But this child is usually an indispensable one within the household's productive structure: normally as a 'plougher' or day-labourer in the case of men or as a *doméstica* or household helper in the case of women. This is why both men and women who have resided natolocally stated that their parents *precisavam dos meus braços* (needed my arms).

Lisón-Tolosana (1971) and Robin Fox (1978) have described similar natolocal residence patterns in Galicia (Northwest Spain) and Tory Island, (off the Donegal coast of Ireland) respectively. The features of both authors'

[26] I am of course only speaking here of the 22 married individuals who did for some time (however short) reside natolocally, and not of *all* married individuals in Fontelas.

descriptions provide remarkable parallels with Fontelas. Both regions are, like Fontelas' area, characterized by tiny rural communities, smallholding farming traditions, poor technology, and distinctly peripheral geographical positions within their national contexts. In Galicia, for instance, Lisón-Tolosana[27] gives one case of 8 married persons in the same generation living in 5 different households: none of these persons was living jointly with his/her spouse (1971:311). Another of his informants spoke of natolocal arrangements in which 'the wife is like an unmarried daughter in the home' (1971:312). Both patterns of the nocturnal visiting husband, as well as the extension of the kin terms mother/father to grandparents, are also reported by Lisón-Tolosana. Finally, precisely the same stress is placed by Galician villagers on the *labour* of married children within their natal households. Numerous peasants in Galicia speak of their natal households needing their arms (*brazos*) and Lisón-Tolosana concludes that 'the separate residence of spouses is also imposed by the need for labouring arms in each respective household' (1971:313).

A distinctly similar pattern is described by Robin Fox for Tory Island (1978/1979).[28] Of 51 current marriages on Tory, Fox analysed 10 which involved natolocal residence, or 20 spouses residing separately. On Tory these husbands also visited their wives at night, their children remaining with the wife's parents (1978:160). Husbands had no major part in repairs of their wives' parents' households (1978:159) and dowries were non-existent (1978:184). Fox also points out that there is a strong pull towards keeping these married children in their own natal households:

> a woman's first duty was to her own people . . . or her 'own' household . . . If she had, for example, brothers or old parents who needed her, she would stay where she was born, even if she married: she should only move when these obligations were fulfilled (1978:158).

In other words, one's obligations towards co-resident kin in the natal household took priority over the newly formed (but de-emphasized) obligations towards one's spouse and affines.[29] Both Lisón-Tolosana and Fox note that the labour and kin obligations of married children towards their

[27] Unfortunately for English-speaking readers, Lisón-Tolosana's original ethnographic study of Galician Spain (*Antropologiá Cultural de Galicia*, 1971) has not yet been translated from the Spanish. To my knowledge, only one of that author's 3 articles in English deals with marriage and inheritance (1976), although even there natolocal residence is not mentioned. Emrys Peters (personal communication, 1981) has informed me, however, that an English translation of the 1971 Spanish edition is currently being carried out through Manchester University Press.

[28] Fox's article 'The Visiting Husband on Tory Island' (1979) seems to be a verbatim copy of his chapter on family and marriage in *The Tory Islanders* (1978): Chapter 7 – Family, Marriage, and Household. The later article does of course stand well on its own, but the reader is recommended the somewhat more complete analysis in the original book.

[29] A similar observation about the conflicting obligations between siblings and affines has been reported for the Ashanti by Meyer Fortes. Fortes speaks of '. . . the contrast between the mutual trust and loyalty of brother and sister and the notorious hazards of marriage' (Fortes 1970:23).

'household of orientation' override those owed to their 'household of procreation'. Long-standing labour and kinship ties within the natal household should not be and indeed are not transformed at marriage. In Fontelas an identical split between natal and marital domestic groups occurs. For the wife of Fontelas the natal and marital households are one and the same, but for the visiting husband they are divided between day and night.

The second explanation offered in Fontelas is that of housing shortage. Most of the individuals I questioned mentioned this as a key factor – 'houses were difficult and costly to build, so each spouse simply remained at home'. Another frequent comment was that it takes many years for a young couple to gather enough materials and capital to construct their own house and that during this time they must live somewhere. As an explanation, this factor seems more plausible with regard to the *jornaleiro* group and perhaps some of the *lavradores*, where land and money (as well as houses) were in short supply. But for the *proprietários* and wealthier *lavradores* it rings less true. Among the latter groups there was an excess of houses at times: the wealthy Conselho household still owns a number of uninhabited houses in the central section of Fontelas (Map 3). These were used as servants' quarters in former years. Many *jornaleiros* have spent successive periods as servants or day-labourers for *proprietários* who rented them houses temporarily. In general then, it is conceivable that among the wealthy the overall shortage of houses in Fontelas did not constitute an absolute barrier to the formation of new houses at marriage.

Both Lisón-Tolosana and Fox also mention this factor, but neither of them deals with it in detail. Nor did their informants always point to it as a major factor underlying natolocal residence. Lisón-Tolosana is more concerned with finding a general tendency in Southern Galicia for 'the perpetuation of the household' through time, whereas Fox is concerned less with limitations of housing than with his islanders' supposed aversion to creating 'a dreaded extended family' (1978:170–1). Neither addresses the problem directly, nor can we construct elaborate comparative analyses without many more detailed ethnographic case-studies. My general impression is, nevertheless, that the problem of housing is a relevant and contributory factor in natolocal arrangements but of varying import in specific cases. However, the difficulties of house construction among the poor of Fontelas have been distinctly more acute. The *jornaleiro* group is today well along the path of modern house construction: an entirely new section has arisen in Fontelas composed of 12 newly built houses. But this is due to the recent wave of emigration and is a relatively recent trend. Quite a different situation existed prior to the 1960s, when the *jornaleiros* as a whole occupied a singularly low and impoverished position within the social hierarchy.

The third major factor frequently cited by villagers is that of the sentimental attachment between parents and children. Both parents as well as their married children spoke of these ties. The most often-quoted comment by the former was: *custa-nos ver um filho sair* (it hurts us to see a child leave). The marriage of a child, especially that of a younger one, threatens these long-established kin ties within the natal household. Natolocal residence thus provides a temporary compromise. Rather than departing for their spouse's household or a newly built one, the married children will simply stay put. Temporary accommodation is provided (at night) for the visiting husband in his wife's parents' household, but each spouse's household retains its daily rhythms of labour and cooking. A married daughter or son does not thus 'leave home' at marriage, and traumas of separation are spared the parents on both sides. The sense of intrusion by an in-marrying affine is also avoided, or at least limited to the husband's nightly visits at the hearth of his parents-in-law. From the married children's respective points of view, the potential split at marriage was also viewed as sentimentally problematic. It was repeatedly stated to me that the idea of leaving one's parent(s) alone was a horrid thought. Again, natolocal residence was one means of postponing this split and avoiding major changes in domestic arrangements.

Fox spends more time on these ties of sentiment than does Lisón-Tolosana, but the latter does mention this factor. In particular, Fox speaks of an outright 'hostility to the idea of marriage from both parents and siblings' on Tory Island (1978:185). Natolocal residence there is most likely to occur in cases of children living in 'incomplete' households either with a widowed parent or one or more unmarried siblings. The sibling bond is elevated by Fox to a central principle around which many Tory substructures and cycles revolve (1978:186–7). On Tory, natolocal residence is simply one more aspect of *nonmarriage*: see also Brettell (1981) for another application of the term 'nonmarriage' for North-west Portugal and Brandes (1976) for an analysis of nonmarriage and celibacy in Central Spain. Separate residence is thus an acceptable and customary arrangement likely to occur at specific periods in a domestic group's developmental cycle. Fox concludes that it is not land ownership but rather pressure on housing as well as sentiment which are the major conditioning factors underlying natolocal residence (1978:188). Kin ties above all, and their moral elements of obligation and assistance, shape the pattern of separate residence. They insulate both parental and sibling bonds from the threat of intrusive marriage.

A fourth explanation is also possible, and here I return to the theme of matrimony and patrimony. Underlying the three explanations of informants outlined above, I see a principle of descent linked to a specific mode of *post-mortem* inheritance. I use the term 'descent' in a cautious way, and will discuss it further in Chapter 7. 'Filiation' would be another possible term. Here I employ descent merely to stress vertical or consanguineal relations between parents and children (or grandchildren) as well as relations between siblings within a natal household. As on Tory Island and in Galicia these relations, linked to the transmission of a natal patrimony, take priority over the conjugal and affinal ties established through marriage. Closely related to the demands of parents upon the labour of their married children is the fact of *post-mortem* inheritance: there is simply no way in Fontelas for a married couple to obtain sufficient capital in either land, cash, or houses to be able to set up neolocal residence. This is not to say that such residence is never established (there are some cases) but rather that it is not a common practice and that residence arrangements certainly do not favour such a setup. The parental generation retains control not only of its patrimony (land, houses, and tools) but also of the labour of its married children.

While the often-quoted phrase *quem casa, casa quer* (whoever marries, wants a house) is clearly a stated ideal, it is not frequently realized in practice. This is in large part due to the brakes upon the conjugal tie imposed by the structure of *post-mortem* inheritance. Children, and especially younger children in natolocal arrangements, simply must fulfil these obligations towards their parents and (to a lesser extent) their unmarried siblings by caring for them as they age. No major property transferral to the younger generation occurs at marriage, nor prior to the death of a parent. Even favoured heirs do not normally inherit any property prior to the death of a parent, although the favoured child may informally take on much of the household's daily management. There is, then, a built-in form of old-age security within the strict system of inheritance at death, and it is this system which underlies the shape of separate residence. The kin and labour ties formed around a natal patrimony remain as it were untouched by the potential dispersal implied by marriage.

Clear evidence for this pattern and for the strengh of relations of descent is provided by the fact that many natolocal situations usually collapse precisely at the moment of the partition of a patrimony. This occurred in the examples in Figure 23 above, and a number of further cases I studied followed the same pattern. The *lavrador* Elias, for example, explained that his own natolocal residence (lasting 6 years) terminated immediately following the deaths of his parents (close to each other in time) and the partition of their natal landholding. It was at this time only that he ceased to be a visiting husband in his wife's father's household and established uxorilocal residence. Both Fox and Lisón-Tolosana have also noted this timing in the shift of residence: Fox states that spouses already married 'might, afterwards, move in together when the parents of one or the other had died' (1978:162). Lisón-Tolosana also describes a similar sequence of events:

> Normally upon the death of the last of their parents the sons and daughters begin to think of dividing the capital and joining their husband or wife under the same roof. 'On partitioning, they join each other. On partitioning, the husband and wife always move in together'. 'When the older ones die, husband and wife unite . . .'
>
> (1971:319; my translation from Spanish and Galician).

Again in Galicia, one informant explicitly indicated the material rationale behind natolocal residence by commenting that 'they live separately in order not to partition their capital, to keep that capital together' (1971:318).

All of these examples focus on the crucial point in a household's cycle at which such a residence pattern is likely to culminate: at the death of a parent (usually the last one) when a natal patrimony is divided. This division of property is almost always accompanied by a major rearrangement of people. This is why in Figure 22 above (where both spouses came from land-poor households) as well as in the households in Figure 23 (all wealthy in land) the same pattern of separate residence appears. Natolocal residence occurs in all of the social groups in Fontelas – among the wealthy, the middling, and the poor. It is not land alone that conditions this form of residence but a combination of factors which together form a far stronger orientation towards descent and filial relations than towards conjugal and affinal ones.

Lisón-Tolosana goes as far as to term natolocal residence a form of 'symbolic suppression of the intermediate generation' (1971:329). In this sense, the illusion of the continuity of a household line is achieved through the suppression of the married child. The grandparental generation thus 'jumps' past the second generation directly to the third (the grandchildren) by skipping the marriage in between. The marriage thus remains hidden and a continuous line of descent is perpetuated through alternating generations. Grandparents (called mother and father) become social parents, while grandchildren are elevated to the level of children: the intermediate generation is symbolically annihilated. Natolocal residence thus provides an extreme example of the process through which a patrimony and its line of descent is preserved by means of the suppression of matrimony. The potential dispersal of labouring arms as well as land is blocked at marriage by the law of *post-mortem* inheritance. Obviously, specific cases of natolocal marriages involve the three main factors (labour, housing, and sentiment) in different ways, but this fourth factor underlies them all. The strings of the patrimony are held firmly by the eldest generation (parental or grandparental) and they cannot be pulled by the young.

I do not mean to imply here that counter-strategies are absent among the younger generation: quite the contrary is the case. But the parental hand of cards is dealt in their favour from the start. There are of course always some possibilities for forming new households by a newly married couple, but the checks on this step are too many and too strong for it to be taken in most cases until after the deaths of the parents. Clearly, time is of great significance here. Once the natal landholding and domestic group are broken up, the married couple themselves (previously the suppressed generation) ultimately take on the role of the former grandparental generation. A succession of different households is thus reproduced over the generations, but a considerable delay occurs in the transfer of control from one generation to the next. Late marriage is in this sense a close correlate of *post-mortem* inheritance, and it is this form of delayed inheritance that also conditions natolocal residence.

The apotheosis of 'suppressed marriage' can be found in the pattern of secret weddings and the association of marriage with the night. This point brings us back to the beginning of this chapter, where I stressed the minimal emphasis placed on wedding ritual in Fontelas. Firstly, we recall the morning wedding of Pedro and Laura in 1977, and secondly the nocturnal visits of husbands to wives in natolocal situations. A third pattern is evident in the satirical night marriages or *casamentos de noite* carried out in Fontelas towards the end of Lent. These 'marriages' were a kind of recited verse sung at the conclusion of the Shrove Tuesday festival (Photo 22). A group of male youths would gather around midnight just outside the centre of Fontelas upon a hill facing the hamlet in the *Outeiro* section. The youths would create a cacophonous din of mixed noises with various objects (sticks, tin cans, iron tools) while shouting *Casamos F. com. S.* (We marry F. with S.). These marriages have been recently discontinued, but many villagers spoke of them humorously and described the manner in which they were performed. The principal aspect of the choices of spouses was that those who were married verbally by the youths were always incongruous matches: very old women with young boys or vice versa, or two elderly celibate villagers. Widows and widowers were also 're-married'.

The date of these satirical weddings, taking place during the last costume festival of *Carnaval* before the beginning of Lent, partook of the symbolic reversals of the pre-Lenten winter months. In fact, as they began around midnight and lasted for an hour or so, these marriages actually extended the *Carnaval* antics past the temporal division point separating Shrove Tuesday from Ash Wednesday. This was part of the 'challenging' element of *Carnaval* activities. The normal order of things is upturned, and the hamlet's non-marrieds are wedded at night. This is a third example, then, of the association of marriage and the Night. Matrimony is a socially dangerous affair, and all attempts are made to hide it from daylight view.[30]

Both Lisón-Tolosana and Fox also report different forms of night-marriage which invite comparison with Fontelas. Lisón-Tolosana mentions one informant's description of natolocal arrangements in the following terms: 'in reality weddings are all for convenience and all planned. They would try to

[30] The entire topic of night-marriage and its relation to the nocturnal visiting husband invites further study. While further comparative work in Northern Iberia would be particularly interesting, I have limited myself here to the barest outlines. Benjamim Pereira (1973:126) describes similar satirical night-marriages in another part of Trás-os-Montes province, and some excellent visual and textual analysis of this custom is available in the marvellous ethnographic film by Noémia Delgado (*Máscaras*, 1976) filmed in hamlets very close to Fontelas. The film has excellent English subtitles. A useful summary of Portuguese cinema from 1896 to 1980 (including descriptions of many ethnographic films) is available in *Framework: A Film Journal*: London, Issue 15/16/17, Summer 1981; pp. 40–73 and 113–122.

22 Shrove Tuesday (*Carnaval*): a group of men and youths accompany the *Entrudo* figure (on donkey) around the hamlet, playing music and collecting door-to-door donations of food and money.

marry at night . . . [or] at dawn, without anyone knowing . . . It was the [religious] ceremony and nothing more, without a banquet and with no one invited. They performed it at dawn so that in the morning they would be working, *each one on his/her farm, as if nothing had happened*' (1971:325; Lisón-Tolosana's emphasis). The same author also states that in the general Spanish context, it is in rural Galicia that marriage is *least* celebrated and ritualized (1971:325). Fox also mentions the brief wedding service on Tory Island and the fact that marriage 'is not a matter for celebration' (1978:162). His most brilliant example is of a nocturnal wedding celebrated across the sea from Tory to the Irish mainland by firelight:

> Sometimes a mainland priest would agree to conduct a strange long-distance marriage ceremony at night. A fire would be lit on Bloody Foreland and one on the cliffs of Tory. On a clear, calm night these could be easily seen. The priest on the mainland would read a portion of the marriage service and then his assistant would put a blanket in front of the fire, cutting off its light. This was the signal for the couple on the island to make their response, after which they would in turn cover their fire, and so on . . . (1978:161).

Marriage then, is systematically relegated to the night in these three cases – Tory Island, Galicia, and Fontelas. The stakes of patrimony are simply too high to allow matrimony full daytime reign.

Consequently, marriage is limited and suppressed to a part-time visiting arrangement. All potential threats to the division of a natal patrimony or the dispersal of a natal labour group must be controlled and postponed through time, in the interests of the perpetuation of a family line through descent. Given the prevailing power of patrimony and such ties of descent, all attempts are made to grant marriage only the most *minimal* role possible within domestic arrangements.

Although Lisón-Tolosana's and Fox's analyses are the two most detailed examinations of natolocal residence in recent European ethnographic literature, I doubt that the pattern is limited solely to these regions. In fact, there are three further sources which mention the pattern, however briefly. For Central Spain, Susan Tax Freeman remarks that one year's separate residence (until the first harvest) was common in Valdemora (1970:75–7). Further, Pierre Bourdieu cites the pattern in passing for the French Pyrenees:

> This type of marriage tended to create a permanent back-and-forth between the two houses or even led the spouses to maintain their separate residences. What was at stake in this open or hidden conflict over the place of residence was, again, the predominance of one or the other lineage and the extinction of a 'house' and its name (1976:135).

For Trás-os-Montes in Portugal, Joaquim Pais de Brito (1977) has reported 12 natolocal marriages (24 spouses living separately) in the border hamlet of Rio de Onor over the past two decades, a number of these cases being natolocal marriages between spouses on opposite sides of the border (the Portuguese Rio de Onor and the Spanish Rihonor). I suspect that the pattern is hardly a rarefied one but rather merely understudied.[31]

Such rigid control over land division and the concomitant deferral of marriage are, I think, likely to be quite acute in smallholding regions where land is in short supply and partition potentially destructive. My hunch is that in other mountainous regions of Portugal and Spain where smallholdings prevail, and particularly where strict laws of *post-mortem* inheritance are practiced, natolocal residence may well not be so unusual. It is a *practical* arrangement within a particular kind of social structure where the needs of patrimony rule over those of matrimony.

[31] Both Maurice Bloch and Sandra Ott (personal communications) have mentioned to me the occurrence of natolocal residence arrangements in Southwest France.

7

The fulcrum of inheritance

In Fontelas, all major property transferrals occur at death. This rite of passage is systematically emphasized, and it occupies a central position within the process of inheritance over the generations. Death is of extreme importance here not only because it brings about abrupt changes in affective and residential arrangements between the living, but also because it is only at death (not at marriage) that the transmission of authority and property rights occurs.

As all major property (land, houses, tools, and other movables) is redistributed following a person's death, we might expect that the specific timing of this property transfer has repercussions throughout the social structure (Goody 1976b). This is indeed the case. In this chapter I shall bring together a number of strands of argument already presented in Chapters 5 and 6. First, I briefly describe the event of death and the accompanying vigil and funeral, and secondly the actual division of property occurring after death at the *partilha*. Finally, I draw some conclusions about the long-term effects of *post-mortem* inheritance on the hamlet's social hierarchy.

Mortuary ritual

Two deaths that occurred in Fontelas will provide us with some comparative details. At the time of each of these, the respective households involved were in very different situations with regard to inheritance: the contrast between the ritual events following each death was quite pronounced. While the events following the first were standard, those following the second were a dramatic case of an inheritance dispute seeping into the very structure of mortuary ritual. The comparison will also provide an excellent example of Bourdieu's point that countless inventions and strategies are also possible within even the 'rigorously stereotyped sequences of a rite' (1977:15). It is crucial to the argument of this book that we grasp the significance of these strategies with regard to death and the inheritance of property.

Shortly after my arrival in Fontelas, one of the hamlet's elderly villagers developed a cancerous infection in his mouth. Benigno, a former *lavrador* living alone at the age of 82, apparently 'burned his lip with a cigarette' and stubbornly proceeded to ignore the course of his infection. By October of 1976 his condition had grown worse, and two attempts by his daughter-in-law to have him treated in hospital were fruitless. Benigno continued to walk around the hamlet with a makeshift cloth tied around his neck and mouth. Shortly prior to his death, visits by other villagers to Benigno's household (H12 on Map 3) began, while his daughter-in-law Juliana (H6) began to take total care of him in bed. On 16 November he died in a Porto hospital, bringing general relief in the community that such a case of needless suffering had ended.[1]

Church bells are rung in successions of three chimes following a death: within minutes most of the hamlet knows of the death and visits are made to the household of the deceased. During these visits, one pays one's respects to the close relatives of the dead person. Those villagers not closely related to the deceased shake the hands of close kin and say *dou-lhe os meus sentimentos* (I give you my condolences). These visits are short, as the members of this household must prepare the coffin and have it placed in a large room for the vigil to follow that night or the next. As Benigno died in the morning and both of his two sons are emigrants respectively in France and West Germany, the funeral was set for two days later. Visits began on 16 November, continued on the 17th, and culminated in the vigil on the night of the 17th.

Following the death, a close relative (in this case Benigno's daughter-in-law Juliana) washes the body and dresses it in the deceased's best clothing. Kin and close friends of both Benigno and Juliana assisted her in this. The coffin (*urna*) was purchased in a neighbouring hamlet to the South of Fontelas, where only one kind of casket (although at various prices) is available. The shopkeeper selling the coffin always delivers it to the household of the deceased, where he sets it up within a central room. This shopkeeper's *taberna* is located on the main road to the municipal town, and provides the coffins for about 10 of the more isolated hamlets around Fontelas. The deceased is then placed inside the casket and draped with a transparent white veil embroidered with the words 'Rest in Peace' (*Descansa em Paz*). The hands of the deceased are crossed over his chest, the veil covering him from head to foot. The body is then left for viewing in the centre of the household's largest room (Photo 23). Four sets of candlesticks (*castiçais*), each with three candles, are stood on the four corners of the coffin. Flowers, a crucifix, and three wreaths (*grinaldas*) also accompany the coffin and a carpet is placed beneath it. At the foot of the casket stands a bowl of holy water which visitors sprinkle in three places over the corpse upon arrival. In most cases the deceased remains in his or her own household, but in Benigno's case the corpse was moved for viewing and the vigil to his daughter-

[1] I attended 8 vigils in Fontelas during my fieldwork and another one in March of 1981. The description of Benigno's vigil and funeral is quite representative of most of the earlier ones. However, 2 of the 8 funerals differed somewhat in that the households involved were quite wealthy, the vigils larger and longer, and the masses performed by 5 priests rather than one. Both of these deaths occurred in *proprietário* households (H29 and H38).

23 The *mortório* (vigil): one of the first visitors sits beside the open coffin. Later that night, the room will fill as other co-villagers arrive to accompany the deceased.

in-law's household. At no point during all of these steps is the coffin closed: it remains constantly open with the corpse in full view.

On the following night a vigil, or *mortório*,[2] was held. Vigils usually begin in the early evening around 8 or 9 p.m. While most villagers leave by 2 a.m., some close relatives usually remain throughout the next morning. The vigil is very much a total hamlet affair, and all households are obliged to send at least one

[2] The use of the word *mortório* is itself revealing. The standard Portuguese words for vigil or wake are *velório* (stressing candlelight) and *vigília* (stressing the process of waiting). Neither of these words is used by villagers in Fontelas, although the priest occasionally employs the latter. Vigils are universally referred to as *mortórios*, thus placing the verbal emphasis upon the word *morte*, or 'death'.

person to the household of the deceased. At around midnight during Benigno's vigil about 60 individuals were present. Funerals, on the other hand, always involve many individuals from neighbouring and distant hamlets. There are three key spatial divisions at all vigils. The first of these is at the coffin itself. On arriving, each visitor sprinkles holy water over the corpse and expresses condolences to the relatives of the deceased. The visitor then remains for a short while (rarely more than 10–15 minutes) beside the casket: at this time the visitor may pray or simply view the corpse quietly. Two wooden benches are provided on both sides of the coffin. The group here at any one moment rarely exceeds 6 or 7. One person (not necessarily kin) normally remains beside the casket as successive guests arrive and then leave the area around it.

Following this, the visitor moves to the second spatial area. This is usually in another room but normally also encompasses the hallways in between. Here the level of conversation is markedly different and may even reach quite loud proportions. The bulk of most visitors' time is spent here among the other attenders. It is always the case that this conversation is not solely limited to comments on the deceased. A number of routine phrases are initially exchanged, such as: *todos temos que morrer* (we must all die) and *nascemos para isto* (we are born for this). But immediately after these initial phrases are uttered, along with some talk about the deceased and the manner of his death, conversation rapidly shifts. Other matters are discussed. These may include literally anything: the weather, the day's activities, relatives abroad, the news, national politics, or the state of one's cows and pigs. No attempt is made to keep the level of speaking very low, and occasional laughs and exclamations can be heard. Messages are given from one villager to another for a third, as at any other time of day, and normal gossip is continued about any and all everyday affairs. It is not what these visitors say but rather their presence that counts.

At certain intervals a woman visitor (again not necessarily kin of the deceased) will commence a series of prayers for the deceased. At these points the chattering stops and all visitors accompany the prayers. These are recited in such manner roughly once every hour. A number of villagers mentioned the former practice of hiring a group of women criers (*choradeiras/carpideiras*) to attend a vigil, but that this has been discontinued for some years. Seats are provided for elderly villagers, and wine, bread, and biscuits are set out on a table in the main visiting room. I was quite struck by the forwardness of speaking at the first few vigils I attended: were it not for the black clothing and the corpse in the other room, this conversation seldom seemed any different from that in any other context of hamlet life.[3]

The third spatial area is that around the hearth. In this area gather those

[3] Both Douglass (1969:26–8) and Brandes (1975:172) have noted similar attitudes towards conversation during vigils in Spanish rural communities, where laughter is not out of place and where a 'stonefaced solemnity' is absent. Douglass interprets this as a sign of a matter-of-fact attitude towards death in Murélaga.

visitors (kin, friends, or co-villagers) who wish to accompany the deceased's relatives in a more intimate fashion. Some visitors may of course move from the coffin to the hearth and then to the larger hallway group. But those remaining at the hearth are generally quieter and wish to comfort the kin of the deceased to a greater extent. Again, conversation may wander, but here it generally remains rather discrete and subdued. As many people gather here as there is space on the benches around the hearth – in small households around 10 and in larger ones up to 20 people. There is no separation between the sexes either here or in the other two areas; men, women, and children gather in all spatial areas. It is here at the hearth that the villagers remaining throughout the night and the following morning will stay, after the larger group of visitors begins to leave at around 2 a.m.

The members of the deceased's household are quite observant throughout the vigil of precisely who has come and exactly which households are represented. A strict reciprocity of vigil-visits is operative, wherein unrelated co-villagers 'exchange' vigils. There are occasionally households which do not send representatives to a vigil, perhaps due to strained relations with the deceased or to distant non-speaking relations with any member of the deceased's household. For instance, one villager refused to attend either Benigno's vigil or his funeral because he simply thought that Benigno 'was bad' (*era mau*) and used to beat children. The two were on speaking terms but not particularly close, and the former felt that Benigno had killed himself through his stubbornness. Although a grudge was not held by Benigno's daughter-in-law towards this villager, his absence at the vigil was noted. In general then, there is an obligation to attend a co-villager's *mortório* and funeral unless the former living relationship was one of extreme enmity.

The funeral and burial (*enterro*) of a dead person is one of the few events in Fontelas that involves the whole hamlet. On the day following the vigil the church bells are rung early in the morning to announce the later procession which will carry the coffin to the church. This usually occurs in mid-afternoon around 2 or 3 o'clock. Villagers from Fontelas as well as outsiders gather outside the deceased's household. A short religious service is held inside the house, while three men dressed in red robes wait outside to lead the funeral procession. These three men represent the one and only religious voluntary association in Fontelas: the *confraria* (lay brotherhood or confraternity). Obsequies are the only occasions at which members of this entity actually do anything. One of these men holds a pole with a large crucifix from which hangs an embroidered tapestry. To his left and right walk the two other men, each carrying poles with lanterns on top. The coffin is then closed temporarily while it is carried to the church behind these three men.

No specific spatial structure governs the procession either from the household of the deceased to the church or from the church to the cemetery. While the three men representing the confraternity always lead the procession, other villagers will walk in front of, beside, and behind the casket and pallbearers. The priest, swinging a censer and reciting prayers as he walks, always follows immediately behind the coffin. Close kin of the deceased usually walk next to or close behind the priest. Behind these walk the rest of the participants in the procession, with no separation of any kind according to age or sex. While it is usual for four men to carry the casket to the church and then to the cemetery, on occasion a fifth or sixth man may assist voluntarily on either side of it. These four men are normally asked to carry the coffin by the deceased's close kin, but this is not a rigid rule. Kin or even close friends or neighbours of the deceased may offer to carry it themselves.

In church the coffin is opened again for viewing during the mass, which is termed a *missa de corpo presente* (mass with the body present). The casket is placed in precisely the same manner as in the household of the deceased, but here the deceased's head lies towards the altar and the feet towards the entrance doorway. In the case of Benigno, the mass was a *missa cantada* (high mass) for which five priests were hired. Towards the end of the service a bench is brought out and placed near the head of the deceased: this is for contributions towards payment for some of the responsories sung by the priests for the deceased during the final part of the ceremony. Most people attending this funeral service placed a small amount of money in a pile on the bench: these amounts begin at $2\frac{1}{2}$ *escudos* but rarely exceed 20-*escudo* notes (£0.33).

Following the service, the coffin is again closed and carried to the cemetery. The path followed by the procession to the cemetery is always the same (Map 3). It turns left immediately outside the church doors and proceeds along the dirt road past H16. The procession then turns sharply left again just to the right of H15 down a steep rocky path towards the *Fundo da Aldeia* section. Here it turns right and follows the wider dirt road in a leftwards curve past an uninhabited house (opposite H11) and around into the cemetery, where the coffin is placed on a large rectangular construction and once again opened (Photo 24). Here the priest(s) recites the last rites before the casket is closed and lowered with two ropes into the grave. Again, there are no sex divisions within the cemetery: any and all individuals of both sexes may enter the cemetery during this service and the positions they take inside are entirely *ad hoc*.

Following the lowering of the closed coffin, the group begins to disperse. Close kin are usually utterly distraught by this time and many must be restrained and held on their feet by other co-villagers. Quite rapidly, close relatives and friends of the deceased retire together while other villagers return home or go about other business. Outside the cemetery a table is set up with wine, bread, and small snacks of sandwiches for those who have attended the funeral but who must walk fair distances home. Here the process ends: there is no banquet (although I was told of funeral banquets in the past). There are no *sepulturies* or house-specific burial plots in the church to be looked after following the person's death (Douglass 1969). Formerly in Fontelas corpses were buried inside the church itself, after which they were then buried in the churchyard (*adro*). Only in 1956, according to Fontelas' current parish priest, did burials begin in the cemetery at the South-west end of the hamlet. Some hamlets in the area still have no separate cemetery, and corpses are buried directly outside the church walls. In fact, wooden coffins themselves are quite new: until recently (I was unable to date this precisely) corpses were simply wrapped in a large white sheet. They were then carried to the church and later turned into the grave on an open wooden stretcher-board (*esquife*).

Formal mourning rules in Fontelas are not rigid, and villagers seem to think that today even these minimal periods are being shortened further. For a husband or wife the prescribed term is two years, although widows may continue to wear black clothing for many years afterwards. For a deceased father, mother, sibling, or child the period is one year; for aunts, uncles, or grandparents 6 months; for more distant kin (cousins, nephews/nieces, brothers- or sisters-in-law, godchildren, etc.) 3 months. A number of villagers stated that the latter periods of mourning (less than 1 year) continue to be shortened, such that in many cases today, mourning for distant relatives does not last for the prescribed term of months. While women wear black continually during these spans of time, men tend to place a black cloth armband around one of the sleeves of a jacket or sweater. The wearing of black, however, is less rigidly adhered to than a general avoidance of household celebrations or participation in other hamlet festivities. Following a death, three masses for the deceased are customarily held: these are the first week's mass (*missa do sétimo dia*), the first month's mass (*missa do primeiro mês*), and the first year's mass (*missa do primeiro ano*). Following the last of these three, the period of formal religious services terminates, but further masses said for the soul of the deceased may occur at any time or frequency. The only other duty owed to the deceased by his closest relatives is that of All Souls' Day on 2 November of each year. On this day a special mass is held for all of the dead of Fontelas: the women of each household then place candles, flowers, and petals in patterned designs upon their relatives' graves. The sight is quite a striking one in Fontelas' neighbouring hamlet Mosteiro, where particular care is taken to decorate the cemetery on All Souls' Day. Following the 'first year's mass', this is the only day of the year when formal religious obligations to the dead are prescribed.

There are three aspects of mortuary ritual that reveal a conspicuous inequality between the deaths of the wealthy and those of the poor, and these deserve brief mention here. The first is the size and duration of the vigil – a large and crowded vigil clearly reflects a highly respected social position on the part of the deceased. The second is the dimension of the funeral itself, defined not solely in terms of size but also in terms of expense (to have one priest is normal but to have five is quite rare). In Benigno's case, villagers explained the presence of five priests through Juliana's husband's emigrant savings: the household had become wealthy through long years of effort and had bought a substantial amount of land. Juliana herself enumerated her total expenses: £37 were paid to the five priests (£13 of which was in fact an 8-year debt of unpaid yearly fees to Fontelas' priest). On top of this, £98 were spent on the coffin, Benigno's shoes, and bread and marmalade for visitors after the funeral, and an additional £100 for the ambulance and taxi which drove Benigno from the Porto hospital to Fontelas. Her total expenses (less the 8-year debt to Fontelas' priest) were thus 13,300 *escudos*, or £222. This was quite a sizeable sum by hamlet standards. In fact, some villagers termed the funeral presumptuous in scale: 'she can afford a big mass with five priests because she has lots of money sent from Germany'. Some also stressed that Benigno possessed no conspicuous qualities (reputation, political influence) deserving of such a large and prestigious funeral ceremony. As one villager put it: Juliana's family 'wanted to be more than they really were'. Benigno himself, although formerly a middling landed *lavrador*, had none of the social poise or prestige of the *proprietário* group.

The third aspect of hierarchy in death is the presence of two privately owned tombs (*jazigos*) in the cemetery. These tombs pertain to the large *lavrador* households of Miguel (H30) and Delfim (H40). All other corpses are buried in the earth in other parts of the cemetery. Many villagers object to this reserving of public space by these two wealthier households. Apart from these three areas of differentiation, however, funerary ritual in Fontelas is quite uniform.

The impact of death upon the living is a theme which recurs repeatedly in songs and verses from the hamlet's oral literature. The songs below, which I recorded in 1976, give some idea of the force with which death affects the living, and the lingering feelings of loss.

Why do you want to go to the cemetery, If you have no one there? Leave me, Mr Grave-digger, Leave me, Mr Grave-digger.	*Que queres ir ò cemitério,* *Su tu lá não tens ninguém?* *Deixe-me, Senhor Coveiro,* *Deixe-me, Senhor Coveiro.*
I have my beloved mother, Leave me, Mr Grave-digger, Leave me, Mr Grave-digger, I have my beloved mother.	*Tenho a minha querida mãe,* *Deixe-me, Senhor Coveiro,* *Deixe-me, Senhor Coveiro,* *Tenho a minha querida mãe.*
On arriving at the cemetery, The mother's grave opened, The tears were so many, The tears were so many.	*Ò chegar ao cemitério,* *A campa da mãe se abriu,* *Eram as lágrimas tantas,* *Eram as lágrimas tantas.*
When her beloved mother arose, The tears were so many, The tears were so many, When her beloved mother arose.	*Quando a querida mãe subiu,* *Eram as lágrimas tantas,* *Eram as lágrimas tantas,* *Quando a querida mãe subiu.*

Listen you, who has no father, Your mother has also died, Tell me with whom you live, Tell me with whom you live.	*Olha tu, já não tens pai, Tua mãe também morreu, Diz-me com quem vives tu, Diz-me com quem vives tu.*
I live with a brother of mine, Tell me then what you do, In order to give him food, Begging at people's doors.	*Eu vivo com um irmão meu, Diz-me lá como lhe fazes, Para lhe dar de comer, Mandengando* pelas portas.*
Begging at people's doors, When there is nothing to do, I wanted to go to the cemetery, And I am frightened all alone.	*Mandengando pelas portas, Quando não há que fazer, Queria ir ao cemitério, E eu sozinha tenho medo.*
I wanted to kiss the grave, I wanted to kiss the grave, Where I have my secret.	*Queria ir beijar a campa, Queria ir beijar a campa, Onde tenho o meu segredo.*
I wanted to kiss the grave, I wanted to kiss the grave, Where I have my secret.	*Queria ir beijar a campa, Queria ir beijar a campa, Onde tenho o meu segredo.*

* i.e., *mendigando*

Particularly noteworthy is the fact that each of the songs refers to a parent/child relationship: the first is about a daughter and her deceased mother and the second concerns a daughter and her two deceased parents. In both cases, the loss of a parent is portrayed traumatically: in the second song the living person attempts to recover her parents by trying to break through the barrier between the living and the dead (the grave or cemetery).

Although the second song mentions a daughter 'living with her brother', both songs assume a particularly strong vertical tie between parent and child. Neither refers to ties between spouses or lovers. Why then is the descent tie between parents and children (and its severance at death) so consistently expressed in these songs?[4]

Let us look briefly at a second vigil, as this will reveal the structure of inheritance and property relations which underlies this concern with death and descent. While I was in Fontelas in March of 1981, the mother of one of the hamlet's wealthiest *lavradores* died. In 1978 Benedita (aged 68) had already been growing old, and continued to live with her son Julião (H19) and his wife and 7 children, assisting with household tasks and particularly with the care of her youngest grandchildren. The events following Benedita's death were unusual. The vigil itself was the smallest I have ever seen in Fontelas, and was

[4] For Tory Island, also a society where strong 'descent' ties and sibling bonds exist, Fox gives an exceptional example of the difficulty in accepting the departure of a deceased relative: 'An extreme expression of grief on the death of a parent is quite common; grief that goes beyond anything considered "normal" even by the islanders afflicts some young people. One young man went to the graveyard gate and wept every day for several years after the death of his mother' (Fox 1978:161).

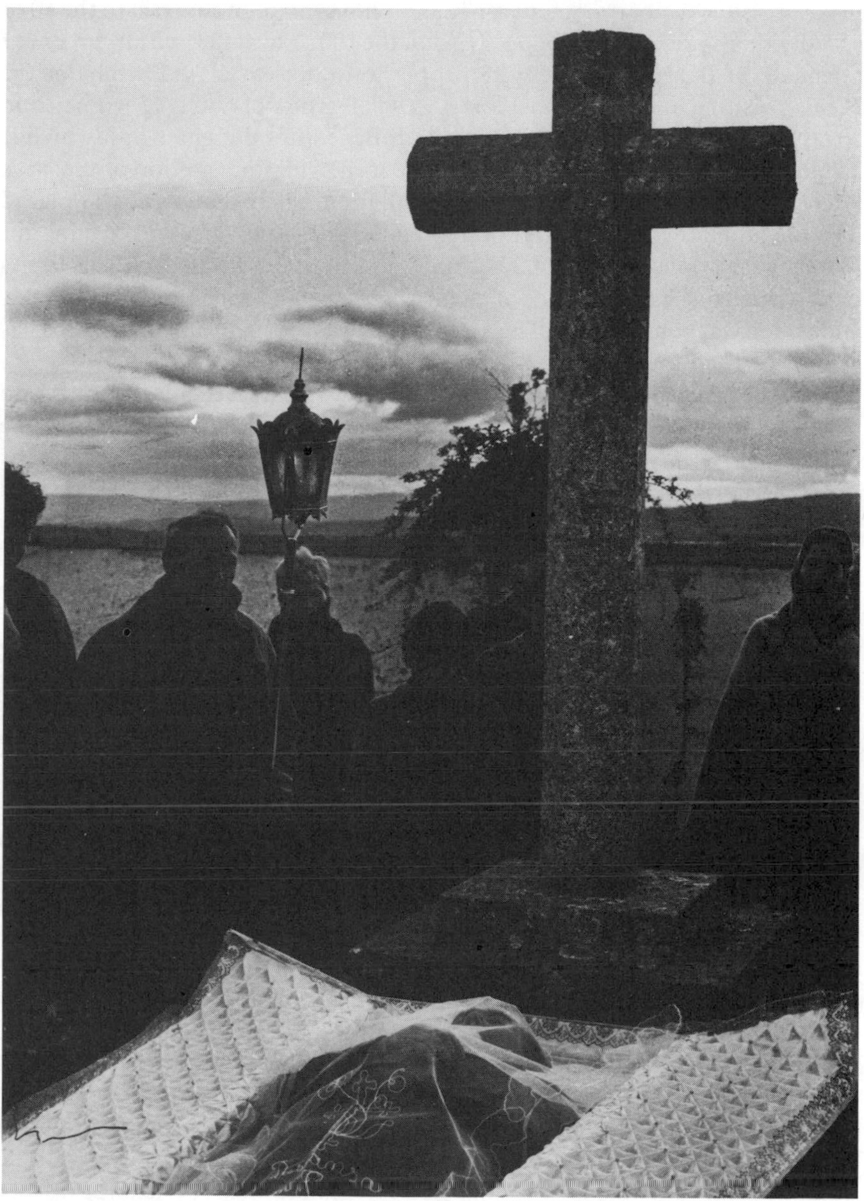

24 Burial in the cemetery: the obsequies.

in fact a distinct embarrassment for Julião's household. In contrast to the 60 or so individuals present at Benigno's vigil or the 100 or so at the two largest ones I attended, at Benedita's barely 25 people were present at the height of the evening visiting hours (9 p.m.–1 a.m.). A small group of about 15 women and some children sat around the hearth with Benedita's daughter-in-law, while Julião himself mingled with around 10–12 men in another section of the large kitchen. Visitors thus moved from the small room where the corpse was placed into the adjoining kitchen. (Although Julião is a large *lavrador* farming his mother's large landholding of 27 hectares, his mother's house itself – H19 – is quite a small one.) The absence of members of most of the hamlet's households at this vigil was conspicuous. The atmosphere was distinctly uncomfortable, as everyone noted the small number of people present.

The funeral itself (which I could not attend) was also particularly small, and villagers stressed this fact. The most striking detail occurred following the church service: at the time the coffin was to be closed and carried to the cemetery, not one individual present offered to pick it up. The priest was forced to ask three men (including Julião himself) to lift the casket and carry it to the cemetery. Further, Julião's half-sister Anastácia from H40 (Benedita's illegitimate daughter by another father) did not set foot in her mother's household during the vigil. Nor did she attend the service in the church or enter the cemetery at any point during the funeral. An inheritance dispute had long since estranged Anastácia from both her half-brother Julião as well as from her mother Benedita. This rift was so deep-seated that following the death of Anastácia's own husband in 1980, Benedita only reluctantly attended the latter's funeral. Instead of wearing a black shawl, she deliberately wore a white one.

The following events in large part explain the rather unusual patterns within the structure of Benedita's funeral. While the latter was in hospital a few days prior to her death, Julião had a will drawn up and signed by her. Villagers understood this action to have willed all the old woman's property to Julião alone, despite the legal fact that Benedita could legally only bequeath her son (or anyone else) a maximum of 1/3 of her total patrimony. There are five other surviving (full) siblings of Julião's in addition to his elder half-sister, Anastácia, two of whom are mentally retarded to some degree. One of Julião's full sisters lives in the household adjoining his own (H20) while the remaining four live in a neighbouring hamlet. Only one of these four siblings attended Benedita's funeral and none was present at the vigil on the preceding night. The sister who did attend made a conspicuous gesture of not speaking to her brother Julião. Comments concurred in criticizing Julião for 'taking advantage of his mother's infirmity' by having a will made out to himself. This was seen as a device for Julião's acquisition of property – an outright *roubo* (robbery) of his five siblings' rightful shares. Despite the fact that Julião had been looking after his mother as she aged, her will of even 1/3 of her patrimony broke the unwritten law of equal partition by instituting Julião as a favoured heir.

The case is now in court in the municipal town, where the other five siblings will dispute the will. A legal inventory of Benedita's total patrimony will recall any portion of her five children's legal inheritance (*legítima*) of 2/3 of their mother's property. Whether the will actually transmitted more than 1/3 of Benedita's patrimony to Julião will only be discovered after the court case is closed. The latter may well have succeeded in including most of Benedita's property in the will. But the key point is that even a will of 1/3 of her possessions was seen by villagers to be an unjust theft of the other siblings' legal shares: they repeatedly emphasized that Julião's retarded sister and brother, despite their infirmities, deserved their 1/6 shares in their mother's inheritance. (Note that upon the death of Benedita's husband a partition was not effected between Benedita and her children – the division of his patrimony was postponed until Benedita's death.) Finally, villagers saw in this case yet another example of a classic pattern always spoken of with extreme bitterness: the use by an individual of a parent's senility or sickness for purposes of personal gain. The two culprits were both the greedy heir Julião as well as the equally devious notary who wangled the crucial documents in town. This is why Benedita's vigil and funeral were so poorly attended, and why no one would offer to lift her coffin.

Benedita's funeral illustrates some of the deep conflicts that can arise from a death. This is the crucial moment in Fontelas when social relations and property relations converge, and when the potential for outright clashes is greatest. Inheritance disputes can and often do result in complete ruptures between individuals and entire households.

The *partilha*

We have observed some of the processes which occur following a death in Fontelas – let us now look at the specific forms of the division of a patrimony. This occurs at the time of partition, called the *partilha*. There are four major ways through which this can be effected in Fontelas: it is instructive to look at each of these in turn.

1. *De boca* (orally): This is by far the most frequent form of division of a patrimony. Upon the death of an individual (assuming for the moment that there are children) 1/2 of the patrimony is distributed in equal shares among the person's direct descendants: this half of the individual's property is divided between the children, while the surviving spouse inherits the other half (I will clarify this below). Each heir has legal rights to a certain share of the total patrimony – this includes land, tools, movables, livestock, and a portion of the house. There is an absolute equality between male and female heirs both in local hamlet custom as well as in the Portuguese Civil Code, and there is no

informal preference within the inheritance system for either sons or daughters. With respect to land, three main types of distribution occur:

(a) plots may be partitioned into smaller plots with boundary stones placed at the borders;
(b) different heirs may each obtain whole separate plots comprising a total share of roughly equal value to the total shares of the other heirs (this practice is called *inteirar* or *osmar*);
(c) heirs remaining in agricultural activities may borrow, rent, or purchase the plots of their non-resident co-heirs.

Except in cases of very large plots of land, (b) and (c) are the most frequent choices, as these lead to a more practical distribution of farming land among those siblings remaining permanently in Fontelas. Obviously, an extreme adherence to (a) through continual subdivisions of shrinking plots would lead eventually to joint economic suicide. Thus (b) and (c) are resorted to in order to circumvent this.

This form of partition is termed by villagers *de boca* simply because that is precisely how it is done – by word of mouth. Nothing is written down anywhere, and each heir inherits his or her share. This is why the town Tax Bureau has such difficulty in keeping track of who owns what in each of the 95 hamlets within its jurisdiction. Plots frequently remain registered in the name of a villager's parent or grandparent. This may temporarily avoid both a minimal inheritance tax as well as a yearly land tax, but it may lead later to problems in cases of sale or disputed ownership rights. Such disputes force an heir to obtain a proper legal title to the plot(s) in question. Alternatively, in other cases all of the plots of a group of heirs may be listed at the time of inheritance in each of their names. The partition is still nevertheless termed an oral one because formal recourse to assessors or lawyers is not resorted to. This is why the term *amigável* (friendly) is used to refer to this form of division: all of the heirs partition the patrimony *amigavelmente*, or 'in a friendly way'. Each heir registers his/her plots (or new portions of plots) and all remain on good terms.

Following the 8 deaths occurring during my fieldwork, 6 oral partitions were effected. Of the 2 remaining cases, one woman's property was left undivided by her three children (two are emigrants) while their father continues to live. In the second case, a widower (Plácido Veiga) died in 1978 leaving only his acquired possessions (movables) to be divided among his six children. Plácido had married into Fontelas, and upon the death of his wife in 1973 the couple's six children immediately orally partitioned all of their mother's land. *De boca* division is the ideal form of a *partilha* in Fontelas and indeed the most common.

2. *Sortes* (by lot): This form of partition was described to me by a number of villagers, although I did not observe it. It is similar to oral partition, except that

a mediator, or witness, is called in from outside the household in question in order to assure an equitable division. The word *sorte* (share/lot) refers firstly to the small slips of paper on which the locations of a series of plots of land are written. These slips of paper are placed in a hat and drawn randomly by the heirs (*tirar sortes*). Secondly, the plots or sub-plots are themselves called *sortes* from this point on. Any field in the hamlet can thus be termed 'my *sorte*' or 'my brother's *sorte*'. But the original and precise meaning of the term refers to the slips of paper put in the hat and drawn by the heirs.

The lot system implies a certain degree of caution on the part of the heirs, otherwise no outside witness would be called in and the heirs could effect the partition orally. It also implies a certain amount of equally distributed luck in the drawing. The witness is usually a villager of high social standing with a good knowledge of the hamlet's terrain, although in some cases the person designated to draw the paper lots is a child. Along with the heirs, the witness draws up a list of all the deceased's land. (I am not sure whether movables are also written on the paper slips; they may have been distributed orally.) It is at this point, shortly prior to the drawing, that the value of the fields must be decided and that disagreements are most likely to occur. A landholding consisting of 20 plots to be divided among 4 heirs may, theoretically, be partitioned into 4 portions of 5 plots each. But subdivisions may also be made, or alternatively three less fertile grain fields put on one slip of paper and one very fertile meadow on another. Each heir thus draws a slip of paper with a series of listed plots whose total value is roughly equal.

The essential point about this 'lottery' is that it is a variant of the friendly oral partition. Although not as straightforward as the latter, such divisions by lot do not go as far as the courts. This is why they are relatively rare: either the heirs basically agree and opt for an entirely oral partition, or they disagree to such an extent that one (or more) of them demands recourse to judicial bodies. A partition by *sortes* is thus a form of compromise between an entirely 'friendly' agreement among co-heirs and disagreements strong enough to commence legal action.

3. *Escritura* (will or donation): This third form of inheritance involves the making of a will (*testamento*) or a donation (*doação*). Both of these forms of transfer are termed inheritance 'by writing' (*por escritura*) and both are considered by villagers to be processes quite distinct from purely oral or lot divisions. A will or a donation both inject a written document into the process of property transfer. According to Portuguese law (*Código Civil* 1966) a person may only freely dispose of 1/3 of his or her patrimony through a will (the percentage is 1/2 if there is only one child). This portion is termed the 'third' or *terço* in Fontelas. In legal terms this constitutes the testator's free quota or *quota disponível*. The remaining 2/3 constitutes the legitimate inheritance (*legítima*) of the testator's heirs, and cannot be included in a will.

If the heirs feel that their *legítima* has been mistakenly or wrongfully encroached on by a will, they may dispute this in court and recover the portions of their patrimony incorrectly included in the will. This is precisely what is in question today in the case of Benedita's will discussed above. The other five heirs feel that all of their mother's property and not merely her free quota of 1/3 was illegally written into the will by Julião and the notary. Even in cases of legally correct testaments, however, there is a strong feeling in Fontelas that wills subvert the law of equal partition between all siblings. As discussed in Chapter 5, this constitutes a fundamental contradiction within this society, and I will return to it below.

In a will, a testator may bequeath any or all of his/her free quota to anyone – these may be one or more of the legal heirs, a spouse, or an entirely unrelated person. A donation, or *doação*, is another matter. This is a *pre-mortem* transfer of property and as such the closest thing to a dowry in Fontelas. It is really a kind of pseudo-will, or advance on inheritance, as the portion of property disposed of through a donation already dips into the testator's free quota. The donation thus leaves less property to dispose of through a later will. It is virtually the only means available in this society (apart from sales and purchases) to transfer property *inter vivos* and avoid the strict rule of *post-mortem* inheritance.

Villagers were very reluctant to discuss donations involving themselves, although they are constantly speculating about the contents of those of others. Such phrases as *deixou-lhe aquela leira* (he left him that field) or *a tia fez-lhe doação da casa* (her aunt donated the house to her) are endlessly on people's lips. Such gossip usually circulates in quiet, whispered tones. Much of this talk is fabrication and fascination about other villagers' property rights rather than precise knowledge of the legal facts, a situation quite apparent in the formulation of questions by lawyers to peasant witnesses in court. Upon interrogation, the latter tend to respond with the nebulous phrases *dizem que sim* (they say so) or 'whether it is true, I don't know – but I heard it said . . .' Indeed, the heirs themselves are not always clear as to the specific juridical details of inheritance in their own cases. However, this fabrication about others is of interest in itself: land and the devolution of property are virtually an obsession of villagers in Fontelas.[5] Particular attention is given to wills and donations, because these lend an aura of suspicion and hidden calculation to the partition. Who has obtained what, and through which means? Did a specific person really deserve to inherit through a will? Or did he/she fiddle the documents or play up to the owner purely for personal interest? Nor are parents the only objects of an avaricious heir's intentions: an unmarried uncle

[5] The villagers' obsession with *terras* (plots of land) is the priest's most often-cited reason for desiring to give up his job and leave Fontelas altogether. Padre Gregório sees this excessive concern with land and inheritance as a degenerate form of materialism. He has for many years sought to escape this 'vicious circle of stingy peasants' by requesting the Bishop to transfer him to Angola or Mozambique as a missionary.

or aunt is always a potential target. Hidden plans and schemes may lurk beneath the honest exteriors of caring children, as expressed in the phrase:

The meek little lamb,	*O cordeirinho manso,*
Sucks from its mother and others too.	*Mama a sua mãe e alheia.*

The inclusion of a will at the time of a partition does occasionally occur in Fontelas, although my impression is that it is an exception among households with direct descendants and more common in cases of elderly unmarried individuals. In none of the 8 cases of the individuals who died during my fieldwork was a written will drawn up. Following my fieldwork, one woman in 1981 left a will (Benedita) and another unmarried villager (Dona Elvira) died later in 1981 also leaving a will. In general, villagers in Fontelas view the making of a will with great suspicion. This is due not only to a general aversion to institutionalized favouritism but also to a deeply rooted fear of the legal manipulations of ambitious heirs and bribed notaries. Conflicts are most likely to arise in cases of wills and not in cases of oral or lottery partitions, although this is not to say that in the latter there is necessarily an absence of quarrels. Of course, a will need not be disputed in all cases, and the heirs of the remaining 2/3 of the patrimony may divide that 2/3 orally and amicably between themselves. Nevertheless a suspect will, in writing and legally binding, is more likely to explode latent disagreements and resentments and to shift the whole affair to the town court.[6]

4. *Justiça* (court): In extreme cases, inheritance discords will force a legal partition in court. Villagers term this process simply one of inheritance by law or 'through justice' (*por justiça*). I observed a number of cases of disputed inheritance in the town court involving individuals from Fontelas as well as from other hamlets in the municipality. When this occurs, heirs as well as their witnesses may completely sever all social relations. The partition itself may require *in situ* valuations of the plots in question by land assessors, the lawyers involved, and the judge. As legal costs are high, recourse to lawyers and the court is an expensive affair and in villagers' eyes must involve enough property to merit the various expenses incurred. There is even a bit of suspicion of the lawyers themselves, whom villagers view as 'liars' and smooth talkers who manipulate the law for their own and their clients' interests. Nevertheless, in cases of deadlock in inheritance the court provides a last resort. Although

[6] The legal processes glossed over here are obviously more complex than I have made out. I have not gone into detail concerning the juridical particulars of inheritance for two reasons. Firstly, the topic requires greater length to describe (many points of family law are comparable to those operative in Pisticci – see Davis 1973). Secondly, what is essential for the argument of this study are not the legal details of inheritance but the *social* and long-term effects of *post-mortem* transfer upon the social structure and internal hierarchy of Fontelas: I close this chapter with this topic. Knowledge of the legal rules of inheritance is of course only of limited use in following the actual practices and specific 'moves' of individuals on the ground, as Bourdieu's brilliant analysis has shown (1976). For further specifics on processes of inheritance, see *Código Civil Português* (1867; 1966; 1977) as well as Graça Branco (1970).

expensive, a juridical division (often lasting for years) usually succeeds in resolving the original dispute.

A second form of inheritance through the court arises in cases of minor children whose parents die before their reaching majority. In these cases, a mandatory probate inventory (*inventário de menores*) is effected in court. This can be a tricky matter, as the following case illustrates. A young villager from a smallholder household (owning barely over 4 hectares) had long suspected one of the hamlet's *proprietários* of having 'robbed' his father of a number of plots and chestnut-trees many years ago. The youth's grandparents had both died before his father reached the age of 10. The youth's suspicion was that the father of this *proprietário* (now dead) had fiddled the probate inventory with one of the court officials so as to acquire much of the land which should have legally gone to the youth's father. The *proprietário* increased his already large holding even further, while the smallholder remained yet poorer. Indeed, the youth's father has not been on speaking terms with the entire *proprietário* household for decades.

Finding the situation unbearable, the youth (aged 18 in 1977) decided to confront the *proprietários* openly. He picked up an axe, walked to a field he knew to be legally his father's, and started to chop one of the plot's chestnut-trees. As he suspected, the *proprietários* said absolutely nothing and lodged no formal complaint anywhere for damage to private property. In fact, they attempted to hush the entire affair, but this was precisely the reaction the youth sought. The *proprietários'* silence was conclusive proof that the tree and the plot (and by implication other plots as well) had in fact been stolen from his father many years ago. Had the *proprietários* obtained a complete legal title to the plot, they would have taken the youth to court. The case caused a scandal in Fontelas in 1978, and when I left the hamlet villagers spoke of a pending court case in which the smallholder's property would be legally recovered. The case was illustrative not only of the exploitation of the poor by the rich but also of the opposition between (a) amicable oral partitions limited to the hamlet context, and (b) those bringing into play legal documents and the suspicious machinations of corrupt town clerks.

Given these four types of partition in Fontelas, two essential characteristics of the hamlet's inheritance system are: (1) its stress on descent, and (2) the weak position of the surviving spouse. These characteristics are features of all four of the forms which a partition may take, and they underlie not only the transferral of property but the entire system of bilateral kin reckoning as well.[7] Let us look briefly at both of these elements.

[7] Kin reckoning in Fontelas is strictly bilateral or cognatic. All kin terms have male and female equivalents: paternal as well as maternal aunts are both called *tias* and uncles on both sides are termed *tios*. The same extension applies to grandparents (*avô*/*avó*), grandchildren (*neto*/*neta*), cousins (*primo*/*prima*), and other relatives. Marriages between first cousins (*primos carnais*)

Both patterns are evident in the legal system determining the order of heirs in inheritance. Until substantial alterations in the Civil Code were introduced on paper in 1977,[8] the patrimony of an individual dying intestate was inherited by the following persons (*Código Civil* 1966: article 2133):

1. Descendants;
2. Ascendants;
3. Siblings and their descendants;
4. Spouse;
5. Other collaterals to the 6th degree;
6. The State.

Note that the surviving spouse figures only fourth in line following three other categories of legitimate heirs. At marriage, in the absence of pre-marital agreements (*escrituras antenupciais*), one of three forms of conjugal property may be chosen: firstly, joint property (*comunhão de bens*); secondly, separate property (*separação de bens*); or thirdly, acquired property (*comunhão de adquiridos*). The second arrangement is chosen principally in cases of remarriage, in order to retain separate inheritance rights for a person's children by a former marriage. Similarly, the acquired property regime has rarely been chosen by villagers, at least in recent decades. It is important to note that this second arrangement only applies to goods acquired by the couple after their marriage: each spouse's possessions prior to the marriage remain legally separate, although formally under the administration of the male head of household. Thus, the most frequently selected form of contract in Fontelas is that of joint marital property, or *comunhão geral de bens*.

and second cousins (*primos segundos*) necessitate ecclesiastical dispensations, but those between third cousins (*primos terceiros*) do not. Beyond this, all cousins are termed *primos afastados* (distant cousins) and reckoning becomes vague. Third cousins constitute the limits of an individual's *familia* or total group of relatives (*parentes*). Affines are frequently referred to as relatives but with qualifying phrases: for instance, an individual's uncle's wife would not be termed *tia* (aunt) without the additional comment that she is an 'aunt by marriage' (*tia por casamento*). Until 1977, extreme stress in inheritance rules has been placed by Portuguese law on relations of consanguinity and not affinity. Irregular kinship relations, involving step-parental ties and consensual unions, provide particularly intricate analytical problems, and must be dealt with separately. For a summary of Portuguese kinship reckoning, see Callier-Boisvert (1968), although some of her comments are not directly applicable to this zone of Trás-os-Montes.

[8] The alterations in the Civil Code following the 1974 Portuguese Revolution have rearranged this order of heirs (at least on paper) and substantially improved the position of the surviving spouse. The order of heirs today proceeds as follows:
1. Spouse and descendants;
2. Spouse and ascendants;
3. Siblings and their descendants;
4. Other collaterals to the 4th degree;
5. The State.

The implementation of these new rules of succession at the municipal level only began towards the very end of my fieldwork. To what extent these legal changes will further affect local customs of inheritance is a question beyond the scope of this study.

This is why two successive partitions of property may theoretically be effected by a couple's children, each following the death of one of the parents. Upon the death of the first parent half of the patrimony may be inherited immediately and directly by the descendants, while the surviving spouse inherits the other half; this second half is divided later after the death of the surviving spouse. For example, in the case of Benigno two partitions did in fact occur. Upon the death of Benigno's wife in 1969, half of the patrimony was inherited by the couple's two sons, while the other half remained with Benigno. (Although divided, acquired goods may of course remain within the original household.) Upon Benigno's death in 1976, Benigno's own property (including a rather large holding of 15 hectares) was divided by Benigno's two sons. As both of these are emigrants abroad but only one maintains a landholding in Fontelas (farmed by Juliana), the latter's current holding includes a number of plots lent from one brother to the other. No overt conflicts over inheritance occurred in this case, nor was there excessive competition for land between these two heirs.

The implications of this system are that the surviving spouse is left in a particularly weak position, half of his/her partner's property being transferred downwards rather than sideways (Goody 1970b). Of course, the children (or other heirs) may and often do delay the partition of the first parent's patrimony until the death of the second parent. However, if a couple remain childless, upon the first partner's death his/her property is not inherited by the surviving spouse (although a maximum of a third may be willed or donated). Rather, the person's property reverts to his/her family line following the principle of *paterna paternis/materna maternis* (the father's property to the father's kin/the mother's property to the mother's kin – Le Roy Ladurie 1976:56). Thus only half of the goods acquired following the marriage (these may include land) is inherited by the surviving spouse: the bulk of the patrimony of the first spouse reverts to his or her natal family. Precisely as described for the regions of Western France, inheritance customs in Fontelas

> attach only slight importance to the act of marriage which they seem to regard as an ephemeral union of two perishable creatures, each issued from a different line whose own value lies in its permanence. Therefore these western customs give first priority to the strict calculation of inheritance along the genealogical method
> (Le Roy Ladurie 1976:56).

In other words, the inheritance system in Fontelas places an extreme emphasis upon the transfer of property at death and not at marriage, and upon relations of descent over those of affinity. A surviving spouse is as it were left out on a limb. Ideally, property should pass downwards rather than sideways and in the absence of a new family line (a childless couple) each spouse's property should return to their original families. These are usually a person's siblings and their descendants (nephews/nieces) or alternatively more distant cousins to the 6th degree. Only in the absence of all of these potential heirs does the spouse or the State inherit. In the absence of wills, this is how property 'descends'.

Another situation that highlights the fragile position of the surviving spouse arises when, following the death of the first spouse, a partition of the entire patrimony is effected between the surviving spouse and the descendants. In such cases, legally only half of the couple's property should be divided, but the surviving spouse allows each of the childen to 'inherit' prematurely his/her share of the remaining half. This practice is called *dar a partilha*. Such divisions benefit those heirs who control larger shares (two partitions are avoided) but leave the widow or widower in a potentially precarious position. Although my impression is that this form of inheritance is rare, it does constitute a variant of the oral partition particularly in cases of widowed persons who maintain amicable relations with their descendants.

It is not surprising that relations of affinity are generally de-emphasized in this system. Natolocal residence provides a particularly clear instance of this. Another example is the absence of a stress upon horizontal links of spiritual kinship. The *compadrio* tie established at a baptism between the parents of the child and the two sponsors is not significant in Fontelas. The only occasion at which relations between *compadres* (male co-parents) and *comadres* (female co-parents) are activated is during labour exchanges, particularly at harvests. Co-parents merely constitute one further extension of potential cooperators, and they could equally be substituted by friends, neighbours, or distant cousins.[9] Of far greater importance in this community are the vertical relationships established between the baptized child and the godparents: one's *padrinho* (godfather) and *madrinha* (godmother) occupy rather more significant positions. In the event of the deaths of both of a child's parents, in the absence of other close kin the godparents must ideally assume responsibility for its upbringing. Formerly in Fontelas, a child encountering a godparent in public was obliged to fold his/her hands in a gesture of prayer and recite the following phrase: *Ó Senhor Padrinho, deia-me a sua bênção* (Oh Godfather, give me your blessing). The godparent would reply by making a sign of the cross with the accompanying words: *Que Deus lhe abençoe* (May God bless you). Although currently defunct, this formerly stylized encounter was mentioned to me by a number of villagers.

[9] A similar lack of stress upon *compadrazgo* ritual kinship has been reported for three Northern Spanish communities. Brandes states that 'the *compadrazgo*, as it is known in Latin America and southern Spain, is virtually nonexistent in the peasant communities of Castile. In Becedas at least friendship and neighborship are the main avenues through which nonfamilial ties are expressed; they are, as it were, functional equivalents of the *compadrazgo*' (1975:133). In the same vein, among the Basques Douglass has noted that 'there is little emphasis placed upon the tie established between the godparents and the natural parents of the child. The elaborate godparenthood relationship, which exists in other parts of Spain [Pitt-Rivers 1958], is not a feature of the social organization of Murélaga' (1969:188). Yet more extreme is the Castilian hamlet studied by Freeman, where 'the term *compadre*, stressing the ties between the adults in the contract, is not in use in Valdemora' (1970:141).

In general then, it is the vertical inter-generational tie of the godparents with the godchild that assumes a significant role, and not the horizontal intra-generational one between the ritual co-parents. The strong parent/child ties of descent which we have been examining are here mimicked by the vertical tie between the godparent and the godchild.

The differing positions of favoured heirs and secondary heirs with respect to a natal patrimony are now clear. Although inheritance in Fontelas is legally partible, its actual shape is really one of *indirect unigeniture*. As we have seen in Chapter 5, among the landed groups a favoured heir usually remains within the natal household and can in some cases unite much of the patrimony by circumventing partition. It is important to note that nowhere are any hard and fast rules of unigeniture operative in this society. The selection of a favoured heir is an informal process, and indeed there are households in which no heir is favoured above any of the other co-heirs. We repeat that no co-heir is ever paid a monetary compensation or dowry in return for leaving the household and relinquishing rights to his or her share of the natal patrimony. Unless they are disinherited (and I have heard of no recent cases of this) all co-heirs retain rights to a portion of the 2/3 *legítima* of each of their parents' patrimonies. They are in no sense residual heirs because they do not legally inherit a residue of the patrimony but truly equal shares. Nor are they really 'secondary' heirs except in social terms. Theoretically, a villager's sibling who has resided for a number of decades in Brazil may return to Fontelas upon a parent's death and claim his or her rightful share (this may then be lent, rented, or sold). Ties with the natal landholding are thus never entirely severed.

This is why the system is indirect. All heirs do not normally stay in Fontelas in agriculture: some emigrate, some marry out, and yet others may remain celibate. But indirectly one of these heirs manages to consolidate much of the patrimony in the interests of avoiding both excessive partitions of land and the dispersal of labouring arms. Each co-heir theoretically inherits a share in the natal house but such division among six siblings, for instance, would obviously be impractical. In fact, there have been only two cases of house-partitions in Fontelas in recent years: H28 and H29 were formerly one, as were H18 and H19. In most cases one heir remains in a central role within the family line and it is this heir who is informally chosen to manage the household and the landholding over time.[10] This may be either a son or a daughter, or as we have seen, even an adopted servant.

[10] This same system of indirect unigeniture through one heir has also been reported by a number of ethnographers for the Swiss Alps, where partible inheritance is also operative (Friedl 1974; Netting 1979). Predictably, both of these Swiss regions are characterized by late ages at marriage, high proportions of celibates, and low-yielding smallholding agriculture. Another possible term for this form of inheritance is *preferential partibility* (Berkner and Mendels 1978), suggesting some kind of selection of an heir, even within a legal system of equitable property division. See also Rainer Bauer's distinction between 'major' and 'minor' heirs in Spanish Galicia (1980).

There are various ways through which this favoured heir is selected. He or she may be the first sibling to marry (at a young age) and produce grandchildren within the household, or the parents may select the most hard-working or honest son or daughter and simply 'rear' this child into a special role of responsibility and dedication to farming. One parent (or both) may even will a portion of property to this favoured heir, although this may create friction or overt conflicts among the other co-heirs. But the practical needs of the household necessitate the elimination of competing claims to the house from the other co-heirs. The marriages of these co-heirs will clearly add to the force of their claims. But the delay or thwarting of their marriages, either by the parents or later by the favoured heir, may diminish their claims and will tend to relegate them to secondary, celibate positions within the household. An intriguing analysis of heir selection in rural Ireland (County Kerry) is contained in Scheper-Hughes' extraordinary monograph (Chapter Six – 'Breeding Breaks Out in the Eye of the Cat: Sex Roles, Birth Order, and the Irish Double Bind' 1979:163–85). There, it is the youngest son who is negatively earmarked to fail at all extra-village pursuits, and it is he who will normally inherit and manage the farm as the parents grow older. The critical selection period occurs during late adolescence and early adulthood, a phase through which, significantly, *elder* sons and daughters pass with greater ease (1979:166). The Portuguese case is somewhat different and the overall context of rural society in Trás-os-Montes exhibits little of the anomie and social disintegration described by Scheper-Hughes for Southwest Ireland. At least at the time of my fieldwork, I found no clear evidence of such negative selection processes in heirship.

The major strategy of the favoured heir is thus to postpone the partition, or if this is unavoidable, to buy out the shares of the other co-heirs in order to consolidate the total holding. As marriage in Fontelas is quite late, by the time a division takes place many co-heirs are already well into their 30's and long established somewhere or other. The varying life circumstances of each of these co-heirs at the time of the *partilha* is crucial. Who has remained in Fontelas? Who has left the hamlet? Who will press for partition and who is likely to claim a share of the patrimony for immediate use? While all co-heirs are in this sense legally equal, socially their positions as claimants to the patrimony at the moment of partition may be distinctly unequal. If we were to emphasize merely the *ideal* legal equality between heirs, the entire complex of *practical* inequality between favoured heirs and secondary co-heirs would be missed. As one woman put it so aptly, the ultimate result of the partition is not always 'equitable':

Some get the vineyards, And others the wine-barrels.	*Uns ficam com as vinhas,* *E outros com as pipas.*

Parallels with societies with systems of formal unigeniture and primogeniture should not be carried too far however, despite the similarities in key features of social structure. Regions of single-heir inheritance in Europe are frequently characterized by late marriage, celibacy, institutionalized emigration, and a stress upon the transmission of a patrimony intact through the generations. Three recent comparative studies of regional variations in inheritance also stress these differences: Le Roy Ladurie (1976) develops Jean Yver's typology of three grand régimes of succession in France, Rogers and Salamon (1983) compare inheritance processes in four rural communities in France and the United States, and Augustins (1982) provides a particularly useful four-fold classification of inheritance and headship systems in France. Fontelas could clearly exemplify Augustins' Type 3: *succession unique, héritage égalitaire* (1982:55–7). One essential difference between inheritance in Fontelas and rigid systems of unigeniture is the complete absence in this community of a full-scale transfer of property at the marriage of the selected heir. This transfer *inter vivos* has been reported for Western Ireland (Arensberg and Kimball 1940), the Basque Country in Spain (Douglass 1969), Galician Spain (Lisón-Tolosana 1971/Iturra 1980), and the Italian Alps (Wolf and Cole 1974). In all of these cases an heir is selected and the bulk of the patrimony is transmitted intact to this heir at his/her marriage (usually his). Thus Douglass maintains that 'the transmission of property rights and authority is not tied in Murélaga to *one* rite of passage' (1969:215). Rather, death in Murélaga seals a process which already begins at the marriage of the selected heir. Excluded heirs must settle for a cash payment or remain celibate.

But in Fontelas, there is no such transfer of property at marriage and no institutionalized means through which the parents or favoured heir can force other co-heirs to leave the hamlet entirely or relinquish their shares. The most a parent can do legally is to favour one of the heirs with 1/3 (the *terço*) of his or her patrimony and a stronger social claim to retain management of the domestic group. There are no fixed house-names in Fontelas except that of the wealthy Conselho household, but even in this case there is no formal link between the house and its undivided fields. Although excessive partition is generally avoided, some portion of most landholdings is bound to be split eventually. Thus land as well as houses pass from individual to individual and they are not a kind of impartible corporate whole as in regions of formal unigeniture.

Another stark contrast between Fontelas' system of inheritance and those reported for regions with more rigid forms of transmission through one heir is the quality of sibling ties. For St Felix in the Tyrol, John Cole stresses that: 'Once the transfer of property took place, social links between siblings were often terminated. In fact many village residents lost track of their absent brothers and sisters, even to the point of not knowing whether they were alive or dead' (1977a:126). In contrast, the second village studied by Cole – in the same region but with a very different (partible) inheritance system – resembles Fontelas with regard to the proliferation of legal heirs to property: in Tret this situation '. . . could get completely out of hand so that in a generation or two a fractional share of a holding might have literally dozens of owners, scattered over entire continents, some perhaps unaware that they ever had an ancestor who came from a place called Tret' (1977a:128). The absence in Fontelas of a *pre-mortem* property transfer such as that described for St Felix leads to continuing and long-lasting ties between siblings (indeed these ties are by definition extended to nephews, nieces, and grandchildren) thus militating against the abrupt severing or atrophy reported for St Felix, but nevertheless reproducing a form of latent legal competition for the practical managerial control of inheritance shares. This *de facto* control of the bulk of a parental landholding by one heir in Fontelas, and the concomitant exclusion of co-heirs from this role, remains within the sphere of subtle, informal social strategies.

Thus, in Fontelas a limitation of the claims of co-heirs is achieved through informal heir-control. If co-heirs cannot be formally expelled, they may at least be cajoled into paths other than that of the favoured heir. Although the prospects for their marriage may be limited and strictly controlled if they stay, their sexuality need not. The society's general de-emphasis of marriage in part accomplishes this, and the tradition of non-marital unions and acceptance of illegitimacy lend further possible avenues for these co-heirs. Never entirely excluded from the natal patrimony in legal terms, and not all emigrants, these co-heirs simply hang around within the hamlet. They retain legal rights to a share of the patrimony, but the actual use to which these rights are put are a function of their specific circumstances at the time of the *partilha*.

In contrast to regions where unigeniture is practiced, in Fontelas inheritance is in fact tied to one sole rite of passage – death. One further element of crucial significance here is the link between death (the critical moment of property transfer) and the care of elderly parents. As Goody has noted, 'the link between stratification and the economy is by means of the system of inheritance, which organises the transmission of property from generation to generation, at death, at marriage or at some other point in the development cycle' (1976a:65). *Post-mortem* transmission implies not only a delay in the acquisition of property by the young, but also a prolongation of the retention of property rights by the old. The fact that a formal transmission of an intact patrimony does not occur at marriage in Fontelas implies that the parental generation does not in any sense lose control of the holding. Nor do they enter any form of retirement from farming, unless utterly senile. The structure of inheritance demands that one or more of the parents' children (or other kin) look after them with special care as they age. Favoured heirs in particular will also provide for the parents' funeral expenses, look after the graves on All Souls' Day, and have at least the prescribed series of three masses said for their souls. The parental generation thus holds the strings of both land and labour while they remain alive.

The selection of a favoured heir may ensure this care. But in the absence of a favoured heir, one or more co-heirs must assume this role of care and assistance. Indeed, one elderly villager quoted an appropriate saying:

Who is your heir?	*Quem é teu herdeiro?*
The one who cleans your behind.	*Quem te limpa o traseiro.*

In systems of formal unigeniture this old-age security is ensured through the selection of a single heir: this is the heir who will maintain control of the patrimony and who will care for the aging parents. In Fontelas, however, ideally all of the children (as equal legal co-heirs) should care for their parents as they age, but this ideal is not always achieved in practice. Villagers are constantly evaluating the attentions of others towards elderly parents. Suspicion is always hovering that the future heir is merely pressing through self-interest for a reciprocal gift of property through a will. In general however, the system of inheritance retains a built-in social welfare element: aging parents are in no sense in retreat from the ownership or control of their landholding.

What is accomplished in unigeniture at the marriage of the selected heir is only ever achieved in Fontelas at death. Here the aging parents retain control of their property until their dying day, much like the 'King Lear principle' to which Leyton refers for a Northern Irish community, where custom warns that no property should be transferred until the death of the owner (1970:1380). In this vein, villagers in Fontelas cite the verse *O que dá o seu antes que morra/ Merece com uma porra* (Those who give away their things before dying/ Deserve a cudgelling). Elderly villagers who cede property rights to their children before they die are frowned upon – I was told of a number of cases of widows and widowers who, after having effected such a *pre-mortem* partition, were 'kicked out' (*postos na rua*) and maltreated by their heirs. Cases such as these, however, are rare. But a certain price must be paid for old-age security. The cost is an excessive postponement for the younger generation: their acquisition of *de facto* rights to their shares of the natal patrimony is excessively delayed. Late marriage, celibacy, and bastardy are further results of this delay.

The implications of inheritance

How then does inheritance shape the form of this hamlet's social inequalities as a whole? How have indirect unigeniture and *post-mortem* division affected the contours of this society over the generations? Two final points will provide us with some answers. These are: (a) the persistence of high proportions of illegitimacy, and (b) the maintenance of an overall social hierarchy through time.

We have seen that the following features have characterized the social structure of Fontelas at least since the late nineteenth century:

Late marriage;
High proportions never marrying;
Large households (many non-nuclear in form);
Stress on descent over affinity;
Natolocal residence;
High illegitimacy ratios.

We have also seen that underlying these patterns is the practice of delayed *post-mortem* inheritance and (among the landed groups) an attempt to preserve patrimonies through indirect unigeniture. Let us now look at the last of the six features enumerated above. In Table 18 I have compiled the illegitimacy ratios for Fontelas from 1870 through 1978; the data are derived from the Parish Register's baptismal entries. In Appendix V I have compiled a sample of baptismal entries: there I have listed every baptism that has taken place in Fontelas over three decades (1880–, 1910–, and 1950–) along with the occupations of each child's mother and father. A perusal of this appendix will clarify how the figures in Table 18 were tallied.

The overall illegitimacy ratios in Fontelas are extraordinarily high, ranging in the late nineteenth century from over 1/3 to almost 1/2 of all baptisms. Although this sample is statistically limited in size, we can nevertheless detect some changes over the decades. The mean illegitimacy ratio (bastards baptized as a percentage of all children baptized) over the century since 1870 has been 47.4 per cent. In other words, throughout the past century, virtually one half of all children baptized in Fontelas have been bastards. In the decade from 1910 through 1919 natural children accounted for 73.6 per cent of all children baptized: three out of four children baptized during that decade were illegitimate. From 1920 through 1929 this percentage remained almost as high, at 67.9 per cent.[11]

Such high rates have not been reported for any European community in my entire bibliography, though clearly not all of the authors I cite have carried out such counts of baptisms in parish registers. The highest figure I have come across was 68.1 per cent from 1870–4 in an Eastern Alpine region of Austria (Mitterauer 1981). These high proportions in Fontelas continued through the

[11] This abrupt rise in illegitimacy may have had to do with the general political climate of the First Republic (1910–26), bearing in mind however that it is difficult to arrive at conclusions without a larger sample from various hamlets. A Monarchist incursion took place in the mountains around Fontelas in 1911–12, and journalists' accounts stress the chaotic developments in the region during those years (Magro 1912; Malheiro Dias 1912; Valente 1912). There was also an epidemic in the summer and autumn of 1918, when the deaths recorded in the Parish Register soared well above previous rates. During the decade from 1910 through 1930, however, there was no substantial imbalance between the sexes in the parish, according to national census figures (p. 39, n. 15). Finally, national legislation following 1910 instituted the possibility of divorce and civil marriage, and a few of the baptisms during those decades specify that the parents were *registados civilmente*, or 'married by civil law'. The connections between all of these factors are not entirely clear, and require further demographic research.

1930s and 1940s at 52.6 per cent and 57.8 per cent respectively, dropping only slightly during the 1950s to 47.5 per cent. The figures for Fontelas are however merely an extreme local example of a general regional trend:

> it has to be noted that the rate of illegitimate fertility in Portugal is very high, and remains relatively stable until 1940, showing a slight decline thereafter. Comparable levels of illegitimacy can be found only in the countries of central and northern Europe, such as Austria, Eastern Germany, and Sweden, in contrast to the very low illegitimacy prevailing in Spain and Italy (Livi Bacci 1971:60).

Some similar comments on regional variations within specific countries can also be found in Laslett (1980a:1–65). Also within the latter's introduction to the topic is a treatment of the more common and simplistic classic explanations of illegitimacy.

A significant decrease occurred in the 1960s to the rather low ratio (for Fontelas) of 23.4 per cent – there was also a smaller total number of baptisms in this decade. Finally, in the 1970s the ratio plummetted to a minuscule 7.4 per cent: only two natural children among 25 legitimate ones were baptized between 1970 and September of 1978. The drop in total baptisms corresponds almost exactly with the wave of emigration to France and West Germany which started around 1960 and gained enormous (clandestine) proportions following 1964. The baptismal entries for 1977 include a series of emigrant baptisms which took place in the month of August when emigrants customarily return to Fontelas. The parents of these children are explicitly registered as 'resident in France'. Recent emigration, in which the *jornaleiro* group played a major role, may in part explain the dramatic decline in illegitimacy in the 1960s and 1970s, but it does not provide an explanation for the consistently high ratios of former decades. For that earlier period the answer must lie elsewhere.

The clearest pattern over the decades (as I have shown with specific examples in Chapter 5) has been the very close link between bastard children and the occupation of 'single woman' in the *jornaleiro* group. Almost as consistent has been the tendency among *lavrador* women to bear legitimate children within legal marriage. A simple sum of the baptisms of illegitimate and legitimate children within these two social groups is instructive:

172 illegitimate children of unmarried *jornaleiras*
87 legitimate children of married *jornaleiras*
259

10 illegitimate children of unmarried *lavradoras*
102 legitimate children of married *lavradoras*
112

(Total children baptized in these two social groups since 1870 = 371)

Table 18. *Illegitimacy ratios in Fontelas, 1870–1978*

Years	Legitimate children (1)	Bastard children (2)	Total baptisms (3)	Illegitimacy ratio (2÷3) %
1870–1879	41	22	63	*34.9*
1880–1889	40	30	70	*42.9*
1890–1899	51	30	81	*37.0*
1900–1909	39	28	67	*41.8*
1910–1919	19	53	72	*73.6*
1920–1929	26	55	81	*67.9*
1930–1939	27	30	57	*52.6*
1940–1949	27	37	64	*57.8*
1950–1959	31	28	59	*47.5*
1960–1969	36	11	47	*23.4*
1970–1978	25	2	27	*7.4*
Totals	362	326	688	*47.4*

Source: Parish Register – Baptismal entries.

* Note that these ratios are calculated on the basis of the baptismal date and not the birth date of each child; the ratios thus refer to children ecclesiastically illegitimate or natural on the date of their baptism. Civil marriages are also recorded in the baptismal entries (there were only 6) but there is no uniform classification of the children of these marriages: twice in 1923 and once in 1926 the children of such unions were registered as 'illegitimate', but twice in 1930 and once in 1977 the children of such civil unions were listed as 'legitimate'.

Of the total of 326 natural children baptized in Fontelas since 1870, the 172 born to single *jornaleiras* accounted for 52 per cent of all bastard baptisms (Table 22 in Appendix V). Although not all *jornaleiras* have borne bastards (87 baptisms were of legitimate children) the trend among the day-labourer women is clearly towards illegitimate births. In striking contrast, there have been extremely few baptisms of natural children born to *lavradora* women: only 10 of 112 baptisms in this group were of bastards. The vast majority of children born to *lavradoras* were legitimate on the date of their baptism. (Some may of course have been born illegitimately, as it is not uncommon for a month or more to pass between the dates of birth and baptism.) Further, more than twice as many children were born to *jornaleira* women as a whole (259) than to *lavradora* women (112).

I have not considered here the large number of other occupations of mothers (Appendix V) but rather have concentrated on the contrast between mothers in the land-poor *jornaleiro* group and those in the landed *lavrador* group. Obviously, far more detailed calculations (and family reconstitutions) could be carried out using the rich baptismal data, but I am interested here in the overall trends revealed by these figures.[12] The basic pattern of the illegitimacy figures points overwhelmingly to bastard births among the poor, and to legitimate ones among the landed.

The Parish Register data suggest that Fontelas contains not merely a 'sub-society' prone to illegitimacy (Laslett *et al* 1980) but that the entire hamlet has been prone to the bearing and at least tacit social acceptance of bastard children. This is a rather different point from that made by Viazzo (1986) for an Italian Alpine village, where an immigrant mining group seems to have constituted a clear example of Laslett's idea of a sub-society of bastardy prone individuals. Pina-Cabral records illegitimacy ratios of over 20 per cent for two parishes in Northwest Portugal during the first three decades of the 20th century (1984a:86), although his use of Laslett's concept of the bastardy prone sub-society is also somewhat different from my own. In the Barroso region of Trás-os-Montes, Fontes has noted that 'this system of single-heir inheritance (*morgado*) explains the existence of large numbers of illegitimate children in each hamlet. All children did not marry, even in wealthy houses . . . But it is certain that single mothers are well accepted by the society' (1977:20; my translation). Similarly, Livi Bacci speaks of high illegitimacy rates in Northern Portugal and notes that 'since a large fraction of the female population was forcibly excluded from marriage, it is not surprising to find a high number of illegitimate conceptions, often tolerated by the family and the society' (1971:72). Fontelas is thus not a bastardy prone sub-society, but an entire bastardy prone *society*.[13] A much more appropriate model, in my view, can be found in Laslett's brief but extremely perceptive analysis (1981) of the presence in the same community of *two* different kinds of 'procreative career' for women, simultaneously interacting in close relation to a sort of black market of unofficial or illegitimate marriages. The latter model – unlike that of the bastardy prone sub-society – has the advantage of locating multiple forms of sexual and moral behaviour in dynamic tension and conflict within the same population or village.

The specific mode of inheritance in Fontelas suggests why this hamlet as a whole constitutes something more complex than a mere sub-society. Household 14 is a case in point. This domestic group is at the peak of its developmental cycle – the elder couple is still active in agriculture, the younger couple is in their 30s, and the unmarried Justiniano is an added asset to the

[12] Again, the use of the term *doméstica* as a woman's occupation following 1946 makes it very difficult to classify these women as *jornaleiras*, *lavradoras*, or as members of any other social group. The occupations of the fathers of legitimate children provide a clue to their wives' occupations, but the fathers of bastards are usually not listed. Another potential problem is the change of priests who did the actual recording of the occupations. In the absence of strictly defined occupational categories, then, we must be content with overall trends.

[13] Enlarging the scope of our sample to include the four hamlets in the parish, we obtain the simple illegitimacy ratios indicated below. Throughout the decades up to 1959, the total number of baptisms in the parish was over 200: in the 1960s this total decreased to 143, and

household's labour. But we recall that Justiniano fathered an illegitimate child by his father's half-sister. In time, the direction of household management will in all likelihood pass to Benta and Avelino rather than Justiniano (see Figure 24). In the next generation it is also likely that the young Leonarda will remain within the household. But what of Justiniano and his bastard son?

Should Justiniano legally recognize the child as his own, this would give the child (resident in another section of the hamlet) a legal claim to a portion of Justiniano's property at his death. Should the latter die intestate after his parents' deaths, it is his sister Benta and niece Leonarda who would inherit his acquired goods as well as his share of both parents' patrimonies. The recognition of the bastard child would thus pose a threat to part of the natal patrimony. Indeed, the Parish Register entries indicate that of the 326 illegitimate children baptized since 1870, the vast majority of 275 (84 per cent) were born to legally 'unknown fathers' (Table 23 in Appendix V). Once affiliated, Justiniano's child would inherit half the property going to Justiniano's sister and niece. (Illegitimate children who are affiliated inherit half-shares in relation to legitimate heirs.) A further threat to the patrimony would arise in the event of Justiniano's marrying someone else from Fontelas: with legitimate children, his later claim to a share of his parents' patrimony

between 1970 and 1978 there were a mere 95. We should note however that although the percentages for Fontelas and Lousada are the highest, the overall proportion throughout the 11 decades in the parish has remained consistently high, at 37.8%.

Illegitimacy ratios in Mosteiro parish, 1870–1978

Years	Mosteiro (head village) %	Fontelas %	Lousada %	Portelinha %	Parish total %
1870–79	29.3	34.9	26.0	22.7	29.2
1880–89	27.8	42.9	43.9	5.9	35.2
1890–99	32.6	37.0	64.6	37.0	40.8
1900–09	31.5	41.8	76.0	18.2	44.1
1910–19	22.5	73.6	50.0	15.8	46.0
1920–29	25.8	67.9	42.9	18.5	42.3
1930–39	30.4	52.6	59.6	—	42.0
1940–49	19.8	57.8	46.9	11.8	37.2
1950–59	27.5	47.5	52.8	22.2	39.6
1960–69	27.1	23.4	37.2	20.0	28.7
1970–78	3.6	7.4	24.3	33.3	13.7
TOTAL (%)	26.8	47.4	47.6	19.2	37.8
Total Bastards:	223	326	289	34	872
Total Baptisms:	833	688	607	177	2,305

Source: Parish Register – Baptismal entries.

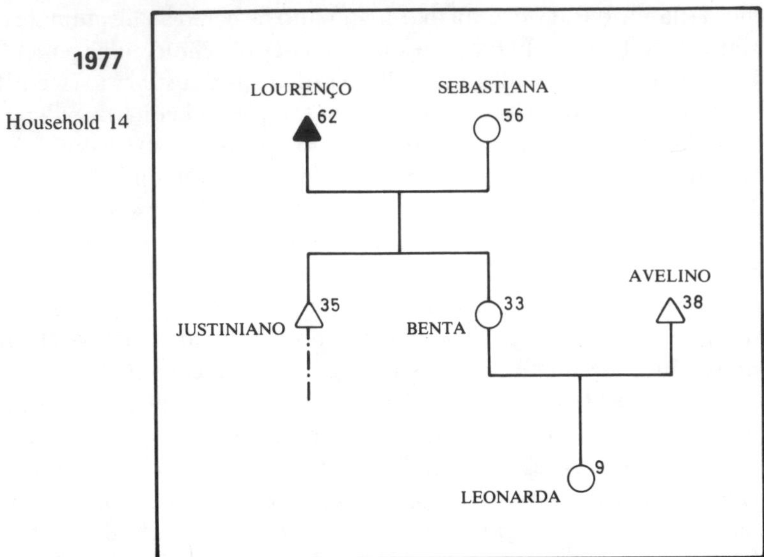

Figure 24. *Lavrador* household (Household 14)

would be greater, and he would be likely to press for equal partition with his sister.

Here then lies the essence of the connection between matrimonial strategies and illegitimacy. Justiniano's marriage is postponed and his labour retained within the natal household. His marriage would threaten future division, but his remaining 'celibate' will not. Two birds are killed with one stone: the natal household thus retains his labour as well as his property, but only at the cost of the limitation of marriage. Of course, Justiniano could marry out or emigrate permanently (he did in fact emigrate to France for a few years in the 1960s). Neither of these choices would pose a serious threat to the patrimony. Or he could marry very late after both of his parents have died, but his claim at that point will be a weak one compared with that of his sister Benta. Benta's marriage was significantly both an early one (she was 18 and Avelino 23) and a strategic one as well. In contrast, Justiniano is likely to remain unmarried: an added hand around the house and the socially distant father of his bastard son. Like the younger sons in seventeenth-century England upon whose efforts the great fortunes of eldest sons were built, these co-heirs and the single mothers of their natural children 'hung around at home, idle, bored, and increasingly resentful' (Thirsk 1969:368). That they should remain so, socially subordinated as dependents of their favoured siblings, is crucial to the maintenance of viable farming units in Fontelas. The actual legal equality of co-heirs is thus hidden beneath the favoured heir's social attempts to delay the marriages and to suppress the inheritance claims of the others.

The unmarried mothers of illegitimate children are in a different position.

Their exclusion from both matrimony and patrimony has been quite evident as far back as local records go. Villagers themselves produce apparently contradictory explanations for illegitimacy. The wealthy and the poor view the problem from opposite ends, and both sides systematically blame the other. The poor, especially many single mothers themselves, blame wealthy men for 'exploiting us as servants or day-labourers' and burdening them with bastard children. Yet the wealthy blame the poor simply for being poor – 'how can they help themselves, those poor souls?' One side seeks economic and political causes while the other finds moral ones. My point is that neither side is entirely correct, but that the entire problem is shaped from the start by a specific mode of inheritance. Not all fathers of bastards are wealthy, nor are all of the relations leading to illegitimate children necessarily exploitative; many fathers were simply co-heirs left outside (or pushed outside) the main lines of property transmission in their natal households. Yet for poorer women, children are always an asset as their labour is highly valued. Better a bastard child than none at all. Even among the poor, descent and sibling ties are strong and ties of marriage and affinity comparatively weak. As Le Roy Ladurie has noted for the West of France (1976:58), the inheritance customs of this region of Portugal 'smile on children, but not on love'.[14]

The very high proportions of illegitimacy over the decades provide ample evidence of a peristent pattern of the social reproduction of a bastard group over time. The maintenance of a group of day-labouring women (the *jornaleiras*) and their illegitimate children has provided a source of temporary hired labour for wealthy landed households. Many servants in these wealthy households have come from this group. But the key point is that the wealthy and the landed have also managed to retain this source of wage labour *without* posing threats to the bulk of the hamlet's patrimonies. The illegitimacy ratios are so high, and bastard births so common, that the society's general level of tolerance for illegitimacy must also be quite high. Even today in Fontelas, over one-third of the hamlet's adult women over 21 have borne at least one natural child at some point in their lives. Bastard children and single mothers, although low in social status, are accepted as social individuals and non-marital unions are openly tolerated.[15] This does not mean that some stigma is

[14] One extreme example of this stress on children was a song I recorded about a mother who buried her bastard child alive. The tune was composed a few years ago and was based on a true incident in one of Fontelas' neighbouring hamlets. The song relates that 'a mother in order to marry/buried her child alive' and that 'it was due to her *namoro*/that the evil woman buried him'. The child was 28 months old and 'already talked well' and the mother buried it 'under a pile of stones'. In villagers' eyes, the mother's real crime was not to have borne the child illegitimately in the first place, but to have buried him 'for love' or to have killed him merely in order to marry.

[15] It is significant that the word *puta* (whore) is never used to refer to these single mothers: villagers only use the latter term in conversations about the behaviour of 'city women' (implying Bragança, Porto, and Lisbon). Even with respect to single mothers with various bastard children of different fathers, I never heard anyone speak of rural prostitution or of any kind of monetary payment.

not also present. As we have seen, bastards are called *zorros* or *zorras*, while other sayings indicate the inheritance of poor mothers' low status: *Da ovelha ruim/Não sai cordeiro bom* (From a bad ewe/A good lamb does not come). Clearly, the term *zorro* does in certain circumstances acquire a note of censure, but it must be borne in mind that such censure derives exclusively from the upper social groups: among *jornaleiros* and other smallholders the word merely refers to a child not affiliated by his/her father. Once legally recognized (even if the father does not marry the mother) the illegitimate child is no longer a *zorro*. Thus the 'malicious' connotation of the term, and the infra-human position alluded to by its association with an animal (fox), suggest a highly ambiguous concept. Both of the latter meanings are constantly brought into play. A bastard always runs the risk of behaving badly, and should he/she do so, villagers may invoke the term reprehensibly. But if not, the bastard is accepted socially within the community on a par with any legitimate child. Irregular sex (including illicit unions, concubinage, and the censure of *zorros*) is thus in the long run a mechanism, or a somewhat indirect path, for the satisfaction of sexuality and the reproduction of labour *outside* the central spheres of marriage and property. From the point of view of the wealthy, a large part of the population must remain marginal to the delicate balance between prestigious matrimony and undivided patrimony. The problem is thus not illegitimacy but marriage itself.

A distinct social hierarchy is continually maintained in this manner. Earlier chapters have shown how this hierarchy is structured with regard to land tenure and unequal labour exchanges. These three chapters (5, 6, and 7) have revealed concomitant evidence of a third form of inequality separating the wealthy from the poor with respect to marriage and inheritance. This differentiation is less visible in patterns of intra-group marriage than in the division between heirs in inheritance. In general, the very wealthy also marry the very wealthy and the poor marry the poor. But *proprietários* do marry *lavradores* and *lavradores* do marry *jornaleiros*, although marriages between the upper group and the lowest one are extremely rare. The crucial division in Fontelas is not between groups which may or may not intermarry: there is some fluidity between the groups and people do move up and down, thus preventing a rigid scale of strictly class-endogamous marriages. The crucial division is rather between individual heirs who may or may not inherit. Although co-heirs are legally equal, the practical concerns of patrimony institute a real inequality between the circumstances of favoured heirs and tacitly excluded secondary heirs. An attempt to pass a patrimony intact through the generations is partially achieved through indirect unigeniture and the general de-emphasis of marriage. Few are those who obtain both prestigious matrimony and a large share of patrimony, but many are those who obtain neither. The latter are however allowed a considerable amount of choice in sexual partners. In this sense, the structure of inheritance favours a few and ousts the rest.

These latter are truly 'underprivileged offspring who run the risk of falling into the proletariat, if they are of the people; or into the church, if they come from the middle or upper classes' (Le Roy Ladurie 1976:63). There is thus an almost continual falling out of co-heirs from the positions their households occupy in the hierarchy (e.g. Rufina). Many more individuals fall downwards in the social echelon through exclusion than those who manage to climb upwards.[16] This is why the fundamental concern of maintaining patrimonies intact is one of heir-control and not merely population control: the lower group of *jornaleiros* and bastard children may continually expand in numbers without threatening the basis of the inheritance of patrimony. Too many *heirs* with valid claims will threaten partition. But for a large number of people (the *jornaleiro* group) with weak claims or none at all, this path is out of the question from the start. In other words, the top and bottom of the social hierarchy mutually support each other, just as favoured heirs and their secondary co-heirs complement each other. Here lies the fulcrum of the inheritance system: each side is dependent on the other's position. The only way in which the society's fundamental contradiction between the legal equality of heirs and the practical inequality between favoured heirs and secondary co-heirs is ever resolved is through the illicit link between these co-heirs and unmarried mothers. A 'bastard class' is the final result. The chosen few hold onto land, while the excluded many are progressively elbowed out.

In consequence, there must be an actual approval (however indirect) of illegitimacy and non-marital sexuality for the purpose of keeping patrimonies together. Like the *proprietários* as a whole, favoured heirs connect marriage, property, and sexuality. But for the rest, these three are disconnected. If an acceptable level of non-marital sex can exist (although *jornaleiras* have borne most of the burden) then a substantial number of people can be kept out of competition for patrimony. In this sense, neither bastards nor excluded heirs are really marginal to the social system – to the contrary, they become indispensable for the reproduction of the very system itself. But this long-term 'integration' lies to a certain degree hidden, given that the social roles of secondary heirs and *zorros* appear so frequently with negative connotations.

[16] The mass emigration of the 1960s has provided a perfect exit (and ultimate re-entry) for these excluded villagers. As ties with natal patrimonies in Fontelas are always retained, regardless of the meagre size of some individuals' shares, emigration constitutes an excellent solution to the problem of pressure on land. Natal holdings benefit from cash remittances (and future technical and housing improvements) while a large proportion of the population formerly relegated to marginal positions has at last the potential for upward mobility. This upward mobility is circuitous and delayed in that emigrants must first move *out* of the hamlet before moving *up* within it. But the long-term effects will provide the *jornaleiros* and some of the *lavradores* with their first really ascendant route *as a social group*. Emigration has not yet overturned the social hierarchy entirely, although today a kind of reversal of the former situation seems to be developing: the really favoured children are those who leave the hamlet successfully rather than those who stay. Only a further and posterior study of emigration and return migration in Fontelas will be able to afford materials capable of depicting this process more clearly.

But the general limitation of matrimony in the society still allows for a few favoured and estimable matches. It is in this sense that the two sides of the coin support each other: prestigious marriage could not remain prestigious without the reproduction of a group of people systematically locked out of both matrimony and patrimony.

The social hierarchy of Fontelas is constituted then, of these major social groups (*proprietários*, *lavradores*, and *jornaleiros*) a small core of which has maintained control of most of the hamlet's land over a number of generations. This core includes the fourth group of large *lavradores*. The fringes of day-labourers have formed the opposite side. At the household level, this opposition is reflected in the distinction between favoured heirs and excluded co-heirs. Both spheres (the household and the hamlet) are thus characterized by an institutionalized inequality which reserves matrimony and patrimony as prizes for the few at the expense of the many. A dual system thus constitutes the internal dynamic of the hamlet's structure over time: a small group of individuals are advantaged and have access to property and prestigious marriage, while a larger group is disadvantaged and remains on the fringes at the bottom of the social scale. This recalls my point in Chapter 3 that the real division within the hamlet is that between the land-rich and the land-poor. Much like the myriad branches of a tree, many more villagers fall outwards from their natal landholdings than those who retain control of the central trunk of the patrimony.

For most Fontelans the overriding power of patrimony, within a system of smallholding agriculture, imposes a strict limitation upon matrimony. One of the most glaring consequences of this limitation is a high ratio of illegitimacy and the social reproduction of a bastard group over time. Underlying these processes, and providing them with their basic structural shape, is the fact of partible inheritance at death: the transmission of all major patrimony is tied to this one rite. It is this system of delayed inheritance that has left its indelible mark on the hamlet's entire social structure.

8

Conclusion

Throughout this book I have been placing great emphasis upon economic and social distinctions within a small Portuguese rural community. Rather than summarize or repeat the major arguments, let me synthesize a few of the main strands woven within my principal theme. Three points are of particular relevance here.

Firstly, the question of egalitarian social structures. My major aim in this study has been to 'deconstruct' the image of the harmonious rural community. This has been done through a shift of focus from aspects of equality to aspects of inequality and social hierarchy. Alan Macfarlane has pointed, for the case of England, to erroneous assumptions about the existence of 'less mobility' and less social contact in the rural communities of the past. He states that the solution to this problem (such assumptions) 'does not lie in finding more archetypal secluded communities' (1977a:635–6). I have attempted to tackle the same problem in an Iberian context but from another angle, by demonstrating that *even within* such an archetypal secluded community forms of rigid economic and social differentiation prevail. In other words, I have deliberately used precisely the same object of study (a small mountain hamlet) as that analysed by previous ethnographers of the Northern Iberian Peninsula, but have come up with a substantially altered picture.

One of the more elegant illustrations of this problem can be found in a passage from the *Travels of the Duke de Chatelet in Portugal* (1809). The Duke's journeys throughout Portugal in 1777–8 were commented on in the Editor's Supplement to that volume in the following fashion. In Chapter XII the Duke had enumerated an entire string of agricultural problems in eighteenth-century Portugal: excessively large estates, badly kept roads, uncleaned river courses, insufficient numbers of labourers, feudal services and impositions, 'oppressions of every sort', decreasing herds, and vagabonds. The Editor then stated that:

. . . these account for two-thirds of Portugal being, still, uncultivated, and why the part which is cultivated in vines, olives, corn, herbs, wood &c. is not brought to the degree of perfection to which it might be brought, and in which it, in fact, was, towards the end of the thirteenth century (Duke de Chatelet 1809:293).

This is of course an extreme example of the way in which discontent with the deterioration of contemporary conditions produces a rather far-fetched idealization of the past. Much as this passage indicates a fantasizing of the past as a harmonious or 'more perfect' time, so the image of the small mountain village created by the Iberian ethnographers has succeeded in cementing a model of the community of equals in the past: whether in the thirteenth century or the nineteenth, things up in the mountains *must* have been harmonious and egalitarian. Through the reports of the authors quoted in Chapter 1 of this book, we have indeed been 'lulled into a spurious sense of community which we impose on the past' (Macfarlane 1977a:647). Thus, in the absence of precise and useful definitions, the term 'egalitarian' should either be eliminated from our scientific vocabulary or very carefully redefined with respect to specific empirical cases.

Much the same confusion has surrounded the concept of the household. Like the hypothetically egalitarian village, the household has been the target of myriad attempts at clear definitions. Very few of these definitions fit the actual cases of domestic group structure in Fontelas, and my efforts to link them with real households (both today and in the past) usually ended up in even greater terminological entanglement. Any number of households at any point in time extracted from the Fontelas Confessional Rolls would serve to question severely the entire system of household diagrams devised by Laslett (1972:31, 41–2), particularly with respect to the delineation of 'conjugal groups' and illegitimacies. I was confronted with a situation astonishingly similar to that described by Raymond T. Smith for the Caribbean: 'The lower class West Indian family is not based on marriage or on the nuclear family, and our informants show no concern about implementing some abstract norm, or value, of nuclear family solidarity . . . once we abandon the *a priori* assumption that the complex household and mating patterns are distorted forms of a basic nuclear family system, then many of the supposed problems of interpretation disappear' (1973:139). Can we simply explain away this pocket of Caribbean-like matrifocality right at the heart of rural Europe?

Thus, a rigid application of terms such as the Nuclear Family Household to Fontelas would only push the data into an even deeper mess and create greater analytical chaos. In fact, the wide variety of domestic arrangements in Fontelas seem to provide more examples of the mythical extended family household than of properly nuclear structures. In other words, households in this hamlet reveal precisely those family structures that Laslett *et al* attempted to relegate to a less prominent theoretical position in *Household and Family in Past Time* (1972). (See, however, Laslett's recent comparative tables on varying household structure and organization in four different regions of traditional Europe – 1983:526–7 and 1984:360–1.) This is not to say that the myth of the extended family household need be revived, but merely to point to the danger of a too-universal application of the 'nuclear family hypothesis' to regions of rural Europe where it does not fit. A similar point concerning the conjugal tie was made long ago by Löfgren and is now confirmed by my Portuguese data on natolocal residence: 'It is, for example, quite evident that a married couple often did not constitute a very strong emotional dyad in peasant society . . . The emergence of the conjugal dyad as an emotionally strong and socially primary unit may be a late development in Scandinavian society' (1974:46). Like purportedly egalitarian villages, households as well as married couples in the European past may not have been as nuclear as our contemporary vision has led us to believe.

The second point concerns religion, or rather, the supposed relation between illegitimacy and the Church. Religion in itself has not been treated directly in this study, mainly due to my primary concern with hidden structures within specific spheres of hamlet life, particularly with regard to economic inequalities, patterns of marriage, and inheritance customs. Of necessity, this has meant that a wide range of 'ideological' elements of daily life has had to remain unfathomed – specifically, greater details concerning emotional and psychological dimensions of villagers' interpersonal relationships, of which religious behaviour constitutes merely one aspect.

By all standards (including the priest's) Fontelas' population participates in the religious activities of the Catholic Church in only the most cursory manner. Attendance at Sunday masses follows a fairly regular pattern, but during each Easter period the priest must literally scold his flock in church in order to get more than a handful of villagers (particularly men) to confess and take at least one yearly communion. (This may well be a recent trend, but more supplementary materials would be necessary to prove this.) The major life-cycle rites are followed by most households but particularly noteworthy is the attitude that, once beyond the church doors, these celebrations are entirely familial and not pious affairs. In fact, this is precisely the aspect of these celebrations that the priest criticizes most vehemently. He views most Fontelans as being excessively concerned with material elements: food, alcohol, clothing, and other aspects of conspicuous display. Indeed, the priest constantly refers to villagers' materialistic religious vows to the saints as not only selfish but utterly 'pagan'.

One statement I heard innumerable times was the following: 'That a God controls us, I believe; but I want nothing to do with all of that priestly nonsense!' For most villagers (except the priest and his close relatives) the rites of the Church are accepted as part of life, but they are not viewed as dominating that life entirely. There are only two villagers (one is a cousin of the priest) who are considered religious fanatics, and even the priest himself occasionally laughs at these two for their rather idiosyncratic behaviour. Unlike the villagers in the Greek mountain community of Ambéli (Du Boulay 1974), people in Fontelas do not go around incessantly making the sign of the cross before, during, and after meals. In fact, the only household in which I ever saw anyone cross themselves prior to a meal was the priest's. A general tone of anticlericalism can be felt in Fontelas as well as its neighbouring hamlets, although the situation in Fontelas today may be rather unusual. Many adult villagers knew the current priest as a child before he studied for a religious career, and this has coloured their view of his sacred role with a note of secular resentment. As the priest comes from a very wealthy *proprietário* household, some amount of indirect envy and distrust is to be expected. A strong current of criticism is discernible in many villagers' comments on persons who 'pray too much' or feign excessive religious zeal:

At the door of someone who prays a lot,	*À porta do rezador,*
Don't leave your wheat out in the sun.	*Não ponhas o trigo ao sol.*

The implication of the saying is, of course, that 'those who make a show of being devout, are likely to be the worst thieves'.

The obvious question here concerning religion, however, is the following: how can this community's very high rates of illegitimacy be reconciled with the 'Catholic' traditions of Northern Portugal? The fallacy here, I suggest, lies in the language of the question itself. There need *not* be any direct link at all between high illegitimacy and a 'weak' Church. In fact, the two are not even necessarily antagonistic. One marvellous passage, again from the Duke de Chatelet's travel account, suggests this point:

> It may, easily, be conceived that monks lead a life of the most unbridled licentiousness; but it must excite some astonishment to be informed, that every nunnery is a sort of seraglio, where the most shameless debauchery readily finds gratification. The convent of Odivelas, during the reign of John V. contained three hundred nuns, all young and beautiful. Each of them had her professed lover; they were seldom dressed in the habit of the order. The most refined gallantry was their occupation, and they were accounted the most accomplished courtezans in the kingdom. Hence issued the numerous illegitimate children of King John V. who made a real harem of this convent. The Marquis of Pombal, who disapproved generally of the multiplicity of convents, made this notorious circumstance a pretext for suppressing a great number, and incorporating them with other religious houses of not quite so bad a character. Still, however, the convents of both sexes in Portugal may be considered the most depraved in Christendom (Duke de Chatelet 1809:91–2).

Despite appearances, the role of the Church may have very little to do with non-marital fertility. Or, to phrase the problem in a more appropriate way with regard to Fontelas – the key link may lie in the relation between illegitimacy and inheritance. As long as most of the burden of bastardy falls on the lower orders of society (the *jornaleiras*) the Church may simply turn a deaf ear.

Indeed, Goody's recent provocative analysis of the complex links between family structures, marriage, and the Church in Europe (1983) seems only to confirm the glaring failure of Portuguese ecclesiastical institutions to obtain a firm grip on 'indigenous' or customary kinship practices in this rural region of the country. Goody's argument appears to have found a perfect example in Fontelas of the apparent survival into the twentieth century of an extremely resistant and resilient constellation of attitudes and practices regarding the control of family property, unorthodox sexual behaviour, natural kinship as contrasted to civil-legal or ecclesiastical definitions of kindred ties, and the conscious or subliminal refusal to abide by formal religious codes. In any case, however much the clergy may shout in this kind of community, the practical needs of the smallholding household prevail over the ideal moral precepts of the Church. In crude terms, it is not that the villagers do not understand the teachings and rules of the Church, but rather that for most of them these lessons and maxims simply go in one ear and out of the other: they are openly and systematically ignored. A case in point is the sacrament of matrimony: in practice and in spite of the Church, only a few may marry in Fontelas – the rest must settle for irregular unions, celibacy, or bastardy.

The third point concerns the antithesis of the image of rural equality – a hierarchy of ranked social groups. Despite the recent wave of emigration from Fontelas, the social processes depicted in the preceding chapters reveal the continuity of stratification over time, at least since the mid-nineteenth century. The 1960s exodus does not appear to have totally transformed, or levelled, this deeply embedded hierarchy. Emigration has not descended upon the hamlet as a *deus ex machina*, hailing the arrival of the light-bulb of Progress amidst these last survivors of the Dark Ages. Certainly, emigration has begun to 'open' the hamlet somewhat more to external influences, but this process should not be overemphasized or granted exaggerated importance. For example, to stress excessively recent changes brought about by emigration would tend to slant our attention towards a purported process of modernization which, in the case of Fontelas, is only now beginning to affect the rural community significantly. Such a slant would blind us to a whole series of characteristics – Fontelas' historical continuity – inherited from past social structure. That social structure, in spite of recent modifications, continues to reveal aspects of extreme poverty: despite the numerous references in this book to abundant harvest meals, villagers themselves incessantly emphasized that a few decades ago not everyone had a pig to kill in winter, and that shepherds went entire days up in the hills with a bare 'slice of pig-fat and rye-bread crust'. Others, in search of petty earnings, joined the nocturnal network of coffee contraband groups (*o trelo*) and carried enormous heavy sacks on their shoulders across the mountains and valleys into Spain.

Whether this hamlet (or any of the hamlets in the area) was ever really a closed community in the past is highly questionable, and without concrete historical evidence it is fruitless to speculate. If we search hard enough for ideal-types, we will probably find them in one form or another. We *can* state with reasonable authority however, on the basis of the wealth of information culled from the various sources examined here, that the social structure of Fontelas has been characterized for at least a century by unmistakable features of social differentiation and economic inequality.

My analysis, especially in the later chapters, may seem to give an excessively powerful role to an abstract system of inheritance, rather than to a particular group of real people. There is a specific reason for this, related to the concept of social hierarchy. In his opening pages to the volume *Family and Inheritance: Rural Society in Western Europe 1200–1800* (1976), Jack Goody places great stress upon the effects which distinct modes of property transmission have upon the shape of varying social structures. Fontelas provides a perfect test case for Goody's wider comparative statements about rural Europe. The features I have described – late marriage, illegitimacy, preferential inheritance – point together towards an extreme form of the repression of marriage for the purpose of maintaining viable landholdings. The timing of the transfer of property from generation to generation (in this case only at death) produces a remarkably weird set of characteristics, particularly if we persist in viewing this community through Mediterranean eyes. Clearly, other alternatives are available to face the problem of maintaining viable landholdings within a context of limited resources and population pressure. For example, holdings could theoretically be fragmented and reunited in alternate generations (usually precluded in Fontelas by the avoidance of partition and the absence of property transfers at marriage), cash dowries could remove wealthy daughters to local cities (a rare practice in this region), and formal primogeniture might be combined with parental retirement and contracts ensuring the heir's later support of the parents (a process not entirely applicable to Fontelas). I believe that the particular mixture of factors observable in this hamlet is less the result of purely cultural preferences or conscious choices and more the product of a specific mode of property devolution, in which local custom prevails over the nineteenth-century State-promulgated Civil Code.

The crux of the matter thus lies in the mode of property transfer, which itself almost takes on a life of its own. By splitting the entire hamlet into two spheres – the inheritors and the disadvantaged – this mode of transfer by definition maintains a distinct social hierarchy which separates the haves from the have-nots. This split can be unveiled (as I have shown) not only inside the structure of households and sibling groups, but also at the hamlet level in the layered structure of *proprietários*, *lavradores*, and *jornaleiros*. Yet further, the split can also be viewed in a diachronic dimension, as entire social groups (particularly bastard-bearing women) are reproduced over the generations in precisely the same niches within the hierarchy.

But how can this system of inheritance attain such a powerful conditioning role? The answer here lies in the link between social relations and property relations. The social structure I have described implies in itself a certain internal dynamic through which the wealthy stay on top and the poor are kept down. This is precisely what is suggested by the following saying, quoted to me by a smallholder woman:

Grapes can be compared,	*As uvas são comparadas,*
To the lives of many people:	*À vida de muita gente:*

They were born to be trodden,	*Nasceram para ser pisadas,*
By the feet of those who do not feel.	*Pelos pés de quem não sente.*

This internal dynamic between social groups also operates at the level of the kinship system. Quite pertinently, Goody highlights the close link between kinship and property: 'The manner of splitting property is a manner of splitting people; it creates (or in some cases reflects) a particular constellation of ties and cleavages between husband and wife, parents and children, sibling and sibling, as well as between wider kin' (1976b:3). It is precisely this 'particular constellation of ties and cleavages' which I have tried to unmask, by granting special prominence to the process of *post-mortem* inheritance.

But the 'trick' of the wealthy has been to disguise this dynamic of domination under the costume of egalitarian relations. As Bourdieu has put it, 'domination . . . must be disguised under the veil of enchanted relationships, the official model of which is presented by relations between kinsmen' (1977:191). This domination occurs not only between individuals in alternate generations but also between entire social groups, and the nexus around which this domination operates is the ownership of land. Sigrid Khera has noted precisely the same pattern for rural Austria: 'Thus, it appears that social interaction among relatives in these central European peasant societies is conditioned primarily by the ownership of land and other patrimony. It is not the kin tie per se that is of importance. It is the property connected with it that determines the social significance or insignificance of the kin tie' (1972b:363). Much of my data points toward the existence of profound structural tensions between individuals and groups – tensions which usually surface or explode at key moments in the developmental cycle when major transfers of property occur. One of the clearest examples of such structural tensions is that between matrimony and patrimony, which I have demonstrated from a number of angles. It is in this sense that property itself takes on an almost personalized role in Fontelas, much as Bourdieu (1976:117) points to Marx's clever phrase concerning the inheritance of land: 'The beneficiary of the entail, the eldest son, belongs to the land. The land inherits him.'

The link between social relations and property relations is thus visible at the critical moment of property transfer – death. Marriage, residence, and matrimony (in the widest sense of the term) fade into insignificance in the face of death and the domination of patrimony. This is why the contradiction between the ideal of partible inheritance and the reality of the split between favoured heirs and excluded siblings is never entirely resolved. The purely legal equality between co-heirs is a disguise under which a whole series of inequalities clash. These inequalities surface, as it were, at the moment of death, when a major re-ordering of personal and property relations usually takes place. As this re-ordering does not occur in this society at marriage, a kind of delayed, double rupture takes place at death: all sorts of property are stored up until the critical moment of partition. It is precisely this tie between death and the transfer of property that has shaped many of the major features of Fontelas' social structure.

A number of years ago Jack Goody made the following statement about kinship and property:

> . . . while anthropologists have given most attention to kinship factors, there are a number of important areas of social life where the mode of distributing property appears to be more significant. This is not a matter of trying to substitute one monolithic form of explanation for another . . . My interest is in attempting to specify the way in which they are associated, particularly with a view to ascertaining the influence of differences in systems of transmission upon kinship relations
>
> (Goody 1969:70).

Carrying Goody's statement one step further, we might actually converge kinship relations with property relations altogether. This is what I have suggested here, and why I have concentrated such attention on land and *post-mortem* inheritance. Social relations and property relations do not only converge in this society at the moment of death; they are continually intertwined all along. Part of the reason for this lies in the precarious mountain economy of Fontelas: landholdings simply must be maintained as viable productive units through the limitation of excessive marital reproduction and multiple inheritance claims. Amidst this delicate balance between land and labour, the needs of the land and the household (patrimony) take priority over the needs of people as individual agents (matrimony), thus conferring a highly conflictual character upon the internal structure of the domestic group. But death is the key event around which this crucial transfer of property revolves, and at which kin relations and their material elements of property are reorganized. In this sense, kinship relations in Fontelas *are* property relations.

In conclusion, let me close by pointing to some implications raised by my argument in this book. Firstly, the topic of night-marriage, and in particular natolocal residence, invites further comparative work within rural Europe. Secondly, illegitimacy in this region of Portugal deserves specific, detailed study on its own. The rates reported here are some of the highest yet encountered for the entire Iberian area, and the link between bastardy and forms of preferential inheritance is an especially clear one. Many of the details described for Fontelas thus reflect the wider Eurasian patterns treated by Goody in his *Production and Reproduction* (1976). Furthermore, we should be able to penetrate much deeper into the more profound differences between, on the one hand the *jornaleiras* and their bastards, and on the other the landed peasant groups. This may lead us towards a model somewhat akin to Sidney Mintz's idea of the 'concealment' of a proletarian or semi-proletarian social group within a rural community of apparently self-sufficient, landowning peasants (Mintz 1974). Such a model might prove quite useful in locating real economic and social tensions hidden beneath immediately visible 'anomalies' such as highly mobile day-labouring women, bastards, servants, and other near-propertyless individuals circulating within an otherwise classic peasant society.

Thirdly, the whole topic of rural sexuality itself emerges as a problematic question. How does sexuality function within the very different contexts of, firstly, the relationships of favoured heirs and, secondly, those of excluded (bastard-bearing) siblings? The latter reveal almost schizophrenic behaviour in relation to their natal domestic groups: while they may *produce* within their own households, they are forced to *reproduce* outside them. It may well be that a substantively different code of sexuality (as distinct from 'love' and legal marriage) may be operative in communities such as Fontelas. This code may be quite a separate one from that with which we are familiar in the Mediterranean region (or indeed in urban Europe as a whole). Perhaps we are dealing with an isolated region of rural Europe where the Church never succeeded totally in obtaining control over popular morality and sexuality, which seem quite resistant to external impositions. Fontelas provides a number of illustrations of Flandrin's theory (1972:1351) of two archetypal modes of sexuality in the West: on the one hand *la procréation* and on the other *la passion amoureuse*. These two modes appear to apply clearly to two divisions within this hamlet: firstly that between respectable sexuality and illicit love, and secondly that between the 'procreative' orientation of favoured heirs and the 'amorous' sexuality of excluded co-heirs. The two forms of conduct are not always separable in daily practice or in the analysis of this rural society, but I suggest that it is within the dynamic between these two codes of behaviour that we will find a possible explanation for bastardy. Beneath this dynamic, we discover another – a structural one – generated by the inheritance system.

Fourthly, the wealth of information contained within the Parish Registers and Confessional Rolls may assist in correcting our blurred vision of rural communities in the past. Closed, bounded, and 'harmonious' mountain hamlets may turn out to be precisely the opposite of what they seemed to myopic modern eyes. A longer span of time and a larger field of hamlets (or parishes) may yield even richer and more conclusive data than that initially offered in this book. Nevertheless, the method adopted here – in the sense of joining anthropology and history – opens a number of analytical paths even with respect to such a minuscule settlement as Fontelas. In general it may be true that historical sources contain large gaps of information on '. . . the "invisible poor", the highly mobile and record-less section of pre-industrial society' (Macfarlane 1980b:81). But in the case of the Portuguese parish records examined here, the poor are quite as well documented as the middling and the wealthy. This study should be seen as one step towards the bringing to light of these formerly invisible poor.

Appendix I: The landholding survey

There is no codified Cadaster (Fr. *cadastre*) of the land owned in Fontelas either in Mosteiro or in the municipal town, or even in the offices of the Instituto Geográfico e Cadastral in Lisbon. The latter body has hanging inside the entrance to its Lisbon office a large map of Portugal which divides the country into two Southern and Northern halves. The completion of a new land-tax register (*cadastro*) is still in progress at the national level but has only reached the Central region of Portugal, having started in the South and proceeding Northwards. While Cutileiro's calculation of the distribution of land in Vila Velha (1971:41–4) was in part based upon the Instituto's cadastral maps of the South (personal communication) no such maps were available for the North.

The Tax Bureau in town does however have an entire room filled with a series of books which are together termed not a Cadaster but *matrizes* (land registers). These registers consist of listings of all of the parcels of land within each named area of each of the municipality's 95 hamlets. All of the parcels in each area of one hamlet, for example, are listed along with the names of their owners and an estimate of their area in 'ploughing days' (*jeiras*) or fractions of a day needed to plough the parcel. One full ploughing day is equivalent in this region to about 0.3 hectare. In surface area this would be about 3.3 ares, or 3,300 square metres. Slicher Van Bath describes similar ploughing-day measurements in various parts of medieval Western Europe: in one day a man with one team of animals ploughed 0.35 hectare in Henley, and 0.36 hectare in Switzerland (1963:183, 299). Loizos has noted a similar form of measurement for Cyprus *donums*: about 2/3 of an acre (0.27 hectare) is ploughed per day in the village of Kalo (1975b:62). As mentioned earlier in Chapter 2 (n. 35) this form of measurement is rarely used today in Fontelas.

No pictorial map of any hamlet or any smaller area within each hamlet's terrain accompanies the land registers, which are in fact so old that many of the parcels listed in them are farmed today by the children and grandchildren of the parcels' recorded owners. This situation is partly due to the system of partible inheritance in the region, which customarily grants siblings equal portions of plots or separate plots of equal value. The great majority of partitions are effected by word of mouth (*de boca*) and not in writing (*por escritura*), except in occasional cases of written wills which allocate specific portions of land to various legatees. Partitions are thus only formally registered in cases of disputes reaching the town court, where the legal division is effected and recorded. The land register is thus quite outdated (the most precise estimate I obtained for the date of its compilation was '100 years ago') and the job of reconstructing even one individual's landholding seemed a nearly impossible task.

A second set of alphabetical tax listings (*verbetes*) are also archived in the Tax Bureau, but these have been updated several times since the original land registers were compiled. Each listing contains a breakdown of each individual owner's plots along with their taxable value in *escudos* but not their surface area. Each owner has a sum of 'taxable income' on land, or *rendimento colectável*, according to the total estimated value of his or her parcels. (A similar listing was compiled in Mosteiro parish in 1892: see Appendix II.) Although somewhat more recent, some of these listings also suffer from inexact recordings of partitions and they are strictly confidential. In any case, it would be an equally difficult task to connect the older estimates of specific parcels' areas in 'ploughing days' with these more recent listings of the same parcels' tax values. One would have to locate every parcel in X's name mentioned in the newer tax listings in the older land register. This could only be done by searching first for all of X's parcels within all of the constituent areas of terrain comprising X's hamlet. Further, these listings themselves are continually falling out of date as villagers make unrecorded improvements on their land (planting of trees, use of fertilizers). Each individual's annual *contribuição* (tax) is a percentage of the total value of his or her land, but the amount of this tax may well be far lower than the ideal current taxable value of the land due to such unregistered changes.

An entirely new cadastral assessment of the municipality's land, however, was begun in mid-1978 and the parish of Mosteiro was one of the first to be surveyed. Part of a national program, each assessment was carried out by a team of three assessors who resided in each hamlet for the time necessary to survey its land. The value of each parcel (1st, 2nd, or 3rd class) was recorded along with the name of its owner, and a precise measurement was obtained through the use of a 10-metre rope. Where possible, the team attempted to make recordings with the help of one or two villagers recommended for their good general knowledge of the hamlet's terrain. This was done in order to ensure correct notation of the owners' names (especially emigrants and other non-resident villagers) in cases where the actual owners could not accompany the assessors through all of their own plots. The new *cadastro* will clearly bring the area and value measurements of land up to date through 1978, but I was told by the assessors that the project as a whole will take about three years to complete.

Confronted with this difficult archival situation, I used the following method to estimate landholding sizes. I calculated the total sizes of landholdings according to the number of *alqueires* of sowing capacity in each constituent plot. The *alqueire* is a standard dry capacity measure equivalent in this region to 17 litres. This is just under 1/2 of an English bushel, or about 2 pecks (4 pecks = 1 bushel = 36.4 litres). Note that the capacity of an *alqueire* of rye grain in this region is somewhat larger than that of an *alqueire* of wheat in a parish of the Southern Alentejo province, where it is equivalent to 1/3 of an English bushel (Cutileiro 1971:16). One hectare of unirrigated land in Fontelas has a capacity of about 12 sown *alqueires* of rye (204 litres or 5.6 English bushels). Thus, for example, a holding containing a number of parcels of land sown with a total of 36 *alqueires* of rye would be equivalent in surface area to 3.0 hectares (36 ÷ 12).

I based this estimate initially upon various local sources, particularly the Forestry Service and *Grémio da Lavoura* (Landowners' Guild) in town, whose representatives were either from this area themselves or familiar with the agricultural practices of Fontelas and its surrounding hamlets. I confirmed these estimates myself with the help of a number of villagers by measuring the sowing capacity of a series of plots with a 20-metre tape-measure. One *alqueire* of sown rye occupied approximately 820 square metres, thus yielding just over 12 *alqueires* per hectare (820 × 12 = 9,840 square metres). There is obviously some variation in the amount of grain sown: firstly, differing terrain may require lighter or heavier sowing, and secondly, different individuals may sow different quantities. These variations, however, do not constitute excessive sources of error, and rarely vary from person to person or from field to field by more than a few litres of grain or at most 1 *alqueire*. Although the productivity of any specific grain field may vary each time it is sown (every other year) its sowing capacity always remains constant. Very few villagers in fact ever use the word 'hectare' and even fewer (some *proprietários* and wealthy *lavradores*) were able to estimate its area (10,000 square metres). All measurements of land by the villagers themselves use the method adopted here of sowing capacity in *alqueires*.

Obtaining estimates of the sowing capacity of grainfields was quite straightforward, as the fields are sown successively every two years. Measurements of non-arable meadows, vineyards, and gardens, however, were more difficult. I measured the areas of these types of land by obtaining estimates from the owners of how many *alqueires* of grain could be sown on these portions of land *if they were ploughed and sown with rye*. The total size of the holding in sowing capacity was then divided by 12, thus yielding the total surface area in hectares. I am quite sure that most of the villagers' plot-by-plot estimates are accurate at least to the nearest 1/2 *alqueire* (0.04 hectare) as many of them have worked extensively and repeatedly not only in their own fields but in many of those of their kin, neighbours, and other co-villagers. As these measurements are estimates only and are not intended to compare with precise cadastral computations, I have taken into account a slight source of error and have rounded the total sum of hectares in each holding to the nearest 0.01 hectare. We recall that a large amount of grain land is left fallow each year due to the two-course system of rye cultivation on the hamlet's two sides. However, whether fallow for one year or uncultivated for a number of years, all land owned by current hamlet residents has been included in the estimates.

Using this method, I was able to gather detailed estimates for all of the hamlet's 55 landholdings. Bento's son Bernardo (H31) farms his father's land and the bus-driver (H17) owns no land in Fontelas, thus accounting for the hamlet's 57 households but only 55 landholdings. I suspect one household's total (the large *lavrador* Gabriel) of being a considerable underestimate, while the task of calculating the precise sizes of the four largest *proprietário* holdings was particularly difficult. In the latter cases, I supplemented each household's own estimates with those of a number of other villagers who were familiar with these four households' land, thereby deriving a probable average. All of the remaining families gave me comprehensive breakdowns of their amounts of grain land (sown and fallow), irrigated arable fields, meadows, gardens, vineyards, chestnut-groves, and land temporarily uncultivated or devoted to shrub growth. In many cases (29 households) this breakdown included a plot-by-plot listing of the total number and size of each specific parcel of land farmed in the holding. Another 26 households estimated the total amounts of each type of land they farmed, and the portions of land they owned, rented, and cleared on the *baldios*. In the absence of a land Cadaster describing the hamlet's terrain, this was the only reliable method available for estimating the sizes of plots and holdings short of metre-by-metre measurements.

As I had carried out just over two years' fieldwork when I conducted the land survey, which itself took five months to complete, I am relatively confident that the estimates of most households were accurate and honest (all suspicion of my being a tax-spy occurred only during the very early months of fieldwork). I most emphatically do *not* recommend the kind of in-depth landholding survey of the type I describe here for anyone in the early (or middle) stages of fieldwork. When I began the survey I had long been entirely accepted by and incorporated in the community and had worked physically alongside most villagers at one time or another in their own or others' fields. By this time informants were quite accustomed to my myriad questions and notations and most had a clear idea of what my study of them involved. In fact, once I had begun estimating a number of households' landholdings, a few others asked me: 'when are you going to do ours?'.

Table 19. *Internal structure of a smallholding (Household 22)*

Parcels of land (location)	Owner	Sowing capacity (in *alqueires*)	Rent paid (in *alqueires*)	Area (ha)
ARABLE FIELDS				
Pereiro	Felícia	3	–	0.25
Val da Breia	Felícia	2	–	0.17
Vinhas Velhas	Felícia	2	–	0.17
Pipa	Felícia	1	–	0.08
Rio de Algoso	Felícia	3	–	0.25
Bouças	Felícia	2	–	0.17
Outeiro	Felícia	2	–	0.17
Chãos (*baldio*)	Felícia	1	–	0.08
Bouças (irrigated)	Felícia	2.5	–	0.20
Val da Breia (irrig.)	Felícia	2	–	0.17
		20.5		1.71
Pendo do Pereiro	Diogo	5	5	0.42
Apanhadas	Diogo	5	2.5	0.42
Mouta	Diogo	4	2	0.33
Mouta	Diogo	4	2	0.33
Bouças	non-resident	2	2	0.17
Seixaragal	non-resident	3	1.5	0.25
Rio de Nuzedo	Gabriel	4	2	0.33
Bouças	emigrant	3	1.5	0.25
Os Tocos (irrig.)	Sância	1	4	0.08
		31		2.58
MEADOWS				
Os Tocos	Felícia	3	–	0.37 (Os Tocos, Carvalho, Albergue)
Carvalho	Felícia	0.5	–	
Albergue	Felícia	1	–	
Rio de Algoso	Sância	10	20	0.83
(6 meadows used as pastures for shared flock)	(Dona Sofia)	(26)	–	(2.17)
GROVES				
Cabancão	Felícia	2	–	0.17
VINEYARDS				
Vinhago	Felícia	0.5		0.04
GARDENS				
Castelo	Felícia	1	–	0.17 (Castelo, Fundo da Aldeia)
Fundo da Aldeia	Felícia	1	–	
Total: 17 parcels owned		29.5	–	2.46 ha
10 parcels rented		41.0	42.5	3.41 ha
27 parcels farmed		70.5	42.5	5.87 ha

Appendix I

A sample of one holding's constituent plots is included in Table 19. The table lists the smallholder Felícia's holding and includes land owned by herself as well as land rented from others. Also in the table there are some meadows borrowed for the pasturage of a joint flock of sheep tended by her husband Eduardo, but these meadows are not included in the totals.

Appendix II: Social groups in 1851 and 1892

How did the current distribution of land in Fontelas come about? Can local historical records indicate any long-term trends with regard to the size of landholdings or the composition of the hamlet's social groups?

This appendix deals with two administrative records compiled in Mosteiro which provide information on the past structure of social groups in Fontelas. The first is an Electoral Census of Adult Males compiled in 1851, and the second a Parish Tax Listing compiled in 1892. Each listing affords a specific picture of the occupational structure of the community in a particular year, but one must turn to Portuguese social and economic history in order to connect these successive pictures with larger regional and national developments. The latter task is beyond the scope of this book. However, both of the images provided by the two sources are in themselves illuminating despite their limited field of view. Let us look briefly at the two sources in order to obtain an idea of the proportions of Fontelas' inhabitants who were *proprietários*, *lavradores*, and *jornaleiros* in former years.

Prior to the 1851 Census, one of the earliest sources enumerating the social groups present in Fontelas was a Census of Trás-os-Montes province compiled in 1796 (Ribeiro de Castro 1796). At that time, the hamlet had 26 *lavradores* and 10 *jornaleiros*: the term *proprietário* was nowhere used in the document. In addition, Fontelas also had a priest, a blacksmith, a tailor, a shepherd, 2 stone-masons, 4 servants (2 male and 2 female), and 5 persons 'of no specific occupation' (*sem ocupação*). A total of 40 households was listed, with 181 people (91 men and 90 women). We do not know if young children were included. This is all that the 1796 Census tells us about Fontelas: a wider comparison of these proportions in many hamlets of the province would of course yield more information (Amado Mendes 1980; 1981). Although Fontelas had a few specialists at the time the Census was compiled, its population was predominantly an agricultural one: the figures suggest that the bulk of its households were *lavradores*. In the area which seems to correspond to the municipality as a whole in 1796, there were 594 *lavradores*, 373 *jornaleiros*, 201 servants, 60 shepherds, and a large variety of artisans. Of particular interest was the use of the term *jornaleiro*, indicating that at least some of Fontelas' residents were day-labourers at the time. The term may of course have had a different meaning in 1796. But its use in the Census suggests even then that a distinction was made (by the enumerator or the villagers, or both) between 'ploughers' and 'day-labourers'.

In 1851 the Câmara of Mosteiro compiled an Electoral Census of Adult Males in the municipality's 8 parishes, which at the time comprised a total of 35 hamlets. (We recall that Mosteiro was elevated to the level of a town from 1837 through 1854.) One sample page from the Census is reproduced here. Following this, Table 20 sets out the figures for Mosteiro parish, and includes those pertaining to Fontelas. The Census is a particularly useful source as it lists not only the names, ages, marital status, and hamlets of birth of the individuals listed, but also their occupations, literacy qualifications, and the precise amount of each man's yearly tithe, or *décima*. This was a general tax on property from which some of the clergy were exempt.

The Electoral Census as a whole was composed of four separate lists of individuals, the first of which was a 'preliminary census'. This initial listing recorded all male parish voters (*eleitores de Parochia*) for the *Assembleias Primárias* in each parish. There is no way of verifying whether all adult males in Fontelas were registered: some may not have owned any land and thus paid no tithe. Further, we do not know if the listing included only male *heads* of household or additional property-owning males as well. Most of the men listed were over the age of 24, although two men in other parishes were listed with the ages of 20 and 22. No rule seems to be operative for these younger men: individuals in their 20s did not have to be married in order to be registered (many were single).

This preliminary census was followed by two shorter listings. The first of these was a listing of those individuals qualified to be electors (*deputados*) who appear to have been representatives of the municipality to the Lisbon Assembly, while the second included only those qualified themselves to become elected representatives. These three listings were compiled in the same book, entitled *Recenseamento dos Eleitores de Parochia nas Assembleas Primarias, dos Eleitores de Deputados, e dos Elegiveis para Deputados*. For example, in the parish of Mosteiro the initial census of voters included 91 names but only 16 of these were eligible to become electors of the parish's representatives to Lisbon. A property qualification of a minimum tithe of 1,800 *réis* determined the choice of these 16 electors (Table 20), two of whom were priests. Only one individual of these 16 was finally eligible to become a representative: with a tithe of 6,000 *réis* the *lavrador* Miguel Pires (Dona Elvira's great-grandfather) was the only person on the second list for Mosteiro parish. At the municipal level (all 8 parishes) these property qualifications were also instructive. Of a total of 853 men registered, only 77 were qualified to be electors. Of these 77 only 12 were finally selected as eligible to become elected representatives, and of these 12, 7 were *proprietários* and 5 were *lavradores*.

A fourth list (in a separate book) was compiled of those individuals eligible to hold further municipal offices locally within the municipality. This book was entitled *Caderno de Recenseamento dos Eleitores e Elegiveis para os Cargos Municipaes*. This listing also had a minimum property qualification: a tithe of 1,000 *réis* (Table 20). As this qualification was lower than the first one, more men were eligible to be elected to such offices – 36 in all. The amount of one's tithe (probably calculated with regard to each individual's landholding) thus had direct bearing not only on one's eligibility for municipal office but even upon one's eligibility to cast a vote in the first place. Of the 91 men from the parish in the 1851 Census, there were 10 cases (21 individuals) of identical names being listed, but only in two of these cases were both individuals with the same name living in the same hamlet. Although the small size of the hamlet (and even of the entire parish) may render this sample statistically insignificant, the reduced size of the population studied provides fewer sources of error in the identification of individuals.

Despite this minor flaw, the 1851 Census provides a detailed view of economic stratification within the parish of Mosteiro and its 7 surrounding parishes. In Table 20, I have classified the adult males listed in the Census according to their occupations, literacy qualifications, and tithes. Let us look first at the figures for the parish as a whole.

The upper group of *proprietários* and Câmara Officials accounted for 16 per cent of the parish's tithes, and four of these men were literate to some degree. (In fact, of the total number of 26 priests – *presbiteros* – listed in the 8 parishes at the time, 17 were also registered as *proprietários*.) Three of the five wealthiest taxpayers were resident in

Mosteiro: the remaining two lived in Fontelas. (The Câmara Official may also have been literate as any position on the Câmara was a high administrative post usually involving a minimal amount of written work.)

51 individuals were registered as *lavradores*, and together they paid 71 per cent of the parish's total tithes. However, only 11 of these 51 were qualified to elect parish representatives to Lisbon, while 31 were eligible to elect municipal officers. As stated earlier, these two property qualifications were respectively a minimum of 1,800 and 1,000 *réis*. A large portion of the *lavradores* thus had voting rights for municipal officers.

The third group – the *jornaleiros* – accounted for only 10 per cent of the parish's wealth, and their average tithe (420 *réis*) was considerably lower than that of the *lavradores* (1,632). A large number of men in this group (17 of 27) paid very small tithes of less than 400 *réis*. We cannot of course rule out the possibility that there were more *jornaleiros* at the time with no tithe, who were therefore not registered. Only 3 of these 27 men (and one stone-mason) paid tithes of over 1,000 *réis* and were thus the only members of this group eligible to elect municipal officers. However, none of the *jornaleiros* nor any of the artisan specialists were qualified to elect parish representatives to Lisbon. Further, only two of the *jornaleiros* and none of the specialists were listed as being literate. Of the total of 91 men registered, only 15 were literate: these were predominantly the *proprietários* and wealthier *lavradores*.

How do the figures for Fontelas alone compare with those for the parish as a whole? Let us look at the column in Table 20 referring to Fontelas alone. While only one *proprietário* was listed in Fontelas, 18 men were registered as *lavradores*. Four of these were indicated as being literate. Three further divisions could be drawn within this group at the time. The first group included only those 4 men paying tithes of over 1,800 *réis*, who were thus eligible along with the *proprietário* and Câmara Official to be electors of representatives.

A second group included those paying tithes of over 1,000 *réis*: these accounted for 14 of Fontelas' 18 *lavradores*, and they were eligible to elect municipal officers. The remaining 4 with tithes of less than 1,000 *réis* formed part of the initial census but had no qualifications for voting. Together, these 18 *lavradores* paid most of Fontelas' tithes: 89.5 per cent. Most men in this group paid high tithes, and Fontelas' total tithes accounted for 1/3 of the total wealth of the parish's four hamlets. It is significant that Fontelas had a particularly large percentage of the total number of *proprietários* and wealthier *lavradores* in the parish at the time.

Finally, five artisan specialists were registered in Fontelas, including only one *journaleiro* paying a tithe of 500 *réis*. These specialists accounted for only 6.5 per cent of Fontelas' total of tithes amounting to 36,660 *réis*. The average tithe paid by a specialist was substantially lower than that of a *lavrador*. Reflecting the situation in the rest of the parish, none of the specialists in Fontelas was listed as being literate.

While the 1851 Electoral Census cannot be considered an entirely reliable record of population or household structure, it does afford evidence of a clear division of the peasantry into three major occupational groups: *proprietários*, *lavradores*, and *jornaleiros*. The *lavradores* themselves were further split internally by the property qualifications of 1,000 and 1,800 *réis*, thus highlighting a separate group of particularly wealthy peasants. Along with specialists (stone-masons, carpenters) these four groups have continued to constitute the basic classifications within Fontelas and the parish until today. Only the last of these three occupational terms has recently fallen out of use, and this is indicative of the recent disappearance of the social group of day-labourers. While the document itself does not define precisely what constituted a *jornaleiro* or a *lavrador* in social terms, it does reveal that day-labourers on the whole possessed a far

Alfaiate: Tailor
Annos de idade: Years of age
Casado: Married
Data da Naturalização: Date of Citizenship [acquired]
Décima: Tithe
Escr.^{am} da Camara: Câmara notary
Estado: Marital Status
Instruido: Educated
Jornº (Jornaleiro): Day-labourer
Labrº (Labrador): Peasant
Le e escreve: Reads and writes
Logar do Nascimento: Place of birth
Nomes: Names
Off.^{al} da Camara: Câmara Official
Presbitero: Priest
Profisão: Occupation
Proprietrº (Proprietário): Large landowner
Qualificação Literaria: Literacy qualification
Soltº (Solteiro): Single
Vencimento: Salary
Vº (Viúvo): Widower

Nomes	Logar do Nascimt.º	Data da Naturalização	Ann. de id.e
João Affonso			52
Manoel João			5
Manoel Neves			5
Manoel Affº Portella			6
Manoel Pires			6
Manoel Seuane			4
Mauricio Affonso			5
Manoel de Campos			4
P.e Manoel Pires			5
Manoel Affonso			3
Manoel Gonçalves			2
Manoel Domingues			8
Marçal Domingues			4
Manoel Affonso			6
Manoel Jose			7
Marçal Martins			4
Mathias Pires			6
Manoel Ferreira			4
Manoel Pires			8
Miguel Pires			8
Manoel Antonio			8
Manoel Diegues			7
Marcelino Rodrigues			3
Pedro Gonçalves			5
Pedro Rodrigues			4
Pedro Martins			6
Pedro Gonçalves			7
Pedro Miguel Domingues			6
Simão Martins			8

...tado	Profisão	Qualificação liter.a	Decima ou vencim.to: Decima	Vencim.to	
...asado	Lab.r		1$100		
"	Jorn.o		$200		
"	Lab.r		1$400		
"	"		2$000		
"	"		1$200		
"	Alfaiate		$320		
"	Jorn.o		1$100		
...lt.o	"		$600		
...abitero	Propriet.o	Instruido	3$000		
...sado	Lab.r		$200		
...asado	Jorn.o		$600		
	"		1$000		
	"		$600		
...sado	"		$320		
...lt.o	"		1$400		
...asado	"		$400		
...isso	Lab.r		$900		
...sado	Jorn.o		$120		
...sado	Lab.r		2$400		
...sado	"	Le escreve	6$000		
...iuvo	Jorn.o		$500		
...iuvo	Lab.r		1$170		Morto
...lt.o	Off.al de lamora		1$440		
...sado	Lab.r		$440		
...sado	"		2$600		
	Jorn.o		$300		
...sado	Lab.r		1$200		
...sado	Escr.am de lamora	Le escreve e conta	7$500		
	Lab.r		$800		

Appendix II

Table 20. *Distribution of tithes in Mosteiro parish, 1851*

	Occupation	(Fontelas taxpayers)	Parish taxpayers	Literacy* qualification	Tithe (in *réis*)	Average tithe	Total %
	Proprietário (priest)		1	'Educated'	3,000		
	Proprietário (priest)	(1)	1	('Educated')	–		
5	Câmara Notary		1	RWC	7,500	4,495	17,980
	Court Notary		1	RWC	6,040		*16%*
	Câmara Official	(1)	1		1,440		
		(1)	1		6,280		
		(1)	1	(RW)	6,000		
			2		2,500–3,000		
		(2)	4		2,000–2,500		
			3		1,800–2,000		
		(2)	5	1 RW	1,500–1,800		
		(8)	15	(1 RWC); 2 R	1,000–1,500		
51	Lavradores	(1)	4	(1 R)	900–1,000	1,632	79,990
		(1)	2	(1RW); 1 R	800–900		*71%*
		(1)	1		700–800		
		(1)	3		600–700		
			0		500–600		
			2	1 R	400–500		
			4		300–400		
			1		200–300		
			1		100–200		
			2		no tithe listed		
		(18)	51				
			3		1,000–1,500		
			0		900–1,000		
			0		800–900		
			1	RWC	700–800		
			3		600–700		
27	Jornaleiros	(1)	1		500–600	420	11,350
			2		400–500		*10%*
			8	1RW	300–400		
			4		200–300		
			4		100–200		
			1		0–100		
		(1)	27				
	Stone-mason	(1)	1		1,000		
	Carpenter		1		850		
	Carpenter	(1)	1		600		
8	Wool carder		1		400	519	3,630
	Tailor		1		320		*3%*
	Weaver	(1)	1		300		
	Stone-mason		1		160		
	Stone-mason	(1)	1		–		
	Total parish		91	15 literate			112,950 *100%*
	Total (Fontelas)	(25)		(6 literate)			(36,660 *32%*)

Source: Câmara Municipal of Mosteiro *Recenseamento dos Eleitores* (1851).
* R – reads; W – writes; C – counts.

smaller amount of taxable wealth than did peasants. Furthermore, most of the former group did not in 1851 possess the minimal property qualifications necessary for electing local officers. At least in formal terms, their voice in public affairs was a relatively mute one.

The distinction between the poorer *lavradores* and the better-off *jornaleiros* is not entirely clear. For instance, a number of the former paid tithes of 100–1,000 *réis* while some of the latter paid higher tithes of 400–1,500 *réis*. This is not inconsistent with my own materials from 1978, in that many individuals who are currently *lavradores* have themselves been *jornaleiros* or servants in former years. Further, a certain quantity of land in itself may not have been an entirely determinant factor in the classification of occupations. In other words, there was in 1851 some overlap between the tithes of these two groups, which prevents our concluding that *all* of the members of one group were necessarily wealthier or owned more land than *all* of the members of the other.

Another factor evident from a comparison of Fontelas' tithes with those of the parish (Table 20) was the larger number of *jornaleiros* in the other three hamlets. We recall that Mosteiro has historically possessed fewer *baldios* as well as fewer and less fertile meadows than Fontelas. The total sum of the latter community's tithes suggests a concentration of large and highly valued landholdings among Fontelas' 14 wealthier *lavradores*. However, in the absence of further information on the compiler(s) of the Census, such conclusions concerning the overall amount and value of land at the time must remain speculative. Despite these shortcomings and possible inaccuracies, the Census remains a rich source for the analysis of economic stratification within the peasantry, and it offers further evidence of the continuity of a ranked social hierarchy over time.

The second source providing detailed information on social groups is the Parish Tax Listing of 1892: *Lançamento Parochial de Impostos Directos e para a Instrucção Primaria para o Anno de 1892*. This Tax Listing offers a useful point of comparison with the earlier tithes registered in the 1851 Electoral Census. The 1892 listing was compiled with each taxpayer's name, hamlet of birth, and total taxable wealth. 18 per cent of this wealth was paid in taxes to the State, while 17 per cent of this 18 per cent constituted the total parish tax. From the latter was deducted a general parish tax (14 per cent) and the small school tax (3 per cent). As the listing does not include each individual's occupation, I have linked most of the taxpayers' names with their occupations as registered in the Parish Confessional Roll of the same year. (This document is described at the beginning of Chapter 5.) Most of the individuals in the Tax Listing can be located in the Confessional Roll, and as the hamlet is so small no cases arose in 1892 of the confusion of two or more individuals with the same name. There were nevertheless a few 'missing people' – individuals present in one listing but not in the other. The question marks in Table 21 thus indicate taxpayers in the Tax Listing who were not found in the Confessional Roll, and whom I have classified within their probable social group given the amounts of their taxable wealth.

The number of *proprietários* in Fontelas was somewhat larger in 1892 than in 1851, but this may well be due to differences in the compilers' categories of occupations. Note that the *proprietários* and wealthier *lavradores* accounted for the hiring of 17 of the hamlet's 20 servants in that year. Four of the *proprietários* and two of the wealthier *lavradores* were the only individuals with taxable non-agricultural earnings and taxable wealth derived from rent (Notes b & c to Table 21).

There was some overlap within the range of taxable wealth in each social group, and I see no immediate explanation for this. The compilers' categories may not have coincided with the villagers' own criteria of differentiation. Furthermore, here again the activities involved in distinct occupations (ploughing, wage labour) may have been

Numero de ordem	NOMES DOS CONTRIBUINTES	Moradas	Rendimento collectavel para a contribuição parochial	
	Transporte		218	370
33	Bonifacio Alves			640
34	Candido Borges		6	060
35	Carlos Gonçalves		7	770
36	Carlos Manoel Branco (Pe)		101	330
37	Carolina Gonçalves		1	540
38	Catharina Diegues		30	620
39	Cecilia Affonso Pereira		2	280
40	Crispim Affonso Simão		1	240
41	Crispim Pello			780
42	Claudio Gonçalves		6	250
43	Clemente de Carvalho		4	590
44	Clemente Gomes		5	140
45	Dárida Gonçalves			820
46	Delfina do Espirito Santo		1	450
47	Domingos Antonio Pires		6	030
48	Domingos Caiado		1	960
49	Domingos Gomes		6	070
50	Domingos Gonçalves Caiado		1	870
51	Domingos Gonçalves do Valle		1	080
52	Domingos Lourada		18	570
53	Domingos Pires		5	910
54	Domingos Pires		90	430
55	Emilia Martins		1	820
56	Engracia Rodrigues			850
57	Ermelinda Rosa		1	310
58	Facundo Borges		3	160
59	Felisbina Pires			500
60	Francisco Affonso		8	740
61	Francisco Annes		8	780
62	Francisco Borges		8	780
63	Francisco Domingues		1	570
			550	310

Nomes dos Contribuintes: Names of Taxpayers
Moradas: Addresses (Hamlets of residence)
Rendimento Collectavel para a contribuição parochial: Taxable wealth for the parish tax
Importancia das contribuições: Amount of the taxes
Predial: House rates
De renda de casas e sumptuaria: House rental and sumptuary

Importancia das contribuições						Total das contribuições do Estado sobre que recae a contribuição parochial	Importancia da contribuição parochial directa na razão de 14 por %	Importancia da C. parochial directa para I. Primaria na razão de 3 por %	Total 17%
Predial	N.os dos artigos da matriz da contribuição predial	Industrial	N.os dos artigos da matriz da contribuição indust.	De renda de casas e sumptuaria	N.os dos artigos da matriz das contribuições de renda de casas e sump.				
				1$010		3$350	//	//	//
						$110			$018
						1$033			[illegible]75
						1$325			$225
						17$330			2$946
						$260			$044
						5$233			$889
						$390			$066
						$210			$035
$130				$670		$800			$136
						1$070			$18[illegible]
						$785			$135
						$880			$149
						$140			$025
						$245			$041
						1$030			$175
						$335			$060
						1$035			$175
						$320			$054
						$185			$030
						3$165			$538
						1$010			$170
15$465				1$010		16$475			2$800
						$310			$052
						$145			$024
						$225			$038
						$540			$094
						$085			$014
						1$495			$255
						1$500			$255
						1$500			$255
						$280			$048
				2$690		97$820			

Total das contribuições do Estado sobre que recae a contribuição parochial: Total State taxes from which the parish tax is subtracted

Importancia da contribuição parochial directa na razão de .. 14 .. por %: Amount of the direct parish tax at the rate of 14%

Importancia da C. parochial directa para I. Primaria na razão de 3 por %: Amount of the direct parish tax for Primary Schooling at the rate of 3%

Table 21. *Taxable wealth in Fontelas, 1892*

	Taxpayer's occupation[a]	Servants	Taxable wealth (in *réis*)	Average tithe	Total %
	Proprietário	1 servant	179,410[b]		
	Proprietário (priest)		41,360		
	Proprietário		27,000[c]		
	Proprietário	1 servant	19,440		
9	Proprietário	6 servants	17,440[c]	35,798	322,180
	Proprietário		14,130[b]		*48.2%*
	Proprietário	1 servant	11,450		
	Proprietária (woman)	2 servants	8,040		
	Proprietário		3,910		
	Lavrador	4 servants	90,430[c]		
	Lavrador		40,090[c]		
	Lavrador	2 servants	33,100		
	Lavrador	1 servant	18,440		
	Labrador		18,420		
	Lavrador	1 servant	15,130		
	Lavradora (woman)		12,690		
	?		10,230		
17	Lavrador		9,960	17,182	292,100
	Lavrador		8,740		*43.7%*
	Lavrador		7,580		
	Lavrador		6,840		
	?		6,180		
	Lavrador		4,640		
	Lavrador		4,590		
	?		4,300		
	Lavrador		740		
	Jornaleiro	1 servant	7,770		
	Jornaleiro		6,250		
	?		3,890		

	?		2,400		
	?		2,130		
	Jornaleira (woman)		2,000		
20	Jornaleiro		1,910	2,285	45,690 *6.8%*
	Jornaleiro		1,800		
	?		1,350		
	?		1,130		
	?		1,000		
	?		940		
	?		800		
	?		710		
	?		550		
	Jornaleira (woman)		500		
	Jornaleira (woman)		500		
1	Blacksmith		8,780		8,780 *1.3%*
Fontelas totals: 47		20	668,750 (35% of parish total)		*100%*
Parish totals:	176 Taxpayers resident in the parish		1,664,210		*88%*
	48 Non-resident taxpayers		225,680		*12%*
	224 Total taxpayers in the parish		1,889,890		*100%*

a – These occupations are derived from the 1892 Confessional Roll.
b – A portion of these individuals' taxable wealth was derived from occupations with substantial earnings (*contribuição industrial*) as well as their land.
c – A portion of these individuals' taxable wealth was derived from the rental of houses to others (*renda de casa*).

Heads of household on the 1892 Confessional Roll but not in the 1892 tax listing	Taxable wealth
1 Proprietário	–
1 Proprietária (woman)	–
1 Lavrador	–
14 Jornaleiras (women)	–
5 Jornaleiros	–
1 Blacksmith	–
1 Weaver	–

Sources: 1892 *Lançamento Parochial de Impostos Directos . . .*
1892 *Rol dos Confessados da Freguezia de Mosteiro.*

of greater significance for these classifications than landed wealth alone. For example (as is the case today) a *jornaleiro* in 1892 with 4 hectares of land may have paid the same tax as another villager who also owned 4 hectares, but the latter may have rented another 4 hectares of land and thus in fact have become a *lavrador*, cultivating a total of 8 hectares. Yet the two villagers may have paid precisely the same tax. Occasionally a *proprietário* in one Confessional Roll is listed in another as a *lavrador* and vice versa. An individual may of course have changed his or her occupation from one year to the next. Furthermore, the general definition by villagers themselves of these occupational terms in 1851 may have changed by 1892, thus bringing about a conceptual shift not entirely attributable to the individual compilers of the listings.

Like the 1851 Census, this listing is a poor guide to the hamlet's *total* population at the time. The Confessional Roll listed 24 domestic groups whose heads of household were not in the Tax Listing (bottom of Table 21). Similarly, 15 taxpayers were not possible to locate in the Confessional Roll. This may have been due either to: (a) these taxpayers' residing outside the parish and thus accounting for some of the 48 non-resident taxpayers, or (b) it is conceivable that some of the *jornaleira* women had portions of land so small as to be un-taxable.

Despite these problems of record linkage, the two sources together provide an approximation of the taxable wealth (principally land) owned by the four major social groups at the time. The *jornaleiro* group in 1892 again constituted a large number of taxpaying households (20 of 47) but they owned only 6.8 per cent of the taxable wealth. In contrast, 8 *proprietário* households together owned 48.2 per cent. The continuity of occupations and landholdings within these groups can be traced up until today. For instance, the priest in 1892 was a co-resident of the *proprietário* household with 6 servants, this family thus owning jointly a sum of 58,000 *réis* of taxable wealth. Some of this wealth was derived from the rental of houses to others. This household is today that of its sole heir, Dona Elvira. The *lavrador* household with the taxable wealth of 90,430 *réis* is today that of the parish priest. If there were means through which we could link the occupations in the 1851 Census with those in the 1892 listing, a process of the concentration of the land within the *proprietário* group could be suggested. This would not be inconsistent with the sharp rise in the number of *jornaleiros* in the hamlet following 1902 (Table 12 in Chapter 5). The *lavrador* group, meanwhile, owned in 1892 far less (43.7 per cent) of the total taxable wealth than it did in 1851 (89.5 per cent).

While these processes remain merely sketched by this series of separate local records, the 1892 Tax Listing again affords evidence of an internal differentiation within the peasantry. Eight *proprietário* households owned almost half of the hamlet's land, while 20 *jornaleiro* households owned barely more than 1/20. The pattern of land ownership was undergoing change between 1851 and 1892, but the overall structure of the control of land by *proprietários* and large *lavradores* was maintained. In broad terms, the process seems to have reduced the size of the 'middle peasantry' of *lavradores*, concentrating more land among the *proprietários*. In other words, the sources suggest that between 1851 and 1892 the hamlet (in relative terms) had become progressively more polarized between the land-rich and the land-poor. While this process of possible land concentration cannot be traced with great precision, the two listings together do depict with absolute clarity the presence of a definite social hierarchy in former years.

Appendix III: The Parish Register

Much of the information presented in this book is derived from the Mosteiro Parish Register of baptisms, marriages, and deaths. Not only are the entries in the Parish Register consecutive without interruption from 1870 through 1978, but the entries themselves are extraordinarily detailed. Baptismal entries, for instance, include various particulars concerning the birth and baptism of the child, its legal status (legitimate or illegitimate), as well as the names, occupations, and hamlets of origin of the child's parents *and* both sets of grandparents. The chosen godparents are also noted along with their marital statuses, occupations, and hamlets of origin. I have transcribed below the texts of four entries exactly as they appear in the Parish Register: a baptismal entry for a legitimate child, a baptismal entry for an illegitimate child, a marriage entry, and a death entry. Beneath each transcription I have included an English translation.

Following each transcription I have also compiled an outline of precisely how I copied all of the entries for Fontelas. Also included below, then, are translations of the four entries' basic skeletal structures following each sample entry. Although throughout this study I have used pseudonyms, here I have copied all names in these sample entries (with the exception only of the place names 'Fontelas', 'Mosteiro', and the municipality of 'M'.) exactly as they appear in the Parish Register. I have also added punctuation in the English translations to assist in the reading of the texts. I copied most of the entries in handwriting, following a specific pattern that would later make it easy to locate individuals quickly. The actual text of each entry was of course not copied – the structure remained constant, so that each entry could be reduced to its basic information of names, ages, places, and dates. It was this essential information that I catalogued. I copied all of the information in the entries in Portuguese, following their original orthography.

I was very careful to copy *all* of the information in each entry, as in the case of baptisms a number of important annotations (*averbamentos*) are frequently written in the left-hand margin. In the first baptismal entry below, the word *morto* (dead) was thus written in the margin. Many other entries include the date and place of death of the baptized child, especially in cases of infant mortality. Others contain elaborate annotations of the later date at which the baptized child married, the spouse's name, and the place of marriage. Many individuals who have married out of Fontelas or died elsewhere can be traced in this fashion, as the priests from other parishes communicate these events to the Mosteiro parish priest for such annotation.

As in the case of the landholding survey I conducted, I do not recommend similar documentary work on Parish Registers (or Confessional Rolls) for any fieldworker not possessed of ample funds, abundant time, and a strong dose of patience. Firstly, the documents must be perused for continuity. This of course presumes their existence in the first place. Secondly, access to copying the entries must be granted by local

Appendix III

1871 BAPTISMAL ENTRY: Legitimate child

No. 15 dia 11 de Julho Perfirio Hernesto Fontelas 'morto'	Aos onze dias do mes de Julho do anno de mil oito centos e setenta e ũm na Igreja de Fontelas anexa desta freguesia de Mosteiro Concelho de M. diocese de Bragança eu o Padre Francisco Joze Rodrigues Cura coadjutor desta freguesia baptisei solemnemente ũm individuo do sexo mascolino a quem dei o nome de Perfirio Hernesto que nasceo nesta freguesia de Mosteiro na povoação de Fontelas as sete horas da manhã do dia vinte e oito de Junho do dito anno Era ut supra filho legitimo de Paulo Pires trabalhador jornaleiro natural de Fontelas desta freguesia de Mosteiro Concelho de M. diocese de Bragança e de Antonia Vasques de Manzanal Reino de Gualiza* recebidos parochianos e moradores em Fontelas anexa desta freguesia de Mosteiro Concelho de M. diocese de Bragança neto paterno de Joze Pires e Justina Gomes esta de Lavradas e aquelle de Fontelas jornaleiros desta freguesia de Mosteiro Concelho de M. diocese de Bragança e materno de Domingos Vasques e Joana Lidia jornaleiros estes de Manzanal Reino de Gualiza foi padrinho Padre Venancio de Fontelas e sua sobrinha Maria Archangela solteira lavradora os quais sei serem os propios E para constar lavrei em duplicado este assento que depois de ser lido e comfrido parante os padrinhos comingo assignou o padrinho e a madrinha não assignou por não saber escrever Era ut supra.
	O padrinho – Venancio Joze Pires, Presbitero O cura coadjutor – Francisco Joze Rodrigues

No. 15 11 July Perfirio Hernesto Fontelas 'dead'	On the eleventh day of the month of July of the year eighteen hundred and seventy one in the church of Fontelas, annex of this parish of Mosteiro, Municipality of M., diocese of Bragança, I, Father Francisco Jozé Rodrigues, vicar's assistant of this parish, solemnly baptized an individual of the masculine sex to whom I gave the name of Perfírio Hernesto, who was born in this parish of Mosteiro in the hamlet of Fontelas at seven o'clock in the morning, on the twenty-eighth of June of the said year, *Era ut supra*; legitimate son of Paulo Pires, day-labourer, born in Fontelas of this parish of Mosteiro, Municipality of M., diocese of Bragança, and of Antónia Vásques of Manzanal, Kingdom of Gualiza, married, parishioners, and residents of Fontelas, annex of this parish of Mosteiro, Municipality of M., diocese of Bragança; paternal grandson of Jozé Pires and Justina Gomes, the latter of Lavradas and the former of Fontelas, day-labourers in this parish of Mosteiro, Municipality of M., diocese of Bragança, and maternal [grandson] of Domingos Vásques and Joana Lídia, day-labourers of Manzanal, Kingdom of Gualiza. His godfather was Father Venâncio of Fontelas, and [his godmother was] his niece Maria Archângela, single, peasant, whom I acknowledge. And in proof of this I made this entry in duplicate, which, after having been read and checked in the presence of the godparents, the godfather signed with me; the godmother did not sign as she cannot write. *Era ut supra.*
[Signatures]	The godfather – Venâncio Jozé Pires The vicar's assistant – Francisco Jozé Rodrigues

* Galicia: the North-west region of Spain bordering Northern Portugal.

1871 BAPTISMAL ENTRY: Legitimate child (basic information)

1871

No. 15

PERFIRIO HERNESTO

nasceu: 28 Junho 1871, Fontelas, 7 da manhã — baptizado: 11 Julho 1871, Igreja de Fontelas

filho legítimo de:

Paulo Pires (natural de Fontelas) trabalhador jornaleiro	Antónia Vásques (natural de Manzanal, jornaleira Gualiza, Espanha)

(recebidos, parochianos, e moradores em Fontelas)

neto paterno de:	neto materno de:
Jozé Pires (Fontelas) Justina Gomes (Lavradas) (jornaleiros desta freguesia de Mosteiro)	Domingos Vásques Joana Lídia (Manzanal) (jornaleiros de Manzanal)

Padrinho: Padre Venâncio Pires (Fontelas/padre)
Madrinha: Maria Archângela (Fontelas/solteira, lavradora) (sua sobrinha)

Assinaturas: Padre Venâncio & Padre Rodrigues

1871

No. 15

PERFIRIO HERNESTO

born: 28 June 1871, in Fontelas, at 7 a.m. — baptized: 11 July 1871, Church of Fontelas

legitimate son of:

Paulo Pires (born in Fontelas) day-labourer	Antónia Vásques (born in Manzanal, Gualiza, Spain)

(married in, parishioners of, and residents of Fontelas)

paternal grandson of:	maternal grandson of:
Jozé Pires (Fontelas)* Justina Gomes (Lavradas) (day-labourers in this parish of Mosteiro)	Domingos Vásques Joana Lídia (Manzanal) (day-labourers in Manzanal)

Godfather: Father Venâncio Pires (Fontelas/priest)
Godmother: Maria Archângela (Fontelas/single, peasant) (his niece)

Signatures: Father Venâncio & Father Rodrigues

* In the case of grandparents, it is unclear sometimes whether the hamlets listed are their hamlets of origin or hamlets of residence.

Appendix III

1872 BAPTISMAL ENTRY: Illegitimate child

No. 18
dia 2 de Julho
João Batista
Fontelas

Aos dois dias do mes de Julho do anno de mil oito centos e setenta e dois na Igreja Paroquial desta freguesia de Mosteiro Concelho de M. diocese de Bragança eu o Padre Francisco Joze Rodrigues Cura coadjutor desta freguesia baptisei solemnemente ũm individuo do sexo mascolino a quem dei o nome de João Batista que nasceo nesta freguesia de Mosteiro na povoação de Fontelas no dia vinte e quatro de Junho do dito anno Era ut supra filho natural de pai incógnito e de Juliana Diegues jornaleira natural de Fontelas desta freguesia de Mosteiro Concelho de M. diocese de Bragança neto paterno de avôs incógnitos e materno de avô incógnito e de Margarida Diegues jornaleira desta povoação de Fontelas foi padrinho Inocencio Pires de Fontelas solteiro jornaleiro e foi madrinha Maria Joze Diegues de Fontelas solteira lavradora os quais sei serem os propios E para constar lavrei em duplicado este assento que depois de ser lido e comfrido perante os padrinhos assignei Os padrinhos não assignaram por não saber escrever Era ut supra.

O cura coadjutor – Francisco Joze Rodrigues

No. 18
2 July
João Batista
Fontelas

On the second day of the month of July of the year eighteen hundred and seventy two in the Parish Church of this parish of Mosteiro, Municipality of M., diocese of Bragança, I, Father Francisco Jozé Rodrigues, vicar's assistant of this parish, solemnly baptized an individual of the masculine sex to whom I gave the name João Batista, who was born in this parish of Mosteiro in the hamlet of Fontelas on the twenty-fourth of June of the said year, *Era ut supra*; natural son of an unknown father and of Juliana Diegues, day-labourer, born in Fontelas of this parish of Mosteiro, Municipality of M., diocese of Bragança; paternal grandson of unknown grandparents, and maternal [grandson] of an unknown grandfather and of Margarida Diegues, day-labourer, of this hamlet of Fontelas. His godfather was Inocêncio Pires of Fontelas, single, day-labourer, and his godmother was Maria Jozé Diegues of Fontelas, single, peasant, whom I acknowledge.

And in proof of this I made this entry in duplicate, which after having been read and checked in the presence of the godparents, I signed. The godparents did not sign as they cannot write. *Era ut supra.*

The vicar's assistant – Francisco Jozé Rodrigues

1872 BAPTISMAL ENTRY: Illegitimate child (basic information)

1872

No. 18

JOÃO BATISTA

nasceu: 24 Junho 1872 Fontelas 7 de manhã — baptizado: 2 Julho 1872 Igreja de Mosteiro

filho natural de:

pai incógnito | Juliana Diegues (Fontelas) jornaleira

neto paterno de: | neto materno de:

avôs incógnitos | avô incógnito
Margerida Diegues (Fontelas) jornaleira

Padrinho: Inocêncio Pires (Fontelas/solteiro, jornaleiro)
Madrinha: Maria Jozé Diegues (Fontelas/solteira, lavradora)

Assinaturas: Padre Francisco Rodrigues

1872

No. 18

JOÃO BATISTA

born: 24 June 1872 in Fontelas at 7 a.m. — baptized: 2 July 1872 Church of Mosteiro

natural son of:

unknown father | Juliana Diegues (Fontelas) day-labourer

paternal grandson of: | maternal grandson of:

unknown grandparents | unknown grandfather
Margarida Diegues (Fontelas) day-labourer

Godfather: Inocêncio Pires (Fontelas/single, day-labourer)
Godmother: Maria Jozé Diegues (Fontelas/single, peasant)

Signatures: Father Francisco Rodrigues

Appendix III

1870 MARRIAGE ENTRY

No. 4

dia 21 de Dezembro

Joze Ignacio e Lucrecia Nunes

Fontelas

Aos vinte e um dias do mes de Dezembro do anno de mil oito centos e setenta nesta igreja paroquial de Mosteiro Concelho de M. diocese de Bragança eu Padre Francisco Jose Rodrigues Cura coadjutor desta freguesia na minha presença comparecerão os nubentes Joze Ignácio e Lucrecia Nunes os quaes sei serem os propios com todos os papeis do estilo corentes sem empedimento algum canonico ou civil para o cazamento elle de idade de vinte e sete annos solteiro lavrador natural de Paradela Concelho de M. diocese de Bragança morador em Paradela e baptizado na mesma freguesia Concelho de M. diocese de Bragança filho natural de Barbara Gomes de Paradela Concelho de M. diocese de Bragança ella de idade de trinta a sete annos solteira lavradora natural e moradora de Fontelas Concelho de M. diocese de Bragança baptizada na freguesia de Mosteiro filha legitima de Silvestre Nunes de Algoso e de Albina Diegues de Fontelas Concelho de M. diocese de Bragança os quaes nubentes se receberão por marido e mulher e os uni em matrimonio procedendo em todo este acto comforme o rito da santa madre igreja Catholica appostolica romana sendo testemunhas Jose Sevane geireiro e Gregorio Pires lavrador moradores em Mosteiro os quaes sei serem os propios E para constar lavrei em duplicado este assento que dipois de ser lido e comfrido perante os conjuges e testemunhas comigo não assignarão por não saber escrever Era ut supra.

O Cura coadjutor – Francisco Jose Rodrigues

No. 4

21 December

Jozé Ignacio & Lucrécia Nunes

Fontelas

On the twenty-first day of the month of December of the year eighteen hundred and seventy in this Parish Church of Mosteiro, Municipality of M., diocese of Bragança, I, Father Francisco José Rodrigues, vicar's assistant of this parish, in my presence received the betrothed José Ignácio and Lucrécia Nunes, whom I acknowledge and who obtained all the necessary papers, without impediments either canonical or civil for the marriage. He is of the age of twenty-seven, single, peasant, and born in Paradela, Municipality of M., diocese of Bragança, resident in Paradela and baptized in the same parish, Municipality of M., diocese of Bragança, natural son of Barbara Gomes of Paradela, Municipality of M., diocese of Bragança. She is of the age of thirty-seven, single, peasant, born and resident in Fontelas, Municipality of M., diocese of Bragança, baptized in the parish of Mosteiro, legitimate daughter of Silvestre Nunes of Algoso and Albina Diegues of Fontelas, Municipality of M., diocese of Bragança; the betrothed received each other as husband and wife and I joined them in matrimony following in all of this process the rites of the holy Roman Apostolic Catholic Church. The witnesses were José Sevane, day-labourer, and Gregório Pires, peasant, both residents of Mosteiro, whom I acknowledge. In proof of this I made this entry in duplicate, which, after having been read and checked in the presence of the spouses and witnesses and myself, was not signed by them as they do not know how to write. *Era ut supra.*

The vicar's assistant – Francisco José Rodrigues

1870 MARRIAGE ENTRY (basic information)

1870 Fontelas 21 Dezembro Igreja de Mosteiro	<u>JOSÉ IGNÁCIO</u> (27 annos) solteiro, lavrador	<u>LUCRÉCIA NUNES</u> (37 annos) solteira, lavradora
	(sem impedimento canónico ou civil)	
	(natural, morador, e baptizado em Paradela)	(natural e morador em Fontelas, baptizada na freguesia de Mosteiro)
	filho natural de: Barbara Gomes (Paradela)	filha legítima de: Silvestre Nunes (Algoso) Albina Diegues (Fontelas)
	testemunhas: José Sevane (geireiro) Gregório Pires (lavrador)	moradores em Mosteiro
	Assinaturas: Padre Francisco José Rodrigues	

1870 Fontelas 21 December Church of Mosteiro	<u>JOSÉ IGNÁCIO</u> (27 years old) single, peasant	<u>LUCRÉCIA NUNES</u> (37 years old) single, peasant
	(without canonical or civil impediments)	
	(born, resident and baptized in Panadela)	(born and resident in Fontelas, baptized in the parish of Mosteiro)
	natural son of: Barbara Gomes (Paradela)	legitimate daughter of: Silvestre Nunes (Algoso)* Albina Diegues (Fontelas)
	witnesses: José Sevane (day-labourer) Gregório Pires (peasant)	residents of Mosteiro
	Signatures: Father Francisco José Rodrigues	

* The occupations of the spouses' parents are not always listed.

Appendix III

1871 DEATH ENTRY

No. 2
dia 22 de Fevereiro
Maria Gonçalves
Fontelas

Aos vinte e dois dias do mes de Fevereiro do anno de mil oito centos setenta e um, ao meio dia na povoação de Fontelas annexa desta freguesia de Mosteiro Concelho de M. diocese de Bragança falleçeo tendo recebido os sacramentos da santa madre igreja um individuo do sexo femenino, por nome Maria Gonçalves de idade de noventa annos lavradora viuva de Agostinho Gonçalves natural de Fontelas desta freguesia Concelho de M. diocese de Bragança, filha legitima de Clemente Gonçalves lavrador natural de Fontelas desta freguesia Concelho de M. diocese de Bragança, e de Maria Jose Annes lavradora, natural de Telhado freguesia de Argozelo Concelho de M. diocese de Bragança, fes testamento, não deixou filhos e foi sepultada no cemiterio de Fontelas. E para constar lavrei em duplicado este assento que assigno. Era ut supra.

O Reitor – Carlos Manuel Branco

No. 2
22 February
Maria Gonçalves
Fontelas

On the twenty-second day of the month of February of the year eighteen hundred and seventy one, at midday in the hamlet of Fontelas, annex of this parish of Mosteiro, Municipality of M., diocese of Bragança, having received the sacraments of the Holy Mother Church, an individual of the feminine sex died, named Maria Gonçalves, of the age of ninety years, peasant, widow of Agostino Gonçalves, born in Fontelas of this parish, Municipality of M., diocese of Bragança, legitimate daughter of Clemente Gonçalves, peasant, born in Fontelas of this parish, Municipality of M., diocese of Bragança, and of Maria José Annes, peasant, born in Telhado, parish of Argozelo , Municipality of M., diocese of Bragança; leaving a will, she did not leave children* and was buried in the cemetery of Fontelas. In proof of this I made this entry in duplicate, which I sign. *Era ut supra.*

The Vicar – Carlos Manuel Branco

* It is not clear whether this means that the deceased bore no children at any time in her life, or whether it means that none of her children were still alive at the date of her death (i.e. she could perhaps have had a child or children who died prior to her own death).

1871 DEATH ENTRY (basic information)

1871 No. 2 22 de Fevereiro Maria Gonçalves Fontelas	MARIA GONÇALVES (90 annos) lavradora natural de Fontelas viúva de Agostinho Gonçalves filha legítima de: Clemente Gonçalves (Fontelas) lavrador	faleceu: 22 Fevereiro 1871 ao meio-dia em Fontelas recebeu os sacramentos Maria José Annes (Telhado) lavradora
	Fez testamento/não deixou filhos Sepultado no cemitério de Fontelas Assinatura: Reitor Carlos Manoel Branco	

1871 No. 2 22 February Maria Gonçalves Fontelas	MARIA GONÇALVES peasant born in Fontelas widow of Agostinho Gonçalves legitimate daughter of: Clemente Gonçalves (Fontelas) peasant	died on: 22 February 1871 at noon in Fontelas received the sacraments Maria José Annes (Telhado) peasant
	Left a will/did not leave children Buried in the Fontelas cemetery Signature: Vicar Carlos Manoel Branco	

ecclesiastical officials; these are local priests in most cases, as the registers are customarily archived in each parish church. (Copies of each entry are required to be sent to a second, centralized archive in the Bishopric of each district.) Thirdly, a method of copying must be devised along with some form of selection. I succeeded in copying every marriage and death entry since 1870 for the four hamlets in the parish. The baptismal entries were another story: they were so detailed that I completed only those for Fontelas. I gave up an attempt to copy all of the baptisms for the parish's other three hamlets. No doubt the latter task may have been necessary had I selected the parish, rather than one hamlet alone, as my locus of study.

Finally, reasonable conditions for copy-work must be available. I began my copying in the hamlet itself after having completed 18 months of ethnographic fieldwork. This posed problems, principally for my eyes. The hamlet did not have electricity, and I had to work at first (at night) by kerosene lamps and candlelight. Most of the copying thus necessitated my moving to the town, where a room with electricity granted me reasonable working conditions. I returned to Fontelas on weekends, and occasionally for a week at a time, while continuing the steady copy-work. The entire task of copying took just under a year to complete, and I was obliged towards the end of my fieldwork to microfilm the books containing entries for the most recent decades. Much assistance in the interpretation of the entries was granted me by officials in the town's Civil Registry Office (*Conservatória do Registo Civil*). It was there that the first four decades of the Parish Register entries were archived (1870–1911); following years were in the Mosteiro parish church. An earlier series of entries was available in Mosteiro for the years 1703–33, but these were considerably more skeletal and less detailed than the later entries, besides remaining outside the temporal scope of this study. Particular thanks are also given to my supervisor Peter Loizos, who at a crucial point in the copy-work advised my continuation of it rather than its abandonment or postponement.

The value of such consecutive and detailed Parish Registers is incalculable for a number of disciplines: particularly social anthropology, social history, and historical demography. Both Peter Laslett *et al* (1972/1977) as well as Alan Macfarlane (1977a/1977b) have stressed the utility of parish records as well as other types of local historical sources for the reconstruction of past social structures in Western Europe. The excellent quality and breadth of the Portuguese registers has, however, to my knowledge not yet been noted by British or American anthropology. For the case of Spain, Lisón-Tolosana has pointed to their utility, although his use of them in *Belmonte de los Caballeros* (1966) was subsumed within a broader analysis based on a wider variety of historical records. As I have shown in this book, the Parish Registers themselves need not be subject to an exhaustive statistical study or computer programming in order to prove useful for other ends. My own suggestion has been to incorporate some of the information in the records within the community-study approach, in order to examine generational change (and continuity) within a specific number of selected households. The registers permit a certain degree of reconstruction of processes of marriage and inheritance over the generations. Further, they provide abundant evidence of a ranked social hierarchy over time within this small hamlet community. The sources reveal widely varying patterns among the wealthier and poorer social groups with respect to household size and structure, marriage alliances, and illegitimacy.

More than this, I must leave for future work and for more sophisticated demographic techniques. Throughout this analysis, nevertheless, I have argued implicitly for the utility of such Parish Registers for social-anthropological research in Europe. This has implied a stance stressing the *equal* importance of these records alongside data collected from the ethnographic present.

Appendix IV: Household structure, 1977

The following diagrams represent the structure of every household in Fontelas in mid-1977. They are based partly on Peter Laslett's ideographic scheme for the pictorial representation of domestic groups (1972:31, 41–2). A summary table of the types of domestic group drawn here is included at the beginning of Chapter 6 (Table 13): the diagrams should be viewed along with that table. All of the households have been numbered by myself and may be located in two further places in this book: in Table 3 where landholdings are listed, and on Map 3 where I have drawn the spatial organization of the hamlet.

In examining the diagrams, the following points should be noted. Firstly, the structure of each household comprises those members of the domestic group present on 1 July 1977. At that time, Fontelas consisted of 57 resident households and a total of 187 people. However, a number of individuals have been included in the diagrams with dashed lines, who were not resident on that date but who resided in the household at some time between early 1976 and late 1978. Also included are 5 people who died during my fieldwork prior to 1 July 1977, as well as a number of marriages which took place after that date. All of these inclusions are noted in the diagrams. These additions allow us a glimpse of some of the short-term changes in household structure over a $2\frac{1}{2}$ year period, and thus avoid the static snapshot quality of household listings pegged to one specific date.

Secondly, all personal names have been changed. None of the names used here duplicate any of the real names of individuals currently living in Fontelas. Rather, all of them have been selected randomly from the Parish Register or from other sources referring to individuals living in the eighteenth or nineteenth centuries. Within this study, however, there is internal consistency. For instance, an individual I have called Valentim in Chapter 3 can be located in the landholding table as well as here in the household diagrams.

Thirdly, let me call attention once again to the order in which kin and affinal relations are drawn in the diagrams. In Household 21, for example, Leocádia gave birth to her illegitimate daughter Emília (by an unknown father) *prior* to her marriage to Elias, who himself had fathered an illegitimate daughter prior to the marriage. This order in relationships is of crucial significance. All irregular relations (including cohabitation) are drawn with a dotted/dashed line, but note that this symbol – in the case of natural filiation – does not discriminate between a formally affiliated bastard child (rare) and a bastard not legally recognized by his/her biological father (more common). Dotted and dashed lines extending downwards from a male villager indicate an illegitimate child (or children) living elsewhere. Barren marriages are noted, as are marriages whose children are resident elsewhere. The latter are shown by a short vertical line under the marriage line (see H12 and H32). Obviously, the diagrams show only those villagers resident in

Appendix IV

Figure 25. Household diagrams, 1977 (57 ideographs)

HOUSEHOLD 1

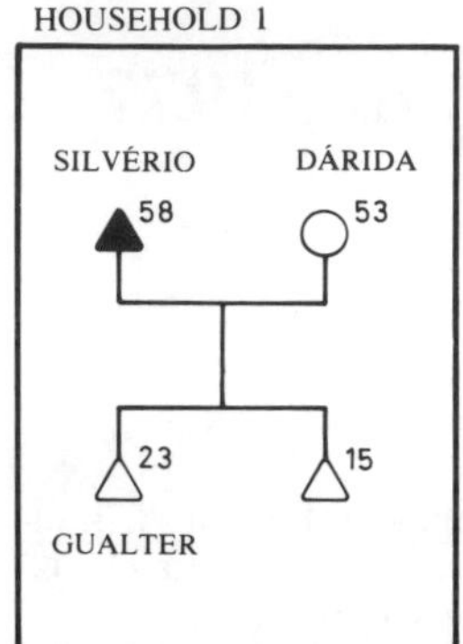

HOUSEHOLD 2

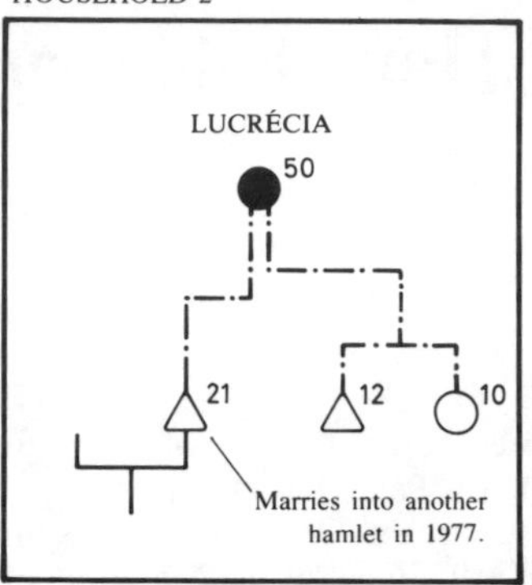

HOUSEHOLD 3

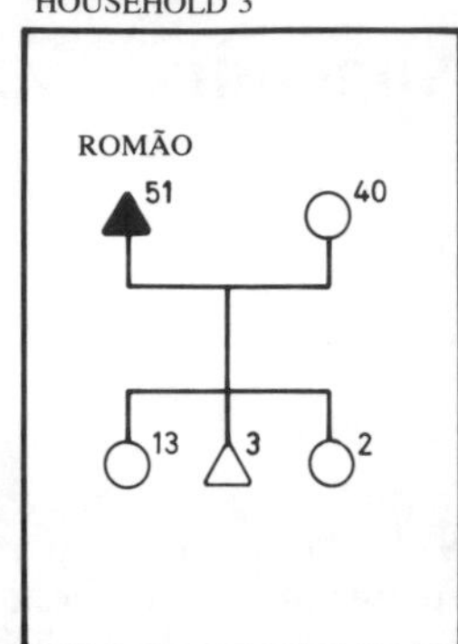

HOUSEHOLD 4

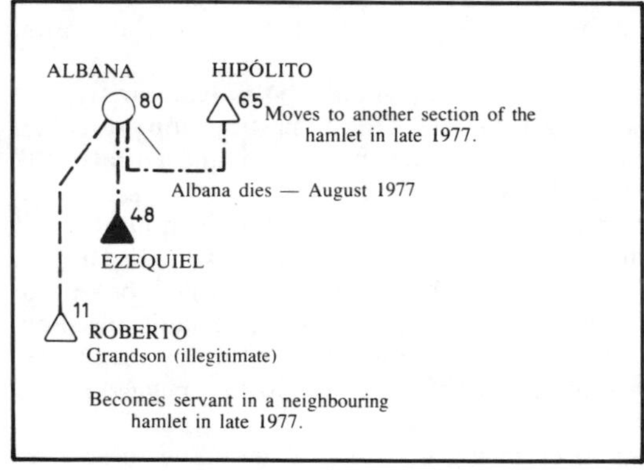

HOUSEHOLD 5

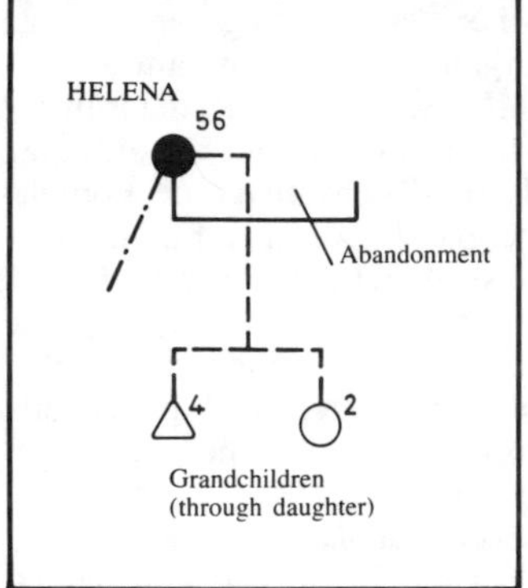

HOUSEHOLD 6

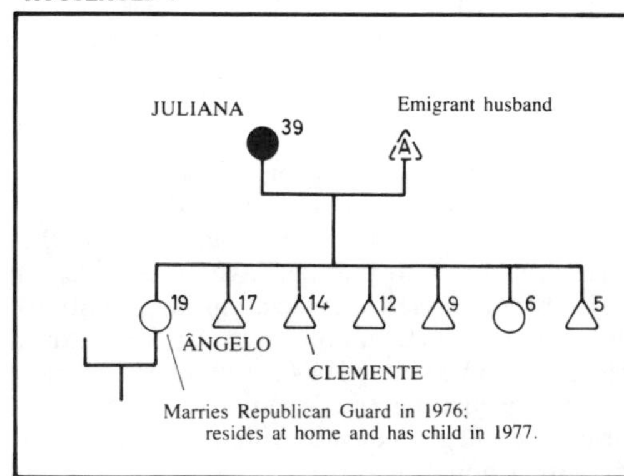

HOUSEHOLD 7

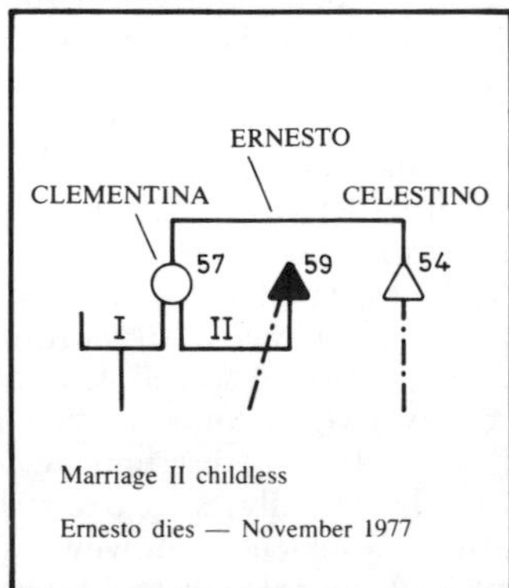

HOUSEHOLD 8

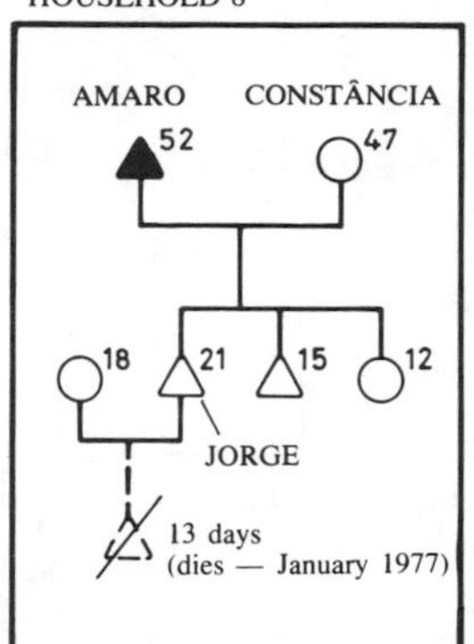

HOUSEHOLD 9

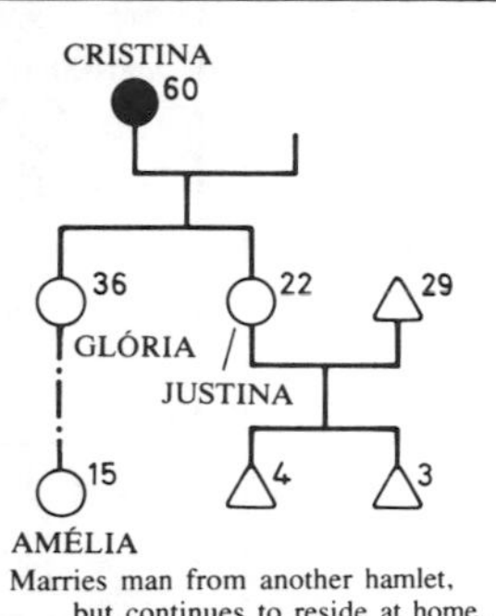

HOUSEHOLD 10

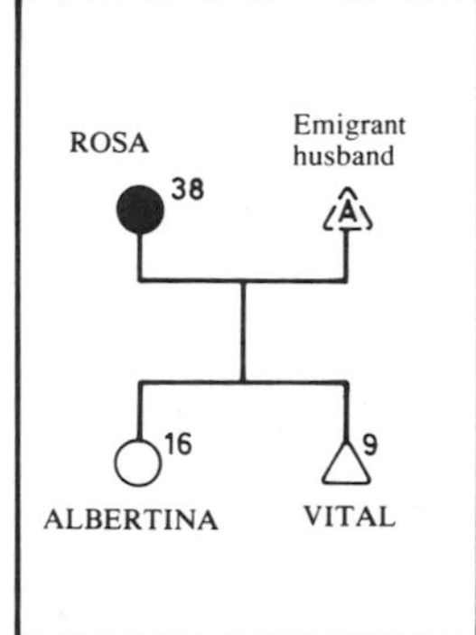

HOUSEHOLD 11

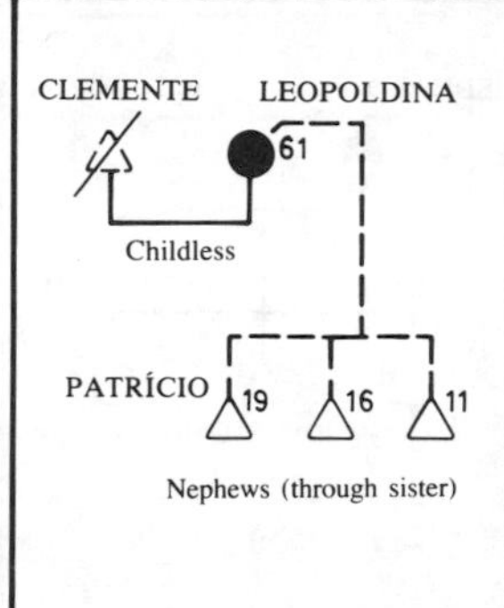

HOUSEHOLD 12

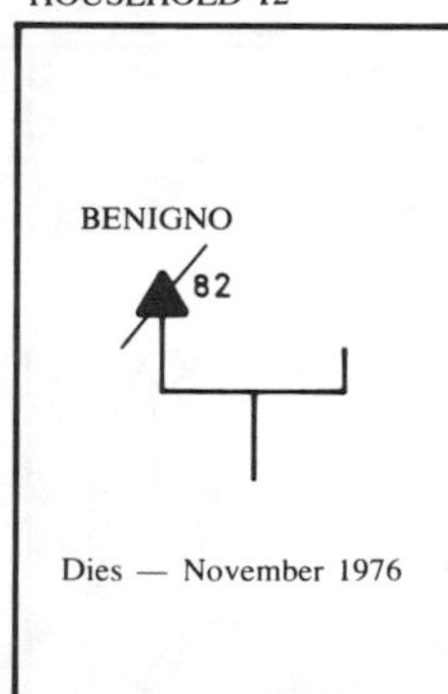

HOUSEHOLD 13

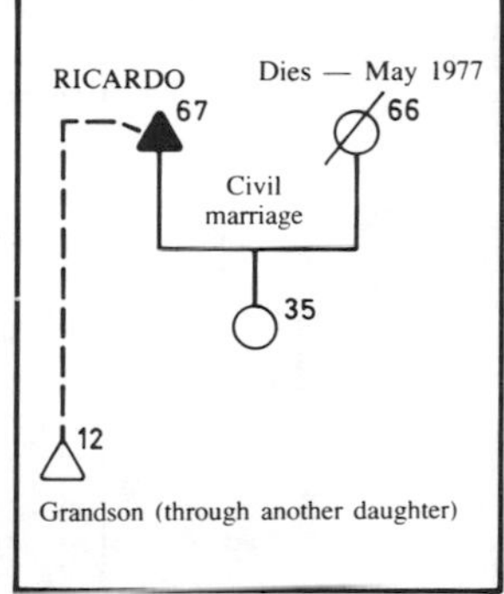

HOUSEHOLD 14

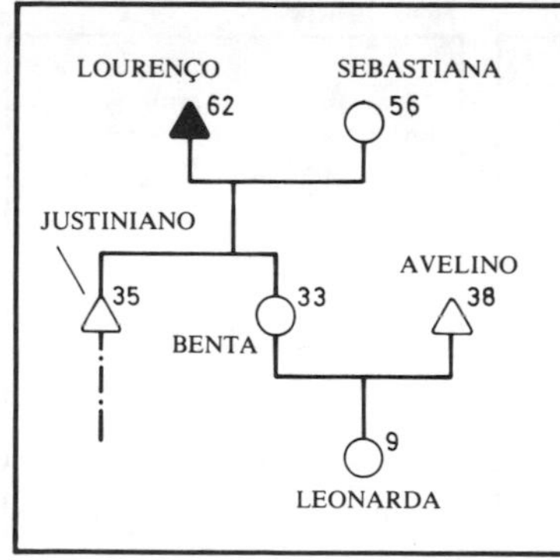

HOUSEHOLD 15

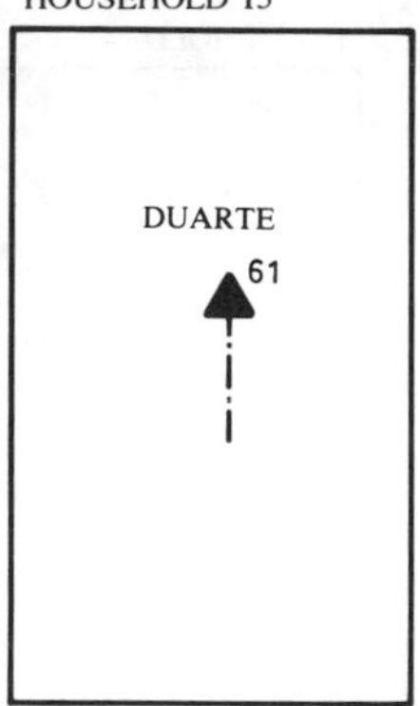

HOUSEHOLD 16

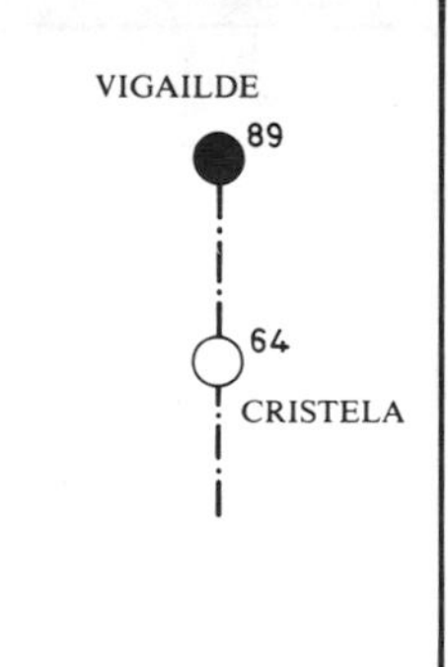

Appendix IV

HOUSEHOLD 17

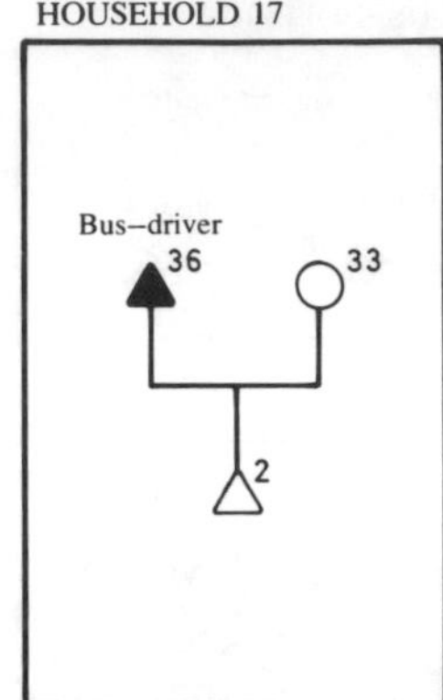

HOUSEHOLD 18

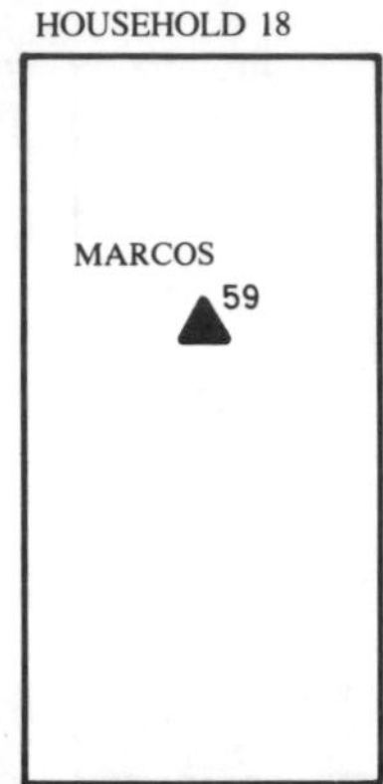

HOUSEHOLD 19

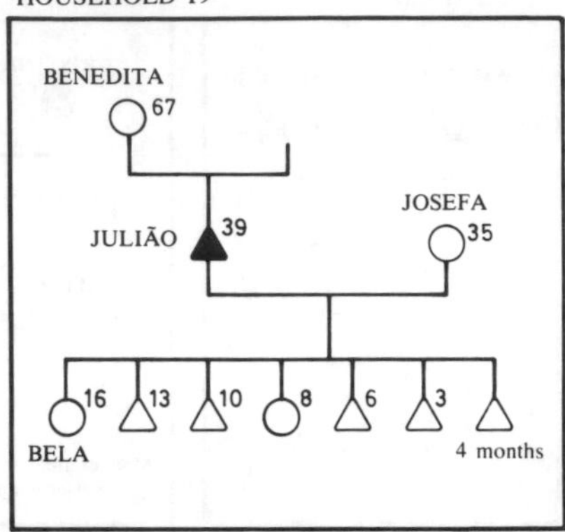

HOUSEHOLD 20

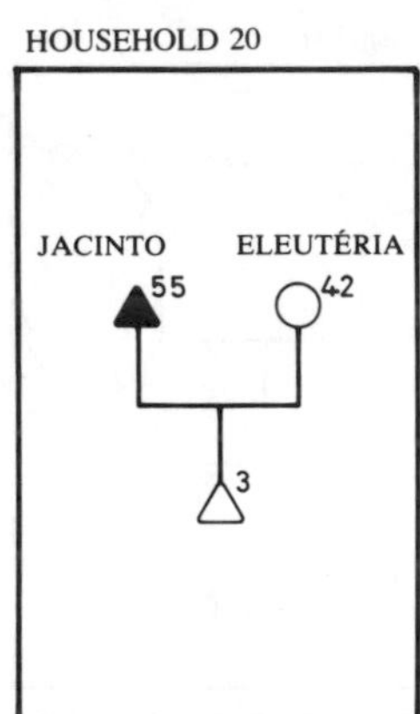

HOUSEHOLD 21

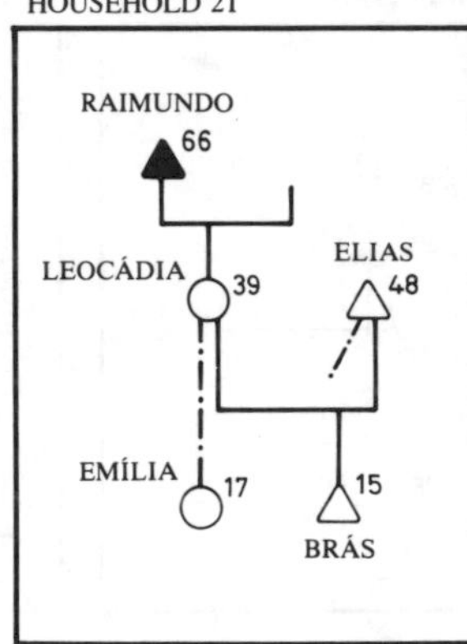

HOUSEHOLD 22

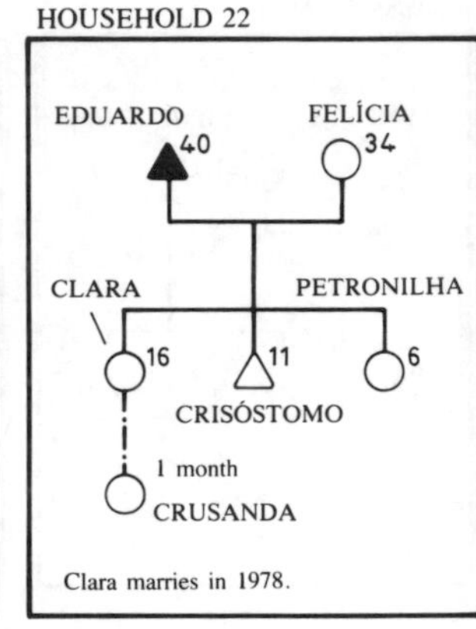

HOUSEHOLD 23

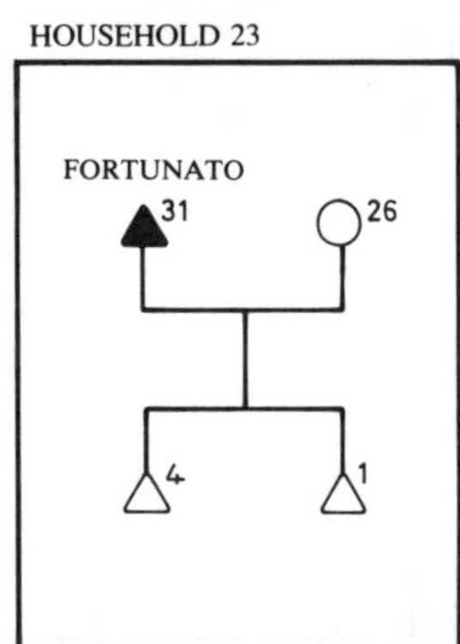

HOUSEHOLD 24

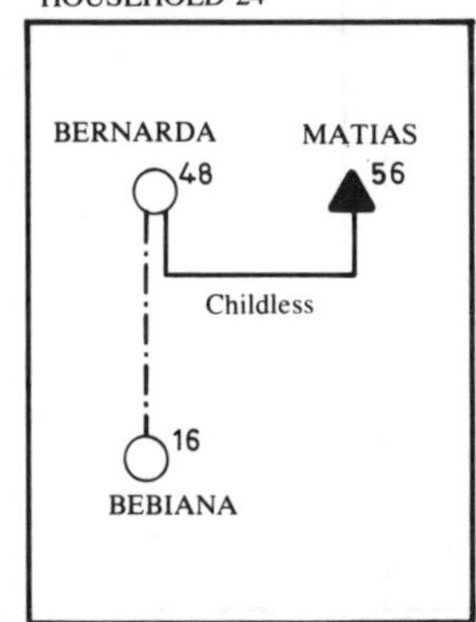

HOUSEHOLD 25

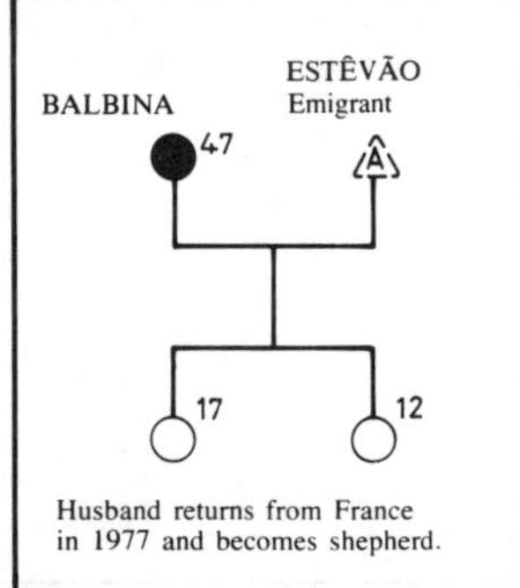

HOUSEHOLD 26

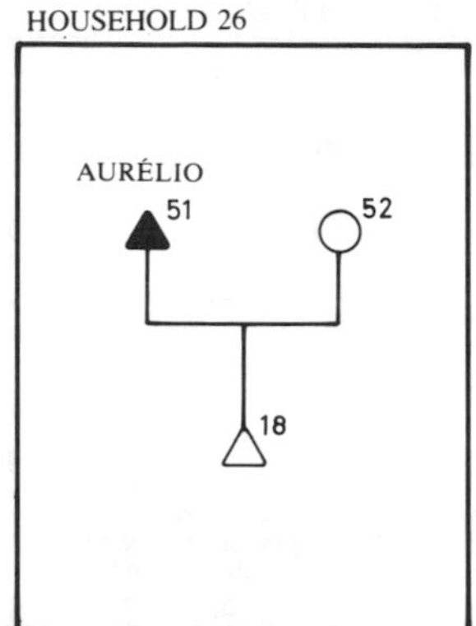

HOUSEHOLD 27

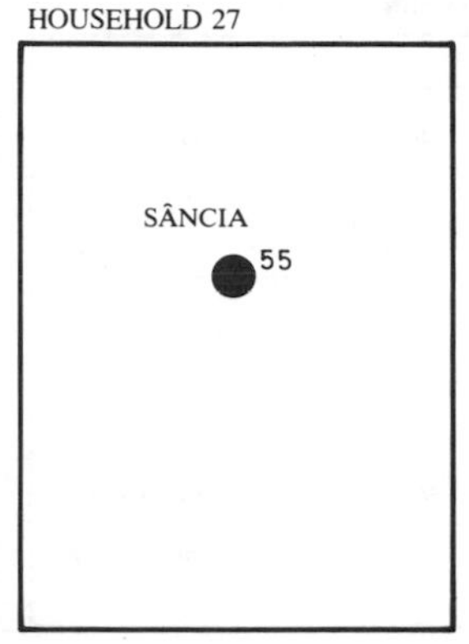

HOUSEHOLD 28

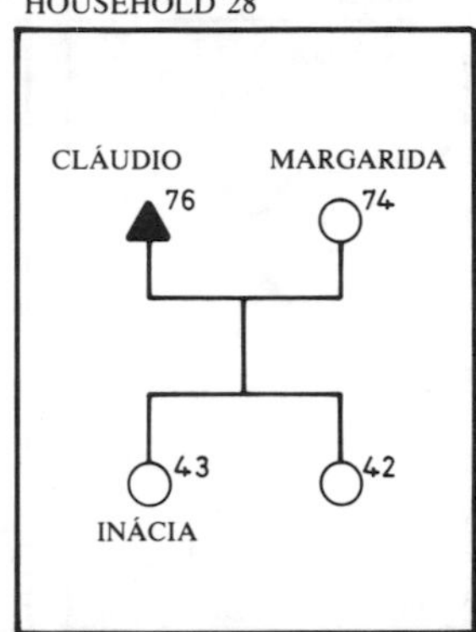

HOUSEHOLD 29

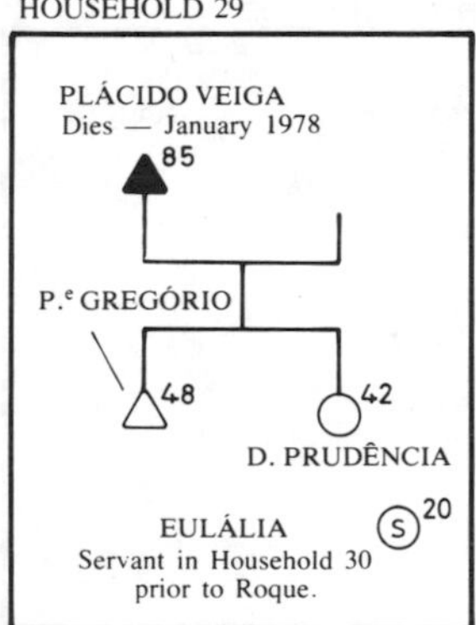

HOUSEHOLD 30

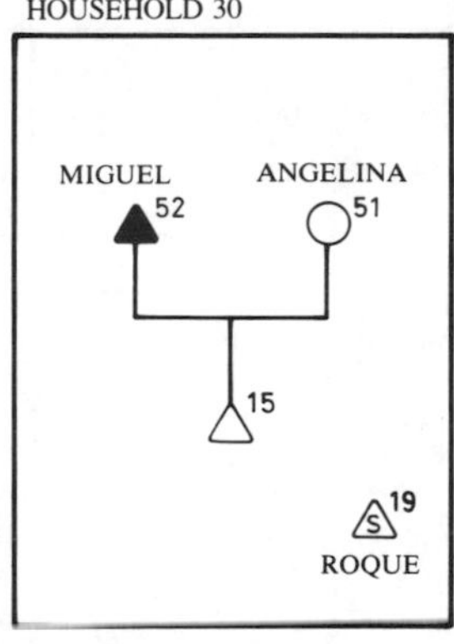

HOUSEHOLD 31

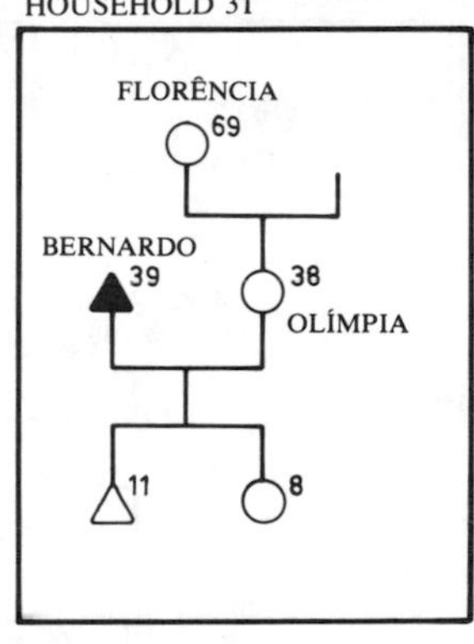

HOUSEHOLD 32

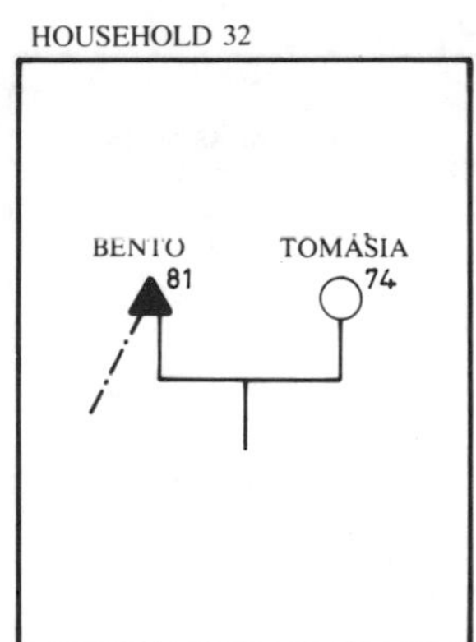

HOUSEHOLD 33

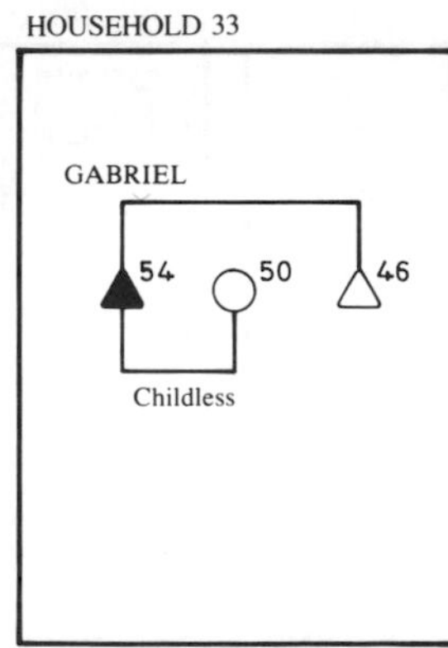

HOUSEHOLD 34

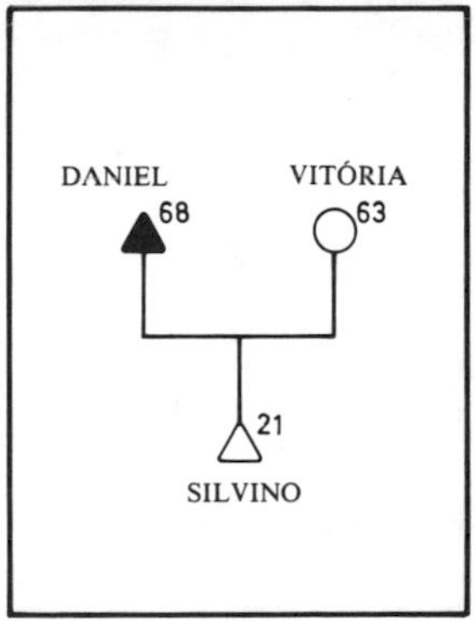

Appendix IV

HOUSEHOLD 35

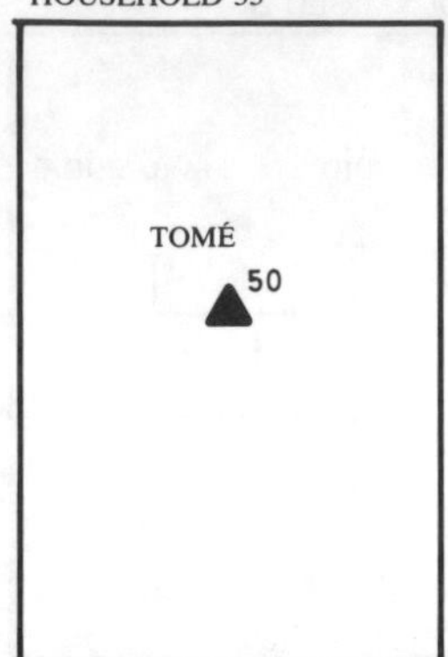

HOUSEHOLD 36

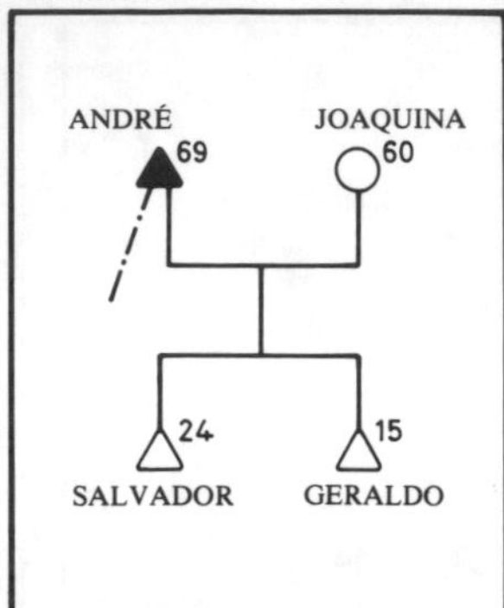

HOUSEHOLD 37

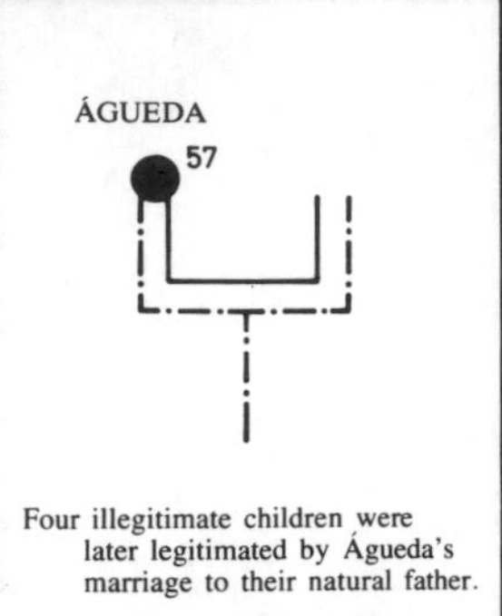

ÁGUEDA
57
Four illegitimate children were later legitimated by Águeda's marriage to their natural father.

HOUSEHOLD 38

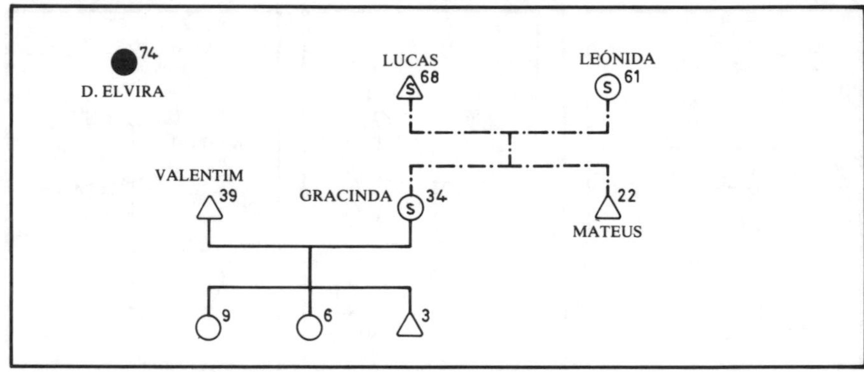

HOUSEHOLD 39

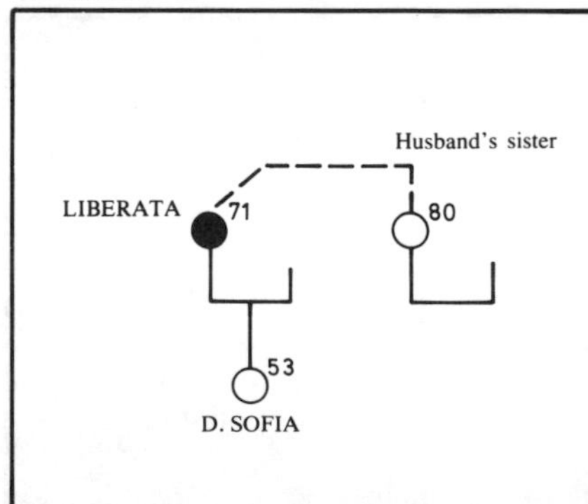

Husband's sister

HOUSEHOLD 40

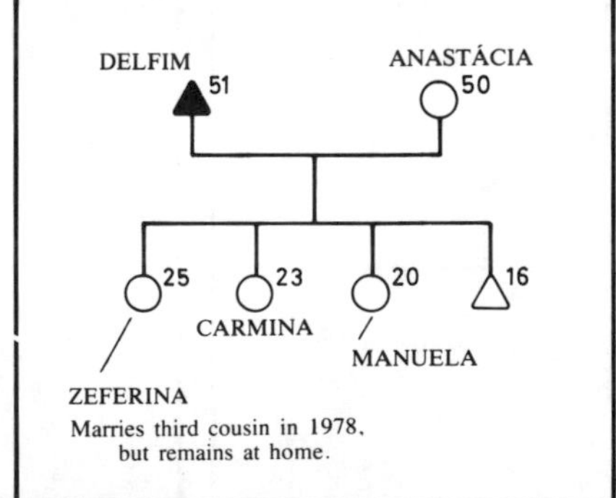

Marries third cousin in 1978, but remains at home.

HOUSEHOLD 41

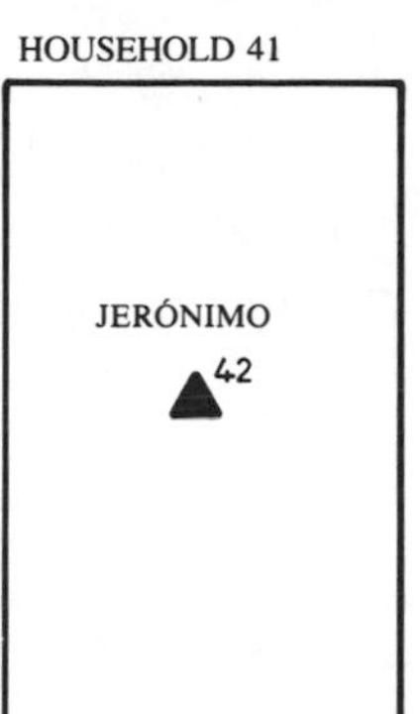

HOUSEHOLD 42

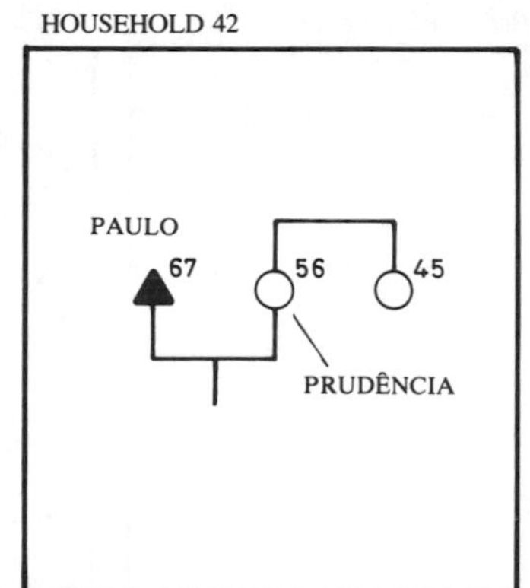

HOUSEHOLD 43

HOUSEHOLD 44

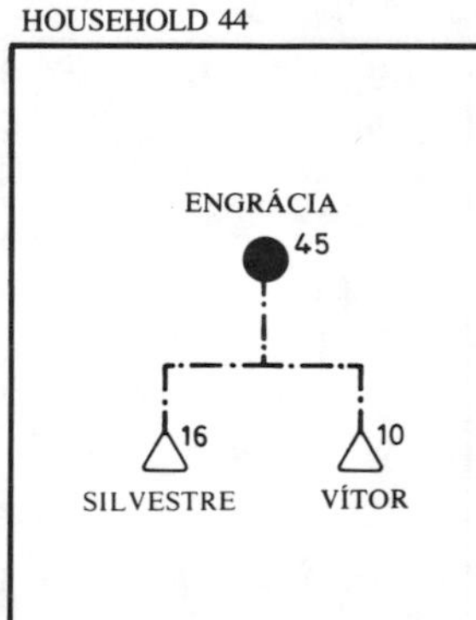

HOUSEHOLD 45

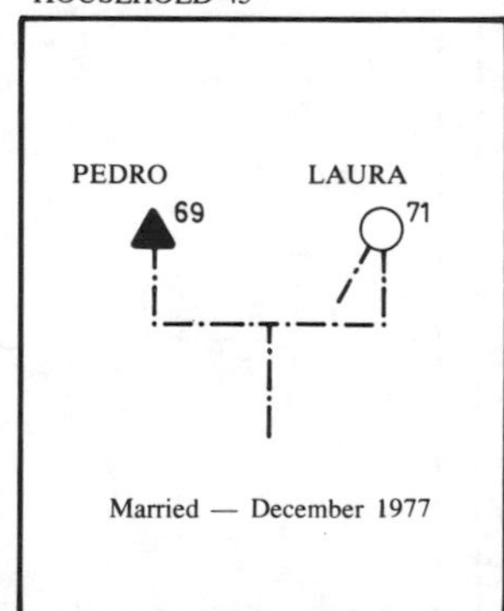

HOUSEHOLD 46

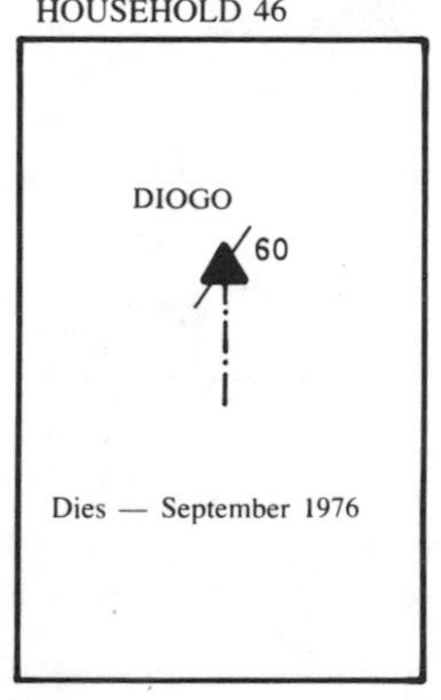

HOUSEHOLD 47

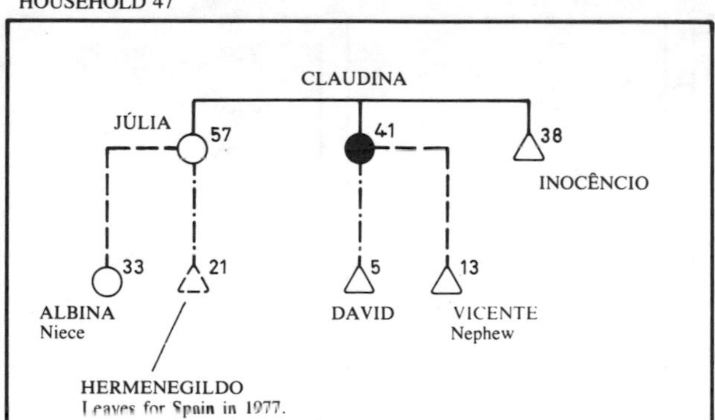

HOUSEHOLD 48

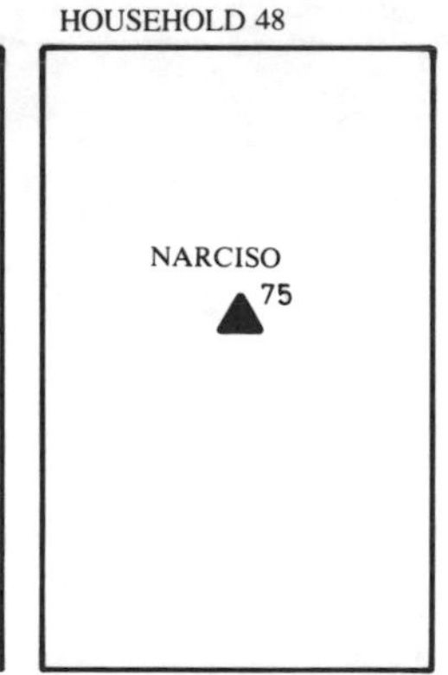

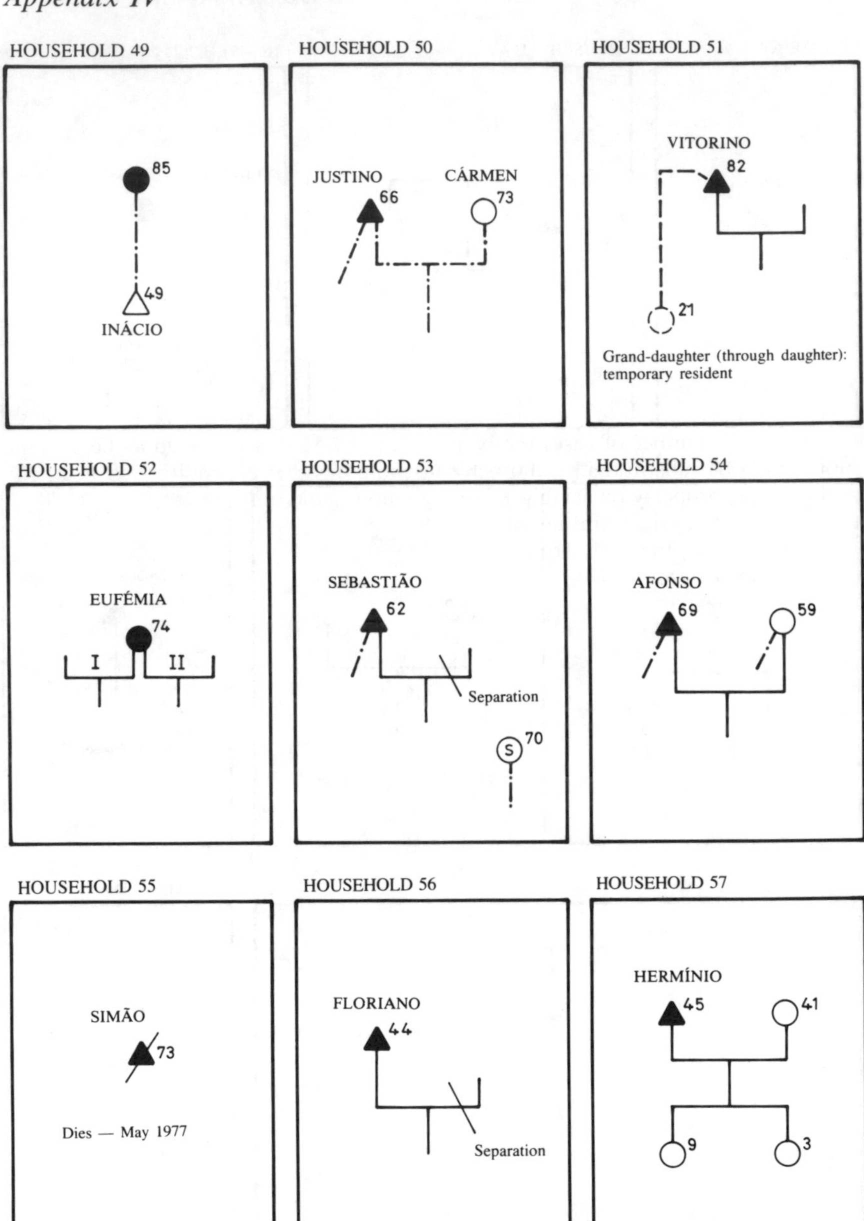
HOUSEHOLD 49
85
49
INÁCIO
HOUSEHOLD 50
JUSTINO
66
CÁRMEN
73
HOUSEHOLD 51
VITORINO
82
21
Grand-daughter (through daughter): temporary resident
HOUSEHOLD 52
EUFÉMIA
74
I
II
HOUSEHOLD 53
SEBASTIÃO
62
Separation
S
70
HOUSEHOLD 54
AFONSO
69
59
HOUSEHOLD 55
SIMÃO
73
Dies — May 1977
HOUSEHOLD 56
FLORIANO
44
Separation
HOUSEHOLD 57
HERMÍNIO
45
41
9
3

1976–8 and not all of a couple's children or siblings. Also not shown are the large number of visiting emigrants who return to Fontelas each August, when household sizes are temporarily expanded.

Fourthly, I have adapted Laslett's diagrams to fit the social structure of Fontelas. I could just as well have based my diagrams on another system or have devised my own. However, as the diagrams do provide a useful method for visually representing the relationships listed in Confessional Rolls and similar archival listings, I have followed them throughout. Nevertheless, I have not circled each conjugal group according to Laslett's system, as this seems to me to place undue emphasis upon the legal marital tie. This would seriously distort the real nature of family structure in Fontelas (Chapter 6), where a systematic de-emphasis of marriage pervades the social structure. Another problematic element in Laslett's scheme is the definition of *household head.* In Fontelas it is not always clear who plays this role: the very institution may be purely nominal, thus hiding subtle aspects of behaviour of various members within the domestic group. In this sense, my indications of household heads in the diagrams should be interpreted flexibly – in a number of cases the blackened individual represented as head could theoretically be substituted by another household member depending on the criteria used (age/sex/property ownership/hamlet opinion/name order in Confessional Roll/role in directing agricultural tasks).

Finally, due to the high proportion of illegitimate births in the hamlet, I have stretched Laslett's category of Multiple Family Households to include illegitimate mother/child ties. This may suggest the question of whether matrifocal ties between single mothers and their bastard children do or do not constitute a 'family'. As this question has not been resolved in European ethnographic literature (indeed it is hardly ever posed) I have had to transpose into the diagrams as close a representation of real social relationships as is possible. In this sense, relations involving bastardy or non-marital unions are just as 'social' as those arising from formal marriage, although their legal content may be quite different. Irregular relationships (see Note 19, Chapter 3) thus pose problems for Laslett's classification. But as they are so common in Fontelas, I have moulded the classifying system in order to include illegitimacies rather than discard it entirely. The diagrams are thus provisional working tools rather than definitive models.

Appendix V: Baptisms of bastards, 1870–1978

Illegitimacy ratios in Fontelas are so high that they tempt a complete questioning of the reliability of the Parish Register data. I have compiled this appendix in order to dispel such doubts. The first two tables below (22 and 23) list the occupations of the mothers and fathers of illegitimate children since 1870. Following these tables I have listed all of the baptisms recorded in Fontelas over the three decades beginning in 1880, 1910, and 1950. These three decades provide a good sample of the completeness of the recording of bastard baptisms over the last century. I have compiled similar lists for all 11 decades since 1870, but include only three here. The baptismal entries are extraordinarily detailed and to a great degree reliable. Furthermore, they can be supplemented through a simple record linkage of named individuals with three further documentary sources: the marriage entries, the death entries, and the Confessional Rolls. The baptismal entries thus provide us with a mine of information concerning bastardy and its occurrence within various social groups over time.

There are six major ways to confirm that the status of a natural child has been correctly recorded in the baptismal entry. Firstly, the standard phrase *pai incógnito* (unknown father) is normally written in the entry immediately following the words 'illegitimate child of . . .' Thus a bastard will be described as an 'illegitimate son of T.P., single, *jornaleira*, born and resident in Fontelas, and of an unknown father . . .' (see the transcription of a complete sample entry of a bastard baptism in Appendix III). If the father is listed as an unknown father then his own parents are also listed as the child's 'unknown grandparents' (*avôs incógnitos*).

Secondly, the marital status of the mother is always given: in cases of illegitimate children the mother is usually listed as *solteira* (single). The only exceptions are bastard-bearing widows or the mothers of adulterine children. Even in these cases the mothers are explicitly listed respectively as *viúva* (widow) or *casada* (married).

Thirdly, the father may occasionally be listed along with his occupation and marital status. In such cases both the father and the mother are listed as single.

Fourthly, the marriage entries in the Parish Register may be checked against the baptismal entries, in order to locate the same individuals in two sources. An unmarried mother bearing a bastard may later marry the child's father, thus legitimating the child. The dates of the child's birth and baptism may thus be linked with the marriage date, and this can confirm that the child was born and baptized as a bastard although later legitimated.

Fifthly, unmarried mothers can usually be located in the death entries, where their marital status is also registered. The vast majority of unmarried *jornaleiras* who have borne bastards have also died unmarried.

Sixthly, yet another check on the baptismal entry is provided by the Confessional Rolls of 1886–1909 and the *Status Animarum* Listing of 1940. Here an unmarried mother may again be located: her marital status (usually 'single') is also registered there. The bastard child(ren) will then later appear at the age of 8 or 9, the mother remaining listed as single. In Chapter 5, the case-study of Rufina and her successive bastard-bearing daughters and granddaughters has shown how these household listings can yield this information correctly.

In other words, there are a whole series of checks both within the baptismal entries themselves as well as in their linkage with other key sources. If any one element of information is missing with regard to a particular mother or child, it can be checked and found in another place through the other sources. This provides conclusive evidence that the baptismal entries are accurate in their recording of bastard baptisms.

A wealth of further patterns could be studied on the basis of the baptismal information: these include godparent selection, literacy, the hamlets of origin of grandparents, and the interval between birth and baptism (frequently over 1 month). Two interesting details afforded by the entries over the past century are, firstly, the number of widows (7) who have borne illegitimate children (some of these may of course have borne more than one child). Secondly, only a very *small* percentage of bastards were later legitimated by the subsequent marriage of their biological parents: 18 of 326 total natural children. (The marriage entries, however, have recorded 39 legitimated children: see Table 14.) Furthermore, Tables 22 and 23 below show definitively that: (a) the majority of mothers of illegitimate children (172) were unmarried *jornaleiras*, and that (b) almost all of the fathers of illegitimate children (275) were registered as 'unknown fathers'. A number of other occupations mentioned in the entries include temporary residents of Fontelas – gypsies, itinerant tinkers, travelling merchants, and one rather ambiguous case of two unmarried parents listed simply as transients (*tranzeuntes*).

In my list of baptisms in Table 24, summary totals for each decade have been included. Note that although the sample is numerically small, in 3 years (1916, 1919, and 1921) not a single legitimate child was baptized in Fontelas. The letters *NG* (not given) indicate that a parent was named and registered but that his or her occupation was not recorded. These individuals' occupations may of course be traced through other sources, but I have not done this here due to questions of space. A question mark (?) indicates an unnamed parent: these were usually unknown fathers or both of the parents of a foundling.

Appendix V

Table 22. *Mothers of illegitimate children, 1870–1978*

Mother's occupation	Illegitimate children	%
Jornaleira	172	*52.8*
Doméstica	79	*24.2*
Lavradora	10	*3.1*
Cottager	9	*2.8*
Proprietária	4	*1.2*
Foundling	3	*0.9*
Minor	3	*0.9*
Travelling merchant	3	*0.9*
Gypsy	1	*0.3*
Servant	1	*0.3*
Spinner	1	*0.3*
Itinerant tinker	1	*0.3*
Transient	1	*0.3*
Identified, but no occupation given	33	*10.1*
—	5*	*1.5*
Total	326	*99.9*

Source: Parish Register – Baptismal entries.
* Foundlings

Table 23. *Fathers of illegitimate children, 1870–1978*

Father's occupation	Illegitimate children	%
'Unknown father'	275	*84.4*
Jornaleiro	16	*4.9*
Lavrador	7	*2.1*
Barber	2	*0.6*
Gypsy	2	*0.6*
Travelling merchant	2	*0.6*
Castrator (mostly pigs)	1	*0.3*
Servant	1	*0.3*
Blacksmith	1	*0.3*
Itinerant tinker	1	*0.3*
Motorist	1	*0.3*
Shopkeeper	1	*0.3*
Gypsy merchant	1	*0.3*
Sawyer	1	*0.3*
Identified, but no occupation given	9	*2.8*
—	5*	*1.5*
Total	326	*99.9*

Source: Parish Register – Baptismal entries.
* Foundlings

Table 24. *Baptisms in Fontelas over three decades*

Year	Status of child	Mother's occupation	Father's occupation	Observations
1880	legitimate	seamstress	jornaleiro	
	legitimate	cottager	stone-mason	
	legitimate	cottager	jornaleiro	
	legitimate	cottager	jornaleiro	
	legitimate	lavradora	lavrador	
	– natural *	– cottager	?	*twins
	– natural *	– cottager	?	
	– natural	– cottager	?	
	– natural	– lavradora	?	
	– adulterine	– NG	?	
	– natural	– lavradora	?	
1881	legitin ate	lavradora	lavrador	
	legitimate	lavradora	lavrador	
	legitimate	lavradora	lavrador	
	legitimate	schoolmistress*	lavrador	*'private tutor of little girls'
1882	legitimate	lavradora	blacksmith	
	legitimate	lavradora	lavrador	
	– natural	– cottager	?	
	legitimate	lavradora	lavrador	
	– natural	– cottager	?	
	legitimate	cottager	cottager	
1883	– natural	– foundling	?	
	legitimate	jornaleira	jornaleiro	
	legitimate	schoolmistress	lavrador	
	legitimate	lavradora	lavrador	
1884	– natural	– jornaleira	?	
	legitimate	jornaleira	jornaleiro	
	legitimate	jornaleira	jornaleiro	
	– foundling	?	?	
	– natural*	– lavradora	?	*legitimated 1896
1885	legitimate	lavradora	lavrador	
	legitimate	jornaleira	jornaleiro	
	legitimate	schoolmistress	jornaleiro	
	legitimate	lavradora	lavrador	

	– natural	– jornaleira	?	
	– natural	– lavradora*	– lavrador*	*both widowed
	– natural	– jornaleira	?	
	– natural	– proprietária*	?	*widow
	– natural	– jornaleira	?	
1886	– natural*	– jornaleira	?	*legitimated 1887
	legitimate	jornaleira	jornaleiro	
	legitimate	lavradora	lavrador	
	legitimate	jornaleira	jornaleiro	
	legitimate	jornaleira	jornaleiro	
	legitimate	jornaleira	jornaleiro	
	– natural*	– jornaleira	?	*legitimated 1896
1887	legitimate	jornaleira	jornaleiro	
	legitimate	lavradora	lavrador	
	– natural	– jornaleira	?	
	legitimate	lavradora	lavrador	
	– natural*	– jornaleira	?	*legitimated 1888
	legitimate	proprietária	proprietário	
1888	– natural	– jornaleira	?	
	– natural	– proprietária*	?	*widow
	– natural	– jornaleira	?	
	– natural	– jornaleira	?	
	– natural	– jornaleira	?	
	– natural	– jornaleira	?	
	legitimate	jornaleira	jornaleiro	
	legitimate	jornaleira	jornaleiro	
	legitimate	jornaleira	jornaleiro	
	legitimate	jornaleira	jornaleiro	
1889	– natural	– jornaleira	?	
	legitimate	jornaleira	jornaleiro	
	– natural	– jornaleira	?	
	legitimate	jornaleira	jornaleiro	
	legitimate	jornaleira	jornaleiro	
	– natural*	– jornaleira	?	*legitimated 1896
	egitimate	lavradora	lavrador	
	egitimate	jornaleira	jornaleiro	

Total legitimate:	40	Illegitimacy ratio: *42.9%*
Total illegitimate:	30	
	70	

NG – Individual named but occupation not given.
? – Unknown father (or unknown mother in cases of foundlings).

Table 24 (*cont.*)

1910	legitimate	jornaleira	jornaleiro	
	legitimate	lavradora	lavrador	
	– illegitimate	– jornaleira	?	
	– illegitimate	– jornaleira	?	
	legitimate	jornaleira	jornaleiro	
	– illegitimate	– jornaleira	?	
	– illegitimate*	– doméstica	?	*legitimated 1946
	– illegitimate	– jornaleira	?	
	legitimate	jornaleira	jornaleiro	
	– illegitimate	– jornaleira	?	
	legitimate	jornaleira	jornaleiro	
1911	– illegitimate	– doméstica	?	
	legitimate	lavradora	lavrador	
	– illegitimate	– jornaleira	?	
	– illegitimate	– jornaleira	?	
	– illegitimate	– jornaleira*	?	*widow
	– illegitimate	– jornaleira	?	
	– illegitimate	– jornaleira	?	
	– illegitimate	– jornaleira	?	
1912	legitimate	lavradora	lavrador	
	legitimate	jornaleira	jornaleiro	
	– illegitimate	– jornaleira	?	
	legitimate	lavradora	lavrador	
	– illegitimate	– jornaleira	?	
1913	– illegitimate	– doméstica	?	
	– illegitimate	– jornaleira	?	
	– illegitimate	– doméstica	?	
	– illegitimate	– doméstica	?	
	legitimate	proprietária	proprietário	
	legitimate	lavradora	lavrador	
	– illegitimate	– jornaleira	?	
1914	– illegitimate	– jornaleira	?	
	– illegitimate	– jornaleira	?	
	legitimate	lavradora	lavrador	
	– illegitimate	– jornaleira	?	
	– illegitimate	– jornaleira	?	
	– illegitimate	– jornaleira	?	

1915	– illegitimate	– jornaleira	?	
	– illegitimate	– jornaleira	?	
	legitimate	lavradora	lavrador	
	– illegitimate	– jornaleira	?	
	– illegitimate	– doméstica	?	
1916	– illegitimate	– jornaleira	?	
	– illegitimate	– jornaleira	?	
	– illegitimate	– jornaleira	?	
	– illegitimate	– jornaleira	?	
	– illegitimate	– jornaleira	?	
1917	legitimate	lavradora	lavrador	
	– illegitimate	– jornaleira	?	
	legitimate	NG	NG	
	– illegitimate	– jornaleira	?	
	legitimate	jornaleira	jornaleiro	
	– illegitimate	– jornaleira	?	
	legitimate	lavradora	lavrador	
	– illegitimate	– jornaleira	?	
	– illegitimate	– jornaleira	?	
	– illegitimate	– jornaleira	?	
1918	– illegitimate	– jornaleira	?	
	– illegitimate	– jornaleira	?	
	– illegitimate	– jornaleira	?	
	legitimate	lavradora	lavrador	
	legitimate	jornaleira	jornaleiro	
	– illegitimate	– jornaleira	?	
	– illegitimate	– jornaleira	?	
	– illegitimate	– jornaleira	?	
	– illegitimate	– jornaleira	?	
1919	– illegitimate	– doméstica	?	
	– illegitimate	– jornaleira	?	
	– illegitimate	– jornaleira	?	
	– illegitimate	– jornaleira	– jornaleiro	
	– illegitimate	– jornaleira	?	
	– illegitimate*	– jornaleira	?	*legitimated 1962

Total legitimate: 19
Total illegitimate: 53
72

Illegitimacy ratio: *73.6%*

Table 24 (*cont.*)

1950	legitimate	doméstica	jornaleiro	
	– illegitimate	– doméstica	?	
	– illegitimate	– doméstica	?	
	– illegitimate*	– doméstica	?	*legitimated (no date)
	legitimate	doméstica	lavrador	
	– illegitimate	– doméstica	?	
1951	– illegitimate	– doméstica	– lavrador	
	legitimate	doméstica	lavrador	
	– illegitimate	– doméstica	?	
	– illegitimate	– doméstica	?	
	– illegitimate	– doméstica	?	
	– illegitimate	– doméstica	?	
1952	– illegitimate	– doméstica	– jornaleiro	
	– illegitimate	– doméstica	?	
	legitimate	doméstica	lavrador	
	– illegitimate	– doméstica	– barber	
	legitimate	doméstica	jornaleiro	
1953	legitimate	doméstica	jornaleiro	
	legitimate	doméstica	lavrador	
	– illegitimate	– doméstica	?	
	– illegitimate	– doméstica	– jornaleiro	
	legitimate	doméstica	blacksmith	
1954	– illegitimate	– doméstica	– barber	
	legitimate	doméstica	lavrador	
	legitimate	doméstica	jornaleiro	
	– illegitimate	– doméstica	– jornaleiro	
	legitimate	doméstica	jornaleiro	
	– illegitimate	– doméstica	?	
1955	legitimate	doméstica	lavrador	
	– illegitimate	– doméstica	?	
	legitimate*	doméstica	lavrador	*born 1953 baptized on
	legitimate**	doméstica	lavrador	**born 1955 the same day
	– illegitimate	– doméstica	– jornaleiro	
	– illegitimate	– doméstica	?	
	– illegitimate	– doméstica	?	
	– illegitimate	– doméstica	?	

	legitimate	doméstica	jornaleiro
	legitimate	doméstica	jornaleiro
	– illegitimate	– doméstica	– lavrador
1956	legitimate	doméstica	lavrador
	– illegitimate	– doméstica	?
	legitimate	doméstica	jornaleiro
	– illegitimate	– doméstica	– gypsy merchant
	legitimate	doméstica	jornaleiro
1957	legitimate	doméstica	lavrador
	– illegitimate	– doméstica	?
	legitimate	doméstica	lavrador
	legitimate	doméstica	lavrador
	legitimate	doméstica	jornaleiro
1958	legitimate	doméstica	jornaleiro
	– illegitimate	– doméstica	?
	legitimate	doméstica	shopkeeper
	legitimate	doméstica	journaleiro
1959	legitimate	doméstica	lavrador
	legitimate	doméstica	jornaleiro
	legitimate	doméstica	lavrador
	legitimate	doméstica	jornaleiro
	legitimate	doméstica	jornaleiro
	– illegitimate	– doméstica	?

Total legitimate: 31
Total illegitimate: 28
59

Illegitimacy ratio: *47.5%*

Source: Parish Register – Baptismal entries.

Glossary of Portuguese terms

Aldeia: Village. Rural settlement of considerable size. In this region, any community with a population over about 400 is considered a large 'village'. Smaller settlements are *lugares*, or hamlets, although the borderline between hamlet and village is not of course a rigid one.

Alqueire: Dry capacity measure for grain equivalent in Fontelas to 17 litres, or just under an English bushel. This measure varies from region to region, and indeed from hamlet to hamlet, and is used by villagers for calculating the productive capacity and surface area of unirrigated cereal plots.

Azinheira (*Quercus Ilex*): Holm-oak or evergreen oak, uncommon or entirely absent in the area around Fontelas.

Bairro: Hamlet section or neighbourhood comprising a group of houses which are either physically connected to one another or located relatively close together.

Baldio: Common-land. Terrain which is either uncultivated or entirely uncultivable and suitable only for pasturage, firewood, or the collection of shrub plants for litter and stones for house construction. Common-land is usually under the tacit *de facto* control of the residents of each hamlet, although in legal terms the land may actually be owned and administered *de jure* by a parish, municipal, or even a national administrative body.

Cabaneiro/a: Cottager. Villager working for other villagers for payment in kind or wages. This obsolete term referred formerly both to the small *cabanas* or cottages of these villagers as well as to their manual digging labour (*cavar*) performed with hoes and picks.

Cabo de polícia: Chief of police. Administrative official at the hamlet level, responsible for reporting minor infractions and misdemeanours to the parish Junta or the town Câmara. This post carries little actual weight in social terms within specific hamlets.

Câmara Municipal (Câmara): Town Council. Local government body at the municipal level, above the level of the Junta, or Parish Council. Mosteiro parish was elevated to municipal level from 1837 to 1854, and all references to the Mosterio Câmara in this book refer exclusively to those years. To avoid confusion, the term 'town Câmara' refers to the corresponding contemporary body in the municipal town, as distinct from the defunct nineteenth-century Mosteiro Câmara.

Carnaval: Shrove Tuesday Masquerade. Winter festival marking the beginning of Lent, at which children and adults parade the hamlet in masks, collecting donations of food and money from door to door.

Carqueja (*Pterospartum tridentatum*): Broom plant, somewhat less common in Fontelas than the broom plant *giesta*.

Carvalho da Beira (*Quercus tozza*): Black-oak or Pyrenees oak, abundant in Fontelas and providing firewood, leaves for litter, and acorns for pig-feed.

Carvalho negral (*Quercus tozza*/*Quercus pyrenaica*): Black-oak or Pyrenees oak, abundant in Fontelas and used for the same purpose as the *Carvalho da Beira*.

Carvalho Português/*Carvalho velano* (*Quercus lusitânica*): Portuguese oak, less common in Fontelas than the black-oak, but used occasionally for the same purpose as the latter.

Castanheiro (*Castanea sativa*): Sweet chestnut-tree, very abundant in and around Fontelas.

Compadre/*comadre*: Co-parent. Two villagers become co-parents when one of them is chosen as the godfather or godmother of a child at a baptism. This horizontal *compadrio* (co-parenthood) tie between the co-parents is distinct from (and indeed much more diffuse than) the vertical relations established between each godparent and the baptized child.

Concelho: Municipality. Portuguese administrative division between the levels of the district and the parish. Mosteiro was temporarily elevated to the level of a municipality comprising 8 parishes from 1837 to 1854.

Conselho: Hamlet council. This institution is called together to discuss and implement public works of common concern to all or most villagers. Meetings of the council are attended by one male representative from each resident household, but female-headed households are always consulted prior to any definitive collective action.

Cortinha: Kitchen-garden. Small plot of highly fertile, irrigated land used to grow household vegetables. These plots are located just outside or close by their owners' houses.

Couto: A plot of land either leased out under seigneurial tenure, or any portion of land temporarily restricted for specific use by a given hamlet. This term is rarely used today in Fontelas but appears in parish records from the nineteenth century.

Doméstica: Housewife or 'woman engaged in housework'. Less commonly used in Fontelas today, this term referred in parish records to women (of all social groups) engaged in their own housework as distinct from wage labour *outside* the household.

Estêva (*Cistus ladaniferus*): Cistus or rock-rose. A shrub plant used occasionally as firewood and litter in animal stables.

Folha: One of the two sides (literally 'leaf'/'page') of the hamlet's terrain devoted to cereal production. Each side of the hamlet's dry grain land is cultivated every other year, thus continually alternating sown and fallow periods.

Freguesia: Parish. Portuguese administrative division below the municipal level, formerly termed a *paróquia*. Several hamlets or villages usually comprise each rural parish.

Giesta (genus *Genista* and *Cytisus*): Broom plant, used in large quantities as firewood and as litter in animal stables.

Guarda-fiscal: Border Guard. Local municipal official stationed in a hamlet close to the Portuguese–Spanish border. These guards are responsible for checking all traffic across the frontier, and particularly for patrolling the more isolated border areas between hamlets for contraband.

Guarda-republicano: Republican Guard. Municipal official concerned with 'law and order' in a general sense (civil and criminal offences). These guards are normally stationed in each municipal town and are responsible for patrolling all of the hamlets and villages of each municipality: their appearance in Fontelas is relatively sporadic.

Herdeiro: Heir or Co-owner. Male or female inheritor of property upon the death of a parent. Also any co-owner of a semi-communal resource such as sectional ovens, threshing-floors, and corporate water-pools. Rights in the use of the latter resources are 'inherited' by children from parents, and co-owners may jointly exclude any owner not contributing to repairs and reconstruction.

Jeira: A day's labour. One day of labour performed for payment in wages (or kind). Also an archaic form of measuring the surface area of land: a *jeira* was equivalent to the amount of unirrigated land (about 1/3 hectare) that could be ploughed by one man in one day with a team of draught animals.

Jornaleiro/a: Day-labourer. Villager working on a fairly regular basis for other villagers for payment in kind or wages. Day-labourers constituted a large part of Fontelas' population formerly, but are much less numerous today. This occupational category does *not* necessarily imply 'landlessness'.

Junta de Freguesia (Junta): Parish Council. Local government body administering all of the hamlets and villages comprising a parish. This body is subordinate to the town Câmara and is concerned generally with the public affairs of the parish. The Junta is located and holds meetings in Mosteiro, 3 kilometres from Fontelas.

Junta de Parochia: Parish Council. Former term for the present-day *Junta de Freguesia*.

Latifúndia: Very large rural estates usually of a few hundred hectares or more in area, typically devoted to extensive commercial production of one crop through the employment of large numbers of wage labourers. This term is never used in Fontelas except in reference to Southern Portugal.

Lavrador/a: 'Plougher-peasant'. Villager owning a plough team of draught animals. The term suggests the English 'peasant' or 'cultivator' and refers to a form of relatively independent household production *not* involving wage labour.

Legítima: Legitim. 'Legitimate inheritance' belonging by law to the legal heirs of a deceased individual, normally consisting of 2/3 of the deceased's total property (or 1/2 in the case of an only child or childless individuals). Only 1/3 (the 'free quota') of the deceased's patrimony may be disposed of in a will, and this 1/3 must remain separate from the legitim.

Lugar: Hamlet. Rural settlement of small size, comprising anywhere from a few houses to about 400 people. Most annex hamlets (like Fontelas) lack any significant administrative bodies and they usually have simple chapels rather than churches.

Madrasta: Stepmother. This term refers either to the relation between a widower's second wife and the widower's legitimate children, or (more rarely) to that between a widower's legitimate children and the widower's common-law wife.

Minifúndio: Rural smallholding usually characterized by 'subsistence' polyculture. These holdings are relatively small in size by national standards, although there is no general agreement on the average size of a typical *minifundium* (this size varies from region to region). The term is commonly used with reference to Northern Portugal and Northern Spain, and implicitly suggests forms of 'family' labour (not wage labour).

Misericórdia: Technically a lay brotherhood in the municipal town, this term is commonly used to refer to the town hospital, whose origins were linked to religious institutions. The *Misericórdia* has no current function in Fontelas itself.

Mortório: Vigil held from about 8 p.m. to 2 a.m. on the night immediately following an individual's death.

Nogueira (*Juglans regia*): Walnut-tree, present in sparse numbers in Fontelas, but highly valued due to lucrative sales of walnuts.

Padrasto: Stepfather. The term refers technically to the relation between the second husband of a widow and the widow's former children, but it is more commonly used by a bastard child to refer to his/her mother's legal husband (who is not the bastard's biological father). It may also refer to a man cohabiting with a bastard's mother, and who is not the bastard's natural father.

Partilha: Partition of property following an individual's death. Various forms of amicable (and hostile) partitions occur in Fontelas, but the most frequent is the unwritten division of a patrimony 'by word of mouth' between all co-heirs.

Patrão: Patron/boss. Literally, a patron or influential local figure, particularly in the municipal town. The term is used in Fontelas either to refer to such outside individuals or more commonly to refer to any host or organizer of a labour-team within the hamlet.

Perfilhação: Affiliation. Legal process through which the biological father of a bastard child recognizes the latter and assumes responsibility for some form of economic support, irrespective of the nature of the tie between the father and the mother. Marriage automatically legitimates bastard children (thus precluding affiliation), but a natural child(ren) of the mother by a prior biological father may be 'concealed' as legitimated within such a marriage, while in reality remaining legally illegitimate and unaffiliated.

Pinheiro bravo (*Pinus pinaster*): Cluster pine or maritime pine, abundant in Fontelas and its surrounding area.

Poulo: Small communal meadow, normally used only for the pasturage of pigs due to the minuscule quantities of grass and hay provided. As this kind of meadow is truly communal property, technically only the entire hamlet (or the hamlet council) may regulate its use.

Proprietário/a: Large landowner. Villager with significantly large landholding and high social rank in the eyes of co-villagers. These landowners continue to constitute the élite of local notables, and they customarily hold important parish and municipal administrative posts, hire wage labourers and servants, and own most of the available agricultural machinery.

Sobreiro (*Quercus suber*): Cork-oak, uncommon or entirely absent in the area around Fontelas.

Souto: Chestnut-grove containing either wild or planted chestnut-trees. Also a coppice of any kind of shrub plant, grown for periodical cutting in order to provide firewood and litter for manure compost mixtures.

Taberna: Small shop or tavern, serving two purposes in Fontelas: (a) the provision of some daily goods needed by villagers, and (b) a public site for drinking and socializing.

Terço: 'Third' or free quota. Portion of an individual's property which may be freely disposed of through a will. This quota cannot legally include any portion of the legitim pertaining to the individual's legitimate heirs (this legitim usually constitutes 2/3 of the property if the individual has two or more children, and 1/2 if the individual is childless or has only one child).

Terra fria: 'Cold land'. Geographical term referring to the Northern, more isolated part of Trás-os-Montes province, stressing the region's mountainous terrain and cold climate.

Terra quente: 'Hot land'. Geographical term referring to the Central and Southern parts of Trás-os-Montes province, stressing this region's lower plains and warmer climate.

Tojo (*Ulex Europaeus*): Furze or common gorse, used in large quantities as firewood and as litter in animal stables.

Tornajeira: 'Day-labour exchange'. An unpaid exchange of labour between two villagers or two households, usually of the same task (threshing for threshing, vintage for vintage).

Touça: Thicket or dense woodland. Also (less commonly) a chestnut-grove.

Urze (*Calluna vulgaris*): Heather plant, used as firewood and less frequently as litter in animal stables.

Vila: Town. Municipal centre of substantial size (usually a few thousand people), administering all of the parishes and hamlets comprising a municipality. Major administrative, legal, ecclesiastical, and educational institutions are normally all concentrated within each municipal town.

Zorro/a: Bastard child. This term implies both 'fox' as well as a 'rascal' or mischief-maker on a symbolic level. On a socio-legal level, the word ceases to refer to a natural child who has been formally affiliated by his/her biological father.

Bibliography

Documentary Sources

1703–33	*Registo Paroquial* (1 book). Parish Register of baptisms, marriages, and deaths. Compiled by various parish priests of Mosteiro.
1758	*Diccionário Geográfico* (*Memórias Paroquiaes*). Compiled by Padre Luis Cardoso; 43 volumes. Ms. in Arquivo Nacional da Torre do Tombo, Lisbon.
1796	Ribeiro de Castro, Columbano Pinto (Compiler). *Mappa do Estado Actual da Provincia de Tras-os-Montes em 1796* . . . Ms. in Biblioteca Nacional, Lisbon: Códice 10 473.
1835–1968	*Minutes* (*Actas*) (5 books). Junta de Parochia of Mosteiro.
1837–54	*Minutes* (*Actas*) (6 books). Câmara Municipal of Mosteiro.
1851	*Recenseamento dos Eleitores de Parochia nas Assembleas Primarias, dos Eleitores de Deputados, e dos Elegiveis para Deputados.* Electoral Census of Adult Males. Compiled by the Câmara Municipal of Mosteiro.
1851	*Caderno de Recenseamento dos Eleitores e Elegiveis para os Cargos Municipaes.* Compiled by the Câmara Municipal of Mosteiro.
1870–1978	*Registo Paroquial* (various books). Parish Register of baptisms, marriages, and deaths. Compiled by various parish priests of Mosteiro.
1886–1909	*Rol dos Confessados da Freguezia de Mosteiro* (15 listings). Confessional Rolls. Compiled by parish priests of Mosteiro: Padres Azevedo, Moraes, and Melo.
1892	*Lançamento Parochial de Impostos Directos e para a Instrucção Primaria para o Anno 1892.* Parish Tax Listing. Compiled by the Junta de Parochia of Mosteiro.
1940	*Status Animarum da Freguezia de Mosteiro, 1940–1944* (1 listing) Compiled by the parish priest of Mosteiro: Padre Lopes.
1941–77	*Minutes* (9 books). *Grémio da Lavoura* (municipal town).
1951–78	*Livro de Contas da Igreja de Fontelas* (1 book). Church Accounts Book. Compiled by various parish priests.
1955–78	*Livro de Registo de Processos de Emigrantes* (1 book). Emigrants' Register. Compiled by the town Câmara.

Bibliography

Published works

Abrams, Philip 1982. *Historical Sociology*. Somerset: Open Books.

Adams, Paul 1971. 'Public and Private Interests in Hogar' in F.G. Bailey (ed.) *Gifts and Poison: The Politics of Reputation*. Oxford: Basil Blackwell; 167–81.

Admiralty 1942. *Spain and Portugal* (Vol. II). Oxford: Naval Intelligence Division – Geographical Handbook Series.

Aguilera, Francisco Enrique 1978. *Santa Eulalia's People: Ritual Structure and Process in an Andalucian Multicommunity*. St. Paul, Minnesota: West Publishing Co (American Ethnological Society Monograph No. 63).

Amado Mendes, José Maria 1980. 'A Província de Trás-os-Montes nos Finais do Século XVIII (Alguns Aspectos Económico-sociais)' in *Estudos Contemporâneos* No. 1: 9–44.

1981. *Trás-os-Montes nos Fins do Século XVIII segundo um Manuscrito de 1796*. Coimbra: Instituto Nacional de Investigação Científica/Centro de História da Sociedade e Cultura da Universidade de Coimbra.

Amorim, Maria Norberta de Simas Bettencourt 1973. *Rebordãos e a sua População nos Séculos XVII e XVIII (Estudo Demográfico)*. Lisboa: Imprensa Nacional/Casa da Moeda – Centro de Estudos Demográficos.

Anderson, Robert T. 1973. *Modern Europe: An Anthropological Perspective*. Pacific Palisades: Goodyear Publishing Co.

Anderson, Robert T. and Gallatin Anderson 1962. 'The Indirect Social Structure of European Village Communities' in *American Anthropologist* 64, 5 (Part 1 – October): 1016–27.

Arensberg, Conrad M. 1963. 'The Old World Peoples: The Place of European Cultures in World Ethnography' in *Anthropological Quarterly* 36, 3 (July): 75–99.

Arensberg, Conrad M. and Solon T. Kimball 1968 (1940). *Family and Community in Ireland*. Cambridge, Massachusetts: Harvard University Press.

Augustins, Georges 1981. 'Maison et Société dans les Baronnies au XIX Siècle' in Georges Augustins and Rolande Bonnain *Maisons, Mode de Vie, Société*. Tome 1 of I. Chiva and J. Goy (eds.) *Les Baronnies des Pyrénées: Anthropologie et Histoire, Permanences et Changements*. Paris: École des Hautes Études en Sciences Sociales/ Centre de Recherches Historiques; 21–122.

1982. 'Esquisse d'une Comparaison des Systèmes de Perpétuation des Groupes Domestiques dans les Sociétés Paysannes Européennes' in *Archives Européennes de Sociologie* XXIII, 1: 39–69.

Bailey, F.G. 1971 (ed.). *Gifts and Poison: The Politics of Reputation*. Oxford: Basil Blackwell.

Barlett, Peggy F. 1982. *Agricultural Choice and Change: Decision Making in a Costa Rican Community*. New Brunswick: Rutgers University Press.

Barnes, R.H., Daniel de Coppet, and R.J. Parkin (1985) (eds.) *Contexts and Levels: Anthropological Essays on Hierarchy*. Oxford: JASO Occasional Papers No. 4.

Barrett, Richard 1972. 'Social Hierarchy and Intimacy in a Spanish Town' in *Ethnology* XI, 4 (October): 386–98.

Bauer, Rainer Lutz 1980. 'Labor Migration and Depopulation in a Mountain District of Spanish Galicia'. Paper presented at the 79th Annual Meeting of the American Anthropological Association, Washington D.C., 3–7 December.

1983. 'Family Politics in a Spanish Galician Community 1750–1850'. Paper presented at the 8th Annual Meeting of the Social Science History Association, Washington D.C., 27–30 October.

Bennema, Jan Willem 1978. *Traditions of Communal Co-operation Among Portuguese*

Peasants (Preliminary Report). Amsterdam: Universiteit van Amsterdam/ Antropologisch-Sociologisch Centrum – Papers on European and Mediterranean Societies No. 11.

Berkner, Lutz K. 1972a. 'The Stem Family and the Developmental Cycle of the Peasant Household: An Eighteenth-century Austrian Example' in *American Historical Review* 77, 2 (April): 398–418.

1972b. 'Rural Family Organization in Europe: A Problem in Comparative History' in *Peasant Studies Newsletter*, 1, 4 (October): 145–56.

1975. 'The Use and Misuse of Census Data for the Historical Analysis of Family Structure' (Review article) in *Journal of Interdisciplinary History* v, 4 (Spring): 721–38.

1976. 'Inheritance, Land Tenure and Peasant Family Structure: A German Regional Comparison' in Jack Goody, Joan Thirsk, and E.P. Thompson (eds.) *Family and Inheritance: Rural Society in Western Europe 1200–1800*. Cambridge: Cambridge University Press; 71–95.

Berkner, Lutz K. and Franklin F. Mendels 1978. 'Inheritance Systems, Family Structure, and Demographic Patterns in Western Europe, 1700–1900' in Charles Tilly (ed.) *Historical Studies of Changing Fertility*. Princeton: Princeton University Press; 209–23.

Berreman, Gerald D. 1981. 'Social Inequality: A Cross-Cultural Analysis' in Gerald D. Berreman (ed.) *Social Inequality: Comparative and Developmental Approaches*. New York: Academic Press; 3–40.

Béteille, André 1976 (1969) (ed.). *Social Inequality: Selected Readings*. Harmondsworth: Penguin Books.

Birot, Pierre n.d. (1950). *Portugal*. Lisboa: Livros Horizonte.

Black, Jacob 1972. 'Tyranny as a Strategy for Survival in an "Egalitarian" Society: Luri Facts versus an Anthropological Mystique' in *Man* 7, 4 (December): 614–34.

Bloch, Marc 1966 (1941). 'The Rise of Dependent Cultivation and Seignorial Institutions' in M.M. Postan (ed.) *The Cambridge Economic History of Europe* (Vol. I: *The Agrarian Life of the Middle Ages*). Cambridge: Cambridge University Press; 235–90.

1978 (1931). *French Rural History: An Essay on its Basic Characteristics*. London: Routledge & Kegan Paul (translated by Janet Sondheimer).

Bloch, Maurice 1973. 'The Long Term and the Short Term: The Economic and Political Significance of the Morality of Kinship' in Jack Goody (ed.) *The Character of Kinship*. Cambridge: Cambridge University Press; 75–87.

1975. 'Property and the End of Affinity' in Maurice Bloch (ed.) *Marxist Analyses and Social Anthropology*. London: Malaby Press (ASA Studies No. 2); 203–28.

Blok, Anton 1974. *The Mafia of a Sicilian Village 1860–1960: A Study of Violent Peasant Entrepreneurs*. Oxford: Basil Blackwell.

Blok, Anton and Henk Driessen 1984. 'Mediterranean Agro-Towns as a Form of Cultural Dominance, with Special Reference to Sicily and Andalusia' in *Ethnologia Europaea* XIV, 2: 111–24.

Blum, Jerome 1971. 'The Internal Structure and Polity of the European Village Community from the Fifteenth to the Nineteenth Century' in *Journal of Modern History* 43, 4 (December): 541–76.

Boissevain, Jeremy 1975. 'Introduction: Towards a Social Anthropology of Europe' in Jeremy Boissevain and John Friedl (eds.) *Beyond the Community: Social Process in Europe*. The Hague: Department of Educational Science of the Netherlands; 9–17.

1979. 'Towards a Social Anthropology of the Mediterranean' in *Current Anthropology* 20, 1 (March): 81–5 and 85–93 (commentary and reply).

Bouquet, Mary R. 1982. 'Production and Reproduction of Family Farms in South-West England' in *Sociologia Ruralis* xxii, 3/4: 227–44.

1984a. 'Women's Work in Rural South-west England' in Norman Long (ed.) *Family and Work in Rural Societies: Perspectives on Non-wage Labour*. London: Tavistock; 142–59.

1984b. 'The Differential Integration of the Rural Family' in *Sociologia Ruralis* xxiv, 1: 65–78.

Bourdieu, Pierre 1962. 'Célibat et Condition Paysanne' in *Études Rurales* 5/6 (Avril–Septembre): 32–135.

1966. 'Condition de Classe et Position de Classe' in *Archives Européennes de Sociologie* vii: 201–23.

1976 (1972). 'Marriage Strategies as Strategies of Social Reproduction' in Robert Forster and Orest Ranum (eds.) *Family and Society: Selections from the Annales*. Baltimore: Johns Hopkins University Press; 117–44 [originally published as 'Les Stratégies Matrimoniales dans le Système de Reproduction' in *Annales E.S.C.* 27, 4/5 (Juillet–Octobre) 1972: Numéro Spécial – Famille et Société; 1105–27].

1977 (1972). *Outline of a Theory of Practice*. Cambridge: Cambridge University Press (originally published as *Esquisse d'une Théorie de la Pratique, Précédé de Trois Études d'Ethnologie Kabyle*. Geneva: Librairie Droz, 1972).

Brandão Fátima 1983. 'Death and the Survival of the Rural Household in a Northwestern Municipality' in Rui Feijó, Hermínio Martins, and João de Pina-Cabral (eds.) *Death in Portugal: Studies in Portuguese Anthropology and Modern History*. Oxford: JASO Occasional Papers No. 2; 75–87.

1985. 'Práticas de Herança no Concelho de Vieira do Minho (1870–1930)' in Albert-Alain Bourdon (ed.) *Les Campagnes Portugaises de 1870 à 1930: Image et Réalité* (Actes du Colloque, Aix-en-Provence, 2–4 Décembre 1982). Paris: Fondation Calouste Gulbenkian/Centre Culturel Portugais; 143–72.

Brandão, Fátima and Robert Rowland 1980. 'História da Propriedade e Comunidade Rural: Questões de Método' in *Análise Social* xvi, 61/62: 173–207.

Brandão, Fátima and Rui Feijó 1984. 'Entre Textos e Contextos: Os Estudos de Comunidade e as suas Fontes Históricas' in *Análise Social* xx, 83: 489–503.

Brandes, Stanley 1975. *Migration, Kinship and Community: Tradition and Transition in a Spanish Village*. New York: Academic Press.

1976. '*La Soltería*, or Why People Remain Single in Rural Spain' in *Journal of Anthropological Research* 32, 3 (Fall): 205–33.

Braudel, Fernand 1973 (1967). *Capitalism and Material Life*. London: Fontana/Collins.

Brettell, Caroline B. 1979a. 'Emigration from Rural Portugal: A Case Study and an Analysis'. Paper presented to the II International Conference on Modern Portugal, Durham, New Hampshire, 21–4 June.

1979b. 'Emigration and its Implications for the Revolution in Northern Portugal' in Lawrence S. Graham and Harry M. Makler (eds.) *Contemporary Portugal: The Revolution and its Antecedents*. Austin: Univerity of Texas Press; 281–98.

1981. 'Late Marriage, Non-marriage, and Emigration in a Northern Portuguese Village'. Paper presented at the 6th Annual Meeting of the Social Science History Association, Nashville, 22–5 October.

Burns, Robert K. 1963. 'The Circum-Alpine Culture Area: a Preliminary View' in *Anthropological Quarterly* 36, 3 (July): 130–55.

Cabral, Manuel Villaverde 1974 (ed.). *Materiais para a História da Questão Agrária em Portugal – Séculos XIX e XX*. Porto: Editorial Inova.

1976. *O Desenvolvimento do Capitalismo em Portugal no Século XIX*. Porto: A Regra do Jogo.

1978. 'Agrarian Structures and Recent Rural Movements in Portugal' in *Journal of Peasant Studies* 5, 4 (July): 411–45.

Cabral, Manuel Villaverde, Eduardo de Freitas, and João Ferreira de Almeida 1976. *Modalidades de Penetração do Capitalismo na Agricultura: Estruturas Agrárias em Portugal Continental, 1950–1970*. Lisboa: Editorial Presença.

Calhoun, C.J. 1978. 'History, Anthropology and the Study of Communities: Some Problems in Macfarlane's Proposal' in *Social History* 3, 3 (October): 363–73.

Callier-Boisvert, Collette 1966. 'Soajo: Une Communauté Féminine Rurale de l'Alto Minho' in *Bulletin des Études Portugaises* XXVII: 237–78.

1967. 'La Vie Rurale au Portugal: Panorama des Travaux en Langue Portugaise' in *Études Rurales* 27 (Juillet–Septembre): 95–134.

1968. 'Remarques sur le Système de Parenté et sur la Famille au Portugal' in *l'Homme* VIII, 2 (Avril–Juin): 87–103.

Cancian, Frank 1976. 'Social Stratification' in *Annual Review of Anthropology* 5: 227–48.

Carmo, Bento Pereira do 1834. *Mappa No. 1 Contendo os Concelhos, Parochias, e numero de Individuos de cada uma, segundo os recenseamentos enviados á Commissão de Estadistica, pelos respectivos Parochos, até ao anno de 1828; distribuidos segundo a Nova Divisão do territorio do Reino de Portugal, em oito Provincias, e quarenta Comarcas, determinado pelo Decreto No. 65 de 28 de Junho de 1833*. Lisboa: Imprensa Nacional.

Carter, Anthony T. 1984. 'Household Histories' in Robert McC. Netting, Richard R. Wilk, and Eric J. Arnould (eds.) *Households: Comparative and Historical Studies of the Domestic Group*. Berkeley: University of California Press; 44–83.

Carvalho da Costa, P.e António 1706, 1708, 1712. *Corografia Portugueza, e Descripçam Topografica do Famoso Reyno de Portugal, com as Noticias das fundações das Cidades, Villas, e Lugares, que contém; Varões illustres, Genealogias das Familias nobres, fundações de Conventos, Catalogos dos Bispos, antiguidades, maravilhas da natureza, edificios, e outras curiosas observaçoẽns*. 3 Volumes. Lisboa: Oficina de Valentim da Costa Deslandes/Oficina Real Deslandesiana.

Castro, Armando de 1973. *A Economia Portuguesa do Século XX (1900–1925)*. Lisboa: Edições Setenta.

Cervantes. Miguel de 1604, 1615. *Don Quixote de la Mancha*. Harmondsworth: Penguin Books (translated by J.M. Cohen, 1970).

Cervin, Vladimir 1953. 'The Ancient Swiss Cooperative Community' in *American Sociological Review* 18, 3 (June): 260–71.

Chayanov, A.V. 1966 (1925). *On the Theory of Peasant Economy* (Edition compiled by Daniel Thorner, Basile Kerblay, and R.E.F. Smith) Homewood, Illinois: Richard D. Irwin.

Christian, William 1972. *Person and God in a Spanish Valley*. New York: Seminar Press.

Código Civil Portuguez de 1867. 1870. Lisboa: Imprensa Nacional (Terceira edição oficial).

Código Civil Português de 1966. 1971. Porto: Porto Editora.

Código Civil Português de 1966. 1977. Com as Novas Alterações introduzidas pelo Decreto-Lei No. 496/77 de 25 de Novembro; Anotações de Carlos Adrião Rodrigues. Lisboa: Moraes Editores.

Cole, John W. 1977a. 'Inheritance Processes in the Italian Alps' in *Ethnohistory* 24, 2 (Spring): 117–32.

1977b. 'Anthropology Comes Part-way Home: Community Studies in Europe' in *Annual Review of Anthropology* 6: 349–78.

Comas, Dolors 1980. 'Sistema d'Herència i Estratificació Social: Les Estratègies Hereditàries en el Pirineu Aragonès' in *Quaderns de l'Institut Català d'Antropologia* 2 (Novembre): 25–55.

Concise Oxford Dictionary of Current English 1978. Oxford: Clarendon Press (Sixth edition, edited by J.B. Sykes).

Connell, K.H. 1968. *Irish Peasant Society: Four Historical Essays*. Oxford: Clarendon Press.

Crawfurd, Oswald 1880. *Portugal Old and New*. London: C. Kegan Paul and Co.

Cuisenier, Jean 1979 (ed.) *Europe as a Cultural Area*. The Hague: Mouton.

Cutileiro, José 1971. *A Portuguese Rural Society*. Oxford: Clarendon Press.

1973. 'The Anthropologist in His Own Society' in *Proceedings of the 10th Annual ASA Conference*, St John's College, Oxford, July.

1977. *Ricos e Pobres no Alentejo (Uma Sociedade Rural Portuguesa)*. Lisboa: Livraria Sá da Costa.

Davis, John 1973. *Land and Family in Pisticci*. London: Athlone Press (LSE Monographs on Social Anthropology No. 48).

1977. *People of the Mediterranean: An Essay in Comparative Social Anthropology*. London: Routledge & Kegan Paul.

Descamps, Paul 1935 *Le Portugal: La Vie Sociale Actuelle*. Paris: Firmin-Didot.

DGSF (Direcção Geral de Serviços Florestais e Aquícolas) 1950. *Projecto de Arborização do Perímetro Florestal da "Serra da P."* Bragança.

Dias, António Jorge 1948. *Vilarinho da Furna: Uma Aldeia Comunitária*. Porto: Instituto para a Alta Cultura/Centro de Estudos de Etnologia Peninsular.

1961. *Portuguese Contribution to Cultural Anthropology*. Johannesburg: Witwatersrand University Press.

1973–4. 'Aspects of Ethnology' in *Ethnologia Europaea* VII, 2: 133–82.

1981 (1953). *Rio de Onor: Comunitarismo Agro-pastoril*. Lisboa: Editorial Presença – Second edition (original edition – Porto: Instituto para a Alta Cultura/Centro de Estudos de Etnologia Peninsular, 1953).

1982 (1948). *Os Arados Portugueses e as Suas Prováveis Origens*. Lisboa: Imprensa Nacional/Casa da Moeda.

Diskin, Martin 1979. 'The Peasant Family Archive: Sources for an Ethnohistory of the Present' in *Ethnohistory* 26, 3 (Summer): 209–29.

Douglass, William A. 1969. *Death in Murélaga: Funerary Ritual in a Spanish Basque Village*. Seattle: University of Washington Press.

1980. 'The South Italian Family: A Critique' in *Journal of Family History* 5, 4 (Winter): 338–59.

1984. 'Sheep Ranchers and Sugar Growers: Property Transmission in the Basque Immigrant Family of the American West and Australia' in Robert McC. Netting, Richard R. Wilk, and Eric J. Arnould (eds.) *Households: Comparative and Historical Studies of the Domestic Group*. Berkeley: University of California Press; 109–29.

Dovring, Folke 1965 (1955). *Land and Labor in Europe in the Twentieth Century: A Comparative Survey of Recent Agrarian History*. The Hague: Martinus Nijhoff.

Duby, Georges 1978 (1969). 'Medieval Agriculture 900–1500' in Carlo M. Cipolla (ed.) *The Fontana Economic History of Europe* (Vol. I: *The Middle Ages*). London: Fontana/Collins; 175–220.

1978. *Medieval Marriage: Two Models from Twelfth-Century France*. Baltimore: Johns Hopkins University Press.

Du Boulay, Juliet 1974. *Portrait of a Greek Mountain Village*. Oxford: Clarendon Press.

Duke de Chatelet 1809. *Travels of the Duke de Chatelet in Portugal. Comprehending Interesting Particulars relative to the Colonies; the Earthquake of Lisbon; the Marquis of Pombal, and the Court*. 2 Volumes. London: J.J. Stockdale (translated from the French by John Joseph Stockdale).

Dumont, René 1964. *Types of Rural Economy: Studies in World Agriculture*. London: Methuen.

East, Gordon 1966. *An Historical Geography of Europe*. London: Methuen.

Erasmus, Charles 1956. 'Culture Structure and Process: The Occurrence and Disappearance of Reciprocal Farm Labor' in *Southwestern Journal of Anthropology* 12, 4 (Winter): 444–69.

Evans, E. Estyn 1970 (1956) 'The Ecology of Peasant Life in Western Europe' in William L. Thomas, Jr. (ed.) *Man's Role in Changing the Face of the Earth* (Vol. I). Chicago: University of Chicago Press; 217–39.

Evans-Pritchard, E.E. 1961. *Anthropology and History: A Lecture*. Manchester: Manchester University Press.

Fél, Edit and Tamás Hofer 1969. *Proper Peasants: Traditional Life in a Hungarian Village*. Chicago: Aldine (Viking Fund Publications in Anthropology No. 46).

Fernandez, James W. 1981. 'The Call to the Commons'. Paper presented at the SSRC Conference on 'Institutionalized Forms of Cooperation and Reciprocity in Europe' organized by Sandra Ott and John Campbell, St Antony's College, Oxford, 9–11 September.

1983. 'Consciousness and Class in southern Spain' (Review article) in *American Ethnologist* 10, 1 (February): 165–73.

Filipović, Mil S. 1958. 'Vicarious Paternity among Serbs and Croats' in *Southwestern Journal of Anthropology* 14, 2 (Summer): 156–67.

Flandrin, Jean-Louis 1972. 'Mariage Tardif et Vie Sexuelle: Discussions et Hypothèses de Recherche' in *Annales E.S.C.* 27, 6 (Novembre–Décembre): 1351–78.

Floud, Roderick 1984. 'Quantitative History and People's History: Two Methods in Conflict?' in *History Workshop* 17 (Spring): 113–24.

Fontes, António Lourenço 1974. *Etnografia Transmontana I: Crenças e Tradições do Barroso*. Montalegre: Edição do autor.

1977. *Etnografia Transmontana II: O Comunitarismo de Barroso*. Montalegre: Edição do autor.

Fortes, Meyer 1970 (1949). 'Time and Social Structure: An Ashanti Case Study' in Meyer Fortes (ed.) *Time and Social Structure and Other Essays*. London: Athlone Press (LSE Monographs on Social Anthropology No. 40); 1–32.

Fox, Robin 1978. *The Tory Islanders: A People of the Celtic Fringe*. Cambridge: Cambridge University Press.

1979. 'The Visiting Husband on Tory Island' in *Journal of Comparative Family Studies* x, 2 (Summer): 163–90.

Franklin, S.H. 1969. *The European Peasantry: The Final Phase*. London: Methuen.

Freeman, Susan Tax 1968. 'Corporate Village Organisation in the Sierra Ministra: An Iberian Structural Type' in *Man* 3, 3 (September): 477–84.

1970. *Neighbors: The Social Contract in a Castilian Hamlet*. Chicago: University of Chicago Press.

1973. 'Introduction: Studies in Rural European Social Organization' in *American Anthropologist* 75, 3 (June): 743–50.

1979. *The Pasiegos: Spaniards in No Man's Land*. Chicago: University of Chicago Press.

Fried, Morton H. 1967. *The Evolution of Political Society: An Essay in Political*

Anthropology. New York: Random House.
1975. *The Notion of Tribe*. Menlo Park: Cummings Publishing Co.
Friedl, Ernestine 1962. *Vasilika: A Village in Modern Greece*. New York: Holt, Rinehart & Winston.
Friedl, John 1974. *Kippel: A Changing Village in the Alps*. New York: Holt, Rinehart & Winston.
Gaunt, David 1982. *Memoir on History and Anthropology*. Stockholm: Swedish Council for Research in the Humanities and Social Sciences (HSFR).
Geertz, Clifford 1961. 'Studies in Peasant Life: Community and Society' in *Biennial Review of Anthropology*: 1–41.
1972. 'The Wet and the Dry: Traditional Irrigation in Bali and Morocco' in *Human Ecology* 1, 1: 23–39.
Gellner, Ernest and John Waterbury 1977 (eds.). *Patrons and Clients in Mediterranean Societies*. London: Duckworth.
Gilmore, David 1977a. 'The Class Consciousness of the Andalusian Rural Proletarians in Historical Perspective' in *Ethnohistory* 24, 2 (Spring): 149–61.
1980. *The People of the Plain: Class and Community in Lower Andalusia*. New York: Columbia University Press.
1982. 'Anthropology of the Mediterranean Area' in *Annual Review of Anthropology* 11: 175–205.
Gilsenan, Michael 1977. 'Against Patron-client Relations' in Ernest Gellner and John Waterbury (eds.) *Patrons and Clients in Mediterranean Societies*. London: Duckworth; 167–83.
Goldey, Patricia 1983. 'Migração e Relações de Produção: A Terra e o Trabalho numa Aldeia do Minho: 1876–1976' in *Análise Social* XIX, 77/78/79: 995–1021.
Goldschmidt, Walter and Evalyn Jacobson Kunkel 1971. 'The Structure of the Peasant Family' in *American Anthropologist* 73, 5 (October): 1058–76.
Goody, Jack 1958 (ed.) *The Developmental Cycle of Domestic Groups*. Cambridge: Cambridge University Press.
1969. 'Inheritance, Property and Marriage in Africa and Eurasia' in *Sociology* 3, 1 (January): 55–76.
1970a. 'Marriage Prestations, Inheritance and Descent in Pre-industrial Societies' in *Journal of Comparative Family Studies* 1, 1 (Autumn): 37–54.
1970b. 'Sideways or Downwards? Lateral and Vertical Succession, Inheritance and Descent in Africa and Eurasia' in *Man* 5, 4 (December): 627–38.
1971. 'Class and Marriage in Africa and Eurasia' in *American Journal of Sociology* 76, 4 (January): 585–603.
1972a. 'Domestic Groups'. Reading, Massachusetts: Addison-Wesley Module in Anthropology No. 28: 1–32.
1972b. 'The Evolution of the Family' in Peter Laslett (ed.) *Household and Family in Past Time*. Cambridge: Cambridge University Press; 103–24.
1973a. 'Bridewealth and Dowry in Africa and Eurasia' in Jack Goody and S.J. Tambiah *Bridewealth and Dowry*. Cambridge: Cambridge University Press; 1–58.
1973b. 'Strategies of Heirship' in *Comparative Studies in Society and History* XV: 3–20.
1976a. *Production and Reproduction: A Comparative Study of the Domestic Domain*. Cambridge: Cambridge University Press.
1976b. 'Introduction' and 'Inheritance, Property and Women: Some Comparative Considerations' in Jack Goody, Joan Thirsk, and E.P. Thompson (eds.) *Family and Inheritance: Rural Society in Western Europe 1200–1800*. Cambridge: Cambridge University Press; 1–9 and 10–36.

1983. *The Development of the Family and Marriage in Europe*. Cambridge: Cambridge University Press.

Goody, Jack and Esther Goody 1967. 'The Circulation of Women and Children in Northern Ghana' in *Man* 2, 2 (June): 226–48.

Goody, Jack, Barrie Irving, and Nicky Tahany 1971. 'Causal Inferences Concerning Inheritance and Property' in *Human Relations* 24, 4 (August): 295–314.

Goubert, Pierre 1977. 'Family and Province: A Contribution to the Knowledge of Family Structures in Early Modern France' in *Journal of Family History* 2, 3 (Fall): 179–95.

Graça Branco, Vasco Hernâni da 1970. *Guia Prático da Divisão da Herança*. Porto: Tipografia A Portuense.

Guillet, David 1983. 'Toward a Cultural Ecology of Mountains: The Central Andes and the Himalayas Compared' in *Current Anthropology* 24, 5 (December): 561–74.

Habakkuk, H.J. 1955. 'Family Structure and Economic Change in Nineteenth-century Europe' in *Journal of Economic History* 15: 1–12.

Hajnal, John 1965. 'European Marriage Patterns in Perspective' in D.V. Glass and D.E.C. Eversley (eds.) *Population in History: Essays in Historical Demography*. London: Edward Arnold; 101–43.

1982. 'Two Kinds of Preindustrial Household Formation System' in *Population and Development Review* 8, 3 (September): 449–94.

Hammel, Eugene A. and Peter Laslett 1974. 'Comparing Household Structure Over Time and Between Cultures' in *Comparative Studies in Society and History* 16, 1 (January): 73–109.

Hanssen, Börje 1979/80. 'Household, Classes, and Integration Processes in a Scandinavian Village over 300 Years' in *Ethnologia Europaea* XI, 1: 76–118.

Herzfeld, Michael 1980. 'Honour and Shame: Problems in the Comparative Analysis of Moral Systems' in *Man* 15, 2 (June): 339–51.

Hilton, Rodney 1978. 'Reasons for Inequality among Medieval Peasants' in *Journal of Peasant Studies* 5, 3 (April): 271–84.

Hobsbawm, Eric 1965 (1959). *Primitive Rebels: Studies in Archaic Forms of Social Movement in the 19th and 20th Centuries*. New York: W.W. Norton.

1972 (1969). *Bandits*. Harmondsworth: Penguin Books.

Hoffman, Richard C. 1975. 'Medieval Origins of the Common Fields' in W. Parker and E.L. Jones (eds.) *European Peasants and their Markets: Essays in Agrarian Economic History*. Princeton: Princeton University Press; 23–71.

Houston, J.M. 1964. *The Western Mediterranean World: An Introduction to its Regional Landscapes*. London: Longmans.

Instituto de Alta Cultura 1974. *In Memoriam António Jorge Dias*. 3 Volumes. Lisboa: Junta de Investigações Científicas do Ultramar.

IGC (Instituto Geográfico e Cadastral) 1960. *Carta Corográfica de Portugal na Escala 1/50,000*. Lisboa: Edição de 1960.

INE (Instituto Nacional de Estatística) 1864–. *Recenseamento Geral da População*. Lisboa: 1864, 1878, 1890, 1900, 1911, 1920, 1930, 1940, 1950, 1960, 1970.

1955. *Inquérito às Explorações Agrícolas do Continente em 1954*. (Vol. III. Províncias do Minho, Trás-os-Montes e Alto Douro). Lisboa.

1968. *Inquérito às Explorações Agrícolas do Continente em 1968*. Lisboa.

Iszaevich, Abraham 1975. 'Emigrants, Spinsters and Priests: The Dynamics of Demography in Spanish Peasant Societies' in *Journal of Peasant Studies* 2, 3 (April): 292–312.

Iturra, Raúl 1977. 'Strategies of Social Recruitment: A Case of Mutual Help in Rural

Galicia' in Milan Stuchlik (ed.) *The Queen's University Papers in Social Anthropology* (Vol. 2 – Goals and Behaviour); 75–93.

1980. 'Strategies in the Domestic Organization of Production in Rural Galicia (N.W. Spain)' in *Cambridge Anthropology* 6, 1/2 (Spring/Summer: Double Issue – Studies in European Ethnography): 88–129.

1985. 'Marriage, Ritual and Profit: The Production of Producers in a Portuguese Village' in *Social Compass* XXXII, 1: 73–92.

Jenkins, Robin 1979. *The Road to Alto: An Account of Peasants, Capitalists and the Soil in the Mountains of Southern Portugal*. London: Pluto Press.

Jones, Anne M. 1983. 'Extending the Family: Family Household Structures and Patriline Continuity in Haute Savoie, 1561–1968'. Paper presented at the Seminar on 'Social Reproduction: Population, Family and Property', Gulbenkian Institute of Science, Oeiras, Portugal, 11–24 September.

JCI (Junta de Colonização Interna) 1939. *Reconhecimento dos Baldios do Continente*. 2 Volumes. Lisboa: Ministério da Agricultura.

Khera, Sigrid 1972a. 'An Austrian Peasant Village Under Rural Industrialization' in *Behavior Science Notes* 7, 1: 29–36.

1972b. 'Kin Ties and Social Interaction in an Austrian Peasant Village with Divided Land Inheritance' in *Behavior Science Notes* 7, 4: 349–65.

1973. 'Social Stratification and Land Inheritance among Austrian Peasants' in *American Anthropologist* 75, 3 (June): 814–23.

1981. 'Illegitimacy and Mode of Land Inheritance among Austrian Peasants' in *Ethnology* XX, 4 (October): 307–23.

Kimball, Solon T. 1949. 'Rural Social Organization and Co-operative Labor' in *American Journal of Sociology* 55, 1 (July): 38–49.

Kussmaul, Ann 1981. *Servants in Husbandry in Early Modern England*. Cambridge: Cambridge University Press.

Laslett, Peter (with the assistance of Richard Wall) 1972 (ed.) *Household and Family in Past Time*. Cambridge: Cambridge University Press.

1977a. 'Characteristics of the Western Family Considered Over Time' in *Journal of Family History* 2, 2 (Summer): 89–115.

1977b. *Family Life and Illicit Love in Earlier Generations*. Cambridge: Cambridge University Press.

1980a. 'Introduction: Comparing Illegitimacy Over Time and Between Cultures' in Peter Laslett, Karla Oosterveen, and Richard Smith (eds.) *Bastardy and its Comparative History*. London: Edward Arnold; 1–65.

1980b. 'The Bastardy Prone Sub-society' in Peter Laslett, Karla Oosterveen, and Richard Smith (eds.) *Bastardy and its Comparative History*. London: Edward Arnold; 217–40.

1981. 'Illegitimate Fertility and the Matrimonial Market' in J. Dupâquier *et al* (eds.) *Marriage and Remarriage in Populations of the Past*. New York: Academic Press; 461–71.

1983. 'Family and Household as Work Group and Kin Group: Areas of Traditional Europe Compared' in Richard Wall (in collaboration with Jean Robin and Peter Laslett) (eds.) *Family Forms in Historic Europe*. Cambridge: Cambridge University Press; 513–63.

1984. 'The Family as a Knot of Individual Interests' in Robert McC. Netting, Richard R. Wilk, and Eric J. Arnould (eds.) *Households: Comparative and Historical Studies of the Domestic Group*. Berkeley: University of California Press; 353–79.

Lawrence, Denise L. 1982. 'Reconsidering the Menstrual Taboo: A Portuguese Case' in *Anthropological Quarterly* 55, 2 (April): 84–98.

Leach, Edmund 1961. *Pul Eliya – A Village in Ceylon: A Study of Land Tenure and Kinship*. Cambridge: Cambridge University Press.

Lee, William R. 1977. 'Bastardy and the Socioeconomic Structure of South Germany' in *Journal of Interdisciplinary History* VII, 3 (Winter): 403–25.

Leitão, Joaquim 1908, 1909, 1910 (ed.). *Illustração Trasmontana: Archivo Pittoresco, Litterario e Scientifico das Terras Trasmontanas*. Porto: Typographia Occidental.

Le Play, Frédéric 1982. *On Family, Work, and Social Change*. Edited, translated, and with an Introduction by Catherine Bodard Silver. Chicago: University of Chicago Press.

Le Roy Ladurie, Emmanuel 1976 (1972). 'Family Structures and Inheritance Customs in Sixteenth-century France' in Jack Goody, Joan Thirsk, and E.P. Thompson (eds.) *Family and Inheritance: Rural Society in Western Europe 1200–1800*. Cambridge: Cambridge University Press; 37–70.

1978 (1975). *Montaillou: Cathars and Catholics in a French Village, 1294–1324*. Harmondsworth: Penguin Books.

Lévi-Strauss, Claude 1973. 'The Story of Asdiwal' in Edmund Leach (ed.) *The Structural Study of Myth and Totemism*. London: Tavistock; 1–47.

Lewis, Bernard 1982. *The Muslim Discovery of Europe*. New York: W.W. Norton.

Leyton, Elliott H. 1970. 'Spheres of Inheritance in Aughnaboy' in *American Anthropologist* 72, 6 (December): 1378–88.

Lisón-Tolosana, Carmelo 1966. *Belmonte de los Caballeros: A Sociological Study of a Spanish Town*. Oxford: Clarendon Press (reprinted as *Belmonte de los Caballeros: Anthropology and History in an Aragonese Community*, Princeton: Princeton University Press; with a Foreword by James W. Fernandez, 1983).

1971. *Antropología Cultural de Galicia*. Madrid: Siglo XXI Editores.

1976. 'The Ethics of Inheritance' in J.G. Peristiany (ed.) *Mediterranean Family Structures*. Cambridge: Cambridge University Press; 305–15.

Livermore, Harold V. 1971. *The Origins of Spain and Portugal*. London: George Allen & Unwin.

Livi Bacci, Massimo 1971. *A Century of Portuguese Fertility*. Princeton: Princeton University Press.

Löfgren, Orvar 1974. 'Family and Household among Scandinavian Peasants: An Exploratory Essay' in *Ethnologia Scandinavica* 2: 17–52 (reprinted in Michael Anderson (ed.) *Sociology of the Family: Selected Readings*, Harmondsworth: Penguin Books, 2nd edition, 1980; 80–124).

Loizos, Peter 1975a. 'Changes in Property Transfer among Greek Cypriot Villagers' in *Man* 10, 4 (December): 503–23.

1975b. *The Greek Gift: Politics in a Cypriot Village*. Oxford: Basil Blackwell.

Macedo dos Santos, M., R.C. dos Santos, and J.F. Pitão (eds.) 1978. *Reforma Agrária Anotada (Arrendamento Rural. Baldios – Legislação Actualizada)*. Coimbra: Parâmetro.

Macfarlane, Alan 1977a. 'History, Anthropology, and the Study of Communities' in *Social History* 5 (May): 631–52.

1977b. 'Historical Anthropology' (Frazer Memorial Lecture – 1973) in *Cambridge Anthropology* 3, 3: 1–21.

1977c. *Reconstructing Historical Communities* (with the assistance of Sarah Harrison and Charles Jardine). Cambridge: Cambridge University Press.

1980a. 'Demographic Structures and Cultural Regions in Europe' in *Cambridge*

Anthropology 6, 1/2 (Spring/Summer: Double Issue – Studies in European Ethnography): 1–17.

1980b. 'Illegitimacy and Illegitimates in English History' in Peter Laslett, Karla Oosterveen, and Richard Smith (eds.) *Bastardy and its Comparative History*. London: Edward Arnold; 71–85.

Magro, Abílio 1912. *A Revolução de Couceiro: Revelações Escandalosas, Confidencias, Crimes*. Porto: Imprensa Moderna.

Malheiro Dias, Carlos 1912. *Do Desafio à Debandada*. 2 Volumes. Lisboa: Livraria Clássica Editora.

Martinez-Alier, Juan 1971. *Labourers and Landowners in Southern Spain*. London: George Allen & Unwin.

Martins, Pe. Firmino 1928. *Folklore do Concelho de Vinhais*. Coimbra: Imprensa da Universidade.

1939. *Folklore de Concelho de Vinhais* (Vol. II). Lisboa: Imprensa Nacional.

Marx, Karl 1852. 'The Eighteenth Brumaire of Louis Bonaparte' in Karl Marx and Frederick Engels *Selected Works*. New York: International Publishers, 1968; 95–180.

McArdle, Frank 1978. *Altopascio: A Study in Tuscan Rural Society, 1587–1784*. Cambridge: Cambridge University Press.

Medeiros, Fernando 1985. 'Groupes Domestiques et Habitat Rural dans le Nord du Portugal: La Contribution de l'École de Le Play (1908–1934)' in Albert-Alain Bourdon (ed.) *Les Campagnes Portugaises de 1870 à 1930: Image et Réalité* (Actes du Colloque, Aix-en-Provence, 2–4 Décembre 1982). Paris: Fondation Calouste Gulbenkian/Centre Culturel Portugais; 215–41.

Medick, Hans and David Warren Sabean 1984 (eds.). *Interest and Emotion: Essays on the Study of Family and Kinship*. Cambridge and Paris: Cambridge University Press/Maison des Sciences de l'Homme.

Mendras, Henri and Ioan Mihailescu 1982 (eds.). *Theories and Methods in Rural Community Studies*. Oxford: Pergamon Press/European Coordination Centre for Research and Documentation in Social Sciences (Vienna).

Ministério da Administração Interna 1976a. *Eleição para a Assembleia da República – 1976*. Lisboa: Imprensa Nacional/Casa da Moeda.

1976b. *Eleição para a Presidência da República – 1976*. Lisboa: Imprensa Nacional/ Casa da Moeda.

1977. *Eleições para os Órgãos das Autarquias Locais – 1976*. Lisboa: Imprensa Nacional/Casa da Moeda.

Mintz, Sidney W. 1974. 'The Rural Proletariat and the Problem of Rural Proletarian Consciousness' in *Journal of Peasant Studies* 1, 3 (April): 291–325.

Mitterauer, Michael 1981. 'Marriage Without Co-residence: A Special Type of Historic Family Forms in Rural Carinthia' in *Journal of Family History* 6, 2 (Summer): 177–81.

Mitterauer, Michael and Reinhard Sieder 1979. 'The Developmental Process of Domestic Groups: Problems of Reconstruction and Possibilities of Interpretation' in *Journal of Family History* 4, 3 (Fall): 257–84.

1982 (1977). *The European Family: Patriarchy to Partnership from the Middle Ages to the Present*. Oxford: Basil Blackwell.

Muller, Viana 1985. 'Origins of Class and Gender Hierarchy in Northwest Europe' in *Dialectical Anthropology* 10, 1/2 (July): 93–105.

Murphy, Robert F. 1979. *An Overture to Social Anthropology*. Englewood Cliffs: Prentice Hall.

Murray, Alexander Callander 1983. *Germanic Kinship Structure; Studies in Law and Society in Antiquity and the Early Middle Ages*. Toronto: Pontifical Institute of Mediaeval Studies.

Netting, Robert McC. 1972. 'Of Men and Meadows: Strategies of Alpine Land Use' in *Anthropological Quarterly* 45, 3 (July): 132–44.

1974. 'The System Nobody Knows: Village Irrigation in the Swiss Alps' in Theodore E. Downing and McGuire Gibson (eds.) *Irrigation's Impact on Society*. Tucson: University of Arizona Press; 67–75.

1976. 'What Alpine Peasants Have in Common: Observations on Communal Tenure in a Swiss Village' in *Human Ecology* 4, 2: 135–46.

1979a. 'Patterns of Marriage in a Swiss Alpine Village' in *Ethnologia Europaea* XI, 1:139–55.

1979b. 'Household Dynamics in a Nineteenth Century Swiss Village' in *Journal of Family History* 4, 1 (Spring): 39–58.

1981. *Balancing on an Alp: Ecological Change and Continuity in a Swiss Mountain Community*. Cambridge: Cambridge University Press.

1982. 'Some Home Truths on Household Size and Wealth' in *American Behavioral Scientist* 25, 6 (July/August): 641–62.

1984. 'Reflections on an Alpine Village as Ecosystem' in Emilio F. Moran (ed.) *The Ecosystem Concept in Anthropology*. Boulder, Colorado: Westview Press; 225–35.

Netting, Robert McC. and Randall McGuire 1982. 'Leveling Peasants? the Maintenance of Equality in a Swiss Alpine Community' in *American Ethnologist* 9, 2 (May): 269–90.

Niederer, Arnold 1965. 'Corvées Communales et Entraide Paysanne au Portugal et en Suisse; in *Actas do Congresso Internacional de Etnografia*. Vol. III (Santo Tirso, 10–18 July 1963) Lisboa: Junta de Investigações do Ultramar; 385–92.

O'Neill, Brian Juan 1974. *Oral Literature and Social Change in a Galician Peasant Village*. M.A. Thesis: Department of Literature, University of Essex.

1982a. 'Trabalho Cooperativo numa Aldeia do Norte de Portugal' in *Análise Social* XVIII, 70: 7–34.

1982b. *Social Hierarchy in a Northern Portuguese Hamlet, 1870–1978*. Ph.D. Thesis: Department of Anthropology, London School of Economics and Political Science.

1983. 'Dying and Inheriting in Rural Trás-os-Montes' in *Journal of the Anthropological Society of Oxford* XIV, 1 (Hilary Term): 44–74 (reprinted in Rui Feijó, Hermínio Martins, and João de Pina-Cabral [eds.] *Death in Portugal: Studies in Portuguese Anthropology and Modern History*. Oxford: JASO Occasional Papers No. 2; 44–74).

1984a. 'Social Conflict in the Galician Folktale' in *Cahiers de Littérature Orale* 14 (En Quête d'Identité): 13–51.

1984b. *Proprietários, Lavradores e Jornaleiras: Desigualdade Social numa Aldeia Transmontana, 1870–1978*. Lisboa: Publicações Dom Quixote – Colecção 'Portugal de Perto' No. 7 (Portuguese edition of 1982 Doctoral Thesis).

1985. 'Family Cycles and Inheritance in Rural Portugal' in *Peasant Studies* 12, 3 (Spring): 199–213.

O'Neill, Brian Juan and Sandra McAdam Clark 1980. 'Agrarian Reform in Southern Portugal' in *Critique of Anthropology* 4, 15 (Spring): 47–74.

O'Neill, Nena and George O'Neill 1984 (1972). *Open Marriage: A New Life Style for Couples*. New York: M. Evans.

Orlove, Benjamin S. 1977. 'Inequality Among Peasants: The Forms and Uses of

Reciprocal Exchange in Andean Peru' in Rhoda Halperin and James Dow (eds.) *Peasant Livelihood: Studies in Economic Anthropology and Cultural Ecology*. New York: St Martin's Press; 201–14.

1980. 'Ecological Anthropology' in *Annual Review of Anthropology* 9: 325–73.

Ott, Sandra 1980. 'Blessed Bread, "First Neighbours" and Asymmetric Exchange in the Basque Country' in *Archives Européennes de Sociologie* XXI, 1: 40–58.

Pais de Brito, Joaquim 1977. 'Primeiras Notas Sobre o Conselho em Rio de Onor' Unpublished Research Report.

1981. 'L'Ordre de l'Ordre: Rotativité dans les Travaux et Organisation de l'Espace dans un Village du Nordest de Portugal'. Paper presented at the Colloque d'*Ethnologia Europaea*, Montmajou, Octobre.

1983. 'La Maison et les Stratégies de l'Identité sur l'Usage des Noms a Rio de Onor' in *L'Uomo* VII, 1/2 (Sistemi di Denominazione nelle Società Europee e Cicli di Sviluppo Familiare: Atti de Primo Seminario degli 'Incontri Mediterranei di Etnologia', Siena, 25–6 Febbraio 1982): 145–54.

1987. *Les Maisons, Le Village: Organisation Communautaire et Reproduction Sociale d'un Village de Montagne – Rio de Onor*. Thèse de Doctorat d'État: Université d'Aix-en-Provence.

Peixoto, Rocha 1908. 'Formas de Vida Comunalista' in Manuel Villaverde Cabral (ed.) *Materiais para a História da Questão Agrária em Portugal – Séculos XIX e XX*. Porto: Editorial Inova, 1974; 391–405.

Pereira, Benjamim 1965. *Bibliografia Analítica de Etnografia Portuguesa*. Lisboa: Instituto de Alta Cultura/Centro de Estudos de Etnologia Peninsular.

1973. *Máscaras Portuguesas*. Lisboa: Junta de Investigações do Ultramar/Museu de Etnologia do Ultramar.

Peristiany, J.G. 1966. (ed.) *Honour and Shame: The Values of Mediterranean Society*. London: Weidenfeld & Nicolson.

Pfeifer, Gottfried 1970 (1956). 'The Quality of Peasant Living in Central Europe' in William L. Thomas, Jr. (ed.) *Man's Role in Changing the Face of the Earth* Vol. I. Chicago: University of Chicago Press; 240–77.

Pina-Cabral, João de 1984a. 'Female Power and the Inequality of Wealth and Motherhood in Northwestern Portugal' in Renée Hirschon (ed.) *Women and Property – Women as Property*. London: Croom Helm; 75–91.

1984b. 'Comentários Críticos sobre a Casa e a Família no Alto Minho Rural' in *Análise Social* XX, 81/82: 263–84.

Pitkin, Donald S. 1963. 'Mediterranean Europe' in *Anthropological Quarterly* 36, 3 (July): 120–9.

Pitt-Rivers, Julian 1972 (1954). *The People of the Sierra*. Chicago: University of Chicago Press.

1977 (1963). (ed.) *Mediterranean Countrymen: Essays in the Social Anthropology of the Mediterranean*. Westport, Connecticut; Greenwood Press.

Plakans, Andrejs 1981. 'Anthropology, History, and the European Joint Family: Reflections on Modes of Research' in *Ethnologia Europaea* XII, 2: 117–32.

1984. *Kinship in the Past: An Anthropology of European Family Life 1500–1900*. Oxford: Basil Blackwell.

Plotnicov, Leonard and Arthur Tuden 1970 (eds.). *Essays in Comparative Social Stratification*. Pittsburgh: University of Pittsburgh Press.

Polonah, Luis 1985. 'Algumas Reflexões sobre o Comunitarismo em Rio de Onor' in *Factos e Ideias: Revista do Centro de Estudos de Relações Internacionais da Universidade do Minho* I, 1: 123–52.

Portela, José F.G. 1981. 'Fragueiro – Notas sobre a Agricultura Local' in *Revista*

Crítica de Ciências Sociais 7/8 (Dezembro): 217–46.
1983. 'Continuidade e Mudança em Fontim – Alguns Elementos Sobre o Modo de Vida Rural' in *Análise Social* XIX, 77/78/79: 611–33.
Pounds, Norman J.G. 1973. *An Historical Geography of Europe, 450 B.C.–A.D. 1330* (Vol. I). Cambridge: Cambridge University Press.
1979. *An Historical Geography of Europe, 1550–1840* (Vol. II). Cambridge: Cambridge University Press.
Price, Richard and Sally Price (1966a). 'Noviazgo in an Andalusian Pueblo' in *Southwestern Journal of Anthropology* 22, 3 (Autumn): 302–22.
1966b. 'Stratification and Courtship in an Andalusian Village' in *Man* I, 4 (December): 526–33.
Redclift, Michael R. 1973. 'The Future of Agriculture in a Spanish Pyrenean Village and the Decline of Communal Institutions' in *Ethnology* XII, 2 (April): 193–202.
Redfield, Robert 1973 (1953/1956). *The Little Community/Peasant Society and Culture*. Chicago: University of Chicago Press.
Rhoades, Robert E. and Stephen I. Thompson 1975. 'Adaptive Strategies in Alpine Environments: Beyond Ecological Particularism' in *American Ethnologist* 2, 3 (August): 535–51.
Ribeiro, Orlando 1967 (1945). *Portugal, O Mediterrâneo e o Atlântico: Estudo Geográfico*. Lisboa: Livraria Sá da Costa.
1968. *Mediterrâneo: Ambiente e Tradição*. Lisboa: Fundação Calouste Gulbenkian.
Ribeiro, René 1945. 'On the *Amaziado* Relationship, and other Aspects of the Family in Recife (Brazil)' in *American Sociological Review* 10, 1 (February): 44–51.
Riegelhaupt, Joyce F. 1967. 'Saloio Women: An Analysis of Informal and Formal Political and Economic Roles of Portuguese Peasant Women' in *Anthropological Quarterly* 40, 3 (July): 109–26.
1973. 'Festas and Padres: The Organization of Religious Action in a Portuguese Parish' in *American Anthropologist* 75, 3 (June): 835–52.
Rogers, Susan Carol and Sonya Salamon 1983. 'Inheritance and Social Organization among Family Farmers' in *American Ethnologist* 10, 3 (August): 529–50.
Rowland, Robert 1981. 'Âncora e Montaria, 1827: Duas Freguesias do Noroeste segundo os Livros de Registo das Companhias de Ordenanças' in *Estudos Contemporâneos* 2/3 (Número Especial: Perspectivas sobre o Norte de Portugal): 199–242.
1984. 'Sistemas Familiares e Padrões Demográficos em Portugal: Questões para uma Investigação Comparada' in *Ler História* 3: 13–32.
in press. 'Sistemas Matrimoniales en la Península Ibérica: Una Perspectiva Regional' in V. Perez Moreda and David Reher (eds.) *La Demografía Histórica de la Península Ibérica, Siglos XVI–XX* (provisional title) (Actas de las I Jornadas de Demografía Histórica, Madrid, Diciembre 1983). Madrid: Editorial Tecnos.
Rutledge, Ian 1977. 'Land Reform and the Portuguese Revolution' in *Journal of Peasant Studies* 5, 1 (October): 79–98.
Sahlins, Marshall 1972 (1965). 'On the Sociology of Primitive Exchange' in Marshall Sahlins *Stone Age Economics*. Chicago: Aldine; 185–275.
Sampaio, Alberto 1923. 'As Vilas do Norte de Portugal' in *Estudos Históricos e Económicos* (Vol. I). Porto: Livraria Chardron de Lello e Irmão; 3–254.
Sanders, Irwin T. 1955. 'Selection of Participants in a Mutual Aid Group in Rural Greece' in *Sociometry* 18, 4: 582–5 (326–9).
Scheper-Hughes, Nancy 1982 (1979). *Saints, Scholars, and Schizophrenics: Mental Illness in Rural Ireland*. Berkeley: University of California Press.
Schneider, Jane 1971. 'Of Vigilance and Virgins: Honor, Shame and Access to

Resources in Mediterranean Societies' in *Ethnology* x, 1 (January): 1–24.
1980. 'Trousseau as Treasure: Some Contradictions of Late Nineteenth-century Change in Sicily' in Eric B. Ross (ed.) *Beyond the Myths of Culture: Essays in Cultural Materialism.* New York: Academic Press; 323–56.

Segalen, Martine 1977. 'The Family Cycle and Household Structure: Five Generations in a French Village' in *Journal of Family History* 2, 3 (Fall): 223–36.

Shanin, Teodor 1971 (ed.). *Peasants and Peasant Societies: Selected Readings.* Harmondsworth: Penguin Books.
1972. *The Awkward Class – Political Sociology of Peasantry in a Developing Society: Russia 1910–1925.* Oxford: Clarendon Press.

Shorter, Edward 1971. 'Illegitimacy, Sexual Revolution, and Social Change in Modern Europe' in *Journal of Interdisciplinary History* II, 2 (Autumn): 237–72.

Shorter, Edward, John Knodel, and Etienne van de Walle 1971. 'The Decline of Non-Marital Fertility in Europe, 1880–1940' in *Population Studies* XXV, 3 (November): 375–93.

Siddle, David 1983. 'Strategies of Inheritance and Domestic Group Formation in Eighteenth-Century Savoie'. Paper presented at the Seminar on 'Social Reproduction: Population, Family and Property', Gulbenkian Institute of Science, Oeiras, Portugal: 11–24 September.

Siddle, David and Anne M. Jones 1982. 'Sources for the Reconstruction of Peasant Systems in an Upland Area of Europe 1561–1975'. University of Liverpool: Liverpool Papers in Human Geography (Working Paper No. 3).

Silbert, Albert 1977 (1960). 'O Colectivismo Agrário em Portugal: História de um Problema' in Albert Silbert *Do Portugal de Antigo Regime ao Portugal Oitocentista.* Lisboa: Livros Horizonte; 199–281.

Silverman, Sydel F. 1966.'An Ethnographic Approach to Social Stratification: Prestige in a Central Italian Community' in *American Anthropologist* 68, 4 (August): 899–921.
1967. 'The Life Crisis as a Clue to Social Functions' in *Anthropological Quarterly* 40, 3 (July): 127–38.
1968. 'Agricultural Organization, Social Structure, and Values in Italy: Amoral Familism Reconsidered' in *American Anthropologist* 70, 1 (February): 1–20.
1970. 'Stratification in Italian Communities: A Regional Contrast' in Leonard Plotnicov and Arthur Tuden (eds.) *Essays in Comparative Social Stratification.* Pittsburgh: University of Pittsburgh Press, 211–29.

Slicher Van Bath, B.H. 1963. *The Agrarian History of Western Europe: A.D. 500–1850.* London: Edward Arnold (translated by Olive Ordish).

Smith, Catherine Delano 1979. *Western Mediterranean Europe: A Historical Geography of Italy, Spain, and southern France since the Neolithic.* New York: Academic Press.

Smith, C.T. 1969. *An Historical Geography of Western Europe Before 1800.* London: Longmans.

Smith, Raymond T. 1973. 'The Matrifocal Family' in Jack Goody (ed.) *The Character of Kinship.* Cambridge: Cambridge University Press; 121–44.

Smith, Richard M. 1979. 'Kin and Neighbors in a Thirteenth-century Suffolk Community' in *Journal of Family History* 4, 3 (Fall): 219–56.
1981. 'The People of Tuscany and Their Families in the Fifteenth Century: Medieval or Mediterranean?' (Review article) in *Journal of Family History* 6, 1 (Spring): 107–28.

Sobral, José Manuel and Raúl Iturra 1984. "A Domesticação do Comportamento Selvagem dos Europeus' (Review article) in *Ler História* 3: 81–94.

Stanlislawski, Dan 1959. *The Individuality of Portugal: A Study in Historical-Political Geography*. Austin: University of Texas Press.

Sweet, Louise E. and Timothy J. O'Leary 1969 (eds.). *Circum-Mediterranean Peasantry: Introductory Bibliographies*. New Haven: Human Relations Area Files.

Taborda, Vergílio 1932. *Alto Trás-os-Montes (Estudo Geográfico)*. Coimbra: Imprensa da Universidade.

Theodoratus, Robert J. 1969. *Europe: A Selected Ethnographic Bibliography*. New Haven: Human Relations Area Files.

Thirsk, Joan 1969. 'Younger Sons in the Seventeenth Century' in *History* LIV, 182 (October): 358–77.

Tilly, Charles 1978. 'Anthropology, History, and the *Annales*' in *Review* I, 3/4 (Winter/Spring – The Impact of the *Annales* School on the Social Sciences): 207–13.

Toennies, Ferdinand 1971. *On Sociology: Pure, Applied, and Empirical* (Selected Writings edited and with an Introduction by Werner J. Cahnman and Rudolf Heberle) Chicago: University of Chicago Press.

Tönnies, Ferdinand 1974 (1887). *Community and Association (Gemeinschaft und Gesellschaft)*. London: Routledge & Kegan Paul (translated and supplemented by Charles P. Loomis).

Valente, Manoel 1912. *A Contra-revolução Monarchica: Revelações, Critica, um Pedaço de Historia*. Porto: Typografia Silva Mendonça.

Veiga de Oliveira, Ernesto 1955. 'Trabalhos Coletivos Gratuítos e Recíprocos em Portugal e no Brasil' in *Revista de Antropologia* 3, 1 (Junho): 21–43.

Veiga de Oliveira, Ernesto, Fernando Galhano, and Benjamim Pereira 1974. 'Rio de Onor 1974' in Instituto de Alta Cultura (ed.) *In Memoriam António Jorge Dias*. Lisboa: Junta de Investigações Científicas do Ultramar/Centro de Estudos de Etnologia e de Antropologia Cultural; Vol. III: 285–312.

1976. *Alfaia Agrícola Portuguesa*. Lisboa: Instituto de Alta Cultura/Centro de Estudos de Etnologia.

Veloso, Francisco José 1953. 'Baldios, Maninhos, e Exploração Silvo-pastoril em Comum' in *Scientia Jurídica* III, 10 (Outubro–Dezembro): 123–48.

Verdon, Michel 1979. 'The Stem Family: Toward a General Theory' in *Journal of Interdisciplinary History* X, 1 (Summer): 87–105.

Viazzo, Pier Paolo 1986. 'Illegitimacy and the European Marriage Pattern: Comparative Evidence from the Alpine Area' in Lloyd Bonfield, Richard Smith, and Keith Wrightson (eds.) *The World We Have Gained: Histories of Population and Social Structure*. Oxford: Basil Blackwell.

Wall, Richard (ed. in collaboration with Jean Robin and Peter Laslett) 1984. *Family Forms in Historic Europe*. Cambridge: Cambridge University Press.

Way, Ruth 1962. *A Geography of Spain and Portugal*. London: Methuen.

Weigandt, Ellen 1977. 'Inheritance and Demography in the Swiss Alps' in *Ethnohistory* 24, 2 (Spring): 133–48.

Weisser, Michael R. 1976 (1972). *The Peasants of the Montes: The Roots of Rural Rebellion in Spain*. Chicago: University of Chicago Press.

Wheaton, Robert 1975. 'Family and Kinship in Western Europe: The Problem of the Joint Family Household' in *Journal of Interdisciplinary History* V, 4 (Spring): 601–28.

White, Lynn 1964 (1962). *Medieval Technology and Social Change*. Oxford: Oxford University Press.

Wilk, Richard R. and Robert McC. Netting 1984. 'Households: Changing Forms and Functions' in Robert McC. Netting, Richard R. Wilk, and Eric J. Arnould (eds.) *Households: Comparative and Historical Studies of the Domestic Group*. Berkeley:

University of California Press; 1–28.
Willems, Emílio 1955. 'A Família Portuguêsa Contemporânea'. São Paulo: Publicações Avulsas da Revista *Sociologia* No. 1: 1–59.
1962. 'On Portuguese Family Structure' in *International Journal of Comparative Sociology* III, 1 (September): 65–79.
Wolf, Eric R. 1955. 'Types of Latin American Peasantry: A Preliminary Discussion' in *American Anthropologist* 57, 3 (June): 452–71.
1957. 'Closed Corporate Peasant Communities in Mesoamerica and Central Java' in *Southwestern Journal of Anthropology* 13, 1 (Spring): 1–18 (reprinted in Jack Potter, George Foster, and May Diaz (eds.) *Peasant Society: A Reader*. Boston: Little, Brown, and Co. 1967; 230–46).
1966. *Peasants*. Englewood Cliffs: Prentice Hall.
1967. 'Levels of Communal Relations' in Manning Nash (volume editor) *Handbook of Middle American Indians* (Vol. 6) (general editor, R. Wauchope). Austin: University of Texas Press; 299–316.
1973 (1966). 'Kinship, Friendship, and Patron-client Relations in Complex Societies' in Michael Banton (ed.) *The Social Anthropology of Complex Societies*. London: Tavistock (ASA Monographs No. 4); 1–22.
1981. 'The Mills of Inequality: A Marxian Approach' in Gerald D. Berreman (ed.) *Social Inequality: Comparative and Developmental Approaches*. New York: Academic Press; 41–57.
1983. 'The Vicissitudes of the Closed Corporate Community'. Paper presented at the 82nd Annual Meeting of the American Anthropological Association, Chicago, 16–20 November.
Wolf, Eric and John Cole 1974. *The Hidden Frontier: Ecology and Ethnicity in an Alpine Valley*. New York: Academic Press.
Woodburn, James 1982. 'Egalitarian Societies' (Malinowski Memorial Lecture for 1981) in *Man* 17, 3 (September): 431–51.
Wrigley, E.A. 1973 (ed.). *Identifying People in the Past*. London: Edward Arnold.
1977. 'Reflections on the History of the Family' in *Daedalus* 106, 2 (Spring): 71–85.

Index

Index

Cambridge Studies in Social Anthropology

Editor: JACK GOODY

1 The Political Organisation of Unyamwezi
R.G. ABRAHAMS
2 Buddhism and the Spirit Cults in North-East Thailand*
S.J. TAMBIAH
3 Kalahari Village Politics: An African Democracy
ADAM KUPER
4 The Rope of Moka: Big-Men and Ceremonial Exchange in Mount Hagen, New Guinea*
ANDREW STRATHERN
5 The Majangir: Ecology and Society of a Southwest Ethiopian People
JACK STAUDER
6 Buddhist Monk, Buddhist Layman: A Study of Urban Monastic Organisation in Central Thailand
JANE BUNNAG
7 Contexts of Kinship: An Essay in the Family Sociology of the Gonja of Northern Ghana
ESTHER N. GOODY
8 Marriage among a Matrilineal Elite: A Family Study of Ghanian Senior Civil Servants
CHRISTINE OPPONG
9 Elite Politics in Rural India: Political Stratification and Political Alliances in Western Maharashtra
ANTHONY T. CARTER
10 Women and Property in Morocco: Their Changing Relation to the Process of Social Stratification in the Middle Atlas
VANESSA MAHER
11 Rethinking Symbolism*
DAN SPERBER, *translated by Alice L. Morton*
12 Resources and Population: A Study of the Gurungs of Nepal
ALAN MACFARLANE
13 Mediterranean Family Structures
Edited by J.G. PERISTIANY
14 Spirits of Protest: Spirit-Mediums and the Articulation of Consensus among the Zezuru of Southern Rhodesia (Zimbabwe)
PETER FRY
15 World Conqueror and World Renouncer: A Study of Buddhism and Polity in Thailand against a Historical Background*
S.J. TAMBIAH

16 Outline of a Theory of Practice*
PIERRE BOURDIEU, *translated by Richard Nice*

17 Production and Reproduction: A Comparative Study of the Domestic Domain*
JACK GOODY

18 Perspectives in Marxist Anthropology*
MAURICE GODELIER, *translated by Robert Brain*

19 The Fate of Schechem, or the Politics of Sex: Essays in the Anthropology of the Mediterranean
JULIAN PITT-RIVERS

20 People of the Zongo: The Transformation of Ethnic Identities in Ghana
ENID SCHILDKROUT

21 Casting out Anger: Religion among the Taita of Kenya
GRACE HARRIS

22 Rituals of the Kandyan State
H.L. SENEVIRATNE

23 Australian Kin Classification
HAROLD W. SCHEFFLER

24 The Palm and the Pleiades: Initiation and Cosmology in Northwest Arizona
STEPHEN HUGH-JONES

25 Nomads of South Siberia: The Pastoral Economies of Tuva
S.I. VAINSHTEIN, *translated by Michael Colenso*

26 From the Milk River: Spatial and Temporal Processes in Northwest Amazonia
CHRISTINE HUGH-JONES

27 Day of Shining Red: An Essay on Understanding Ritual
GILBERT LEWIS

28 Hunters, Pastoralists and Ranchers: Reindeer Economies and their Transformations
TIM INGOLD

29 The Wood-Carvers of Hong Kong: Craft Production in the World Capitalist Periphery
EUGENE COOPER

30 Minangkabau Social formations: Indonesian Peasants and the World Economy
JOEL S. KAHN

31 Patrons and Partisans: A Study of Politics in Two Southern Italian *Comuni*
CAROLINE WHITE

32 Muslim Society*
ERNEST GELLNER

33 Why Marry Her? Society and Symbolic Structures
LUC DE HEUSCH, *translated by Janet Lloyd*

34 Chinese Ritual and Politics
EMILY MARTIN AHERN

35 Parenthood and Social Reproduction: Fostering and Occupational Roles in West Africa
ESTHER N. GOODY

36 Dravidian Kinship
THOMAS R. TRAUTMANN

37 The Anthropological Circle: Symbol, Function, History*
MARC AUGE, *translated by Martin Thom*

38 Rural Society in Southeast India
KATHLEEN GOUGH

39 The Fish People: Linguistic Exogamy and Tukanoan Identity in Northwest Amazonia
JEAN E. JACKSON
40 Karl Marx Collective: Economy, Society and Religion in a Siberian Collective Farm*
CAROLINE HUMPHREY
41 Ecology and Exchange in the Andes
Edited by DAVID LEHMANN
42 Traders without Trade: Responses to Trade in two Dyula Communities
ROBERT LAUNAY
43 The Political Economy of West African Agriculture*
KEITH HART
44 Nomads and the Outside World
A.M. KHAZANOV, *translated by Julia Crookenden*
45 Actions, Norms and Representations: Foundations of Anthropological Inquiry*
LADISLAV HOLY *and* MILAN STUCHLIK
46 Structural Models in Anthropology*
PER HAGE *and* FRANK HARARY
47 Servants of the Goddess: The Priests of a South Indian Temple
C.J. FULLER
48 Oedipus and Job in West African Religion*
MEYER FORTES
with an essay by ROBIN HORTON
49 The Buddhist Saints of the Forest and the Cult of Amulets: A Study in Charisma, Hagiography, Sectarianism, and Millennial Buddhism*
S.J. TAMBIAH
50 Kinship and Marriage: An Anthropological Perspective
ROBIN FOX
(* paperback available in U.S.A. only)
51 Individual and Society in Guiana: A Comparative Study of Amerindian Social Organization*
PETER RIVIERE
52 People and the State: An Anthropology of Planned Development*
A.F. ROBERTSON
53 Inequality among Brothers: Class and Kinship in South China
RUBIE S. WATSON
54 On Anthropological Knowledge*
DAN SPERBER
55 Tales of the Yanomami: Daily Life in the Venezuelan Forest*
JACQUES LIZOT, *translated by Ernest Simon*
56 The Making of Great Men: Male Domination and Power among the New Guinea Baruya*
MAURICE GODELIER, *translated by Rupert Swyer*
57 Age Class Systems: Social Institutions and Polities Based on Age*
BERNARDO BERNARDI, *translated by David I. Kertzer*
58 Strategies and Norms in a Changing Matrilineal Society: Descent, Succession and Inheritance among the Toka of Zambia
LADISLAV HOLY
59 Native Lords of Quito in the Age of the Incas: The Political Economy of North-Andean Chiefdoms
FRANK SALOMON

60 Culture and Class in Anthropology and History: A Newfoundland Illustration
GERALD SIDER
61 From Blessing to Violence: History and Ideology in the Circumcision Ritual of the Merina of Madagascar*
MAURICE BLOCH
62 The Huli Response to Illness
STEPHEN FRANKEL

*ALSO AVAILABLE AS A PAPERBACK